VW Golf & Jetta
Service and Repair Manual

I M Coomber and Christopher Rogers

Models covered
VW Golf & Jetta Mk 2 models with petrol engines, including fuel injection, catalytic converter, Formel E, 16-valve and special/limited edition models 1043 cc, 1272 cc, 1595 cc & 1781 cc

Covers mechanical features of Van. Does not cover Convertible, Rallye, Caddy, diesel engine, 4-wheel drive, Mk 1 models or new Golf range introduced in February 1992

(1081 - 344 - 11AF14)

© Haynes Publishing 2003

ABCDE
FGHIJ
KL
4

A book in the **Haynes Service and Repair Manual Series**

All rights reserved. No part of this book may be reproduced or transmitted in any form or by any means, electronic or mechanical, including photocopying, recording or by any information storage or retrieval system, without permission in writing from the copyright holder.

ISBN **978 0 85733 867 9**

British Library Cataloguing in Publication Data
A catalogue record for this book is available from the British Library

Printed in the UK

Haynes Publishing
Sparkford Yeovil, Somerset BA22 7JJ England

Haynes North America, Inc
859 Lawrence Drive, Newbury Park, California 91320 USA

Contents

LIVING WITH YOUR VOLKSWAGEN GOLF OR JETTA

Introduction	Page	0•4
Safety First!	Page	0•5

Roadside Repairs

Introduction	Page	0•6
If your car won't start	Page	0•6
Jump starting	Page	0•7
Wheel changing	Page	0•8
Identifying leaks	Page	0•9
Towing	Page	0•9

Weekly Checks

Introduction	Page	0•10
Underbonnet check points	Page	0•10
Engine oil level	Page	0•11
Coolant level	Page	0•11
Brake fluid level	Page	0•12
Power steering fluid level	Page	0•12
Screen/headlamp washer fluid level	Page	0•13
Wiper blades	Page	0•13
Tyre condition and pressure	Page	0•14
Battery	Page	0•15
Electrical systems	Page	0•15

Lubricants and fluids

	Page	0•16

Capacities and tyre pressures

	Page	0•17

MAINTENANCE

Routine Maintenance and Servicing

Servicing specifications	Page	1•2
Maintenance schedule:		
Vehicles manufactured before August 1985	Page	1•5
Vehicles manufactured after August 1985	Page	1•6
Maintenance - component location	Page	1•7
Maintenance procedures	Page	1•10

Contents

REPAIRS & OVERHAUL

Engine and Associated Systems

Engine repair procedures - 1.05 and 1.3 litre - pre August 1985	Page 2A•1
Engine repair procedures - 1.05 and 1.3 litre - post August 1985	Page 2B•1
Engine repair procedures - 1.6 and 1.8 litre 8 valve	Page 2C•1
Engine repair procedures - 1.8 litre 16 valve	Page 2D•1
Cooling, heating and air conditioning systems	Page 3•1
Fuel and exhaust systems - carburettor models	Page 4A•1
Fuel and exhaust systems - K-Jetronic fuel injection - 8 valve engines	Page 4B•1
Fuel and exhaust systems - K-Jetronic fuel injection - 16 valve engines	Page 4C•1
Fuel and exhaust systems - Mono Jetronic fuel injection	Page 4D•1
Fuel and exhaust systems - Digijet fuel injection	Page 4E•1
Fuel and exhaust systems - Digifant fuel injection	Page 4F•1
Ignition system - contact breaker type	Page 5A•1
Ignition system - transistorised type	Page 5B•1
Ignition system - fully electronic type	Page 5C•1
Starting and charging systems	Page 5D•1

Transmission

Clutch	Page 6•1
Manual gearbox	Page 7A•1
Automatic transmission	Page 7B•1
Driveshafts	Page 8•1

Brakes and Suspension

Braking system	Page 9•1
Suspension and steering	Page 10•1

Body Equipment

Bodywork and fittings	Page 11•1
Body electrical systems	Page 12•1

Wiring Diagrams

Page 12•17

REFERENCE

Dimensions and Weights	Page REF•1
Conversion Factors	Page REF•2
Buying Spare Parts and Vehicle Identification	Page REF•3
General Repair Procedures	Page REF•4
Jacking and Vehicle Support	Page REF•5
Tools and Working Facilities	Page REF•6
MOT test checks	Page REF•8
Fault Finding	Page REF•12
Glossary of Technical Terms	Page REF•20

Index

Page REF•25

Introduction

The Mk. II Volkswagen Golf and Jetta range of models was introduced in March 1984, revised body and trim features being the main visual difference to the earlier range of models.

The engine/transmission is mounted transversely at the front of the vehicle, drive being to the front wheels. Detailed improvements have been made throughout the years of manufacture to improve power output and economy. These include the introduction of hydraulic bucket tappets, the Digifant, Digijet and Mono-Jetronic fuel injection systems, the 16-valve engine fitted to the GTi variant, the fully electronic ignition system (FEI), the 085 5-speed gearbox and several other minor modifications and revisions.

As with earlier models the new range is proving popular, giving economy, reliability, comfort and, if previous models can be used as a yardstick, long life.

VW Golf

VW Jetta

The VW Golf & Jetta Team

Haynes manuals are produced by dedicated and enthusiastic people working in close co-operation. The team responsible for the creation of this book included:

Authors	Ian Coomber
	Cristopher Rogers
Sub-editors	Carole Turk
	Sophie Yar
Editor & Page Make-up	Steve Churchill
Workshop manager	Paul Buckland
Photo Scans	John Martin
	Paul Tanswell
	Steve Tanswell
Cover illustration & Line Art	Roger Healing

We hope the book will help you to get the maximum enjoyment from your car. By carrying out routine maintenance as described you will ensure your car's reliability and preserve its resale value.

Your Golf and Jetta Manual

The aim of this Manual is to help you get the best value from your vehicle. It can do so in several ways. It can help you decide what work must be done (even should you choose to get it done by a garage), provide information on routine maintenance and servicing, and give a logical course of action and diagnosis when random faults occur. However, it is hoped that you will use the Manual by tackling the work yourself. On simpler jobs it may even be quicker than booking the car into a garage and going there twice, to leave and collect it. Perhaps most important, a lot of money can be saved by avoiding the costs a garage must charge to cover its labour and overheads.

The Manual has drawings and descriptions to show the function of the various components so that their layout can be understood. Then the tasks are described and photographed in a clear step-by-step sequence.

References to the 'left' or 'right' are in the sense of a person in the driver's seat, facing forward.

Acknowledgements

Thanks are due to Draper Tools Limited, who supplied some of the workshop tools, and to all those people at Sparkford who helped in the production of this Manual.

This manual is not a direct reproduction of the vehicle manufacturer's data, and its publication should not be taken as implying any technical approval by the vehicle manufacturers or importers.

We take great pride in the accuracy of information given in this Manual, but vehicle manufacturers make alterations and design changes during the production run of a particular vehicle of which they do not inform us. No liability can be accepted by the authors or publishers for loss, damage or injury caused by any errors in, or omissions from the information given.

Safety first!

Working on your car can be dangerous. This page shows just some of the potential risks and hazards, with the aim of creating a safety-conscious attitude.

General hazards

Scalding
- Don't remove the radiator or expansion tank cap while the engine is hot.
- Engine oil, automatic transmission fluid or power steering fluid may also be dangerously hot if the engine has recently been running.

Burning
- Beware of burns from the exhaust system and from any part of the engine. Brake discs and drums can also be extremely hot immediately after use.

Crushing
- When working under or near a raised vehicle, always supplement the jack with axle stands, or use drive-on ramps. *Never venture under a car which is only supported by a jack.*
- Take care if loosening or tightening high-torque nuts when the vehicle is on stands. Initial loosening and final tightening should be done with the wheels on the ground.

Fire
- Fuel is highly flammable; fuel vapour is explosive.
- Don't let fuel spill onto a hot engine.
- Do not smoke or allow naked lights (including pilot lights) anywhere near a vehicle being worked on. Also beware of creating sparks (electrically or by use of tools).
- Fuel vapour is heavier than air, so don't work on the fuel system with the vehicle over an inspection pit.
- Another cause of fire is an electrical overload or short-circuit. Take care when repairing or modifying the vehicle wiring.
- Keep a fire extinguisher handy, of a type suitable for use on fuel and electrical fires.

Electric shock
- Ignition HT voltage can be dangerous, especially to people with heart problems or a pacemaker. Don't work on or near the ignition system with the engine running or the ignition switched on.
- Mains voltage is also dangerous. Make sure that any mains-operated equipment is correctly earthed. Mains power points should be protected by a residual current device (RCD) circuit breaker.

Fume or gas intoxication
- Exhaust fumes are poisonous; they often contain carbon monoxide, which is rapidly fatal if inhaled. Never run the engine in a confined space such as a garage with the doors shut.
- Fuel vapour is also poisonous, as are the vapours from some cleaning solvents and paint thinners.

Poisonous or irritant substances
- Avoid skin contact with battery acid and with any fuel, fluid or lubricant, especially antifreeze, brake hydraulic fluid and Diesel fuel. Don't syphon them by mouth. If such a substance is swallowed or gets into the eyes, seek medical advice.
- Prolonged contact with used engine oil can cause skin cancer. Wear gloves or use a barrier cream if necessary. Change out of oil-soaked clothes and do not keep oily rags in your pocket.
- Air conditioning refrigerant forms a poisonous gas if exposed to a naked flame (including a cigarette). It can also cause skin burns on contact.

Asbestos
- Asbestos dust can cause cancer if inhaled or swallowed. Asbestos may be found in gaskets and in brake and clutch linings. When dealing with such components it is safest to assume that they contain asbestos.

Special hazards

Hydrofluoric acid
- This extremely corrosive acid is formed when certain types of synthetic rubber, found in some O-rings, oil seals, fuel hoses etc, are exposed to temperatures above 400°C. The rubber changes into a charred or sticky substance containing the acid. *Once formed, the acid remains dangerous for years. If it gets onto the skin, it may be necessary to amputate the limb concerned.*
- When dealing with a vehicle which has suffered a fire, or with components salvaged from such a vehicle, wear protective gloves and discard them after use.

The battery
- Batteries contain sulphuric acid, which attacks clothing, eyes and skin. Take care when topping-up or carrying the battery.
- The hydrogen gas given off by the battery is highly explosive. Never cause a spark or allow a naked light nearby. Be careful when connecting and disconnecting battery chargers or jump leads.

Air bags
- Air bags can cause injury if they go off accidentally. Take care when removing the steering wheel and/or facia. Special storage instructions may apply.

Diesel injection equipment
- Diesel injection pumps supply fuel at very high pressure. Take care when working on the fuel injectors and fuel pipes.

⚠️ ***Warning: Never expose the hands, face or any other part of the body to injector spray; the fuel can penetrate the skin with potentially fatal results.***

Remember...

DO
- Do use eye protection when using power tools, and when working under the vehicle.
- Do wear gloves or use barrier cream to protect your hands when necessary.
- Do get someone to check periodically that all is well when working alone on the vehicle.
- Do keep loose clothing and long hair well out of the way of moving mechanical parts.
- Do remove rings, wristwatch etc, before working on the vehicle – especially the electrical system.
- Do ensure that any lifting or jacking equipment has a safe working load rating adequate for the job.

DON'T
- Don't attempt to lift a heavy component which may be beyond your capability – get assistance.
- Don't rush to finish a job, or take unverified short cuts.
- Don't use ill-fitting tools which may slip and cause injury.
- Don't leave tools or parts lying around where someone can trip over them. Mop up oil and fuel spills at once.
- Don't allow children or pets to play in or near a vehicle being worked on.

0•6 Roadside repairs

The following pages are intended to help in dealing with common roadside emergencies and breakdowns. You will find more detailed fault finding information at the back of the manual, and repair information in the main chapters.

If your car won't start and the starter motor doesn't turn

- [ ] If it's a model with automatic transmission, make sure the selector is in 'P' or 'N'.
- [ ] Open the bonnet and make sure that the battery terminals are clean and tight.
- [ ] Switch on the headlights and try to start the engine. If the headlights go very dim when you're trying to start, the battery is probably flat. Get out of trouble by jump starting (see next page) using a friend's car.

If your car won't start even though the starter motor turns as normal

- [ ] Is there fuel in the tank?
- [ ] Is there moisture on electrical components under the bonnet? Switch off the ignition, then wipe off any obvious dampness with a dry cloth. Spray a water-repellent aerosol product (WD-40 or equivalent) on ignition and fuel system electrical connectors like those shown in the photos. Pay special attention to the ignition coil wiring connector and HT leads.

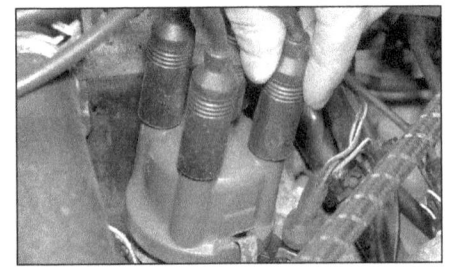

A Check that the HT lead connections at the distributor are clean and make sure they are secure by pushing them onto the cap.

B Check that the HT lead connections at the spark plugs are secure by pushing them onto the plugs.

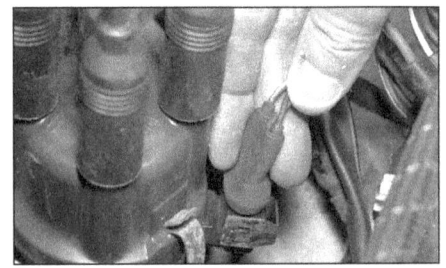

C Check that the LT lead connections are clean and secure.

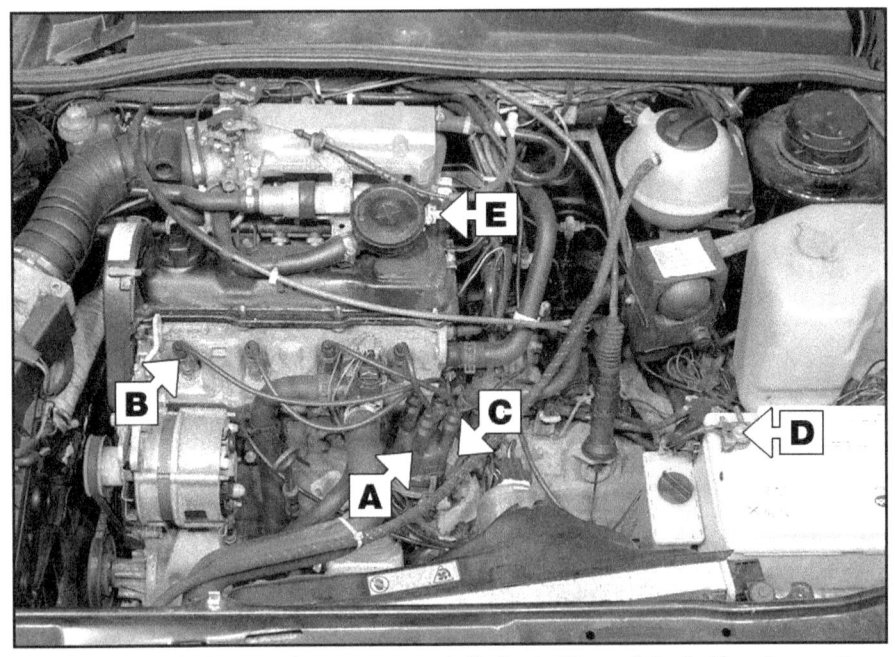

Check that electrical connections are secure (with the ignition switched off) and spray them with a water dispersant spray like WD40 if you suspect a problem due to damp

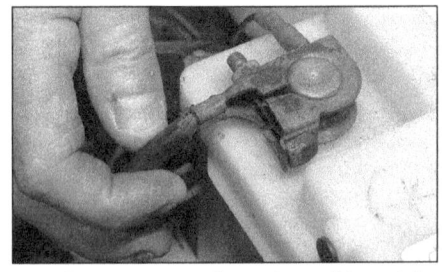

D Check the security and condition of the battery connections.

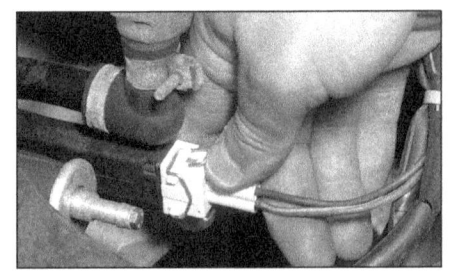

E Wiring plugs may cause problems if dirty or not connected properly.

Roadside repairs 0•7

Jump starting

HAYNES HiNT

Jump starting will get you out of trouble, but you must correct whatever made the battery go flat in the first place. There are three possibilities:

1 *The battery has been drained by repeated attempts to start, or by leaving the lights on.*

2 *The charging system is not working properly (alternator drivebelt slack or broken, alternator wiring fault or alternator itself faulty).*

3 *The battery itself is at fault (electrolyte low, or battery worn out).*

When jump-starting a car using a booster battery, observe the following precautions:

✔ Before connecting the booster battery, make sure that the ignition is switched off.

✔ Ensure that all electrical equipment (lights, heater, wipers, etc) is switched off.

✔ Take note of any special precautions printed on the battery case.

✔ Make sure that the booster battery is the same voltage as the discharged one in the vehicle.

✔ If the battery is being jump-started from the battery in another vehicle, the two vehicles MUST NOT TOUCH each other.

✔ Make sure that the transmission is in neutral (or PARK, in the case of automatic transmission).

1 Connect one end of the red jump lead to the positive (+) terminal of the flat battery

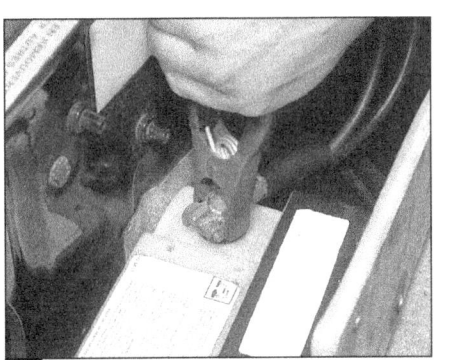

2 Connect the other end of the red lead to the positive (+) terminal of the booster battery.

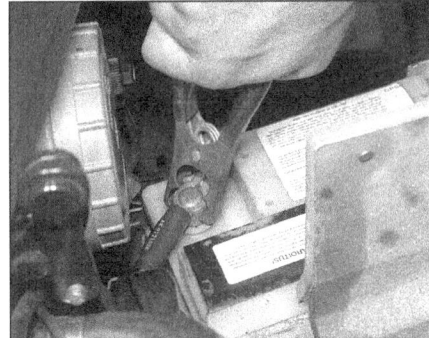

3 Connect one end of the black jump lead to the negative (-) terminal of the booster battery

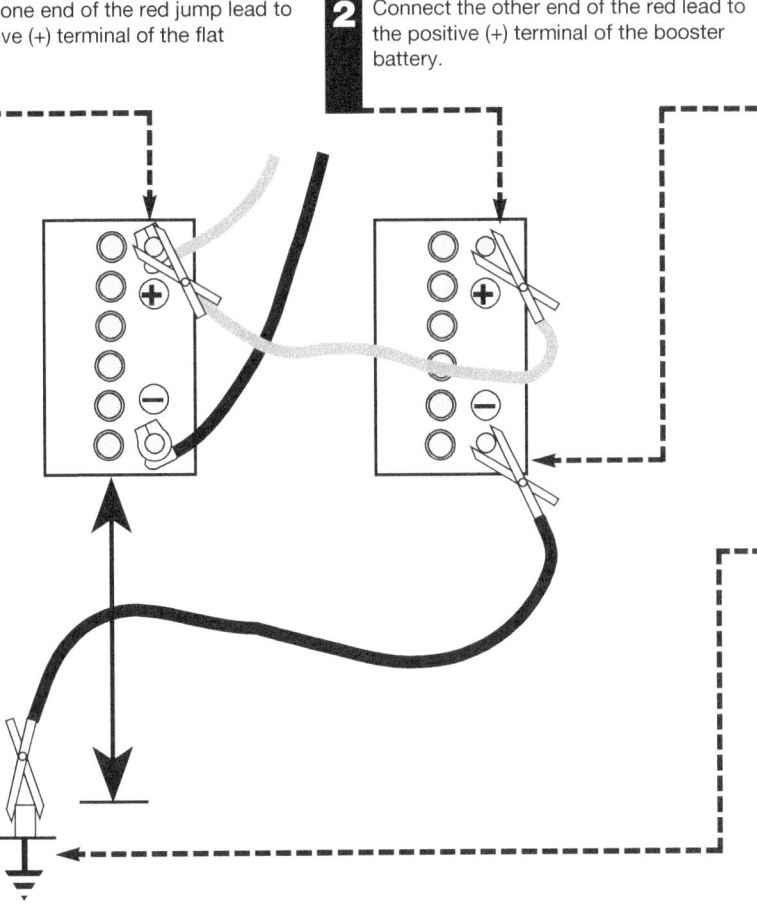

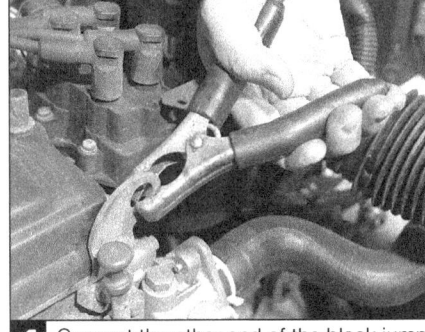

4 Connect the other end of the black jump lead to a bolt or bracket on the engine block, well away from the battery, on the vehicle to be started.

5 Make sure that the jump leads will not come into contact with the fan, drive-belts or other moving parts of the engine.

6 Start the engine using the booster battery and run it at idle speed. Switch on the lights, rear window demister and heater blower motor, then disconnect the jump leads in the reverse order of connection. Turn off the lights etc.

0•8 Roadside repairs

Wheel changing

Some of the details shown here will vary according to model. For instance, the location of the spare wheel and jack is not the same on all cars. However, the basic principles apply to all vehicles.

> **Warning:** Do not change a wheel in a situation where you risk being hit by another vehicle. On busy roads, try to stop in a lay-by or a gateway. Be wary of passing traffic while changing the wheel - it is easy to become distracted by the job in hand.

Preparation

- [ ] When a puncture occurs, stop as soon as it is safe to do so.
- [ ] Park on firm level ground, if possible, and well out of the way of other traffic.
- [ ] Use hazard warning lights if necessary.
- [ ] If you have one, use a warning triangle to alert other drivers of your presence.
- [ ] Apply the handbrake and engage first or reverse gear (or Park on models with automatic transmission.
- [ ] Chock the wheel diagonally opposite the one being removed – a couple of large stones will do for this.
- [ ] If the ground is soft, use a flat piece of wood to spread the load under the jack.

Changing the wheel

1 The spare wheels and tools are stored in the luggage compartment. Release the retaining strap and lift out the jack and tools from the centre of the wheel.

2 Unscrew the retaining nut and lift the wheel out of the vehicle.

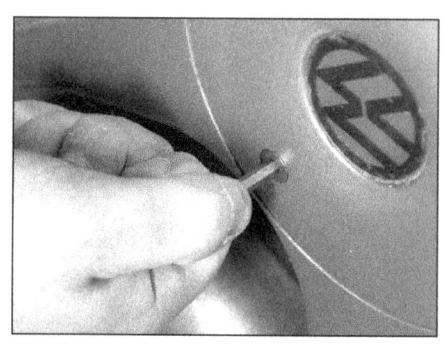

3 Remove the wheel trim/hub cap from the wheel (some trims have retaining screws which must be undone first). Slacken each wheel bolt by half a turn.

4 Locate the jack below the reinforced point on the sill and on firm ground. Turn the jack handle to raise the car until the wheel is clear of the ground.

5 Unscrew the wheel bolts and remove the wheel. Fit the spare wheel and screw in the wheel bolts. Lightly tighten them using the wheelbrace, then lower the car to the ground.

6 Once the car is on the ground, tighten the wheel bolts securely in a diagonal pattern using the wheelbrace. At the earliest possible opportunity, have the wheel bolts slackened and then tightened to the correct torque wrench setting.

Finally...

- [ ] Remove the wheel chocks.
- [ ] Stow the jack and tools in the correct locations in the car.
- [ ] Check the tyre pressure on the wheel just fitted. If it is low, or if you don't have a pressure gauge with you, drive slowly to the nearest garage and inflate the tyre to the right pressure.
- [ ] Have the damaged tyre or wheel repaired as soon as possible.

Roadside repairs 0•9

Identifying leaks

Puddles on the garage floor or drive, or obvious wetness under the bonnet or underneath the car, suggest a leak that needs investigating. It can sometimes be difficult to decide where the leak is coming from, especially if the engine bay is very dirty already. Leaking oil or fluid can also be blown rearwards by the passage of air under the car, giving a false impression of where the problem lies.

Warning: Most automotive oils and fluids are poisonous. Wash them off skin, and change out of contaminated clothing, without delay.

HAYNES HiNT *The smell of a fluid leaking from the car may provide a clue to what's leaking. Some fluids are distinctively coloured. It may help to clean the car carefully and to park it over some clean paper overnight as an aid to locating the source of the leak.*
Remember that some leaks may only occur while the engine is running.

Sump oil

Engine oil may leak from the drain plug...

Oil from filter

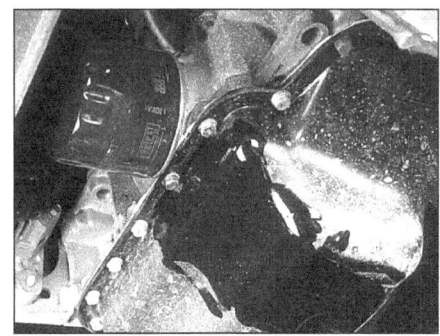

...or from the base of the oil filter.

Gearbox oil

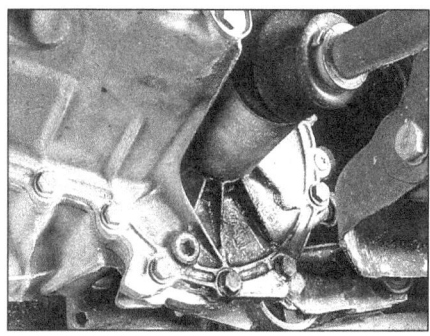

Gearbox oil can leak from the seals at the inboard ends of the driveshafts.

Antifreeze

Leaking antifreeze often leaves a crystalline deposit like this.

Brake fluid

A leak occurring at a wheel is almost certainly brake fluid.

Power steering fluid

Power steering fluid may leak from the pipe connectors on the steering rack.

Towing

When all else fails, you may find yourself having to get a tow home – or of course you may be helping somebody else. Long-distance recovery should only be done by a garage or breakdown service. For shorter distances, DIY towing using another car is easy enough, but observe the following points:

☐ Use a proper tow-rope – they are not expensive. The vehicle being towed must display an 'ON TOW' sign in its rear window.
☐ Always turn the ignition key to the 'on' position when the vehicle is being towed, so that the steering lock is released, and that the direction indicator and brake lights will work.
☐ Only attach the tow-rope to the towing eyes provided.
☐ Before being towed, release the handbrake and select neutral on the transmission.
☐ Note that greater-than-usual pedal pressure will be required to operate the brakes, since the vacuum servo unit is only operational with the engine running.
☐ On models with power steering, greater-than-usual steering effort will also be required.

☐ The driver of the car being towed must keep the tow-rope taut at all times to avoid snatching.
☐ Make sure that both drivers know the route before setting off.
☐ Only drive at moderate speeds and keep the distance towed to a minimum. Drive smoothly and allow plenty of time for slowing down at junctions.
☐ On models with automatic transmission, special precautions apply. If in doubt, do not tow, or transmission damage may result.

Weekly checks

Introduction

There are some very simple checks which need only take a few minutes to carry out, but which could save you a lot of inconvenience and expense.

These "Weekly checks" require no great skill or special tools, and the small amount of time they take to perform could prove to be very well spent, for example;

☐ Keeping an eye on tyre condition and pressures, will not only help to stop them wearing out prematurely, but could also save your life.

☐ Many breakdowns are caused by electrical problems. Battery-related faults are particularly common, and a quick check on a regular basis will often prevent the majority of these.

☐ If your car develops a brake fluid leak, the first time you might know about it is when your brakes don't work properly. Checking the level regularly will give advance warning of this kind of problem.

☐ If the oil or coolant levels run low, the cost of repairing any engine damage will be far greater than fixing the leak, for example.

Underbonnet check points

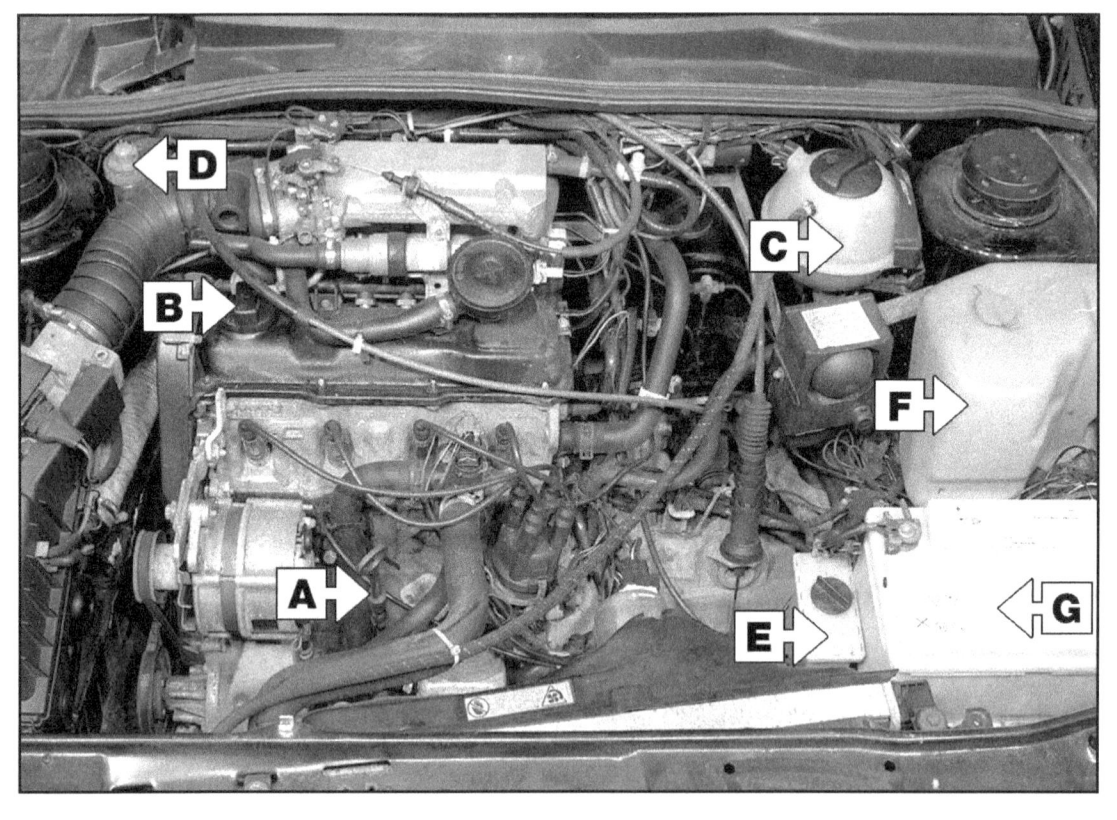

◀ **All models (typical)**

A Engine oil level dipstick
B Engine oil filler cap
C Coolant expansion tank
D Brake fluid reservoir
E Power steering fluid reservoir
F Screen washer fluid reservoir
G Battery

Weekly checks 0•11

Engine oil level

Before you start
✔ Make sure that your car is on level ground.
✔ Check the oil level before the car is driven, or at least 5 minutes after the engine has been switched off.

HAYNES HiNT *If the oil is checked immediately after driving the vehicle, some of the oil will remain in the upper engine components, resulting in an inaccurate reading on the dipstick!*

The correct oil
Modern engines place great demands on their oil. It is very important that the correct oil for your car is used (See "Lubricants, fluids and capacities").

Car Care
● If you have to add oil frequently, you should check whether you have any oil leaks. Place some clean paper under the car overnight, and check for stains in the morning. If there are no leaks, the engine may be burning oil.

● Always maintain the level between the upper and lower dipstick marks (see photo 3). If the level is too low severe engine damage may occur. Oil seal failure may result if the engine is overfilled by adding too much oil.

1 The dipstick is located at the right-hand end of the engine (see "Underbonnet check points" on page 0•10 for exact location). Withdraw the dipstick.

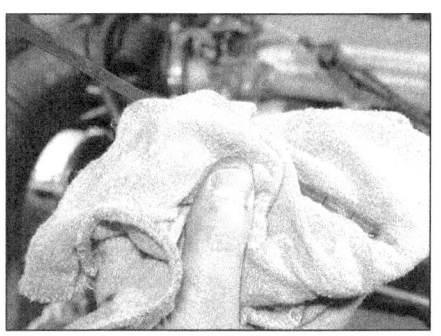

2 Using a clean rag or paper towel remove all oil from the dipstick. Insert the clean dipstick into the tube as far as it will go, then withdraw it again.

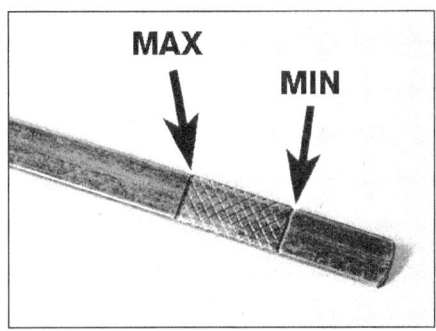

3 Note the oil level on the end of the dipstick, which should be between the upper ("MAX") mark and lower ("MIN") mark. Approximately 1.0 litre of oil will raise the level from the lower mark to the upper mark.

4 Oil is added through the filler cap. Unscrew the cap and top-up the level; a funnel may help to reduce spillage. Add the oil slowly, checking the level on the dipstick often. Don't overfill (see "Car Care" left).

Coolant level

⚠ **Warning: DO NOT attempt to remove the expansion tank pressure cap when the engine is hot, as there is a very great risk of scalding. Do not leave open containers of coolant about, as it is poisonous.**

Car Care
● With a sealed-type cooling system, adding coolant should not be necessary on a regular basis. If frequent topping-up is required, it is likely there is a leak. Check the radiator, all hoses and joint faces for signs of staining or wetness, and rectify as necessary.

● It is important that antifreeze is used in the cooling system all year round, not just during the winter months. Don't top-up with water alone, as the antifreeze will become too diluted.

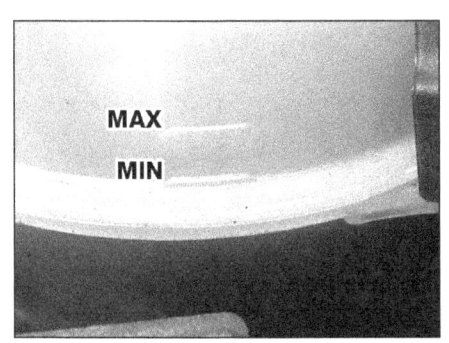

1 The coolant level varies with the temperature of the engine. When the engine is cold, the coolant level should be between the MAX and MIN marks on the side of the expansion tank. When the engine is hot, the level may rise slightly.

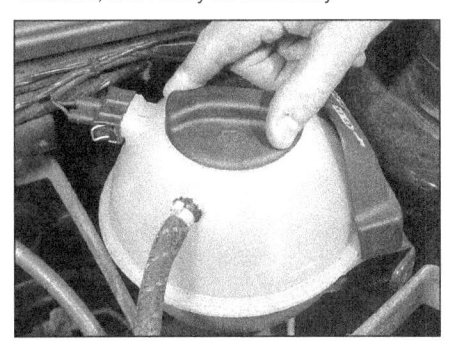

2 If topping up is necessary, **wait until the engine is cold**. Slowly unscrew the expansion tank cap, to release any pressure present in the cooling system, and remove it.

3 Add the recommended mixture of water and antifreeze through the expansion tank filler neck, until the coolant is up to the MAX level mark. Refit the cap, turning it clockwise as far as it will go until it is secure.

Weekly checks

Brake fluid level

⚠️ *Warning:*
● *Brake fluid can harm your eyes and damage painted surfaces, so use extreme caution when handling and pouring it.*
● *Do not use fluid that has been standing open for some time, as it absorbs moisture from the air, which can cause a dangerous loss of braking effectiveness.*

HAYNES HiNT
● *Make sure that your car is on level ground.*
● *The fluid level in the reservoir will drop slightly as the brake pads wear down, but the fluid level must never be allowed to drop below the "MIN" mark.*

Safety First!
● If the reservoir requires repeated topping-up this is an indication of a fluid leak somewhere in the system, which should be investigated immediately.

● If a leak is suspected, the car should not be driven until the braking system has been checked. Never take any risks where brakes are concerned.

1 The "MAX" and "MIN" marks are indicated on the front of the reservoir. The fluid level must be kept between the marks at all times.

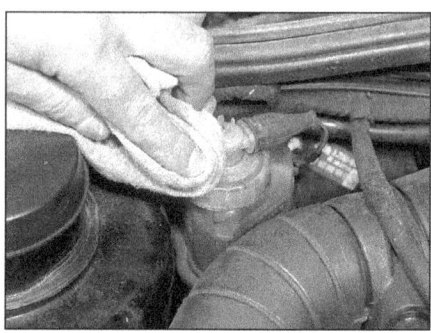

2 If topping-up is necessary, first wipe clean the area around the filler cap to prevent dirt entering the hydraulic system.

3 Unscrew the reservoir cap and carefully lift it out of position, taking care not to damage the level switch float. Inspect the reservoir, if the fluid is dirty the hydraulic system should be drained and refilled (see Chapter 1).

4 Carefully add fluid, taking care not to spill it onto the surrounding components. Use only the specified fluid; mixing different types can cause damage to the system. After topping-up to the correct level, securely refit the cap and wipe off any spilt fluid.

Power steering fluid level

Before you start:
✔ Park the vehicle on level ground.
✔ Set the steering wheel straight-ahead.
✔ The engine should be turned off.

HAYNES HiNT *For the check to be accurate, the steering must not be turned once the engine has been stopped.*

Safety First!
● The need for frequent topping-up indicates a leak, which should be investigated immediately.

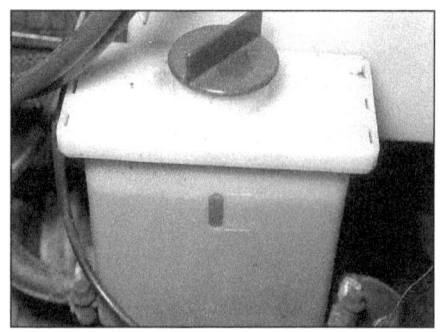

1 The fluid reservoir is mounted next to the battery in the engine compartment. "MAX" and "MIN" level marks are indicated on the side of the reservoir. The fluid level should be maintained between these marks at all times.

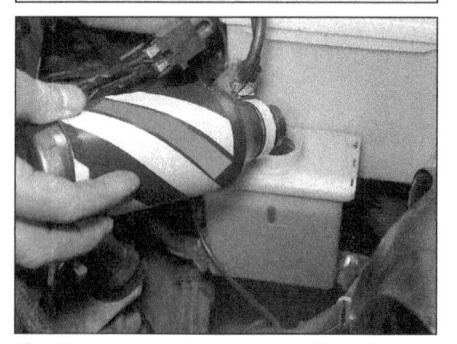

2 If topping-up is necessary, first wipe the area around the filler cap with a clean rag before removing the cap. When adding fluid, pour it carefully into the reservoir to avoid spillage. Be sure to use only the specified fluid.

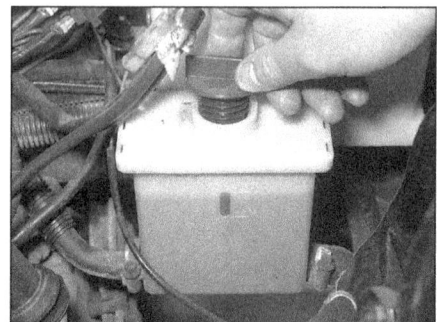

3 After filling the reservoir to the proper level, make sure that the cap is refitted securely to avoid leaks and the entry of foreign matter into the reservoir.

Weekly checks 0•13

Screen/headlamp washer fluid level

Screenwash additives not only keep the winscreen clean during foul weather, they also prevent the washer system freezing in cold weather - which is when you are likely to need it most. Don't top up using plain water as the screenwash will become too diluted, and will freeze during cold weather. *On no account use coolant antifreeze in the washer system - this could discolour or damage paintwork.*

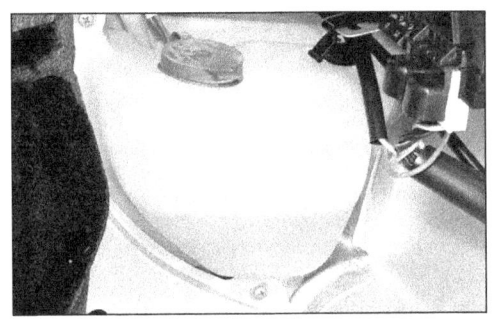

1 The reservoir for the windscreen and headlamp washer systems is located on the left-hand side of the engine compartment, forward of the suspension turret. The rear screen washer system reservoir is located on the right-hand side rear corner of the luggage compartment. Later systems have a single reservoir located in the engine compartment.

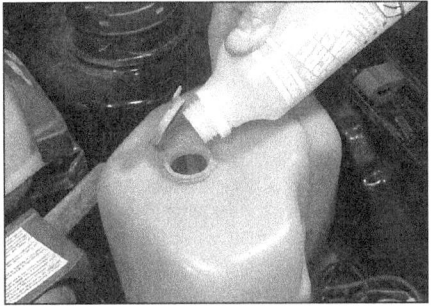

2 When topping-up the reservoir(s) a screenwash additive should be added in the quantities recommended on the bottle.

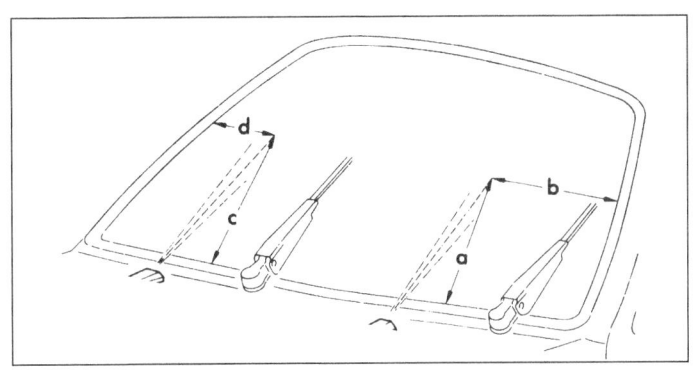

3 Check the operation of both screen and headlamp washers. Adjust the nozzles using a pin if necessary, aiming the spray to a point slightly above the centre of the swept area.
a = 345 mm   b = 420 mm   c = 320 mm   d = 300 mm

Wiper blades

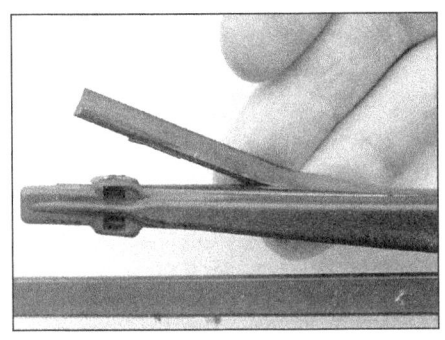

1 Check the condition of the wiper blades; if they are cracked or show any signs of deterioration, or if the glass swept area is smeared, renew them. Wiper blades should be renewed annually.

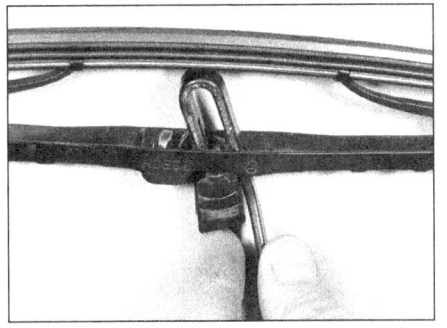

2 To remove a windscreen wiper blade, pull the arm fully away from the screen until it locks. Swivel the blade through 90°, press the locking tab with your fingers and slide the blade out of the arm's hooked end.

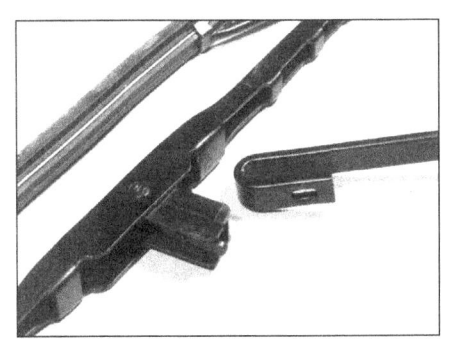

3 Don't forget to check the tailgate wiper blade as well. To remove the blade, depress the retaining tab and slide the blade out of the hooked end of the arm.

Weekly checks

Tyre condition and pressure

It is very important that tyres are in good condition, and at the correct pressure - having a tyre failure at any speed is highly dangerous. Tyre wear is influenced by driving style - harsh braking and acceleration, or fast cornering, will all produce more rapid tyre wear. As a general rule, the front tyres wear out faster than the rears. Interchanging the tyres from front to rear ("rotating" the tyres) may result in more even wear. However, if this is completely effective, you may have the expense of replacing all four tyres at once!

Remove any nails or stones embedded in the tread before they penetrate the tyre to cause deflation. If removal of a nail does reveal that the tyre has been punctured, refit the nail so that its point of penetration is marked. Then immediately change the wheel, and have the tyre repaired by a tyre dealer.

Regularly check the tyres for damage in the form of cuts or bulges, especially in the sidewalls. Periodically remove the wheels, and clean any dirt or mud from the inside and outside surfaces. Examine the wheel rims for signs of rusting, corrosion or other damage. Light alloy wheels are easily damaged by "kerbing" whilst parking; steel wheels may also become dented or buckled. A new wheel is very often the only way to overcome severe damage.

New tyres should be balanced when they are fitted, but it may become necessary to re-balance them as they wear, or if the balance weights fitted to the wheel rim should fall off. Unbalanced tyres will wear more quickly, as will the steering and suspension components. Wheel imbalance is normally signified by vibration, particularly at a certain speed (typically around 50 mph). If this vibration is felt only through the steering, then it is likely that just the front wheels need balancing. If, however, the vibration is felt through the whole car, the rear wheels could be out of balance. Wheel balancing should be carried out by a tyre dealer or garage.

1 Tread Depth - visual check
The original tyres have tread wear safety bands (B), which will appear when the tread depth reaches approximately 1.6 mm. The band positions are indicated by a triangular mark on the tyre sidewall (A).

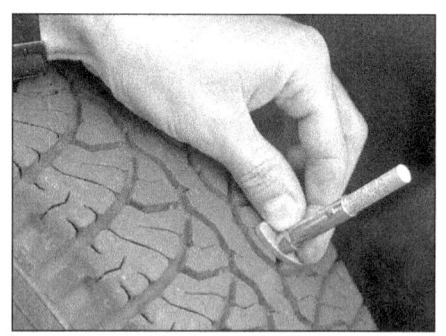

2 Tread Depth - manual check
Alternatively, tread wear can be monitored with a simple, inexpensive device known as a tread depth indicator gauge.

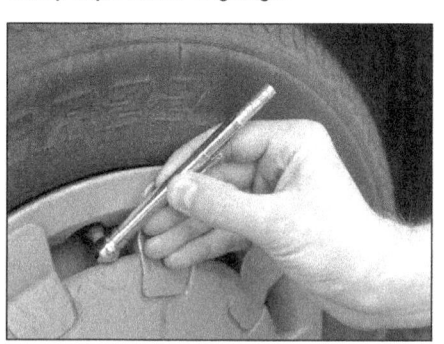

3 Tyre Pressure Check
Check the tyre pressures regularly with the tyres cold. Do not adjust the tyre pressures immediately after the vehicle has been used, or an inaccurate setting will result.

Tyre tread wear patterns

Shoulder Wear

Underinflation (wear on both sides)
Under-inflation will cause overheating of the tyre, because the tyre will flex too much, and the tread will not sit correctly on the road surface. This will cause a loss of grip and excessive wear, not to mention the danger of sudden tyre failure due to heat build-up.
Check and adjust pressures
Incorrect wheel camber (wear on one side)
Repair or renew suspension parts
Hard cornering
Reduce speed!

Centre Wear

Overinflation
Over-inflation will cause rapid wear of the centre part of the tyre tread, coupled with reduced grip, harsher ride, and the danger of shock damage occurring in the tyre casing.
Check and adjust pressures

If you sometimes have to inflate your car's tyres to the higher pressures specified for maximum load or sustained high speed, don't forget to reduce the pressures to normal afterwards.

Uneven Wear

Front tyres may wear unevenly as a result of wheel misalignment. Most tyre dealers and garages can check and adjust the wheel alignment (or "tracking") for a modest charge.
Incorrect camber or castor
Repair or renew suspension parts
Malfunctioning suspension
Repair or renew suspension parts
Unbalanced wheel
Balance tyres
Incorrect toe setting
Adjust front wheel alignment
Note: *The feathered edge of the tread which typifies toe wear is best checked by feel.*

Weekly checks 0•15

Battery

Caution: *Before carrying out any work on the vehicle battery, read the precautions given in "Safety first" at the start of this manual.*

✔ Make sure that the battery tray is in good condition, and that the clamp is tight. Corrosion on the tray, retaining clamp and the battery itself can be removed with a solution of water and baking soda. Thoroughly rinse all cleaned areas with water. Any metal parts damaged by corrosion should be covered with a zinc-based primer, then painted.

✔ Periodically (approximately every three months), check the charge condition of the battery as described in Chapter 5A.

✔ If the battery is flat, and you need to jump start your vehicle, see **Roadside Repairs**.

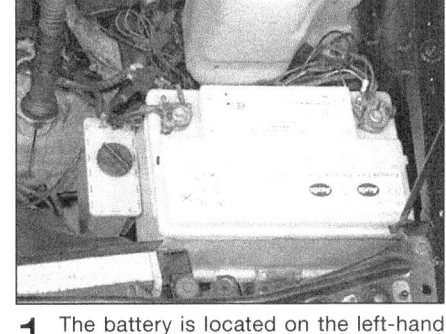

1 The battery is located on the left-hand side of the engine compartment. The exterior of the battery should be inspected periodically for damage such as a cracked case or cover.

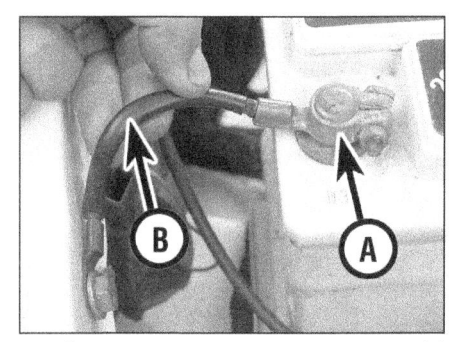

2 Check the tightness of battery clamps (A) to ensure good electrical connections. You should not be able to move them. Also check each cable (B) for cracks and frayed conductors.

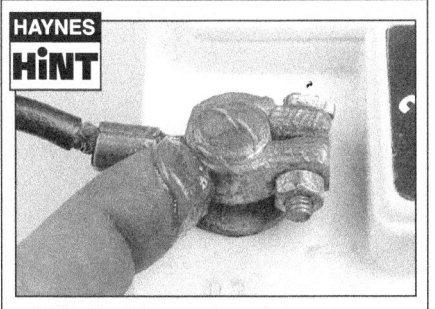

HAYNES HiNT
Battery corrosion can be kept to a minimum by applying a layer of petroleum jelly to the clamps and terminals after they are reconnected.

3 If corrosion (white, fluffy deposits) is evident, remove the cables from the battery terminals, clean them with a small wire brush, then refit them. Automotive stores sell a tool for cleaning the battery post . . .

4 . . . as well as the battery cable clamps

Electrical systems

✔ Check all external lights and the horn. Refer to the appropriate Sections of Chapter 12 for details if any of the circuits are found to be inoperative.

✔ Visually check all accessible wiring connectors, harnesses and retaining clips for security, and for signs of chafing or damage.

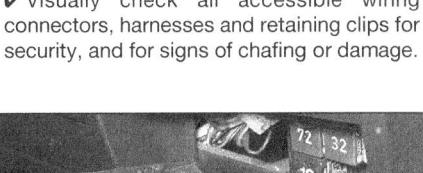

HAYNES HiNT
If you need to check your brake lights and indicators unaided, back up to a wall or garage door and operate the lights. The reflected light should show if they are working properly.

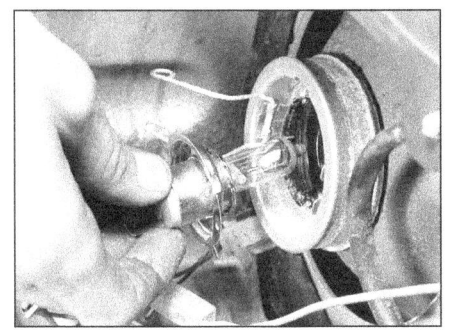

1 If a single indicator light, stop-light or headlight has failed, it is likely that a bulb has blown and will need to be replaced. Refer to Chapter 12 for details. If both stop-lights have failed, it is possible that the switch has failed.

2 If more than one indicator light or tail light has failed it is likely that either a fuse has blown or that there is a fault in the circuit (see Chapter 12). The fuses are located under the facia panel, on the right-hand side, behind a removable cover.

3 To replace a blown fuse, simply pull it out and fit a new fuse of the correct rating (see Chapter 12). If the fuse blows again, it is important that you find out why - a complete checking procedure is given in Chapter 12.

0•16 Lubricants and fluids

Lubricants and fluids

Component or system	Lubricant or fluid
Engine	Multigrade engine oil, viscosity SAE 10W/40, 15W/40, 15W/50 or 20W/50
Cooling system	Ethylene glycol-based antifreeze with corrosion inhibitors
Manual gearbox	Gear oil, viscosity SAE 80, to API GL4
Automatic transmission	Dexron type ATF
Final drive:	
Manual gearbox	Gear oil, viscosity SAE 80
Automatic transmission	Gear oil, viscosity SAE 90EP
Brake hydraulic system	Hydraulic fluid to FMVSS 116 DOT 4
Power steering:	
Pre-April 1989	Dexron type ATF
Post-April 1989	VW hydraulic oil G 002 000

Choosing your engine oil

Engines need oil, not only to lubricate moving parts and minimise wear, but also to maximise power output and to improve fuel economy.

HOW ENGINE OIL WORKS

• Beating friction

Without oil, the moving surfaces inside your engine will rub together, heat up and melt, quickly causing the engine to seize. Engine oil creates a film which separates these moving parts, preventing wear and heat build-up.

• Cooling hot-spots

Temperatures inside the engine can exceed 1000° C. The engine oil circulates and acts as a coolant, transferring heat from the hot-spots to the sump.

• Cleaning the engine internally

Good quality engine oils clean the inside of your engine, collecting and dispersing combustion deposits and controlling them until they are trapped by the oil filter or flushed out at oil change.

OIL CARE - FOLLOW THE CODE

To handle and dispose of used engine oil safely, always:

- Avoid skin contact with used engine oil. Repeated or prolonged contact can be harmful.
- Dispose of used oil and empty packs in a responsible manner in an authorised disposal site. Call 0800 663366 to find the one nearest to you. Never tip oil down drains or onto the ground.

0800 66 33 66
www.oilbankline.org.uk

Capacities and tyre pressures 0•17

Capacities

Component or system	Capacity
Engine:	
1.05 & 1.3 litre:	
rocker-finger type	3.0 litres with filter change
	2.5 litres without filter change
hydraulic tappet type	3.5 litres with filter change
	3.0 litres without filter change
1.6 & 1.8 litre:	
pre-August 1985	3.5 litres with filter change
	3.0 litres without filter change
post-August 1985	4.0 litres with filter change
	3.5 litres without filter change
Cooling system	6.3 litres
Manual gearbox:	
084 type	2.2 litres
085 type	3.1 litres
020 4-speed	1.5 litres
020 5-speed	2.0 litres
Automatic transmission	6.0 litres from dry
	3.0 litres service drain & fill
Final drive:	
Manual gearbox	Included in gearbox capacity
Automatic	0.75 litre
Fuel tank	55.0 litres

Tyre pressures *(tyres cold)*

	Front	Rear
1.05 & 1.3 litre models:		
Half load	1.8 bar (26 lbf/in^2)	1.8 bar (26 lbf/in^2)
Full load	1.8 bar (26 lbf/in^2)	2.4 bar (35 lbf/in^2)
1.6 & 1.8 litre models:		
Half load	2.0 bar (29 lbf/in^2)	1.8 bar (26 lbf/in^2)
Full load	2.0 bar (29 lbf/in^2)	2.4 bar (35 lbf/in^2)

Advanced driving

Many people see the words 'advanced driving' and believe that it won't interest them or that it is a style of driving beyond their own abilities. Nothing could be further from the truth. Advanced driving is straightforward safe, sensible driving - the sort of driving we should all do every time we get behind the wheel.

An average of 10 people are killed every day on UK roads and 870 more are injured, some seriously. Lives are ruined daily, usually because somebody did something stupid. Something like 95% of all accidents are due to human error, mostly driver failure. Sometimes we make genuine mistakes - everyone does. Sometimes we have lapses of concentration. Sometimes we deliberately take risks.

For many people, the process of 'learning to drive' doesn't go much further than learning how to pass the driving test because of a common belief that good drivers are made by 'experience'.

Learning to drive by 'experience' teaches three driving skills:

- Quick reactions. (Whoops, that was close!)
- Good handling skills. (Horn, swerve, brake, horn).
- Reliance on vehicle technology. (Great stuff this ABS, stop in no distance even in the wet...)

Drivers whose skills are 'experience based' generally have a lot of near misses and the odd accident. The results can be seen every day in our courts and our hospital casualty departments.

Advanced drivers have learnt to control the risks by controlling the position and speed of their vehicle. They avoid accidents and near misses, even if the drivers around them make mistakes.

The key skills of advanced driving are **concentration**, effective all-round **observation, anticipation** and **planning.** When **good vehicle handling** is added to these skills, all driving situations can be approached and negotiated in a safe, methodical way, leaving nothing to chance.

Concentration means applying your mind to safe driving, completely excluding anything that's not relevant. Driving is usually the most dangerous activity that most of us undertake in our daily routines. It deserves our full attention.

Observation means not just looking, but seeing and seeking out the information found in the driving environment.

Anticipation means asking yourself what is happening, what you can reasonably expect to happen and what could happen unexpectedly. (One of the commonest words used in compiling accident reports is 'suddenly'.)

Planning is the link between seeing something and taking the appropriate action. For many drivers, planning is the missing link.

If you want to become a safer and more skilful driver and you want to enjoy your driving more, contact the Institute of Advanced Motorists at www.iam.org.uk, phone 0208 996 9600, or write to IAM House, 510 Chiswick High Road, London W4 5RG for an information pack.

Chapter 1
Routine maintenance and servicing

Contents

Air cleaner element renewal 32	Fuel filter renewal 33
Air conditioning system check 8	Fuel system control linkage check 9
Alternator, power steering pump and air conditioner compressor	Gearbox oil level check 22
drivebelt(s) check 13	Headlight beam alignment check 27
Antifreeze concentration check 14	Hinge and catch lubrication 30
Automatic transmission and final drive fluid renewal 35	Ignition timing check 17
Automatic transmission fluid level check 23	Intensive maintenance 2
Battery electrolyte level check 7	Introduction 1
Brake check 5	Light, direction indicator and horn check 10
Brake fluid renewal 36	Lock, hinge and latch mechanism check 3
Brake pad and rear shoe lining check 26	Seat belt check 4
Clutch operation check 21	Slow running adjustment 20
Contact breaker point renewal and adjustment 16	Spark plug renewal 15
Contact breaker point check 11	Steering gear check 28
CV joint and boot check 24	Sunroof guide rails cleaning and lubrication 34
Engine oil and filter renewal 18	Suspension check 29
Exhaust system check 19	Timing belt renewal 37
Fluid leakage and engine electrical system check 6	Valve clearance check 12
Fuel and brake line, hose and union check 25	Vehicle underbody check 31

Degrees of difficulty

Easy, suitable for novice with little experience	**Fairly easy,** suitable for beginner with some experience	**Fairly difficult,** suitable for competent DIY mechanic	**Difficult,** suitable for experienced DIY mechanic	**Very difficult,** suitable for expert DIY or professional

Servicing specifications

Lubricants, fluids and capacities
Refer to the end of "Weekly checks"

Engine

Valve clearances

1.05 and 1.3 litre engines - pre August 1985: | **Inlet** | **Exhaust**
Warm | 0.15 to 0.20 mm | 0.25 to 0.30 mm
Cold | 0.10 to 0.15 mm | 0.20 to 0.25 mm

Hydraulic tappet free travel

1.05 and 1.3 litre - post August 1985, 1.6 and 1.8 litre (Maximum travel) ... 0.1 mm

Cooling system
Antifreeze mixture .... 50 % antifreeze (by volume) with water

Air conditioning system
Compressor drivebelt tension .... 5.0 to 10.0 mm deflection on longest run

Fuel system

Idle speed

1.05 litre carburettor engines:
- Pierburg/Solex 31 PIC-7 .... 900 to 1000 rpm
- Pierburg/Solex 1B3 and Weber 32 TLA .... 750 to 850 rpm

1.3 litre carburettor engines:
- Pierburg/Solex 2E3 .... 750 to 850 rpm

1.6 litre carburettor engines:
- Pierburg/Solex 2E2 - engine code EZ .... 900 to 1000 rpm
- Pierburg/Solex 2E2 - engine code RF .... 700 to 800 rpm

1.8 litre carburettor engines:
- Pierburg/Solex 2E2 .... 900 to 1000 rpm

K-Jetronic fuel-injected engine:
- 8 valve:
  - Pre Sept. 1984 .... 900 to 1000 rpm
  - From Sept. 1984 .... 800 to 1000 rpm
  - Air conditioned models .... 850 to 1000 rpm
- 16 valve .... 900 to 1000 rpm

Mono Jetronic fuel-injected engine .... 750 to 950 rpm (not adjustable)

Digijet fuel-injected engine:
- Up to July 1989 .... 750 to 850 rpm
- July 1989 .... 880 to 980 rpm

Digifant fuel-injected engine .... 750 to 850 rpm

CO content (%)

1.05 litre carburettor engines:
- Pierburg/Solex 31 PIC-7 .... 0.5 to 1.5
- Pierburg/Solex 1B3 and Weber 32 TLA .... 1.5 to 2.5

1.3 litre carburettor engines (Pierburg/Solex 2E3) .... 1.5 to 2.5

1.6 litre carburettor engines:
- Pierburg/Solex 2E2 - engine code EZ .... 0.5 to 1.5
- Pierburg/Solex 2E2 - engine code RF .... 1.0 to 1.5

1.8 litre carburettor engines (Pierburg/Solex 2E2) .... 0.5 to 1.5

K-Jetronic fuel-injected engine .... 0.5 to 1.5

Mono Jetronic fuel-injected engine .... 0.2 to 1.2

Digijet fuel-injected engine:
- Up to July 1989 .... 0.3 to 1.1
- July 1989 .... 0.3 to 1.5

Digifant fuel-injected engine .... 0.5 to 1.5

Servicing specifications 1•3

Ignition system

Firing order (all engines) .... 1-3-4-2 (No. 1 cylinder at crankshaft pulley end)

Contact breaker system
Distributor:
  Contact breaker gap (initial setting only) .... 0.4 mm
  Dwell angle (1.05, 1.3 and 1.6 litre):
    Setting .... 44 to 50° (50 to 56%)
    Wear limit .... 42 to 58° (47 to 64%)
Ignition timing (at idle):
  1.05 and 1.3 litre .... 4 to 6° BTDC
  1.6 and 1.8 litre (carburettor engine) .... 17 to 19° BTDC
  1.8 litre (fuel injection engine) .... 5 to 7° BTDC

Transistorised system
Distributor:
  Dwell angle (1.05,1.3 and 1.6 litre):
    Setting .... 44 to 50° (50 to 56%)
    Wear limit .... 42 to 58° (47 to 64%)
Ignition timing:
  1.3 litre (code NZ) - TCI-H .... 4 to 6° BTDC at 750 to 850 rpm, with vacuum hose disconnected
  1.6 litre (code RF and EZ) - TCI-H .... 17 to 19° BTDC at 700 to 800 rpm, with vacuum hose disconnected
  1.8 litre:
    Code PB and PF - Digifant .... 1 to 6° BTDC at 2000 to 2500 rpm, with temperature sender disconnected
    Code GU and RH - TCI-H .... 17 to 19° BTDC at 675 to 825 rpm, with vacuum hose connected
    Code RP - TCI-H .... 5 to 7° BTDC at 950 rpm, with vacuum hose disconnected

Fully electronic system
All Specifications as for Transistorised System except for:
Ignition timing:
  1.8 litre 16 valve engine .... 5 to 7° BTDC at 950 to 1050 rpm, with vacuum hose connected

Spark plugs

	Type	Electrode gap
1.05 litre engine:		
Code GN	Bosch W 6 DP	0.8 mm
Code HZ:		
Green ignition coil	Bosch WR 7 LT+	1.0 mm
Grey ignition coil	Bosch WR 7 D+	0.8 mm
1.3 litre engine:		
Code HK	Bosch WR 7 D+	0.8 mm
Codes MH, NZ and 2G:		
Green ignition coil	Bosch WR 7 LT+	1.0 mm
Grey ignition coil	Bosch WR 7 D+	0.8 mm
1.6 litre engine:		
Codes EZ and RF:		
Green ignition coil	Bosch WR 8 LT+	1.0 mm
Grey ignition coil	Bosch WR 8 D+	0.8 mm
1.8 litre engine:		
Codes GU, RP and EV	Bosch WR 7 LT+	1.0 mm
Code RH, PB and PF:		
Green ignition coil	Bosch WR 7 LT+	1.0 mm
Grey ignition coil	Bosch WR 7 D+	0.8 mm
Code KR	Bosch FR 56	Not adjustable

Servicing specifications

Charging system

Alternator drivebelt tension
Initial adjustment for new drivebelt .... 2.0 mm deflection under finger pressure at point midway between alternator and crankshaft pulleys
Adjustment after 500 miles (750 km) .... 5.0 mm deflection under finger pressure at same point
Models after early 1985 fitted with rack type adjustment link .... 8 to 10 Nm (6 to 7 lbf ft) torque loading on adjuster bolt

Clutch
Free play at clutch pedal .... 15 to 20 mm

Braking system

Pad thickness
Front disc brakes:
  New - excluding backplate:
    1.05 and 1.3 litre .... 12.0 mm
    1.6 and 1.8 litre .... 14.0 mm
    1.8 litre with ventilated discs .... 10.0 mm
  Minimum - including backplate:
    All models .... 7.0 mm
Rear disc brakes:
  New - including backplate .... 12.0 mm
  Minimum - including backplate .... 7.0 mm

Shoe lining thickness
Rear drum brakes:
  Minimum - including shoe .... 5.0 mm
  Minimum - excluding shoe .... 2.5 mm

Steering
Power steering pump drivebelt tension .... 10.0 mm deflection under firm finger pressure at point midway between pump and crankshaft pulleys

Tyre pressures
Refer to the end of "Weekly checks"

Torque wrench settings

	Nm	lbf ft
Engine		
Sump drain plug	30	22
Valve cover	10	7
Ignition system		
Contact breaker system:		
Spark plugs	20	15
Distributor clamp bolt:		
1.05 and 1.3 litre	10	7
1.6 and 1.8 litre	25	18
Transistorised and fully electronic systems:		
Spark plugs:		
1.05 and 1.3 litre	25	18
1.6 and 1.8 litre	20	15
Charging system		
Alternator mounting/pivot bolt	45	33
Alternator adjuster link bolts	25	18
Manual gearbox		
Oil filler plug	25	18
Oil drain plug	25	18
Automatic transmission		
Oil pan bolts	20	15
Oil strainer (filter) cover bolts	3	2
Steering		
Power steering pump/swivel bracket bolts	20	15
Power steering pump tensioner/bracket	20	15
Roadwheels		
Roadwheel bolts	110	81
Body fittings		
Seat belt anchor bolts	40	30

Maintenance schedule

The maintenance intervals in this Manual are provided with the assumption that you will be carrying out the work yourself. These are the minimum maintenance intervals recommended by the manufacturer for vehicles driven daily. If you wish to keep your vehicle in peak condition at all times, you may wish to perform some of these procedures more often. We encourage frequent maintenance, because it enhances the efficiency, performance and resale value of your vehicle.

If the vehicle is driven in dusty areas, used to tow a trailer, or driven frequently at slow speeds (idling in traffic) or on short journeys, then more frequent maintenance intervals are recommended.

When the vehicle is new, it should be serviced by a factory-authorised dealer service department, in order to preserve the factory warranty.

Vehicles manufactured before August 1985

Every 250 miles (400 km) or weekly
- [ ] see *"Weekly checks"*

Every 1000 miles (1500 km) or monthly
- [ ] Check lock, hinge and latch mechanisms (Section 3)
- [ ] Check seat belts (Section 4)
- [ ] Check brakes (Section 5)
- [ ] Check for fluid leakage and engine electrical system security (Section 6)
- [ ] Check battery electrolyte level (Section 7)
- [ ] Check air conditioning system (Section 8)
- [ ] Check and lubricate fuel system control linkage (Section 9)
- [ ] Check operation of lights, direction indicators and horns (Section 10)

Every 5000 miles (7500 km) or 6 months
- [ ] Check contact breaker points (Section 11)

Every 10 000 miles (15 000 km) or 12 months
- [ ] Check valve clearances (Section 12)
- [ ] Check alternator, power steering pump and air conditioner compressor drivebelt(s) adjustment and condition (Section 13)
- [ ] Check antifreeze concentration (Section 14)
- [ ] Renew spark plugs (Section 15)
- [ ] Renew and adjust contact breaker points (Section 16)
- [ ] Check ignition timing (Section 17)
- [ ] Renew engine oil and filter (Section 18)

Note: *Frequent oil and filter changes are beneficial for the engine. We recommend changing the oil at half the mileage specified here or at least twice a year.*

- [ ] Check exhaust system (Section 19)
- [ ] Adjust slow running (Section 20)
- [ ] Check clutch operation (Section 21)
- [ ] Check gearbox oil level (Section 22)
- [ ] Check automatic transmission fluid level (Section 23)
- [ ] Check CV joints and boots (Section 24)
- [ ] Check fuel and brake lines, hoses and unions (Section 25)
- [ ] Check brake pads and rear shoe linings (Section 26)
- [ ] Check headlight beam alignment (Section 27)
- [ ] Check steering gear (Section 28)
- [ ] Check suspension (Section 29)
- [ ] Lubricate hinges and catches (Section 30)
- [ ] Check vehicle underbody (Section 31)

Every 20 000 miles (30 000 km) or 24 months
- [ ] Renew air cleaner element (Section 32)
- [ ] Renew fuel filter (Section 33)

Every 30 000 miles (45 000 km)
- [ ] Renew automatic transmission and final drive fluid (Section 35)

Every 2 years
- [ ] Renew brake fluid (Section 36)

Every 40 000 miles (60 000 km)
- [ ] Renew timing belt (Section 37)

Maintenance schedule

Vehicles manufactured after August 1985

Every 250 miles (400 km) or weekly
☐ See "Weekly checks"

Every 1000 miles (1500 km) or monthly
☐ Check lock, hinge and latch mechanisms (Section 3)
☐ Check seat belts (Section 4)
☐ Check brakes (Section 5)
☐ Check for fluid leakage and engine electrical system security (Section 6)
☐ Check battery electrolyte level (Section 7)
☐ Check air conditioning system (Section 8)
☐ Check and lubricate fuel system control linkage (Section 9)
☐ Check operation of lights, direction indicators and horns (Section 10)

Every 12 months
☐ Check antifreeze concentration (Section 14)
☐ Renew engine oil and filter (Section 18)
Note: *Frequent oil and filter changes are beneficial for the engine. We recommend changing the oil at least twice a year.*
☐ Check exhaust system (Section 19)
☐ Check idling speed and mixture (Section 20)
☐ Check clutch operation (Section 21)
☐ Check automatic transmission fluid level (Section 23)
☐ Check CV joints and boots (Section 24)
☐ Check fuel and brake lines, hoses and unions (Section 25)
☐ Check brake pads and rear shoe linings (Section 26)
☐ Check headlight beam alignment (Section 27)
☐ Check steering gear (Section 28)
☐ Check suspension (Section 29)
☐ Lubricate hinges and catches (Section 30)
☐ Check vehicle underbody (Section 31)

Every 10 000 miles (15 000 km) - if completing more than 10 000 miles (15 000 km) per annum
☐ Renew engine oil and filter (Section 18)
Note: *Frequent oil and filter changes are beneficial for the engine. We recommend changing the oil at half the mileage specified here or at least twice a year.*
☐ Check brake pad linings (Section 26)

Every 20 000 miles (30 000 km)
☐ Check alternator, power steering pump and air conditioner compressor drivebelt(s) adjustment and condition (Section 13)
☐ Renew spark plugs (Section 15)
☐ Renew air cleaner element (Section 32)
☐ Renew fuel filter (Section 33)
☐ Clean and lubricate sunroof guide rails (Section 34)
☐ Renew automatic transmission and final drive fluid (Section 35)

Every 2 years
☐ Renew brake fluid (Section 36)

Every 40 000 miles (60 000 km)
☐ Renew timing belt (Section 37)

Maintenance - component location 1•7

Underbonnet view – 1.3 litre model (air cleaner removed)

1 Engine oil dipstick
2 Fuel line filter
3 Brake master cylinder reservoir
4 Carburettor
5 Ignition coil
6 Cooling system expansion tank
7 Windscreen/headlight washer reservoir
8 Ignition distributor
9 Battery
10 Cooling fan
11 Engine oil filler cap

Underbonnet view – fuel injection model

1 Engine oil dipstick
2 Compressor (air conditioning)
3 Fuel distributor
4 Alternator
5 Engine oil filler cap
6 Brake master cylinder reservoir
7 Throttle housing
8 Ignition coil
9 Cooling system expansion tank
10 Windscreen/headlamp washer reservoir
11 Battery
12 Clutch cable
13 Cooling fan
14 Ignition distributor

Maintenance - component location

Front underbody view - 1.3 litre model

1 Alternator
2 Oil filter
3 Driveshaft
4 Front mounting
5 Cooling system bottom hose
6 Gearbox
7 Track control arm
8 Tie-rod
9 Exhaust
10 Engine sump

Front underbody view - fuel injected model

1 Driveshaft
2 Front mounting
3 Starter motor
4 Gearbox
5 Track control arm
6 Tie-rod
7 Anti-roll bar
8 Exhaust system
9 Engine sump

Maintenance - component location

Rear underbody view - 1.3 litre model

1. Exhaust
2. Fuel tank
3. Rear shock absorber lower mounting
4. Axle beam
5. Handbrake cable (right-hand)
6. Handbrake cable (left-hand)
7. Rear drum brake

Rear underbody view - fuel injected model

1. Exhaust
2. Fuel tank
3. Rear shock absorber lower mounting
4. Axle beam
5. Fuel pump and associated fittings
6. Brake pressure regulator
7. Rear disc brake

Maintenance procedures

1 Introduction

This Chapter is designed to help the home mechanic maintain his/her vehicle for safety, economy, long life and peak performance.

The Chapter contains a master maintenance schedule, followed by Sections dealing specifically with each task in the schedule. Visual checks, adjustments, component renewal and other helpful items are included. Refer to the accompanying illustrations of the engine compartment and the underside of the vehicle for the locations of the various components.

Servicing your vehicle in accordance with the mileage/time maintenance schedule and the following Sections will provide a planned maintenance programme, which should result in a long and reliable service life. This is a comprehensive plan, so maintaining some items but not others at the specified service intervals, will not produce the same results.

As you service your vehicle, you will discover that many of the procedures can - and should - be grouped together, because of the particular procedure being performed, or because of the close proximity of two otherwise-unrelated components to one another. For example, if the vehicle is raised for any reason, the exhaust can be inspected at the same time as the suspension and steering components.

The first step in this maintenance programme is to prepare yourself before the actual work begins. Read through all the Sections relevant to the work to be carried out, then make a list and gather together all the parts and tools required. If a problem is encountered, seek advice from a parts specialist, or a dealer service department.

2 Intensive maintenance

1 If, from the time the vehicle is new, the routine maintenance schedule is followed closely, and frequent checks are made of fluid levels and high-wear items, as suggested throughout this Manual, the engine will be kept in relatively good running condition, and the need for additional work will be minimised.
2 It is possible that there will be times when the engine is running poorly due to the lack of regular maintenance. This is even more likely if a used vehicle, which has not received regular and frequent maintenance checks, is purchased. In such cases, additional work may need to be carried out, outside of the regular maintenance intervals.
3 If engine wear is suspected, a compression test will provide valuable information regarding the overall performance of the main internal components. Such a test can be used as a basis to decide on the extent of the work to be carried out. If, for example, a compression test indicates serious internal engine wear, conventional maintenance as described in this Chapter will not greatly improve the performance of the engine, and may prove a waste of time and money, unless extensive overhaul work is carried out first.
4 The following series of operations are those most often required to improve the performance of a generally poor-running engine:

Primary operations

a) Clean, inspect and test the battery
b) Check all the engine-related fluids
c) Check the condition and tension of the auxiliary drivebelt
d) Renew the spark plugs
e) Inspect the distributor cap and HT leads - as applicable
f) Check the condition of the air cleaner filter element, and renew if necessary
g) Renew the fuel filter (if fitted)
h) Check the condition of all hoses, and check for fluid leaks
i) Check the idle speed and mixture settings - as applicable

5 If the above operations do not prove fully effective, carry out the following secondary operations:

Secondary operations

a) Check the charging system
b) Check the ignition system
c) Check the fuel system
d) Renew the distributor cap and rotor arm - as applicable
f) Renew the ignition HT leads - as applicable

Every 1000 miles (1500 km) or monthly

3 Lock, hinge and latch mechanism check

Check the security and operation of all hinges, latches and locks.
Check the condition and operation of the tailgate struts, renewing them if either is leaking or is no longer able to support the tailgate securely when raised.

4 Seat belt check

1 Check the webbing of each belt for signs of fraying, cuts or other damage, pulling the belt out to its full extent to check its entire length. Check the operation of the buckles by fitting the belt tongue plate and pulling hard to ensure that it remains locked, then check the retractor mechanism (inertia reel only) by pulling out the belt to the halfway point and jerking hard. The mechanism must lock immediately to prevent any further unreeling but must allow free movement during normal driving.

2 Ensure that all belt mounting bolts are securely tightened. Note that the bolts are shouldered so that the belt anchor points are free to rotate.
3 If there is any sign of damage, or any doubt about a belt's condition, it must be renewed. If the vehicle has been involved in a collision any belts in use at the time must be renewed as a matter of course and all other belts should be checked carefully.
4 Use only warm water and non-detergent soap to clean the belts. Never use any chemical cleaners, strong detergents, dyes or bleaches. Keep the belts fully extended until they have dried naturally; do not apply heat to dry them.

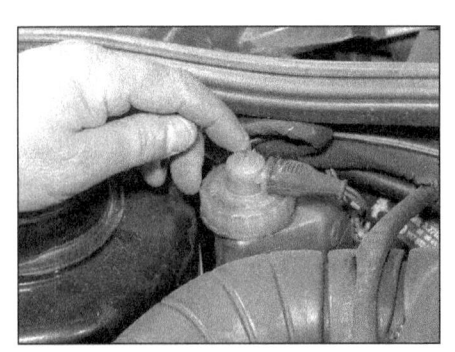

5 Brake check

1 Make sure that the vehicle does not pull to one side when braking and that the wheels do not lock prematurely when braking hard.
2 Check that there is no vibration through the steering when braking.
3 Check that the handbrake operates correctly without excessive movement of the lever and that it holds the vehicle stationary on a slope.
4 Check the brake warning device for correct operation by switching the ignition on and releasing the handbrake. Now press the contact on the reservoir filler cap down and get an assistant to check that the handbrake and dual circuit warning lamp light up **(see illustration)**.

5.4 Check brake fluid level warning device

Every 1000 miles or monthly

6 Fluid leakage and engine electrical system check

1 Open the bonnet and inspect the engine joint faces, gaskets and seals for any signs of coolant or oil leaks. Pay particular attention to the areas around the rocker cover, cylinder head, oil filter and sump joint faces. Bear in mind that over a period of time some very slight seepage from these areas is to be expected but what you are really looking for is any indication of a serious leak. Should a leak be found, renew the offending gasket or oil seal.

2 Carefully check the condition and security of all under bonnet coolant, fuel, power steering and brake pipes and hoses. Renew any hose which is cracked, swollen or deteriorated. Cracks will show up better if the hose is squeezed. Pay close attention to the hose clips that secure the hoses to the system components. Hose clips can pinch and puncture hoses, resulting in leaks. If wire type hose clips are used, it may be a good idea to replace them with screw-type clips **(see Haynes Hint)**.

HAYNES HiNT

A leak in the cooling system will usually show up as white or rust coloured deposits on the area adjoining the leak

3 Check the condition of all exposed wiring harnesses. Ensure that all cable-ties are in place and in good condition. Ties which are broken or missing can lead to chafing of the wiring which could cause serious problems in the future.

4 Wipe away any dirt which has accumulated on the outside of the alternator and check that its cable connector is pushed firmly onto its terminals.

5 Clean the ignition system HT and LT leads by wiping along their length with a fuel-moistened cloth. Inspect each lead for damage and renew if defective in any way. Ensure that all lead connections are secure and where applicable, protected **(see illustration)**.

6 Check that all HT and LT leads are correctly routed and clear of moving or hot engine components.

7 Any corroded HT or LT lead connection

6.5 Ensure all HT lead connections are secure

must be cleaned. A smear of petroleum jelly (not grease) applied to the cleaned connection will help to prevent further corrosion.

8 Check the transmission for obvious oil leaks and investigate and rectify any problems found.

9 Where accessible, inspect the fuel filler neck for punctures, cracks and other damage. Sometimes a rubber filler neck or connecting hose will leak due to loose retaining clamps or deteriorated rubber.

7 Battery electrolyte level check

1 A "maintenance-free" (sealed for life) battery is standard equipment on all vehicles covered by this Manual. Although this type of battery has many advantages over the older refillable type and should never require the addition of distilled water, it should still be routinely checked. The electrolyte level can be seen through the battery's translucent case and must be between the MINIMUM and MAXIMUM level marks. Although it should not alter in normal use, if the level has lowered (for example, due to electrolyte having boiled away as a result of overcharging) it is permissible to gently prise up the cell cover(s) and to top-up the level.

2 If a conventional battery has been fitted as a replacement, the electrolyte level of each cell should be checked and, if necessary, topped up until the separators are just covered. On some batteries the case is translucent and incorporates MINIMUM and MAXIMUM level marks. The check should be made more often if the vehicle is operated in high ambient temperature conditions.

3 Top-up the electrolyte level using distilled or de-ionised water **(see illustrations)**.

HAYNES HiNT *If regular topping-up becomes necessary and the battery case is not fractured, the battery is being overcharged and the voltage regulator and/or alternator will have to be checked.*

8 Air conditioning system check

During winter months, operate the air conditioner for a few minutes each week to keep the system in good order.

Check that the condenser is free of dirt and insects. If necessary, clean it either by rinsing with a cold water hose or by blowing it clean with an air hose. Use a soft bristle brush to assist removal of dirt jammed in the condenser fins.

9 Fuel system control linkage check

Check all parts of the fuel system control linkage for free movement throughout its complete operating range.

Clean all linkage joints and then lubricate with a light machine oil.

10 Light, direction indicator and horn check

Check that the horn and all vehicle lights are functioning correctly. Renew any defective bulbs.

The headlights and (where applicable) the foglights should be in correct alignment.

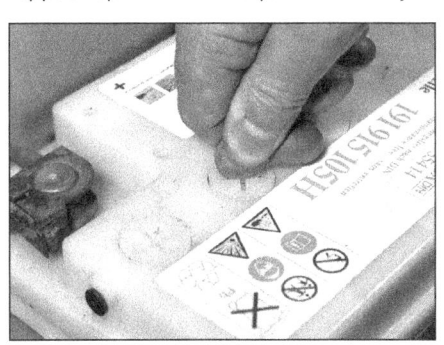

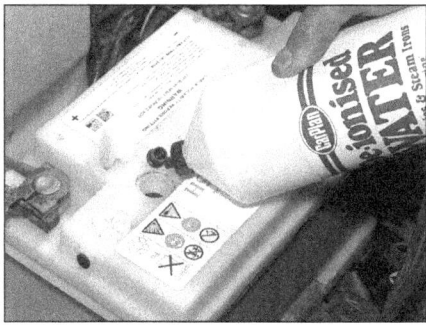

7.3a Remove battery filler caps . . .

7.3b . . . and top up electrolyte level using distilled or de-ionised water

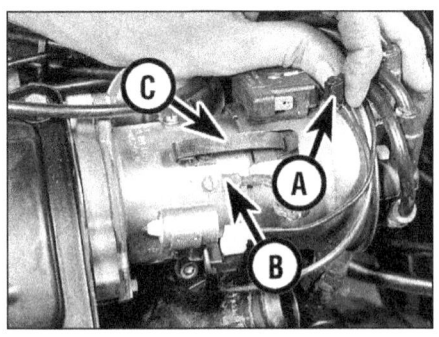

1•12 Maintenance procedures

11.1 Disconnect LT lead (A) earth strap (B) and release securing clips (C)

11.2 Withdraw distributor cap and screen ring

11.3 Pull off the rotor arm

Every 5000 miles (7500 km) or 6 months

11 Contact breaker point check

1 Disconnect the LT lead from the terminal block on the screening ring, then the earth strap spade connector on the distributor body **(see illustration)**.
2 Release the two retaining clips and withdraw the distributor cap, complete with screen ring, from the distributor **(see illustration)**.
3 Pull off the rotor arm and remove the dust cover **(see illustration)**.
4 Using a screwdriver, prise open the points and inspect the condition of their faces **(see illustration)**. If they are pitted and discoloured, remove them and dress them using emery tape or a grindstone whilst ensuring that their surfaces are flat and parallel. If the points are worn excessively, renew them. If the points are in good condition, then check their adjustment.

11.4 Contact breaker points viewed through window in bearing plate (arrowed) - Ducellier

Every 10 000 miles (15 000 km) or 12 months

12 Valve clearance check

1.05 and 1.3 litre engines

1 Run the engine up to its normal operating temperature. Stop the engine and remove the valve cover.
2 Turn the engine until both cam peaks for No 1 cylinder are pointing upwards.
3 Insert a feeler blade of the correct thickness (specified "Warm" clearance) between the cam and cam follower. If the blade is not a firm sliding fit, proceed as follows:
4 Turn the adjustable ball-stud using an Allen key **(see illustration)**. The valves from the timing belt end of the engine are in the following order:
Inlet - Exhaust - Inlet - Exhaust - Inlet - Exhaust - Inlet - Exhaust
5 Repeat the procedure given in paragraphs 2 and 3 for the remaining valves. If the engine is rotated in its normal direction, adjust the valves of No 3 cylinder followed by No 4 cylinder and No 2 cylinder.
6 Refit the valve cover, together with a new gasket.

TOOL TiP

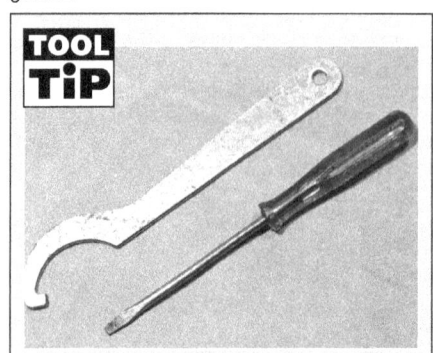

Ideally VW tools 2078 and 10.208 should be used to remove the valve shims, but we managed quite well with these tools; a small electrician's screwdriver and a C-spanner which was just the right size to push the bucket down without pushing the tappet shim (ie pushing the rim down).

1.6 and 1.8 litre 8 valve engines

Note: *Ideally VW tools 2078 and 10.208 should be used to remove the valve shims, but alternatives can be used (see Tool Tip)*
Note: *The following procedure applies only to engines fitted with shim bucket tappets - that is, those manufactured before August, 1985*
7 Run the engine up to its normal operating temperature. Stop the engine and remove the valve cover.
8 Check each valve clearance in turn by rotating the engine so that the valve to be checked has the cam lobe facing upwards. In this position, the valve in question is fully closed and a feeler blade inserted between the heel of the cam lobe and the valve tappet shim within the tappet bucket will give the clearance present **(see illustration)**.

12.4 Adjusting a valve clearance - 1.05 and 1.3 litre

12.8 Checking a valve clearance - 1.6 and 1.8 litre

Every 10 000 miles or 12 months

9 The engine will turn over more easily if the spark plugs are removed. Do not rotate the engine by turning the camshaft sprocket as this will stretch the timing belt. Use the alternator drivebelt (V-belt) or jack up one front wheel and with the engine in gear rotate the roadwheel. Do not turn the engine with any of the shims removed, otherwise the camshaft may foul the rim at the top of the bucket.

10 Repeat this measurement for all valves in turn and then compare the measurements with those specified ("Warm" clearance).

11 Make a table of the actual clearances and then calculate the error from those specified. Suppose on No 1 exhaust valve, the measured clearance is 0.15 mm. It is 0.3 mm too small so it must be adjusted and a shim 0.3 mm thinner fitted instead of the present one. As the shims are in steps of 0.05 mm variation, the required shim can be selected once the size of the shim at present installed is known. If you have dismantled and reassembled the head, then you know the size etched on the back of the shim but if you do not, then the shim must be removed to find out.

12 With the cam turned to give maximum clearance, the tappet is pushed down against the valve springs while the shim is levered out and removed by the VW tool or a screwdriver. Be careful, because if the spanner slips when the shim is halfway out, the shim will fly out sharply (see illustration).

13 Once all the shim sizes are known, a table may be constructed and the sizes of the new shims required may be calculated. Going back to the example, if the present shim is marked 3.60 then one marked 3.30 is required. Bucket

12.12 Removing a tappet bucket shim - 1.6 and 1.8 litre

shims are available in 26 different thicknesses which increase in increments of 0.05 mm, from 3.00 mm to 4.25 mm.

14 As it is unlikely that you will have the required shims readily available, it will be necessary to wait until they have been obtained before the tappets can be adjusted.

15 When inserting the shims, the thickness etching faces should be facing downwards.

16 Once the correct clearances have been achieved, refit the spark plugs and the valve cover.

13 Alternator, power steering pump and air conditioner compressor drivebelt(s) check

1 Check all drivebelts along their full length for cracks, splitting, fraying or damage. Check also for signs of glazing (shiny patches) and for separation of the belt plies. Renew the belt if worn or damaged.

> **HAYNES HiNT** *Always recheck the tension of a new drivebelt after the engine has been run for ten minutes.*

Alternator

Pre 1985

2 Depress the alternator drivebelt firmly with a finger midway between the alternator and crankshaft pulleys (see illustration). The belt should deflect approximately 5.0 mm.

3 If a new drivebelt has been fitted, then initial adjustment should give a deflection of 2.0 mm. After a suitable running in period of about 500 miles (750 km), belt adjustment should be rechecked and adjusted to deflect 5.0 mm.

4 To adjust the drivebelt, loosen the nut on the adjusting link and pivot bolt (see illustrations), then lever the alternator away from the cylinder block by using a lever at the pulley end of the alternator, until the belt is tensioned correctly.

5 Tighten the nut and bolt on completion of drivebelt adjustment.

From 1985

6 From early 1985, some models are fitted with a rack type alternator adjustment link (see illustration). To adjust drivebelt tension, first fully loosen the adjustment locknut and bolt, the link pivot bolt and the alternator pivot bolt, so that the alternator falls to one side under its own weight.

7 Using a socket and torque wrench on the adjustment bolt, apply a torque of 8 to 10 Nm (6 to 7 lbf ft), then secure the adjustment bolt in the set position by tightening its locknut to 35 Nm (26 lbf ft).

8 If the special VW tool is being used, then the adjustment bolt can now be tightened. If not, tighten the pivot bolt then remove the socket and immediately tighten the adjustment bolt, making sure that the alternator does not move.

9 Tighten the link pivot bolt and alternator pivot bolt.

Power steering pump

10 Loosen the power steering pump unit retaining nuts and bolts and the adjuster bolt locknut on the pump bracket.

11 Turn the tensioning bolt until the belt can be depressed approximately 10.0 mm under firm finger pressure midway between the crankshaft and pump pulleys.

12 When tension is correct, tighten the adjusting bolt locknut and the pump retaining nuts and bolts.

Air conditioner compressor

13 Drivebelt tension is adjusted by adding or subtracting shims from between the halves of the compressor pulley.

14 When correctly adjusted, the belt should give a deflection of 5 to 10 mm on its longest run.

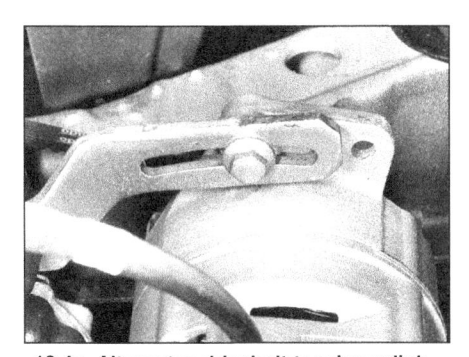

13.2 Checking alternator drivebelt tension

13.4a Alternator drivebelt tensioner link - 1.3 litre

13.4b Alternator drivebelt tensioner link - 1.8 litre

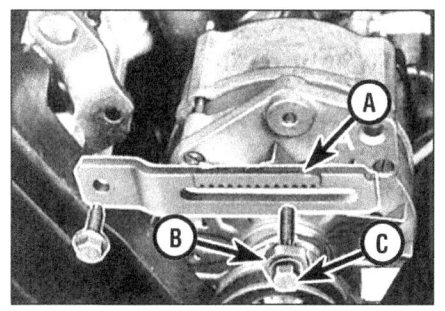

13.6 Rack type alternator drivebelt tensioner link (A) adjustment nut (B) and lockbolt (C)

1•14 Every 10 000 miles or 12 months

14 Antifreeze concentration check

Warning: *Wait until the engine is cold before checking antifreeze. Do not allow antifreeze to come in contact with your skin or painted surfaces of the vehicle. Rinse off spills immediately with plenty of water. Never leave antifreeze lying around in an open container or in a puddle in the driveway or on the garage floor. Children and pets are attracted by its sweet smell. Antifreeze is fatal if ingested.*

1 The concentration of antifreeze in the cooling system should be checked and made good if necessary. Most garages can do this check, or an instrument similar to a battery hydrometer can be purchased for making the check at home.

2 It is essential that an antifreeze mixture is retained in the cooling system at all times to act as a corrosion inhibitor and to protect the engine against freezing in winter months. The mixture should be made up from clean water with a low lime content (preferably rainwater) and a good quality ethylene glycol based antifreeze which contains a corrosion inhibitor and is suitable for use in aluminium engines.

3 The proportion of antifreeze to water must be 50/50 and give protection down to approximately -30ºC.

4 In climates which render frost protection redundant, it is still necessary to use a corrosion inhibitor in the cooling system. Suitable inhibitors should be available from a local VW agent or other reputable specialist.

15 Spark plug renewal

Note: *Some models are fitted with a modified ignition coil and single earth electrode spark plugs. This modified coil is identified by a grey (rather than green) sticker. Refer to the Servicing Specifications at the start of this Chapter for the recommended plug types. It is not permissible to use new plugs with an old coil, or vice versa.*

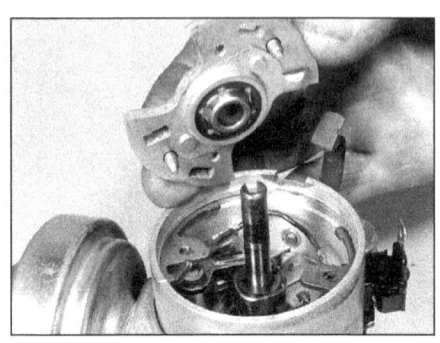

16.3 Removing the bearing plate - 1.05 and 1.3 litre

15.2 Hold the suppresser cap when pulling each HT lead from its spark plug

1 Where applicable, remove the air cleaner.
2 Pull the HT lead and fittings from each spark plug, identifying them for location if necessary (see illustration). On the 16V engine, the end fittings incorporate extensions, as the plugs are deeply recessed in the cylinder head.
3 Using compressed air or a vacuum cleaner, remove any debris from around the spark plugs.
4 Unscrew the plugs using a plug socket, preferably with a rubber insert to grip the plug.
5 Refitting is a reversal of removal. Tighten each spark plug to the specified torque (see Haynes Hint).

16 Contact breaker point renewal and adjustment

Renewal

1 Disconnect the LT lead from the terminal block on the screening ring, then the earth strap spade connector on the distributor body.
2 Release the two retaining clips and withdraw the distributor cap, complete with screen ring, from the distributor.
3 On 1.05 and 1.3 litre engines, remove the screws and withdraw the bearing plate (see illustration).
4 Disconnect the moving contact LT lead from the terminal then remove the retaining screw and withdraw the contact breaker set from the distributor.

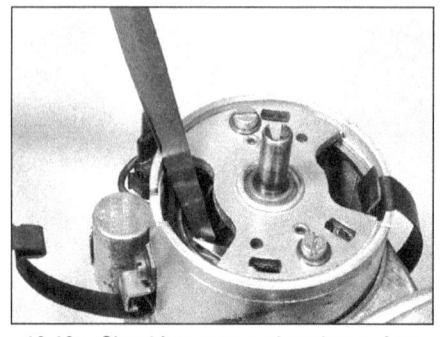

16.10a Checking contact breaker points gap

HAYNES HINT

It is very often difficult to insert spark plugs into their holes without cross-threading them. To avoid this possibility, fit a short length of 5/16 inch internal diameter rubber hose over the end of the spark plug. The flexible hose acts as a universal joint to help align the plug with the plug hole. Should the plug begin to cross-thread, the hose will slip on the spark plug, preventing thread damage to the aluminium cylinder head.

5 Wipe clean the contact breaker plate in the distributor and make sure that the contact surfaces of the new contact breaker set are clean. Lubricate the arm surface and moving contact pivot with a little multi-purpose grease. Use only a small amount, otherwise the contact points may become contaminated.
6 Fit the contact set on the baseplate and refit the retaining screw. Connect the LT lead to the terminal.
7 Refit the bearing plate and tighten the screws (where applicable).
8 Adjust the contact breaker points as follows.

Adjustment

9 Turn the engine with a spanner on the crankshaft pulley bolt until the moving contact point is fully open with its contact heel on the peak of one of the cam lobes.
10 Using a feeler blade, check that the gap between the two points is as specified. If not, loosen the fixed contact screw and reposition the fixed contact until the feeler blade is a firm sliding fit between the two points. In order to make a fine adjustment, slightly loosen the screw then position the screwdriver in the fixed contact notch and the two pips on the contact plate. With the gap adjusted, tighten the screw (see illustrations).
11 Using a dwell meter, check that the dwell angle of the contact points is as specified while spinning the engine on the starter. If not, readjust the points gap as necessary. Reduce the gap in order to increase the dwell angle, or increase the gap in order to reduce the dwell angle.
12 Clean the dust cover and rotor arm then refit them. Do not remove any metal from the rotor arm segment.

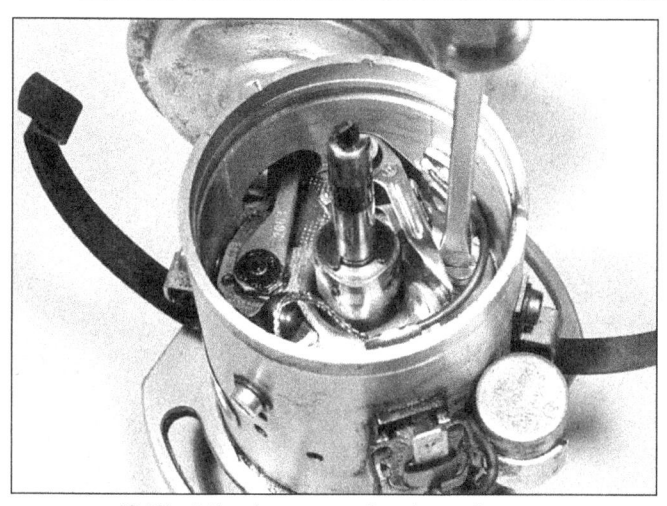

Every 10 000 miles or 12 months

16.10b Adjusting contact breaker points gap

16.10c Two pips and notch (arrowed) for inserting screwdriver when adjusting contact breaker points gap

13 Wipe clean the distributor cap and make sure that the carbon brush moves freely against the tension of the spring. Clean the metal segments in the distributor cap but do not scrape away any metal, otherwise the HT spark at the spark plugs will be reduced. Also clean the HT leads and coil tower.

14 Refit the distributor cap and interference screen.

15 Start the engine and check that the dwell angle is as specified, both at idling and higher engine speeds. A decrease in dwell angle at high engine speeds indicates a weak spring on the moving contact points.

16 After making any adjustment to the contact breaker points, check and adjust the ignition timing.

17 Ignition timing check

Contact breaker system

Note: Accurate ignition timing is only possible using a stroboscopic timing light, although on some models a DC sender unit is located on the top of the gearbox casing and may be used with a special VW tester to give an instant read-out. However, this tester will not normally be available to the home mechanic. For initial setting-up purposes, the test bulb method can be used but this must always be followed by the stroboscopic timing light method

Test bulb method

1 Remove No. 1 spark plug (crankshaft pulley end) and place a thumb over the aperture.

2 Turn the engine in the normal running direction (clockwise viewed from the crankshaft pulley end) until pressure is felt in No. 1 cylinder, indicating that the piston is commencing its compression stroke. Use a spanner on the crankshaft pulley bolt, or engage top gear and pull the vehicle forwards.

3 Continue turning the engine until the line on the crankshaft pulley is aligned with the pointer on the timing cover. If there are no marks on the timing cover, unscrew and remove the DC sensor or blanking plug from the top of the gearbox and align the timing mark (see *Specifications*) with the timing pointer **(see illustrations)**.

4 Remove the distributor cap and check that the rotor arm is pointing toward the No. 1 HT lead location in the cap.

5 Connect a 12 volt test bulb between the coil LT negative terminal and a suitable earthing point on the engine.

6 Loosen the distributor clamp retaining bolt.

7 Switch on the ignition. If the bulb is already lit, turn the distributor body slightly clockwise until the bulb goes out.

8 Turn the distributor body anti-clockwise until the bulb just lights up, indicating that the points have just opened. Tighten the clamp retaining bolt.

9 Switch off the ignition and remove the test bulb.

10 Refit the distributor cap and No. 1 spark plug and HT lead. Once the engine has been started, check the timing stroboscopically.

Stroboscopic timing light method

11 Run the engine until its normal operating temperature is reached.

12 On fuel injection engines, disconnect and plug the distributor vacuum hose.

13 If there are no timing marks on the timing cover and crankshaft pulley, unscrew and remove the TDC sensor or blanking plug from the top of the gearbox.

14 Connect the timing light in accordance with the manufacturer's instructions.

17.3a Crankshaft pulley mark (A) timing mark (B) and TDC mark (C) (timing cover removed) - 1.3 litre

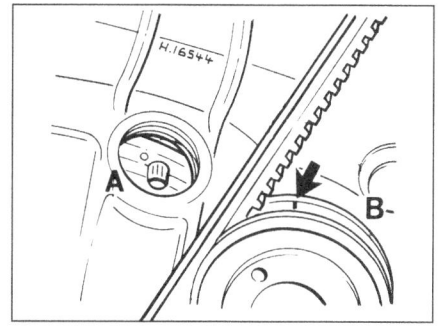

17.3b TDC timing marks - 1.6 and 1.8 litre
A Flywheel/driveplate
B Crankshaft pulley

17.3c Rotor arm aligned with TDC mark on distributor body – 1.6 and 1.8 litre

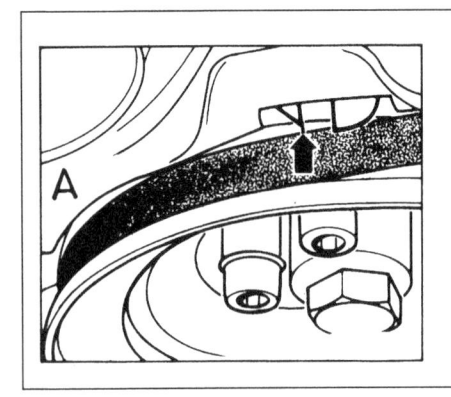

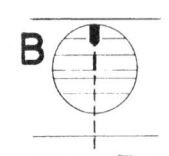

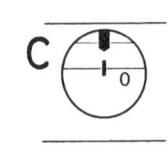

1•16 Every 10 000 miles or 12 months

17.17 Ignition timing marks

A 1.05 and 1.3 litre
B 1.6 and 1.8 litre (carburettor models)
C 1.8 litre (fuel injection models)

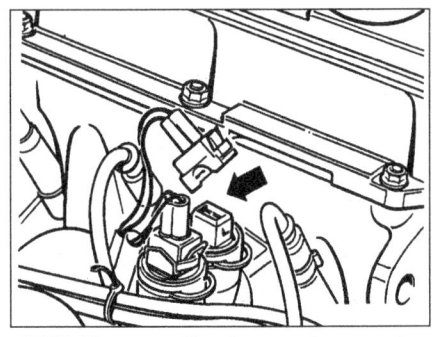

17.34 Disconnecting temperature sender wire

15 Connect a tachometer in accordance with the manufacturer's instructions.
16 Start the engine and run it at idling speed.
17 Point the timing light at the timing mark and pointer which should appear to be stationary and aligned. If adjustment is necessary (ie. the marks are not aligned), loosen the clamp retaining bolt and turn the distributor body to correct the ignition timing **(see illustration)**.
18 Gradually increase the engine speed while still pointing the timing light at the timing marks. The mark on the flywheel or pulley should appear to move opposite to the direction of rotation, proving that the centrifugal weights are operating correctly. If not, the centrifugal mechanism is faulty and the distributor should be renewed.
19 Accurate checking of the vacuum advance (and retard where fitted) requires the use of a vacuum pump and gauge. However, providing that the diaphragm unit is serviceable, the vacuum hose(s) firmly fitted, and the internal mechanism not seized, the system should work correctly.
20 Switch off the engine, remove the timing light and tachometer, and refit the vacuum hose (where applicable).

Transistorised systems

Note: *Accurate ignition timing is only possible using a stroboscopic timing light, although on some models a DC sender unit is located on the top of the gearbox casing and may be used with a special VW tester to give an instant read-out. However, this tester will not normally be available to the home mechanic*

TCI-H

21 Run the engine until its normal operating temperature is reached.
22 On fuel injection engines, disconnect and plug the distributor vacuum hose.
23 If there are no timing marks on the timing cover and crankshaft pulley, unscrew and remove the TDC sensor or blanking plug from the top of the gearbox.
24 Connect a timing light in accordance with the manufacturer's instructions.
25 Connect a tachometer in accordance with the manufacturer's instructions.
26 Start the engine and run it at idling speed.

27 Point the timing light at the timing mark and pointer which should appear to be stationary and aligned. If adjustment is necessary (ie. the marks are not aligned), loosen the clamp retaining bolt and turn the distributor body to correct the ignition timing **(see illustration 17.17)**.
28 Gradually increase the engine speed while still pointing the timing light at the timing marks. The mark on the flywheel or pulley should appear to move opposite to the direction of rotation, proving that the centrifugal weights are operating correctly. If not, the centrifugal mechanism is faulty and the distributor should be renewed.
29 Accurate checking of the vacuum advance (and retard where fitted) requires the use of a vacuum pump and gauge. However, providing that the diaphragm unit is serviceable, the vacuum hose(s) firmly fitted, and the internal mechanism not seized, the system should work correctly.
30 Switch off the engine, remove the timing light and tachometer, and refit the vacuum hose (where applicable).

Digifant

31 Run the engine to normal operating temperature, then switch off the ignition.
32 Connect a stroboscopic timing light to the engine.
33 Run the engine at idle speed.
34 Disconnect the wiring from the temperature sender **(see illustration)**.
35 Increase the engine speed to between 2000 and 2500 rpm, then point the timing light at the aperture over the flywheel. The timing marks should be aligned **(see illustration 17.17)**, but if not, loosen the clamp bolt, turn the distributor as required and retighten the bolt.
36 While checking the ignition timing, the opportunity should be taken to check the temperature and knock sensor controls.
37 With the temperature sender wiring disconnected, increase the engine speed to 2300 rpm and note the exact ignition timing. Hold the engine speed at 2300 rpm, then reconnect the wiring and check that the ignition timing advances by 30° ± 3° from the previously noted value.
38 If the ignition timing only advances about 20°, slacken the knock sensor securing bolt,

retighten to 20 Nm (15 lbf ft) and repeat the test. If there is no difference, check the associated wiring for an open-circuit, or as a last resort, renew the knock sensor.
39 If there is no advance in ignition timing, check the temperature sender wiring for an open-circuit. A fault is indicated in the Digifant control unit if there is no open-circuit.

18 Engine oil and filter renewal

Oil renewal

1 Before starting this procedure, gather together all necessary tools and materials. Ensure that you have plenty of clean rags and newspapers handy to mop up any spills. Ideally, the engine oil should be warm as it will drain better and more built-up sludge will be removed with it. Take care not to touch the exhaust or any other hot parts of the engine when working under the vehicle. To avoid any possibility of scalding and to protect yourself from possible skin irritants and other harmful contaminants in used engine oils, it is advisable to wear gloves when carrying out this work.
2 With the vehicle standing on level ground, position a suitable container under the sump drain plug **(see illustration)**. Remove the drain plug from the sump.
3 Allow some time for the old oil to drain, noting that it may be necessary to reposition the container as the flow of oil slows to a trickle. Work can be speeded-up by removing

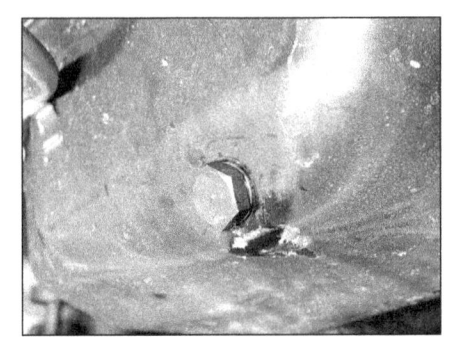

18.2 Sump drain plug

Every 10 000 miles or 12 months

18.13 Using a chain wrench to unscrew oil filter

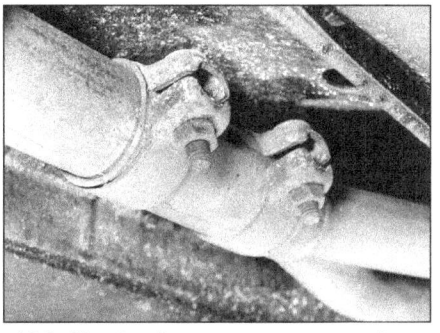

19.2 Check exhaust system connections for leaks and security

19.3 Check exhaust system mountings

the oil filter, as described below, while the oil is draining.

4 After all the oil has drained, wipe off the drain plug with a clean rag and on 1.6 and 1.8 litre models, renew the O-ring. Clean the area around the drain plug opening and refit the plug. Tighten the plug to the specified torque setting.
5 Depending on engine type, refer to the following sub Section and renew the oil filter.
6 Remove the oil container and all tools from under the vehicle.
7 Refill the engine with the specified type of oil. Pour in half the specified quantity of oil first, then wait a few minutes for the oil to drain to the sump. Continue adding oil a small quantity at a time until the level is up to the lower mark on the dipstick (see Weekly checks). Adding a further 1.0 litre will bring the level up to the upper mark on the dipstick.
8 Start the engine and run it for a few minutes while checking for leaks around the oil filter seal and the sump drain plug.
9 Switch off the engine and wait a few minutes for the oil to settle in the sump once more. With the new oil circulated and the filter now completely full, recheck the level on the dipstick and add more oil as necessary.
10 Dispose of the used engine oil safely.

Filter renewal

11 On 1.05 and 1.3 litre engines, the oil filter is located on the front of the engine beside the alternator.
12 On 1.6 and 1.8 litre engines, the oil filter is located on the side of the crankcase beneath the distributor. It is screwed onto a mounting bracket attached to the crankcase. On fuel injection models, an oil cooler is fitted between the mounting bracket and filter cartridge.
13 With the engine oil drained, place a suitable container beneath the filter then, using a suitable tool, unscrew the filter **(see illustration)**. Empty any oil in the old filter into the container and allow any residual oil to drain out of the engine.
14 Check the old filter to make sure that the rubber sealing ring has not stuck to the engine. If it has, then carefully remove it. Wipe clean the sealing face on the cylinder block.
15 Smear the sealing rubber on the new filter with clean engine oil, then fit and tighten the filter by hand only.

16 On completion, replenish the engine oil then wipe clean the filter body. When the engine is restarted, check around the filter joint for any signs of leakage.

19 Exhaust system check

1 With the exhaust system cold, check the complete system from the engine to the end of the tailpipe. Ideally the inspection should be carried out with the vehicle raised and supported on axle stands (see "Jacking and vehicle support") to permit unrestricted access.
2 Check the exhaust pipes and connections for evidence of leaks, severe corrosion and damage **(see illustration)**. Ensure that all brackets and mountings are in good condition and tight. Leakage at any of the joints or in other parts of the system will usually show up as a black sooty stain in the vicinity of the leak.
3 Rattles and other noises can often be traced to the exhaust system, especially the brackets and mountings **(see illustration)**. Try to move the pipes and silencers. If the components can come into contact with the body or suspension parts, secure the system with new mountings or if possible, separate the joints and twist the pipes as necessary to provide additional clearance.

20 Slow running adjustment

To check this adjustment, first determine which fuel system is fitted to the vehicle concerned and then refer to the appropriate Part of Chapter 4 for adjustment of that particular system.

21 Clutch operation check

1 Check that the clutch pedal moves smoothly and easily through its full travel and that the clutch itself functions correctly, with no trace of slip or drag.

2 If excessive effort is required to operate the clutch, check first that the cable is correctly routed and undamaged, then remove the pedal to ensure that its pivot is properly greased before suspecting a fault in the cable itself. If the cable is worn or damaged, or if its adjusting mechanism is no longer effective, then it must be renewed.
3 Refer to Chapter 6 and on those models where it is possible, check that the clutch is correctly adjusted.

22 Gearbox oil level check

Note: *Gearbox oil can foam when hot and give a false level reading. Allow the gearbox to cool before checking the oil level.*

1 The gearbox oil level must be checked before the vehicle is driven, or at least 5 minutes after the engine has been switched off. If the oil is checked immediately after driving, some of the oil will remain distributed around the gearbox components, resulting in an inaccurate level reading.

084 and 085 gearboxes

2 Position the vehicle on level ground.
3 The oil filler/level plug is difficult to reach using the normal hexagon key and it will be much easier to use a nut and bolt as shown **(see illustration)** together with a conventional spanner. Instead of welding a single nut on the bolt, two nuts may be tightened against each other using thread-locking fluid.

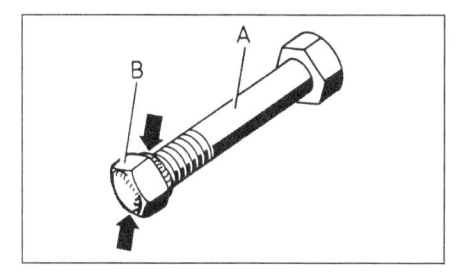

22.3 Nut and bolt welded together to make oil level plug removal tool - 084 gearbox

A Bolt M10 x 100 mm   B Welded nut
Arrows show area of weld

Every 10 000 miles or 12 months

22.4 Gearbox filler/level plug location (arrowed) - 084 gearbox

22.10 Using a key to unscrew level plug - 020 5-speed gearbox

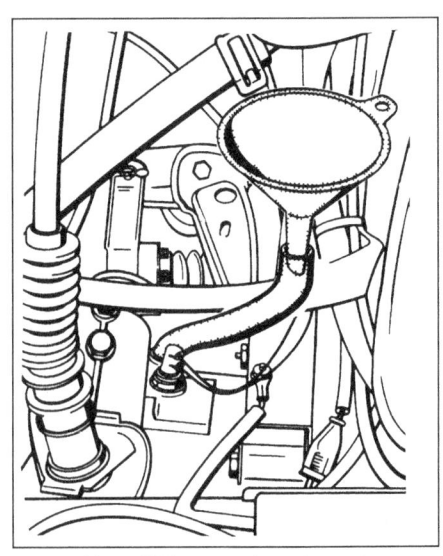

22.11 Filling gearbox through speedometer driveshaft hole - early 020 5-speed gearbox

4 Wipe clean the area around the filler/level plug, then unscrew the plug and clean it. Discard the sealing washer **(see illustration)**.

5 The oil level should reach the lower edge of the filler/level hole. A certain amount of oil will have gathered behind the plug and will trickle out when it is removed - this does not necessarily indicate that the level is correct. To ensure that a true level is established, wait until the initial trickle has stopped, then add oil as necessary until a trickle of new oil can be seen emerging. The level will be correct when the flow ceases. Use only good quality oil of the specified type.

6 If the gearbox has been overfilled so that oil flows out as soon as the filler/level plug is removed, check that the vehicle is completely level (front-to-rear and side-to-side) and allow the surplus to drain off into a suitable container.

7 When the oil level is correct, fit a new sealing washer and refit the filler/level plug, tightening it to the specified torque wrench setting. Clean away any spilt oil.

020 5-speed gearbox

8 Note the basic instructions given for the 084 and 085 gearboxes whilst taking into account the following information.

9 This gearbox was originally designed for an engine/gearbox unit without any inclination. When fitted to the models covered in this Manual a 2° inclination to the left exists, therefore an accurate check cannot be made with the vehicle on ground level.

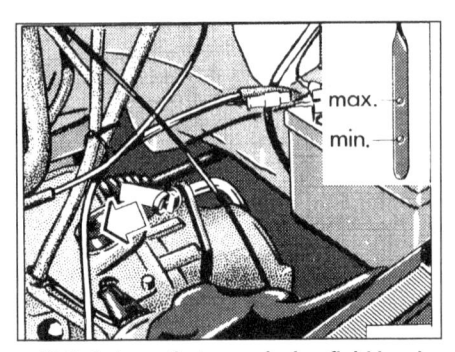

10 When checking the oil level with the vehicle on level ground, unscrew the level plug **(see illustration)** and if there is a thick flow of oil immediately refit the plug. If there is no flow, first top-up to the bottom of the hole then refit the plug.

11 Now add a further 0.5 litre of oil through the speedometer driveshaft hole **(see illustration)**.

12 From October 1987, the oil level plug hole has been relocated 7.0 mm higher than the one on earlier models. Consequently all filling and topping up can be carried out through the oil level hole. Removal of the speedometer drive cable is no longer necessary for final topping up.

23 Automatic transmission fluid level check

1 Check the transmission fluid level with the engine warm and idling, with the selector lever in position N (neutral) and the handbrake firmly applied.

2 With the vehicle on a level surface, withdraw the level dipstick and wipe it clean with a lint-free cloth. Reinsert it and withdraw again. The level must be between the two marks on the dipstick **(see illustration)**. If not, top-up the level through the dipstick tube using the specified fluid.

3 If much topping-up is required, carry out a check for leaks. If no external leaks are visible, check the final drive oil level. If this is found to be too high, it is probable that the transmission fluid is leaking internally into the final drive casing and if this is the case, it must be attended to without delay by your VW dealer.

4 The difference in quantity of fluid between the maximum and minimum marks on the fluid level dipstick is 0.4 litre.

5 On completion, insert the dipstick and switch off the engine.

23.2 Automatic transmission fluid level dipstick - remove in direction of arrow

24 CV joint and boot check

1 With the vehicle raised and supported on axle stands (see "*Jacking and vehicle support*"), turn the steering onto full lock then slowly rotate each roadwheel in turn to facilitate inspection of the CV joints and boots.

2 Inspect the condition of each CV joint boot while squeezing it to open out any folds **(see illustration)**. Check for signs of cracking, splits or deterioration of the rubber which may allow grease to escape and lead to the entry of water and grit into the joint. Also check the security and condition of the boot retaining clips. If any damage or deterioration is found, the boot should be renewed.

3 At the same time, check the general condition of the CV joints themselves by first holding the driveshaft and attempting to rotate the roadwheel. Repeat this check by holding the inner joint and attempting to rotate the driveshaft. Any appreciable movement indicates wear in the joints, in the driveshaft splines, or a loose driveshaft nut.

24.2 Inspect condition of each CV joint boot

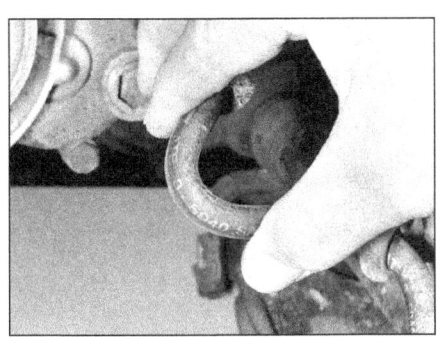

Every 10 000 miles or 12 months

25.3a Bend each brake hose to check for cracks

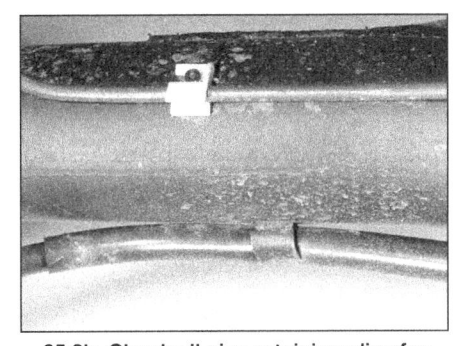

25.3b Check all pipe retaining clips for security

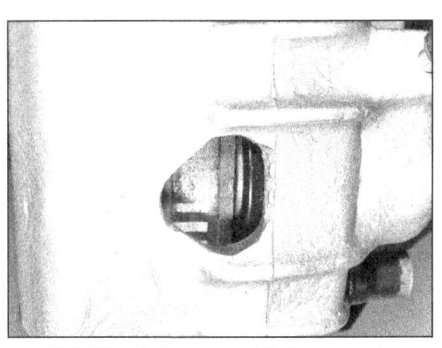

26.1 Check brake pad lining wear by viewing through inspection aperture

25 Fuel and brake line, hose and union check

> **Warning:** Do not drive the vehicle until necessary repair work has been carried out on damaged fuel and brake lines.

1 It is essential for this check to raise the vehicle sufficiently enough to allow a complete uninterrupted view of its underside.
2 Working methodically from one end of the vehicle to the other, carry out the following tasks.
3 Clean the rigid brake lines and flexible hoses, at the same time checking them for damage, leakage, chafing and cracks. If the coating on the rigid pipes is damaged or if rusting is apparent, then they must be renewed. Check all pipe retaining clips for security and clean away any accumulation of dirt **(see illustrations)**.
4 Similarly, inspect all hoses and metal pipes leading away from the fuel tank. Pay particular attention to the vent pipes and hoses which often loop up around the tank filler neck and can become blocked or crimped.
5 Inspect the underside of the fuel tank for punctures, scrapes and other damage.
6 If damage or deterioration is discovered to either system, do not drive the vehicle until the necessary repair work has been carried out.

26 Brake pad and rear shoe lining check

Note: *VW recommend that operation of the brake pressure regulator is checked by one of their garages at the same interval that the disc pads and rear brake linings are checked for wear*

Brake pads

1 Both front and rear brake pad lining wear can be checked by viewing through a hole in the wheel rim **(see illustration)**. Use a mirror placed on the inside of the wheel. The use of a torch may also be necessary.
2 If pad thickness is less than the minimum amount specified, renew the pads as a set.

Rear brake shoes

3 Jack up the rear of the vehicle and support it on axle stands (see "*Jacking and vehicle support*"). Chock the front wheels.
4 Working beneath the vehicle, remove the rubber plugs from the front of the backplates and check with a torch that the linings are not worn below the minimum thickness specified. On completion, refit the plugs.

27 Headlight beam alignment check

Single unit

Caution: It is recommended that headlamp beam alignment is checked by a VW garage using modern beam setting equipment. However, in an emergency, the following procedure will provide an acceptable light pattern.

1 With its tyres correctly inflated, position the vehicle on a level surface, approximately 10 metres in front of a flat wall.
2 Draw a horizontal line on the wall or door at headlamp centre height. Draw a vertical line corresponding to the centre line of the vehicle. Now measure off a point either side of this, on the horizontal line, corresponding with the headlamp centres.

3 Switch on the main beam and check that the areas of maximum illumination coincide with the headlamp centre marks on the wall. If not, turn the upper cross-head adjustment screw to adjust the beam laterally and/or the lower screw to adjust the beam vertically **(see illustration)**.

Twin unit

4 On models with twin headlamps, the inner lamps are adjusted laterally with the lower adjustment screw and vertically with the upper screw.

28 Steering gear check

1 Raise the front of the vehicle and securely support it on axle stands (see "*Jacking and vehicle support*").
2 Visually inspect the balljoint dust covers and the steering gear rubber gaiters for splits, chafing or deterioration **(see illustration)**. Any damage to these components will cause loss of lubricant together with dirt and water entry, resulting in rapid deterioration of the balljoints or steering gear.
3 Grasp the roadwheel at the 9 and 3 o'clock positions and try to rock it. Any movement felt may be caused by wear in the hub bearings or track rod balljoints. If a balljoint is worn, the visual movement will be obvious. If the inner joint is suspect, it can be felt by placing a hand over the steering gear rubber gaiter and

27.3 Turn adjustment screws (arrowed) to adjust headlamp beam alignment

28.2 Inspect balljoint dust covers

1•20 Every 10 000 miles or 12 months

gripping the track rod. If the wheel is now rocked, movement will be felt at the inner joint if wear has taken place.

4 With the vehicle standing on its wheels, have an assistant turn the steering wheel back and forth about an eighth of a turn each way. There should be very little, if any, lost movement between the steering wheel and the roadwheels. If this is not the case, closely observe the joints and mountings previously described, but in addition check for wear of the steering column universal joint and the steering gear itself.

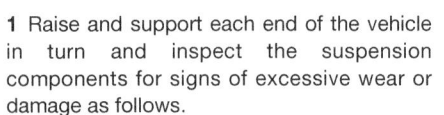

29 Suspension check

1 Raise and support each end of the vehicle in turn and inspect the suspension components for signs of excessive wear or damage as follows.
2 Inspect the suspension balljoints for wear and the dust covers for any signs of splits or deterioration. Renew if necessary.
3 Check the track control arm (wishbone) and anti-roll bar mounting/pivot bushes for signs of excessive wear and/or deterioration and again renew if necessary.
4 Check the shock absorbers for signs of leakage and the suspension to subframe and body mountings for signs of corrosion (see illustration).

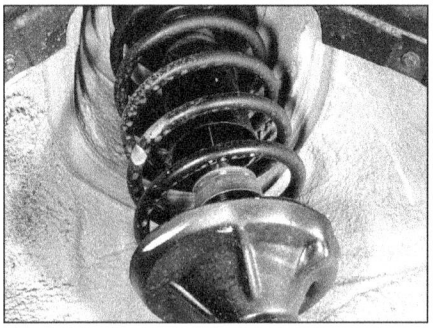

29.4 Check shock absorbers for leakage

30 Hinge and catch lubrication

1 Lubricate the door, bonnet and tailgate hinges with a little light machine oil.
2 Lubricate also the bonnet release mechanism and door, bonnet and tailgate locks. Do not lubricate the steering lock.
3 At the same time lubricate the door check straps with a little multi-purpose grease.

31 Vehicle underbody check

Note: *Steam-cleaning is available at many garages for the purpose of removing any accumulation of oily grime from beneath a vehicle.*

1 Raise the vehicle sufficiently enough to allow a complete uninterrupted view of its underside.
2 Wash the vehicle underbody down as thoroughly as possible.
3 Carefully check all underbody paintwork, looking closely for chips or scratches. Check with particular care vulnerable areas such as the front spoiler and around the wheel arches. Any damage to the paintwork must be rectified to prevent further corrosion.
4 If a chip or light scratch is found that is recent and still free from rust, it can be touched-up using the appropriate paint. More serious damage or rusted stone chips can be repaired as described in Chapter 11. If damage or corrosion is so severe that a panel must be renewed, seek professional advice as soon as possible.
5 The wax-based underbody protective coating should now be inspected to ensure that it is unbroken and any damage to the coating repaired using undershield. If any body panels are disturbed for repair or renewed, do not forget to replace the coating and to inject wax into door panels, sills, box sections etc. so as to maintain the level of protection provided by the manufacturer.
6 Check carefully that all wheel arch liners and underwing shields are in place and securely fastened.
7 Finally, check that all door and ventilator opening drain holes and pipes are completely clear so that water is allowed to drain.

Every 20 000 miles (30 000 km) or 24 months

32 Air cleaner element renewal

Carburettor models

1.05 and 1.3 litre engines

1 Release the spring clips securing the air cleaner lid and remove the lid (see illustration).
2 Cover the carburettor entry port to prevent any dirt entering it when the element is lifted out. Remove the element (see illustration). Wipe the inside of the air cleaner with a moist rag to remove all dust and dirt and then remove the covering from the entry port.
3 Fit the new element. Clean the cover, position it in place, then clip it down whilst ensuring that the two arrows are aligned.

1.6 and 1.8 litre engines

4 Unclip and remove the cover then withdraw the element. Note that on some models, it is necessary to first loosen the front mounting nut (see illustrations).
5 Clean the interior of the air cleaner with a fuel-moistened cloth, then wipe it dry.
6 Fit the new element in the reverse order of removal.

Fuel-injected models

7 Release the spring clips securing the air cleaner cover and separate the cover from the airflow meter (see illustration).

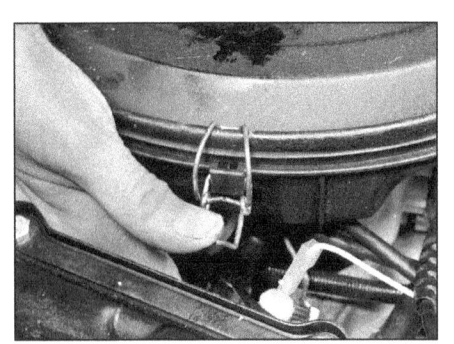

32.1 Unclip the air cleaner lid . . .

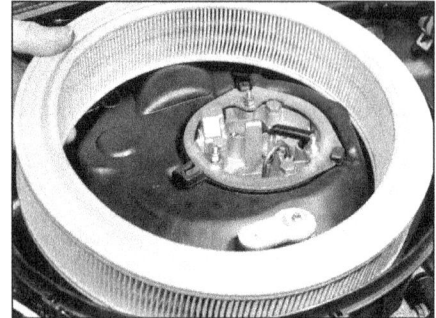

32.2 . . . and remove the element - 1.3 litre, carburettor

32.4a Unclip air cleaner cover . . .

Every 20 000 miles or 24 months 1•21

32.4b ... loosen front mounting nut ...

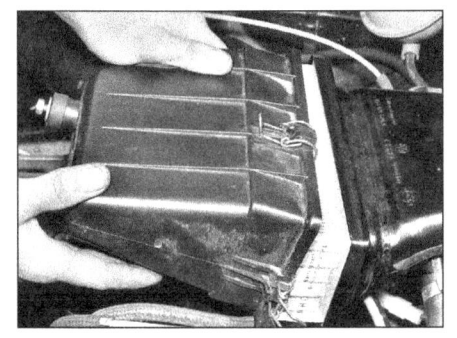

32.4c ... then remove cover to expose element - 1.6 and 1.8 litre, carburettor

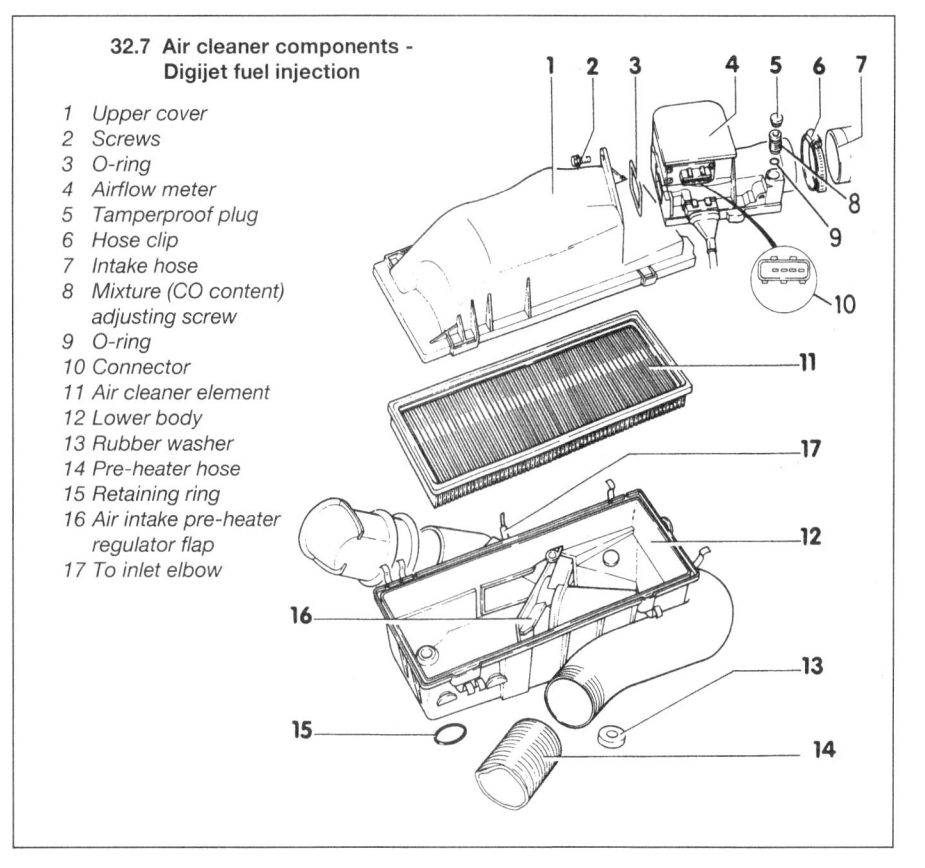

32.7 Air cleaner components - Digijet fuel injection

1. Upper cover
2. Screws
3. O-ring
4. Airflow meter
5. Tamperproof plug
6. Hose clip
7. Intake hose
8. Mixture (CO content) adjusting screw
9. O-ring
10. Connector
11. Air cleaner element
12. Lower body
13. Rubber washer
14. Pre-heater hose
15. Retaining ring
16. Air intake pre-heater regulator flap
17. To inlet elbow

8 Withdraw the element from the housing.
9 Wipe clean the inside of the cover.
10 Fit the new element and secure the cover by pressing the clips home.

33 Fuel filter renewal

Carburettor models

1 To remove the in-line filter, remove its pipe retaining clips, disconnect the pipes and extract the filter **(see illustration)**. If necessary, replace the original crimped type clips with screw type ones.
2 Fit the new filter in a horizontal position with its arrow facing the flow of fuel towards the fuel pump. Ensure that the pipe retaining clips are properly tightened then start the engine and check carefully for any signs of fuel leaks from the pipe ends.
3 Dispose safely of the old filter, it will be highly inflammable and may explode if thrown on a fire.

Fuel-injected models

4 The fuel filter is mounted on the inboard side of the pump reservoir on the underside of the vehicle at the rear just forward of the fuel tank **(see illustration)**.
5 Disconnect the battery earth lead.
6 Raise the vehicle at the rear and support it on axle stands (see "Jacking and vehicle support").
7 At the forward end of the filter, undo the fuel accumulator hose union bolt and detach the union whilst collecting the washer each side of it.
8 At the rear end of the filter, detach the fuel supply hose (to the metering distributor) by undoing the union bolt. Collect the washer each side of the union.
9 Loosen the filter retaining clamp and withdraw the filter.
10 Fitting the new filter is a reversal of the removal procedure. Renew the union washers and tighten the union bolts to the specified torque. Check that the arrow on the filter points in the direction of fuel flow.
11 On completion, check for any signs of fuel leakage with the engine running.
12 Dispose safely of the old filter, it will be highly inflammable and may explode if thrown on a fire.

34 Sunroof guide rail cleaning and lubrication

Open the sunroof and wipe clean its guide rails. Coat each rail very lightly with grease, ensuring that none finds its way onto the interior trim.

Check that the sunroof opens and closes smoothly throughout its complete operating range.

33.1 In-line fuel filter - 1.05 and 1.3 litre, carburettor

33.4 Fuel filter unit clamp (A) hose to accumulator (B) and hose to metering valve (C) - K-Jetronic fuel injection

1•22 Maintenance procedures

Every 30 000 miles (45 000 km)

35 Automatic transmission and final drive fluid renewal

Note: *Under extreme operating conditions, automatic transmission fluid should be changed at more frequent intervals.*

Automatic transmission

1 Whenever the automatic transmission fluid is renewed, the oil pan and strainer must also be cleaned (where applicable). First jack up the vehicle and support it on axle stands (see "*Jacking and vehicle support*").
2 Remove the transmission drain plug and drain the fluid into a container. If there is no drain plug, loosen the oil pan front bolts then unscrew the rear bolts and lower the pan in order to drain the fluid **(see illustration)**. Take care to avoid scalding if the engine has just been run.
3 Unbolt and remove the pan from the transmission and remove the gasket. Clean the inside of the pan.
4 Unbolt the strainer cover and remove the strainer and gasket.
5 Clean the strainer and cover and dry thoroughly.
6 Refit the cover and strainer, together with a new gasket, and tighten the bolts to the specified torque.
7 Refit the pan, together with a new gasket, and tighten the securing bolts to the specified torque. Lower the vehicle.
8 Initially, refill the transmission with 2.5 litres of the specified fluid, then restart the engine. Check that the handbrake is fully applied then move the gear selector lever through the full range of gears finishing at N. With the engine still idling, check the fluid level on the dipstick. The fluid level should at least be visible on the dipstick. If not, add the minimum amount of fluid necessary to bring the level up to be visible on the tip of the dipstick.
9 Take the vehicle on a short drive to warm-up the fluid in the transmission then recheck the fluid level. Top-up if necessary. Do not overfill with fluid or the excess will have to be drained off.

Final drive unit

10 To check the oil level in the final drive unit, the vehicle will need to be over an inspection pit or raised and supported on a level position on axle stands (see "*Jacking and vehicle support*") for access to the filler/level plug **(see illustration)**.
11 Remove the plug and check that the oil is level with the bottom edge of the plug hole. If not, top-up the level through the plug hole then refit the plug. Lower the vehicle.

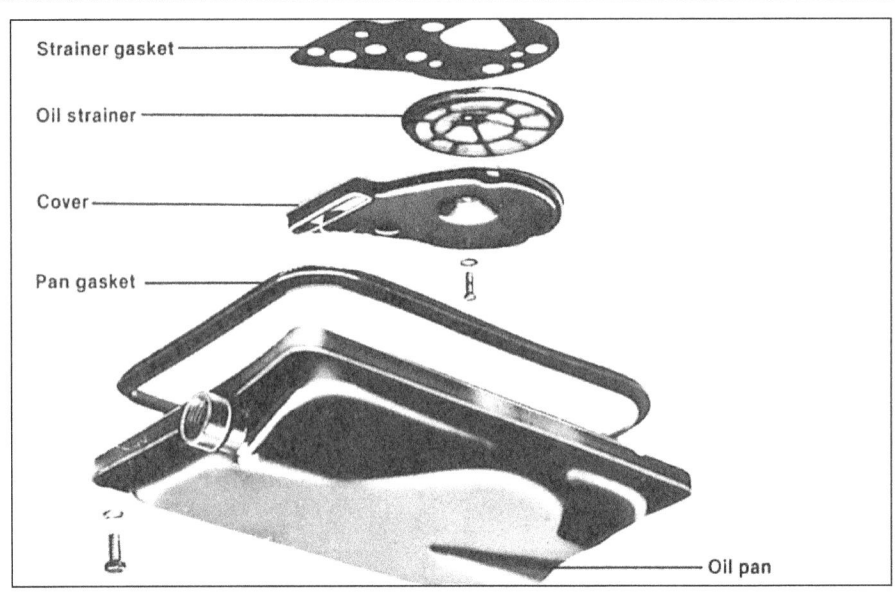

35.2 Automatic transmission oil pan and strainer

35.10 Final drive unit oil filler/level plug (arrowed)

Every 2 years

36 Brake fluid renewal

1 The procedure is similar to that described for bleeding of the hydraulic system in Chapter 9, except that the brake fluid reservoir should be emptied before starting by syphoning, using a clean poultry baster or similar. Also, allowance should be made for the old fluid to be expelled when bleeding a section of the circuit.
2 Working as described in Chapter 9, open the first bleed nipple in the sequence and pump the brake pedal gently until nearly all the old fluid has been emptied from the master cylinder reservoir. Top-up to the MAX level with new fluid and continue pumping until only the new fluid remains in the reservoir and new fluid can be seen emerging from the bleed nipple. Tighten the nipple and top the reservoir level up to the MAX level line.
3 Old hydraulic fluid is invariably much darker in colour than the new, making it easy to distinguish the two.
4 Work through all the remaining nipples in the sequence until new fluid can be seen at all of them. Be careful to keep the master cylinder reservoir topped up to above the MIN level at all times or air may enter the system and greatly increase the length of the task.
5 When the operation is complete, check that all nipples are securely tightened and that their dust caps are refitted. Wash off all traces of spilt fluid and recheck the master cylinder reservoir fluid level.
6 Check the operation of the brakes before taking the vehicle on the road.

Every 40 000 miles (60 000 km)

37 Timing belt renewal

Refer to the appropriate Part of Chapter 2 for the particular engine type concerned.

Chapter 2 Part A:
Engine repair procedures - 1.05 and 1.3 litre pre August 1985

Contents

Camshaft - examination and renovation	27
Camshaft - refitting	35
Camshaft - removal	10
Crankshaft and bearings - examination and renovation	21
Crankshaft and main bearings - refitting	29
Crankshaft and main bearings - removal	18
Crankshaft oil seals - renewal	14
Cylinder block/crankcase - examination and renovation	22
Cylinder head - dismantling and overhaul	11
Cylinder head - reassembly	34
Cylinder head - refitting	36
Cylinder head - removal	9
Engine dismantling - general information	7
Engine reassembly - general information	28
Engine - adjustments after major overhaul	41
Engine ancillary components - removal	8
Engine ancillary components and gearbox - refitting	39
Engine - refitting	40
Engine - removal	5
Engine/gearbox - separation	6
Examination and renovation - general information	20
Flywheel - examination and renovation	25
Flywheel - refitting	33
Flywheel - removal	13
General information	1
Major operation only possible after removal of engine from vehicle	3
Major operations possible with engine in vehicle	2
Method of engine removal	4
Oil filter - renewal	19
Oil pump - examination and renovation	24
Oil pump - refitting	31
Oil pump - removal	16
Pistons and connecting rods - examination and renovation	23
Pistons and connecting rods - refitting	30
Pistons and connecting rods - removal	17
Sump - refitting	32
Sump - removal	15
Timing belt and sprockets - examination and renovation	26
Timing belt and sprockets - refitting	37
Timing belt and sprockets - removal	12
Valve clearances - checking and adjustment	38

Degrees of difficulty

Easy, suitable for novice with little experience
Fairly easy, suitable for beginner with some experience
Fairly difficult, suitable for competent DIY mechanic
Difficult, suitable for experienced DIY mechanic
Very difficult, suitable for expert DIY or professional

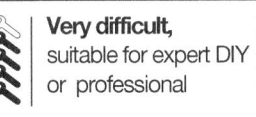

Specifications

General
Type	Four-cylinder in-line, water cooled, overhead camshaft
Code:	
1.05 litre	GN
1.3 litre	HK
Firing order	1-3-4-2 (No 1 at camshaft sprocket end)
Displacement:	
1.05 litre	1043 cc
1.3 litre	1272 cc
Bore:	
1.05 litre	75.0 mm
1.3 litre	75.0 mm
Stroke:	
1.05 litre	59.0 mm
1.3 litre	72.0 mm
Compression ratio:	
1.05 litre	9.5 to 1
1.3 litre	9.5 to 1
Compression pressure:	
New	8 to 10 bar
Minimum	7.0 bar
Maximum permissible difference between any two cylinders	3.0 bar

Crankshaft

Main journal:
  Standard diameter .... 54.0 mm
  Undersizes .... 53.75, 53.50 and 53.25 mm
Crankpin:
  Standard diameter .... 42 mm
  Journal undersizes .... 41.75, 41.50 and 41.25 mm
Endfloat:
  Maximum .... 0.20 mm
  Minimum .... 0.07 mm
Main bearing maximum running clearance .... 0.17 mm

Connecting rods

Big-end:
  Maximum running clearance .... 0.095 mm
  Maximum endfloat .... 0.40 mm

Pistons

Clearance in bore:
  Maximum .... 0.07 mm
  Minimum .... 0.03 mm
Diameter:
  Standard .... 74.98 mm
  Oversize:
    1st oversize .... 75.23 mm
    2nd oversize .... 75.48 mm
    3rd oversize .... 75.98 mm
Wear limit (10 mm from base/ right angles to pin) .... 0.04 mm

Piston rings

Maximum clearance in groove. .... 0.15 mm
End gap:
  Compression rings .... 0.30 to 0.45 mm
  Oil scraper ring .... 0.25 to 0.40 mm

Gudgeon pin

Fit in piston .... Push fit at 60°C

Cylinder head

Maximum allowable face distortion .... 0.1 mm

Camshaft

Run-out at centre bearing .... 0.02 mm
Endfloat .... 0.15 mm

Valves

Seat angle .... 45°
Head diameter:
  Inlet .... 34.0 mm
  Exhaust .... 28.1 mm
Stem diameter:
  Inlet .... 7.97 mm
  Exhaust .... 7.95 mm
Standard overall length:
  Inlet .... 110.5 mm
  Exhaust .... 110.5 mm

Valve guides

Maximum valve rock (stem flush with guide):
  Inlet .... 1.0 mm
  Exhaust .... 1.3 mm

Valve timing

Nil valve clearance at 1.0 mm valve lift
1.05 litre:
  Inlet opens .... 9° ATDC
  Inlet closes .... 13° ABDC
  Exhaust opens .... 15° BBDC
  Exhaust closes .... 11° BTDC

1.3 litre:
  Inlet opens .... 3° BTDC
  Inlet closes .... 38° ABDC
  Exhaust opens .... 41° BBDC
  Exhaust closes .... 3° BTDC

Valve clearances
Warm:
  Inlet .... 0.15 to 0.20 mm
  Exhaust .... 0.25 to 0.30 mm
Cold:
  Inlet .... 0.10 to 0.15 mm
  Exhaust .... 0.20 to 0.25 mm

Lubrication
System type .... Wet sump, pressure feed, full flow filter
Lubricant type/specification/capacity .... Refer to *"Lubricants, fluids and capacities"*
Pump type .... Eccentric gear driven by crankshaft
Pressure (2000 rpm with oil temperature 80°C) .... 2.0 bar minimum

Torque wrench settings	Nm	lbf ft
Engine to gearbox	55	41
Exhaust pipe to manifold	25	18
Flywheel bolts	75	55
Clutch bolts	25	18
Sump bolts	20	15
Sump drain plug	30	22
Main bearing cap bolts	65	48
Oil pump bolts	10	7
Connecting rod big-end cap nuts (oiled):		
Stage 1	30	22
Stage 2*	Tighten further 1/4 turn (90°)	
Oil suction pipe to pump	10	7
Oil relief valve plug	25	18
Oil pressure sender switch	25	18
Timing cover	10	7
Valve cover	10	7
Camshaft sprocket bolt	80	59
Crankshaft sprocket/pulley nut	80	59
Coolant pump bolts	10	7
Distributor flange bolts	20	15
Cylinder head bolts (engine cold):		
Stage 1	40	30
Stage 2	60	44
Stage 3	Tighten further 1/2 turn (180°)	
Engine mountings (with oiled threads):		
Refer to illustrations 40.1a and 40.1b		
(a) M8	25	18
(a) M10	45	33
(b)	35	26
(c)	45	33
(d)	50	37
(e)	60	44
(f)	70	52
(g)	80	59

* When checking the connecting rod-to-crankshaft journal radial clearance using Plastigage, tighten only to 30Nm (22 lbf ft).

1 General information

The 1.05 and 1.3 litre engines are of four-cylinder, in-line, overhead camshaft type, mounted transversely at the front of the vehicle. The transmission is attached to the left-hand side of the engine.

The crankshaft is of five bearing type and separate thrustwashers are fitted to the central main bearing to control crankshaft endfloat.

The camshaft is driven by a toothed belt which also drives the coolant pump. The toothed belt is tensioned by moving the coolant pump in its eccentric mounting. The valves are operated from the camshaft by rocker fingers which pivot on ball-head studs. The distributor is driven by the camshaft and is located on the left-hand end of the cylinder head.

The oil pump is of the eccentric gear type driven from the end of the crankshaft.

The cylinder head is of crossflow design, with the inlet manifold at the rear and the exhaust manifold at the front.

The crankcase ventilation system is of the positive type and consists of an oil separator on the rear (coolant pipe side) of the cylinder block, connected to the air cleaner by a rubber hose. Vacuum from the air cleaner provides a partial vacuum in the crankcase and the piston blow-by gases are drawn through the oil separator and into the engine combustion chambers.

2 Major operations possible with engine in vehicle

The following operations can be carried out without having to remove the engine from the vehicle:
a) Removal and servicing of the cylinder head, camshaft and timing belt
b) Removal of the flywheel and crankshaft rear oil seal (after removal of the gearbox)
c) Removal of the sump
d) Removal of the piston/connecting rod assemblies (after removal of the cylinder head and sump)
e) Renewal of the crankshaft front and rear oil seals and the camshaft front oil seal
f) Renewal of the engine mountings
g) Removal of the oil pump

3 Major operation only possible after removal of engine from vehicle

The following operation can only be carried out after removal of the engine from the vehicle:
a) Renewal of crankshaft main bearings

4 Method of engine removal

1 The engine, together with the gearbox, must be lifted from the engine compartment and the engine separated from the gearbox on the bench. Two people will be needed.

2 A hoist of 150 kg capacity will be needed to lift the engine approximately 1 metre. If the hoist is not portable, then sufficient room must be left behind the vehicle to push it back out of the way so that the engine may be lowered. Blocks will be needed to support the engine after removal.
3 Ideally the vehicle should be over a pit. If this is not possible then the body must be supported on axle stands (see "*Jacking and vehicle support*") so that the front wheels may be turned to undo the driveshaft nuts. The left-hand shaft is accessible from above but the right-hand shaft must be undone from underneath. Removal of the gearshift linkage can only be done from underneath, as can removal of the exhaust pipe bracket. When all tasks are complete, lower the vehicle back onto its wheels.
4 A set of splined keys will be required to remove and refit the socket-head bolts used to secure certain items, such as the cylinder head bolts.
5 Draining of oil and coolant is best done away from the working area if possible. This saves the mess made by spilled oil in the place where you must work.
6 If an air conditioning system is fitted, observe the precautions listed in Chapter 3.

5 Engine - removal

1 Disconnect the battery negative lead.
2 Remove the bonnet.
3 Drain the engine coolant and remove the radiator, complete with cooling fan unit.
4 Remove the air cleaner unit.
5 Loosen the clip and disconnect the top hose from the thermostat housing.
6 Place a container beneath the engine then unscrew the sump drain plug and drain the oil - see Chapter 1. When complete, clean the drain plug and washer and refit it to the sump.

7 Identify the fuel supply and return hoses then disconnect them from the fuel pump **(see illustration)** and fuel reservoir/carburettor. Plug the hoses to prevent fuel leakage.
8 Loosen the clip and disconnect the bottom hose from the coolant pipe at the rear of the engine.
9 Disconnect the accelerator cable and, where applicable, the choke cable.
10 Disconnect the heater hoses from the thermostat housing and rear coolant pipe.
11 Detach the following connections, identifying each lead as it is disconnected to avoid confusion on reassembly:
a) The oil pressure switches on the rear (carburettor side) of the cylinder head
b) Inlet manifold preheating element line connector
c) Thermo-switch leads (coolant hose intermediate piece)
d) Distributor HT and LT leads
e) Starter motor
f) Temperature sender unit (thermostat housing)
g) Fuel cut-off solenoid valve on carburettor
h) Earth strap to gearbox
12 Detach the wiring loom from the location clip on the bottom hose and fold back out of the way.
13 Disconnect and unclip the vacuum hoses from the distributor and inlet manifold as necessary.
14 Disconnect the clutch cable **(see illustration)**.
15 Disconnect the exhaust downpipe from the exhaust manifold.
16 Disconnect the speedometer cable from the gearbox and place it on one side.
17 Apply the handbrake then jack up the front of the vehicle and support it on axle stands (see "*Jacking and vehicle support*").
18 Remove the screw from the shift rod coupling and ease the coupling from the rod **(see illustration)**. The screw threads are coated with a liquid locking agent and if

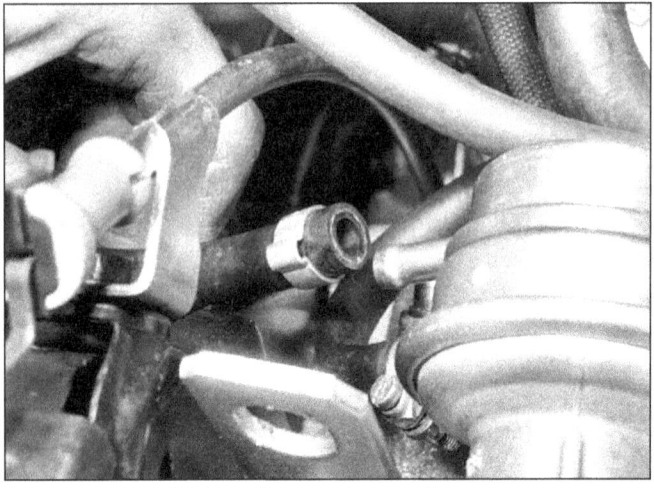

5.7 Detach hoses from fuel pump

5.14 Earth lead (A) and clutch cable (B)

Engine repair procedures - 1.05 and 1.3 litre pre August 1985 2A•5

5.18 Shift rod coupling screw

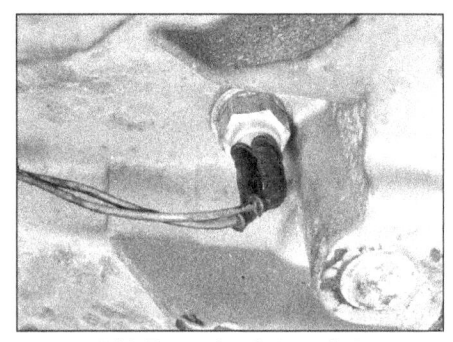

5.21 Reversing light switch

5.23 Engine lifting eye

difficulty is experienced, it may be necessary to heat up the coupling with a blowlamp whilst observing the necessary fire precautions. Note that once removed this screw should be renewed.

19 Note its orientation then withdraw the shift rod coupling.
20 Unbolt the exhaust steady bracket from the downpipe and clutch housing/starter motor.
21 Detach the reversing light switch lead **(see illustration)**.
22 Unbolt the driveshafts from the drive flanges and tie them to one side with wire.
23 Attach a suitable hoist to the engine lifting eye brackets (one at each end of the cylinder head on the carburettor side) **(see illustration)**. Take the weight of the engine/gearbox unit.
24 Working from above, undo the three engine mounting/bearer retaining bolts (underneath the carburettor) **(see illustration)**.
25 Undo and remove the gearbox mounting bolt (rear left side of engine compartment).
26 Undo and remove the front engine mounting bolt and then remove the bolts securing the bracket to the engine. Withdraw the mounting **(see illustrations)**.

5.24 Engine mounting/bearer - right-hand

27 Before lifting out the engine/gearbox unit, get an assistant to hold the engine steady and help guide it clear of surrounding components as it is removed.
28 Lift the engine/gearbox unit from the engine compartment **(see illustration)** while turning it as necessary to clear the internally mounted components. Make sure that all wires, cables and hoses have been disconnected.
29 Lower the unit onto a workbench or large piece of wood placed on the floor.

5.26a Undo front mounting through-bolt

6 Engine/gearbox - separation

1 The engine/gearbox unit must be supported so that the gearbox can be eased away from it. Either support the engine on blocks so that the gearbox overhangs the bench, or do the job while the engine and gearbox are on the hoist.
2 Detach the lead from the alternator then unclip the lead from the locating clips on the sump side walls.

5.26b Unbolt and remove mounting unit

5.28 Lifting out engine/gearbox unit

2A•6 Engine repair procedures - 1.05 and 1.3 litre pre August 1985

6.3 Starter motor and exhaust support bracket

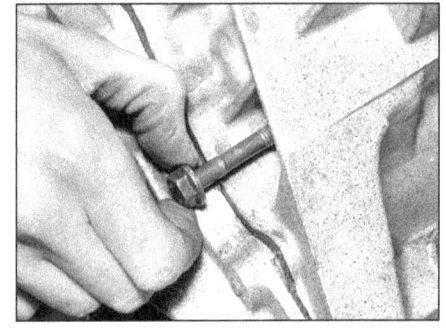

6.6a Undo securing bolts (recessed bolt shown) . . .

6.6b . . . then separate engine and transmission

3 Because the rear bearing of the starter armature is in the bellhousing, it is necessary to remove the starter before separating the engine and gearbox. If not already removed when unbolting the starter motor, also detach the exhaust pipe support bracket **(see illustration)**.
4 Detach the coolant pipe at its flange on the rear side of the coolant pump and at the clutch housing.
5 Undo the clutch housing belly plate bolt and withdraw the plate.
6 Undo and remove the remaining engine-to-gearbox securing bolts then pull the gearbox free. Do not insert wedges or you will damage the facing. Tap the gearbox gently and wriggle it off the two dowels which locate it. The intermediate plate will remain in position **(see illustrations)**.

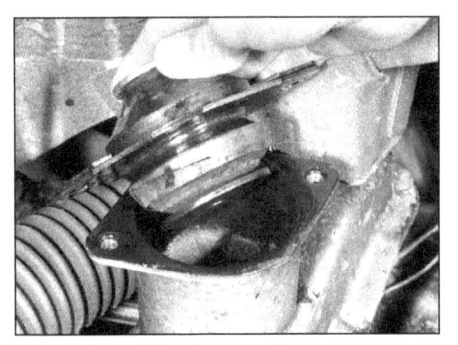

8.1a Lift the mounting away

7 Engine dismantling - general information

1 If possible, mount the engine on a stand for the dismantling procedure, but failing this, support it in an upright position with blocks of wood.
2 Cleanliness is most important. If the engine is dirty, it should be cleaned with paraffin while keeping it in an upright position.
3 Avoid working with the engine directly on a concrete floor as grit presents a real source of trouble.
4 As parts are removed, clean them in a paraffin bath. Do not immerse parts with internal oilways in paraffin as it is difficult to remove. Clean oilways with nylon pipe cleaners.
5 Obtain suitable containers to hold small items. This will help when reassembling the engine and also prevent possible loss.
6 Obtain complete sets of gaskets when the engine is being dismantled but retain the old gaskets with a view to using them as a pattern to make a replacement if a new one is not available.
7 When possible, refit nuts, bolts and washers in their location after being removed. This helps to protect the threads and will also be helpful when reassembling the engine.
8 Retain unserviceable components in order to compare them with the new parts supplied.

8 Engine ancillary components - removal

With the engine removed from the vehicle and separated from the gearbox, the externally mounted ancillary components should now be removed before dismantling begins. The removal sequence need not necessarily follow the order given:
a) Alternator and drivebelt
b) Inlet manifold and carburettor
c) Exhaust manifold
d) Distributor
e) Fuel pump
f) Thermostat
g) Clutch
h) Crankcase ventilation hose
i) Distributor cap and spark plugs
j) Oil filter
k) Engine mountings **(see illustrations)**
l) Dipstick **(see illustration)**
m) Oil pressure switches
n) Coolant temperature thermo-switch
o) Alternator mounting bracket and engine earth lead
p) Engine rear coolant pipe **(see illustration)**

8.1b Right-hand rear mounting viewed from above

8.1c Engine dipstick and tube

8.1d Removing engine rear coolant pipe

Engine repair procedures - 1.05 and 1.3 litre pre August 1985 2A•7

9 Cylinder head - removal

1 If the engine is still in the vehicle, first carry out the following operations:
  a) Disconnect the battery negative lead
  b) Remove the air cleaner and fuel pump
  c) Drain the cooling system and remove the top hose and thermostat
  d) Remove the distributor and spark plugs
  e) Remove the inlet and exhaust manifolds. If necessary, this can be carried out with the cylinder head on the bench
  f) Disconnect the wiring from the coolant temperature sender and oil pressure switch

2 Unscrew the nuts and bolts from the valve cover and remove the cover together with the gasket and reinforcement strips **(see illustrations)**.

3 Turn the engine until the indentation in the camshaft sprocket appears in the TDC hole in the timing cover and the notch in the crankshaft pulley is aligned with the TDC pointer on the front of the oil pump **(see illustrations)**. Now turn the crankshaft one quarter of a turn anti-clockwise so that none of the pistons are at TDC.

9.2a Removing valve cover...

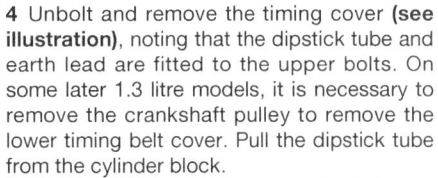

9.2b ...and gasket

4 Unbolt and remove the timing cover **(see illustration)**, noting that the dipstick tube and earth lead are fitted to the upper bolts. On some later 1.3 litre models, it is necessary to remove the crankshaft pulley to remove the lower timing belt cover. Pull the dipstick tube from the cylinder block.

5 Using a socket through the hole in the camshaft sprocket, unscrew the timing cover plate upper retaining bolt.

6 Loosen the coolant pump retaining bolts, then turn the pump body to release the tension from the timing belt. Remove the timing belt from the camshaft sprocket.

7 Remove the bolts and withdraw the timing cover plate, followed by the coolant pump if required.

8 Using a splined key, unscrew the cylinder head bolts half a turn at a time in the reverse order to that shown for tightening. Note the location of the engine lifting hooks.

9 Lift the cylinder head from the block **(see illustration)**. If it is stuck, tap it free with a wooden mallet. Do not insert a lever as damage will occur to the joint faces.

10 Remove the gasket from the cylinder block **(see illustration)**.

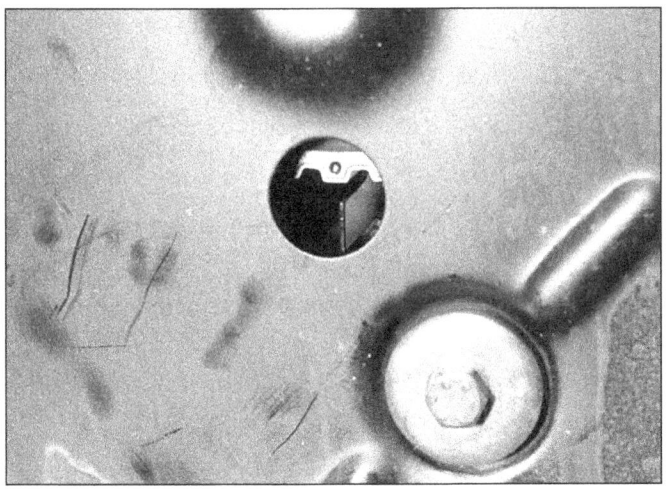

9.3a TDC mark on camshaft sprocket and pointer

9.3b Crankshaft pulley notch aligned with TDC pointer

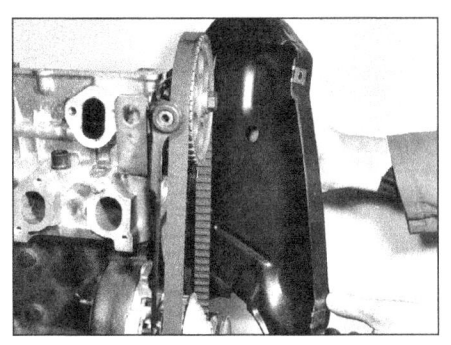

9.4 Removing timing cover

9.9 Removing cylinder head...

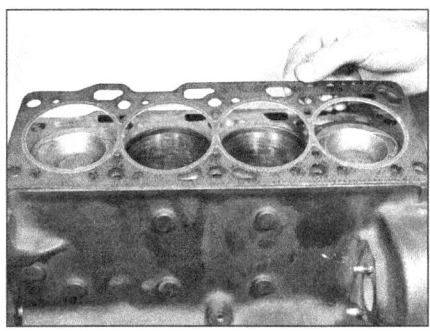

9.10 ...and gasket

2A•8 Engine repair procedures - 1.05 and 1.3 litre pre August 1985

10.7 Removing oil spray tube

10.8 Removing a cam follower clip

10.9 Removing a cam follower

10 Camshaft - removal

1 If the engine is still in the vehicle, first carry out the following operations:
 a) *Disconnect the battery negative lead*
 b) *Remove the air cleaner and fuel pump*
 c) *Remove the distributor and spark plugs*
2 If the cylinder head is still fitted to the engine, first carry out the procedure described in paragraphs 3 to 6 inclusive.
3 Unscrew the nuts and bolts from the valve cover and remove the cover together with the gasket and reinforcement strips.
4 Turn the engine until the indentation in the camshaft sprocket appears in the TDC hole in the timing cover and the notch in the crankshaft pulley is aligned with the TDC pointer on the front of the oil pump. Now turn the crankshaft one quarter of a turn anti-clockwise so that none of the pistons are at TDC.
5 Unbolt and remove the timing cover, noting that the dipstick tube and earth lead are fitted to the upper bolts. On some later 1.3 litre models, it is necessary to remove the crankshaft pulley to remove the lower timing belt cover.
6 Loosen the coolant pump retaining bolts, then turn the pump body clockwise to release the tension from the timing belt. Remove the timing belt from the camshaft sprocket.
7 Prise the oil spray tube from the top of the cylinder head **(see illustration)**.
8 Note how the cam follower clips are fitted then prise them from the ball-studs **(see illustration)**.
9 Identify each cam follower for location then remove each one by levering with a screwdriver. Make sure that the peak of the relevant cam is pointing away from the follower first by turning the camshaft as necessary **(see illustration)**.
10 Unscrew the camshaft sprocket bolt and remove the spacer **(see illustration)**. The sprocket can be held stationary using a metal bar with two bolts, with one bolt inserted in a hole and the other bolt resting on the outer rim of the sprocket.
11 Tap the sprocket from the camshaft with a wooden mallet and prise out the Woodruff key.
12 Using feeler blades, check the camshaft endfloat by inserting the blade between the end of the camshaft and distributor flanges **(see illustration)**. If it is more than the amount specified, the components will have to be checked for wear and renewed as necessary.
13 Using an Allen key, unscrew the bolts and remove the distributor flange **(see illustration)**. Remove the gasket.
14 Carefully slide the camshaft from the cylinder head, taking care not to damage the three bearing surfaces as the lobes of the cams pass through them **(see illustration)**.
15 Prise the camshaft oil seal from the cylinder head **(see illustration)**.

10.10 Removing camshaft sprocket bolt (early type sprocket shown)

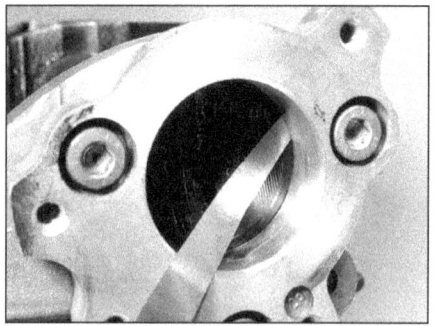

10.12 Checking camshaft endfloat

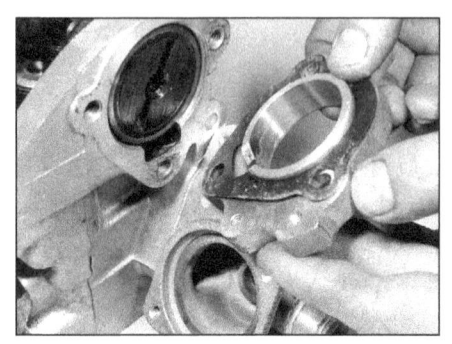

10.13 Removing distributor flange

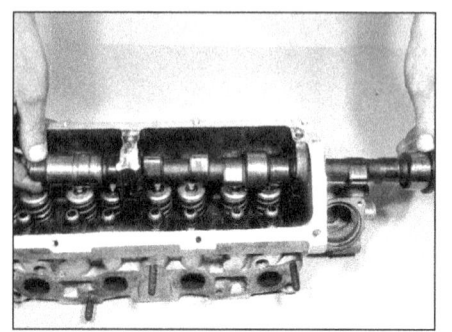

10.14 Withdrawing camshaft

10.15 Removing camshaft oil seal

Engine repair procedures - 1.05 and 1.3 litre pre August 1985 2A•9

11.2a Compressing a valve spring to remove split collets

11.2b Removing valve springs and retainers...

11 Cylinder head - dismantling and overhaul

Dismantling

1 Remove the cylinder head and camshaft, as described in the previous Sections.
2 Using a valve spring compressor, compress each valve spring in turn until the split collets can be removed. Release the compressor and remove the retainers and springs **(see illustrations)**. If the retainers are difficult to remove, do not continue to tighten the compressor but gently tap the top of the tool with a hammer. Always make sure that the compressor is held firmly over the retainer.
3 Remove each valve from the cylinder head, keeping them identified for location.
4 Prise the valve seals from the valve guides and remove the lower spring seats **(see illustration)**.
5 Do not remove the cam follower ball-studs unless they are unserviceable. They are likely to be seized in the head.

Overhaul

6 Use a scraper to carefully remove any carbon from the cylinder head. Remove all traces of gasket then wash the cylinder head thoroughly in paraffin and wipe dry.
7 Use a straight-edge and feeler blade to check that the cylinder head mating surface is not distorted. If it is, then it must be resurfaced by a suitably equipped engineering works. If the cylinder head face is to be resurfaced, this will necessitate the valve seats being re-cut so that they are recessed deeper by an equivalent amount to that machined from the cylinder head. This is necessary to avoid the possibility of the valves coming into contact with the pistons and causing serious damage and is a task to be entrusted to a suitably equipped engine reconditioning specialist. **(see illustration)**.

8 Examine the valve heads for pitting and burning. Renew any valve which is badly burnt. Examine the valve seats at the same time. If the pitting is very slight, it can be removed by grinding the valve heads and seats together with coarse, then fine, grinding paste. Note that the exhaust valves should not be re-cut, they should be renewed if the sealing face is excessively grooved as a result of regrinding.
9 Where excessive pitting has occurred, the valve seats must be re-cut or renewed by a specialist.
10 Valve grinding is carried out as follows. Place the cylinder head upside down on a bench with a block of wood at each end. Smear a trace of coarse carborundum paste on the seat face and press a suction grinding tool onto the valve head. With a semi-rotary action, grind the valve head to its seat, lifting the valve occasionally to redistribute the grinding paste. When a dull matt even surface is produced on both the valve seat and the valve, wipe off the paste and repeat the process with fine carborundum paste as before. A light spring placed under the valve head will greatly ease this operation. When a smooth unbroken ring of light grey matt finish is produced on both the valve and seat, the grinding operation is complete.

11 Scrape away all carbon from the valve head stem and clean away all traces of grinding compound. Clean the valves and seats with a paraffin-soaked rag, then wipe with a clean rag.
12 Check for wear in the valve guides. This may be detected by fitting a new valve in the guide and checking the amount that the rim of the valve will move sideways when the top of the valve stem is flush with the top of the valve guide. The rock limit for the inlet valve is 1.0 mm and 1.3 mm for the exhaust valve. This can be measured with feeler blades if you use a clamp as a datum but it must be with a new valve. If the rock is at or below this limit with your old valve then this indicates that the existing guide(s) do not need renewal. Check each valve guide in turn but note that the inlet and exhaust valve stem dimensions differ, so do not get them confused. If the rock exceeds the limit with a new valve, this will indicate the need for new valve guides as well. The removal and refitting of new guides is a task which must be entrusted to a specialist.

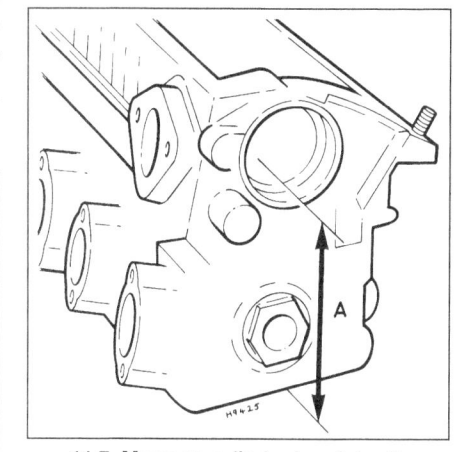

11.4 ... and valve spring lower seats

11.7 Measure cylinder head depth between points indicated

Minimum allowable depth a = 119.3 mm

2A•10 Engine repair procedures - 1.05 and 1.3 litre pre August 1985

13 If possible, compare the length of the valve springs with new ones and renew them as a set if any are shorter.

14 If the engine is still in the vehicle, clean the piston crowns and cylinder bore upper edges but make sure that no carbon drops between the pistons and bores. To do this, locate two of the pistons at the top of their bores and seal off the remaining bores with paper and masking tape. Press a little grease between the two pistons and their bores to collect any carbon dust which can be wiped away when the piston is lowered. To prevent carbon build-up, polish the piston crown with metal polish but remove all traces of the polish afterwards.

12 Timing belt and sprockets - removal

1 If the engine is still in the vehicle, first carry out the following operations:
  a) *Disconnect the battery negative lead*
  b) *Remove the air cleaner*
  c) *Remove the alternator drivebelt*

2 Turn the engine until the indentation in the camshaft sprocket appears in the TDC hole in the timing cover and the notch in the crankshaft pulley is aligned with the TDC pointer on the front of the oil pump.

3 Unbolt and remove the timing cover, noting that the dipstick tube and earth lead are fitted to the upper bolts. On some later 1.3 litre models, it is necessary to remove the crankshaft pulley to remove the lower timing belt cover.

4 Loosen the coolant pump retaining bolts, then turn the pump body to release the tension from the timing belt. Remove the timing belt from the camshaft sprocket **(see illustration)**.

5 Using an Allen key, unbolt the pulley from the crankshaft sprocket then remove the timing belt.

6 To remove the camshaft sprocket, unscrew the bolt and remove the spacer. Tap off the sprocket and remove the Woodruff key. Do not turn the camshaft. The sprocket can be held stationary using a metal bar with two bolts, with one bolt inserted through a sprocket hole and the other bolt resting on the outer rim.

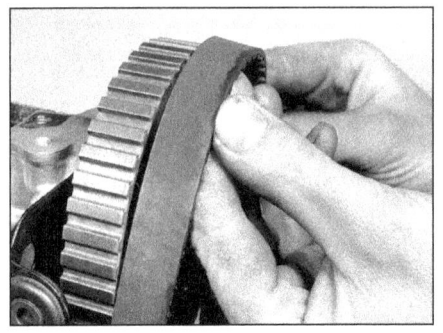

7 To remove the crankshaft sprocket, unscrew the bolt and lever the sprocket from the crankshaft **(see illustration)**. Do not turn the crankshaft otherwise the pistons may touch the valve heads. Hold the crankshaft stationary with a lever inserted in the starter ring gear (remove the starter as applicable). Remove the Woodruff key.

12.4 Releasing timing belt from camshaft sprocket

13 Flywheel - removal

1 Remove the clutch.
2 Hold the flywheel stationary with a lever or angle iron **(see illustration)** engaged with the starter ring gear.
3 Unscrew the bolts and lift the flywheel from the crankshaft **(see illustration)**.
4 Remove the engine plate from the cylinder block **(see illustration)**.
5 The flywheel bolts must be renewed once they are removed.

14 Crankshaft oil seals - renewal

Front seal

1 Remove the crankshaft sprocket.
2 If available, use VW tool 2085 to remove the seal from the oil pump housing. Removal of the seal with the engine and oil pump in position in the vehicle can prove difficult without the special tool. In this instance, an alternative method is to drill two holes, diagonally opposed to each other in the seal, insert two self-tapping screws and then pull on the screws using grips to withdraw the seal. If using this method, care must be taken not to drill into the housing.

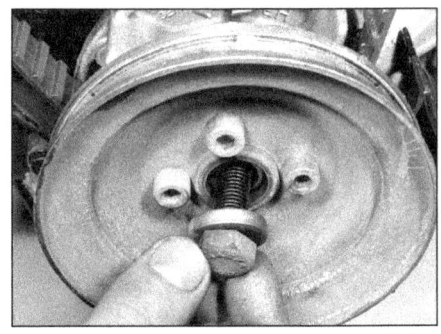

3 If the oil pump is removed from the engine, the seal can be prised out and a new item fitted - see illustration 31.1.
4 Clean the recess in the oil pump.
5 Smear a little clean engine oil on the lip and outer edge of the new seal, then fit it with VW tool 10-203 or by tapping it in with a suitable metal tube.
6 Refit the crankshaft sprocket.

Rear seal

7 Remove the flywheel.

Method 1

8 Drill two diagonally opposite holes in the seal. Insert two self-tapping screws and pull out the seal with grips.
9 Clean the recess in the housing.
10 Smear a little clean engine oil on the lip and outer edge of the new seal then tap it into the housing using a suitable metal tube
11 Refit the flywheel.

Method 2

12 Remove the sump.
13 Unscrew the bolts and withdraw the housing from the dowels on the cylinder block. Remove the gasket **(see illustrations)**.

12.7 Removing crankshaft sprocket bolt and washer

13.2 One method of holding the flywheel stationary

13.3 Removing flywheel

13.4 Removing engine plate

Engine repair procedures - 1.05 and 1.3 litre pre August 1985 2A•11

14.13a Withdrawing crankshaft rear oil seal housing . . .

14.13b . . . and gasket

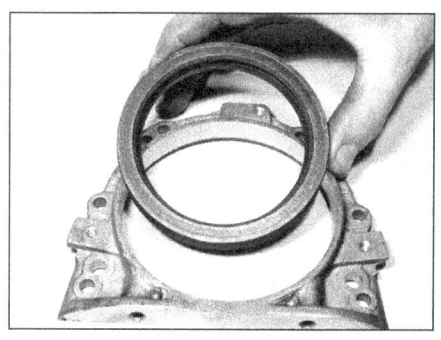

14.14 Remove crankshaft rear oil seal from housing

14 Support the housing and drive out the oil seal **(see illustration)**.
15 Clean the recess in the housing.
16 Smear a little clean engine oil on the lip and outer edge of the new seal then tap it into the housing using a block of wood **(see illustration)**.
17 Clean the mating faces then refit the housing, together with a new gasket, and tighten the bolts evenly in diagonal sequence.
18 Refit the sump and flywheel.

15 Sump - removal

1 If the engine is still in the vehicle, first carry out the following operations:

a) Jack up the front of the vehicle and support it on axle stands (see "Jacking and vehicle support"). Apply the handbrake
b) Disconnect the right-hand side driveshaft and the exhaust system
c) Unclip the alternator wire from the sump **(see illustration)**
d) Drain the engine oil into a suitable container. Clean the drain plug and washer and refit it, tightening to the specified torque

2 Unscrew the bolts and withdraw the sump from the cylinder block **(see illustration)**. If it is stuck, lever it away or cut through the gasket with a knife .
3 Scrape the gasket from the sump and cylinder block.

16 Oil pump - removal

1 Remove the timing belt and crankshaft sprocket.
2 Remove the sump.
3 Unbolt and remove the pick-up tube and strainer from the oil pump and cylinder block. Remove the flange gasket **(see illustration)**.
4 Unscrew the bolts and withdraw the oil pump from the dowels on the front of the cylinder block. Note that the timing pointed bracket is located on the two upper central bolts and the timing belt guard on the two left-hand side bolts. Remove the gasket **(see illustrations)**.

14.16 Installing new crankshaft rear oil seal

15.1 Alternator wire clip on sump

15.2 Removing the sump

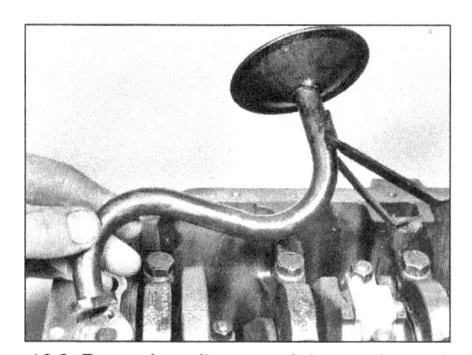

16.3 Removing oil pump pick-up tube and strainer

16.4a Removing oil pump . . .

16.4b . . . and gasket

2A•12 Engine repair procedures - 1.05 and 1.3 litre pre August 1985

17.4 Checking connecting rod endfloat

17.5 Piston crown showing arrow which points to timing belt end of engine

17.7 Withdrawing a big-end cap

17 Pistons and connecting rods - removal

1 Remove the cylinder head.
2 Remove the sump.
3 Unbolt and remove the pick-up tube and strainer from the oil pump and cylinder block. Remove the flange gasket.
4 Using a feeler blade, check that the connecting rod big-end endfloat on each crankpin is within the specified limits **(see illustration)**. If not, the components must be checked for wear and renewed as necessary.
5 Check the big-end caps and connecting rods for identification marks, if necessary use a centre punch to mark them for location and position. Note that the cut-outs in the connecting rods and caps face the timing belt end of the engine. The arrows on the piston crown also face the timing belt **(see illustration)**.
6 Turn the crankshaft so that No 1 crankpin is at its lowest point.
7 Unscrew the big-end nuts and tap free the cap, together with its bearing shell **(see illustration)**.
8 Using the handle of a hammer, tap the piston and connecting rod from the bore and withdraw it from the top of the cylinder block **(see illustration)**.
9 Loosely refit the cap to the connecting rod.
10 Repeat the procedure given in paragraphs 7 to 9 on No 4 piston and connecting rod, then turn the crankshaft through half a turn and repeat the procedure on No 2 and 3 pistons.
11 Note that during reassembly, the connecting rod bolts must be renewed.

18 Crankshaft and main bearings - removal

1 Disconnect the connecting rods from the crankshaft. It is not essential to remove the pistons or, therefore, to remove the cylinder head.
2 Remove the oil pump and the rear oil seal housing.
3 Using a feeler blade, check that the crankshaft endfloat is within the specified limits **(see illustration)**. Insert the feeler blade between the centre crankshaft web and the thrustwashers. This will indicate whether new thrustwashers are required or not.
4 Check that the main bearing caps are identified for location and position. There should be a cast number in the crankcase ventilation pipe/coolant coolant pipe side of the caps, numbered from the timing belt end of the engine **(see illustration)**.
5 Unscrew the bolts and tap the main bearing caps free. Keep the bearing shells and where fitted, the thrustwashers identified for position.
6 Lift the crankshaft from the crankcase and remove the remaining bearing shells and thrustwashers. Keep them identified for position **(see illustration)**.

17.8 Removing a piston

19 Oil filter - renewal

Refer to Chapter 1, Section 18

20 Examination and renovation - general information

With the engine completely stripped, clean all the components and examine them for wear. Each part should be checked and where necessary renewed or renovated, as described in the following Sections. Renew main and big-end shell bearings as a matter of course, unless you know that they have had little wear and are in perfect condition

18.3 Checking crankshaft endfloat

18.4 Crankshaft main bearing cap numbering

18.6 Removing crankshaft

Engine repair procedures - 1.05 and 1.3 litre pre August 1985

21 Crankshaft and bearings - examination and renovation

1 Examine the bearing surfaces of the crankshaft for scratches or scoring. Using a micrometer, check each journal and crankpin for ovality. Where this is found to be in excess of 0.17 mm, the crankshaft will have to be reground and undersize bearings fitted.
2 Crankshaft regrinding should be carried out by a specialist who will normally supply the matching undersize main and big-end shell bearings.
3 If crankshaft endfloat is more than the maximum specified amount, new centre main bearing shells with side flanges will have to be fitted to replace the thrustwashers. These are usually supplied together with the main and big-end bearings on a reground crankshaft.

22 Cylinder block/crankcase - examination and renovation

1 The cylinder bores must be examined for taper, ovality, scoring and scratches. Start by examining the top of the bores. If these are worn, a slight ridge will be found which marks the top of the piston ring travel. If the wear is excessive, the engine will have had a high oil consumption rate accompanied by blue smoke from the exhaust.
2 If available, use an inside dial gauge to measure the bore diameter just below the ridge and compare it with the diameter at the bottom of the bore, which is not subject to wear. If the difference is more than 0.15 mm, the cylinders will normally require reboring with new oversize pistons fitted.
3 If cylinder bore wear does not exceed 0.20 mm, special oil control rings and pistons can be fitted to restore compression and stop the engine burning oil.
4 If new pistons are being fitted to old bores, it is essential to roughen the bore walls slightly with fine glasspaper to enable the new piston rings to bed in properly.
5 Thoroughly examine the crankcase and cylinder block for cracks and damage and use a piece of wire to probe all oilways and waterways to ensure that they are unobstructed.
6 Check the core plugs for leaks and security (see illustration).

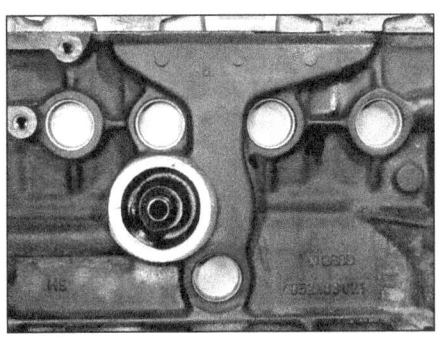

22.6 Core plugs in cylinder block

23 Pistons and connecting rods - examination and renovation

1 Examine the pistons for ovality, scoring and scratches. Check the connecting rods for wear and damage.
2 To remove the pistons from the connecting rods, first mark the two components in relation to each other. The indentation on the bearing end of the connecting rod faces the same way as the arrow on the piston crown (see illustration).
3 Prise out the circlips then dip the piston in hot water. Press out the gudgeon pin and separate the piston from the connecting rod.
4 Assemble the pistons in reverse order.
5 If new rings are to be fitted to the original pistons, expand the old rings over the top of the pistons by using three old feeler blades to prevent the rings dropping into empty grooves.
6 Before fitting the new rings, insert each of them into the cylinder bore approximately 15.0 mm from the bottom and check that the end gaps are as specified (see illustration).
7 When fitting the rings to the pistons, ensure that the TOP markings face towards the piston crown and arrange the end gaps at 120° intervals (see illustration). Using a feeler blade, check that the clearance of each ring in its groove is within the limits specified (see illustration).

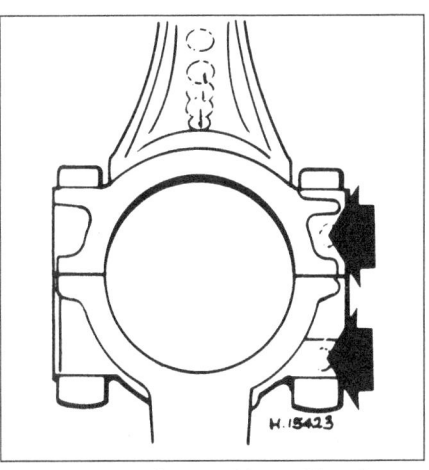

23.2 Indentations on big-end bearings (arrowed) must face same way as arrow on piston crown

24 Oil pump - examination and renovation

Note: *The manufacturer does not supply any clearances for checking oil pump gear wear, so the pump must be assumed to be in good order provided that oil pressure is as specified. Pressure can only be checked with the engine assembled and the task should be entrusted to a VW garage. A visual examination of the oil pump can be made as follows:*

1 Using an Allen key, unscrew the relief valve plug and extract the spring and plunger (see illustrations).
2 Using an impact screwdriver, remove the cross-head screws and withdraw the cover from the pump (see illustration).
3 Remove the rotors, noting that the indentation on the outer rotor faces the cover (see illustrations).

23.6 Checking piston ring gaps

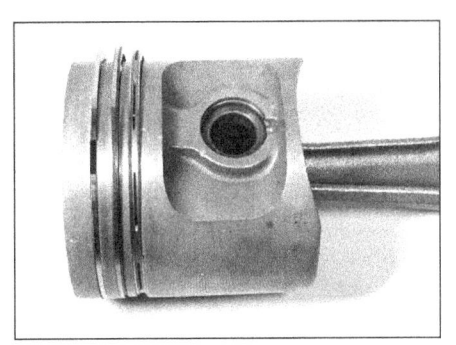

23.7a Space ring gaps at 120° intervals

23.7b Checking piston ring-to-groove wall clearance

2A•14 Engine repair procedures - 1.05 and 1.3 litre pre August 1985

24.1a Unscrew relief valve plug . . .

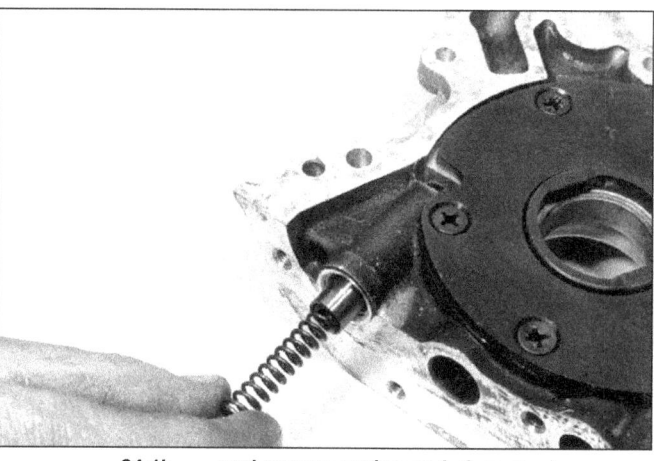

24.1b . . . and remove spring and plunger

24.2 Removing oil pump cover . . .

24.3a . . . and rotors

24.3b Outer rotor indentation (arrowed) must face cover

4 Clean the components in paraffin and wipe dry, then examine them for wear and damage. If evident, renew the oil pump complete but if in good order, reassemble the pump in reverse order and tighten the screws and plug.

25 Flywheel - examination and renovation

1 A damaged flywheel must be renewed.
2 Inspect the starter ring teeth. If these are chipped or worn it is possible to renew the starter ring. This means heating the ring until it may be separated from the flywheel, or alternatively splitting it. A new ring must then be shrunk on. If you know how to do this and you can get a new ring, then the job can be done but it is beyond the capacity of most owners.
3 Serious scoring on the flywheel clutch facing again requires a new flywheel. Do not attempt to clean the scoring off with a scraper or emery.

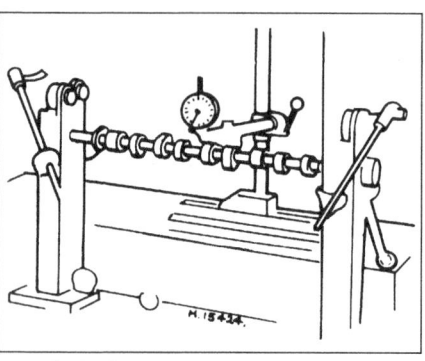

26 Timing belt and sprockets - examination and renovation

1 The timing belt should be renewed as a matter of course at 40 000 miles (60 000 km), see Chapter 1.
2 The full length of the timing belt must be checked for signs of uneven wear, splitting or oil contamination. Renew the belt if there is the slightest doubt about its condition.
3 The camshaft and crankshaft sprockets do not normally require renewal as wear takes place very slowly.

27 Camshaft - examination and renovation

27.2 Checking camshaft run-out

Examine the camshaft bearing surfaces, cam lobes and followers for wear. If wear is excessive, renew the camshaft and followers.

Check the camshaft run-out by turning it between fixed centres with a dial gauge on the centre journal. If the run-out exceeds that specified, renew the shaft (see illustration).

28 Engine reassembly - general information

To ensure maximum life with minimum trouble from a rebuilt engine, adhere to the following:
a) Ensure that all components are spotlessly clean
b) Ensure that all oilways are clear
c) Ensure lockwashers are fitted where indicated
d) Lubricate all bearings and other working surfaces thoroughly with clean engine oil during assembly
e) Renew any bolts or studs with damaged threads.
f) Gather together a torque wrench, oil can and some clean rags
g) Obtain a set of engine gaskets and oil seals, together with a new oil filter

Engine repair procedures - 1.05 and 1.3 litre pre August 1985 2A•15

29.2 Fitting centre main bearing shell

29.3 Thrustwasher location on centre main bearing

29.4 Fitting centre main bearing cap

29 Crankshaft and main bearings - refitting

1 Clean the backs of the bearing shells and the bearing recesses in the cylinder block and main bearing caps.
2 Press the main bearing shells into the cylinder block and caps and oil them liberally (see illustration).
3 Where thrustwashers are being refitted (instead of a shouldered type No 3 main bearing shell, a plain shell is used), smear the washers with grease and stick them into position on the side of the centre main bearing and its cap (see illustration). The washers must be fitted so that their oilways face away from the bearings in the block and cap.
4 Lower the crankshaft into position, then fit the main bearing caps in their previously noted positions (see illustration). Note that the bearing shell lugs are adjacent to each other.
5 Insert the bolts and tighten them evenly to the specified torque. Check that the crankshaft rotates freely then check that the endfloat is within the specified limits by inserting a feeler blade between the centre crankshaft web and the thrustwashers or bearing shoulder, as applicable.
6 Refit the rear oil seal bearing and oil pump and reconnect the connecting rods.

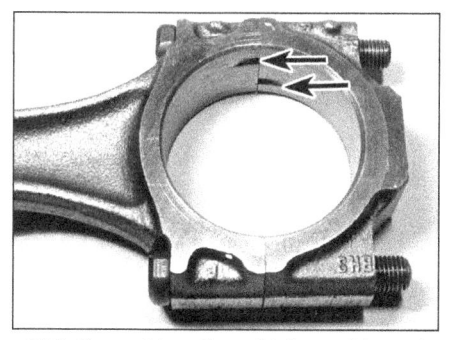

30 Pistons and connecting rods - refitting

1 As mentioned during removal, the manufacturers recommend that the connecting rod bolts be renewed. Assemble the new bolts to the rods.
2 Clean the backs of the bearing shells and the recesses in the connecting rods and big-end caps.
3 Press the big-end bearing shells into the connecting rods and caps in their correct positions and oil them liberally (see illustration).
4 Fit a ring compressor to No 1 piston then insert the piston and connecting rod into No 1 cylinder (see illustration). With No 1 crankpin at its lowest point, drive the piston carefully into the cylinder with the wooden handle of a hammer and at the same time, guide the connecting rod into the crankpin. Make sure that the arrow on the piston crown faces the timing belt end of the engine.
5 Fit the big-end bearing cap in its previously noted position then fit the nuts and tighten them evenly to the specified torque.
6 Check that the crankshaft turns freely and use a feeler blade to check that the connecting rod endfloat is within the specified limits.
7 Repeat the procedure given in paragraphs 3 to 5 for No 4 piston and connecting rod, then turn the crankshaft through half a turn and repeat the procedure for No 2 and 3 pistons.
8 If the engine is in the vehicle, refit the oil pump pick-up tube and strainer, the sump and the cylinder head.

31 Oil pump - refitting

1 Renew the oil seal in the oil pump housing (see illustration).
2 Locate a new gasket on the dowels on the front of the cylinder block.
3 Locate the oil pump on the block, making sure that the inner rotor engages the flats on the crankshaft. Do not damage the oil seal.
4 Insert the bolts, together with the timing pointer bracket and timing belt guard, then tighten them evenly to the specified torque (see illustration).

30.3 Correct location of tabs on big-end bearings (arrowed)

30.4 Using a piston ring compressor

31.1 Prising out oil pump oil seal

31.4 Fitted location of oil pump

2A•16 Engine repair procedures - 1.05 and 1.3 litre pre August 1985

32.3 Fitting sump gasket

5 Locate a new gasket on the flange face then fit the pick-up tube and strainer. Insert the bolts and tighten them to the specified torque.
6 Refit the sump, timing belt and sprocket.

32 Sump - refitting

1 If applicable (ie. the engine has been dismantled), refit the crankshaft rear oil seal and housing.
2 Clean the mating faces of the sump and cylinder block.
3 Locate the new gasket on the block (see illustration) then fit the sump. Insert the sump bolts and tighten them evenly in diagonal sequence to the specified torque. If required, the two bolts at the flywheel end of the sump can be replaced by socket-headed bolts to facilitate their removal with the engine in the vehicle. Note that the tightening torque for the replacement bolts is 8 Nm (6 lbf ft).
4 If the engine is in the vehicle, replenish it with oil, fasten the alternator wire to the sump clip and lower the vehicle to the ground.

33 Flywheel - refitting

1 Locate the engine plate on the cylinder block dowels.
2 Clean the mating faces of the flywheel and crankshaft then locate the flywheel in position. Note that the bolt holes only align in one position as they are offset.
3 Apply locking fluid to the threads of new bolts (see illustration) then insert and tighten them in a diagonal sequence to the specified torque while holding the flywheel stationary.
4 Refit the clutch.

34 Cylinder head - reassembly

1 Fit the valves into their correct locations in the cylinder head.
2 Working on each valve at a time, locate the valve spring lower seat in position.
3 Before fitting each valve seal, locate the special plastic sleeve provided in the gasket set over the valve stem in order to prevent damage to the seal (see illustration).
4 Slide each new seal over the valve stem and press it firmly onto the guide using a metal tube (see illustration). Remove the plastic sleeve.
5 Fit the spring and retainer over each valve stem, then compress the spring with the compressor and insert the split collets. Release the compressor and remove it.
6 Refit the camshaft.

34.3 Locate plastic sleeve on valve stem . . .

34.4 . . . then fit the new oil seal

33.3 Applying liquid locking fluid to flywheel bolts

35 Camshaft - refitting

1 Smear a little clean engine oil on the lip and outer edge of the camshaft oil seal then drive it squarely into the cylinder head with a block of wood.
2 Oil the camshaft bearing surfaces then slide the camshaft into position, taking care not to damage the oil seal.
3 Fit the distributor flange, together with a new gasket, and tighten the socket-head bolts.
4 Using a feeler blade, check that the camshaft endfloat is as specified.
5 Fit the Woodruff key then fit the sprocket to the camshaft followed by the spacer and bolt. Tighten the bolt while holding the sprocket stationary with a metal bar and two bolts (see illustration).
6 Fit the cam followers by turning the camshaft so that the relevant cam lobe peak is pointing away from the valve, then tap the follower between the valve stem and cam and onto the ball-stud.
7 Slide the cam follower clips into the grooves on the ball studs and locate the upper ends on the cam followers (see illustration).

35.5 Method of tightening camshaft sprocket bolt

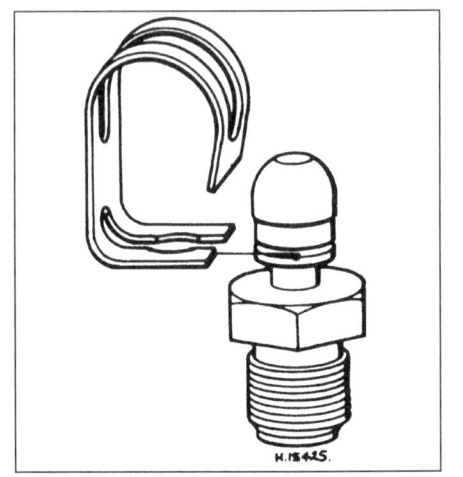

35.7 Cam follower clip and groove in ball-stud

Engine repair procedures - 1.05 and 1.3 litre pre August 1985 2A•17

35.9 Camshaft sprocket (later type) with index mark aligned with timing cover TDC pointer

36.2 Correct fitting of cylinder head gasket

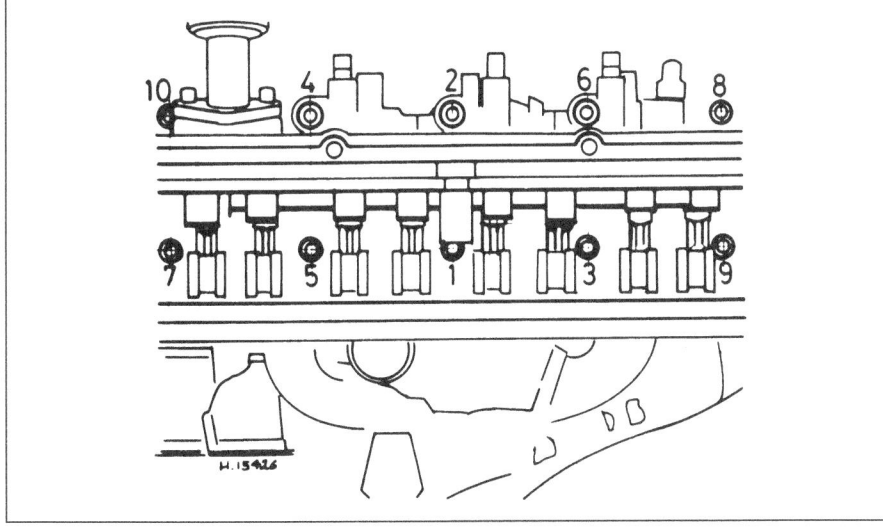

36.4 Cylinder head bolt tightening sequence

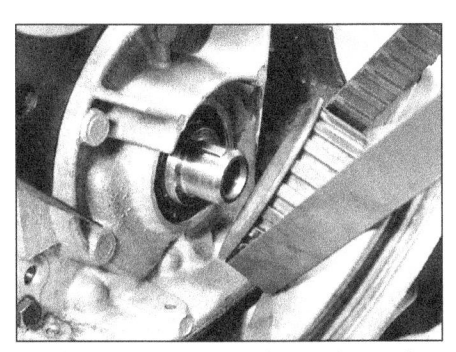

36.9 Fitting crankshaft sprocket and timing belt

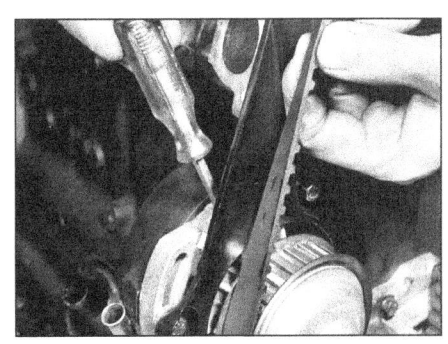

36.13 Tensioning timing belt

8 Adjust the valve clearances.
9 Turn the camshaft so that the indentation in the sprocket is pointing downwards and in line with the pointer on the timing cover plate **(see illustration)**.
10 Turn the crankshaft a quarter of a turn clockwise so that the notch in the crankshaft pulley is aligned with the TDC pointer on the front of the oil pump.
11 Fit the timing belt to the camshaft sprocket and coolant pump.
12 Using a screwdriver in the coolant pump, turn the pump and tension the timing belt until it can just be turned through 90° with the thumb and forefinger midway between the camshaft sprocket and coolant pump.
13 Tighten the coolant pump bolts when the belt tension is correct and check the timing marks are still aligned.
14 Fit the dipstick tube to the cylinder block.
15 Fit the timing cover, insert the bolts with the earth lead and dipstick tube bracket, then tighten the bolts.
16 Press the oil spray tube into the top of the cylinder head.
17 Refit the valve cover with a new gasket, locate the reinforcement strips and tighten the nuts and bolts.
18 If the engine is in the vehicle, reverse the preliminary procedures given in Section 10.

36 Cylinder head - refitting

1 Position Nos 1 and 4 pistons at TDC then turn the crankshaft a quarter of a turn anti-clockwise so that neither of the pistons is at TDC.
2 Ensure that the faces of the cylinder head and block are perfectly clean then locate the new gasket on the block, making sure that all oil and coolant holes are visible. The gasket part number should be uppermost **(see illustration)**.
3 Lower the cylinder head onto the gasket then insert the bolts together with the engine lifting hooks.
4 Using a splined key, tighten the bolts in the stages given in *Specifications*, using the sequence shown **(see illustration)**.
5 Refit the coolant pump, if applicable.
6 Fit the timing cover plate and insert the coolant pump bolts loosely.
7 If required, refit the camshaft.
8 Refit and tighten the timing cover plate upper retaining bolt.
9 If applicable, refit the crankshaft sprocket and timing belt to the crankshaft **(see illustration)**.
10 Turn the camshaft so that the indentation in the sprocket is aligned with the pointer on the timing cover plate.
11 Turn the crankshaft a quarter of a turn clockwise so that the notch in the crankshaft pulley (temporarily refit if necessary) is aligned with the TDC pointer on the front of the oil pump.
12 Fit the timing belt to the camshaft sprocket and coolant pump.
13 Using a screwdriver in the coolant pump, turn the pump and tension the timing belt until it can just be turned through 90° with the thumb and forefinger midway between the camshaft sprocket and coolant pump **(see illustration)**.
14 Tighten the coolant pump bolts when the tension is correct and check that the timing marks are still aligned.
15 Fit the dipstick tube to the cylinder block.
16 Fit the timing cover, insert the bolts with the earth lead and dipstick tube bracket and tighten the bolts.
17 Refit the valve cover with a new gasket, locate the reinforcement strips and tighten the nuts and bolts.
18 If the engine is in the vehicle, reverse the preliminary procedures given in Section 9.

37 Timing belt and sprockets - refitting

1 Fit the Woodruff key in the crankshaft and tap the sprocket into position.
2 Insert the bolt and tighten it to the specified torque while holding the crankshaft stationary with a lever in the starter ring gear.
3 Fit the Woodruff key to the camshaft then fit the sprocket followed by the spacer and bolt. Tighten the bolt while holding the sprocket stationary with a metal bar and two bolts.
4 Locate the timing belt on the crankshaft sprocket then fit the pulley. Insert the bolts and tighten them with an Allen key.
5 Turn the camshaft so that the indentation in the sprocket is aligned with the pointer on the timing cover plate. Check that the notch in the crankshaft pulley is aligned with the TDC pointer on the front of the oil pump
6 Fit the timing belt to the camshaft sprocket and coolant pump.
7 Using a screwdriver in the coolant pump, turn the pump and tension the timing belt until it can just be turned through 90° with the thumb and forefinger midway between the camshaft sprocket and coolant pump.
8 Tighten the coolant pump bolts when the belt tension is correct and check that the timing marks are still aligned.
9 Fit the timing cover, insert the bolts with the earth lead and dipstick tube bracket, then tighten the bolts.
10 If the engine is in the vehicle, reverse the preliminary procedures given in Section 12.

38 Valve clearances - checking and adjustment

1 The valve clearances can be checked and adjusted with the cylinder head removed (prior to refitting after overhaul) or in the normal manner described in Section 12 of Chapter 1.
2 There are two specified valve clearance settings, these being for a cold (cylinder head removed) or warm (engine in vehicle) engine condition.
3 If the valve clearances are adjusted with the engine cold, recheck the clearances again after 600 miles (900 km) with the engine at its normal operating temperature.

39 Engine ancillary components and gearbox - refitting

Refer to Section 8 and refit the listed ancillary components.
Refit the gearbox to the engine, reversing the procedures described in Section 6.

40 Engine - refitting

Reverse the removal procedure given in Section 5 but note the following additional points:
a) *When lowering the engine/gearbox unit into the vehicle, ensure that the driveshafts are aligned with the flanges*
b) *Assemble the engine mountings loosely initially and tighten them only after the unit is central without straining the mountings* **(see illustrations)**
c) *Adjust the clutch*
d) *Adjust the accelerator cable and, where applicable, the choke cable*
e) *Refill the engine with oil and coolant*

41 Engine - adjustments after major overhaul

1 With the engine/gearbox unit fitted to the vehicle, make a final check to ensure that everything has been reconnected and that no rags or tools have been left in the engine compartment.
2 If new pistons or crankshaft bearings have been fitted, turn the carburettor engine speed screw in about half a turn to compensate for the initial tightness of the new components.
3 Fully pull out the choke (manual choke models) and start the engine. This may take a little longer than usual as the fuel pump and carburettor float chamber may be empty.
4 As soon as the engine starts, push in the choke to the detent. Check that the oil pressure light goes out.
5 Check the oil filter, fuel hoses and coolant hoses for leaks.
6 Run the engine to normal operating temperature, then adjust the slow running (idle).
7 If new pistons or crankshaft bearings have been fitted, the engine must be run-in for the first 500 miles (750 km). Do not operate the engine at full throttle or allow the engine to labour in any gear.
8 Although not strictly essential, it is good practice to change the engine oil and filter after the initial running-in period. This will get rid of the small metallic particles which are produced by new components bedding in to each other.

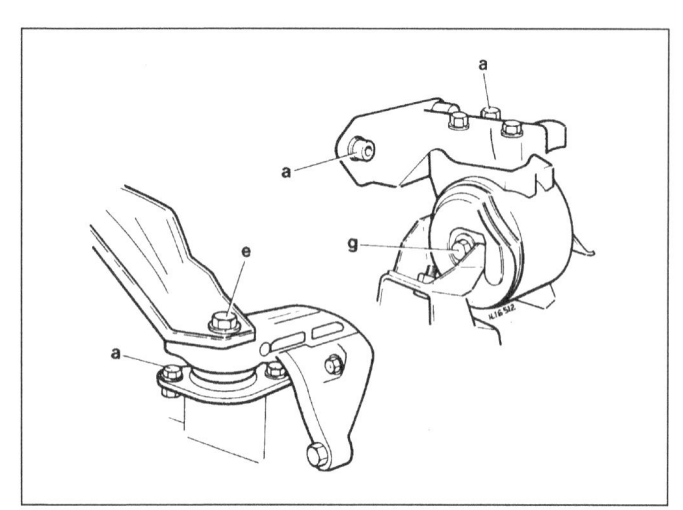

40.1a Engine mounting bolt identification - see Specifications for torque settings

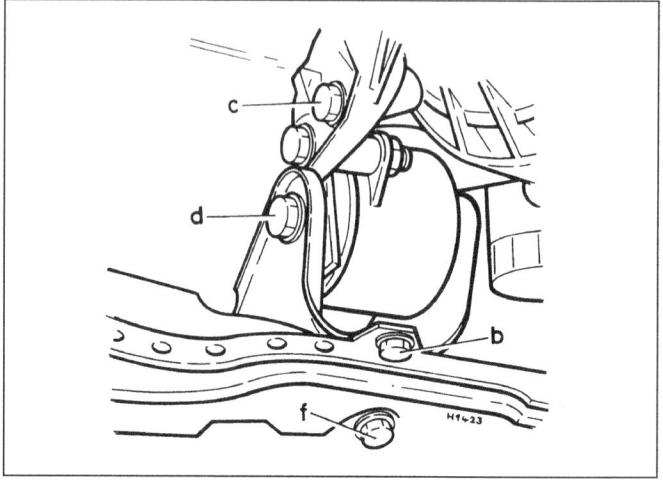

40.1b Engine/transmission mounting bolt identification - see Specifications for torque settings

2B•1

Chapter 2 Part B:
Engine repair procedures - 1.05 and 1.3 litre post August 1985

The following information is a revision of, or supplementary to, that contained in Part A of this Chapter

Contents

Camshaft - examination 8	Engine - adjustments after major overhaul 13
Camshaft - refitting 10	General information 1
Camshaft - removal 4	Hydraulic bucket tappets - checking free travel 12
Camshaft oil seal - renewal 3	Oil pump - refitting 9
Cylinder head - dismantling and overhaul 5	Oil pump - removal and examination 7
Cylinder head - refitting 11	Timing belt and sprockets - removal 6
Cylinder head - removal 2	

Degrees of difficulty

Easy, suitable for novice with little experience	Fairly easy, suitable for beginner with some experience	Fairly difficult, suitable for competent DIY mechanic	Difficult, suitable for experienced DIY mechanic	Very difficult, suitable for expert DIY or professional

Specifications

General
Code:
  1.05 litre .... HZ
  1.3 litre .... MH
  1.3 litre .... NZ
  1.3 litre 2G

Cylinder head
Minimum dimension after machining (skimming) .... 135.6 mm

Camshaft
Maximum run-out .... 0.01 mm
Maximum radial play .... 0.10 mm

Valves
Maximum seat width .... 2.2 mm
Head diameter:
  Inlet .... 36.0 mm
  Exhaust .... 29.0 mm
Valve length:
  Inlet .... 98.9 mm
  Exhaust .... 99.1 mm

Hydraulic tappets
Maximum free travel .... 0.1 mm

Valve timing

Nil valve clearance at 1.0 mm valve lift	MH/NZ/2G	HZ
Inlet opens	12°ATDC	5°ATDC
Inlet closes	28°ABDC	29°ABDC
Exhaust opens	25°BBDC	33°BBDC
Exhaust closes	9°BTDC	9°BTDC

2B•2 Engine repair procedures - 1.05 and 1.3 litre post August 1985

Lubrication system

Pump gear teeth backlash:
- New .... 0.05 mm
- Wear limit .... 0.20 mm

Pump gear teeth axial play (wear limit) .... 0.15 mm
Pump chain drive deflection .... 1.5 to 2.5 mm

Torque wrench settings

	Nm	lbf ft
Camshaft sprocket bolt	80	59.0
Timing belt cover:		
Upper bolt	10	7.3
Lower bolt	20	14.7
Camshaft bearing cap nuts:		
Stage 1	6	4.4
Stage 2	Tighten by further 90°	
Number 5 cap screws	10	7.3
Cylinder head bolts:		
Stage 1	40	29.5
Stage 2	60	44.3
Stage 3	Tighten by further 180°	
Oil pump bolts	20	14.7
Stay bracket bolts	10	7.3
Strainer assembly to pump body	10	7.3
Socket-headed screws in sump (new)	8	5.9
Crankshaft sprocket bolt (oiled) - 1986-on:		
Stage 1	90	66
Stage 2	Tighten by further 180°	
Flywheel bolt (with shoulder)	100	74

1 General information

The 1.05 and 1.3 litre engines produced since August 1985 have a redesigned cylinder head which incorporates hydraulic "bucket" type tappets in place of the previously fitted "rocker finger" tappets.

The oil pump has also been changed from the previously fitted crescent type to a gear type which is driven by chain from the crankshaft.

Additionally, different ancillary components are fitted such as the carburettor and distributor.

Unless otherwise given in the following Sections, all servicing procedures are as given in Part A of this Chapter for the pre-August 1985 1.05 and 1.3 litre engines.

2 Cylinder head - removal

The procedure for removing the cylinder head is basically the same as described in Part A of this Chapter but note the following:
a) The valve cover is different, being held in place by three bolts (see illustration)
b) There is a plastic oil shield located at the distributor end of the engine (see illustration)
c) The fuel and coolant pipes differ, depending on model
d) Spring type re-usable hose clips may be fitted. These are removed by pinching the ends together to expand the clip and then sliding it down the hose
e) The clips on the fuel hoses are designed to be used only once, so obtain new ones or replace them with screw type clips

3 Camshaft oil seal - renewal

1 This is a straightforward task if the camshaft is removed but it is possible to renew the oil seal without removing the camshaft.
2 A VW special tool exists for this job (see illustration) but if it is not available, the old seal will have to be removed by securing self-tapping screws into it and pulling it out with pliers. Note which way round it is fitted.
3 Whichever method is used, the timing cover and camshaft sprocket will have to be removed. Slacken the coolant pump bolts to release the tension in the timing belt.
4 Lightly oil the new seal and slide onto the camshaft. Use a suitable socket and a bolt in the end of the shaft to press the new seal home. Push it in as far as it will go.

2.1a Valve cover

2.1b Plastic oil shield

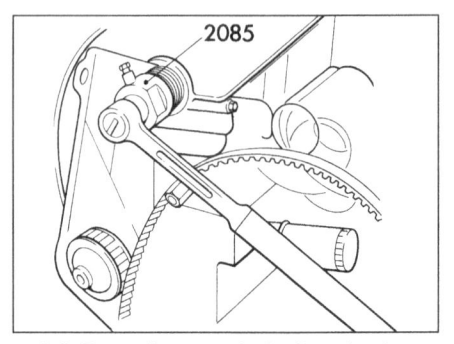

3.2 Renewing camshaft oil seal using VW tool 2085

Engine repair procedures - 1.05 and 1.3 litre post August 1985 2B•3

4.5 Two lengths of metal used to lock camshaft sprocket

4 Camshaft - removal

1 Unscrew the nuts and bolts from the valve cover and remove the cover together with the gasket and reinforcement strips.
2 Turn the engine until the indentation in the camshaft sprocket appears in the TDC hole in the timing cover and the notch in the crankshaft pulley is aligned with the TDC pointer on the front of the oil pump. Now turn the crankshaft one quarter of a turn anti-clockwise so that none of the pistons are at TDC.
3 Unbolt and remove the timing cover, noting that the dipstick tube and earth lead are fitted to the upper bolts. On some later 1.3 litre models, it is necessary to remove the crankshaft pulley to remove the lower timing belt cover.
4 Loosen the coolant pump retaining bolts, then turn the pump body to release the tension from the timing belt. Remove the timing belt from the camshaft sprocket.
5 Devise a method to prevent the camshaft turning and remove the sprocket bolt **(see illustration)**. Remove the camshaft sprocket and where applicable, the Woodruff key.
6 The camshaft bearing caps must be refitted in their original locations and the same way round. They are usually numbered but mark them if necessary, to ensure correct refitting.
7 Remove bearing caps Nos 5, 1 and 3, in that order. Now undo the nuts holding 2 and 4 in a diagonal pattern and the camshaft will lift them up as the pressure of the valve springs is exerted. When they are free, lift the caps off.
8 If the caps are stuck, give them a sharp tap with a soft-faced mallet to loosen them. Do not try to lever them off with a screwdriver.
9 Lift out the camshaft complete with the oil seal.

5 Cylinder head - dismantling and overhaul

Caution: If new tappets are fitted, the engine must not be started after fitting for approximately 30 minutes, or the valves will strike the pistons.

Cylinder head

1 If the valve seats are badly pitted or eroded they can be reworked but this is a specialist job best left to a VW dealer or engine overhaul specialist.
2 Similarly, if the head is warped, its surfaces can be skimmed, again by specialist engineers.
3 If it is found that there are cracks from the valve seats or valve seat inserts to the spark plug threads, the cylinder head may still be serviceable. Consult your VW dealer for advice.

Hydraulic bucket tappets

4 With the camshaft removed, lift out the tappets one by one, ensuring that they are kept in their correct order and can be returned to their original bores **(see illustration)**.
5 Place them, cam contact surface down, on a clean sheet of paper as they are removed.
6 Inspect the tappets for wear (indicated by ridging on the clean surface), pitting and cracks.
7 Tappets cannot be repaired and if worn, must be renewed.
8 Before fitting the tappets, lubricate all parts liberally with clean engine oil and slip each tappet back into its original bore.

Valves

9 With the camshaft and tappets removed, use a valve spring compressor with a deep reach to compress the valve springs. Remove the two cotters and release the compressor and springs.
10 Lift out the upper spring seat **(see illustration)**.
11 Remove the outer and inner valve springs **(see illustrations)**.
12 Lift out the valve **(see illustration)**.
13 The valves should be inspected as described in Part A of this Chapter, Section 11.
14 Valves must be renewed if they are worn and be ground in the normal manner.
15 If possible, check the valve spring lengths against new ones. Renew the whole set if any are too short.
16 Refitting is a reversal of removal.

Valve stem oil seals

17 The valve stem oil seals should be renewed whenever the valves are removed, by prising them from the ends of the valve guides **(see illustration)**.

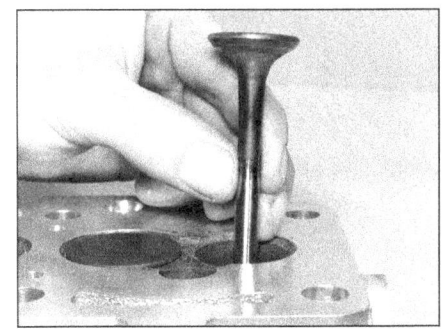

5.4 Removing an hydraulic bucket tappet

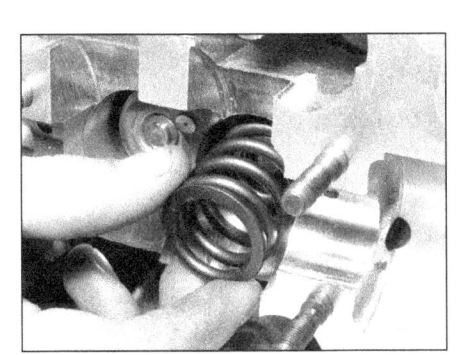

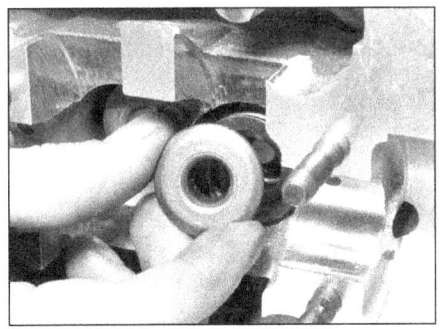

5.10 Removing valve spring upper seat

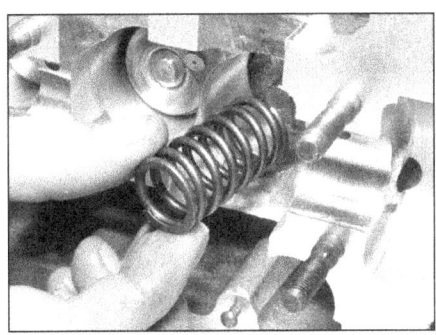

5.11a Removing an outer valve spring

5.11b Removing an inner valve spring

5.12 Removing a valve

2B•4 Engine repair procedures - 1.05 and 1.3 litre post August 1985

5.17 A valve stem oil seal

18 With the seals removed, the lower spring seats can also be lifted out for cleaning. Press the new seals onto the ends of the valve guides.

6 Timing belt and sprockets - removal

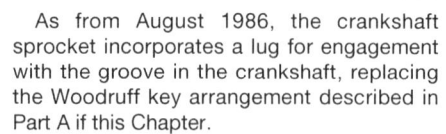

As from August 1986, the crankshaft sprocket incorporates a lug for engagement with the groove in the crankshaft, replacing the Woodruff key arrangement described in Part A if this Chapter.

When tightening the crankshaft sprocket bolt, observe the specified stages.

7 Oil pump - removal and examination

Note: *The oil pump can be removed with the engine still in the vehicle*

1 Drain the engine oil.
2 Disconnect the exhaust downpipe and the inboard end of the right-hand driveshaft to permit sump removal.
3 Remove the sump.
4 If it is only desired to check backlash in the pump gears, this can be done by removing the cover and strainer assembly from the back of the pump **(see illustration)**.

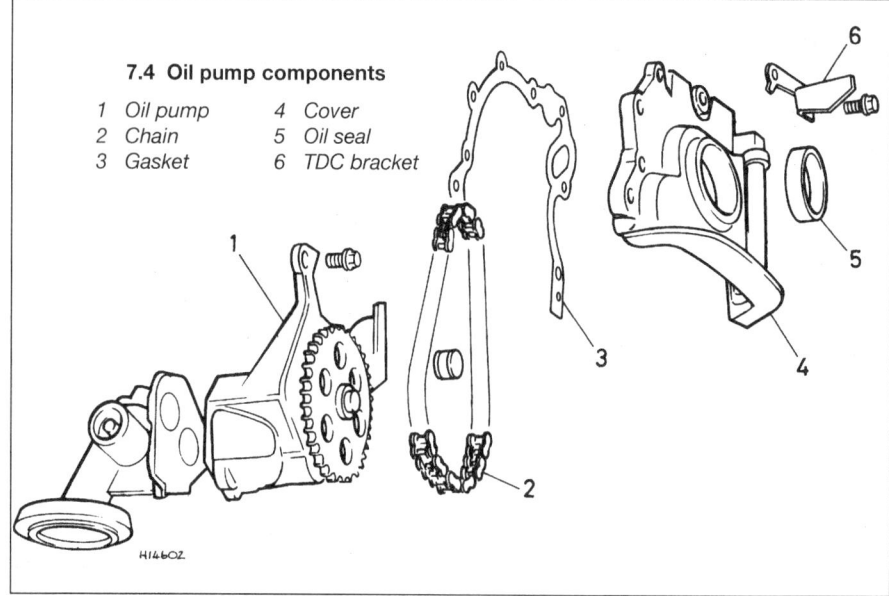

7.4 Oil pump components

1 Oil pump
2 Chain
3 Gasket
4 Cover
5 Oil seal
6 TDC bracket

5 Check backlash and axial play against the specified tolerances **(see illustrations)**.
6 If the tolerances are exceeded then the oil pump must be renewed.
7 To remove the pump, first remove the following components:
 a) Camshaft drivebelt (timing belt)
 b) Alternator drivebelt
 c) Crankshaft pulley
 d) Lower timing belt cover
 e) Front cover and TDC setting bracket
8 If they are still in position, remove the bolts holding the rear stay bracket.
9 Remove the two bolts holding the pump to the cylinder block.
10 This will release the tension on the chain and allow the pump to be removed.
11 If sufficient slack in the chain cannot be achieved by this method, then slide the pump, chain and crankshaft drive sprocket forward together.

12 Check the chain and teeth of the drive sprockets and renew any parts which are worn.
13 If a new pump is being fitted, renew all associated parts at the same time.

8 Camshaft - examination

1 Clean the camshaft in solvent, then inspect its journals and cam peaks for pitting, scoring, cracking and wear.
2 The camshaft bearings are machined directly into the cylinder head and the bearing caps.
3 Radial play in the bearings can be measured using the Plastigage method. Compare the results with the specified dimension.
4 If wear is evident, consult your VW dealer.
5 To check camshaft endfloat, refit the camshaft using only number 3 bearing cap.
6 Set up a dial test indicator or use feeler blades to measure the endfloat **(see illustration)**. If the endfloat is greater than that specified, consult your VW dealer.

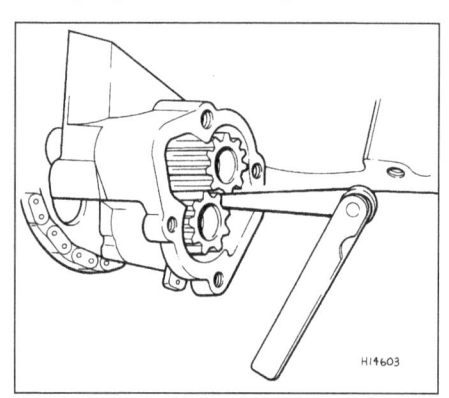

7.5a Checking oil pump backlash

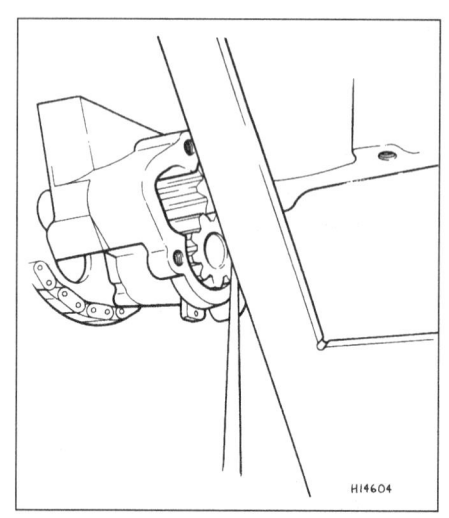

7.5b Checking oil pump axial play

8.6 Measuring camshaft endfloat

9.1 Checking oil pump drive chain tension

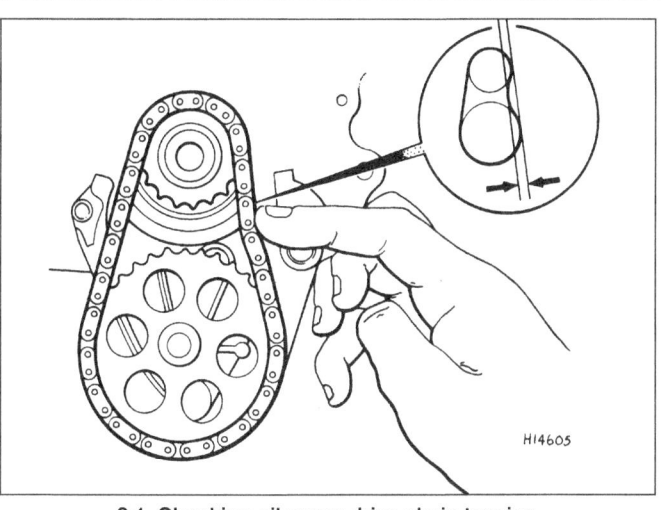

10.2 Refitting the camshaft

9 Oil pump - refitting

Refitting is a reversal of removal, but bear in mind the following points:
a) Use new gaskets on all components.
b) Lubricate all new parts liberally with clean engine oil.
c) If the small plug in the front cover is at all damaged, renew it.
d) Fit a new crankshaft oil seal to the cover. The oil seal can be prised out and a new one pressed fully home.
e) The chain is tensioned by moving the pump housing against its mounting bolts.
f) With light finger pressure exerted on the chain, deflection should be as specified **(see illustration)**.
g) Whenever the sump is removed with the engine in situ, the two hexagon screws in the sealing flange at the flywheel end should be replaced by socket-headed screws and spring washers, and tightened to the specified torque setting.

10 Camshaft - refitting

1 Lubricate the bucket tappets, the camshaft journals and the camshaft liberally with clean engine oil.
2 Place the camshaft in position on the cylinder head **(see illustration)**.
3 Fit a new camshaft oil seal **(see illustration)**.
4 Refit the bearing caps, ensuring that they are the right way and in their correct position (they should be numbered 1 to 5, readable from the exhaust manifold side of the head).
5 Thread on the cap retaining nuts loosely, then tighten the nuts on Nos. 2 and 4 caps in a diagonal sequence to the Stage 1 torque figure specified **(see illustration)**.
6 Tighten the nuts on caps 1, 3 and 5 to the Stage 1 torque.
7 Once all nuts have been tightened to the Stage 1 torque, tighten all nuts a further 90° (Stage 2). Fit and tighten No. 5 cap screws to the correct torque.

8 Refit the Woodruff key into its slot in the camshaft, where applicable. Fit the camshaft sprocket and tighten the bolt to the specified torque **(see illustration)**.
9 If the work is being carried out in the engine compartment, follow the procedure given in Part A of this Chapter, Section 35, paragraphs 9 to 18.
10 Ignore any reference to the oil spray tube and be sure to refit the oil shield at the distributor end of the camshaft before the valve cover is refitted.
11 If the cylinder head is out of the vehicle, it will obviously have to be refitted before the timing belt can be reconnected.

11 Cylinder head - refitting

1 Clean all traces of old gasket from the cylinder block and cylinder head faces, taking great care not to mark the gasket surfaces.
2 Using a new gasket, fit the inlet manifold **(see illustrations)**.

10.3 Camshaft oil seal

10.5 Tightening a camshaft bearing cap nut

10.8 Fitting the camshaft sprocket bolt

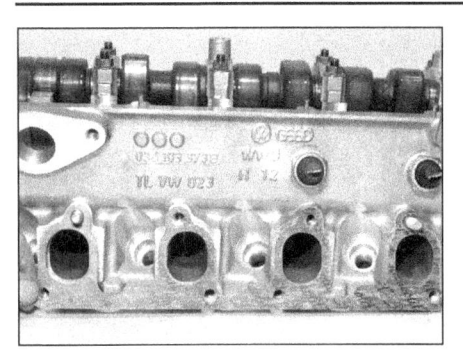

2B•6 Engine repair procedures - 1.05 and 1.3 litre post August 1985

11.2a Fitting a new inlet manifold gasket

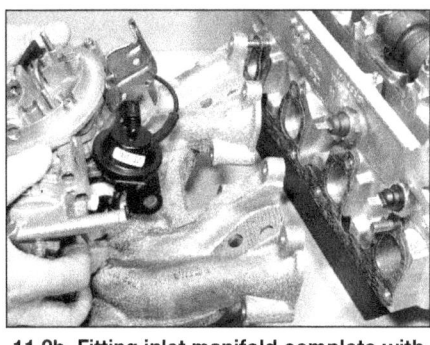

11.2b Fitting inlet manifold complete with carburettor

11.3 Refitting oil pressure switch

3 If they have been removed, refit the oil pressure switches, using new copper sealing washers **(see illustration)**.
4 Refit the thermostat housing, using a new O-ring **(see illustration)**.

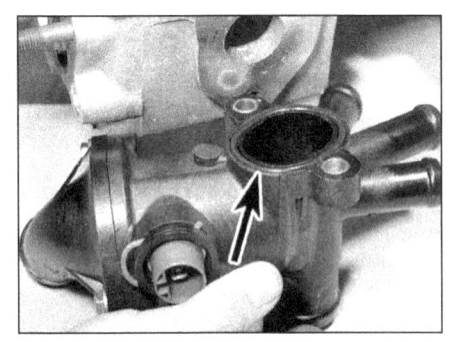

5 Refit the coolant hoses, ensuring that they are connected up in the correct position **(see illustration)**.
6 Lubricate the fuel pump plunger with clean engine oil and slip it into its housing in the cylinder head **(see illustration)**.
7 Refit the fuel pump and fit and tighten the bolts, not forgetting the engine lifting eye **(see illustrations)**.
8 Slide the distributor into position and ensure that it goes fully home **(see illustration)**. Hand-tighten the retaining bolts.
9 Fit the distributor rotor arm **(see illustration)**.
10 Fit the distributor cap and connect up the earth lead **(see illustration)**.
11 Check the timing marks on the cylinder head and camshaft sprocket are lined up.
12 Note that none of the pistons should be at TDC when refitting the cylinder head.
13 Position a new cylinder head gasket on the cylinder block **(see illustration)**.
14 Lower the cylinder head gently into position. Special guides are used by the manufacturer both to line up the gasket and

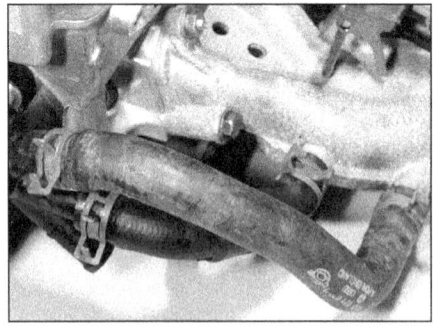

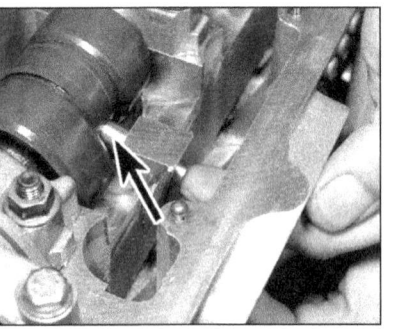

11.4 O-ring (arrowed) in thermostat housing

11.5 Coolant hoses in position

11.6 Fitting fuel pump plunger (arrowed)

11.7a Fitting fuel pump

11.7b Location of engine lifting eye

11.8 Refitting ignition distributor

11.9 Fitting rotor arm

11.10 Fitting distributor cap and earth lead

Engine repair procedures - 1.05 and 1.3 litre post August 1985 2B•7

11.13 Cylinder head gasket in position

11.17 Plastic oil shield correctly located

11.18 Locating dowel for valve cover gasket (arrowed)

guide the cylinder head into position but this can be done using suitable sized rods inserted in two cylinder head bolt holes.
15 Install the cylinder head bolts. Refer to Part A of this Chapter for the tightening sequence but use the torque figures and stages given in the *Specifications* of this Chapter.
16 It is not necessary to retighten the bolts after a period of service, as is normally the case.
17 Refit the plastic oil shield **(see illustration)**.
18 Using a new rubber sealing gasket properly located over the dowels, refit the valve cover **(see illustration)**.
19 Fit a new gasket to the exhaust manifold **(see illustration)**.
20 Fit the exhaust manifold, tightening its nuts securely, then fit the hot air shroud **(see illustration)**.

21 Connect up the exhaust downpipe and any other exhaust brackets loosened during removal.
22 Refit all remaining hoses of the cooling system and fuel system, referring to the relevant Chapter where necessary.
23 Refit all electrical connections disturbed during dismantling (distributor, carburettor, oil pressure and coolant temperature switches, inlet manifold preheater, etc.) **(see illustrations)**. Do not forget the earth lead under the inlet manifold nut.
24 Refit the distributor vacuum hose.
25 With reference to Part A of this Chapter, Section 37, refit the timing belt and covers.
26 Refit the throttle cable.
27 Refit the spark plugs, air cleaner and associated pipework and electrical leads.
28 Check oil and coolant levels, replenishing as necessary, then adjust the ignition timing.

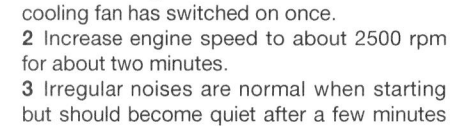

12 Hydraulic bucket tappets - checking free travel

1 Start the engine and run it until the radiator cooling fan has switched on once.
2 Increase engine speed to about 2500 rpm for about two minutes.
3 Irregular noises are normal when starting but should become quiet after a few minutes running.
4 If the valves are still noisy, carry out the following check to identify worn tappets.
5 Stop the engine and remove the valve cover from the cylinder head.
6 Turn the crankshaft clockwise by using a wrench on the crankshaft pulley securing bolt, until the cam of the tappet to be checked is facing upward and is not exerting any pressure on the tappet.

11.19 Fitting a new exhaust manifold gasket

11.20 Fitting hot air shroud

11.23a Ignition distributor electrical connection

11.23b Coolant temperature switch/sender electrical connection

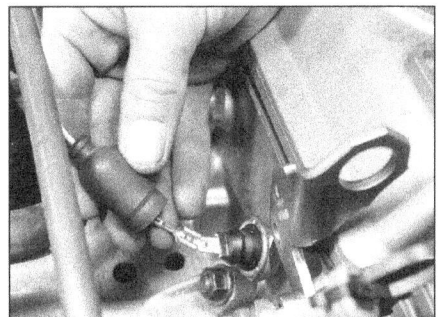

11.23c Oil pressure switch electrical connection

11.23d Earth lead under inlet manifold bolt head

7 Press the tappet down using a wooden or plastic wedge **(see illustration)**.
8 If free travel of the tappet exceeds that specified, the tappet must be renewed.

13 Engine - adjustments after major overhaul

If the valve tappets have been renewed, it is essential that no attempt to restart the engine is made for a minimum period of 30 minutes after installation. Failure to observe this precaution may result in engine damage caused by the valves contacting the pistons.

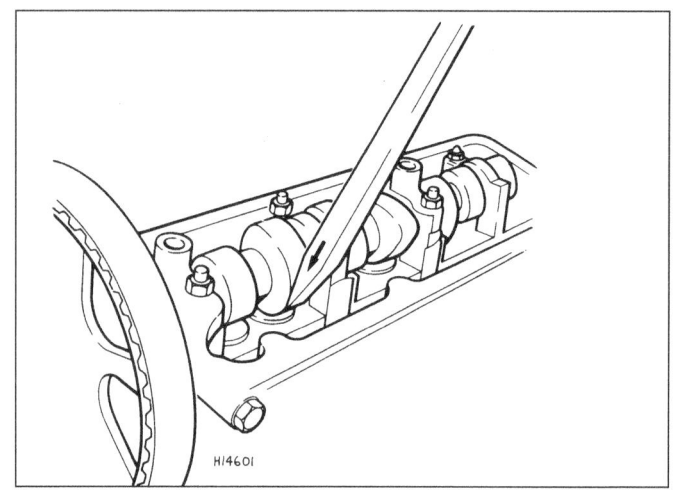

12.7 Checking hydraulic tappet free travel

Chapter 2 Part C:
Engine repair procedures - 1.6 and 1.8 litre 8 valve

Contents

Camshaft - removal, examination and refitting 10
Crankshaft and bearings - examination and renovation 22
Crankshaft and main bearings - refitting 30
Crankshaft and main bearings - removal 15
Cylinder block/crankcase - examination and renovation 23
Cylinder head - dismantling and overhaul 12
Cylinder head - refitting 34
Cylinder head - removal 11
Engine - adjustments after major overhaul 39
Engine - refitting 37
Engine - removal 5
Engine ancillary components - removal 8
Engine ancillary components refitting 36
Engine dismantling - general information 7
Engine reassembly - general information 29
Engine/gearbox - separation and reconnection 6
Examination and renovation - general information 21
Flywheel/driveplate - examination and renovation 27
General information 1
Hydraulic bucket tappets - checking free travel (from August 1985) .. 38
Intermediate shaft - examination and renovation 26
Intermediate shaft - refitting 31
Intermediate shaft - removal 16
Major operations only possible after removal of engine from vehicle .. 3
Major operations possible with engine in vehicle 2
Method of engine removal 4
Oil cooler - removal and refitting 18
Oil filter - renewal 17
Oil filter mounting - removal and refitting 19
Oil pump - examination and renovation 25
Oil seals - renewal 20
Pistons and connecting rods - examination and renovation 24
Pistons and connecting rods - refitting 32
Pistons and connecting rods - removal 14
Sump and oil pump - removal and refitting 13
Timing belt and sprockets - examination and renovation 28
Timing belt and sprockets - refitting 35
Timing belt and sprockets - removal 9
Valve clearances - checking and adjustment (pre August 1985) .. 33

Degrees of difficulty

Easy, suitable for novice with little experience	Fairly easy, suitable for beginner with some experience	Fairly difficult, suitable for competent DIY mechanic	Difficult, suitable for experienced DIY mechanic	Very difficult, suitable for expert DIY or professional

Specifications

General

Type .... Four-cylinder in-line, water cooled, overhead camshaft
Code:
   1.6 litre engines:
      Without catalytic converter .... EZ
      With catalytic converter .... RF
   1.8 litre carburettor engines:
      Without catalytic converter .... GU
      With catalytic converter .... RH
   1.8 litre fuel injection engines:
      Mono-Jetronic .... RP
      K-Jetronic (early GTi models) .... EV
      Digifant (later GTi models, without catalytic converter) .... PB
      Digifant (later GTi models, with catalytic converter) .... PF
Firing order .... 1-3-4-2 (No 1 at camshaft sprocket end)
Displacement:
   1.6 litre .... 1595 cc
   1.8 litre .... 1781 cc
Bore:
   1.6 litre .... 81.0 mm
   1.8 litre .... 81.0 mm
Stroke:
   1.6 litre .... 77.4 mm
   1.8 litre .... 86.4 mm
Compression ratio:
   1.6 litre .... 9.0 to 1
   1.8 litre
      Code RP .... 9.0 to 1
      All other codes .... 10.0 to 1

2C•2 Engine repair procedures - 1.6 and 1.8 litre 8 valve

Compression pressure:
  1.6 litre:
    New .... 9 to 12 bar
    Minimum .... 7.5 bar
    Maximum permissible difference between any two cylinders .... 3.0 bar
  1.8 litre:
    New .... 10 to 13 bar
    Minimum .... 7.5 bar
    Maximum permissible difference between any two cylinders .... 3.0 bar

Crankshaft
Main journal:
  Standard diameter .... 54.0 mm
  Undersizes .... 53.75, 53.50 and 53.25 mm
Crankpin:
  Standard diameter .... 47.80 mm
  Journal undersizes .... 47.55, 47.30 and 47.05 mm
Endfloat:
  Maximum .... 0.25 mm
  Minimum .... 0.07 mm
Main bearing maximum running clearance .... 0.17 mm

Connecting rods
Big-end:
  Maximum running clearance .... 0.012 mm
  Maximum endfloat .... 0.37 mm

Pistons
Clearance in bore:
  Maximum .... 0.07 mm
  Minimum .... 0.03 mm
Diameter:
  Standard .... 80.98 mm
  Oversize:
    1st oversize .... 81.23 mm
    2nd oversize .... 81.48 mm
Wear limit (10 mm from base/ right angles to pin) .... 0.04 mm

Piston rings
Maximum clearance in groove .... 0.15 mm
End gap:
  Compression rings .... 0.30 to 0.45 mm
  Oil scraper ring:
    1 part .... 0.25 to 0.40 mm
    2 part .... 0.25 to 0.45 mm
    3 part .... 0.25 to 0.50 mm
Maximum end gap .... 1.0 mm

Gudgeon pin
Fit in piston .... Push fit at 60°C

Intermediate shaft
Maximum endfloat .... 0.25 mm

Cylinder head
Maximum allowable face distortion .... 0.1 mm
Minimum height .... 132.6 mm

Camshaft
Run-out at centre bearing .... 0.01 mm
Endfloat .... 0.15 mm

Valves
Seat angle .... 45°
Head diameter:
  Inlet:
    Codes PB, PF .... 40.0 mm
    All other codes .... 38.0 mm
  Exhaust .... 33.0 mm

Engine repair procedures - 1.6 and 1.8 litre 8 valve

Stem diameter:
  Inlet .... 7.97 mm
  Exhaust .... 7.95 mm
Standard overall length*:
  Inlet:
    Codes EZ, EV, GU .... 98.70 mm
    All other codes .... 91.0 mm
  Exhaust:
    Codes EZ, EV, GU .... 98.50 mm
    Codes PB, PF, RP .... 90.95 mm
    All other codes .... 90.80 mm
* **Caution**: *Check with manufacturer on valve dimensions before renewing*

Valve guides
Maximum valve rock (stem flush with guide):
  Inlet .... 1.0 mm
  Exhaust .... 1.3 mm

Hydraulic tappets
Maximum free travel .... 0.1 mm

Valve timing
Nil valve clearance at 1.0 mm valve lift
1.6 litre (code EZ - shim bucket tappets):
  Inlet opens .... 5° BTDC
  Inlet closes .... 21° ABDC
  Exhaust opens .... 41° BBDC
  Exhaust closes .... 3° BTDC
1.6 litre (code EZ - hydraulic tappets - August 1985 to March 1986):
  Inlet opens .... 3° BTDC
  Inlet closes .... 19° ABDC
  Exhaust opens .... 27° BBDC
  Exhaust closes .... 5° BTDC
1.6 litre (code EZ - hydraulic tappets - March 1986 on):
  Inlet opens .... TDC
  Inlet closes .... 22° ABDC
  Exhaust opens .... 28° BBDC
  Exhaust closes .... 6° BTDC
1.6 litre (code RF):
  Inlet opens .... TDC
  Inlet closes .... 22° ABDC
  Exhaust opens .... 28° BBDC
  Exhaust closes .... 6° BTDC
1.8 litre (code GU - shim bucket tappets)
  Inlet opens .... 1° BTDC
  Inlet closes .... 37° ABDC
  Exhaust opens .... 42° BBDC
  Exhaust closes .... 2° ATDC
1.8 litre (code GU - hydraulic tappets - August 1985 to March 1986
  Inlet opens .... 3° BTDC
  Inlet closes .... 33° ABDC
  Exhaust opens .... 41° BBDC
  Exhaust closes .... 5° BTDC
1.8 litre (code GU - hydraulic tappets - March 1986 on):
  Inlet opens .... 2° BTDC
  Inlet closes .... 34° ABDC
  Exhaust opens .... 44° BBDC
  Exhaust closes .... 8° BTDC
1.8 litre (code EV):
  Inlet opens .... 2° BTDC
  Inlet closes .... 45° ABDC
  Exhaust opens .... 45° BBDC
  Exhaust closes .... 8° BTDC
1.8 litre (codes PB, PF):
  Inlet opens .... 3° ATDC
  Inlet closes .... 43° ABDC
  Exhaust opens .... 37° BBDC
  Exhaust closes .... 3° ATDC

2C•4 Engine repair procedures - 1.6 and 1.8 litre 8 valve

Valve timing (continued)

Nil valve clearance at 1.0 mm valve lift

1.8 litre (code RH):
- Inlet opens .... 2° BTDC
- Inlet closes .... 34° ABDC
- Exhaust opens .... 44° BBDC
- Exhaust closes .... 8° BTDC

1.8 litre (code RP - pre July 1988):
- Inlet opens .... 2° ATDC
- Inlet closes .... 38° ABDC
- Exhaust opens .... 40° BBDC
- Exhaust closes .... 4° BTDC

1.8 litre (code RP - August 1988 on):
- Inlet opens .... 5° BTDC
- Inlet closes .... 41° ABDC
- Exhaust opens .... 37° BBDC
- Exhaust closes .... 1° BTDC

Valve clearances

Warm:
- Inlet .... 0.20 to 0.30 mm
- Exhaust .... 0.40 to 0.50 m

Cold:
- Inlet .... 0.15 to 0.25 mm
- Exhaust .... 0.35 to 0.45 mm

Lubrication

- System type .... Wet sump, pressure feed, full flow filter
- Lubricant type/specification/capacity .... Refer to *"Lubricants, fluids and capacities"*
- Pump type .... Twin gear, driven by intermediate shaft together with distributor
- Pressure (2000 rpm with oil temperature 80°C) ... 2.0 bar minimum

Torque wrench settings

	Nm	lbf ft
Engine to gearbox:		
M10	45	33
M12	75	55
Exhaust manifold nuts	25	18
Exhaust pipe to manifold	10	7
Flywheel/driveplate bolts	20	15
Clutch pressure plate/washer bolts (renew)	100	74
Sump bolts	20	15
Sump drain plug	30	22
Main bearing cap bolts	65	48
Connecting rod big-end cap nuts:		
Stage 1	30	22
Stage 2*	Further tighten 1/4 turn (90°)	
Oil pump bolts	10	7
Oil pressure switch	25	18
Oil filter flange bolts	25	18
Front seal flange bolts:		
Small	20	15
Large	10	7
Intermediate shaft flange bolts	25	18
Camshaft bearing cap nuts (in sequence)	20	15
Camshaft sprocket bolt	80	59
Valve cover nuts	10	7
Belt tensioner pulley	45	33
Crankshaft sprocket bolt (oiled)	200	148
Intermediate shaft sprocket bolt	80	59
V-belt pulley	20	15
Timing cover	10	7
Rear cover lower bolts	30	22
Rear cover top bolt	10	7
Coolant pump bolts	20	15
Fuel pump bolts	20	15
Distributor clamp bolt	25	18

Engine repair procedures - 1.6 and 1.8 litre 8 valve 2C•5

Cylinder head bolts (engine cold)	As for 1.05 and 1.3 litre engines	
Refer to illustration 5.25b. Also 40.1a and 40.1b in Part A of this Chapter.		
a) M8	25	18
a) M10	45	33
b)	35	26
c)	45	33
d)	50	37
e)	60	44
f)	70	52
g)	80	59

* *When checking the connecting rod-to-crankshaft journal radial clearance using Plastigage, tighten only to 30Nm (22 lbf ft).*

1 General information

The 1.6 and 1.8 litre 8-valve engines are of four-cylinder, in-line, overhead camshaft design, mounted transversely at the front of the vehicle. The transmission is attached to the flywheel end of the engine.

The crankshaft is of five main bearing type, its endfloat being controlled by a shouldered centre bearing or by half thrustwashers located each side of the centre bearing.

The camshaft is driven by a toothed belt which is tensioned by a tensioner on an eccentric bearing. On engines manufactured before August 1985, the valves are operated by bucket type cam followers in direct contact with the camshaft. From August 1985, all engines are fitted with a redesigned cylinder head incorporating hydraulic bucket tappets in place of the previous shim bucket tappets. Camshaft bearing No. 4 is deleted on all single camshaft engines. In order to identify the type of tappets fitted, a sticker is normally affixed to the valve cover indicating that valve clearance adjustment is neither necessary nor possible.

An intermediate shaft (driven by the toothed timing belt) drives the distributor and oil pump and on carburettor equipped engines, the fuel pump.

The oil pump is of twin gear type, driven from the immediate shaft and incorporates a pressure relief valve.

The aluminium cylinder head is of conventional design with the inlet and exhaust manifolds mounted on the rear side (as viewed with the engine in the vehicle).

The crankcase ventilation system comprises a hose from the flywheel end of the valve cover to the side of the air cleaner.

On fuel injection equipped engines, there is a hose to the air inlet manifold and a hose to the air cleaner from a three-way connector on the valve cover.

2 Major operations possible with engine in vehicle

The following operations can be carried out without having to remove the engine from the vehicle:

a) *Removal and servicing of the cylinder head, camshaft and timing belt*
b) *Renewal of the crankshaft rear oil seal (after removal of the transmission, driveplate or clutch as applicable)*
c) *Removal of the sump and oil pump*
d) *Removal of the piston/connecting rod assemblies (after removal of the cylinder head and sump)*
e) *Renewal of the crankshaft front oil seal, intermediate shaft front oil seal and camshaft front oil seal*
f) *Renewal of the engine mountings*

3 Major operations only possible after removal of engine from vehicle

The following operations can only be carried out after removal of the engine from the vehicle:

a) *Renewal of crankshaft main bearings*
b) *Removal and refitting of the crankshaft*
c) *Removal and refitting of the intermediate shaft*

4 Method of engine removal

1 The engine, together with the gearbox, must be lifted from the engine compartment, then the engine separated from the gearbox on the bench. Two people will be needed.
2 A hoist of 150 kg capacity will be needed to lift the engine approximately 1 metre. If the hoist is not portable and the engine is lifted, then sufficient room must be left behind the vehicle to push it back out of the way so that the engine may be lowered. Blocks will be needed to support the engine after removal.
3 Ideally, the vehicle should be over a pit. If this is not possible then the body must be supported on axle stands (see "*Jacking and vehicle support*") so that the front wheels may be turned to undo the driveshaft nuts. The left-hand shaft is accessible from above but the right-hand shaft must be undone from underneath. Removal of the gearshift linkage can only be done from underneath, as can exhaust downpipe-to-manifold detachment.
4 The exhaust downpipe-to-manifold flange connection is secured by special spring clips rather than bolts or studs and nuts. When disconnecting and reconnecting the joint, it will be necessary to use VW tool no. 3049A. Without this tool, detachment and certainly reconnection of the joint and clips is virtually impossible, so make arrangements to borrow or hire the tool in advance.
5 The only other special tools required will be a set of splined key wrenches which will be needed to remove and refit the socket-head bolts used to secure certain items such as the cylinder head bolts.
6 Draining of oil and coolant is best done away from the working area if possible. This saves the mess made by spilled oil in the place where you must work.
7 Although not listed as an optional fitting on UK models, an air conditioning system may have been fitted. Where this is the case, the following precautions must be taken when handling refrigerant lines or system components:

a) *Do not stress or bend flexible hose lines to a radius of less than 101 mm*
b) *Flexible hose lines must be correctly located, must not chafe against adjacent components and must be kept well clear of the exhaust manifold and downpipe*
c) *All metal tubing lines must be kept free of kinks and must be handled with care*
d) *Do not disconnect any of the air conditioning supply lines*
e) *Do not weld or apply heat in the vicinity of the air conditioning lines or equipment*
f) *If any part of the system is to be detached then it must first be depressurised by your VW dealer or a competent air conditioning systems engineer. The only exception is the removal and fitting of the compressor drivebelt which can be achieved in the same manner as for the alternator drivebelt*

5 Engine - removal

Carburettor equipped

1 Disconnect the battery negative lead.
2 Remove the bonnet.
3 Drain the engine coolant.
4 Position a suitable container beneath the engine, undo the sump drain plug and drain the engine oil - see Chapter 1. On completion clean the drain plug and refit it. Renew the O-ring.

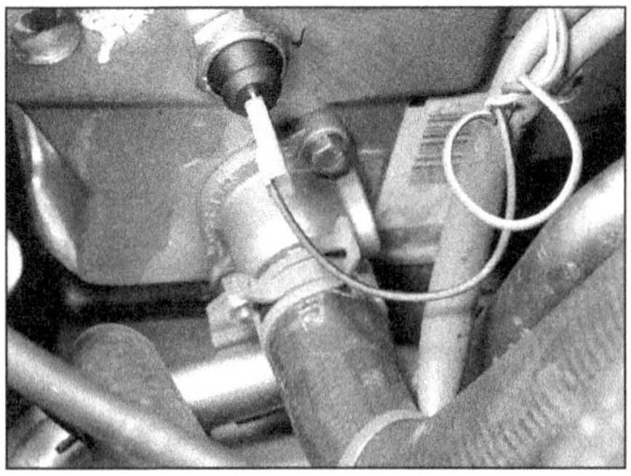

2C•6 Engine repair procedures - 1.6 and 1.8 litre 8 valve

5.8a Oil pressure switch location in rear of cylinder head

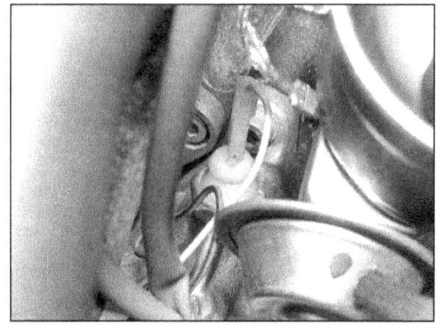

5.8b Oil pressure switch location in filter mounting

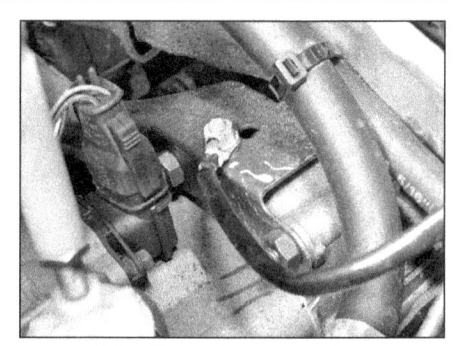

5.8c Earth strap to gearbox

5 Remove the radiator, together with the cooling fan. On models manufactured after 1986, remove the front panel before removing the radiator.

6 Remove the air cleaner unit then disconnect the throttle cable at the carburettor. Position the cable out of the way.

7 Where power steering is fitted, remove the hydraulic pump drivebelt. Unbolt the pump, belt tensioner and fluid reservoir and tie them to one side of the engine compartment.

8 Disconnect the following wiring connections, identifying each lead as it is detached to avoid confusion on reassembly:
   a) Alternator lead
   b) Oil pressure switch lead(s) at cylinder head **(see illustrations)** and oil filter bracket
   c) Inlet manifold preheater thermo-switch lead
   d) Choke cover thermo-switch lead (where applicable)
   e) Ignition HT and LT leads
   f) Choke cover lead separate connector
   g) Coolant temperature sender unit lead
   h) Earth strap to gearbox **(see illustration)** and multi-function switch to gearbox
   i) Starter motor leads

9 Disconnect the fuel supply hose from the fuel pump and the fuel return hose (to the fuel tank). Plug the hoses to prevent fuel leakage.

10 Disconnect the coolant and heater hoses from the engine.

5.24 Engine rear bearer

11 On manual gearbox models, disconnect the clutch cable.

12 Disconnect the following items from around the carburettor. Identify the connections where necessary to avoid confusion on reassembly:
   a) Thermotime valve
   b) Idle/overrun cut-off valve
   c) Inlet manifold preheater separator connector
   d) Part throttle channel heater separate connector

13 Disconnect the speedometer cable from the transmission.

14 Disconnect and remove the vacuum reservoir.

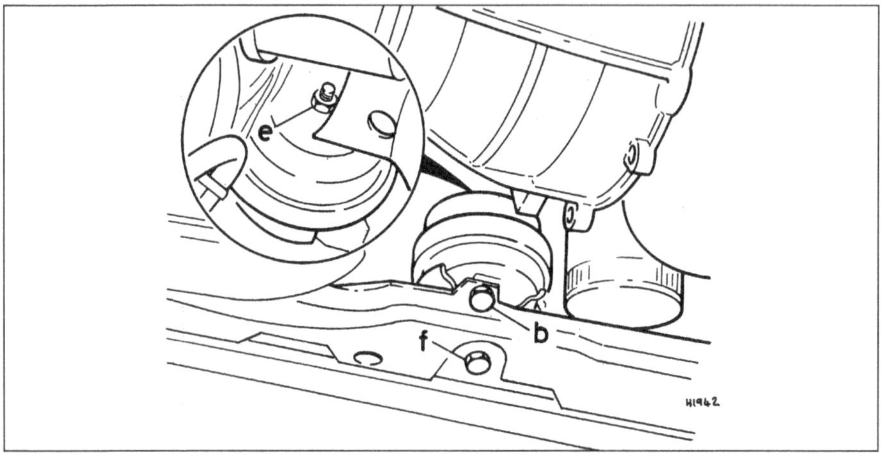

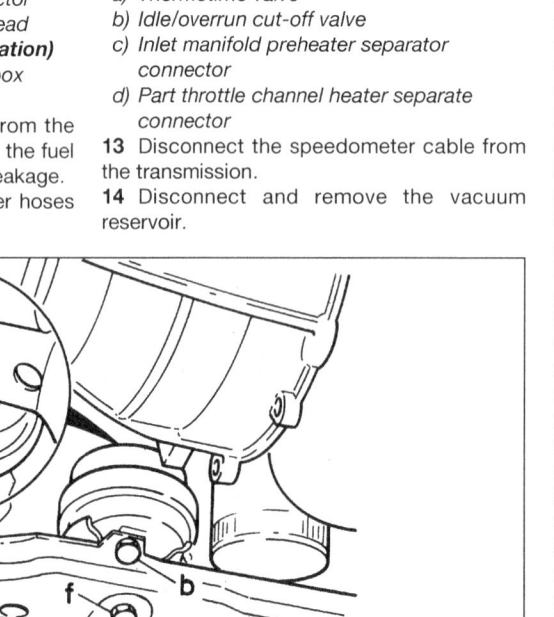

5.25a Engine/gearbox unit front mounting

15 Disconnect the brake vacuum servo hoses and the vacuum hoses from the inlet manifold.

16 Undo and remove the gearbox mounting bolt.

17 Raise and support the vehicle on axle stands (see "Jacking and vehicle support"), allowing sufficient clearance to work underneath.

18 Disconnect the manual gearbox linkage.

19 On automatic transmission models, select P (Park) then disconnect the throttle and selector cables from the transmission.

20 Disconnect the driveshafts from the gearbox and tie them up out of the way.

21 To disconnect the exhaust manifold to downpipe connection, VW tool no. 3049A will be required. Although it may be possible to prise the clips free to separate this joint, the tool will definitely be required to refit the springs.

22 The vehicle can now be lowered, the remaining removal operations being from above.

23 Attach a suitable sling and hoist to the engine/gearbox unit and take its weight.

24 Disconnect the rear engine bearer by undoing the three bolts **(see illustration)**.

25 The engine/gearbox unit front mounting must now be detached by unscrewing and removing the single through-bolt. It may be necessary to further lift, lower or twist the unit to allow the through-bolt to be withdrawn **(see illustration)**. Note that from December 1984, the front mounting is changed from the bonded rubber type to a 'hydro' type with damping action **(see illustration)**.

5.25b Hydro-type front engine mounting
Refer to Specifications for fastener torque wrench settings b, e and f

Engine repair procedures - 1.6 and 1.8 litre 8 valve 2C•7

26 The engine/gearbox unit is now ready for lifting out but first make a final check that all cables, wiring and hoses are clear.

27 Have an assistant at hand to help guide the unit clear of the surrounding components in the engine compartment as it is lifted out. The unit will have to be twisted slightly as it is raised. Once clear of the vehicle, lower it to the work surface.

Fuel injection equipped

28 On fuel injection equipped engines, the removal procedure closely follows that given for carburettor equipped engines. However, disregard those items concerning detachment of the carburettor and associated items. The following injection equipment items will need to be disconnected instead. Refer to Chapter 4 for further details:

29 Disconnect the wires from the warm-up valve (green connector) **(see illustration)**.

30 Disconnect the wiring to the cold start valve (blue connector).

31 Disconnect the wiring to the auxiliary air valve.

32 Disconnect the throttle cable at the fast idle cam and bracket but do not remove the securing clip **(see illustration)**.

33 Remove the cold start valve but leave the fuel lines connected. Place out of the way.

34 Disconnect the air inlet pipe at the flexible ducting attached to the throttle housing.

35 Disconnect the vacuum hoses from the inlet manifold and vacuum booster.

36 Leaving the fuel lines connected, undo the retaining bolts and withdraw the warm-up valve from the cylinder block. Position out of the way.

37 Detach the injectors from the cylinder head and plug the holes. Disconnect the injector lines from the locating bracket on the throttle housing and fold them out of the way.

38 Detach the vacuum hoses to the throttle housing T-piece connector location clip at the bulkhead. Fold the hoses back out of the way.

39 Disconnect the oil temperature switch sender lead **(see illustration)**.

40 When lifting out the engine/gearbox unit, greater care will have to be taken in manoeuvring the unit from the engine compartment due to the close proximity of the air inlet manifold to the bulkhead. The unit will need to be pulled forwards first then twisted and lifted.

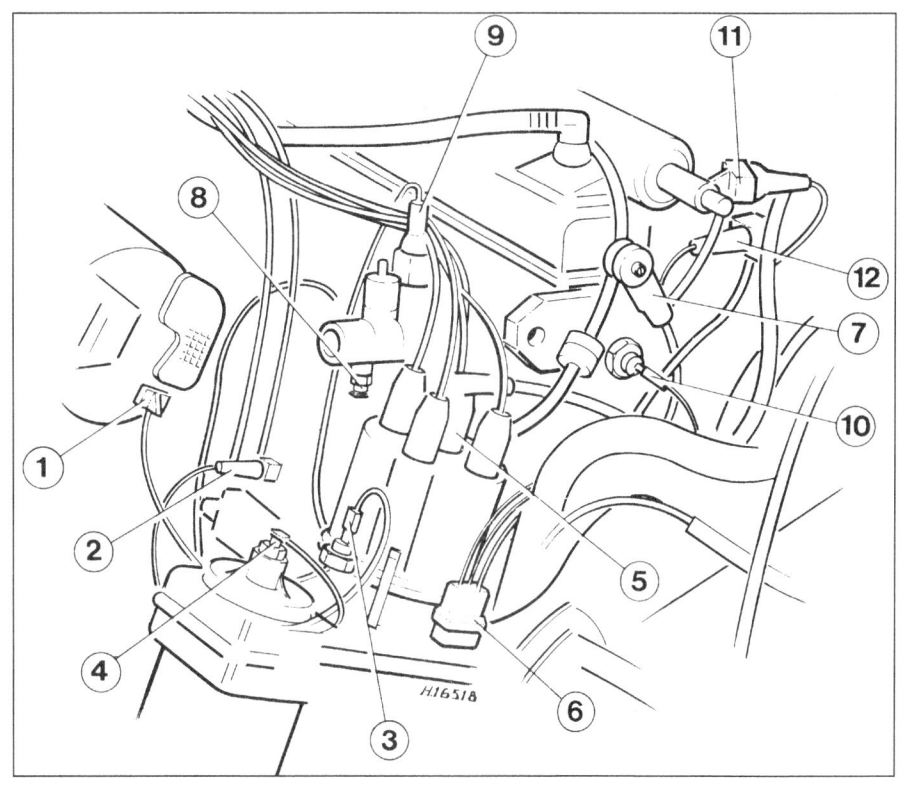

5.29 Wiring connections to be detached - fuel injection models

1 Alternator
2 Warm-up valve
3 1.8 bar oil pressure switch
4 Oil temperature sender
5 Distributor HT cable (terminal 4)
6 Hall sender (distributor)
7 Vacuum switch
8 Coolant temperature sender
9 Thermotime switch
10 0.3 bar oil pressure switch
11 Cold start valve
12 Auxiliary air valve

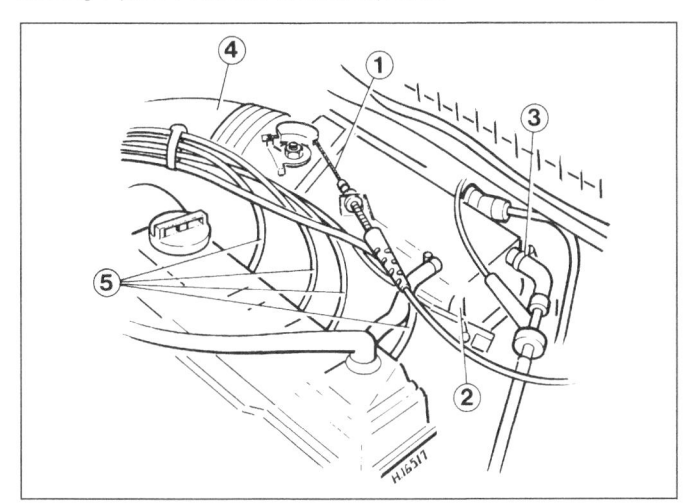

5.32 Fuel injection components to be detached

1 Throttle cable
2 Cold start valve
3 Vacuum hoses
4 Air intake pipe
5 Injectors

5.39 Oil temperature sender (arrowed)

2C•8 Engine repair procedures - 1.6 and 1.8 litre 8 valve

6 Engine/gearbox - separation and reconnection

This procedure is fully described in Chapter 7, Parts A or B, as applicable. It is only necessary to refer to those paragraphs pertinent to the particular method being used. The engine must be supported on blocks, or alternatively the gearbox can be separated with the engine still on the hoist.

7 Engine dismantling - general information

Refer to Section 7 in Part A of this Chapter.

8 Engine ancillary components - removal

With the engine removed from the vehicle and separated from the transmission, the externally mounted ancillary components can be removed prior to engine dismantling. The removal sequence need not necessarily follow the order given:
a) Alternator and drivebelt
b) Inlet manifold and carburettor or inlet manifold and throttle housing (fuel injection)
c) Exhaust manifold
d) Fuel pump
e) Warm-up valve (fuel injection), if still attached
f) Distributor
g) Oil filter with cooler (where applicable) and filter mounting
h) Oil pressure and coolant temperature and sensor switches
i) Coolant pump and coolant hose connectors from cylinder block and head. New O-rings will be required
j) Clutch then intermediate plate (manual gearbox)
k) Driveplate, noting location of spacer and shim(s) (automatic transmission)

9 Timing belt and sprockets - removal

1 If the engine is still in the vehicle, first carry out the following operations:
a) Disconnect the battery earth lead
b) Remove the alternator drivebelt
c) Unbolt and remove the coolant pump pulley

2 Depending on type, undo the retaining bolt(s)/nut(s), release the retaining clips and remove the upper timing cover **(see illustration)**. On some engines it will be necessary to remove the bung from the front

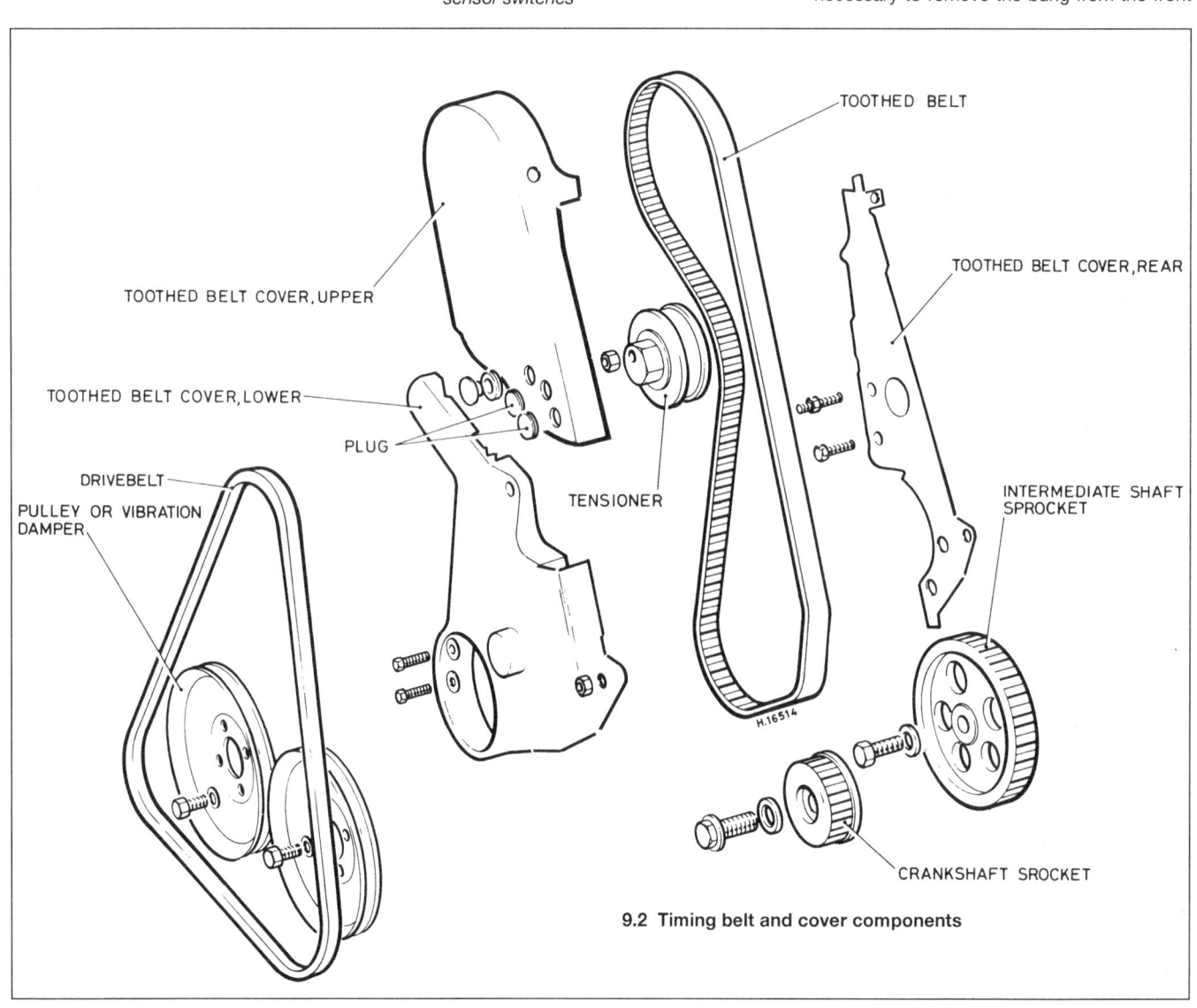

9.2 Timing belt and cover components

Engine repair procedures - 1.6 and 1.8 litre 8 valve 2C•9

9.6 Intermediate sprocket timing mark (arrowed) aligned with notch in crankshaft pulley

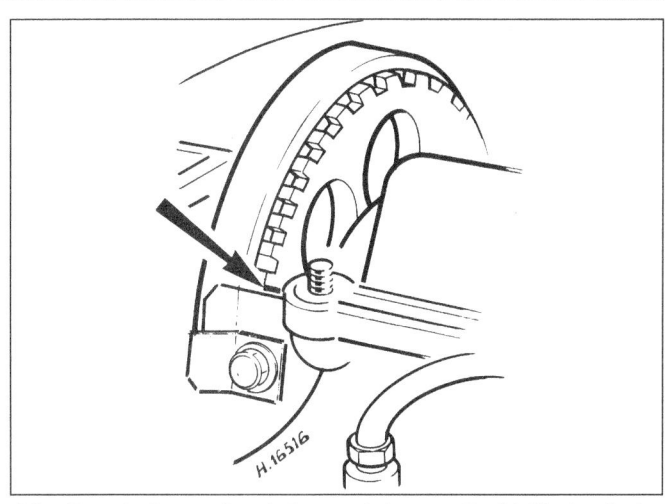

9.7a Camshaft sprocket timing mark (arrowed) with No 1 cylinder at TDC on compression

face of the cover to allow access to the Allen type retaining screw recessed within the cover. On other engines, the retaining screw can be seen but its key slot is deeply recessed (access to it being made via the hole in the centre of the screw surround).

3 Unscrew the nuts and bolts from the valve cover and remove the cover together with the gasket and reinforcement strips. Detach the crankcase emission hose(s) from the rocker cover.

4 Mark the relative positions of the crankshaft pulley and crankshaft sprocket, then undo the four socket-head bolts and withdraw the pulley.

5 Unbolt and withdraw the lower timing cover.

6 The engine must now be set for timing. Temporarily refit the crankshaft pulley. On the intermediate sprocket for the timing belt one tooth has a centre-punch mark. Turn the engine until this mates with a notch on the V-belt pulley bolted to the crankshaft sprocket **(see illustration)**. To turn the engine over, remove the spark plugs then fit a suitable spanner onto the crankshaft sprocket retaining bolt and turn it in the direction of engine rotation.

7 When these marks match, look at the sprocket on the camshaft. One tooth of this has a centre-punch mark. This should be level with the valve cover flange **(see illustration)**. Having turned the engine until these marks agree, now look at the cams for No 1 cylinder (nearest the timing belt). They will both be in the 'valve closed' position **(see illustration)**. Now look through the hole in which the TDC sensor goes where the timing marks show on the periphery of the flywheel and note the reading.

8 Before removing the timing drivebelt, check its correct tension. If held between the finger and thumb halfway between the intermediate shaft and the camshaft it should be just possible to twist it through 90° **(see illustration)**. If it is too slack, adjust it by slackening the bolt holding the eccentric cam on the tensioner wheel. If you are satisfied it can be adjusted to the correct tension, remove it and examine it for wear. Now is the time to order a new one if necessary.

9 Loosen the tensioner then withdraw the timing belt from the camshaft, intermediate and crankshaft sprockets.

10 Each of the timing belt sprockets is secured by a central bolt and washer. The intermediate, camshaft and crankshaft sprocket (the latter in particular) securing bolts are tightened to a substantial torque and the sprockets will therefore need to be firmly held when undoing the bolts.

11 To remove the camshaft sprocket, unscrew the bolt with the sprocket held stationary by inserting a suitable metal bar through a sprocket hole and resting it on the valve cover face of the cylinder head, but take care not to damage the face. Remove the bolt and spacer washer then withdraw the sprocket, tapping it free if necessary. Check the fit of the Woodruff key in the camshaft, it must be renewed if loose in its groove. Lever out the Woodruff key and keep it with the sprocket.

12 To remove the crankshaft sprocket, hold the crankshaft stationary with a lever jammed in the starter ring gear (remove the starter motor as applicable). Do not allow the crankshaft to turn or the pistons may touch the valve heads. Unscrew the retaining bolt and remove it, together with the spacer washer, then lever the sprocket free from the crankshaft. Check the fit of the Woodruff key (if fitted) in the crankshaft, it must be renewed if loose in its groove. Lever out the Woodruff key and keep it with the crankshaft sprocket.

13 The intermediate shaft sprocket is removed in a similar manner to that for the camshaft sprocket.

10 Camshaft - removal, examination and refitting

Removal

1 To remove the camshaft with the engine in the vehicle, first carry out the following operations:
   a) Remove the timing cover and valve cover, then disconnect the timing belt from the camshaft sprocket

9.7b No. 1 cylinder cam lobes in valve closed position

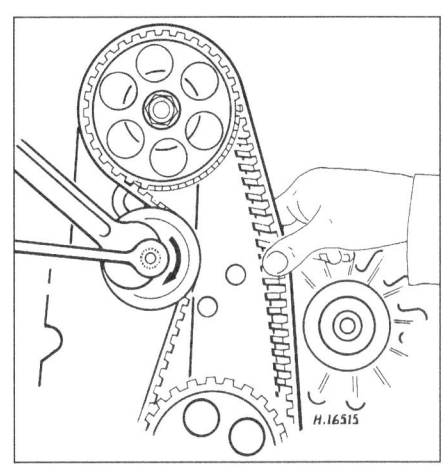

9.8 Timing belt tension check method

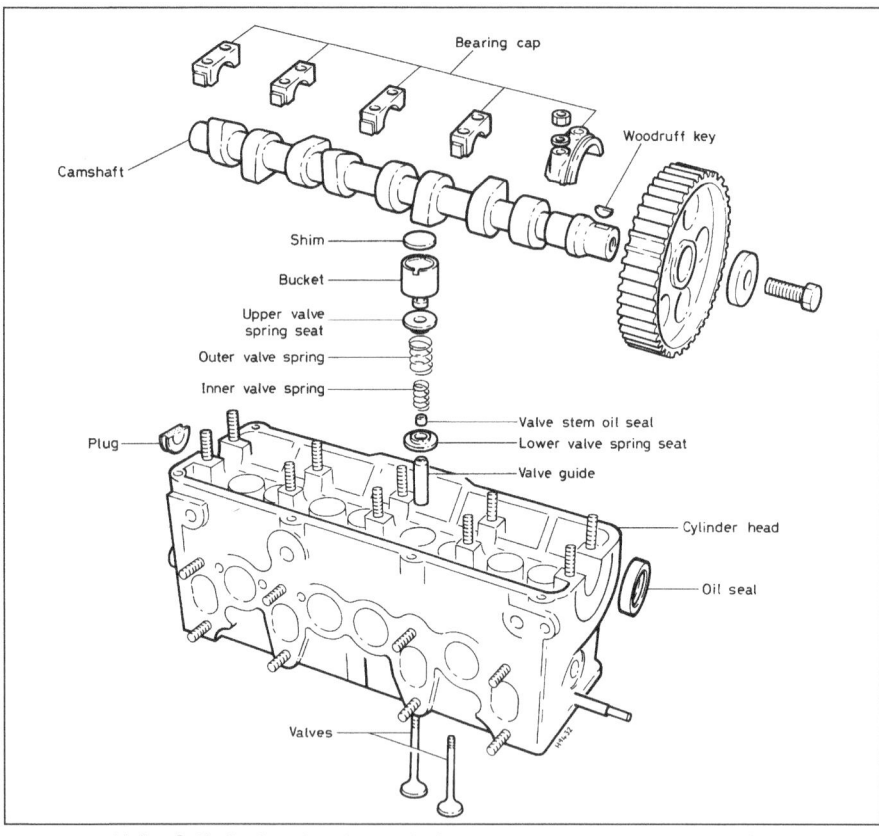

2C•10 Engine repair procedures - 1.6 and 1.8 litre 8 valve

10.2a Cylinder head and camshaft components - carburettor engine

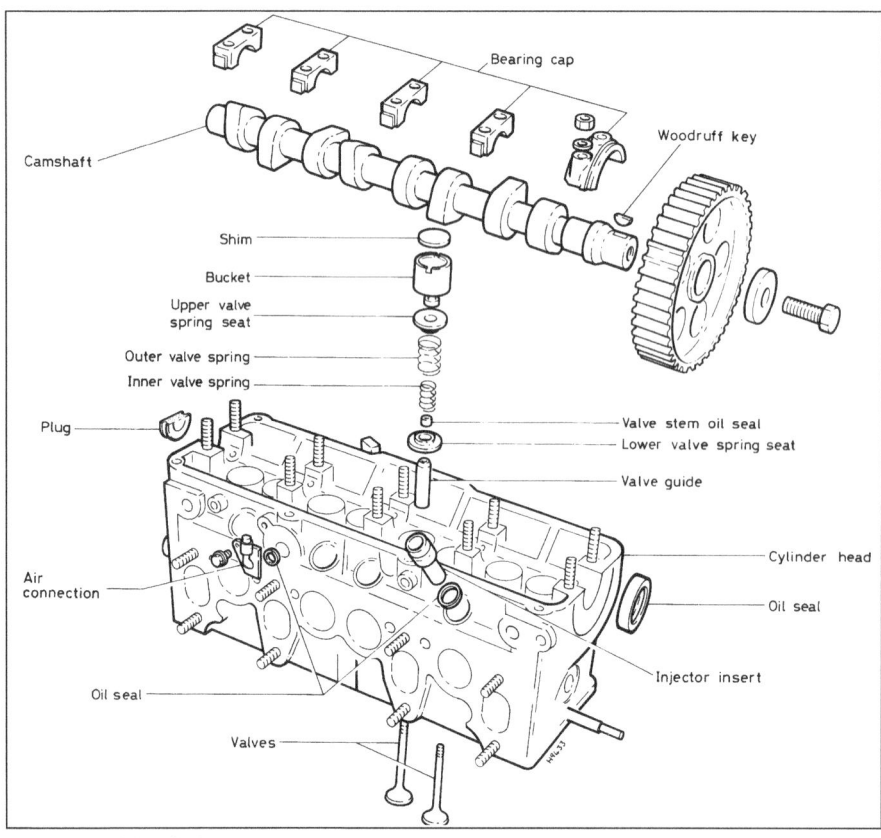

10.2b Cylinder head and camshaft components - fuel injection engine

b) If the camshaft oil seal is to be renewed then the camshaft timing sprocket must be removed

2 Remove the camshaft bearing caps **(see illustrations)**, making a careful note of their fitted positions for reference when refitting. The caps are numbered **(see illustration)** but mark the side nearest the front of the cylinder head. No. 1 cap is the one with a small oil seal on it.

3 Remove cap nos. 5, 1 and 3 in that order. Now undo the nuts holding 2 and 4 in a diagonal pattern. The camshaft will lift the caps up as the pressure of the valve springs is exerted. When they are free, lift the caps off along with the camshaft. The oil seal on the front end of the camshaft will come with it. Depending on tappet type, proceed as follows:

Shim bucket tappets

4 The tappet buckets are now exposed and may be lifted out **(see illustration)**. Take each one out in turn, prising the little disc out of the bucket by inserting a small screwdriver either side and lifting the disc away. On its reverse, each disc is engraved with a size (eg. 3.75). This is its thickness number. Note the number and then clean the disc and refit it, number side down. There are eight of these and they must not be mixed up. On assembly, each disc must go back into the bore from whence it came. This problem exists also for the valves, so a container for each valve assembly

10.2c Camshaft bearing cap number (arrowed)

10.4 Tappet bucket and shim

and tappet is required. Label the containers 1 to 8, as follows:

Containers 1 and 2 will be No 1 cylinder exhaust and inlet respectively
Containers 3 and 4 will be No 2 cylinder exhaust and inlet respectively
Containers 5 and 6 will be No 3 cylinder inlet and exhaust respectively
Containers 7 and 8 will be No 4 cylinder inlet and exhaust respectively

5 Note the thickness of all tappet clearance discs from Nos. 1 to 8 for use during reassembly.

Hydraulic bucket tappets

6 Lift out the tappets one by one, ensuring that they are kept in their correct order and can be returned to their original bores.
7 Place them, cam contact surface down, on a clean sheet of paper as they are removed.
8 Inspect the tappets for wear (indicated by ridging on the clean surface), pitting and cracks.
9 Tappets cannot be repaired and if worn, must be renewed.

Examination

10 Refer to Section 27 in Part A of this Chapter whilst noting that on exchange engines or cylinder heads, the camshaft is supplied with bearing shells instead of running directly in the head and bearing caps. Exchange units supplied by VW may have an undersized camshaft with corresponding bearing shells. Where this is the case, the camshaft will have a yellow paint spot on it and the journal diameter will be 25.75 mm. An unmarked camshaft supplied with bearing shells will be of standard size with a journal diameter of 26.00 mm.

Refitting

11 Refer to Section 12.

11 Cylinder head - removal

All engines

1 If the cylinder head is being removed with the engine out of the vehicle, proceed from paragraph 17. If the cylinder head is being removed with the engine in the vehicle, it is best removed with the inlet and exhaust manifolds. The manifolds can then be detached after removal of the cylinder head but note that a special tool is required to release (and subsequently reconnect) the exhaust downpipe-to-manifold flange retaining clips. A splined key will also be required to undo and tighten the cylinder head bolts.
2 Disconnect the battery earth lead. Drain the cooling system, then disconnect the cooling and heater hoses from the cylinder head.
3 Disconnect the thermoswitch and oil pressure lead connections.
4 On carburettor models, remove the air cleaner unit.
5 Disconnect the alternator from the cylinder head attachment brackets and remove the drivebelt.
6 If removing the manifolds with the cylinder head, disconnect the vacuum hose from the inlet manifold and the accelerator cable (and choke cable if applicable) from the carburettor.
7 Disconnect the HT leads from the spark plugs.

Fuel injection equipped engines

8 Detach the injector lines from the cylinder head and location clips and fold them back out of the way.
9 Disconnect the inlet duct at the flexible hose connection to the throttle valve housing.
10 Detach the vacuum hoses to the throttle valve housing and at the three-way connector on the bulkhead side of the cylinder head. Fold back and secure the hoses out of the way.
11 Disconnect the auxiliary air valve lead from the underside of the inlet manifold and the auxiliary air valve hose to the flexible hose on the throttle valve housing.
12 Disconnect the servo vacuum hose from the green connector on the flexible hose on the throttle housing.
13 If air conditioning is fitted, detach the hoses from the auxiliary air valve and tube connections.
14 Detach the MFI hose at the servo hose valve connection.
15 Detach the wiring connector from the cold start valve.

All engines

16 Remove the timing cover and valve cover, then disconnect the timing belt from the camshaft sprocket.
17 Remove the camshaft.
18 Remove the cylinder head bolts. These are recessed in the well of the cylinder head and are socket-head bolts. They must be removed using the correct splined tool.
19 The cylinder head bolts must be unscrewed in a progressive manner and in the reverse sequence to that shown for tightening.

20 When all ten bolts have been removed, lift the head from the cylinder block. It may need a little tapping to loosen it but do not try to prise it loose by hammering in wedges. Lift off the gasket and, if the engine is not being dismantled, clean the piston crowns and block face. Note that the cylinder head bolts must not be re-used, a new set will need to be obtained when ordering the cylinder head gasket set.

12 Cylinder head - dismantling and overhaul

1 Using a wire brush, scraper and steel wool, clean all carbon from the combustion chambers, valve faces and exhaust ports. Remove the spark plugs for cleaning.
2 The valves are not easy to get out unless a suitable valve spring compressor is available. Because the collets and spring caps are set so far down in the head, a long claw is necessary on the compressor and it must be split sufficiently to enable the collets to be removed and inserted. If such a tool is not to hand then find a piece of steel tube of about 25 mm inside diameter which will fit over the valve stem and press down the spring cover (see illustration). The length will depend on the size of the compressor so fit the compressor over the head fully extended, measure the distance between the claw and the valve spring seat and cut the tube to a suitable length.
3 The next step is to cut two windows of suitable size (approx. 25 mm long and 16 mm wide) in opposite sides of the tube. The tube may then be used with the compressor to extract the collets from each valve stem in turn. Place the valve, springs, collets and seats with the tappet in the appropriate receptacle, keeping them strictly together for refitting in the valve guide from which they were taken (see illustration).

> **HAYNES HiNT** *If your fingers are too big, put a blob of grease on the collet and pick it up with a small screwdriver, then insert it into the slot on the valve stem.*

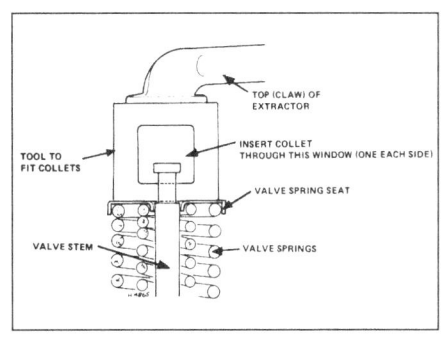

12.2 Improvised tool used to remove and refit collets to valve stems

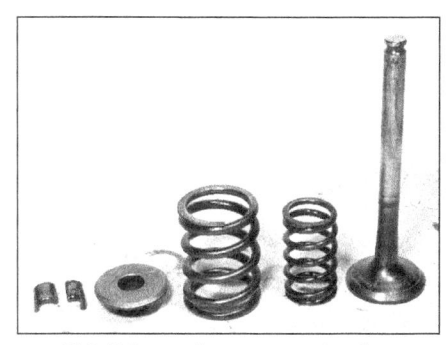

12.3 Valve springs, cap and collets

2C•12 Engine repair procedures - 1.6 and 1.8 litre 8 valve

12.12a Inserting a valve into the cylinder head

12.12b Locating valve springs and cap . . .

12.12c . . . and valve collets

4 The valve springs must be renewed if they are damaged, distorted, or known to have covered a high mileage. If in doubt as to their condition, have your VW dealer check them for compression efficiency using a calibrated valve spring compressor.

5 The valves should be cleaned and checked for signs of wear or burring. Where this has occurred, the inlet valve may be reground on a machine at a dealer. Exhaust valves must not be reground on the machine but ground in by hand. On engines fitted with hydraulic tappets, valves should not be re-cut as this will adversely affect the operation of the tappets.

6 Wear in the valve guides may be detected by fitting a new valve in the guide and checking the amount that the rim of the valve will move sideways when the top of the valve stem is flush with the top of the valve guide. The valve rock limits are given in the *Specifications*. New valve guides must be fitted and reamed by your VW dealer.

7 Do not spend too long grinding in the valves. If the valve seat and valve are not satisfactory after 15 minutes then you will probably do more harm than good by going on. Make sure both surfaces are clean, smear grinding paste onto the valve evenly and using a suction cup, work the valve with an oscillating motion lifting the valve away from the seat occasionally to stop ridging. Clean the seat and valve frequently and carry on until there is an even grey band on both seat and valve then wipe off all the paste.

8 The surface of the head must be checked with a straight-edge and feeler blade. Place the straight-edge along the centre of the machined face of the head. Make sure there are no ridges at the extreme ends and measure the clearance with feelers between each combustion chamber head. This is the area where the narrowest part of the cylinder head gasket comes and where the gasket is most likely to fail. If the straight-edge is firmly in place and feelers in excess of 0.1 mm can be put between the head and the straight-edge, then the head should be taken to a dealer for servicing or replacement.

9 If the cylinder head shows signs of cracking, have it inspected by your VW dealer to assess its condition for reuse.

10 VW recommend that the valve stem oil seals should always be renewed to prevent possible high oil consumption. Pulling off the old seal is simple with pliers. With a packet of new oil seals is a small plastic sleeve. This is fitted over the valve stem and lubricated. The seal should then be pushed over the plastic sleeve until it seats on the guide. This should be done with VW tool 10 204 which fits snugly round the outside of the seal and pushes it on squarely. If the seal is assembled without the plastic sleeve, it will be damaged and oil consumption will become excessive.

11 Before reassembling the cylinder head, check the condition of the camshaft.

12 When all components have been examined, then assembly of the head may commence. Insert the valve in the correct guide, fit the inner seat, valve springs and outer cap, assemble the valve spring compressor and possibly the small tube and compress the valve spring until the collets may be assembled to the valve stem (see illustrations).

13 Assemble the second collet and holding them carefully together in place, ease off the compressor until the spring seats the collets home. Remove the compressor, put a rag over the valve stem and tap the stem with a hammer. This is to ensure that the collets are seated correctly. If they are they will not come out. Repeat until all eight valves are in position in the cylinder head.

14 Refit the tappets in the bores from which they came, lubricating them liberally with clean engine oil (see illustration). Lubricate the camshaft bearing surfaces with oil and fit the camshaft, positioned so that No 1 cylinder cams point upwards.

15 Fit a new oil seal at the sprocket end, lubricate the bearings, set the shaft in position and install bearing caps Nos 2 and 4, tightening the nuts in a diagonal pattern until the shaft is in place (see illustration). Now install the other bearing caps, making sure they are the right way round (marks towards the drive pulley) and tighten the caps down using a diagonal pattern to the specified torque. Install a new rubber seal at the opposite end to the sprocket.

16 On engines equipped with shim bucket tappets, adjust the valve clearances.

13 Sump and oil pump - removal and refitting

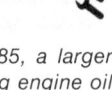

Modification: *From August 1985, a larger sump is fitted thereby increasing engine oil capacity. If renewing the sump, ensure that one of identical capacity is fitted*

Removal

1 If the engine is in the vehicle then drain the engine oil. Note that the sump plug has an O-ring which must be renewed (see illustration).

2 Undo the sump retaining bolts and remove the sump from the lower face of the crankcase. Remove the sump gasket which must also be renewed.

3 To remove the oil pump, undo the two retaining bolts and lower the pump unit,

12.14 Fit the tappet buckets

12.15 Fit the bearing caps

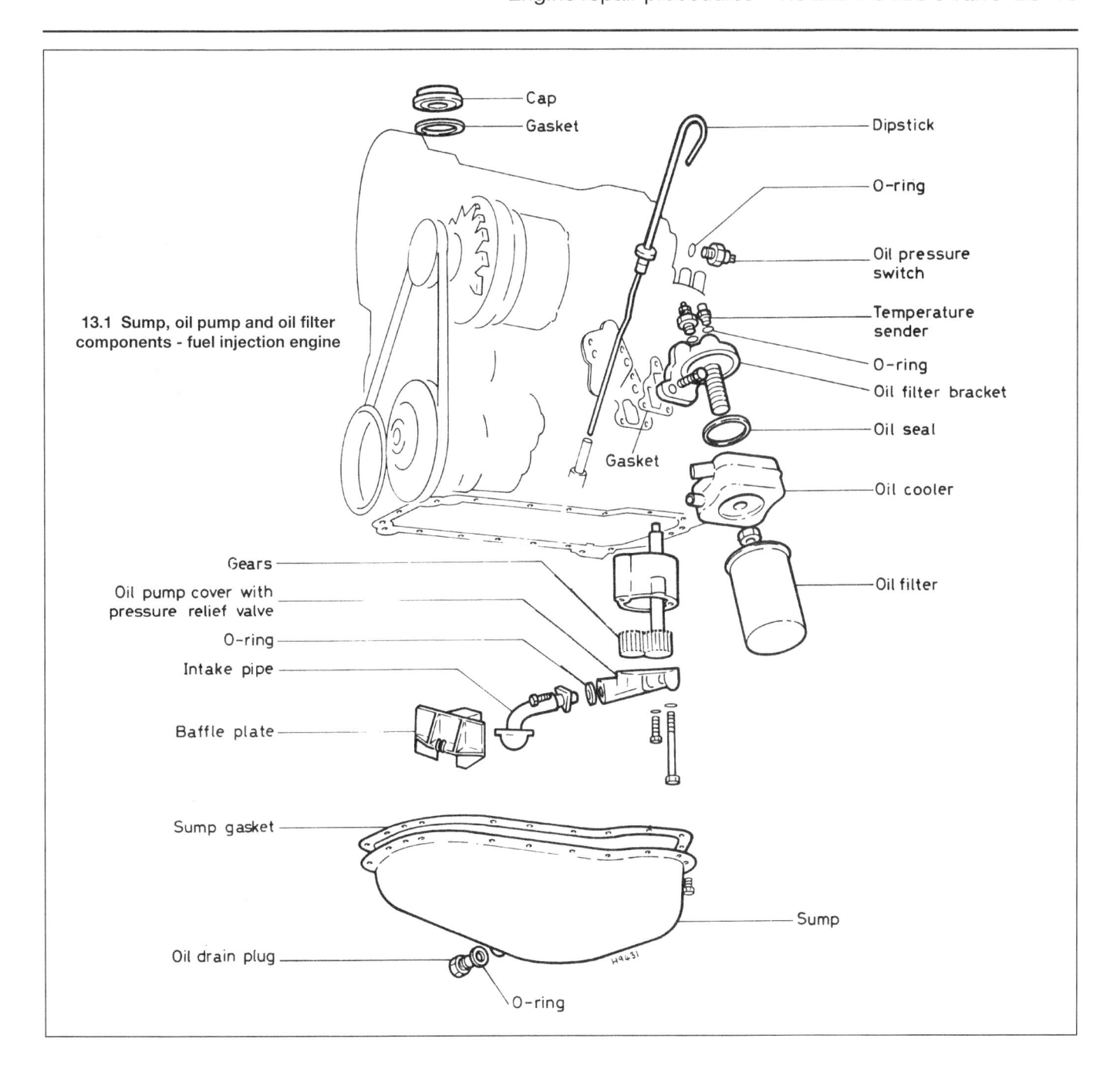

Engine repair procedures - 1.6 and 1.8 litre 8 valve 2C•13

13.1 Sump, oil pump and oil filter components - fuel injection engine

Labels: Cap, Gasket, Dipstick, O-ring, Oil pressure switch, Temperature sender, O-ring, Oil filter bracket, Oil seal, Oil cooler, Oil filter, Gasket, Gears, Oil pump cover with pressure relief valve, O-ring, Intake pipe, Baffle plate, Sump gasket, Sump, Oil drain plug, O-ring

complete with the oil pick-up pipe and strainer.

Refitting

4 To refit the pump, ensure that the mating faces are clean, locate it in position and fit and tighten the securing bolts to the specified torque.
5 Locate the new sump gasket but do not apply an adhesive sealant. Refit the sump and tighten the retaining bolts evenly to the specified torque.
6 Refit the oil drain plug with O-ring and tighten it to the specified torque.

14 Pistons and connecting rods - removal

1 Remove the cylinder head.
2 Remove the sump.
3 Unscrew the two oil pump retaining bolts then lower and remove the pump, complete with oil pick-up pipe from the crankcase. Place it on one side for cleaning and inspection.
4 The piston and connecting rod removal procedure now follows that given for the smaller engine variants in Part A of this Chapter.

15 Crankshaft and main bearings - removal

1 Disconnect the pistons and connecting rods from the crankshaft. Note that, although the engine has to be removed to remove the crankshaft, the cylinder head, pistons and connecting rods can be left in position.
2 At the flywheel end, undo and remove the six bolts securing the oil seal flange to the crankcase **(see illustration)**. Withdraw the flange, seal and gasket.
3 Examine the main bearing caps. It will be

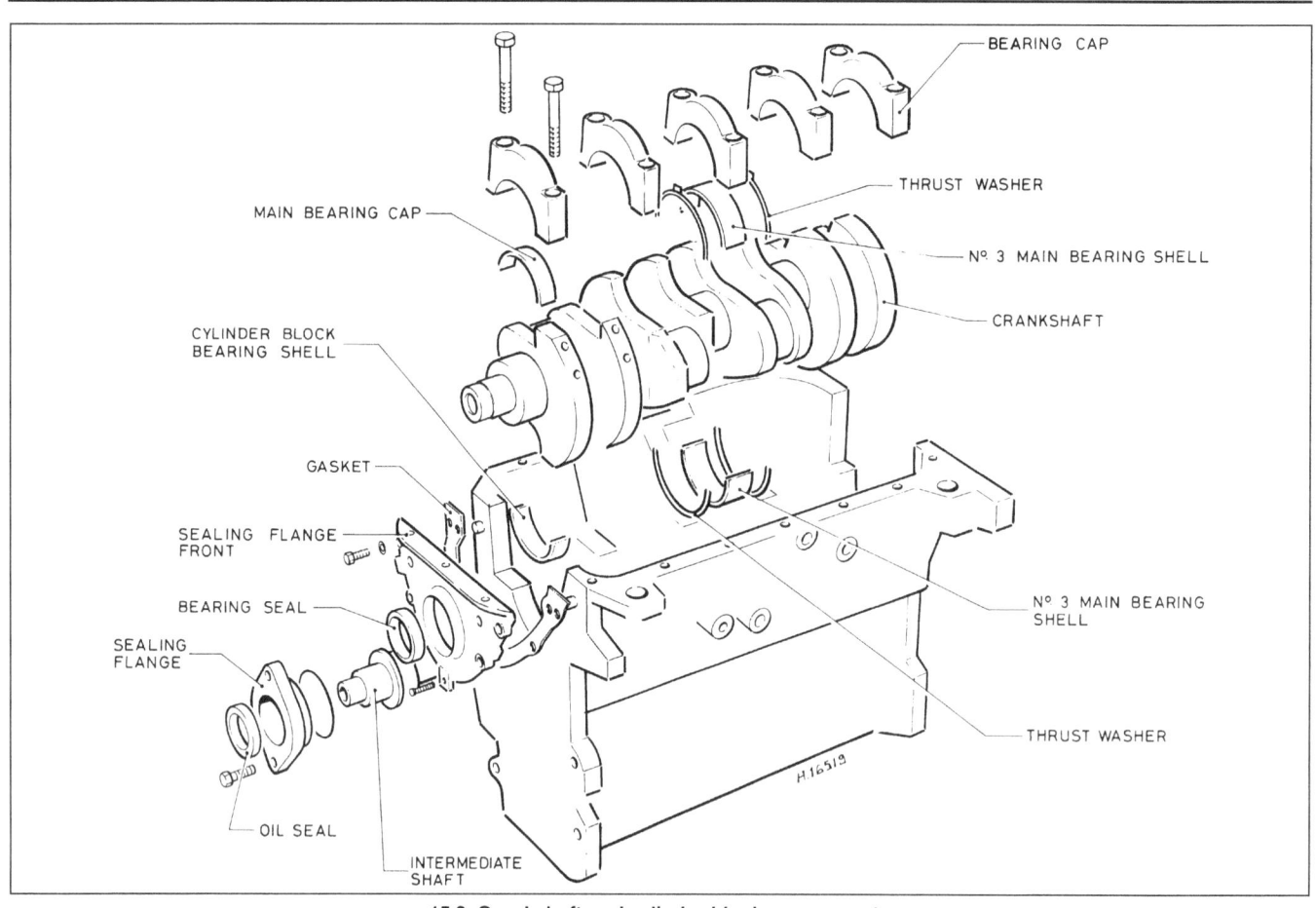

2C•14 Engine repair procedures - 1.6 and 1.8 litre 8 valve

15.2 Crankshaft and cylinder block components

seen that the caps are numbered 1 to 5 and that the number is on the side of the engine opposite the oil pump position. Identify these numbers. If they are obscured, then mark the caps in the same way as the connecting rod caps. Before removing the caps, push the crankshaft to the rear and check the endfloat using a feeler blade between the thrustwasher flanges on No 3 main bearing and the crankshaft web **(see illustration)**. It must not exceed the specified maximum.

4 Remove the bearing cap retaining bolts, remove the bearing caps and lift out the thrustwashers from each side of the centre main bearing.

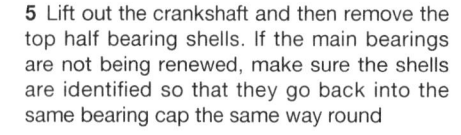

5 Lift out the crankshaft and then remove the top half bearing shells. If the main bearings are not being renewed, make sure the shells are identified so that they go back into the same bearing cap the same way round

16 Intermediate shaft - removal

1 The intermediate shaft can only be withdrawn from the crankcase with the engine removed from the vehicle.
2 Remove the timing belt.

3 Remove the fuel pump on carburettor models and the ignition distributor.
4 Before removing the intermediate shaft, check that the endfloat does not exceed the maximum specified amount.
5 Undo the two sealing flange retaining bolts then withdraw the intermediate shaft, complete with sealing flange **(see illustrations)**.
6 Withdraw the sealing flange from the intermediate shaft. The oil seal within the flange and the O-ring must be renewed on reassembly.

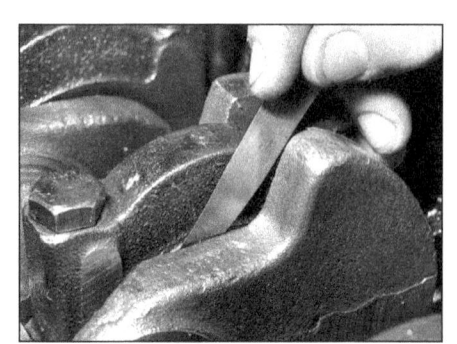

15.3 Checking crankshaft endfloat at No. 3 main bearing

16.5a Intermediate shaft retaining flange bolts (arrowed)

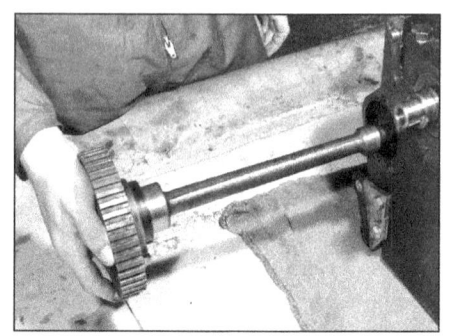

16.5b Withdrawing intermediate shaft

17 Oil filter - renewal

Refer to Chapter 1, Section 18

18 Oil cooler - removal and refitting

1 On fuel injection models, an oil cooler is fitted between the oil filter cartridge and mounting bracket. The cooler must be renewed if the engine oil has been contaminated with metal particles, such as might be the case following total or partial engine seizure. Renew it anyway if it is likely to contain any other harmful contaminant.
2 To remove the cooler, first remove the oil filter cartridge.
3 Drain the cooling system and disconnect the coolant hoses from the cooler.
4 Remove the cooler retaining nut and the cooler. The O-ring between the cooler and mounting must be renewed.
5 Refitting is a reversal of the removal procedure. Wipe clean the sealing faces of the cooler and mounting and smear the O-ring with clean engine oil.
6 On completion, top-up the engine oil and coolant levels. Start the engine and check for any signs of leaks.

19 Oil filter mounting - removal and refitting

1 Remove the oil filter and on fuel injection models, the oil cooler.
2 Disconnect the oil pressure switch lead, undo the oil filter mounting securing bolts and withdraw the mounting and gasket.
3 The oil pressure switch can be unscrewed from the top face of the mounting if required. Renew the switch O-ring.
4 Refitting is a reversal of the removal procedure. Renew the mounting gasket.

20 Oil seals - renewal

Note: *The following procedures were all carried out with the engine in the vehicle*

Crankshaft seals

Flywheel/driveplate end

1 On manual gearbox models, remove the clutch and pressure plate. On automatic transmission models, remove the transmission then unbolt the driveplate from the crankshaft, noting the location of the spacer and shim(s).

2 Carefully prise out the oil seal with a screwdriver or strong wire and wipe clean the recess **(see illustration)**.
3 Fill the space between the lips of the new seal with multi-purpose grease, then drive it squarely into the housing using a block of wood or suitable metal tubing. If at all possible, use VW fitting sleeve No. 2003 to avoid damage to the oil seal lip.
4 Refit the driveplate or clutch.

Timing belt end

5 Remove the alternator, together with its drivebelt.
6 Remove the timing belt cover and timing belt, ensuring that the timing marks are correctly aligned.
7 Unscrew the bolt from the front of the crankshaft, withdraw the pulley and sprocket and remove the Woodruff key. On manual gearbox models, if the belt is difficult to loosen, have an assistant engage top gear and apply the brakes. On automatic transmission models, remove the starter model and restrain the driveplate ring gear with a suitable lever.
8 Prise out the oil seal or extract it with VW tool No. 2085, then wipe clean the recess **(see illustration)**.
9 Fill the space between the lips of the new seal with multi-purpose grease, then drive it squarely into the housing using a block of wood or suitable metal tubing. If available use VW fitting sleeve No. 3083.
10 The remaining refitting procedure is a reversal of removal. Ensure that the timing marks are aligned before refitting the timing belt and tensioning it.

Camshaft front seal

11 Remove the alternator together with its drivebelt.
12 Remove the timing belt cover and timing belt, ensuring that the timing marks are correctly aligned.
13 Hold the camshaft sprocket stationary with a screwdriver inserted through one of its holes, then unscrew the bolt and remove the washer, sprocket and Woodruff key.
14 Prise out the oil seal or alternatively,

20.8 VW tool 2085 for removing crankshaft oil seal (timing belt end) and camshaft oil seal

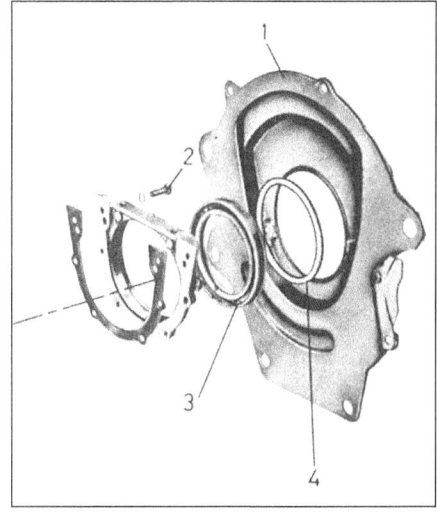

20.2 Flywheel end crankshaft oil seal components

1 Intermediate plate
2 Bolt
3 Oil seal
4 Sealing ring (not fitted to all models)

extract it with VW tool No. 2085, then wipe clean the recess.
15 Fill the space between the lips of the new seal with multi-purpose grease, then drive it squarely into the cylinder head using a block of wood or suitable metal tubing. If available, use VW fitting sleeve No. 10-203.
16 The remaining refitting procedure is a reversal of removal. Ensure that the timing marks are aligned before refitting the timing belt and tensioning it.

Intermediate shaft seal

17 Remove the alternator together with its drivebelt.
18 Remove the timing belt cover and timing belt, ensuring that the timing marks are correctly aligned.
19 Hold the intermediate shaft sprocket stationary with a screwdriver inserted through one of its holes, then unscrew the bolt and remove the washer, sprocket and Woodruff key.
20 Renew the oil seal.
21 The remaining refitting procedure is a reversal of removal. Ensure that the timing marks are aligned before refitting the timing belt and tensioning it.

21 Examination and renovation - general information

Refer to Section 20 in Part A of this Chapter.

22 Crankshaft and bearings - examination and renovation

Refer to Section 21 in Part A of this Chapter.

2C•16 Engine repair procedures - 1.6 and 1.8 litre 8 valve

25.2 Examine face of oil pump cover for scoring

25.3 Checking oil pump gear backlash

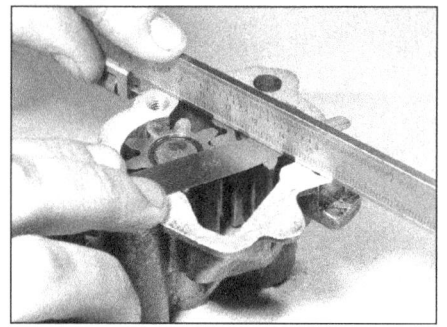

25.4 Checking oil pump gear endfloat

23 Cylinder block/crankcase - examination and renovation

Refer to Section 22 in Part A of this Chapter.

24 Pistons and connecting rods - examination and renovation

Refer to Section 23 in Part A of this Chapter.

25 Oil pump - examination and renovation

1 With the oil pump on the bench, prise off the cap with a screwdriver and clean the strainer gauze in fuel. Refit the gauze and press on the cap.
2 Remove the two small bolts and take the cover away from the body. Examine the face of the cover (see illustration). As seen in the illustration, the gears have marked the cover. If the depth of this marking is significant, then the face of the cover must be machined flat again.
3 Remove the gears and wash them with the body in clean paraffin. Dry and reassemble the gears, lubricating them with clean engine oil. Measure the backlash between the gears with a feeler blade (see illustration). This should be 0.05 to 0.20 mm.
4 Now place a straight-edge over the pump body along the line joining the centre of the two gears and measure with a feeler blade the axial clearance between the gears and the straight-edge (see illustration). This must not exceed 0.15 mm.
5 If all is well, check that the shaft is not slack in its bearings and reassemble the pump for fitting to the engine.
6 If there is any doubt about the pump, it is recommended that a replacement be obtained. Once wear starts in a pump it progresses rapidly. In view of the engine damage that may follow a loss of oil pressure, skimping the oil pump repair is a false economy.

26 Intermediate shaft - examination and renovation

1 Check the fit of the intermediate shaft in its bearing. If there is excessive play, the shaft must be compared with a new one. If the shaft is in good order but the bearings in the block are worn, then seek expert advice.
2 Check the surface of the cam which drives the fuel pump (where applicable). If serious ridging is present, a new shaft is indicated.
3 Check the teeth of the distributor drivegear for scuffing or chipping. Check the condition of the timing belt sprocket.
4 It is unlikely that damage to the shaft has happened but if it has, seek advice from a VW dealer.
5 There is an oil seal in the flange for the intermediate shaft. This may need renewal if there are signs of leakage. To do this, remove the timing belt sprocket and withdraw the flange from the shaft. The oil seal may now be prised out and a new one pressed in. Always fit a new O-ring on the flange before assembling it to the cylinder block.

27 Flywheel/driveplate - examination and renovation

1 Inspect the starter ring teeth. If these are chipped or worn then renew the starter ring. This means heating the ring until it may be withdrawn from the flywheel, or alternatively, splitting it. A new one must then be shrunk on. If you know how to do this and you can get a new ring then the job can be done but it is beyond the capacity of most owners.
2 Serious scoring on the flywheel clutch facing requires a new flywheel. Do not attempt to clean the scoring off with a scraper or emery. The face must be machined.
3 If it is necessary to fit a new flywheel, the ignition timing mark must be made by the owner. The new flywheel has only the TDC mark as an O on the outer face. Punch or scribe the appropriate timing mark for your model to the left of the TDC mark at the appropriate distance (see illustration).

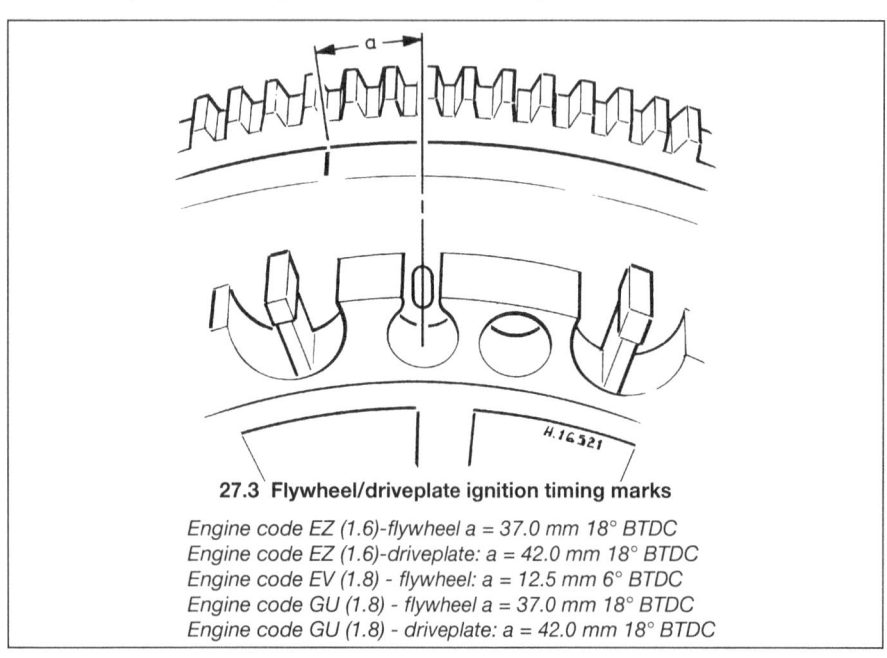

27.3 Flywheel/driveplate ignition timing marks

Engine code EZ (1.6)-flywheel a = 37.0 mm 18° BTDC
Engine code EZ (1.6)-driveplate: a = 42.0 mm 18° BTDC
Engine code EV (1.8) - flywheel: a = 12.5 mm 6° BTDC
Engine code GU (1.8) - flywheel a = 37.0 mm 18° BTDC
Engine code GU (1.8) - driveplate: a = 42.0 mm 18° BTDC

Engine repair procedures - 1.6 and 1.8 litre 8 valve 2C•17

30.3a Fitting flanged type centre main bearing into crankcase

30.3b Fitting alternative type centre main bearing into crankcase . . .

30.3c . . . together with thrustwashers

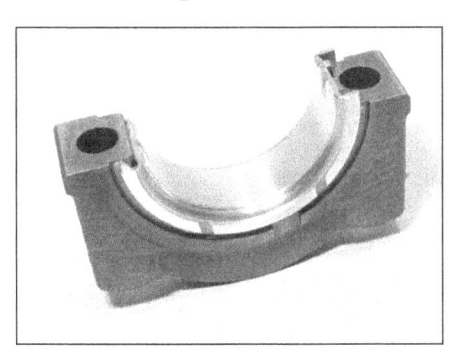

30.3d Fitting flanged type centre main bearing to cap

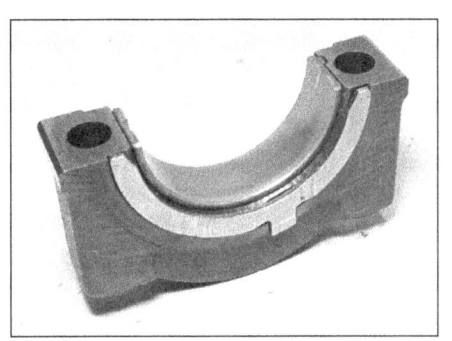

30.3e Fitting centre bearing and separate thrustwashers to cap

30.3f Ensure that ends of bearing are flush with joint face

4 On automatic transmission models, check the driveplate as described for the flywheel. It will also be necessary to mark a new driveplate for ignition timing.

28 Timing belt and sprockets - examination and renovation

Refer to Section 26 in Part A of this Chapter. The information given also applies to the intermediate shaft sprocket.

29 Engine reassembly - general information

Refer to Section 28 in Part A of this Chapter.

30 Crankshaft and main bearings - refitting

Note: *If it is difficult to rotate the crankshaft, check that the bearing shells are seated properly and that the bearing cap is in the correct way round. Rotation will only be difficult if something is incorrect and the fault must be found. Dirt on the back of a bearing shell is sometimes the cause of a tight main bearing.*

1 If a new crankshaft is being fitted to automatic transmission models, the needle roller bearing supplied and fitted by the manufacturer will need to be removed from its aperture in the rear end of the crankshaft. It may already have been removed by the supplier, but check anyway.

2 Clean the crankcase recesses and bearing caps thoroughly and fit the bearing shells so that the tang on the bearing engages in the recess in the crankcase or bearing cap. Ensure that the shells fitted to the crankcase have oil grooves and holes and that these align with the drillings in the bearing housings. When fitting the bearing shells to the caps, note that bearing Nos. 1, 2 and 5 are plain shells whilst No. 4 has an oil groove.

3 The bearing shells of the centre bearing (No. 3) may either be flanged to act as thrustwashers, or may have separate thrustwashers. These should be fitted with oil groove outwards. Fit the bearing shells so that the ends of the bearing are flush with the joint face **(see illustrations)**.

4 Oil the bearings and journals then locate the crankshaft in the crankcase.

5 Fit the main bearing caps (with centre main bearing thrustwashers if applicable) in their correct positions **(see illustration)**.

6 Fit the bolts to the bearing caps and tighten the bolts of the centre cap to the specified torque, then check that the crankshaft rotates freely.

7 Working out from the centre, tighten the remaining bearing caps in turn, checking that the crankshaft rotates freely after each bearing has been tightened.

8 Check that the endfloat of the crankshaft is within specifications by inserting feeler blades between the crankshaft and the centre bearing thrust face/washer while levering the crankshaft first in one direction and then in the other.

9 Lubricate the rear of the crankshaft and using a new gasket, install the rear oil seal and flange. Tighten the six bolts **(see illustration)**.

30.5 Fitting main bearing caps

30.9 Fitting crankshaft rear oil seal and flange

2C•18 Engine repair procedures - 1.6 and 1.8 litre 8 valve

10 Lubricate the front of the crankshaft and fit the front oil seal and flange with a new gasket. Tighten the bolts to the correct torque.

31 Intermediate shaft - refitting

Lubricate the intermediate shaft with clean engine oil then install it in the block.
Fit the O-ring and flange, together with the oil seal, then tighten the bolts. Note that the oil hole must be at the bottom of the flange.

32 Pistons and connecting rods - refitting

Proceed as described in Section 30, Part A of this Chapter, paragraphs 2 to 7 inclusive. When refitting the big-end nuts, oil the threads.
On completion, check the endfloat of each connecting rod in a similar manner to that described for checking the crankshaft endfloat.

33 Valve clearances - checking and adjustment (pre August 1985)

1 If a new or reconditioned cylinder head, complete with camshaft, is being fitted, then the valve clearances will have been preset.
2 Valve clearances can be checked and adjusted with the cylinder head removed (prior to refitting after overhaul) or in the normal manner described in Section 12 of Chapter 1.
3 There are two specified valve clearance settings, these being for a cold (cylinder head removed) or warm (engine in vehicle) engine condition.
4 If valve adjustment is made with the engine cold, then it must be checked again with the engine at normal operating temperature (ie. coolant above 35°C). If the cylinder head has been overhauled, then it should be checked again, hot, after 600 miles (900 km).

34 Cylinder head - refitting

Note: *New cylinder head retaining bolts must be used on refitting*
1 Clean the top face of the block. Clean and inspect the bores and lubricate them with clean engine oil. Turn the crankshaft so that the pistons are in the mid-cylinder position.
2 The engine number is stamped on an inclined surface between No. 3 and No. 4 cylinders on the side above the distributor.

34.2 Cylinder head gasket located on block

Using this as a datum, install a new cylinder head gasket so that the word 'OBEN' on the gasket is over this datum point and on the top side of the gasket **(see illustration)**.
3 Lower the cylinder head into position, locating onto the centring pins where fitted **(see illustration)**. If the cylinder block does not have centring pins, initially refit new No. 8 and No. 10 cylinder head bolts. Do not use jointing compound. Check that the gasket is seating correctly and fit the remainder of the new bolts. Following the sequence shown, tighten the bolts until the head is firmly held. Using a torque wrench, tighten the bolts in stages to the specified torque following the same sequence **(see illustration)**.
4 The cylinder head will not need further tightening.

35 Timing belt and sprockets - refitting

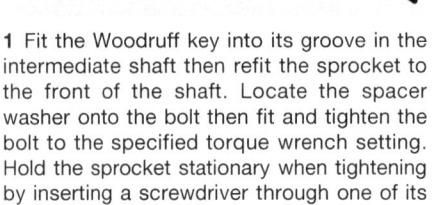

1 Fit the Woodruff key into its groove in the intermediate shaft then refit the sprocket to the front of the shaft. Locate the spacer washer onto the bolt then fit and tighten the bolt to the specified torque wrench setting. Hold the sprocket stationary when tightening by inserting a screwdriver through one of its holes and jamming it against the cylinder block.
2 Locate the Woodruff key (if applicable) to the groove at the front of the crankshaft then

34.3a Lowering cylinder head onto block

refit the timing belt sprocket onto the shaft. Lubricate the retaining bolt with oil, locate the spacer washer onto the bolt then fit and tighten it to the specified torque wrench setting. When tightening the bolt, prevent the crankshaft from turning by using the same method as that for its removal.
3 Locate the Woodruff key into its groove on the front of the camshaft then refit the camshaft sprocket. Refit the retaining bolt together with the spacer washer and tighten to the specified torque wrench setting. Hold the sprocket stationary when tightening by inserting a screwdriver through one of its holes and jamming it against the cylinder block or head.
4 If removed, refit the timing belt rear cover. Apply locking compound to the stud thread.
5 Locate the crankshaft pulley onto the sprocket (aligning the marks made previously) using one bolt to secure it temporarily.
6 Turn the camshaft sprocket so that the lobes of No. 1 cylinder cams are pointing upwards and the mark on the camshaft sprocket is aligned with the valve cover - **see illustration 9.7a**.
7 Rotate the crankshaft sprocket and the intermediate shaft sprocket until the dot on the intermediate sprocket and the mark on the V-belt pulley coincide. Install the timing belt tensioner loosely and then the timing belt. Making sure the marks are still in place, put a spanner on the adjuster and tighten the belt until it will twist only 90 degrees when held between the finger and thumb halfway

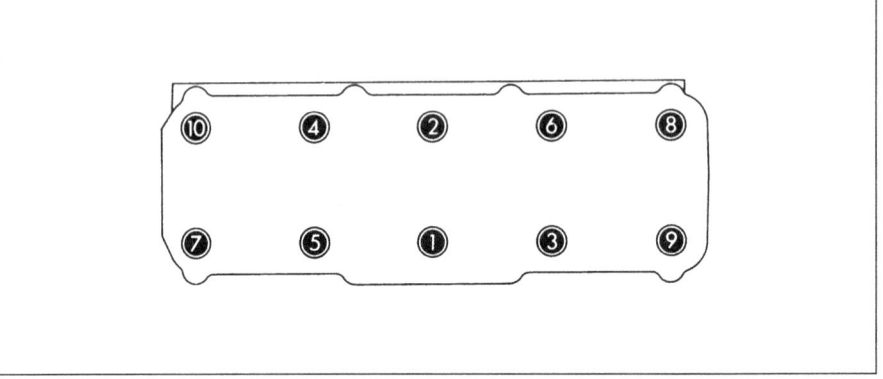

34.3b Cylinder head bolt tightening sequence

between the camshaft and intermediate shaft sprockets. Tighten the eccentric adjuster nut to the specified torque - **see illustration 9.8**.
8 Unbolt and remove the crankshaft V-belt pulley.
9 Fit the lower timing cover then refit the crankshaft V-belt pulley and tighten its retaining bolts to the specified torque.
10 Locate the new valve cover gasket on the cylinder head, the seal to the No. 1 camshaft bearing cap and the half round grommet into its location at the rear end of the cylinder head.
11 Fit the valve cover into position, locate the reinforcement strips then refit and tighten the retaining nuts evenly to the specified torque.
12 Refit the upper timing belt cover.

36 Engine ancillary components - refitting

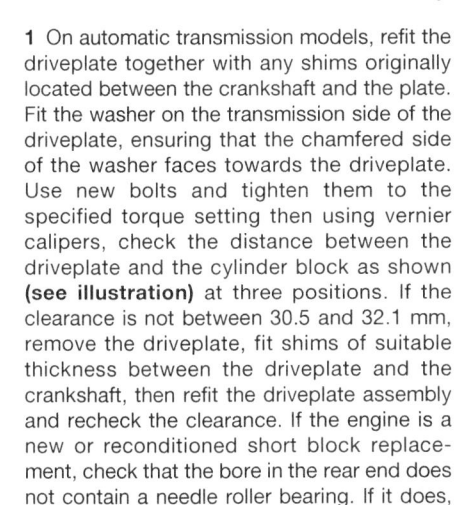

1 On automatic transmission models, refit the driveplate together with any shims originally located between the crankshaft and the plate. Fit the washer on the transmission side of the driveplate, ensuring that the chamfered side of the washer faces towards the driveplate. Use new bolts and tighten them to the specified torque setting then using vernier calipers, check the distance between the driveplate and the cylinder block as shown **(see illustration)** at three positions. If the clearance is not between 30.5 and 32.1 mm, remove the driveplate, fit shims of suitable thickness between the driveplate and the crankshaft, then refit the driveplate assembly and recheck the clearance. If the engine is a new or reconditioned short block replacement, check that the bore in the rear end does not contain a needle roller bearing. If it does, then remove the bearing as this is for manual gearbox models only.
2 On manual gearbox models, refit the clutch together with the intermediate plate.
3 Refit the inlet and exhaust manifolds.
4 Refit the coolant pump and all hoses to the engine.
5 Refit the alternator and drivebelt.
6 Refit the oil pressure switch to the cylinder head or filter mounting as applicable, using a new washer or O-ring. Tighten to the specified torque.
7 Fit the oil filter mounting to the cylinder block, together with a new gasket and tighten the bolts. On models fitted with an oil cooler, refit the supply and return hoses to their correct unions.
8 Fit the oil filter.
9 Refit the distributor.
10 On carburettor models, refit the fuel pump.
11 On fuel injection models, refit the warm-up valve (if the hoses were disconnected).
12 Refit the coolant temperature sender unit and the thermotime switch with new O-rings.

13 Refit the spark plugs, if not already done.
14 Refit the gearbox/transmission to the engine.

37 Engine - refitting

To refit the engine/transmission, reverse the removal procedures but note the following:
a) *When lowering the unit into the engine compartment, align the driveshafts with the flanges prior to attaching the respective mountings*
b) *Assemble the engine mountings loosely initially and tighten them only after the unit is central without straining the mountings*
c) *Adjust the clutch cable (manual gearbox)*
d) *Adjust the throttle and selector cables (automatic transmission)*
e) *Reconnect and adjust the gear selector linkages (manual gearbox)*
f) *Adjust the throttle and choke cables*
g) *Refill the cooling system*
h) *Refill the engine with the correct grade and quantity of oil*
i) *Where necessary, retension the power steering pump drivebelt and replenish the system fluid*

38 Hydraulic bucket tappets - checking free travel (from August 1985)

1 Start the engine and run it until the radiator cooling fan has switched on once.
2 Increase engine speed to about 2500 rpm for about two minutes.
3 Irregular noises are normal when starting but should become quiet after a few minutes running.
4 If the valves are still noisy, carry out the following check to identify worn tappets.
5 Stop the engine and remove the valve cover from the cylinder head.
6 Turn the crankshaft clockwise by using a wrench on the crankshaft pulley securing bolt, until the cam of the tappet to be checked is facing upward and is not exerting any pressure on the tappet.
7 Press the tappet down using a wooden or plastic wedge.
8 If free travel of the tappet exceeds that specified, the tappet must be renewed.

39 Engine - adjustments after major overhaul

Refer to Section 41 in Part A of this Chapter.
If new hydraulic bucket tappets have been fitted, it is essential that no attempt to restart the engine is made for a minimum period of 30 minutes after installation. Failure to observe this precaution may result in engine damage caused by the valves contacting the pistons.

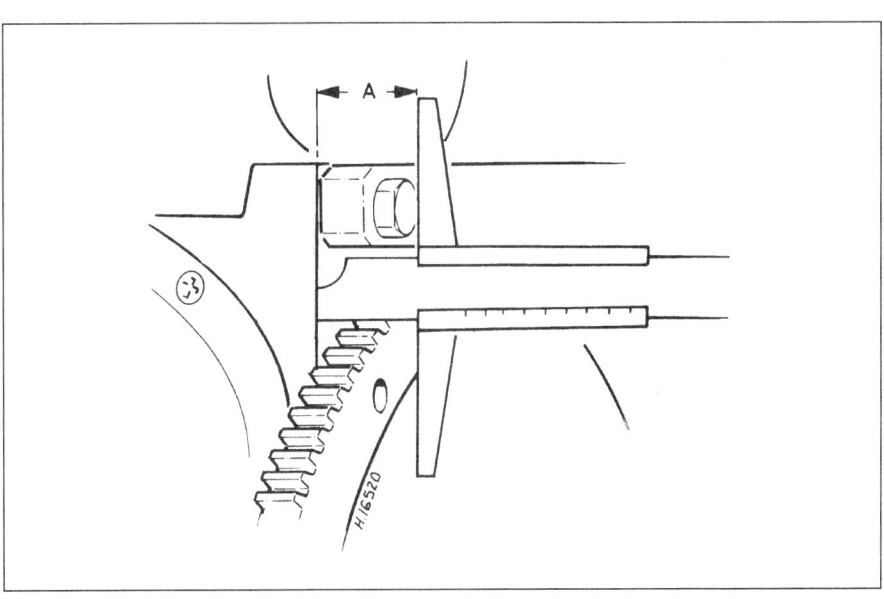

36.1 Checking driveplate-to-cylinder block dimension (A) using vernier calipers

Chapter 2 Part D:
Engine repair procedures 1.8 litre 16 valve

The following information is a revision of, or supplementary to, that given for the 1.8 litre engine in Part C of this Chapter

Contents

Camshafts - removal and refitting 3	Pistons and connecting rods - removal and refitting 5
Cylinder head - dismantling and overhaul 4	Timing belt and sprockets - removal and refitting 2
General information 1	

Degrees of difficulty

Easy, suitable for novice with little experience	Fairly easy, suitable for beginner with some experience	Fairly difficult, suitable for competent DIY mechanic	Difficult, suitable for experienced DIY mechanic	Very difficult, suitable for expert DIY or professional

Specifications

General
Code:
    GTi 16V with catalytic converter .... KR
Compression ratio 10:1

Cylinder head
Minimum height .... 118.1 mm - measured through cylinder head bolt hole

Valves
Head diameter:
    Inlet .... 32.0 mm
    Exhaust .... 28.0 mm
Stem diameter:
    Inlet .... 6.97 mm
    Exhaust .... 6.94 mm
Overall length:
    Inlet .... 95.5 mm
    Exhaust .... 98.2 mm

Valve timing
Nil valve clearance at 1.0 mm valve lift
Inlet opens .... 3° ATDC
Inlet closes .... 35° ABDC
Exhaust opens .... 43° BBDC
Exhaust closes .... 3° BTDC

Torque wrench settings	Nm	lbf ft
Vibration damper	20	15
Intermediate shaft sprocket bolt	65	48
Valve cover	10	7
Oil cooler	25	19
Camshaft sprocket bolt	65	48
Camshaft bearing caps	15	11
Oil temperature sender	10	7
Oil pump cover	10	7
Oil pump mounting bolts	20	15
Oil jet	10	7
Crankshaft sprocket bolt (oiled)	180	133

2D•2 Engine repair procedures 1.8 litre 16 valve

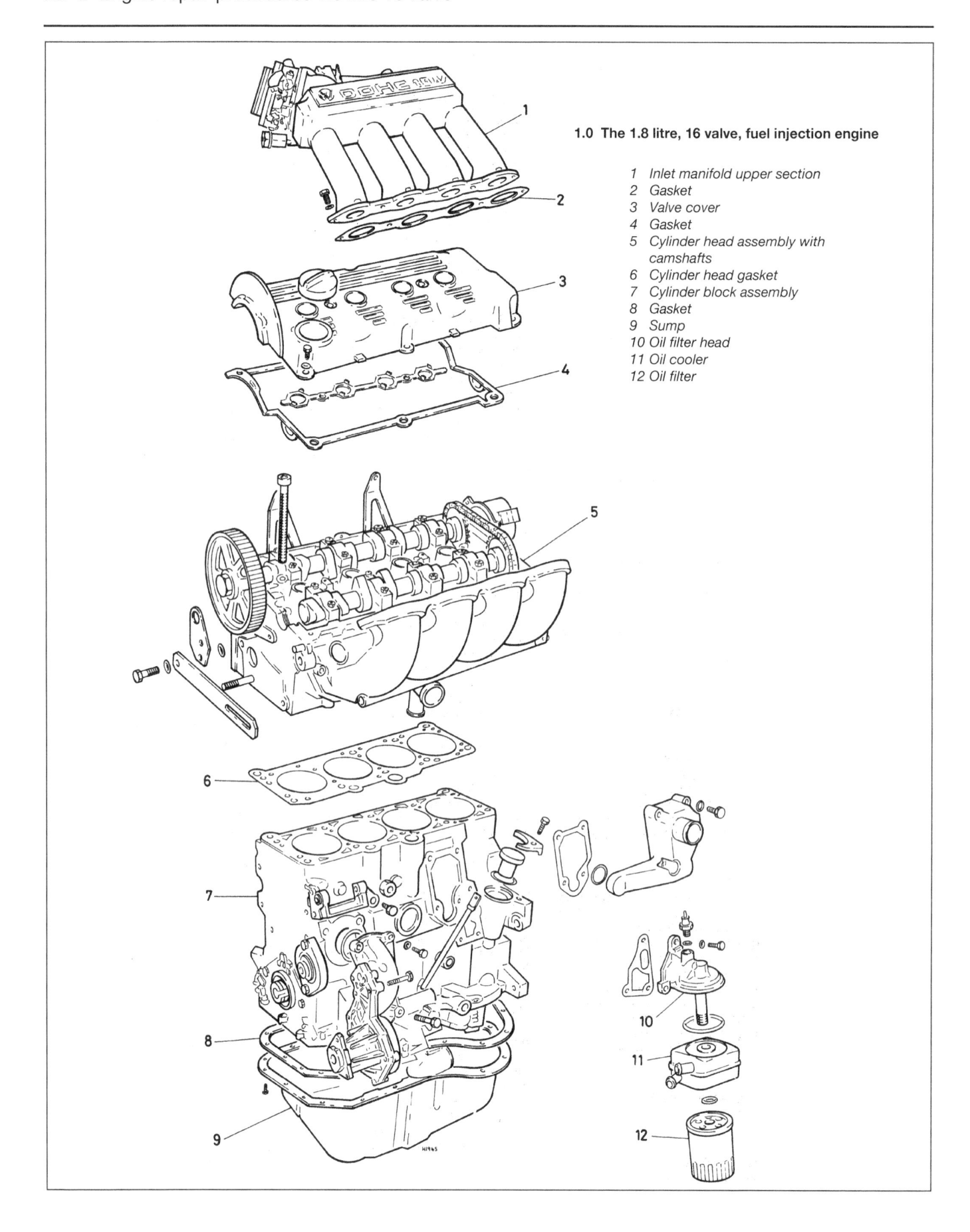

1.0 The 1.8 litre, 16 valve, fuel injection engine

1. Inlet manifold upper section
2. Gasket
3. Valve cover
4. Gasket
5. Cylinder head assembly with camshafts
6. Cylinder head gasket
7. Cylinder block assembly
8. Gasket
9. Sump
10. Oil filter head
11. Oil cooler
12. Oil filter

Engine repair procedures 1.8 litre 16 valve 2D•3

1 General information

The 1.8 litre, 16-valve engine fitted to GTi models from October 1986, incorporates double overhead camshafts, one operating the exhaust valves and the other the inlet valves. There are four valves per cylinder which operate simultaneously in pairs and provide the engine with a much improved breathing capability over the 8-valve version, thus resulting in greater power output. A single camshaft sprocket is attached to the exhaust camshaft and a chain and sprocket at the opposite end of the cylinder head is used to drive the inlet camshaft (see illustration).

Most overhaul procedures for the 16-valve engine are basically the same as those described for the 8-valve engine in Part C of this Chapter. The following Sections describe procedures which differ.

2 Timing belt and sprockets - removal and refitting

Besides the timing mark on the camshaft sprocket referred to in Part C of this Chapter, Section 9, an additional timing mark is provided on the outside of the camshaft sprocket which aligns with a mark on the valve cover (see illustration). This means that if the timing belt alone is being renewed, it is not necessary to remove the valve cover in order to check the alignment marks.

When fitting the timing belt, it is recommended that VW tool 210 is used to set the tension accurately as this is more critical with the DOHC arrangement (see illustration). Using this tool, the tension should be set to record a reading of between 13 and 14 on the scale. The tool can be obtained from a VW dealer.

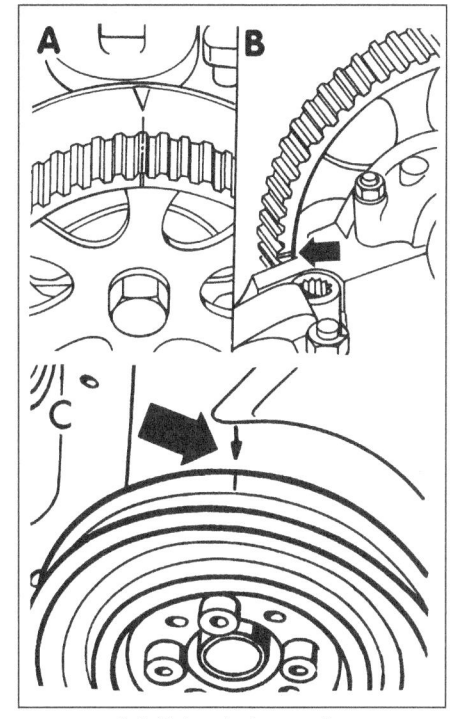

2.1 Valve timing marks

A Camshaft sprocket outer marks
B Camshaft sprocket inner marks
C Crankshaft vibration damper marks

3 Camshafts - removal and refitting

Removal

1 Remove the camshaft sprocket cover.
2 Unbolt and remove the upper section of inlet manifold.
3 Unbolt and remove the valve cover after disconnecting the HT leads from the spark plugs. Remove the main gasket and the central gasket from around the spark plug locations.

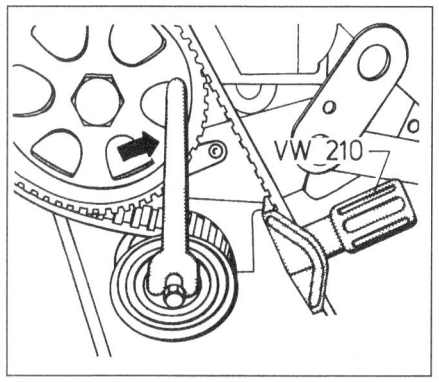

2.2 Adjusting timing belt tension using VW tool 210

4 Align the timing marks with reference to Part C of this Chapter, then check also that the marks on the chain sprockets are aligned (see illustration).
5 Remove the timing belt and camshaft sprocket with reference to Part C of this Chapter.
6 Note the fitted positions of the camshaft bearing caps, if necessary marking them to ensure correct refitting (see illustration).
7 Progressively unscrew the nuts and bolts from the end caps and bearing cap Nos. 1 and 3 on the exhaust camshaft.
8 Progressively unscrew the bolts from bearing cap Nos. 2 and 4. The exhaust valve springs will force the exhaust camshaft up as the bolts are loosened. Remove the bearing caps keeping them identified for position.
9 Working on the inlet camshaft, progressively unscrew the nuts and bolts from the end cap and bearing cap Nos. 5 and 7.
10 Progressively unscrew the bolts from bearing cap Nos. 6 and 8, then remove all the caps keeping them identified for position.
11 Lift both camshafts from the cylinder head then release them from the drive chain.

3.4 TDC timing marks in alignment on camshaft drive chain sprockets

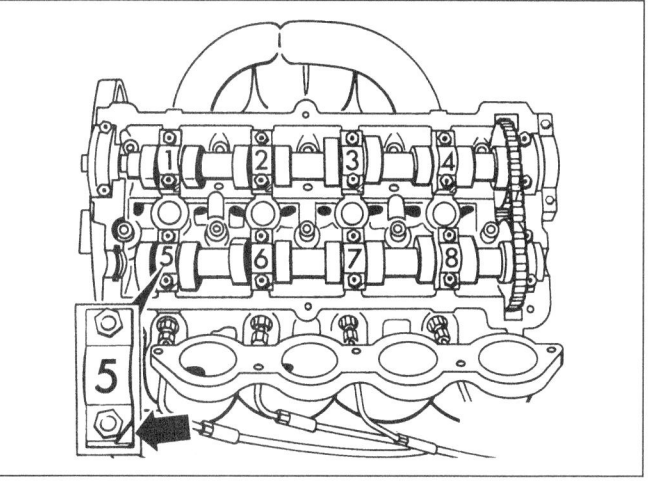

3.6 Camshaft bearing cap identification
Inset shows recessed corner position (arrowed)

2D•4 Engine repair procedures 1.8 litre 16 valve

12 If necessary, remove the hydraulic bucket tappets. Check the camshafts and drive chain for wear.

Refitting

13 Lubricate all bucket tappets and camshaft journals with clean engine oil, then insert the tappets in their original bores.
14 Locate the drive chain on the camshaft sprockets so that the timing marks are aligned as shown in **illustration 3.4**, then lower the camshafts into position on the cylinder head. Recheck the timing mark alignment.
15 Fit a new oil seal to the front end of the exhaust camshaft.
16 When refitting the bearing caps, make sure that they are located the correct way round. The numbers must be readable from the inlet manifold side of the head. The recessed corners of the caps must also face the inlet manifold side of the head.
17 Refit bearing cap Nos. 6 and 8, then progressively tighten the bolts to the specified torque.
18 Refit the inlet camshaft end cap and bearing cap Nos. 5 and 7, then progressively tighten the nuts and bolts to the specified torque.
19 Refit bearing cap Nos. 2 and 4, then progressively tighten the bolts to the specified torque.
20 Refit the exhaust camshaft end caps and bearing cap Nos. 1 and 3, then progressively tighten the nuts and bolts to the specified torque.
21 Refit the camshaft sprocket and timing belt with reference to Part C of this Chapter and Section 2.
22 Check that all timing marks, including the drive chain sprocket marks, are aligned.
23 Refit the valve cover together with new gaskets and reconnect the spark plug HT leads.
24 Refit the inlet manifold upper section and the camshaft sprocket cover.

4 Cylinder head - dismantling and overhaul

Exhaust valves on the 16 valve engine are filled with sodium to provide improved heat dissipation. Special precautions are necessary when disposing of this type of valve, particularly where recycling of scrap metal is concerned.

To render each valve safe, it should be wiped dry then cut through the stem with a hacksaw. Throw the valve into a bucket of water, keeping well away from it until the chemical reaction has subsided.

5 Pistons and connecting rods - removal and refitting

The big-end caps on 16 valve engines are fitted with oil jets which direct a stream of oil to the underside of the pistons, mainly for cooling purposes **(see illustration)**.

The oil jets are secured to the caps by small screws which must be coated with thread-locking fluid before inserting them and tightening to the specified torque.

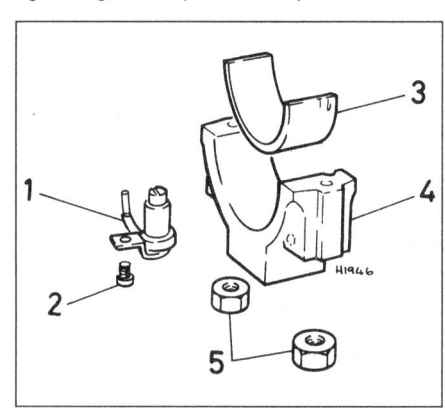

5.1 Big-end cap components

1 Oil jet
2 Screw
3 Bearing shell
4 Cap
5 Nuts

Chapter 3
Cooling, heating and air conditioning systems

Contents

Air conditioning system compressor - drivebelt adjustment 12	General information and precautions 1
Air conditioning system compressor - removal and refitting 11	Heat exchanger/fresh air box - removal and refitting 10
Coolant pump - removal and refitting 6	Heater and fresh air blower unit - removal and refitting 9
Cooling fan and motor- removal and refitting 4	Heater controls - removal and refitting 8
Cooling system - draining, flushing and filling 2	Radiator - removal, inspection and refitting 3
Cooling system electrical switches - removal, testing and refitting . . 7	Thermostat - removal, testing and refitting 5

Degrees of difficulty

Easy, suitable for novice with little experience	**Fairly easy,** suitable for beginner with some experience	**Fairly difficult,** suitable for competent DIY mechanic	**Difficult,** suitable for experienced DIY mechanic	**Very difficult,** suitable for expert DIY or professional

Specifications

Cooling system
Type . . . . Pressurised with pump driven by timing or V-belt. Front mounted radiator with internal or external expansion tank. Electric cooling fan

Radiator/expansion tank
Cap operating pressure . . . . 1.2 to 1.5 bar

Thermostat
Minimum stroke . . . . 7.0 mm
Opening temperature:
    1.05 and 1.3 litre engines:
        Rocker finger tappet type . . . . 92°C
        Hydraulic tappet type . . . . 87°C
    1.6 and 1.8 litre engines . . . . 85°C
Fully open temperature:
    1.05 and 1.3 litre engines:
        Rocker finger tappet type . . . . 108°C
        Hydraulic tappet type . . . . 102°C
    1.6 and 1.8 litre engines . . . . 105°C

Cooling fan thermo-switch
Carburettor engines:
    Switch-on temperature . . . . 93° to 98°C
    Switch-off temperature . . . . 88° to 93°C
Fuel injection engines (except 16 valve):
    Switch-on temperature:
        Single speed and 1st stage of twin speed . . . . 92° to 97°C
        2nd stage of twin speed . . . . 99° to 105°C
    Switch-off temperature:
        Single speed and 1st stage of twin speed . . . . 84° to 91°C
        2nd stage of twin speed . . . . 91° to 98°C
Injector cooling:
    Switch-on temperature . . . . 110°C
    Switch-off temperature . . . . 103°C

3•2 Cooling, heating and air conditioning systems

Torque wrench settings	Nm	lbf ft
All models		
Temperature sender unit	10	7
Cooling fan thermo-switch	25	18
Radiator	10	7
1.05 and 1.3 litre		
Thermostat housing through-bolts	20	14
Thermostat housing-to-pipe bolts	10	7
Coolant pump unit	10	7
1.6 and 1.8 litre		
Coolant pump housing	20	14
Coolant pump cover	10	7
Coolant pump pulley bolts	20	14
Thermostat housing to coolant pump	10	7
Thermo-switch (inlet manifold preheater):		
1.6 and 1.8 litre carburettor	10	7
1.8 litre fuel injection	30	22

1 General information and precautions

General information

Cooling and heating systems

The cooling system is of pressurised type and includes a front mounted radiator, coolant pump, expansion tank and thermostatically operated electric cooling fan **(see illustrations)**.

Coolant circulation through the radiator is controlled by a thermostat, the location of which differs according to engine type. On 1.05 and 1.3 litre engines, it is located in a housing on the rear end of the cylinder head (left side of vehicle) below the distributor. On 1.6 and 1.8 litre engines, the thermostat is located in the base of the coolant pump housing which is mounted low down on the front of the engine (timing case end).

Fuel-injected engines incorporate an oil cooler unit which is located between the oil filter and its mounting bracket.

Cold coolant from the bottom of the radiator circulates through the bottom hose to the coolant pump, where the pump impeller forces it around the cylinder block and head passages. After cooling the cylinder bores, combustion surfaces and valve seats, the coolant reaches the cylinder head outlet and is returned to the pump via the bypass hoses when the thermostat is closed. A further cylinder head outlet allows coolant to circulate through the inlet manifold and heater matrix (with heater control on) and it is then returned to the pump.

When the coolant reaches a predetermined temperature, the thermostat opens and the coolant then circulates through the top hose to the top of the radiator. As the coolant circulates down through the radiator, it is cooled by the inrush of air when the vehicle is in forward motion, supplemented by the action of the electric cooling fan when necessary. Having reached the bottom of the radiator, the coolant is now cooled and the cycle is repeated.

The electric cooling fan is controlled by a thermo-switch located in the left-hand side of the radiator.

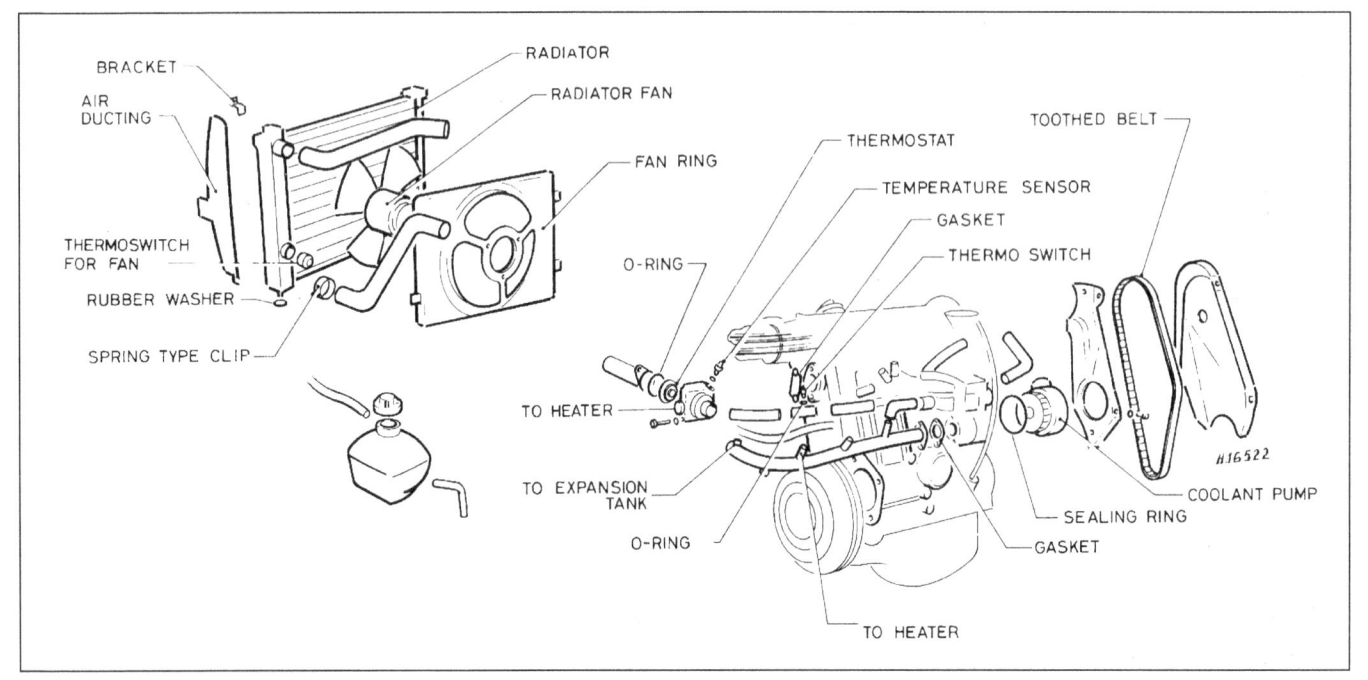

1.0a Cooling system components – 1.05 and 1.3 litre, pre August 1985

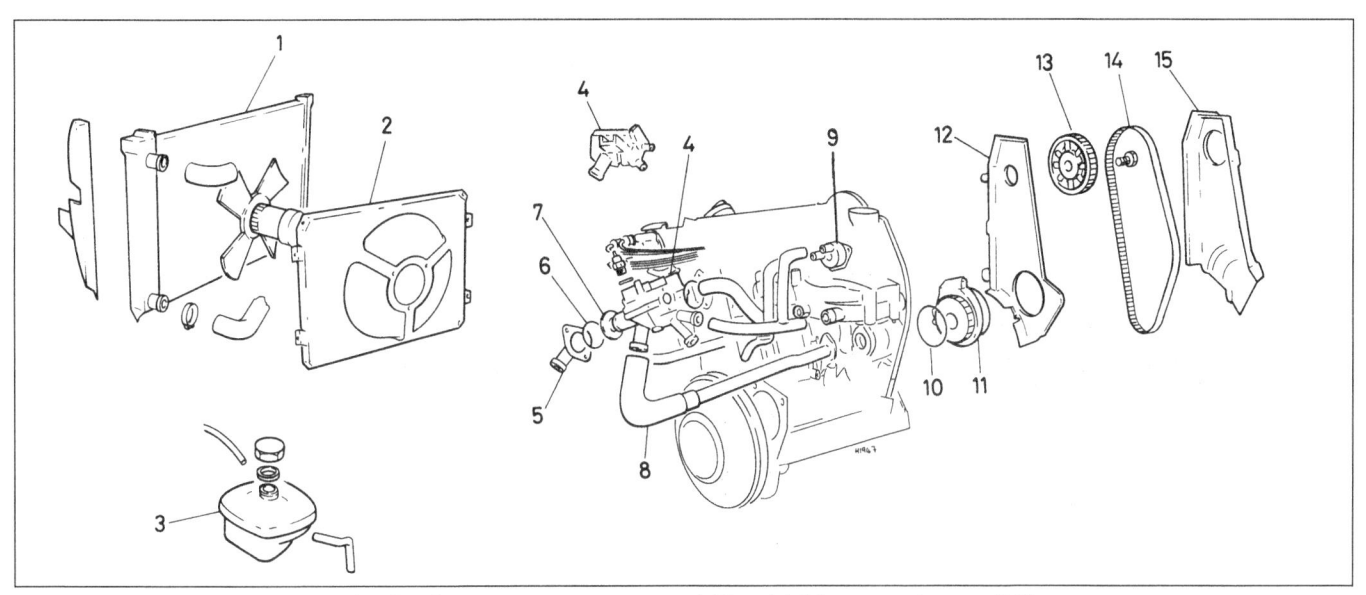

Cooling, heating and air conditioning systems 3•3

1.0b Cooling system components - 1.05 and 1.3 litre, post August 1985

1 Radiator
2 Fan ring
3 Expansion tank
4 Thermostat housing
5 Cover
6 O-ring
7 Thermostat
8 Hose
9 Automatic choke
10 O-ring
11 Coolant pump
12 Inner timing cover
13 Camshaft sprocket
14 Timing belt
15 Outer timing cover

Air conditioning system

The air conditioning unit works on exactly the same principle as a domestic refrigerator, having a compressor, a condenser and an evaporator. The condenser is attached to the vehicle radiator system. The compressor, belt-driven from the crankshaft pulley, is installed on a bracket on the engine. The evaporator is installed in a housing under the dashboard which takes the place of the normal fresh air housing. The housing also contains a normal heat exchanger unit for warming the inlet air. The evaporator has a blower motor to circulate cold air as required.

The system is controlled by a unit on the dashboard similar to the normal heater control in appearance.

The refrigerant used is a dangerous substance in unskilled hands. As a liquid it is very cold and if allowed to touch the skin will cause cold burns. As a gas it is colourless and has no odour. Heavier than air, it displaces oxygen and can cause asphyxiation if pockets of it collect in pits or similar workplaces. It does not burn but even a lighted cigarette causes it to break down into constituent gases, some of which are poisonous to the extent of being fatal.

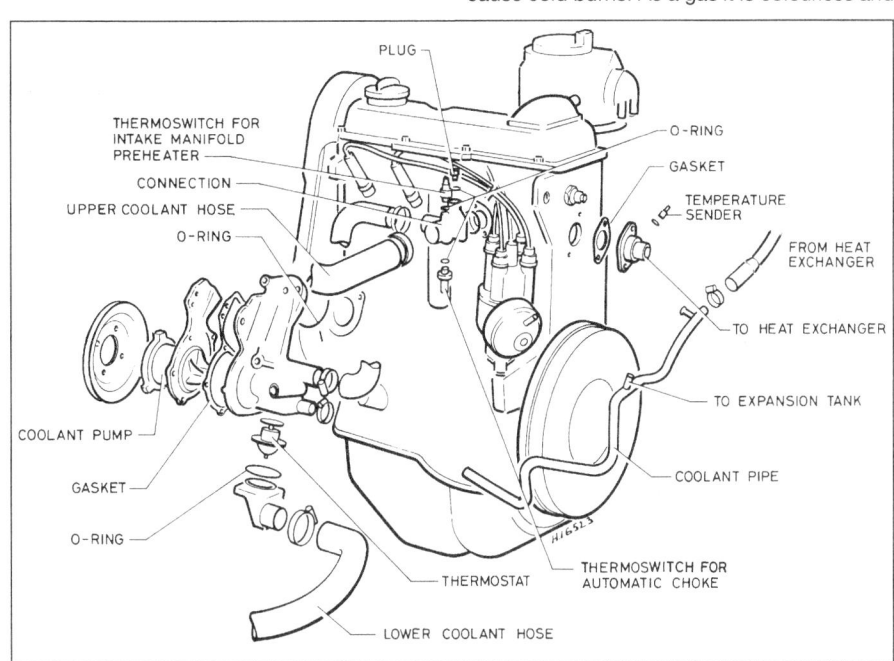

Precautions

Cooling system maintenance

Do not remove the expansion tank filler cap or disturb any part of the cooling system whilst it is hot, as there is a very great risk of scalding. If the filler cap must be removed before the system is cool, then the pressure in the system must first be released. Cover the cap with a thick layer of cloth, to avoid scalding, and slowly unscrew the cap until a hissing sound can be heard. When the hissing has stopped, then system pressure is released. Slowly unscrew the cap until it can be removed. If more hissing sounds are heard, wait until they have stopped before unscrewing the cap completely. At all times keep well away from the filler opening.

If the engine is hot, the electric cooling fan may start rotating even if the engine is not running. Be careful to keep hands, hair and loose clothing well clear of the fan when working in the engine compartment.

Antifreeze mixture

Antifreeze mixture is poisonous. Keep it out of reach of children and pets. Never leave antifreeze lying around, it is fatal if ingested.

Do not allow antifreeze to come in contact with your skin or the painted surfaces of the vehicle. Rinse off spills immediately with plenty of water.

1.0c Cooling system components – 1.6 and 1.8 litre, carburettor

3•4 Cooling, heating and air conditioning systems

Air conditioning refrigerant

Although the refrigerant is not itself toxic, in the presence of a naked flame (or a lighted cigarette) it forms a highly toxic gas. Liquid refrigerant spilled on the skin will cause frostbite. If refrigerant enters the eyes, rinse them with a dilute solution of boric acid and seek medical advice immediately.

In view of the above points, and of the need for specialised equipment for evacuating and recharging the system, any work which requires the disconnection of a refrigerant line must be left to a specialist.

Do not allow refrigerant lines to be exposed to temperatures above 230°F (110°C) - eg. during welding or paint drying operations. Do not operate the air conditioning system if it is known to be short of refrigerant, or further damage may result.

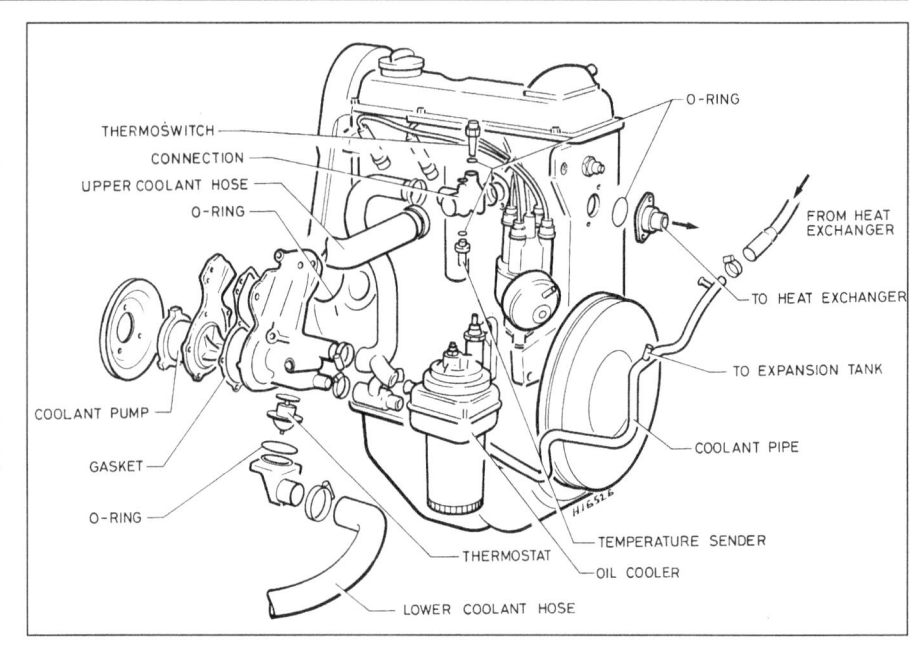

2 Cooling system - draining, flushing and filling

Warning: Never work on the cooling system when it is hot. Take care to avoid any possibility of scalding

Draining

1 It is preferable to drain the cooling system when the engine has cooled. If this is not possible, place a cloth over the expansion tank filler cap and turn it slowly in an anti-clockwise direction until pressure starts to escape.

2 When all pressure has escaped, remove the filler cap **(see illustration)**.
3 Set the heater controls to maximum heat, then place a suitable container beneath the left-hand side of the radiator.
4 Loosen the clip and ease the bottom hose away from the radiator outlet. Drain the coolant into the container **(see illustrations)**.

Flushing

5 After some time, the radiator and engine waterways may become restricted or even blocked with scale or sediment which can reduce the efficiency of the cooling system. When this occurs, the coolant will appear rusty and dark in colour and the system should then be flushed. In severe cases reverse flushing may be required, although if the correct antifreeze has been in constant use, this is unlikely.

6 With the coolant drained, disconnect the top hose from the radiator. Insert a garden

1.0d Cooling system components – 1.8 litre, fuel injection

1.0e Cooling system components - 16 valve engine

1 Alternator bracket
2 Pulley
3 Coolant pump assembly
4 Outlet elbow
5 Thermostat
6 O-ring
7 Cover
8 Oil cooler
9 O-ring
10 Outlet elbow

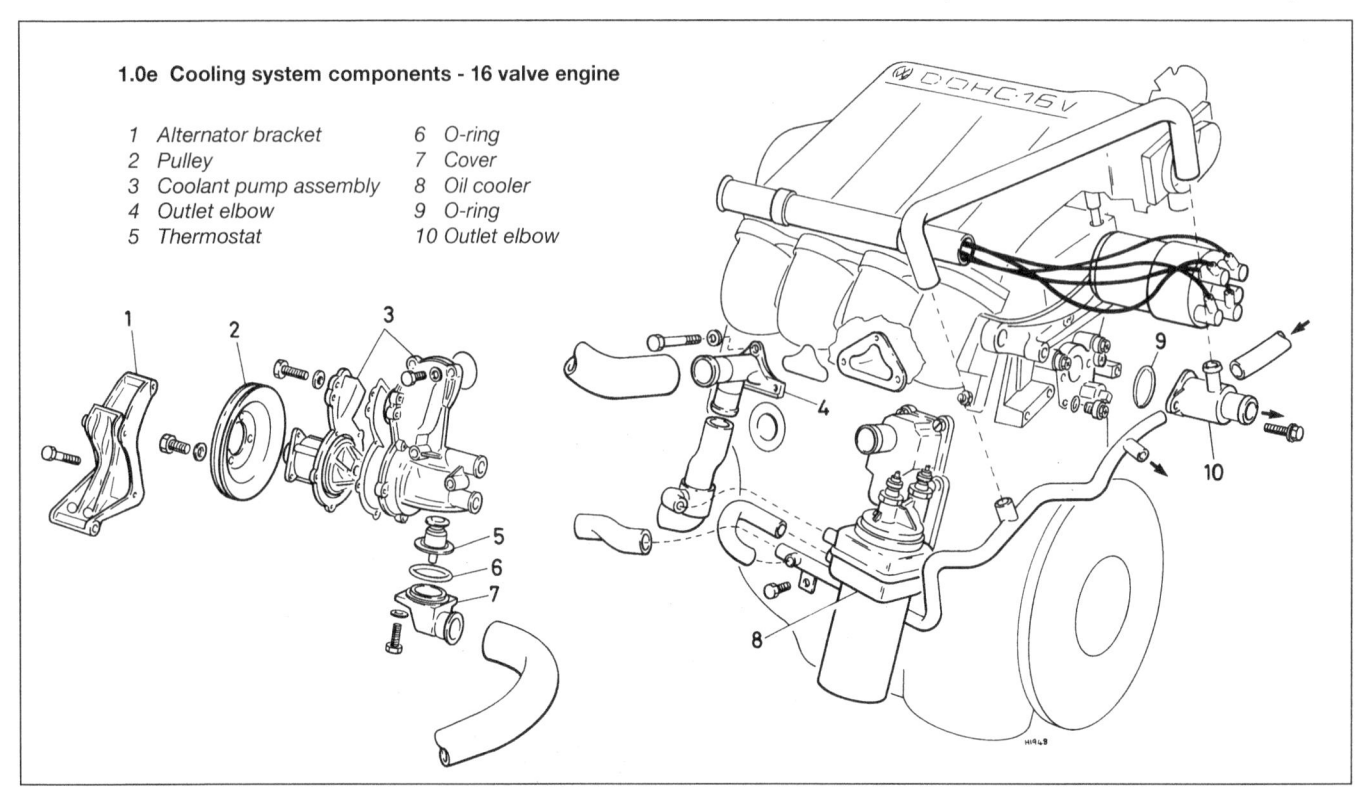

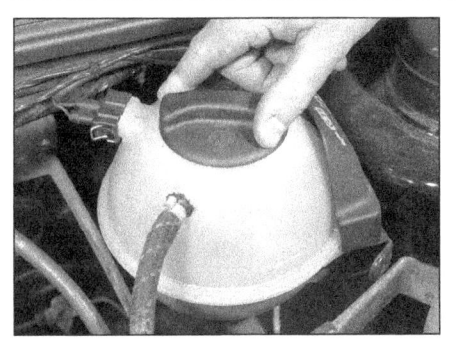

Cooling, heating and air conditioning systems 3•5

2.2 Removing expansion tank cap

2.4a Radiator bottom hose connection - 1.3 litre

2.4b Radiator bottom hose connection - 1.8 litre

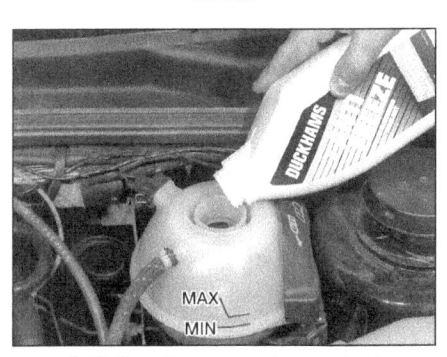

hose and allow the water to circulate through the radiator until it runs clear from the bottom outlet. If, after a reasonable period the water still does not run clear, the radiator can be flushed with a good proprietary cleaning agent.

7 Disconnect the heater hose from the cylinder head outlet and insert a garden hose in the heater hose. With the heater controls set at maximum heat, allow water to circulate through the heater and out through the bottom hose until it runs clear.

8 In severe cases of contamination the system should be reverse flushed. To do this, remove the radiator, invert it and insert a garden hose in the outlet. Continue flushing until clear water runs from the inlet.

9 The engine should also be reverse flushed. To do this, disconnect the heater hose from the cylinder head outlet and insert a garden hose in the outlet. Continue flushing until clear water runs from the bottom hose.

Filling

10 Reconnect all disturbed hoses and check that the heater controls are set to maximum heat.

11 Pour the recommended coolant mixture into the expansion tank until it reaches the MAX level mark.

12 Refit and tighten the filler cap then run the engine at a fast idling speed for a few minutes whilst keeping an eye on the coolant level.

13 Stop the engine and top-up the coolant level, as necessary, to the MAX mark (see illustration). Refit the filler cap.

14 After running the engine up to its normal operating temperature (electric cooling fan cuts into operation), the coolant level should be rechecked. When the engine is warm, the level of the coolant in the reservoir should be at the MAX level mark. When cool, the coolant level should be between the MIN and MAX level marks.

3 Radiator - removal, inspection and refitting

Removal

1 Disconnect the battery negative lead.
2 Drain the cooling system.

2.13 Topping-up engine coolant

3 Disconnect the wiring from the thermo-switch and cooling fan motor (see illustrations).
4 Disconnect the top hose and expansion tank hose from the radiator (see illustration).
5 Undo the two retaining bolts (see illustration) and remove the insulators and L brackets from the top of the radiator. Note that the longer bracket is the centre one.
6 Remove the front grille.
7 Remove the two bolts each side at the front and remove the left and right-hand air ducts.
8 The radiator can now be lifted from the engine compartment whilst taking care not to damage the matrix (see illustration).

Inspection

9 Remove the screws and withdraw the cowling and fan from the radiator.

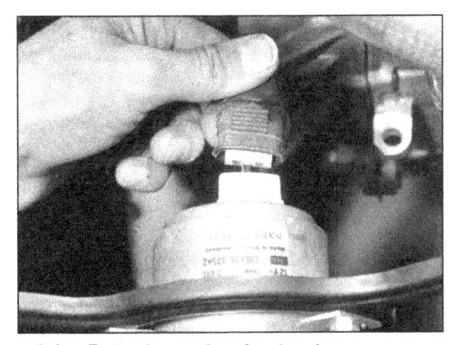

3.3a Radiator thermo-switch - 1.8 litre

3.3b Detach cooling fan lead connector

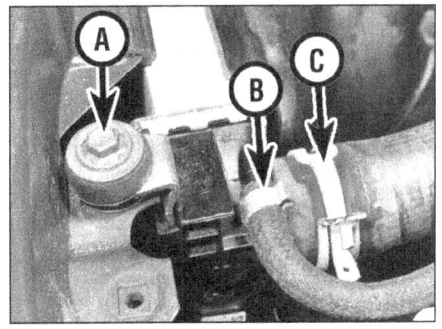

3.4 Radiator securing bolt (A) expansion tank hose connection (B) and top hose connection (C)

3.5 Radiator central retaining bolt and bracket

3•6 Cooling, heating and air conditioning systems

3.8 Lifting out radiator and cooling fan assembly

3.13 Radiator lower mounting rubber

3.15 Secure fan lead with plastic clip (arrowed)

10 Clean the radiator matrix of flies and small leaves with a soft brush or by hosing. At the same time check for signs of damage and coolant leakage.
11 It is not possible to repair this type of radiator without special equipment.
12 Renew any hoses or clips that are damaged.

Refitting

13 Refitting is a reversal of removal. If necessary, renew the radiator lower mounting rubbers **(see illustration)**.
14 Refill the cooling system.
15 When reconnecting the cooling fan motor wiring, secure the lead to the cowling web **(see illustration)**.

4 Cooling fan and motor - removal and refitting

Removal

1 Disconnect the battery negative lead.
2 Disconnect the wiring from the cooling fan motor and cowling. Note that as from January 1986, the wiring on all new cooling fan motors obtained from VW incorporates a standardised connector. Where necessary, the old connector must be cut from the main harness and the standardised part fitted instead. The relevant parts are obtainable from a VW dealer.
3 Remove the retaining bolts and screws and lift the cowling, together with the cooling fan and motor, from the radiator.
4 Remove the retaining nuts and withdraw the cooling fan and motor from the cowling **(see illustration)**.
5 If necessary, the fan can be separated from the motor by prising off the clamp washer. On AEG motors drive out the roll pin. On Bosch motors remove the shake-proof washer. Assemble the components in reverse order using a new clamp washer.

Refitting

6 Refitting is a reversal of removal.

5 Thermostat - removal, testing and refitting

1.05 and 1.3 litre engines

Removal

1 The thermostat is located in the outlet housing on the left-hand (rear) end of the cylinder head. To remove it, first drain the cooling system.
2 Unscrew the bolts and remove the thermostat cover **(see illustrations)**. Place the cover with top hose still attached to one side.
3 Remove the sealing ring **(see illustration)**.
4 Extract the thermostat from the outlet housing.

Testing

5 To test the thermostat, suspend it with a piece of string in a container of water. Gradually heat the water and note the temperature at which the thermostat starts to open. Continue heating the water to the specified fully open temperature then check that the thermostat has opened by at least the minimum specified amount. Remove the thermostat from the water and check that it is fully closed when cold.
6 Renew the thermostat if it fails to operate correctly.
7 Clean the thermostat seating and the mating faces of the outlet housing and cover.

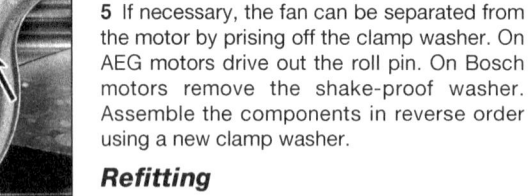

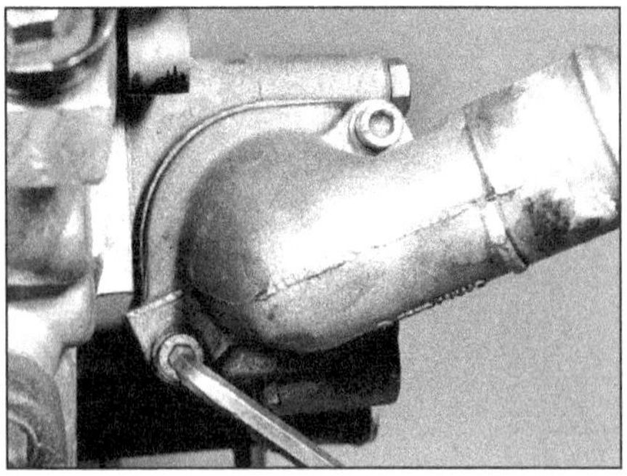

4.4 Cooling fan motor retaining nuts (arrowed)

5.2a Unscrew socket-head bolts . . .

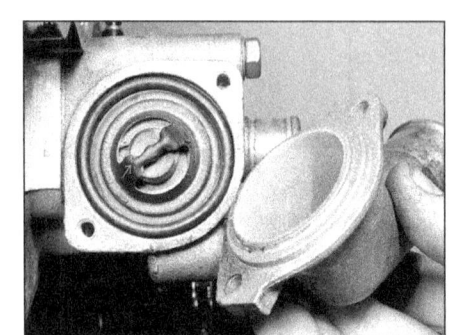

5.2b . . . and remove thermostat cover

5.3 Removing thermostat sealing ring

Cooling, heating and air conditioning systems 3•7

5.11a Undo the retaining bolts...

5.11b ...withdraw thermostat elbow...

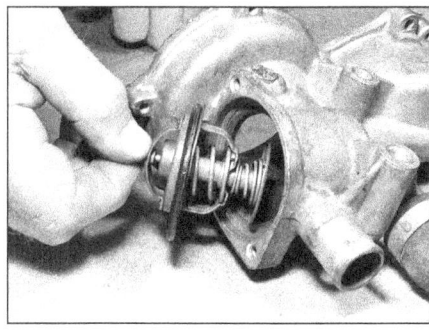

5.11c ...then extract thermostat and seal

Refitting

8 Refitting is a reversal of removal. Fit a new sealing ring and tighten the cover bolts to the specified torque. The breather hole in the thermostat should face upwards.
9 On completion, refill the cooling system.

1.6 and 1.8 litre engines

Removal

10 The thermostat is located in the bottom of the coolant pump behind the inlet elbow. To remove it, first drain the cooling system.
11 Unbolt the inlet elbow from the coolant pump and remove the seal and thermostat (see illustrations).
12 Clean the coolant pump and elbow of any scale or corrosion.

Testing

13 To test the thermostat, proceed as described in paragraphs 5, 6 and 7.

6.5 Disengage timing belt from coolant pump sprocket

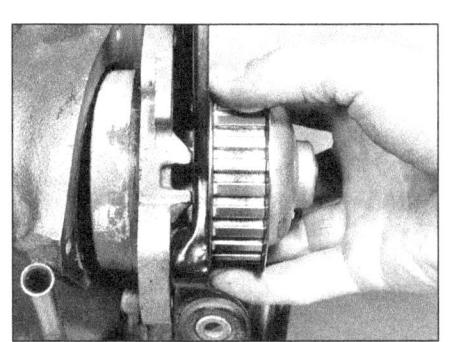

6.6 Withdrawing coolant pump

Refitting

14 Refitting is a reversal of removal procedure. Always fit a new seal.
15 On completion, refill the cooling system.

6 Coolant pump - removal and refitting

1.05 and 1.3 litre engines

Removal

1 Drain the cooling system.
2 Remove the air cleaner and air ducting and disconnect the battery negative lead.
3 Unbolt and remove the timing belt cover. On some later 1.3 litre models, it is necessary to remove the crankshaft pulley to remove the lower timing belt cover.
4 Turn the engine with a spanner on the crankshaft pulley until the timing cover plate upper retaining bolt is visible through the camshaft sprocket hole. Unscrew and remove the bolt.
5 Align the timing marks and release the timing belt from the coolant pump and camshaft sprocket (see illustration).
6 Remove the bolts and withdraw the timing cover plate followed by the coolant pump (see illustration). Remove the sealing ring.
7 It is not possible to repair the coolant pump and if faulty, it must be renewed. Clean the mating faces of the coolant pump and cylinder block.

6.16 Coolant pump location (engine removed from vehicle) - 1.6 and 1.8 litre

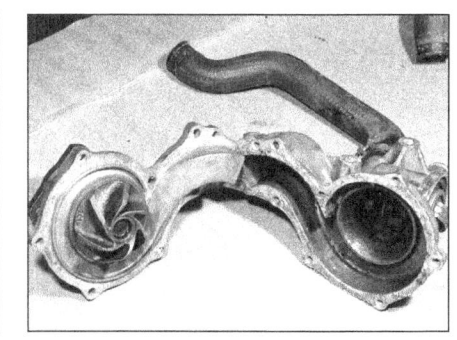

Refitting

8 Refitting is a reversal of removal.
9 When fitting a pump which has been reconditioned by VW, check to see if the sealing ring groove has been reworked. If it has, a 'Y' will be stamped on the pump mounting flange indicating that a 5.0 mm diameter sealing ring should be fitted instead of the normal 4.0 mm diameter ring. Always fit a new sealing ring.
10 Correctly tension the timing belt.
11 On completion, refill the cooling system.

1.6 and 1.8 litre engines

Removal

12 Drain the cooling system.
13 Remove the alternator.
14 On models fitted with power steering, it will be necessary to remove the pump unit and mounting bracket for access to the coolant pump.
15 On models equipped with air conditioning, it will be necessary to move aside the compressor unit and its mounting. Do not detach the air conditioning system hoses.
16 Disconnect the three coolant hoses from the pump, then remove the four bolts holding the pump to the cylinder block (see illustration). The pump will probably be stuck to the block but will come off if tapped gently. Remove the O-ring with the pump.
17 Remove the pulley and then take out the eight bolts which secure the bearing housing and impeller to the coolant pump housing. The two halves may now be separated (see illustration). Do not drive a wedge in to break

6.17 Two halves of coolant pump - 1.6 and 1.8 litre

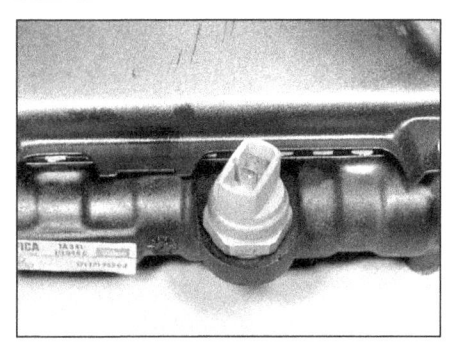

3•8 Cooling, heating and air conditioning systems

7.3 Cooling fan thermo-switch

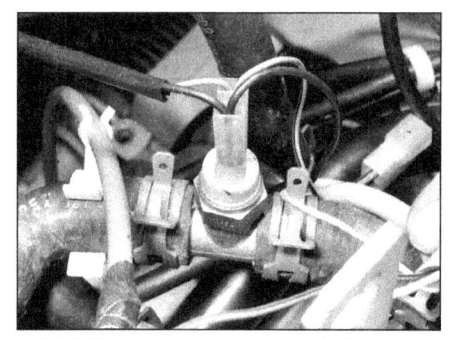

7.11 Temperature sender unit thermo-switch location - 1.05 and 1.3 litre

7.12 Temperature sensor (arrowed) - 1.05 and 1.3 litre

the joint. Clean off the old gasket.
18 Remove the thermostat.
19 The impeller housing and impeller complete with bearings are serviced as one part. If coolant is leaking through the bearing, or the impeller is damaged, the complete assembly must be renewed.
20 Fit a new gasket using jointing compound, then fit the two pump halves together and tighten the bolts evenly.
21 Fit the thermostat.

Refitting
22 Refitting is a reversal of removal. Always fit a new O-ring.
23 On completion, refill the cooling system.
24 Correctly tension the drivebelt(s).

7 Cooling system electrical switches - removal, testing and refitting

Cooling fan motor thermo-switch
1 Disconnect the battery negative lead.
2 Drain the cooling system.
3 Unscrew the thermo-switch from the left-hand side of the radiator and remove the sealing ring (see illustration). Note that from September 1985, on fuel injection engines (except 16V) the switch, located in the bottom of the radiator, is of a 3-pin type, replacing the previous 2-pin type. The new switch has two operation temperature ranges, the first range operating the coolant fan at normal speed and the second range operating the fan at boost speed.
4 To test the thermo-switch, suspend it with a piece of string so that its element is immersed in a container of water. Connect the thermo-switch in series with a 12 volt test lamp and battery. Gradually heat the water and note its temperature with a thermometer. The test lamp should light up at the specified switch-on temperature and go out at the specified switch-off temperature. If not, renew the thermo-switch.
5 Refitting is a reversal of removal. Fit a new sealing ring and tighten the thermo-switch to the specified torque.
6 On completion, refill the cooling system.

Cooling fan temperature sensor
7 From March 1986, the cooling fan is also controlled by a temperature sensor located between injectors 1 and 2. A time relay is also incorporated in the wiring circuit to keep the system functional for 10 to 12 minutes after switching off the ignition.

Temperature sender unit/thermo-switches
8 It is not necessary to drain the cooling system if some form of plug, such as an old sender unit or rubber plug, is available as a substitute for the removed switch.
9 Release any pressure in the system by unscrewing the pressure cap. If the system is still hot, observe the precautions at the start of this Chapter. With all pressure released, retighten the cap.
10 The location of the sender unit or thermo-switch is dependent on engine type. In general, they are as follows:

1.05 and 1.3 litre engines
11 The thermo-switch is located in the intermediate piece in the hoses between the inlet manifold and thermostat housing (see illustration).
12 The temperature sensor is located in the thermostat housing (see illustration).

1.6 and 1.8 litre carburettor engines
13 The temperature sender unit is located in the heat exchanger hose connecting flange on the rear of the cylinder head.
14 The thermo-switch (inlet manifold preheater) is located on the top face of the hose connector

7.16 Temperature sender unit (A) and thermo-switch (B) - 1.8 litre, fuel injection

on the spark plug side of the cylinder head.
15 The thermo-switch (automatic choke) is located in the base of the hose connector on the spark plug side of the cylinder head.

1.8 litre fuel injection engine
16 The temperature sender unit is located in the hose connector on the spark plug side of the cylinder head (see illustration).
17 The thermo-switch is located on the top face of the hose connector on the spark plug side of the cylinder head.

1.8 litre 16V engine
18 The temperature sender is located on the flywheel end of the cylinder block below the outlet elbow and controls the temperature gauge.

All engines
19 Disconnect the wiring lead from the sender unit/switch concerned.
20 Unscrew and remove the sender unit/switch and plug the aperture.
21 Refitting is the reversal of the removal procedure. Tighten the sender unit/thermo-switch to the specified torque.
22 On completion, check and if necessary top-up the cooling system.

8 Heater controls - removal and refitting

Removal
1 Disconnect the battery earth lead.
2 The heater control unit is located in the centre of the dashboard. It is accessible after the radio has been removed or, on vehicles without a radio, the cubby hole.
3 Pull off the control knobs and unclip the trim panel (see illustrations).
4 Remove the three cross-head screws holding the control unit and ease it forward (see illustration).
5 The cables can now be unhooked from the control unit levers and their outer body unclipped from the control unit body.
6 If a cable is to be renewed, unhook it from the control flap at the other end and withdraw it. For access to the flap control valves, it is

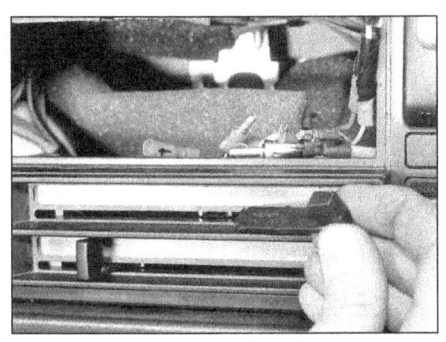

Cooling, heating and air conditioning systems 3•9

8.3a Pulling free heater/ventilation control knobs

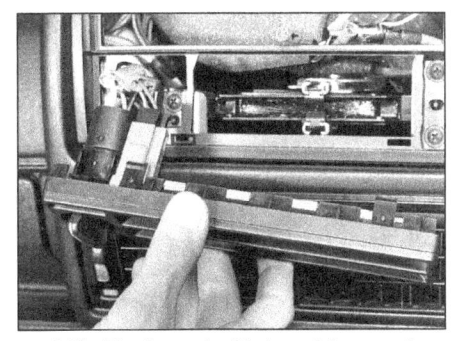

8.3b Unclip and withdraw trim panel

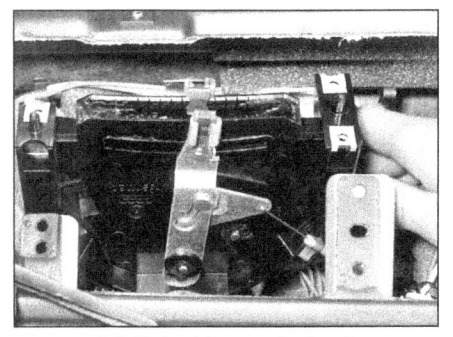

8.4 Detaching control unit

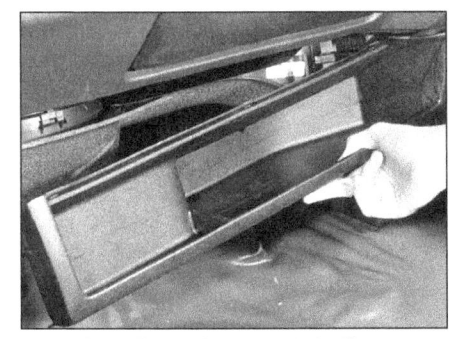

8.6a Removing parcel shelf . . .

8.6b . . . and insulation sheet

8.6c Control cable connections to flap valves at heater distribution box unit (arrowed)

necessary to remove the lower parcel tray on the passenger side and also the insulation sheet **(see illustrations)**.

7 It is best to renew the heater cables completely if the inner cable snaps. In this way the exact length required is obtained. It is a good idea to fit new cable clamps also, as the old ones seem to distort when removed.

Refitting

8 Refitting is a reversal of removal. Ensure that the cables are correctly routed with no sharp bends.

9 Heater and fresh air blower unit - removal and refitting

Removal

1 Disconnect the battery earth lead.
2 Remove the parcel shelf and insulation sheet on the underside of the facia panel on the passenger side.
3 The blower unit is mounted in the left-hand corner. Disconnect the wiring multi-connector **(see illustration)**.
4 Release the retaining tab (carefully) then twist the blower unit in a clockwise direction and withdraw it from the housing **(see illustration)**.
5 The wiring connection plate on the blower can be levered free by inserting a screwdriver blade under the retaining tab at the top.
6 If an ohmmeter is available, the thermo cut-out can be checked as shown.
7 Check that the blower wheel runs freely and that the air ducts are not blocked.

Refitting

8 Refitting is a reversal of removal.

9.3 Blower unit and wiring connection

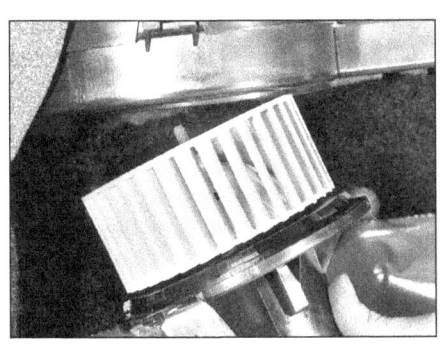

9.4 Blower unit withdrawal from housing

10 Heat exchanger/fresh air box - removal and refitting

Removal

1 Disconnect the battery earth lead.
2 Remove the centre console.
3 Remove the parcel shelf and insulator panel on the passenger side.
4 Drain the engine coolant (heater in ON position).
5 Disconnect the heater coolant hoses at the bulkhead on the engine compartment side **(see illustration)**.

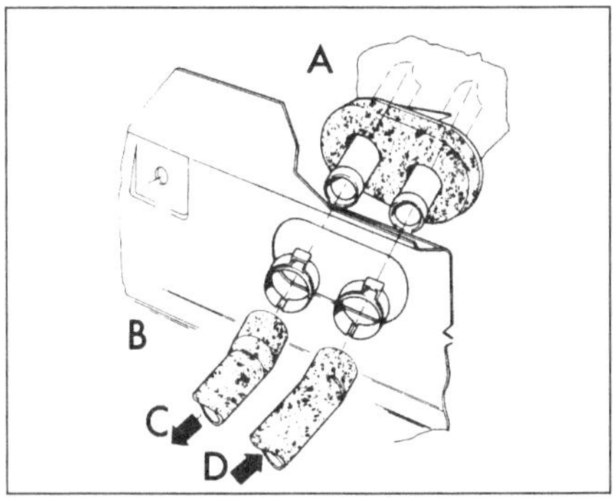

10.5 Bulkhead coolant hose connections

A Passenger compartment
B Engine compartment
C Return hose
D Supply hose

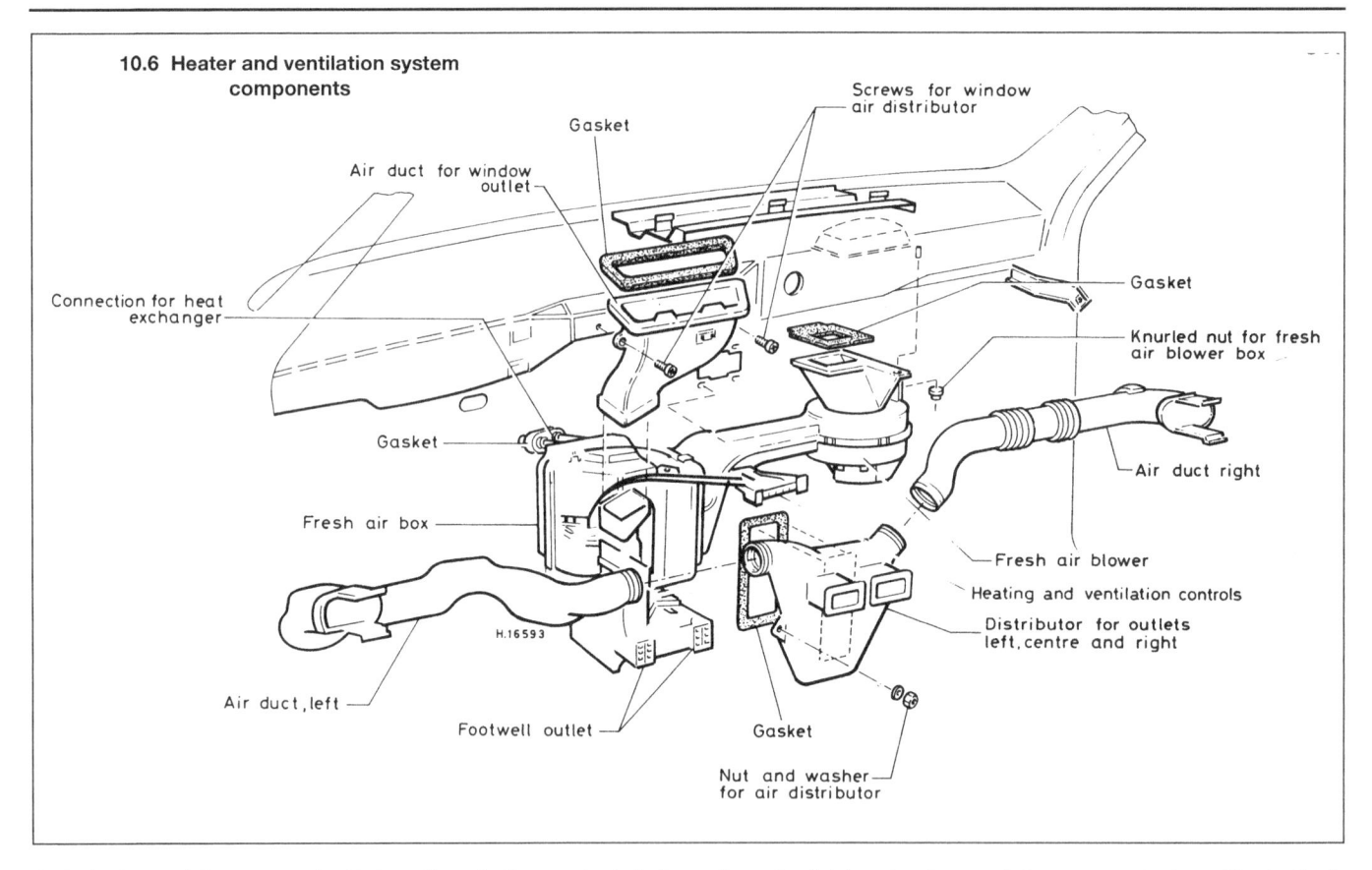

3•10 Cooling, heating and air conditioning systems

10.6 Heater and ventilation system components

- Air duct for window outlet
- Screws for window air distributor
- Gasket
- Connection for heat exchanger
- Gasket
- Knurled nut for fresh air blower box
- Gasket
- Air duct right
- Fresh air box
- Fresh air blower
- Heating and ventilation controls
- Distributor for outlets left, centre and right
- Air duct, left
- Footwell outlet
- Gasket
- Nut and washer for air distributor

6 Undo the retaining nuts and withdraw the outlet distributor from the air box, disconnecting the distributor from the left and right-hand air ducts as it is withdrawn. Remove the gasket **(see illustration)**.

7 Disconnect the control cables at the air box end.

8 Loosen the dash securing screws enough to enable the air box to be withdrawn and removed.

9 Release the clips and withdraw the heat exchanger unit from the air box. Allow for further coolant drainage from the inlet and outlet pipes.

10 The housing upper and lower housing halves can be separated by releasing the securing clips **(see illustration)**. Once separated, the flap valves can be removed. Take care not to split or crack the housings.

Refitting

11 Refitting is a reversal of the removal procedure. When engaging the control cable levers, align the index markings on the outer faces of the segments **(see illustration)**. Renew the heat exchanger cover gasket and ensure that the hose connections are securely made.

12 Before refitting the parcel shelf, top-up the cooling system and run the engine up to its normal operating temperature. Operate the heater and check for any sign of leakage from the heat exchanger hose connections. Check that the controls operate in a satisfactory manner.

10.10 Upper-to-lower housing retaining clips (arrowed)

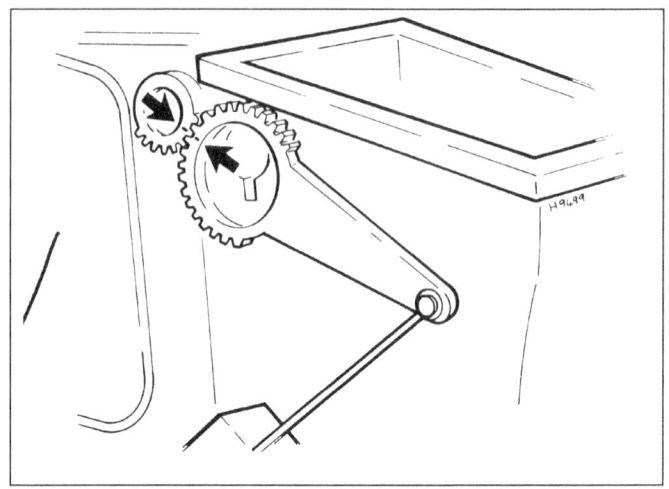

10.11 Align marks to set centre and side outlet flap positions

Cooling, heating and air conditioning systems 3•11

11 Air conditioning system compressor - removal and refitting

Warning: The air conditioning system must be depressurised and drained by a VW dealer or refrigeration specialist. Do not attempt this yourself.

1 Removal and refitting of the air conditioner compressor is straight-forward. However, under no circumstances should the refrigerant circuit be opened (see illustration).

2 Place the compressor on the side of the engine compartment when removing the engine and only move it to the point where the flexible refrigerant hoses are in no danger of being stretched.

3 When a situation arises which calls for the removal of one of the air conditioning system components, have the system discharged by your VW agent or a qualified refrigeration engineer. Similarly have the system recharged by him on completion.

4 Observe the precautions at the start of this Chapter.

12 Air conditioning system compressor - drivebelt adjustment

Refer to Chapter 1, Section 13.

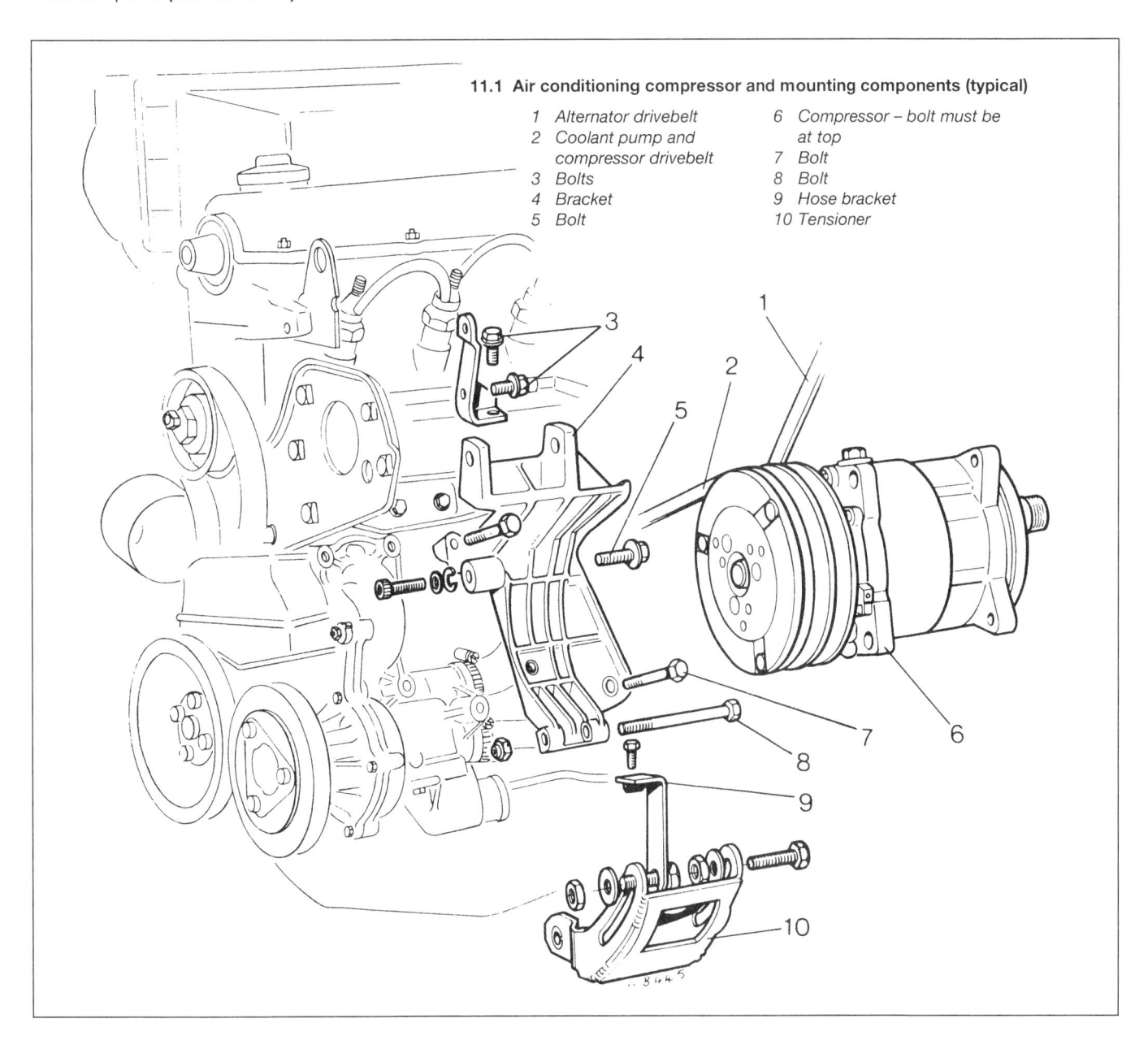

11.1 Air conditioning compressor and mounting components (typical)

1 Alternator drivebelt
2 Coolant pump and compressor drivebelt
3 Bolts
4 Bracket
5 Bolt
6 Compressor – bolt must be at top
7 Bolt
8 Bolt
9 Hose bracket
10 Tensioner

Notes

Chapter 4 Part A:
Fuel and exhaust systems - carburettor models

Contents

Accelerator and throttle cables - removal, refitting and adjustment . 10
Accelerator pedal - removal and refitting 11
Air cleaner element - renewal 2
Air cleaner unit - removal and refitting 3
Automatic air cleaner temperature control - testing 4
Carburettor (1.05 litre engine) - adjustments 15
Carburettor (1.3 litre engine) - adjustments 16
Carburettor (1.6 & 1.8 litre engines) - adjustments 17
Carburettor - overhaul 14
Carburettor - removal and refitting 13
Choke cable (1.05 litre engine) - removal, refitting and adjustment . 12
Exhaust system - inspection, removal and refitting 20
Fuel filler gravity valve - removal, testing and refitting 9
Fuel gauge sender unit - removal and refitting 8
Fuel pump - testing, removal and refitting 5
Fuel reservoir - removal and refitting 6
Fuel tank - removal and refitting 7
General information and precautions 1
Inlet and exhaust manifolds - removal and refitting 19
Inlet manifold preheating - testing 18

Degrees of difficulty

| Easy, suitable for novice with little experience | Fairly easy, suitable for beginner with some experience | Fairly difficult, suitable for competent DIY mechanic | Difficult, suitable for experienced DIY mechanic | Very difficult, suitable for expert DIY or professional |

Specifications

Air cleaner
Type . . . . Automatic air temperature control

Fuel pump
Type:
   1.05 and 1.3 litre . . . . Mechanical, diaphragm, operated by plunger from camshaft
   1.6 and 1.8 litre . . . . Mechanical, diaphragm, operated by eccentric on intermediate shaft

Carburettor - 1.05 litre
Pierburg/Solex 31 PIC-7

Type	Downdraught with manual or automatic choke
Venturi	23 mm
Main jet	X117.5
Air correction jet with emulsion tube	115 Z
Idling fuel jet	45
Idling air jet	135
Auxiliary fuel jet	32.5
Auxiliary air jet	130
Enrichment (primary/secondary)	70/70
Injection capacity (cc/stroke)	1.00 ± 0.15
Float needle valve	1.5
Float needle valve washer thickness	2.0 mm
Fast idle speed	2600 ± 100 rpm
Choke valve gap	1.8 ± 0.2 mm
Throttle valve gap smooth running detent	2.5 ± 0.3 mm
Idle speed	950 ± 50 rpm
CO content %	1.0 ± 0.5

4A•2 Fuel and exhaust systems - carburettor models

Carburettor - 1.05 litre (continued)

Pierburg/Solex 1B3

Venturi	23 mm
Main jet	105
Air correction jet	57.5
Idling fuel/air jet	50/130
Pump injection tube	32.5/150
Needle valve	1.5
Accelerator pump capacity (cc/stroke)	1.0 ± 0.15
Choke valve gap	1.8 ± 0.2 mm
Fast idle speed	2000 ± 100 rpm
Idle speed	800 ± 50 rpm
CO content %	2.0 ± 0.5

Weber 32 TLA

Venturi	22 mm
Main jet:	
Code 030 129 016	105
Code 030 129 016 D	102
Air correction jet:	
Code 030 129 016	80
Code 030 129 016 D	100
Emulsion tube	F96
Idling fuel jet	47
Idling air jet:	
Code 030 129 016	110
Code 030 129 016D	145
Auxiliary fuel jet (code 030 129 016D)	30
Auxiliary air jet (code 030 129 016D)	170
Pump injection tube	0.35/0.35
Needle valve	1.75
Needle valve washer thickness	0.75 mm
Accelerator pump capacity (cc/stroke)	1.05 ± 0.15
Choke valve gap (pull-down):	
Without vacuum	2.5 ± 0.2 mm
With 300 mbar vacuum	2.0 ± 0.2 mm
Choke valve gap (wide open kick):	
Code 030 129 016	2.0 ± 0.5 mm
Code 030 129 01 6D	2.5 ± 0.5 mm
Float level	28.0 ± 1.0 mm
Fast idle speed	2000 ± 100 rpm
Idle speed	800 ± 50 rpm
CO content %	2.0 ± 0.5

Carburettor - 1.3 litre

Pierburg/Solex 2E3

Type	Twin progressive choke, downdraught with automatic choke	

	Stage I	Stage II
Venturi	19	23
Main jet	X95	X110
Air correction jet with emulsion tube	120	130
Idling fuel/air jet	45/130	-
Full throttle enrichment	-	95
Pump injection tube diameter	0.35 mm	-
Choke cover code	276	
Injection capacity (cc/stroke)	1.0 ± 0.15	
Locking lever clearance	0.4 ± 0.15 mm	
Full throttle enrichment - height above atomiser	12.0 mm	
Choke valve gap	2.0 ± 0.1 mm	
Fast idle speed	2000 ± 100 rpm	
Idle speed	800 ± 50 rpm	
C0 content %	2.0 ± 0.5	

Carburettor-1.6 litre

Pierburg/Solex 2E2 - engine code EZ

Type .... Twin progressive choke, downdraught with automatic choke

	Stage I	Stage II
Venturi diameter	22.0 mm	26.0 mm
Main jet	X110	X127
Air correction jet with emulsion tube	0.75/1.05 mm	1.05 mm
Idle fuel/air jet	42.5	-
Full throttle enrichment	-	0.7
Pump injection tube	0.5	-
Injection capacity (cc/stroke)	1.0 ± 0.15	
Choke valve gap with primary throttle open 45°	6.3 ± 0.3 mm	
Fast idle speed	3000 ± 200 rpm	
Idle speed	950 ± 50 rpm	
Increased idle speed:		
Automatic transmission	800 rpm	
Air conditioner	950 ± 50 rpm	
CO content %	1.0 ± 0.5	

Pierburg/Solex 2E2 - engine code RF

	Stage I	Stage II
Venturi	22.0 mm	26.0 mm
Main jet	102.5	127.5
Air correction jet with emulsion tube	80	105
Idle fuel/air jet	42.5	-
Fuel throttle enrichment	-	0.7
Accelerator pump injection tube	0.5	-
Choke valve gap:		
Manual gearbox	2.5 ± 0.15 mm	5.0 ± 0.15 mm
Automatic transmission	1.9 ± 0.15 mm	5.3 ± 0.15 mm
Accelerator pump capacity (cc/stroke)	1.0 ± 0.15	
Fast idle speed	3000 ± 200 rpm	
Idle speed	750 ± 50 rpm	
CO content %	1.0 to 1.5	

Carburettor - 1.8 litre

Pierburg/Solex 2E2

Type .... Twin progressive choke, downdraught with automatic choke

	Stage I	Stage II
Venturi diameter	22.0 mm	26.0 mm
Main jet	X105	X120
Air correction jet with emulsion tube	105 mm	100 mm
Idle fuel/air jet	42.5	-
Full throttle enrichment	-	0.9
Pump injection tube:		
Carburettor part number type 027 129 015	0.35	-
Carburettor part number type 027 129 015 Q	0.5	-
Injection capacity (cc/stroke)	1.1 ± 0.15	
Choke valve gap (measured at lower edge)	2.3 ± 0.15 mm	4.7 ± 0.15 mm
Fast idle speed	3000 ± 200 rpm	
Idle speed	950 ± 50 rpm	
Increased idle speed:		
Automatic transmission	800 rpm	
Air conditioner	950 ± 50 rpm	
CO content %	1.0 ± 0.5	

Torque wrench settings

	Nm	lbf ft
1.05 and 1.3 litre		
Carburettor	10	7
Intermediate flange	10	7
Inlet manifold	25	18
Inlet manifold preheater	10	7
Fuel tank strap bolts	25	18
Exhaust manifold	25	18
Exhaust manifold to downpipe	25	18
Exhaust pipe clamp bolts	25	18

4A•4 Fuel and exhaust systems - carburettor models

Torque wrench settings (continued)

	Nm	lbf ft
1.6 and 1.8 litre		
Carburettor	7	5
Fuel pump	20	15
Inlet manifold	25	18
Inlet manifold preheater	10	7
Fuel tank strap bolts	25	18
Exhaust manifold	25	18
Exhaust pipe clip:		
8 mm	25	18
10 mm	40	30

1 General information and precautions

General information

The fuel system comprises a rear-mounted fuel tank, a mechanical diaphragm fuel pump and a downdraught carburettor.

The pump on 1.05 and 1.3 litre models is operated by means of a plunger activated by the camshaft, whilst on 1.6 and 1.8 litre models, it is operated directly by an eccentric on the intermediate shaft.

The air cleaner unit contains a renewable paper element and incorporates an automatic temperature control.

A conventional exhaust system is used on all models, being fitted in sections for ease of replacement.

Precautions

Fuel warning

Many of the procedures in this Chapter require the removal of fuel lines and connections which may result in some fuel spillage. Before carrying out any operation on the fuel system refer to the precautions given in Safety first! at the beginning of this Manual and follow them implicitly. Petrol is a highly dangerous and volatile liquid and the precautions necessary when handling it cannot be overstressed.

Tamperproof adjustment screws

Certain adjustment points in the fuel system are protected by "tamperproof" caps, plugs or seals. The purpose of such tamperproofing is to discourage, and to detect, adjustment by unqualified operators.

In some EEC countries (though not in the UK), it is an offence to drive a vehicle with missing or broken tamperproof seals. Before disturbing a seal, satisfy yourself that you will not be breaking any anti-pollution regulations by doing so. Fit a new seal when adjustment is complete, if this is required by law.

Do not break tamperproof seals on a vehicle which is still under warranty.

Unleaded petrol - usage

For full information on the use of unleaded petrol, consult your VW dealer who will be able to inform you if your vehicle is capable of running on unleaded fuel and, where possible, of the necessary adjustments required. The use of unleaded fuel in a vehicle not designed, or suitably adjusted, to run on unleaded fuel will lead to serious damage of the valve seats.

2 Air cleaner element - renewal

Refer to Chapter 1, Section 32

3 Air cleaner unit - removal and refitting

1.05 and 1.3 litre engines

1 Remove the element.
2 Unscrew the nut(s) securing the air cleaner body and remove the adapter or retaining ring **(see illustration)**.
3 Note the location of all hoses and tubes then disconnect them. Withdraw the air cleaner body from the carburettor and remove the sealing ring **(see illustrations)**.
4 Refit in the reverse order of removal, ensuring that all hose connections are securely made.

1.6 and 1.8 litre engines

5 Remove the element.
6 Unclip and detach the air hose at the side of the cleaner body **(see illustration)**.
7 Undo the retaining nut at the top and lift the cleaner unit clear, disconnecting the remaining hoses.
8 Refit in the reverse order of removal. Fit a new sealing washer if the old one has perished or distorted.

4 Automatic air cleaner temperature control - testing

1 Unclip and remove the vacuum unit and inlet pipe but leave the vacuum pipe connected **(see illustration)**.
2 Suspend a thermometer in the flow of air through the inlet duct then start the engine. Between -20°C and +20°C, the control flap in the unit should be a maximum of 2/3rds open to admit hot air from the exhaust manifold. Above 20°C, the control flap must close the hot air supply **(see illustration)**.
3 The control flap movement can be checked by sucking on the vacuum inlet.
4 With the engine running and inlet air temperature above 20°C, disconnect the vacuum hose from the vacuum unit. The control flap should fully open within a maximum of 20 seconds.

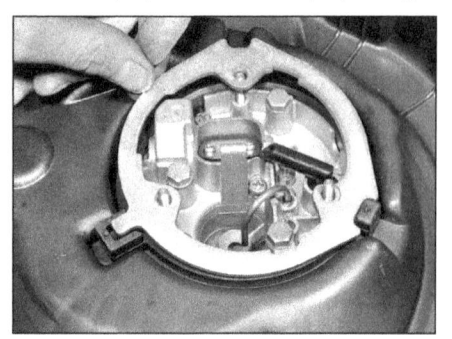

3.2 Removing air cleaner body retaining ring - 1.3 litre

3.3a Disconnecting temperature sensor hose . . .

3.3b . . . and crankcase emission hose - 1.3 litre

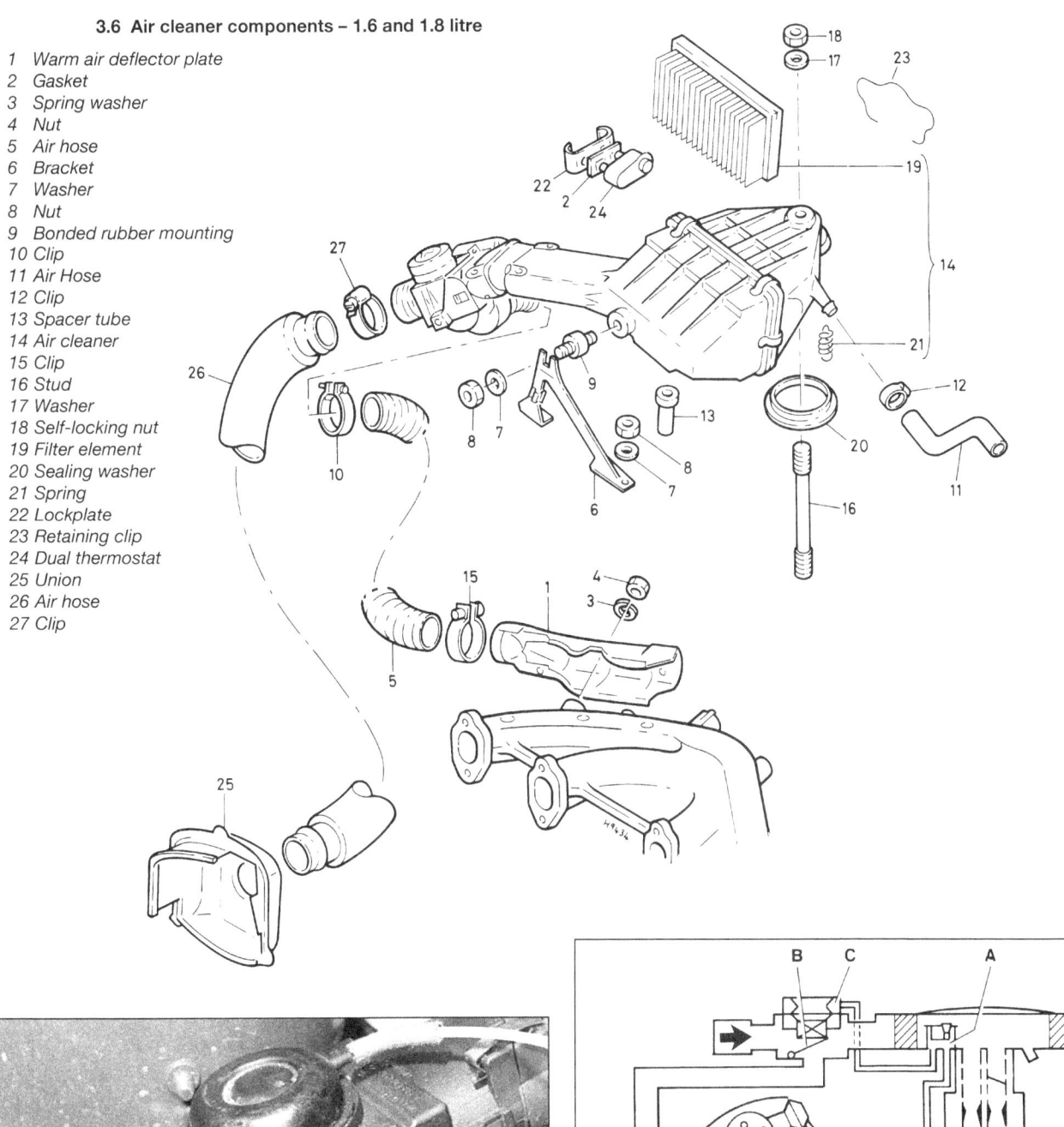

Fuel and exhaust systems - carburettor models 4A•5

3.6 Air cleaner components – 1.6 and 1.8 litre

1. Warm air deflector plate
2. Gasket
3. Spring washer
4. Nut
5. Air hose
6. Bracket
7. Washer
8. Nut
9. Bonded rubber mounting
10. Clip
11. Air Hose
12. Clip
13. Spacer tube
14. Air cleaner
15. Clip
16. Stud
17. Washer
18. Self-locking nut
19. Filter element
20. Sealing washer
21. Spring
22. Lockplate
23. Retaining clip
24. Dual thermostat
25. Union
26. Air hose
27. Clip

4.1 Air cleaner vacuum unit

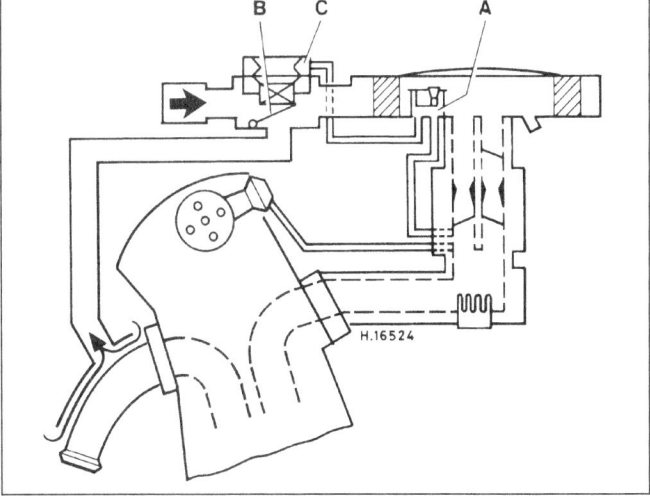

4.2 Air cleaner load and temperature control diagram – 1.05 and 1.3 litre

A Temperature regulator C Vacuum unit
B Intake pipe with thermostat

4A•6 Fuel and exhaust systems - carburettor models

4.5 Upper view of air temperature sensor - 1.3 litre

5 If the control unit does not operate correctly then renew it, together with the temperature sensor **(see illustration)**.

6 Refit the vacuum unit and inlet pipe.

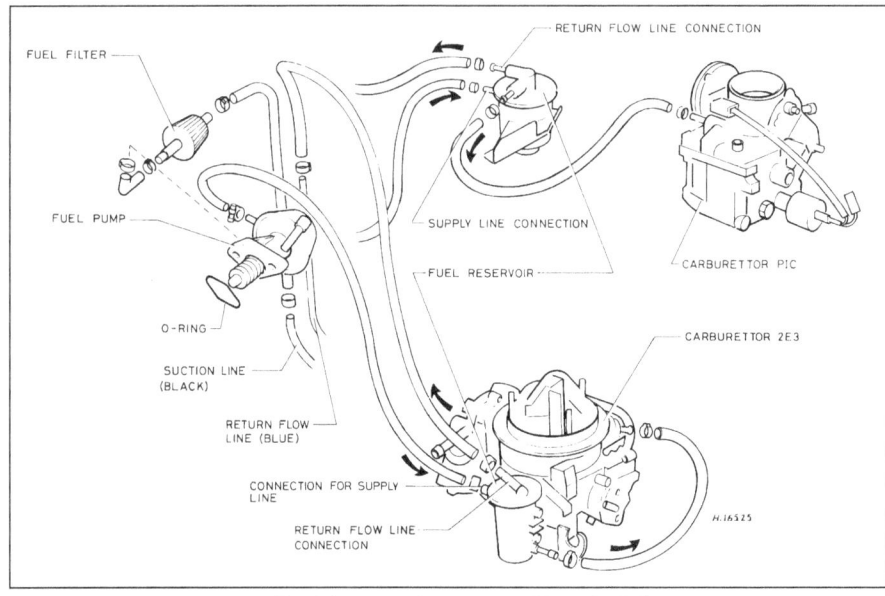

5 Fuel pump - testing, removal and refitting

Testing

1 Pump location is dependent on engine type and is as follows:
 a) *1.05 and 1.3 litre engines - The pump is located on the right-hand side of the engine, forward of the carburettor **(see illustration)**. Mounted on the cylinder head, it is driven indirectly from the camshaft.*
 b) *1.6 and 1.8 litre engines - The pump is located on the side of the cylinder block, next to the oil filter mounting bracket. It is driven direct from the intermediate shaft.*

2 If the pump is suspected of malfunctioning, disconnect the supply pipe from the carburettor (air cleaner removed) and the LT lead from the coil positive terminal. Ensure that there is fuel in the tank. Turn the engine on the starter while holding a wad of rag near the fuel pipe. If the pump is operating correctly, well defined spurts of fuel should be ejected from the pipe.

3 If the pump is malfunctioning then it must be renewed, as it is not possible to service or repair it. However, prior to removal of the pump, check the in-line filter for blockage.

5.1 Fuel pump location - 1.3 litre

5.4a Fuel line attachments – 1.05 and 1.3 litre

Removal

4 To remove the fuel pump, first identify the hoses for position then disconnect them from the pump **(see illustrations)**.

5 Using a suitable splined or Allen key, unscrew the pump retaining bolts and withdraw the unit from the cylinder head or cylinder block (as applicable). Remove the sealing ring and, if applicable, note the earth lead location.

6 Clean the mating faces of the pump and cylinder head or cylinder block/seal flange.

Refitting

7 Refitting is a reversal of the removal procedure. Renew the seal ring and, where crimped type hose clips were used, change them to screw type clips.

8 On completion, check all hose connections with the engine running and look for any sign of fuel leakage.

5.4b Fuel pump and line connections – 1.6 and 1.8 litre

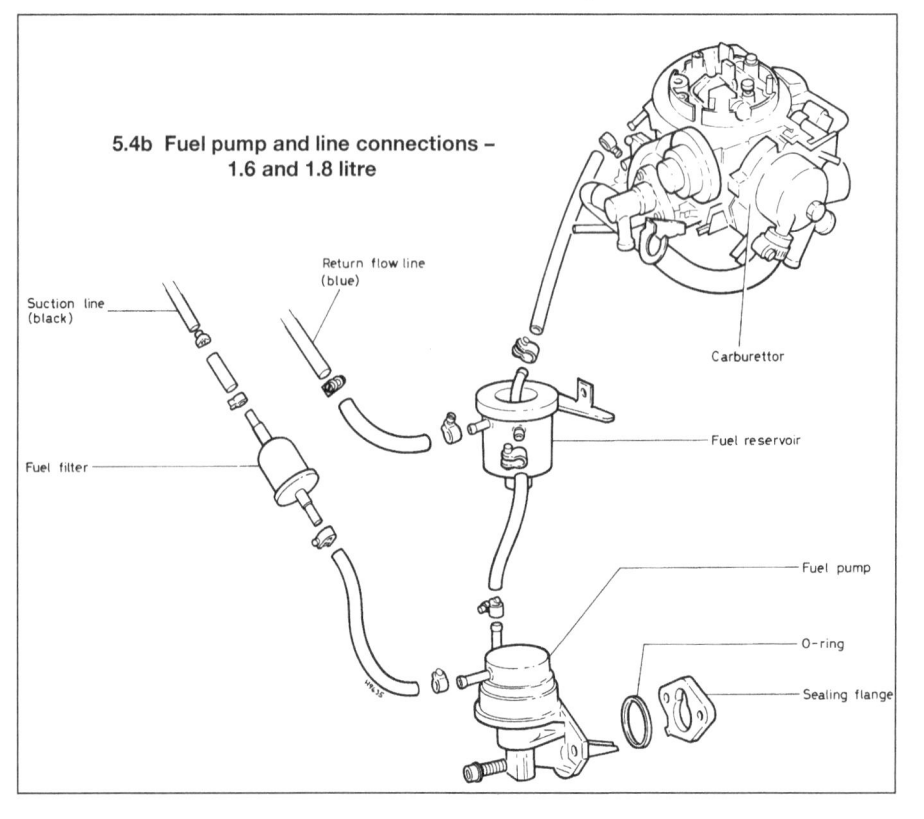

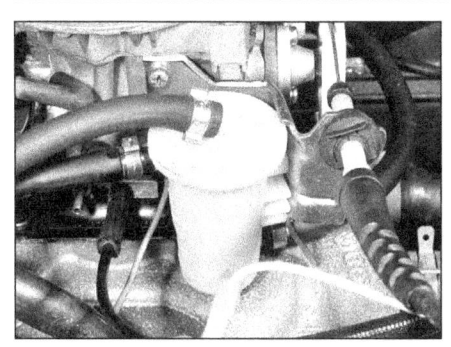

Fuel and exhaust systems - carburettor models 4A•7

6.1 Fuel reservoir location - 1.3 litre

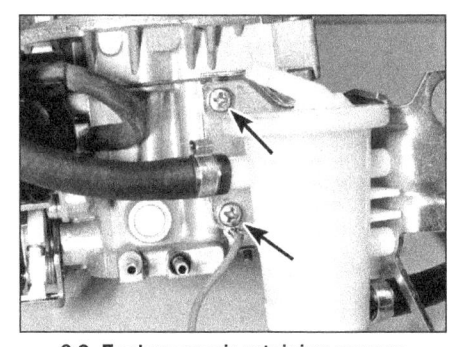

6.3 Fuel reservoir retaining screws (arrowed)
Note earth lead connection to lower screw

6 Fuel reservoir - removal and refitting

1 The fuel reservoir is located between the fuel pump and the carburettor (see illustration). The reservoir has three hose connections which are marked as follows:
a) From the pump - arrow marked
b) To the carburettor - not marked
c) To the fuel return line - marked R
2 To remove the reservoir, disconnect the three hoses and plug them to prevent leakage.
3 Remove the support bracket retaining screws and lift away the reservoir. Note the earth lead connection (see illustration).
4 Refit in the reverse order to removal and then check for any signs of leakage on completion.

7 Fuel tank - removal and refitting

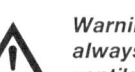

Warning: The fuel tank must always be removed in a well ventilated area and never over a pit

Removal

1 Disconnect the battery negative lead.
2 Siphon or pump all the fuel from the tank (there is no drain plug).
3 Lift the floor covering from the luggage compartment then remove the circular sender unit cover (see illustration).
4 Disconnect the wiring plug from the top of the sender unit, also the fuel feed (to pump) and return (from fuel reservoir) hoses.
5 Jack up the rear of the vehicle and support it on axle stands (see "*Jacking and vehicle support*"). Chock the front wheels, remove the right-hand side rear wheel.
6 Disconnect the breather hose from the filler neck (see illustration).
7 Disconnect the expansion tank-to-filler neck hose and breather pipe.
8 Disconnect the filler neck funnel which is secured by a large C-clip.
9 Support the fuel tank with a trolley jack and length of wood. Unscrew the retaining nuts and bolts, detach the straps (see illustration) and lower the tank to the ground. On GTi models, it will also be necessary to detach the side protector plate.
10 If the expansion reservoir is to be removed, undo the retaining bolt and lower it from the wheel arch.
11 If the tank is contaminated with sediment or water, remove the gauge sender unit and swill the tank out with clean fuel. If the tank is damaged or leaks, it should be repaired professionally or renewed.

Refitting

12 Refitting is a reversal of removal. Make sure that the rubber packing strips are fitted to the retaining straps. Refit the hoses free of any kinks.

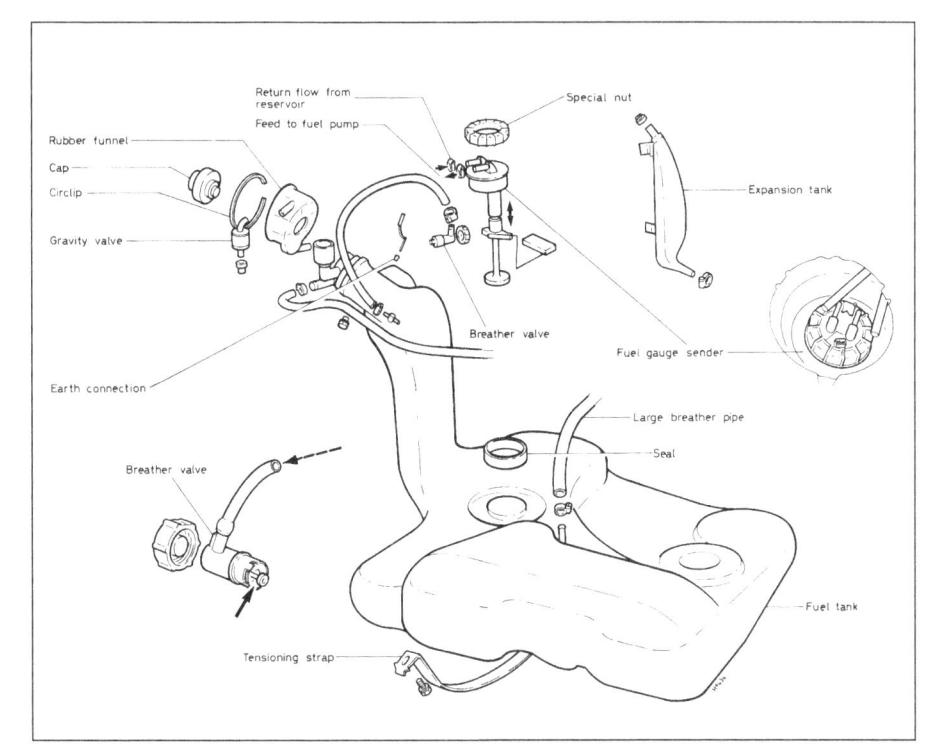

7.3 Fuel tank and associated components

7.6 Fuel filler breather valve and hose

7.9 Fuel tank retaining strap-to-floor bolts

4A•8 Fuel and exhaust systems - carburettor models

10.3 Accelerator cable to carburettor throttle control

10.4 Release cable grommet from support bracket

8 Fuel gauge sender unit - removal and refitting

⚠ **Warning: The fuel gauge sender unit must always be removed in a well ventilated area.**

Removal

1 Disconnect the battery negative lead.
2 Lift the luggage compartment floor covering and remove the circular sender unit cover.
3 Disconnect the wiring connector from the top of the unit then detach the fuel supply and return hoses.
4 Undo the retaining nut and lift out the unit, noting its orientation alignment marking. A suitable wrench may be necessary to loosen the securing nut.
5 Renew the sender unit seal.

Refitting

6 Refit in the reverse order to removal, noting the following:
 a) Check that the unit is correctly aligned with the markings in register
 b) Replace the crimped supply and return line clips with screw type clips
 c) Check that the wiring connection is secure.

9 Fuel filler gravity valve - removal, testing and refitting

1 The gravity valve is located in the fuel filler neck and is accessible from within the right-hand rear wheel arch.
2 To remove the valve, pull it upwards from the fuel filler neck and unclip it.
3 When the valve is held vertically, it must be open. When the valve is angled at 45° then it must shut. Renew the valve if found to be defective.
4 Refit in the reverse order of removal.

10 Accelerator and throttle cables - removal, refitting and adjustment

Manual gearbox

Removal

1 Disconnect the battery earth lead.
2 Remove the air cleaner unit.
3 Prise free and release the inner cable securing clip(s) at the carburettor throttle control, noting their location **(see illustration)**.
4 Release the cable grommet from the support bracket **(see illustration)**.
5 Working inside the vehicle, remove the lower facia panel then unclip the inner cable from the accelerator pedal **(see illustration)**.
6 Withdraw the complete accelerator cable into the engine compartment, together with the rubber grommets.

Refitting

7 Refitting of the accelerator cable is a reversal of removal. Make sure that the cable is free of kinks. Adjust it as follows before refitting the air cleaner.

Adjustment

8 Before adjusting the cable, check that it is correctly aligned over its full length.

10.5 Accelerator cable-to-pedal attachment

9 Have an assistant fully depress the accelerator pedal.
10 Check that the clearance between the throttle lever at the carburettor and the fully open stop is a maximum of 1.0 mm. Note that the throttle lever must not be hard against the fully open stop (ie. there must be a small clearance).
11 There are different cable adjustment arrangements which are as follows:
 a) Where locknuts are provided at the engine end of the outer cable, loosen them then adjust the cable position and tighten the locknuts
 b) Where a ferrule and circlip are provided, extract the circlip, adjust the cable position then refit the circlip so that it is abutting the ferrule guide
 c) On some models, it is necessary to adjust the inner cable by loosening the clamp screw, repositioning the lever while holding the cable taut then tightening the screw
12 After adjustment refit the air cleaner.

Automatic transmission

Removal

13 On automatic transmission models, the accelerator pedal activates the accelerator cable which is attached to the operating lever of the gearbox shift control. This simultaneously operates the throttle cable fitted between the shift mechanism and the carburettor **(see illustration)**.
14 Before removing either cable, select P (Park).
15 To remove the accelerator pedal cable, first loosen the cable adjusting nut then detach the inner cable from the operating lever clevis and the outer cable from its location bracket. The cable can then be disconnected from the pedal and removed in the same manner as that for manual gearbox models.
16 To remove the throttle cable, loosen the adjuster and locknut at the carburettor support bracket, remove the inner cable

Fuel and exhaust systems - carburettor models 4A•9

retaining clip and then disconnect the cable from the carburettor.
17 At the transmission end, prise free the securing clip and detach the cable from the operating lever and the cable support bracket.

Refitting
18 Refitting of both cables is a reversal of the removal procedure.

Adjustment
19 This procedure is described in Chapter 7B.

11 Accelerator pedal - removal and refitting

Removal
1 Remove the lower facia panel.
2 Disconnect the accelerator cable from the pedal
3 Prise out the clip and remove the pivot pin.
4 Remove the accelerator pedal. If necessary press out the pivot pin bushes.

Refitting
5 Refitting is a reversal of removal. Lubricate the bushes with a little grease and check cable adjustment.

12 Choke cable (1.05 litre engine) - removal, refitting and adjustment

Removal
1 Disconnect the battery negative lead.
2 Remove the air cleaner.
3 Using a screwdriver, loosen the inner and outer cable clamps and disconnect the cable from the carburettor.
4 Working inside the vehicle, remove the lower facia panel.
5 Pull out the clip and remove the choke knob.
6 Unscrew the ring and withdraw the cable from the facia.
7 Disconnect the wiring and withdraw the complete cable from inside the vehicle.

Refitting
8 Refitting is a reversal of removal. Make sure that the cable is correctly aligned and that the grommets are firmly fitted in the bulkhead. Adjust it as follows before refitting the air cleaner.

Adjustment
9 Locate the outer cable in the clamp so that its end protrudes by approximately 12.0 mm. Tighten the clamp with the outer cable in this position (see illustration).

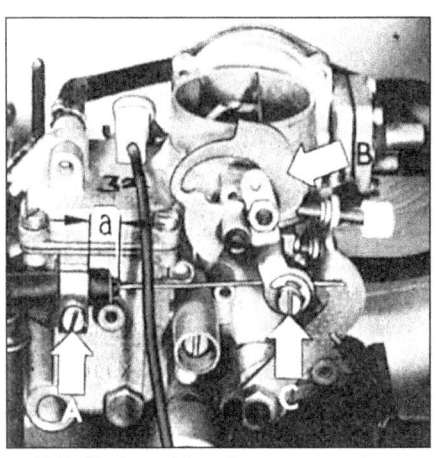

12.9 Choke cable adjustment setting – 1.05 litre

A Outer cable projection
B Cam and stop
C Choke inner cable connection

10 Push the choke knob fully in then pull it out by 3.0 mm. Switch on the ignition and check that the warning lamp is not lit.
11 Insert the inner cable into the choke lever clamp and fully open the choke lever by hand. Tighten the inner cable clamp screw in this position.
12 Refit the air cleaner.

13 Carburettor - removal and refitting

Removal
1 Disconnect the battery earth lead.
2 Remove the air cleaner unit.
3 Disconnect the accelerator cable from the carburettor.
4 Disconnect the wiring from the following, as applicable:
 a) Fuel cut-off solenoid
 b) Bypass air cut-off valve
 c) Part throttle channel heater
 d) Automatic choke control unit
 e) Earth point
5 Drain off half the engine coolant then disconnect the coolant hoses from the automatic choke unit and the expansion element (where applicable) (see illustrations).
6 Disconnect the fuel supply and return hoses at the carburettor/fuel reservoir, as necessary, and plug or clamp the hoses to prevent fuel leakage. Note the connections in case of confusion when refitting.
7 Disconnect the vacuum hoses and note their connections.
8 Unscrew the through-bolts or retaining nuts, as applicable, and carefully remove the carburettor from the inlet manifold (see illustration).
9 To remove the intermediate flange from the manifold, undo the four nuts on the manifold underside and lift the flange clear.

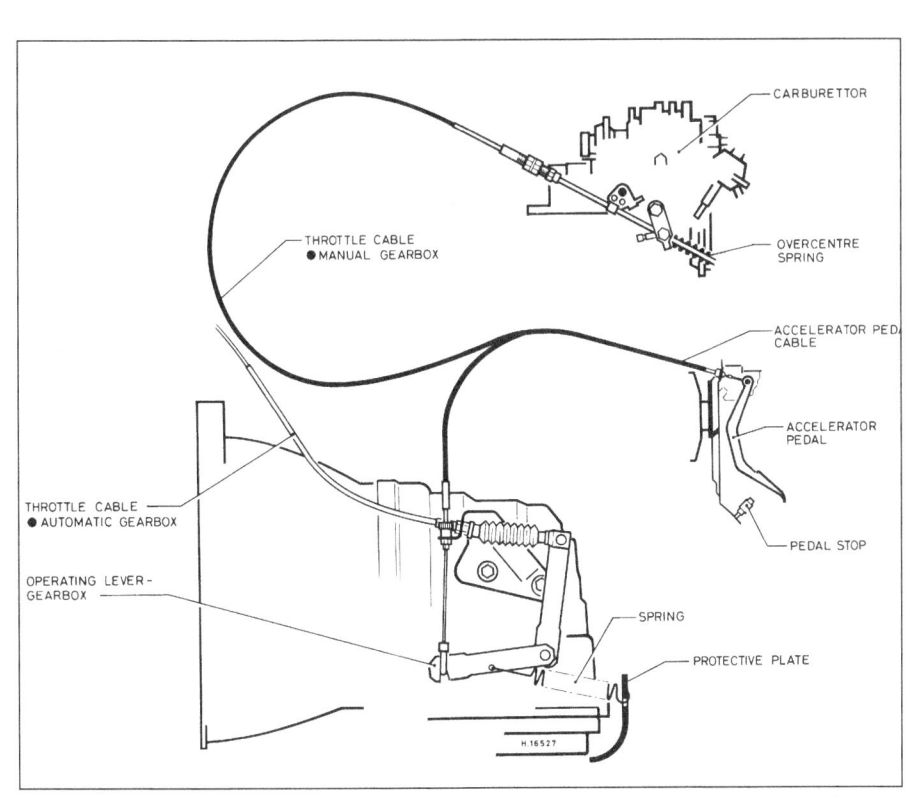

10.13 Accelerator/throttle cable connections – manual gearbox and automatic transmission variants with 2E2 carburettor

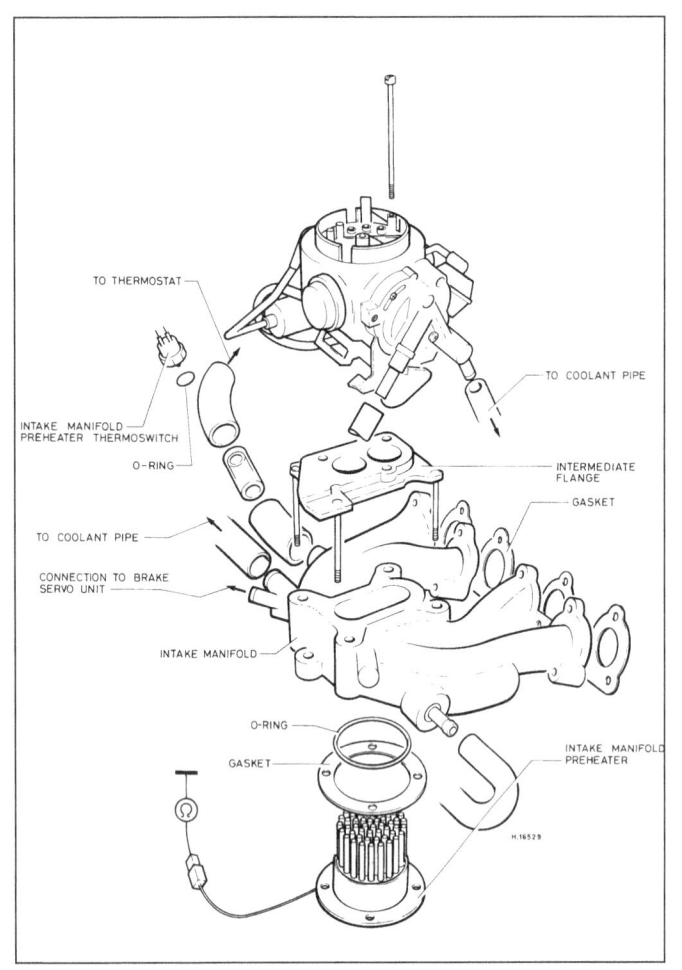

4A•10 Fuel and exhaust systems - carburettor models

13.5a Pierburg/Solex 2E3 carburettor, manifold and associated components

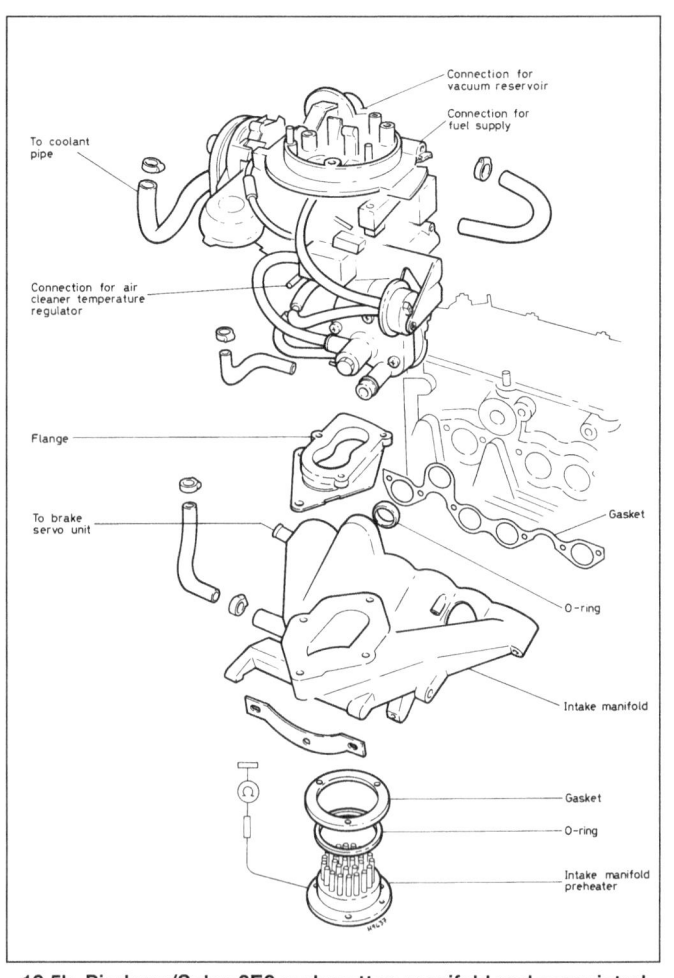

13.5b Pierburg/Solex 2E2 carburettor, manifold and associated components

Refitting

10 Refitting is a reversal of the removal procedure. Ensure that the inlet manifold, intermediate flange and carburettor mating faces are clean and use new gaskets.

13.8 Carburettor securing bolts (arrowed) – Pierburg/Solex 2E3

11 On completion, top-up the cooling system, restart the engine and check for fuel and coolant leaks.
12 Adjust the carburettor as necessary.

14 Carburettor - overhaul

1 A complete strip-down of a carburettor is unlikely to cure a fault which is not immediately obvious without introducing new problems. If persistent carburation problems are encountered, it is recommended that the advice of a VW dealer or carburettor specialist is sought. Most dealers will be able to provide carburettor re-jetting and servicing facilities and if necessary, it should be possible to purchase a reconditioned carburettor of the relevant type.
2 If it is decided to go ahead and service a carburettor, check the cost and availability of spare parts before commencement. Obtain a carburettor repair kit, which will contain the necessary gaskets, diaphragms and other renewable items.
3 When working on carburettors, scrupulous cleanliness must be observed and care must be taken not to introduce any foreign matter into components. Carburettors are delicate instruments and care should be taken not to disturb any components unnecessarily.
4 Referring to the relevant exploded view of the carburettor **(see illustrations)**, remove each component part whilst making a note of its fitted position. Make alignment marks on linkages, etc.
5 Reassemble the carburettor in the reverse order to dismantling, using new gaskets, O-rings etc. Be careful not to kink any diaphragms.

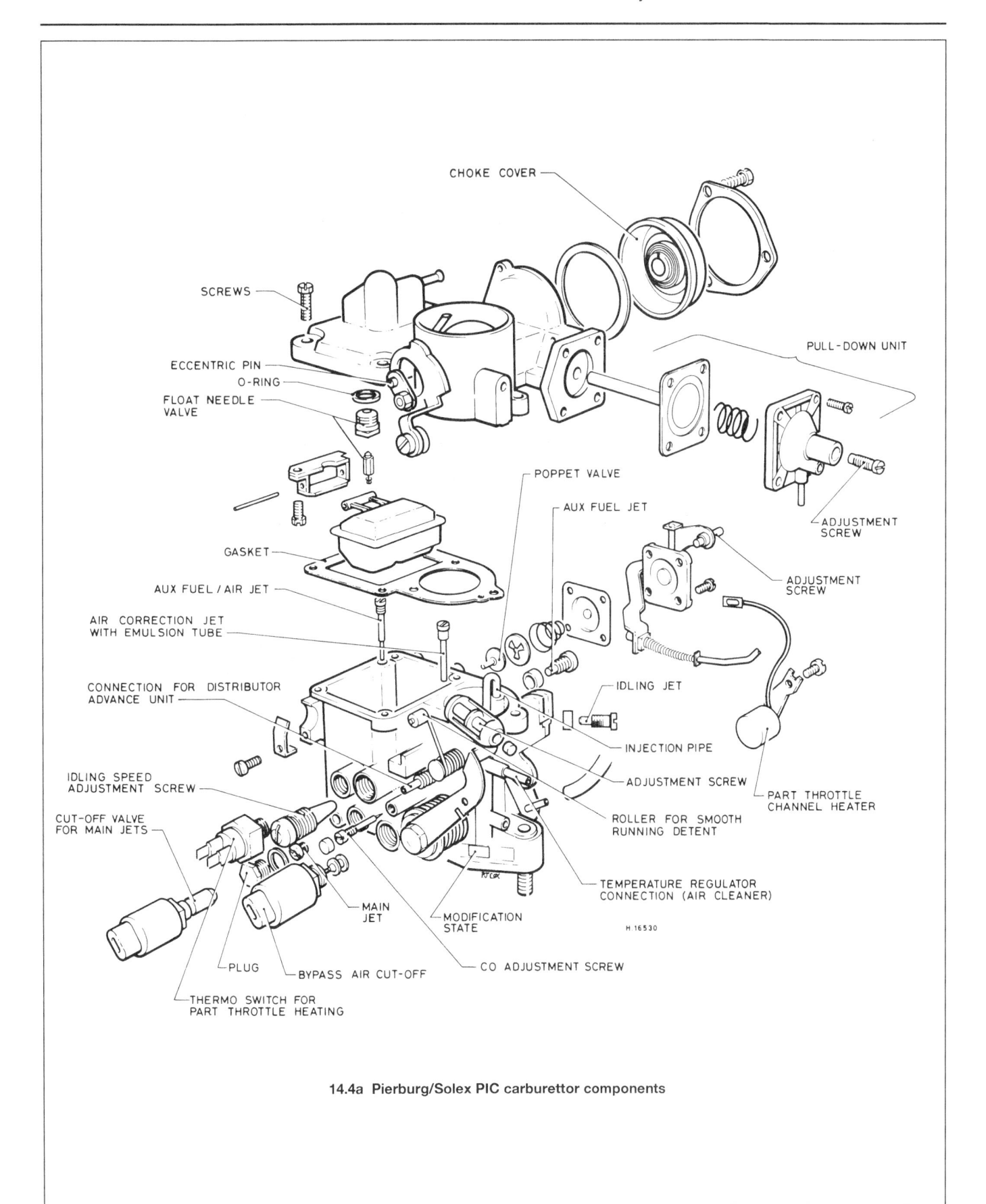

Fuel and exhaust systems - carburettor models 4A•11

14.4a Pierburg/Solex PIC carburettor components

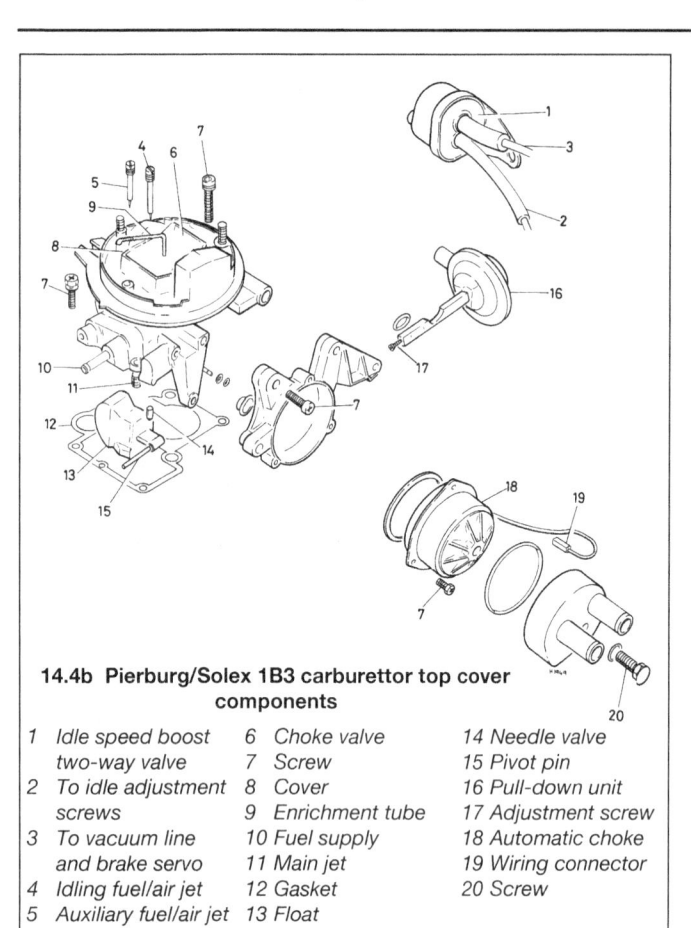

4A•12 Fuel and exhaust systems - carburettor models

14.4b Pierburg/Solex 1B3 carburettor top cover components

1. Idle speed boost two-way valve
2. To idle adjustment screws
3. To vacuum line and brake servo
4. Idling fuel/air jet
5. Auxiliary fuel/air jet
6. Choke valve
7. Screw
8. Cover
9. Enrichment tube
10. Fuel supply
11. Main jet
12. Gasket
13. Float
14. Needle valve
15. Pivot pin
16. Pull-down unit
17. Adjustment screw
18. Automatic choke
19. Wiring connector
20. Screw

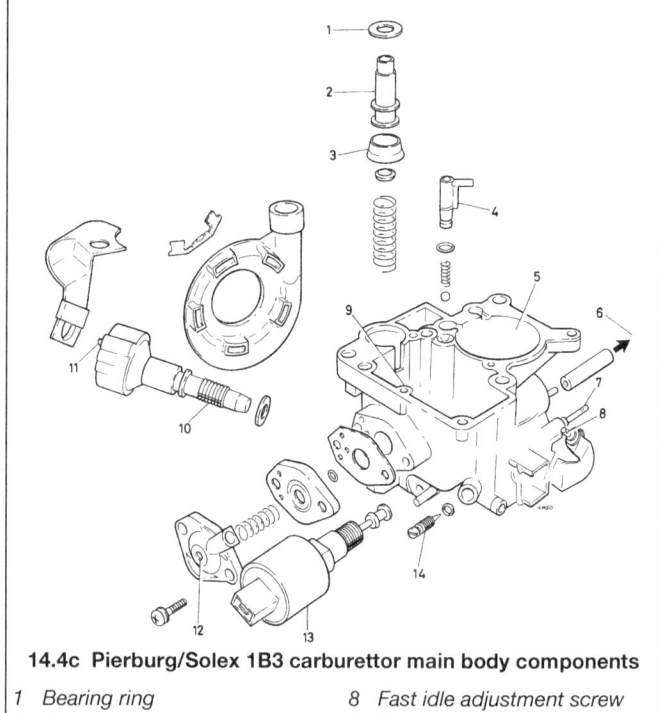

14.4c Pierburg/Solex 1B3 carburettor main body components

1. Bearing ring
2. Pump plunger
3. Seal
4. Injection tube
5. Main body
6. To pull-down unit
7. To air cleaner vacuum control
8. Fast idle adjustment screw
9. Part throttle enrichment jet
10. Idle speed adjustment screw
11. To two-way valve
12. Part throttle enrichment valve
13. Idle cut-off solenoid
14. Mixture adjustment screw

14.4d Pierburg/Solex 2E2 carburettor components

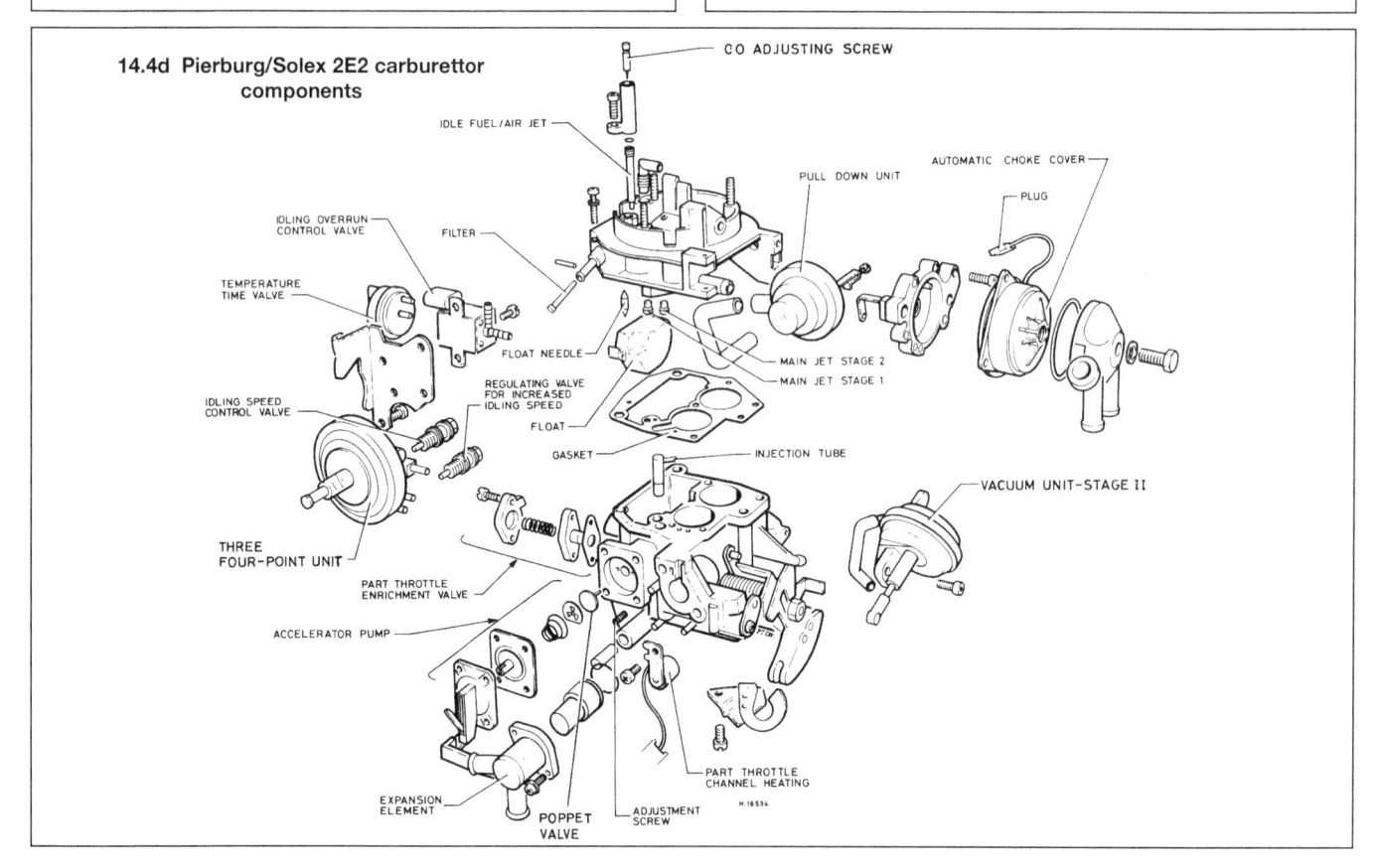

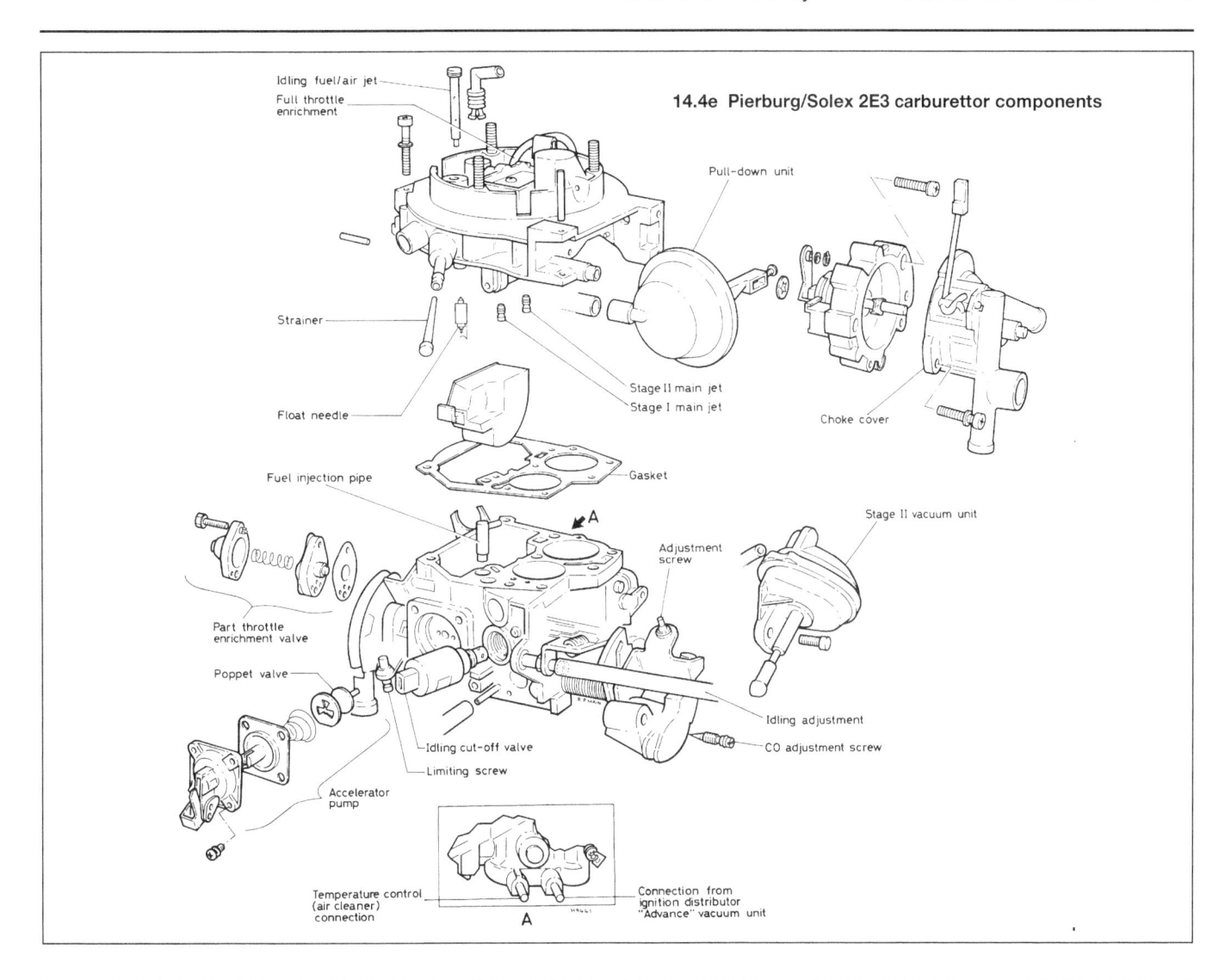

Fuel and exhaust systems - carburettor models 4A•13

14.4e Pierburg/Solex 2E3 carburettor components

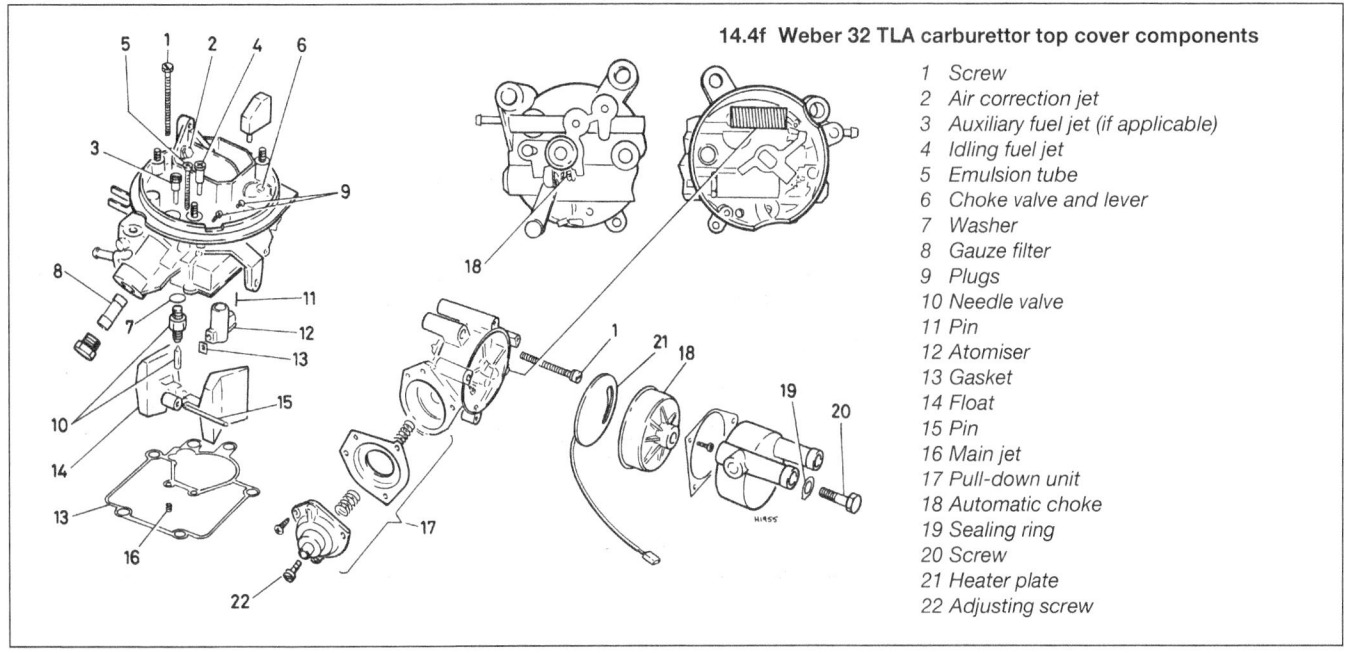

14.4f Weber 32 TLA carburettor top cover components

1 Screw
2 Air correction jet
3 Auxiliary fuel jet (if applicable)
4 Idling fuel jet
5 Emulsion tube
6 Choke valve and lever
7 Washer
8 Gauze filter
9 Plugs
10 Needle valve
11 Pin
12 Atomiser
13 Gasket
14 Float
15 Pin
16 Main jet
17 Pull-down unit
18 Automatic choke
19 Sealing ring
20 Screw
21 Heater plate
22 Adjusting screw

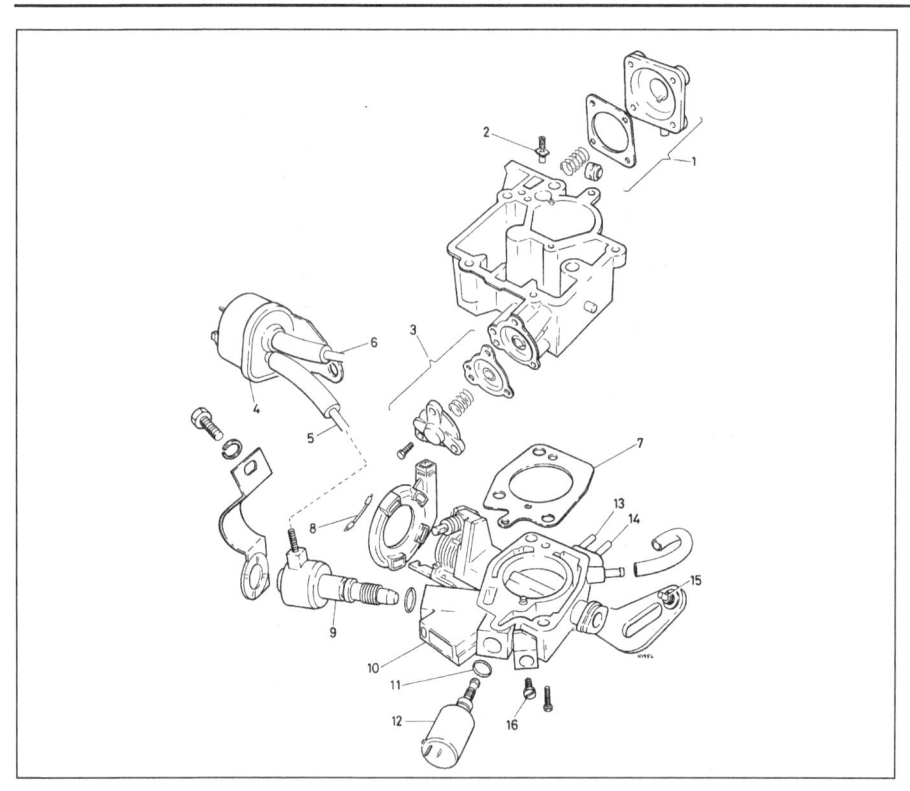

4A•14 Fuel and exhaust systems - carburettor models

14.4g Weber 32 TLA carburettor main body components

1. Accelerator pump
2. Injection pipe
3. Part throttle enrichment valve
4. Idle speed boost two-way valve
5. To idle adjusting screw
6. To vacuum line and brake servo
7. Gasket
8. Clip
9. Idle speed adjustment screw
10. Throttle housing
11. Sealing ring
12. Idle cut-off solenoid
13. To air cleaner
14. To distributor
15. Fast idle adjustment screw
16. Mixture adjustment screw

Accelerator pump injection capacity

5 The accelerator pump injection capacity may be checked with the carburettor fitted or removed. However, the air cleaner must be removed and the float chamber must be full.

6 Open the choke valve and retain it in the open position with a piece of wire, then push a length of close fitting plastic tube over the injection pipe. Operate the throttle until fuel emerges then place the tube in a measuring glass. Operate the throttle fully five times allowing at least three seconds per stroke. Divide the final quantity by five to determine the amount per stroke and compare with the amount specified. If necessary, reposition the adjusting screw on the accelerator pump lever **(see illustration)**. Note that fuel must be injected into the throttle valve gap. If necessary, bend the injection pipe.

Slow running and fast idle

7 Run the engine to normal operating temperature then stop it. Connect a tachometer and, if available, an exhaust gas analyser.

8 Check that all electrical accessories are switched off and note that slow running adjustments should not be made while the radiator cooling fan is running.

9 Disconnect the crankcase ventilation hose from the air cleaner body and plug the air cleaner outlet.

15 Carburettor (1.05 litre engine) - adjustments

Note: *Accurate adjustment of the carburettor is only possible if adjustment of the ignition timing, dwell angle and spark plug gaps is correct. Incorrect valve clearances can also effect carburettor adjustment*

Pierburg/Solex 31 PIC7

Bypass air cut-off valve

1 To check the bypass air cut-off valve when removed, depress the pin approximately 3 to 4 mm then energise it with battery voltage. A click should be heard and the pin should move out.

Cut-off valve

2 To check the cut-off valve for the main jets (where fitted), apply battery voltage. It must be heard to click when the voltage is applied.

Choke valve gap

3 To adjust the choke valve gap, operate the choke lever fully then return it to the smooth running detent and hold it there. With the choke spindle lever against the cam, check that the clearance between the choke valve and barrel is as shown in *Specifications*. Use a twist drill to make the check and if necessary, adjust the clearance by turning the adjusting screw as required **(see illustrations)**.

4 Although the choke valve gap smooth running detent position is preset during manufacture its setting can be checked and if necessary adjusted. Pull the choke out fully, then push it onto the smooth running detent. Press the choke lever against the cam and check the choke valve gap with a twist drill, as in the previous paragraph. If the gap is not as specified, adjust by turning the eccentric pin on the choke spindle lever.

15.3a Checking choke valve gap with twist drill

15.3b Adjusting screw location for choke valve gap (A) and choke valve gap smooth running detent eccentric pin (B)

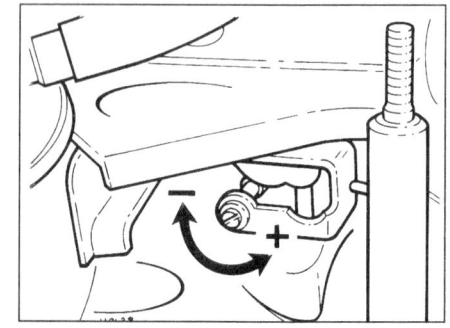

15.6 Accelerator pump adjuster screw

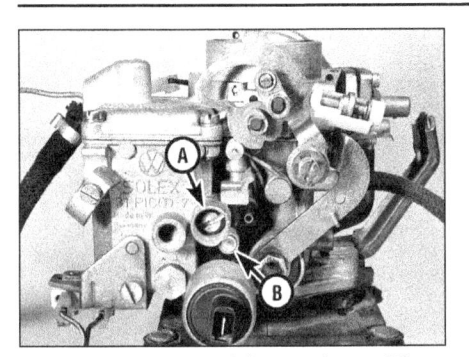

Fuel and exhaust systems - carburettor models 4A•15

15.10 Idle speed (A) and mixture (B) adjusting screw locations

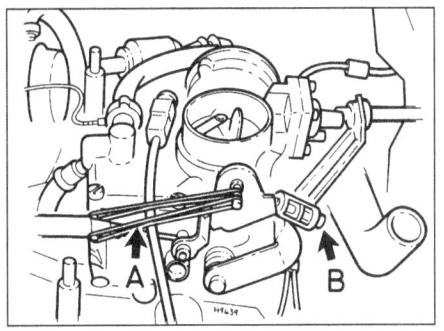

15.17 Fast idle speed setting
A Choke valve held open with rubber band
B Adjustment screw

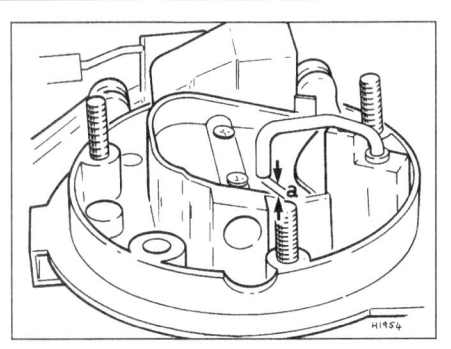

15.20 Enrichment tube adjustment
$a = 1.0 \pm 0.3$ mm

10 Start the engine and let it idle. Check that the engine speed and CO content are as specified. If not, turn the two screws located above the cut-off solenoid alternately as necessary **(see illustration)**.

11 If an exhaust gas analyser is not immediately available, an approximate mixture setting can be made by turning the mixture screw to give the highest engine speed.

12 Reconnect the crankcase ventilation hose. If this results in an increase in the CO content, the engine oil is diluted with fuel and should be renewed. Alternatively, if an oil change is not due, a long fast drive will reduce the amount of fuel in the oil.

13 Stop the engine and remove the tachometer and exhaust gas analyser.

14 To adjust the fast idle speed, first check that the engine is still at normal operating temperature. Remove the air cleaner.

15 With the engine stopped, pull the choke control knob fully out then push it in to the smooth running detent.

16 Retain the choke valve in its open position using an elastic band.

17 Connect a tachometer then start the engine and check that the fast idle speed is as specified. If not, turn the adjustment screw on the side of the choke lever cam. Note that this screw may also have a tamperproof cap **(see illustration)**.

18 Stop the engine, disconnect the tachometer and elastic band, then refit the air cleaner. Push the choke control knob fully in.

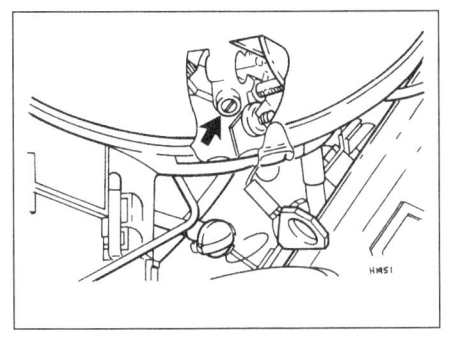

Pierburg/Solex 1B3

19 All adjustments are as described for the Pierburg 2E3 carburettor fitted to the 1.3 litre engine, with the following additions.

Enrichment tube

20 With the choke valve closed, the bottom of the enrichment tube should be 1.0 mm from the valve **(see illustration)**.

Idle speed and mixture

21 Before making any adjustment, ensure that the automatic choke is fully open, otherwise the throttle valve linkage may still be on the fast idle cam.

Idle speed boost valve

22 The idle speed adjustment screw **(see illustration)** incorporates a vacuum-operated valve which opens if the idle speed drops below 700 rpm, thereby causing an increase in the idle speed. The valve is itself controlled by a two-way valve and further control unit. The control unit monitors the engine speed and activates the two-way valve which applies vacuum to the idle valve.

23 To test the system, run the engine at idle speed, then slowly reduce the engine speed by manually closing the choke valve. At 700 rpm there should be vacuum at the hose in the idle valve.

Fast idle speed

24 With the engine at normal operating temperature and switched off, connect a tachometer and remove the air cleaner.

25 Fully open the throttle valve, then turn the fast idle cam and release the throttle valve so that the adjustment screw is positioned on the second highest part of the cam.

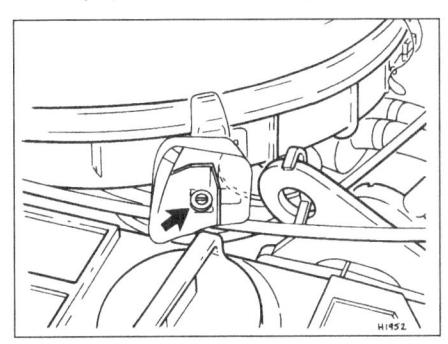

26 Without touching the accelerator pedal, start the engine and check that the fast idle speed is as specified. If not, turn the adjustment screw on the linkage as necessary. If a tamperproof cap is fitted, renew it after making the adjustment **(see illustration)**.

Choke valve gap

27 With the engine cold, fully open the throttle valve, then turn the fast idle cam and release the throttle valve so that the adjustment screw is positioned on the highest part of the cam.

28 Press the choke operating rod as far as possible towards the pull-down unit.

29 Using the shank of a twist drill, check that the distance from the choke valve to the carburettor wall is as specified. If not, adjust the screw behind the automatic choke.

Accelerator pump capacity

30 Hold the carburettor over a funnel and measuring glass.

31 Turn the fast idle cam so that the adjusting screw is off the cam. Hold the cam in this position during the following procedure.

32 Fully open the throttle ten times, allowing at least three seconds per stroke. Divide the total quantity by ten and check that the resultant injection capacity is as specified. If not, loosen the camplate locking screw, turn the camplate as required and tighten the screw **(see illustration)**.

15.22 Idle speed adjustment screw location

15.26 Mixture (CO content) adjustment screw location

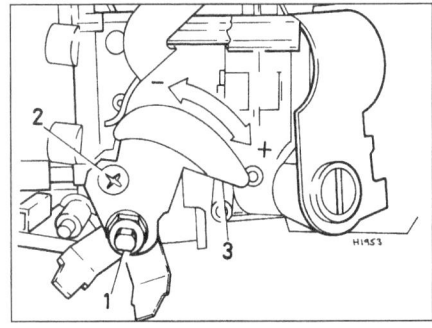

15.32 Accelerator pump adjustment
1 Nut
2 Camplate locking screw
3 Camplate

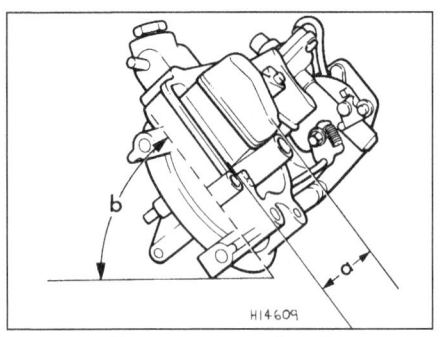

15.36 Float level checking diagram
$a = 28 \pm 1.0$ mm $b = 45°$ angle

33 If difficulty is experienced in making the adjustment, check the pump seal and make sure that the return check valve and injection tube are clear.

Idle cut-off solenoid

34 When the ignition is switched on, the solenoid should be heard to click, indicating that the idle circuit has been opened.

35 If the solenoid is removed for testing, the plunger must first be depressed by 3.0 to 4.0 mm before switching on the unit.

Weber 32 TLA

Float level

36 With the upper part of the carburettor inverted and held at an angle of approximately 45°, the measurement "a" (see illustration) should be as shown. The ball of the float needle should not be pressed in against the spring when making the measurement,

Idle speed and mixture

37 The procedure for checking and adjusting the idle speed and CO content are basically the same as given for the Pierburg 31 PIC-7 carburettor. Refer to the accompanying illustrations for the location of adjustment screws and to the *Specifications* for settings. (see illustrations).

Idle speed boost valve

38 The idle speed boost valve is identical to the unit on the Pierburg 1B3 carburettor.

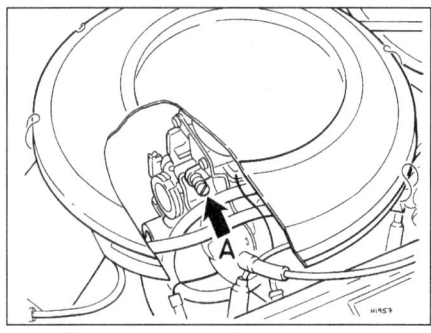

15.37a Idle speed adjusting screw (A) - pre June 1985

Choke valve gap (pull-down)

39 Remove the choke cover.

40 Place the fast idle speed adjusting screw on the highest step of the cam (see illustration). The manufacturer's original instruction was to press the pull rod in the direction of the arrow shown, then to check that the choke valve gap is 2.5 ± 0.2 mm. As from April 1987 however, this instruction is revised and it is now necessary to use a vacuum pump to apply 300 mbar vacuum on the pull-down unit. The choke valve gap in this case must be 2.0 ± 0.2 mm.

41 Adjustment is made on the screw at the end of the pull-down device. Ensure that the spring "2" (see illustration) is not compressed when making the check.

Idle cut-off valve

42 To check the cut-off valve, apply battery voltage. The valve must be heard to click when voltage is applied.

Fast idle speed

43 Before carrying out this check, ensure that the ignition timing and manual idling adjustments are correct. The engine should be at normal operating temperature.

44 Remove the air cleaner.

45 Plug the temperature regulator connection.

46 Connect the tachometer.

47 Remove the choke cover and set the fast

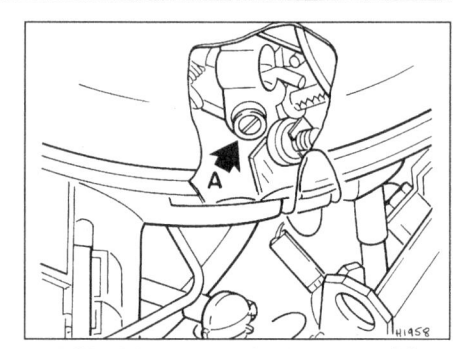

15.37b Idle speed adjusting screw (A) - from July 1985

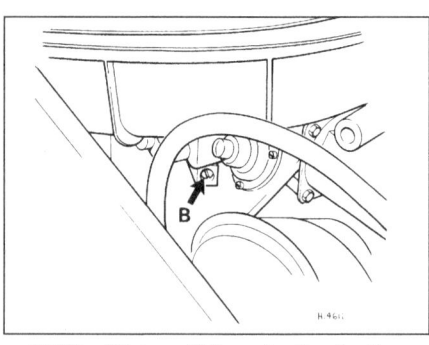

15.37c Mixture (CO content) adjusting screw (B)

idle speed adjusting screw on the second highest step on the cam (see illustration).

48 Tension the operating lever with a rubber band so that the choke valve is fully open.

49 Without touching the accelerator pedal, start the engine, which should run at the fast idle speed specified.

50 Adjust the screw as necessary.

Choke valve gap (wide open kick)

51 Remove the air cleaner.

52 Fully open the throttle and hold it in this position.

53 Press the lever (1) upwards (see illustration).

54 Check the gap with a twist drill. The gap should be as specified. If necessary, adjust by bending the lever (see illustration).

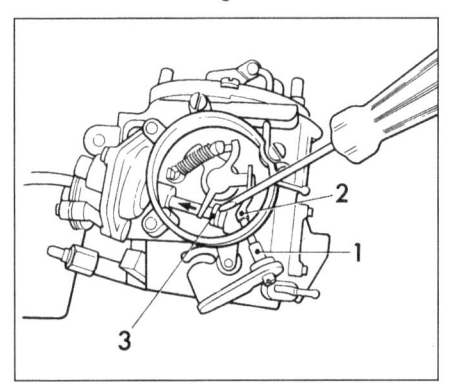

15.40 Choke valve gap adjustment

1 Fast idle adjustment screw
2 Cam 3 Pull rod

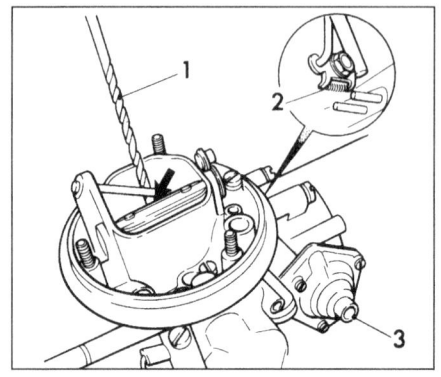

15.41 Checking choke valve gap (pull-down)

1 Twist drill 3 Adjusting screw
2 Spring

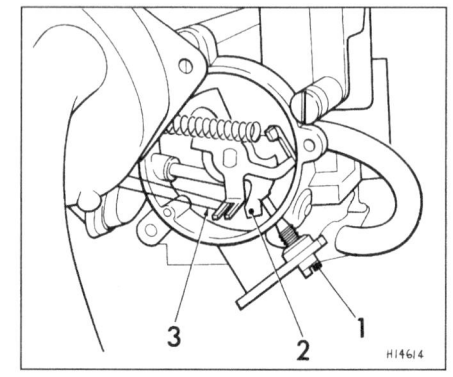

15.47 Adjusting fast idle speed

1 Fast idle adjusting screw
2 Cam 3 Rubber band

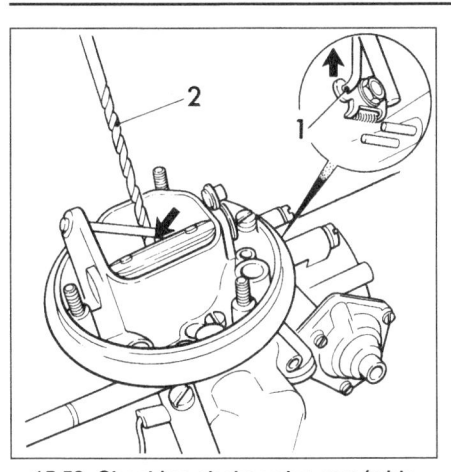

Fuel and exhaust systems - carburettor models 4A•17

15.53 Checking choke valve gap (wide open kick)

1 Pressure applied upwards
2 Twist drill

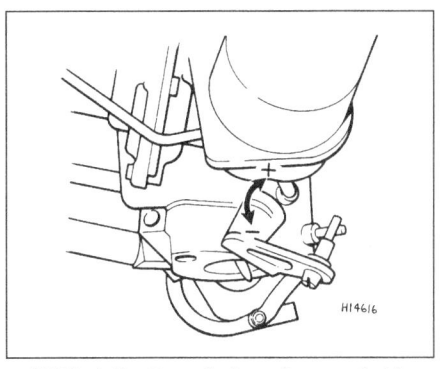

15.54 Adjusting choke valve gap (wide open kick)

Bend lever as required

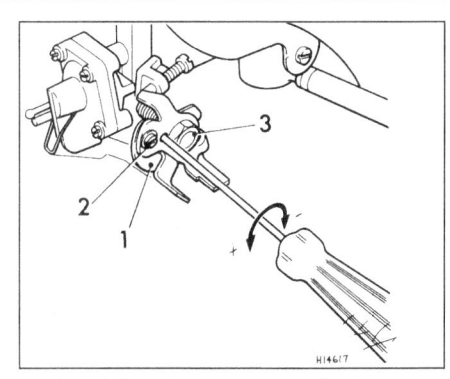

15.57 Accelerator pump adjustment

1 Cam
2 Camplate
3 Camplate locking nut

Accelerator pump capacity

55 This can be checked by following the procedure given for the Pierburg 2E3 carburettor, with the following differences.

56 Open the throttle valve quickly when operating the pump (ie. one second per stroke, with pauses of three seconds between strokes).

57 The amount of fuel injected can be altered, but only very slightly, as follows: **(see illustration)**.

58 Take the accelerator cable cam off the throttle valve lever.

59 Secure the accelerator pump cam with an M4 screw.

60 Loosen the locknut on the camplate securing screw. Loosen the screw and turn the camplate with a screwdriver clockwise to decrease injected fuel and anti-clockwise to increase injected fuel. Tighten the screw and locknut and recheck the injection capacity.

16 Carburettor (1.3 litre engine) - adjustments

Note: *Accurate adjustment of the carburettor is only possible if adjustment of the ignition timing, dwell angle and spark plug gaps is correct. Incorrect valve clearances can also effect carburettor adjustment*

Pierburg/Solex 2E3

Cut-off valve

1 To check the cut-off valve, apply battery voltage. It must be heard to click when the voltage is applied.

Choke valve gap

2 To check the choke valve gap the choke cover must be removed. Move the throttle valve and the fast idle cam so that the adjustment screw is against the highest cam stop. Now push the choke valve operating rod fully towards the adjustment screw (and pull-down unit), then check the choke valve-to-barrel clearance using a twist drill as a gauge. If necessary turn the adjuster screw as required to provide the specified choke valve gap **(see illustrations)**.

Accelerator pump injection capacity

3 The accelerator pump injection capacity can be checked in the same manner as that described for the Pierburg 2E3 carburettor but allow 1 second per stroke and 3 seconds between strokes **(see illustration)**.

Choke

4 The automatic choke cover and choke housing alignment marks should correspond. To check the choke, connect up a test lamp between a battery positive terminal and the choke lead. The test lamp should illuminate. If not, then the choke unit is defective and must be renewed.

5 The choke pulldown unit can be checked when removed but as this requires the use of a vacuum pump and gauge, it is a check best entrusted to your VW dealer. The pulldown unit can also be tested when the carburettor is in position in the vehicle. The air cleaner unit must be removed. Run the engine at idle speed then close the choke valve by hand and check that a resistance is felt over the final 3.0 mm of travel. If no resistance is felt, there may be a leak in the vacuum connections, or the pulldown unit diaphragm is broken, in which case the unit must be renewed.

16.2a Fast idle cam (1) and choke valve gap adjusting screw (2)

16.2b Checking choke valve gap

1 Choke valve operating rod (push in direction of arrow)
2 Twist drill

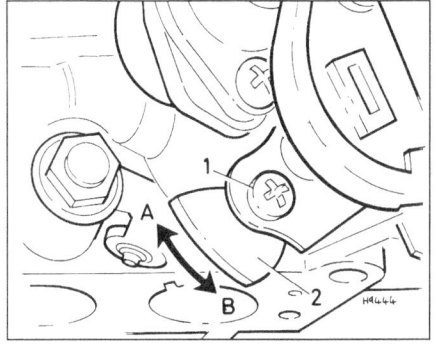

16.3 Accelerator pump adjustment

1 Fast idle cam clamp screw
2 Fast idle cam
A Increase capacity
B Decrease capacity

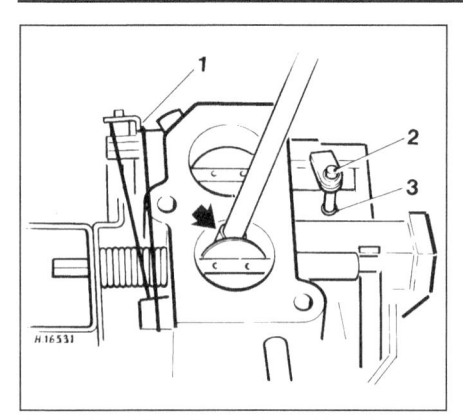

4A•18 Fuel and exhaust systems - carburettor models

16.7a Throttle valve basic setting showing rod to hold valve open (arrowed), lock lever (1) limiting screw (2) and stop (3)

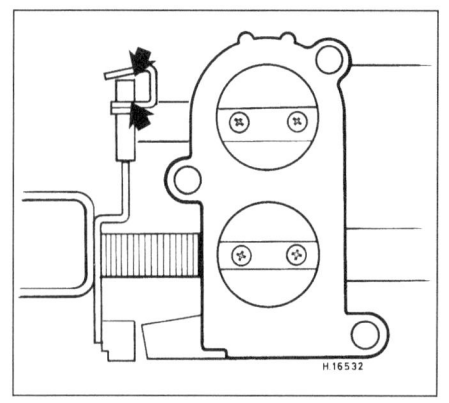

Throttle valve

6 The basic Stage II throttle valve adjustment is made during manufacture and should not require further adjustment. If, for any reason, the limiting screw has been removed or its setting altered, readjust it as follows.

7 Open the throttle valve and hold it in position by inserting a wooden rod or similar implement between the valve and venturi (see illustration). Using a rubber band, pretension the Stage II throttle valve locking lever then unscrew the limiting screw to provide a clearance between the stop and the limiting screw. Now turn the limiting screw in so that it is just in contact with the stop. The limiting screw stop point can be assessed by inserting a thin piece of paper between the stop and screw. When the paper starts to get pinched between the two, the stop point is reached and from this point, tighten the limiting screw a further quarter turn then secure it with locking compound. Close both throttle valves then measure the locking lever clearances (see illustration). If the clearances are not as specified, then bend the levers as necessary.

Slow running and fast idle

8 To check and adjust the slow running setting, refer to Section 15, paragraphs 7 to 13 inclusive (see illustration).

9 To check and adjust the fast idle adjustment, first check that the engine is still at normal operating temperature. The air

16.7b Locking lever clearance with throttle valves closed

Clearance to equal 0.25 to 0.55 mm (each side)

cleaner must be removed and the other provisional conditions must apply as for the slow running adjustment. Plug the air cleaner temperature control hose.

10 Restart the engine and open the throttle to give an engine speed of approx. 2500 rpm. Press down the fast idle cam to its stop then move the throttle valve back so that the adjuster screw is on the second highest stop on the fast idle cam. In this position, the fast idle speed should be as specified. If the setting is incorrect, turn the adjustment screw in the required direction until it is correct (see illustration). Note that the screw may have a tamperproof cap fitted.

11 On completion, unplug the temperature control connector and refit the air cleaner.

17 Carburettor (1.6 & 1.8 litre engines) - adjustments

Note: Accurate adjustment of the carburettor is only possible if adjustment of the ignition timing, dwell angle and spark plug gaps is correct. Incorrect valve clearances can also effect carburettor adjustment

Pierburg/Solex 2E2

1 The adjustment procedures for the 2E2 carburettor closely follow those described for

the 2E3 carburettor. The following checks and adjustments are additional to, or differ from, those given.

Part throttle channel heater unit

2 To check this unit, connect a test lamp between the unit wiring plug and battery positive terminal. Earth the unit. If the test bulb fails to light, the unit is defective and must be renewed.

Choke valve gap (wide open kick)

3 Remove the automatic choke cover and fit a rubber band to the operating pin, so that the choke valve is held in the closed position.

4 Hold the primary throttle valve open 45°. To do this, temporarily insert a 10 mm nut between the fast idling adjustment screw and the vacuum unit plunger.

5 Using a twist drill, check that the gap between the choke valve and carburettor wall is 6.3 ± 0.3 mm. If not, bend the choke operating lever as required (see illustration).

6 After making an adjustment, check and adjust the choke pull-down unit as follows.

Choke pull down unit

7 This unit can be checked in the same manner as that for the choke pull down unit on the 2E3 carburettor but note that the resistance felt must be over the final 5.0 mm of travel.

8 Note also that from February 1987, the choke pull-down unit is both temperature and time-controlled by a thermotime valve. When the valve is open (starting a cold engine) the vacuum to the pull-down unit is reduced, and the choke valve will open by a small amount. After between one and six seconds (depending on ambient temperature), the valve heats up (to approximately 20 to 30°C) and closes. This allows more vacuum to reach the pull-down unit and the choke valve will open by a larger amount. The choke is of course fully released by the heat of the engine coolant and the electric heater acting on the automatic choke bi-metallic spring.

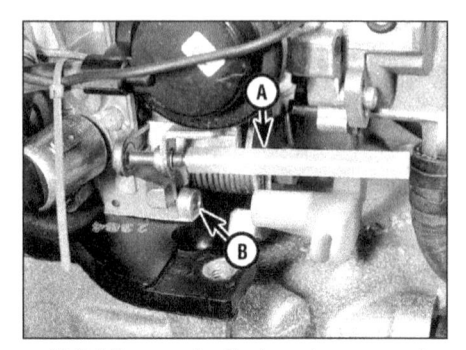

16.8 Idle speed adjustment screw and guide sleeve (A) mixture screw (B)

16.10 Fast idle speed adjustment screw (2)

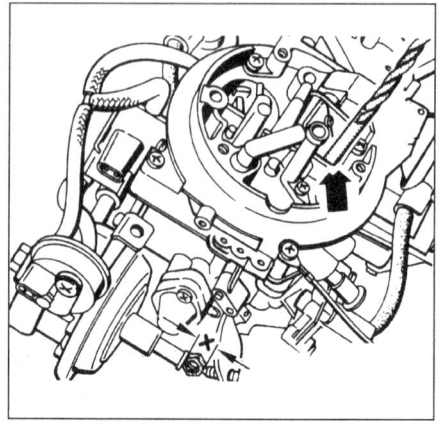

17.5 Checking choke valve gap

Using drill of correct diameter as a gauge (arrowed)
Note dimension x (10.0 mm)

Fuel and exhaust systems - carburettor models 4A•19

17.10 Accelerator pump check preparation

A Vacuum pump connection
B Plug vacuum connection (3-point unit)
C Plug vacuum connection (4-point unit)

Accelerator pump

9 To make this check, the carburettor must be removed and you will need a vacuum pump and an M8 x 20 mm bolt.
10 Detach the vacuum hoses from the three/four point unit then connect up the vacuum pump to the three/four point unit at "A" (see illustration). Plug connection B (and C on four point unit). Apply vacuum with the pump to hold the diaphragm pushrod in the overrun/cut-off position and to give a clearance between the fast idle speed and diaphragm pushrod.

17.13 Loosen screw (A) and turn cam plate (B) in direction required to adjust accelerator pump injection capacity

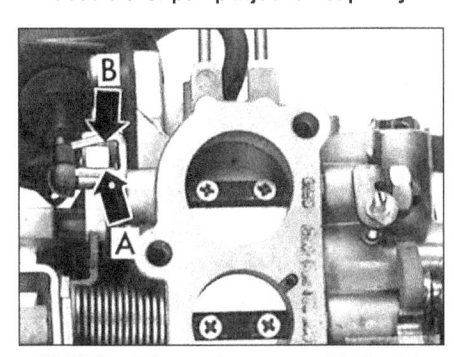

17.15 Lock lever clearance with throttle valves closed

11 Pivot the warm-up lever up to the point where the throttle valve control pin has clearance and insert the M8 x 20 mm bolt to hold the warm-up lever in this position (see illustration).
12 Hold the carburettor over a funnel and measuring glass then slowly open the throttle valve lever fully five times allowing at least 3 seconds per stroke. Divide the total quantity by five and check the resultant injection capacity against that specified.
13 If adjustment is necessary, loosen screw A and rotate the cam plate B in the required direction to increase or decrease the injection capacity (see illustration). On completion, retighten the screw and seal in position with locking compound.
14 The accelerator pump injection capacity can also be checked with the carburettor in the vehicle but as specialised equipment is required, this is a task best entrusted to your VW dealer.

Throttle valve

15 For the basic Stage II valve adjustment, proceed as described in Section 16, paragraphs 6 and 7 whilst referring to the accompanying illustration (see illustration).

Three/four point unit - vacuum pump method

16 Detach the vacuum hoses from the unit and attach a vacuum pump to connection "1" (see illustration). Apply vacuum to pull the diaphragm pushrod to the idle point and then measure the amount of rod protrusion, which must be as specified.
17 To check the overrun cut-off point, plug off the vacuum connection 3, then apply increased vacuum with the vacuum pump. This should cause the diaphragm pushrod to move to the overrun/cut-off point. Measure the rod protrusion (a) which should now be 1.0 mm. The pushrod should hold at this position for one minute.
18 If rod protrusion is incorrect, or will not hold for the specified period, then the diaphragm or three/four point unit are probably leaking and in need of renewal.

17.16 Three or four point unit check preparation

Pushrod to idle point a = 8.5 mm
1 Vacuum connection
2 and 3 Plug these connections

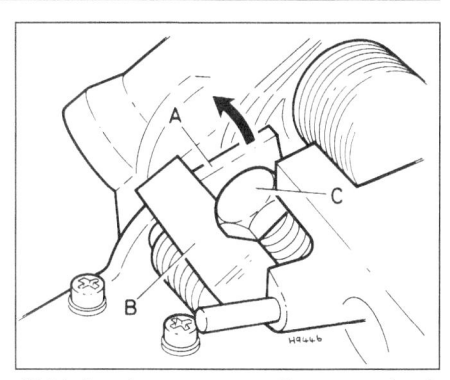

17.11 Accelerator pump adjustment check showing warm-up lever (A) lever (B) and bolt (C)

Three/four point unit - engine vacuum method

19 Run the engine to normal operating temperature then switch it off. Remove the air cleaner and close the vacuum line from the carburettor to the temperature regulator.
20 With the engine stopped, check the diaphragm pushrod (A) (see illustration) is fully extended to approximately 14.5 mm.
21 Start the engine and let it idle. The diaphragm pushrod must now be extended approximately 8.5 mm (three-point unit), or 9.5 mm (four-point unit), and must just contact the fast idle adjustment screw.
22 On models with air conditioning, switch on the air conditioner with the blower on maximum speed. The diaphragm pushrod dimension should be approximately 12.0 mm.
23 To check the overrun cut-off point, run the engine at idle speed.
24 On the four-point unit, disconnect and plug the pink-coloured hose at the control valve.
25 Using a screwdriver, hold the primary throttle valve fully closed to prevent it moving to the overrun cut-off point.
26 Disconnect the plug from the idling/overrun control valve, then check that the diaphragm pushrod dimension is approximately 1.5 mm.
27 To check the unit for leaks, first, on the three-point unit only, pinch the hose between the unit and Y-piece.

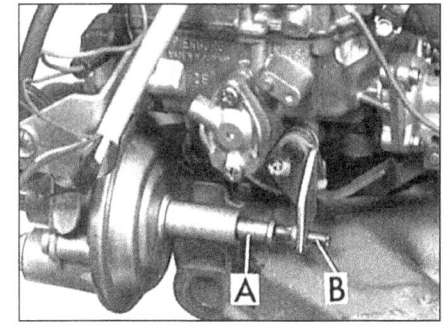

17.20 Three/four point unit with pushrod (A) and cold idling adjusting screw (B) in idling position

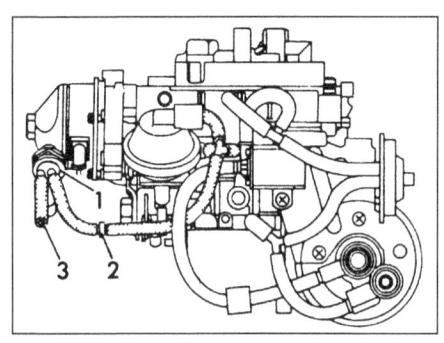

4A•20 Fuel and exhaust systems - carburettor models

17.30 Stage II vacuum unit control

1 Thermo-pneumatic valve
2 Restrictor
3 Straight connection hose

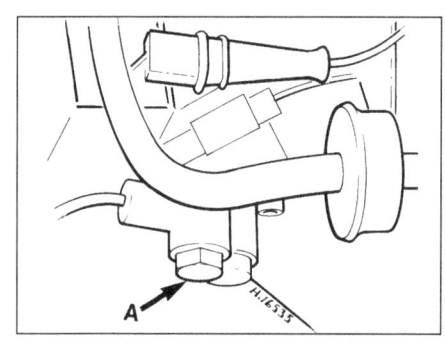

17.34a Idling speed control valve (A)

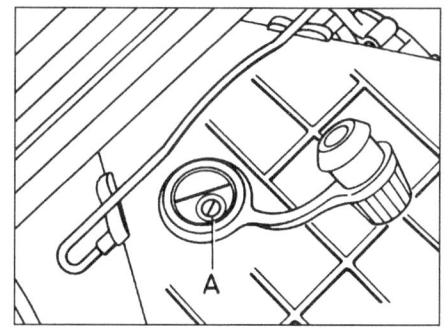

17.34b Mixture (CO) adjustment screw (A)

28 Stop the engine by disconnecting the coil terminal 15, and check that the diaphragm rod remains in the overrun/cut-off position for a minimum of five seconds.

29 Reconnect the coil wiring, control valve plug and hose where applicable. Refit the air cleaner.

Stage II vacuum control unit

30 This device is fitted to 1.6 litre manual gearbox models and 1.8 automatic gearbox models from August 1984 on. Its function is to delay the Stage II opening slightly whilst the coolant temperature is below 18°C. It achieves this by venting the vacuum hose via the thermo-pneumatic valve and the resistor **(see illustration)**.

31 Check that the straight hose at connection 3 on the thermo-pneumatic valve is not blocked and check the valve itself by blowing through it. It should be open at 18°C and close when the temperature rises above 28°C.

Idle/overrun control valve

32 Entrust this operation to your VW dealer as specialised testing equipment is necessary.

Temperature time valve

33 Entrust this operation to your VW dealer as specialised testing equipment is necessary.

Slow running and fast idle

34 To check and adjust the slow running setting, proceed as described in Section 15, paragraphs 7 to 13 inclusive whilst noting the following differences:

a) Before making any adjustments, ensure that the three/four point unit pushrod is in the idling position with the cold idling adjusting screw touching the pushrod
b) If adjustment is necessary, turn the idling speed control valve and CO adjustment screw **(see illustrations)**, as necessary.
c) Access to the CO adjustment screw is gained by prising out the tamperproof plug. If the CO content is difficult to adjust, remove the adjustment screw and clean its point, then refit and adjust it

35 On automatic transmission models, the increased idling speed can be checked and adjusted as follows. In addition to those preliminary requirements necessary when checking the idle speed slow running setting, the hand brake must be fully applied and chocks placed against the wheels.

36 When the engine is started, turn on the fresh air blower (fully), switch on the headlights (high beam) and the heated rear window. Get an assistant to sit in the vehicle and depress the foot brake then select D. Check that the four point unit diaphragm rod is in the increased idling position, the fast idle adjuster screw rests against the diaphragm rod and the engine increased idle speed is not under that specified. Adjust if necessary by altering the regulator valve setting **(see illustration)**.

37 On models fitted with air conditioning, the procedure for checking the increased idling speed is similar to that for automatic transmission models except that it is also necessary to switch on the air conditioner and have the control set at maximum cooling at the highest blower speed. The increased idle speed must be as specified and if adjustment is required, alter the regulator valve setting accordingly.

38 With the slow/increased running idle speed adjustment complete, the fast idle speed can be checked and, if necessary, adjusted. Check that the engine is still at its normal operating temperature.

39 Detach the Y-piece from the vacuum hose and plug the hose **(see illustration)**. Connect a tachometer to the engine. Start and run the engine and check that the fast idle speed is as specified. If not, turn the adjustment screw on the linkage as necessary **(see illustration)**. On completion of adjustment, apply sealant to the screw threads to lock it in position, unplug and reconnect the Y-piece to the vacuum hose and check that the slow running (idle) speed is as specified.

18 Inlet manifold preheating - testing

Heater element

1 The inlet manifold is preheated by coolant from the cooling system and by a heater element located in the bottom of the inlet manifold.

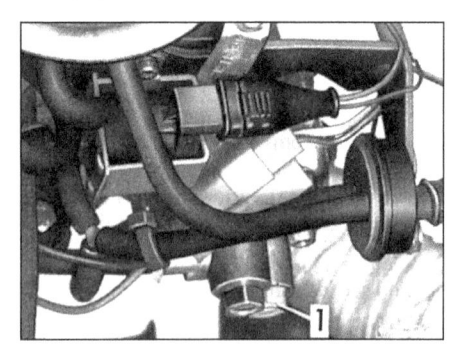

17.36 Engine speed regulator valve (1)

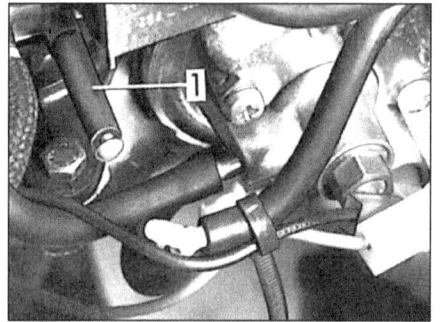

17.39a Disconnect and plug vacuum hose (1) to check/adjust engine fast idle speed adjustment

17.39b Fast idle adjustment screw (A)

Fuel and exhaust systems - carburettor models 4A•21

18.3a Unscrew the bolts . . .

18.3b . . . and remove heater element from inlet manifold

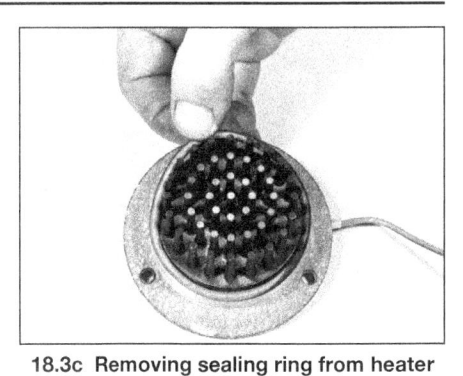

18.3c Removing sealing ring from heater element

2 To check the heater element, the engine should be cold. Disconnect the wire from the element at its in-line connector, then attach an ohmmeter between the wire connector from the element and earth. This should record 0.25 to 0.50 ohm.
3 To remove the element, disconnect the wire then unscrew the bolts and withdraw the unit. Remove the sealing ring and gasket **(see illustrations)**. When refitting, always renew the sealing ring and gasket.

Thermo-switch

4 On 1.05 and 1.3 litre engines, the heater element is controlled by a thermo-switch located in the coolant supply hose to the inlet manifold. On 1.6 and 1.8 litre engines, the thermo-switch is located in the top of the coolant hose connecting piece mounted on the side of the cylinder head.

5 Before removing the thermo-switch, drain off some engine coolant to reduce spillage when the switch is removed.
6 To test the thermo-switch, first detach the lead connector. Unscrew and remove the switch from the housing and plug the hole to stop any leakage of coolant.
7 With an ohmmeter connected to the terminals, gradually heat the base of the switch unit in hot water. Below the following temperatures there should be zero resistance (ie. internal contacts closed):
  1.05 litre engine - 65°C
  1.3, 1.6 and 1.8 litre engines - 55°C
8 Above the following temperatures there should be a maximum resistance (ie. internal contacts open):
  1.05 litre engine - 75°C
  1.3, 1.6 an d 1.8 litre engines - 65°C
9 If defective, the switch must be renewed.

19 Inlet and exhaust manifolds - removal and refitting

Inlet manifold

1 Remove the carburettor.
2 Disconnect the inlet manifold preheater wire at the in-line connector.
3 Drain the cooling system and disconnect the coolant hoses from the manifold.
4 Disconnect the manifold vacuum hoses as necessary **(see illustration)**.
5 Where applicable, disconnect the stay rod between the base of the manifold and the crankcase **(see illustration)**.
6 Undo the manifold retaining nuts and bolts **(see illustration)** whilst noting their respective

19.4 Vacuum hose connections – 1.6 and 1.8 litre with Pierburg/Solex 2E2 carburettor

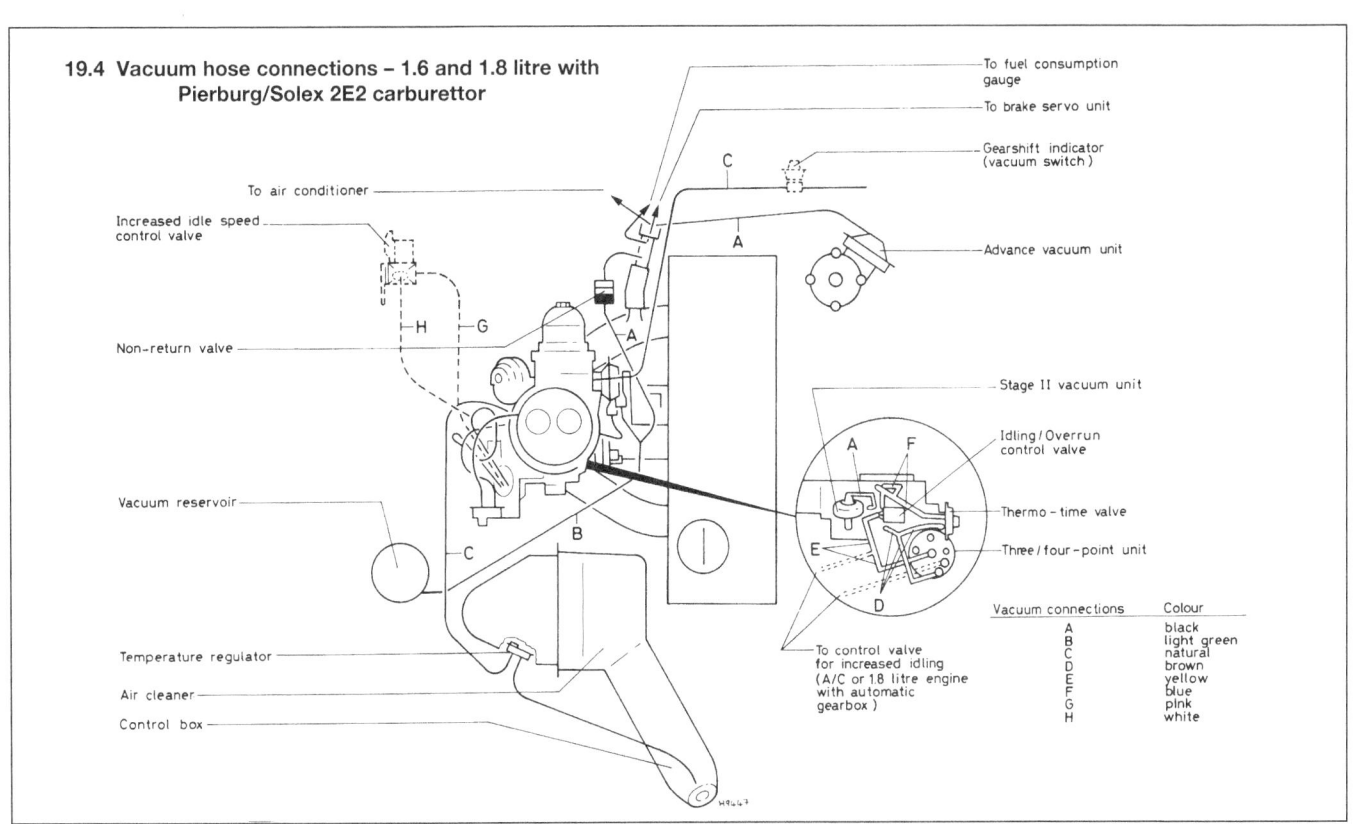

Vacuum connections	Colour
A	black
B	light green
C	natural
D	brown
E	yellow
F	blue
G	pink
H	white

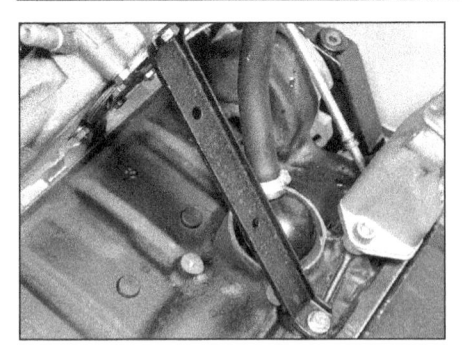

19.5 Inlet manifold support stay - 1.3 litre

19.6 Inlet manifold-to-cylinder head securing nuts and bolts
Note position of earth lead spade connector (arrowed) - 1.3 litre

19.9 Warm air deflector plate - 1.3 litre

locations, then carefully withdraw the manifold from the cylinder head.
7 Remove the gasket and clean the mating faces of the manifold and cylinder head.
8 Refitting is a reversal of the removal procedure. Use a new manifold gasket and tighten the securing nuts and bolts to the specified torque setting.

Exhaust manifold

9 Undo the retaining nut(s) and withdraw the warm air deflector plate from the exhaust manifold **(see illustration)**.
10 On 1.05 and 1.3 litre engines, unbolt and detach the exhaust downpipe from the manifold joint **(see illustration)**.
11 On 1.6 and 1.8 litre engines, refer to Section 20, paragraph 2.
12 Unscrew and remove the remaining manifold retaining bolts/nuts, then carefully withdraw the manifold from the cylinder head. Remove the gasket.
13 Clean the mating faces of the manifold and cylinder head. Also the exhaust downpipe flange connections.
14 Refit in the reverse order of removal. Use a new gasket and tighten the securing nuts/bolts evenly to the specified torque wrench setting.
15 When reconnecting the downpipe to the manifold, smear a little exhaust jointing paste onto the flange prior to connection. This will ensure a good seal at the joint.

20 Exhaust system - inspection, removal and refitting

Inspection

1 Refer to Chapter 1, Section 19

Removal

2 On 1.6 and 1.8 litre engines, it should be noted that if the exhaust system is to be separated at the manifold/downpipe connection, then VW tool No. 3049A will be necessary to release and subsequently refit the joint retaining clips **(see illustration)**. Without this tool, it is virtually impossible to separate and reassemble the joint without distorting the retaining clips. In view of this, removal and refitting of the system will necessitate detachment of the manifold and front pipe section, or manifold and system complete, and then taking the assembly to your VW dealer to separate/reassemble the front joint. If the complete system is in need of replacement, it is probably best entrusted to your VW dealer.
3 On 1.05 and 1.3 litre engines, when removing any part of the exhaust system it is usually easier to undo the manifold-to-front pipe joint and remove the complete system from the vehicle, then separate the various pieces of the system, or cut out the defective part with a hacksaw.
4 Before doing any dismantling work on the exhaust system, wait until the system is cool and then saturate all bolts and joints with a proprietary anti-corrosion fluid **(see illustrations)**. It may be found easier to cut through heavily corroded bolts with a hacksaw, rather than try to unscrew them.

Refitting

5 Refit the system a section at a time starting at the front. If the manifold has been removed its gasket must be renewed. New nuts and bolts should be used throughout the system.
6 Before assembly, smear all joints with a proprietary exhaust sealing compound. This makes it easier to align the pieces and also ensures that the joints will be gas tight. Leave all bolts loose.
7 Run the engine until the exhaust system is at normal temperature and then, with the engine running at idling speed, tighten all the mounting bolts and clips, starting at the manifold and working towards the rear silencer. Take care to avoid touching any part of the system with bare hands because of the danger of painful burns.
8 With all bolts and clips tightened, it is important to ensure that there is no strain on any part of the system.

19.10 Exhaust downpipe-to-manifold flange connection - 1.3 litre

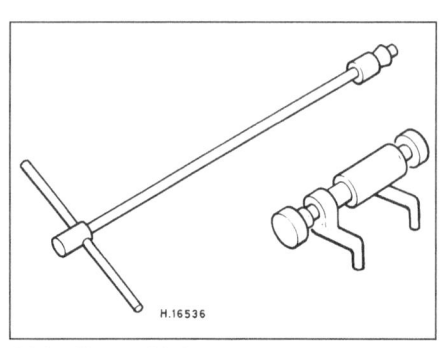

20.2 VW tool 3049A used to release and fit exhaust downpipes to manifold clips - 1.6 and 1.8 litre

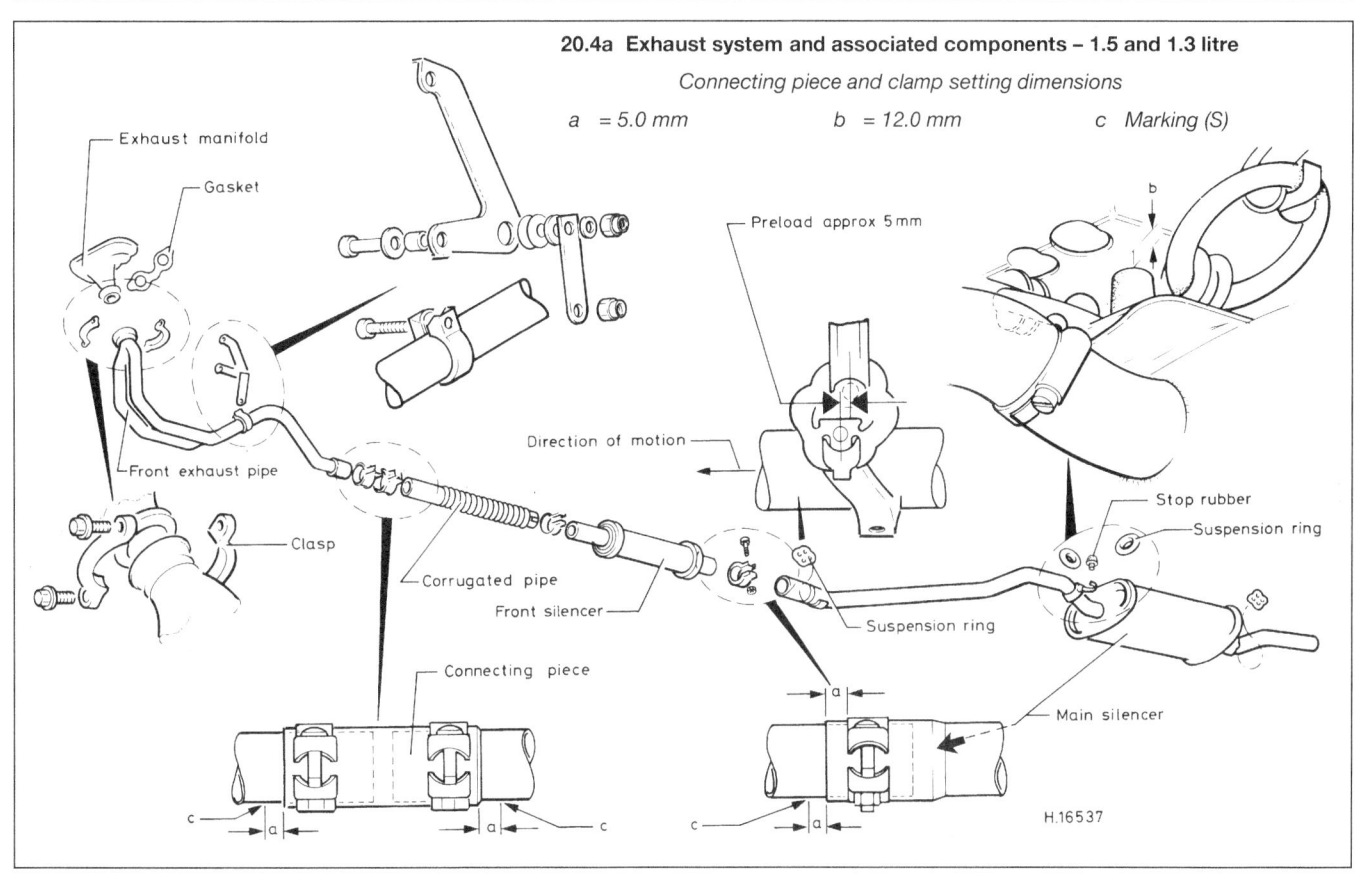

Fuel and exhaust systems - carburettor models 4A•23

20.4a Exhaust system and associated components – 1.5 and 1.3 litre

Connecting piece and clamp setting dimensions

a = 5.0 mm   b = 12.0 mm   c Marking (S)

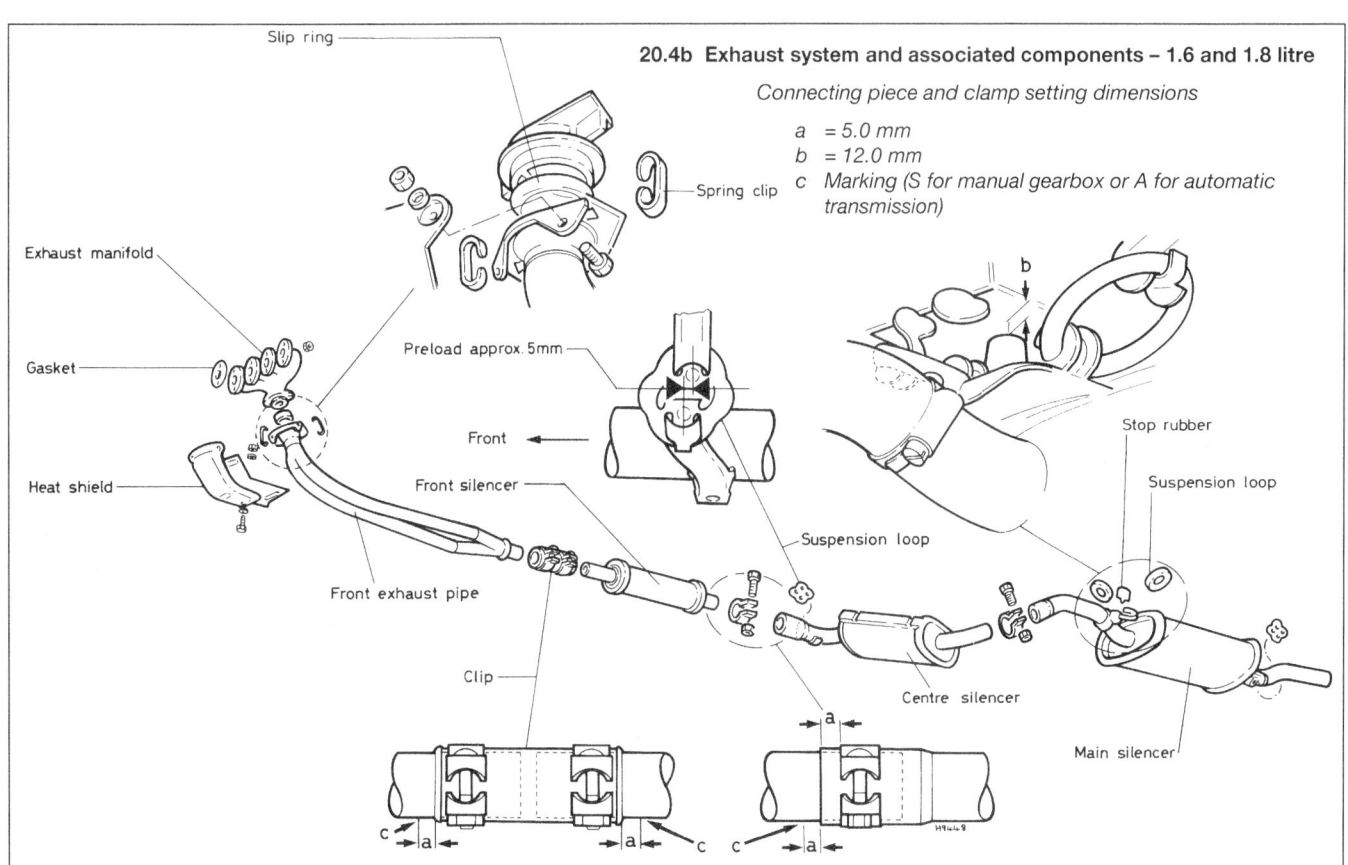

20.4b Exhaust system and associated components – 1.6 and 1.8 litre

Connecting piece and clamp setting dimensions

a = 5.0 mm
b = 12.0 mm
c Marking (S for manual gearbox or A for automatic transmission)

Notes

Chapter 4 Part B:
Fuel and exhaust systems - K-Jetronic fuel injection - 8 valve engines

Contents

Accelerator cable - removal, refitting and adjustment 8
Air cleaner element - renewal 3
Airflow meter - removal and refitting 16
Airflow sensor plate and control plunger - testing 14
Auxiliary air valve - testing 10
Catalytic converters - general information and precautions 2
Cold acceleration enrichment system - testing 12
Cold start valve and thermotime switch - testing 9
Exhaust manifold - removal and refitting 24
Exhaust system - inspection, removal and refitting 25
Fuel accumulator - removal and refitting 21
Fuel filter - removal and refitting 20
Fuel injectors - removal, testing and refitting 13
Fuel lift pump - testing, removal and refitting 18
Fuel metering distributor - removal and refitting 15
Fuel pump - removal and refitting 19
Fuel tank and associated components - removal and refitting 22
General information and precautions 1
Idle mixture - adjustment 7
Idle speed - adjustment 4
Idle speed boost (air conditioned models) - testing and idle speed adjustment 6
Increased idling speed valve (air conditioned models) - testing 5
Inlet manifold - removal and refitting 23
Pressure relief valve - removal, servicing and refitting 17
Warm-up valve - testing 11

Degrees of difficulty

| **Easy,** suitable for novice with little experience | **Fairly easy,** suitable for beginner with some experience | **Fairly difficult,** suitable for competent DIY mechanic | **Difficult,** suitable for experienced DIY mechanic | **Very difficult,** suitable for expert DIY or professional |

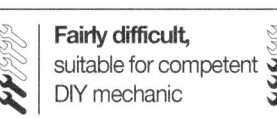

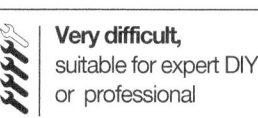

Specifications

Air cleaner
Type .... Automatic air temperature control

Injection system
Type .... K-Jetronic, continuous injection system (CIS)
Application .... 1.8 litre (code EV) engine
System pressure:
  Pre March 1986 .... 4.7 to 5.4 bar
  From March 1986 .... 5.2 to 5.9 bar
Idle speed:
  Pre Sept. 1984 .... 900 to 1000 rpm
  From Sept. 1984 .... 800 to 1000 rpm
  Air conditioned models .... 850 to 1000 rpm
CO content % .... 0.5 to 1.5

4B•2 Fuel and exhaust systems - K-Jetronic fuel injection - 8 valve engines

Torque wrench settings

	Nm	lbf ft
Injector insert	20	15
Injector line to injector	25	18
Injector line to fuel metering distributor	10	7
Thermo-time switch	30	22
System pressure relief valve	20	15
Cold start valve	10	7
Throttle valve housing to manifold	20	15
Inlet manifold	25	18
Fuel filter clamp	10	7
Union bolt at filter (from fuel accumulator)	25	18
Union nut at accumulator (to filter)	20	15
Union bolt at filter (to metering distributor)	20	15
Fuel pump reservoir mounting	10	7
Fuel pump non-return valve	20	15
Fuel pump damper unit	20	15
Inlet manifold nuts/bolts	20	15
Exhaust manifold	25	18
Exhaust heat shield	10	7
Exhaust pipe clamp bolts	40	30

1 General information and precautions

General information

The principle of the K-Jetronic continuous injection system is very simple and there are no specialised electronic components. There is an electrically driven fuel pump and electrical sensors and switches but these are no different from those in general use on vehicles **(see illustration)**.

The following paragraphs describe the system and its various elements. Later Sections describe tests which can be carried out to ascertain whether a particular unit is functioning correctly. Repairs are not generally possible.

The system measures the amount of air entering the engine and determines the amount of fuel which needs to be mixed with the air to give the correct combustion mixture for the particular conditions of engine operation. Fuel is sprayed continuously by an injection nozzle to the inlet port of each cylinder. This fuel/air mixture is drawn into the cylinder when the inlet valves open.

Airflow meter

The airflow meter measures the volume of air entering the engine and comprises an air funnel with a sensor plate mounted on a lever which is supported at its fulcrum. The weight of the airflow sensor plate and its lever are balanced by a counterweight and the upward force on the sensor plate is opposed by a plunger. The plunger, which moves up and down as a result of the variations in air flow, is surrounded by a sleeve having vertical slots in it. The vertical movement of the plunger uncovers a greater or lesser length of the slots, which meters fuel to the injection valves.

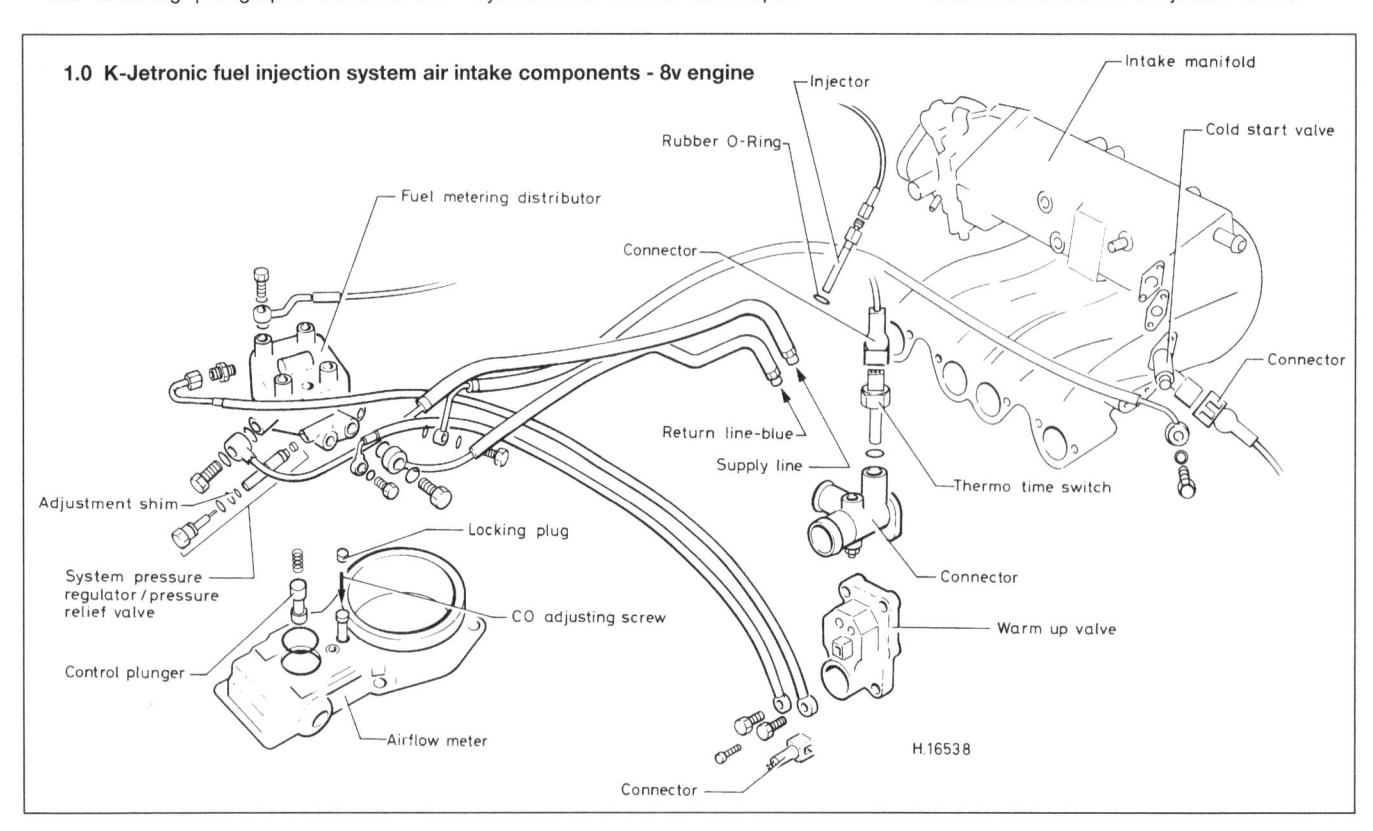

1.0 K-Jetronic fuel injection system air intake components - 8v engine

Fuel supply

The fuel pump operates continuously while the engine is running, excess fuel being returned to the fuel tank. The pump is operated when the ignition switch is in the START position. Once the starter is released, a switch which is connected to the air plate, prevents the pump from operating unless the engine is running.

The fuel line to the fuel supply valve incorporates a filter and also a fuel accumulator. The function of the accumulator is to maintain pressure in the fuel system after the engine has been switched off and so give good hot restarting.

Associated with the accumulator is a pressure regulator which is an integral part of the fuel metering device. When the engine is switched off, the pressure regulator lets the pressure to the injection valves fall rapidly to cut off the fuel flow through them and so prevent the engine from "dieseling" or "running on". The valve closes at just below the opening pressure of the injector valves and this pressure is then maintained by the accumulator.

Fuel distributor

The fuel distributor is mounted on the air metering device and is controlled by the vertical movement of the airflow sensor plate. It comprises a spool valve which moves vertically in a sleeve, the sleeve having as many vertical slots around its circumference as there are cylinders on the engine.

The spool valve is adjusted to hydraulic pressure on the upper end and this balances the pressure on the air plate which is applied to the bottom of the valve by a plunger. As the spool valve rises and falls, it uncovers a greater or lesser length of metering slot and so controls the volume of fuel fed to each injector.

Each metering slot has a differential pressure valve, which ensures that the difference in pressure between the two sides of the slot is always the same. Because the drop in pressure across the metering slot is unaffected by the length of slot exposed, the amount of fuel flowing depends only on the exposed area of the slots.

Cold start valve

The cold start valve is mounted in the inlet manifold and sprays additional fuel into the manifold during cold starting. The valve is solenoid operated and is controlled by a thermotime switch in the engine cooling system. The thermotime switch is actuated for a period which depends upon coolant temperature, the period decreasing with rise in coolant temperature. If the coolant temperature is high enough for the engine not to need additional fuel for starting, the switch does not operate.

Warm-up regulator (valve)

While warming up, the engine needs a richer mixture to compensate for fuel which condenses on the cold walls of the inlet manifold and cylinder walls. It also needs more fuel to compensate for power lost because of increased friction losses and increased oil drag in a cold engine. The mixture is made richer during warming up by the warm-up regulator. This is a pressure regulator which lowers the pressure applied to the control plunger of the fuel regulator during warm-up. This reduced pressure causes the airflow plate to rise higher than it would do otherwise, thus uncovering a greater length of metering slot and making the mixture richer.

The valve is operated by a bi-metallic strip which is heated by an electric heater. When the engine is cold, the bi-metallic strip presses against the delivery valve spring to reduce the pressure on the diaphragm and enlarge the discharge cross-section. This increase in cross-section results in a lowering of the pressure fed to the control plunger.

Auxiliary air device

Compensation for power lost by greater friction is achieved by feeding a larger volume of fuel/air mixture to the engine than is supplied by the normal opening of the throttle. The auxiliary air device bypasses the throttle with a channel having a variable aperture valve in it. The aperture is varied by a pivoted plate controlled by a spring and a bi-metallic strip.

During cold starting, the channel is open and increases the volume of air passing to the engine. As the bi-metallic strip bends, it allows a control spring to pull the plate over the aperture until at normal operating temperature the aperture is closed.

Cold acceleration enrichment

This system is fitted to later models only.

When the engine is cold (below 35°C), acceleration is improved by briefly enriching the fuel mixture for a period of approximately 0.4 seconds. This cold acceleration enrichment will only operate if the thermotime switch, the diaphragm pressure switch and the throttle valve switch are shut off.

Temperature sensor

From March 1986, a temperature sensor is located between injectors 1 and 2. After switching off the ignition, this switches on the cooling fan when the temperature of the cylinder head exceeds 110°C. A time relay is incorporated in the circuit. This switches off the function between ten and twelve minutes after switching off the ignition.

Precautions

Fuel warning

Many of the procedures in this Chapter require the removal of fuel lines and connections which may result in some fuel spillage. Before carrying out any operation on the fuel system, refer to the precautions given in Safety first! at the beginning of this Manual and follow them implicitly. Petrol is a highly dangerous and volatile liquid and the precautions necessary when handling it cannot be overstressed.

Fuel injection system warning

Residual pressure will remain in the fuel lines long after the vehicle was last used, therefore extra care must be taken when disconnecting a fuel line.

Loosen any fuel line slowly to avoid a sudden release of pressure which may cause fuel spray. As an added precaution, place a rag over each union as it is disconnected to catch any fuel which is forcibly expelled.

Take particular care to ensure that no dirt is allowed to enter the system. The ignition must be off and the battery disconnected.

Unleaded petrol - usage

Refer to Part A of this Chapter.

Catalytic converters

Before attempting work on these items, carefully read the precautions listed in the following Section.

2 Catalytic converters - general information and precautions

The catalytic converter is a reliable and simple device which needs no maintenance in itself, but there are some facts of which an owner should be aware if the converter is to function properly for its full service life.

a) *DO NOT use leaded petrol in a vehicle equipped with a catalytic converter - the lead will coat the precious metals, reducing their converting efficiency and will eventually destroy the converter.*

b) *Always keep the ignition and fuel systems well-maintained in accordance with the manufacturer's schedule. Ensure that the air cleaner element, fuel filter and spark plugs are renewed at the correct intervals. If the inlet air/fuel mixture is allowed to become too rich due to neglect, the unburned surplus will enter and burn in the catalytic converter, overheating the element and eventually destroying the converter.*

c) *If the engine develops a misfire, do not drive the vehicle at all (or at least as little as possible) until the fault is cured. The misfire will allow unburned fuel to enter the converter, which will result in its overheating.*

d) *DO NOT push or tow-start the vehicle. This will soak the catalytic converter in unburned fuel, causing it to overheat when the engine does start.*

e) *DO NOT switch off the ignition at high engine speeds. If the ignition is switched off at anything above idle speed, unburned fuel will enter the (very hot) catalytic converter, with the possible risk of its igniting on the element and damaging the converter.*

4B•4 Fuel and exhaust systems - K-Jetronic fuel injection - 8 valve engines

f) DO NOT use fuel or engine oil additives as these may contain substances harmful to the catalytic converter.

g) DO NOT continue to use the vehicle if the engine burns oil to the extent of leaving a visible trail of blue smoke. The unburned carbon deposits will clog the converter passages and reduce its efficiency. In severe cases, the element will overheat.

h) Remember that the catalytic converter operates at very high temperatures, hence the heat shields on the vehicle's underbody. The casing will become hot enough to ignite combustible materials which brush against it. DO NOT, therefore, park the vehicle in dry undergrowth, over long grass or piles of dead leaves.

I) Remember that the catalytic converter is FRAGILE. Do not strike it with tools during servicing work, take great care when working on the exhaust system, ensure that the converter is well clear of any jacks or other lifting gear used to raise the vehicle and do not drive the vehicle over rough ground, road humps etc. in such a way as to 'ground' the exhaust system.

j) In some cases, particularly when the vehicle is new and/or is used for stop/start driving, a sulphurous smell (like that of rotten eggs) may be noticed from the exhaust. This is common to many catalytic converter-equipped vehicles and seems to be due to the small amount of sulphur found in some petrols reacting with hydrogen in the exhaust to produce hydrogen sulphide (H_2S) gas. While this gas is toxic, it is not produced in sufficient amounts to be a problem. Once the vehicle has covered a few thousand miles the problem should disappear. In the meantime, a change of driving style or brand of petrol used may effect a solution.

k) The catalytic converter used on a well-maintained and well-driven vehicle, should last for between 50 000 and 100 000 miles. From this point on, careful checks should be made at all specified service intervals of the CO level to ensure that the converter is still operating efficiently. If the converter is no longer effective, it must be renewed.

3 Air cleaner element - renewal

Refer to Chapter 1, Section 32

4 Idle speed - adjustment

1 Run the engine until the oil temperature is at least 80°C. Do not let the engine coolant temperature rise above normal as the electric radiator fan will run and this should not be operating when checking or adjusting idle speed.

2 Check the ignition timing and adjust if necessary.

3 Except on air conditioned models, the main headlights should be turned on. Disconnect and plug the crankcase breather hose from the valve cover.

4 Where air conditioning is fitted, the system must be switched off during checking and adjustment.

5 If the injector pipes have been reconnected just prior to checking the idle speed, run the engine up to 3000 rpm a few times and then let it idle for a minimum period of two minutes before checking the idle speed.

6 If adjustment to the idle speed is necessary, remove the locking cap from the adjustment screw on the throttle assembly and turn the screw to achieve the specified idle speed **(see illustration)**. Adjustment should be made only when the radiator fan is stationary.

7 If an exhaust gas analyser is available, check the CO reading and compare it with the specified figure. If necessary adjust the idle mixture.

8 Air conditioned models will also be fitted with an increased idle speed valve and, in some instances, a second idle speed boost valve. To check these, refer to Sections 5 or 6, as applicable.

4.6 Idle speed adjustment screw location in throttle valve housing (arrowed)

5 Increased idling speed valve (air conditioned models) - testing

1 Start and run the engine at its normal idle speed.

2 With the air conditioner switched off, pinch the hose at the increased idle speed valve **(see illustration)**. The engine speed should not change.

3 Switch the air conditioning system on and then repeat the test. This time the engine speed should drop. If these tests prove the valve to be faulty then it must be renewed.

4 Disconnect the hose, unclip and detach the wiring connector then unbolt and remove the valve from its support bracket.

5 Refit in the reverse order of removal.

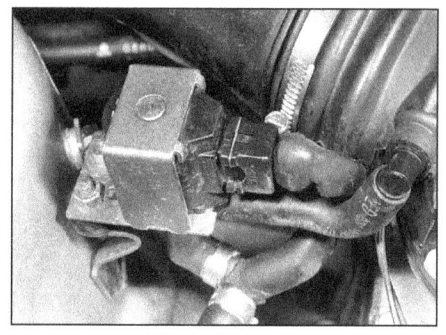

5.2 Increased idling speed valve (air conditioned models)

6 Idle speed boost (air conditioned models) - testing and idle speed adjustment

General

1 The function of this device is to stabilise the engine speed when it drops below 700 rpm under certain operating conditions. This is achieved by increasing the air supply to the engine, which raises the idling speed to approximately 1050 rpm. At this point, the air supply valve is cut off and the idle speed then returns to normal. The two valves which control this system are attached to the right-hand front suspension mounting in the engine compartment **(see illustration)**.

2 Valve No. 1 (inboard side) increases the engine speed when it drops below 700 rpm, whilst valve No. 2 (outboard side) increases the idle speed when the air conditioner is switched on.

Valve 1 - testing and idle speed adjustment

3 Run the engine up to its normal operating temperature, switch off the air conditioner and allow the engine to idle. With the exception of the air conditioner, switch on all electrical consumers (lights, etc.), then adjust the idle speed to 700 rpm. When reaching idle speed, the valve should open and the idle speed increase. Using a pair of pliers, pinch the air hose from the valve then check that the speed drops.

6.1 Idle speed boost valve check

1 Valve No 1   2 Valve No 2   3 Hose

Fuel and exhaust systems - K-Jetronic fuel injection - 8 valve engines 4B•5

7.2 Idle CO adjustment screw location (arrowed)

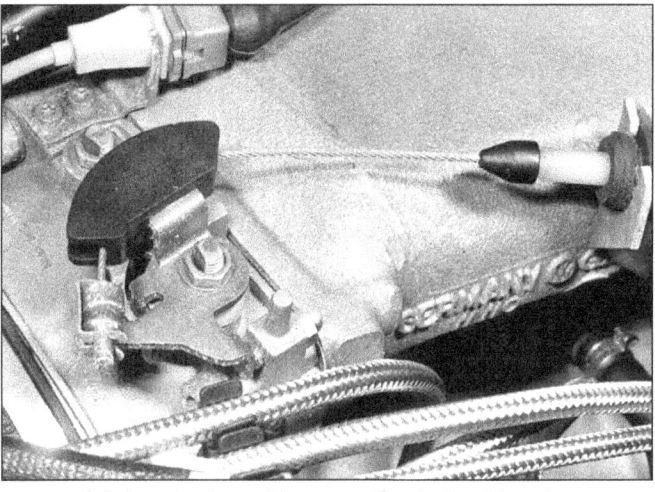

8.2 Accelerator cable connection to throttle valve

4 Switch off all electrical consumers, then pinch the air hose again and adjust idle speed to that specified. When the correct idle speed is reached, unclamp the hose. The idle speed should then increase up to about 1050 rpm at which point the valve will close and the speed drop to the specified idle speed setting.

Valve 2 - checking

5 Run the engine at normal idle speed with the air conditioner switched off. Pinch the air hose and check that the engine speed remains the same.
6 Now switch the air conditioning on and repeat the test. When the hose is pinched, the engine speed should drop.
7 If the air hose and/or valves Nos. 1 or 2 are disconnected or removed for any reason, it is important when refitting to note that the three-way hose connector large hole must go to valve No. 2.

7 Idle mixture - adjustment

Note: *Accurate idle mixture adjustment can only be made using an exhaust gas analyser*
1 The idle CO adjustment screw alters the height of the fuel metering distributor plunger relative to the air control plate of the air flow meter.
2 The screw is accessible by removing the locking plug from between the air duct scoop and the fuel metering distributor on the airflow meter casing **(see illustration)**.
3 Although a special tool is recommended for this adjustment, it can be made using a long, thin screwdriver.
4 Ensure that the engine is running under the same conditions as those necessary for adjusting the idling speed and that the idling speed is correct.
5 Connect an exhaust gas analyser to the tailpipe, as directed by the equipment manufacturer, and read the CO level.

6 Turn the adjusting screw clockwise to raise the percentage of CO and anti-clockwise to lower it. It is important that the adjustment is made without pressing down on the adjusting screw, because this will move the airflow sensor plate and affect the adjustment.
7 Remove the tool, accelerate the engine briefly and re-check. If the tool is not removed before the engine is accelerated, there is a danger of the tool becoming jammed and getting bent.
8 Recheck that the idle speed is correct and further adjust if necessary.
9 When reconnection of the crankcase ventilation hose results in an increase in the CO content, the engine oil is diluted with fuel and should be renewed. Alternatively, if an oil change is not due, a long fast drive will reduce the amount of fuel in the oil.

8 Accelerator cable - removal, refitting and adjustment

Removal

1 Disconnect the battery earth lead.
2 Prise free the inner cable retaining clip from the throttle valve control on the throttle valve housing **(see illustration)**.

3 Release the inner cable from the control quadrant and the outer cable from the location/adjustment bracket on top of the inlet manifold.
4 Prise free and remove the plastic cover from the top of the bulkhead trough.
5 Working inside the vehicle, remove the lower facia panel on the driver's side.
6 Unclip the inner cable from the accelerator pedal, then withdraw the complete cable into the engine compartment, together with the rubber grommets.

Refitting

7 Refitting is a reversal of removal, but ensure that the cable run is not kinked and is correctly aligned, then adjust the cable.

Adjustment

8 Ask an assistant to fully depress the accelerator pedal whilst the cable position is set at the throttle valve housing end.
9 When the throttle valve is fully open, there should be a 1.0 mm clearance between the throttle valve lever and the stop **(see illustration)**.
10 Adjust by altering the cable retainer position at the location/adjustment bracket **(see illustration)**.

8.9 Accelerator cable clearance at full throttle position (arrowed)

8.10 Accelerator cable adjuster and support bracket

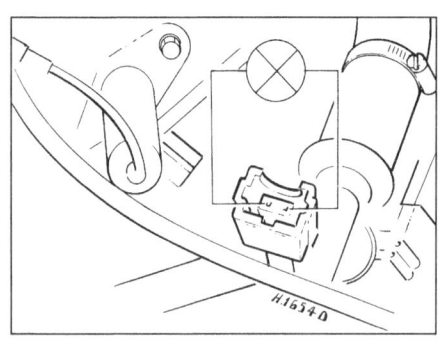

4B•6 Fuel and exhaust systems - K-Jetronic fuel injection - 8 valve engines

9.3 Cold start valve test lamp connections

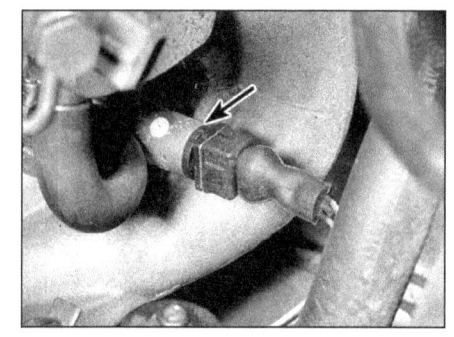

10.3 Auxiliary air valve (arrowed)

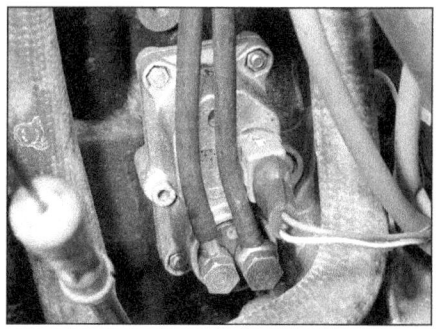

11.2 Warm-up valve

9 Cold start valve and thermotime switch - testing

Cold start valve

1 The thermotime switch energises the cold start valve for a short time on starting. The time for which the valve is switched on depends upon the engine temperature.
2 This check must only be carried out when the coolant temperature is below 30°C.
3 Pull the connector off the cold start valve and connect a test lamp across the contacts of the connector (see illustration).
4 Pull the high tension lead off the centre of the distributor and connect the lead to earth.
5 Pull the connector from the thermotime switch then connect an extension lead from earth to the thermotime switch W terminal (green/white wire). The red/black wire must not be earthed.
6 Operate the starter and check that the test lamp lights up. If it does not, then there is an open circuit which must be located and repaired.
7 To check the cold start valve, leave the thermotime switch W terminal earthed, remove the cold start valve and re-attach its connector. Take care not to break the gasket when withdrawing the cold start valve from the inlet manifold.
8 With fuel line and electrical connections connected to the valve, hold the valve over a glass jar and operate the starter for 10 seconds. The cold start valve should produce an even cone of spray during the time the thermotime switch is on.
9 Wipe dry the cold start valve nozzle with a clean non-fluffy cloth, then check that the valve does not drip or its body become damp over a period of one minute. If proved defective, renew the valve.

Thermotime switch

10 To check the thermotime switch, proceed as described in paragraphs 3 and 4 inclusive. The coolant should be at 30°C. If the switch needs to be cooled down to the temperature specified, remove it and immerse its base in cold water. When cooled, earth the switch to make the test.
11 Operate the starter for 10 seconds. The test lamp should light immediately and stay on for three seconds.
12 Refit the high tension lead onto the distributor and reconnect the lead to the cold start valve.

10 Auxiliary air valve - testing

1 To carry out this test, the engine coolant temperature must be below 30°C.
2 Detach the distributor HT lead.
3 Detach the auxiliary air valve electrical plug and ensure that the contacts in the plug connector are in good condition (see illustration).
4 Connect up a voltmeter across the contacts of the plug connectors, start the engine and run at idle speed. The voltage reading must be a minimum of 11.6 V. If a voltmeter is not available, a test lamp will suffice to check the voltage supply.
5 With the auxiliary air valve electrical plug still detached, leave the engine running at idle speed and pinch the air inlet duct-to-auxiliary valve hose. The engine speed should drop.

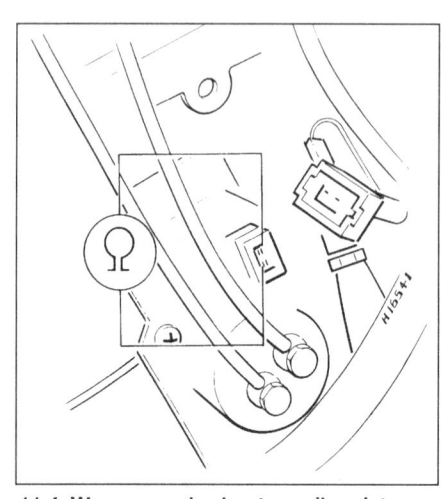

11.4 Warm-up valve heater coil resistance test

6 When the engine is warmed up to normal operating temperature, reconnect the auxiliary valve plug then pinch the hose again. This time the engine speed should remain unaltered.

11 Warm-up valve - testing

1 Detach the distributor HT lead and earth it.
2 With the engine cold, detach the wiring connector from the warm-up valve (see illustration).
3 Connect a voltmeter across the terminals of the warm-up valve connector and operate the starter. The voltage across the terminals should be a minimum of 11.5 volts.
4 Switch the ignition off and connect an ohmmeter across the terminals of the warm-up valve (see illustration). If the meter does not indicate a resistance of about 20 to 26 ohm, the heater coil is defective and a new valve must be fitted.

12 Cold acceleration enrichment system - testing

1 When the engine is cold (below 35°C), acceleration is improved by briefly enriching the fuel mixture for a period of approximately 0.4 seconds. This cold acceleration enrichment will only operate if the thermotime switch, the diaphragm pressure switch and the throttle valve switch are shut off.
2 To check the system, first check that the cold start valve is operational.
3 Detach the wiring connector from the cold start valve and connect up a test lamp to its terminals.
4 Detach the wiring connector from the thermotime switch and connect a length of wire between an earth point and the connector No.2 terminal W (green/white wire). Do not earth terminal G (red/black wire).
5 Run the engine and allow it to idle, at which point the test lamp should not light up. When the engine is quickly accelerated, the test lamp should light up briefly (0.4 seconds) (see illustration).

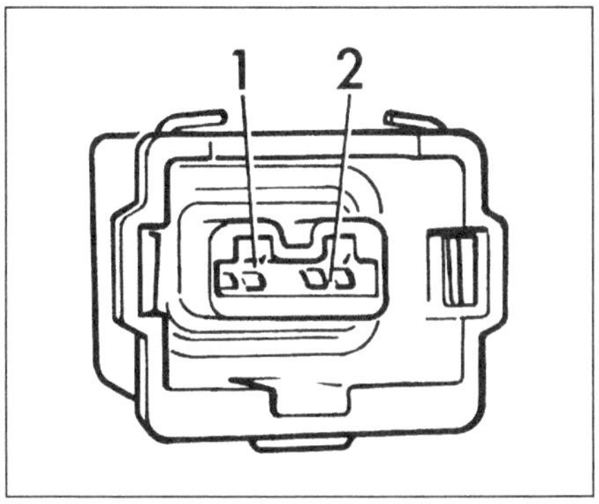

Fuel and exhaust systems - K-Jetronic fuel injection - 8 valve engines 4B•7

12.5 Cold acceleration enrichment system check

Cold start valve connector earth contact (2) (green/white wire to W terminal)
Do not earth contact 1

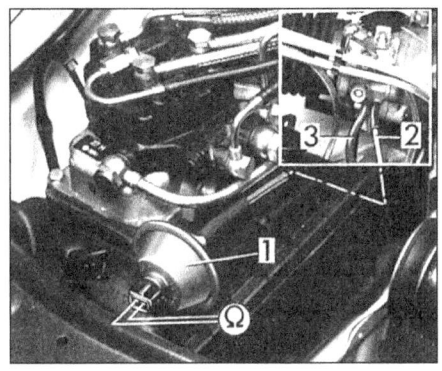

12.8 Diaphragm pressure switch test

1 Diaphragm pressure switch
2 Vacuum connection for switch (yellow)
3 Vacuum connection for spark control

12.10 Throttle valve switch check

1 Throttle valve switch
a = 0.2 to 0.6 mm

6 If a fault is evident, check the wiring connections, the throttle valve switch and the diaphragm pressure switch.
7 The diaphragm pressure switch can be checked using an ohmmeter. Detach the wiring connector from the end of the diaphragm pressure switch, then start the engine and allow it to idle. Using the ohmmeter, check the resistance reading between the contacts. An infinity reading should be given.
8 Accelerate the engine briefly and check that the resistance drops briefly and then returns to infinity **(see illustration)**.
9 To check the throttle valve switch, detach the switch lead connector and measure the resistance between the switch contacts. An infinity reading should be given.
10 Now slowly open the throttle valve to the point where the switch is heard to operate with a click. The ohmmeter should give a 0 ohm reading and the clearance between the throttle lever and the idle stop must be between 0.2 to 0.6 mm **(see illustration)**.
11 If necessary, adjust the switch by loosening the switch (underside of throttle housing) and

positioning a feeler blade of 0.4 mm thickness between the lever and stop. Move the switch towards the lever until the switch is heard to operate, then retighten the switch and check adjustment.
12 If the throttle valve switch is being removed, prise the connector bracket apart to release the connector.

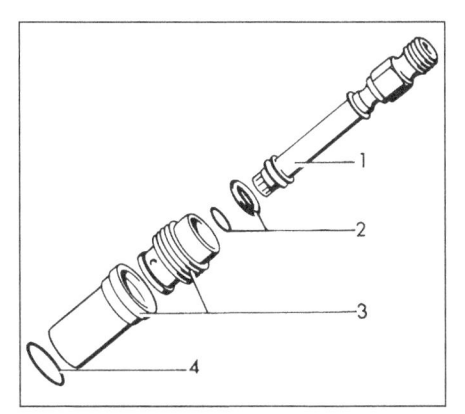

13 Fuel injectors - removal, testing and refitting

1 An injector may give trouble for one of the following reasons:
a) The spray may be irregular in shape
b) The nozzle may not close when the engine is shut down, causing flooding when restarting
c) The nozzle filter may be choked, giving less that the required ration of fuel
d) The seal may be damaged, allowing an air leak

2 To remove an injector for inspection, simply pull it free **(see illustration)**.
3 Inspect the rubber seal. If it shows signs of cracking, distortion or perishing, then it must be renewed. If found to be defective, check the other injector seals as they are likely to be in similar condition.
4 Specialised tools are required for an accurate test of injector performance. However, a basic check can be made as follows.
5 Hold the injector in a suitable measuring glass and plug up the injector location hole. Start the engine and let it idle on three cylinders and look at the shape of the spray. It should be of a symmetrical cone shape. If it is not, then the injector must be changed because the vibrator pin is damaged or the spring is broken. Shut off the engine and wait for 15 seconds. There must be no leak or dribble from the nozzle. If there is, the injector must be renewed, as dribble will cause flooding and difficult starting.

6 An injector cannot be dismantled for cleaning. If an injector is renewed, the line union must be tightened to the specified torque.
7 When inserting an injector, lubricate the seal with fuel before fitting.

14 Airflow sensor plate and control plunger - testing

1 For the correct mixture to be supplied to the engine, it is essential that the sensor plate is central in the venturi and that its height is correct. First run the engine for a period of about one minute.
2 Loosen the hose clips at each end of the air scoop and remove the scoop. If the sensor plate appears to be off-centre, loosen its centre screw and carefully run a 0.10 mm feeler blade round the edge of the plate to centralise it, then re-tighten the bolt **(see illustration)**.
3 Raise the airflow sensor plate and then quickly move it to its rest position. No resistance should be felt on the downward movement. If there is resistance, the airflow meter is defective and a new one must be fitted.

14.2 Top view of airflow sensor plate

13.2 Air shrouded injector assembly (later models)

1 Injector
2 Rubber rings
3 Injector insert
4 Washer

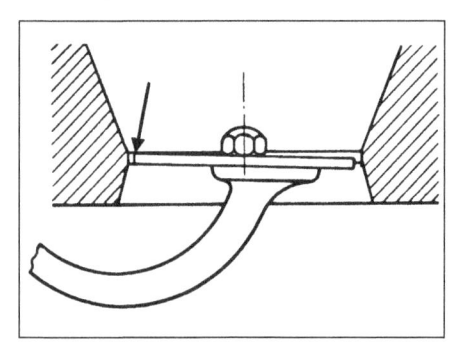

4B•8 Fuel and exhaust systems - K-Jetronic fuel injection - 8 valve engines

14.5 Sensor plate position requirement

Upper edge of plate (arrowed) must be flush with bottom of air cone

4 If the sensor plate can be moved downwards easily but has a strong resistance to upward movement, the control plunger is sticking. Remove the fuel distributor and clean the control plunger in fuel. If this does not cure the problem, a new fuel distributor must be fitted.

5 Release the pressure on the fuel distributor and then check the rest position of the airflow sensor plate. The upper edge of the plate should be flush with the bottom edge of the air cone **(see illustration)**. It is permissible for the plate to be lower than the edge by not more than 0.5 mm but if higher, or lower than the permissible limit, the plate must be adjusted.

6 Adjust the height of the plate by lifting it and bending the wire clips attaching the plate to the balance arm. Take care not to scratch or damage the surface of the air cone **(see illustration)**.

7 After adjustment, tighten the warm-up valve union and check the idle speed and CO content.

14.6 Airflow sensor plate adjustment clip (arrowed)

15 Fuel metering distributor - removal and refitting

Note: *Ensure that the vehicle is in a well ventilated space and away from naked flames or other possible sources of ignition*

Removal

1 Disconnect the battery terminals.
2 While holding a rag over the joint to prevent fuel from being sprayed out, loosen the control pressure line from the warm-up valve. The control pressure line is the one connected to the large union of the valve.
3 Mark each fuel line and its port on the distributor. Carefully clean all dirt from around the fuel unions and distributor ports and then disconnect the lines.
4 Unscrew and remove the connection of the pressure control line to the distributor.
5 Remove the locking plug from the CO adjusting screw, then remove the three screws securing the distributor **(see illustration)**.

6 Lift off the distributor, taking care that the metering plunger does not fall out. If the plunger does fall out accidentally, clean it in fuel and then re-insert it with its chamfered end downwards.

Refitting

7 Before refitting the distributor, ensure that the plunger moves up and down freely. If the plunger sticks, the distributor must be renewed.
8 Refit the distributor, using a new sealing ring. After tightening the screws, lock them with paint.
9 Refit the fuel lines and the cap of the CO adjusting screw then tighten the union on the warm-up valve.

16 Airflow meter - removal and refitting

Removal

1 Remove the fuel lines from the distributor.
2 Loosen the clamps at the air cleaner and throttle assembly ends of the air scoop and take off the air scoop.
3 Remove the bolts securing the airflow meter to the air cleaner and lift off the airflow meter and fuel metering distributor **(see illustration)**.
4 The plunger should be prevented from falling out when the distributor is removed from the airflow meter.

Refitting

5 Refitting is the reverse of removing. It is necessary to use a new gasket between the airflow meter and air cleaner.

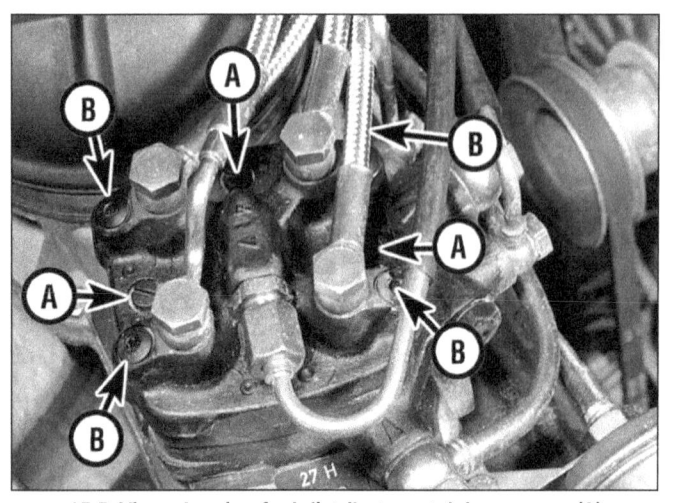

15.5 View showing fuel distributor retaining screws (A)

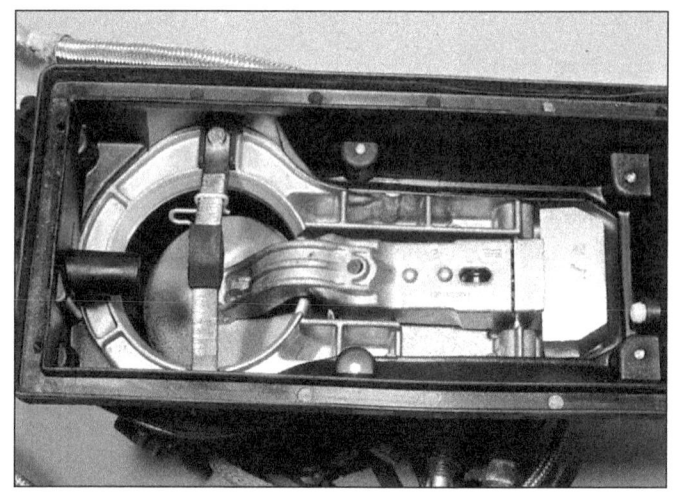

Do not remove screws (B)

16.3 Airflow meter and fuel distributor unit (inverted)

17 Pressure relief valve - removal, servicing and refitting

1 Release the pressure in the fuel system.
2 Unscrew the non-return valve plug and remove the plug and sealing washer.
3 Take out the O-ring, plunger and O-ring, in that order (see illustration).
4 When refitting the assembly, use new O-rings and ensure that all the shims which were removed are refitted.
5 The number of shims fitted determine the system operating pressure. If for any reason the system pressure is suspect, it will be necessary to have a pressure check made by your VW dealer who should have the correct gauge needed to check the pressure in the system. He will know the amount of shims required to correct the pressure should it be necessary.

18 Fuel lift pump - testing, removal and refitting

Testing

1 The fuel lift pump is attached to the base of the fuel gauge sender unit fitted to the fuel tank (see illustration).
2 If the pump is suspected of malfunction, first check that the pump wiring does not have an open circuit. Remove the luggage compartment floor covering and the circular cover in the floor for access to the sender unit and connections. Detach the wiring connector and make a continuity check between the centre wires and the outer (brown) wire of the connector (see illustration).
3 If the wiring proves correct, then check the pump relay and pump fuse (No. 5). Assuming the fuse to be in order, check the relay by first detaching the Hall sender connector from the ignition system distributor.
4 Remove the fusebox and relay plate cover then pull free the pump relay from position 2.
5 Using a voltmeter, switch on the ignition and check the voltage reading between the following:
a) Contact No. 2 and earth
b) Contact Nos. 2 and 1
c) Contact Nos. 4 and 1
d) Contact Nos. 5 and 1
6 In each case, battery voltage should show.
7 Check that when the central connector wire is earthed briefly, there is a voltage drop. If the voltage does not drop, check the ignition (TCI/H switch) unit. If the voltage does drop, renew the fuel pump relay. If the problem still persists, have the ignition Hall sender unit checked.

Removal

8 If after making the above checks the pump still malfunctions, remove the sender unit as described in Part A of this Chapter, Section 8, then detach the pump for renewal.

Refitting

9 Refitting is a reversal of the removal procedure.

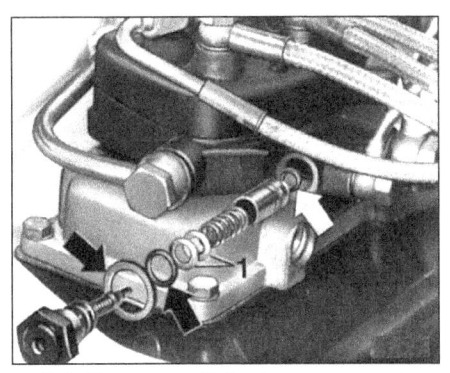

17.3 Pressure relief valve components
1 Shims   Arrows indicate O-rings

19 Fuel pump - removal and refitting

Removal

1 The fuel pump is located on the underside of the vehicle, forwards of the fuel tank on the right-hand side, the pump being housed in the pump reservoir (see illustrations).
2 Disconnect the battery earth lead.
3 Raise the vehicle at the rear and support it on axle stands (see "Jacking and vehicle support").
4 Prise free the retaining clip and detach the pump wiring connector (see illustration).
5 Unscrew the damper unit from the rear end of the pump and detach the hose union, noting the washer each side of the union.
6 Undo the retaining nuts and washers and remove the adapter.
7 Undo the three screws securing the pump retaining ring and withdraw the ring, followed by the pump unit.
8 Remove the O-ring and withdraw the strainer.

Refitting

9 Refitting is a reversal of the removal procedure. Smear the O-ring with fuel when fitting and check that it does not become distorted.
10 When fitting the pump, position it so that its lug engages with the slot in the retaining ring.
11 If the pump non-return valve was removed from the rear end of the pump, refit it using a new seal washer. Also use a new seal washer each side of the hose union. Tighten the damper unit to the specified torque.
12 On completion, start the engine and check for any signs of fuel leakage from the pump connections.

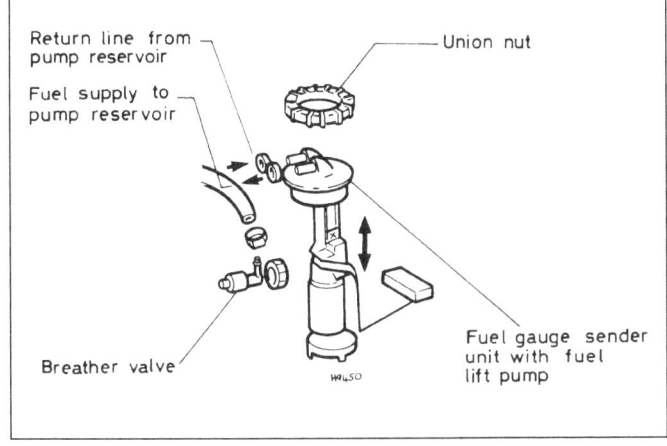

18.1 Fuel tank sender unit
Tank and other associated components are identical to those used for carburettor engines

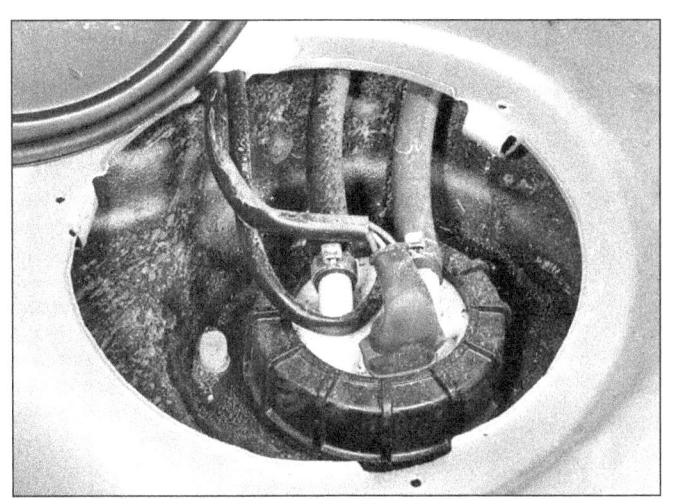

18.2 Fuel tank sender unit and connections

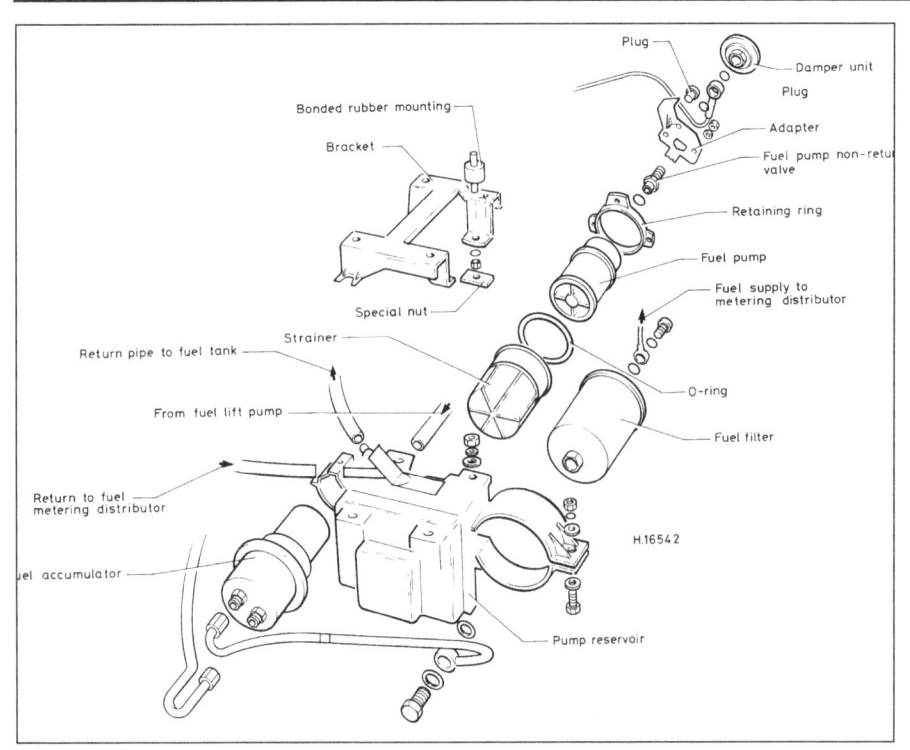

4B•10 Fuel and exhaust systems - K-Jetronic fuel injection - 8 valve engines

19.1a Fuel pump and associated components

19.1b Fuel pump viewed from rear

19.4 Disconnecting wiring connector from fuel pump

20 Fuel filter - removal and refitting

Refer to Chapter 1, Section 33

21 Fuel accumulator - removal and refitting

Removal

1 The fuel accumulator is mounted on the outboard side of the fuel pump reservoir on the underside of the vehicle at the rear, just forward of the fuel tank (see illustration).
2 Disconnect the battery earth lead.
3 Raise the vehicle at the rear and support it on axle stands (see "Jacking and vehicle support").

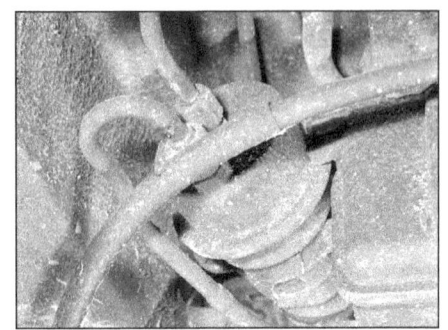

21.1 Fuel accumulator unit location

4 Disconnect the fuel pipes from their connections at the front end of the regulator.
5 Undo the clamp bolt and withdraw the accumulator.

Refitting

6 Refit in the reverse order to removal. Check that the fuel line connections are clean before refitting. On completion, check for fuel leaks with the engine running.

22 Fuel tank and associated components - removal and refitting

The fuel tank and associated components can be removed and refitted in the same manner as described for carburettor models in Part A of this Chapter.

To test the breather valve, blow through the hose (dotted arrow - see illustration 7.3 in Part A of this Chapter) and push the lever in to see if the airflow opens then shuts off as the lever is released. If defective, renew the valve.

23 Inlet manifold - removal and refitting

Note: Access to many of the fastenings and fittings of the manifold, on the bulkhead side in particular, is not good due to the close proximity of adjacent components. It may therefore be found necessary to at least partially disconnect and remove the engine/gearbox unit to gain access to certain items and allow clearance for manifold removal.

Modification: As from September 1984, components associated with the inlet manifold were modified (see illustration). All work procedures remain as follows for engines manufactured before that date (see illustration).

Removal

1 Disconnect the battery earth lead and decompress the fuel system.
2 Disconnect the accelerator cable from the throttle valve and support/adjuster bracket on the manifold.
3 Disconnect the wiring connector and the vacuum hose from the auxiliary air valve.
4 Disconnect the wiring and detach the warm-up valve.
5 Undo the hose clips and detach the vacuum hose from the connection on the end of the manifold (left side) and the rear side of the throttle valve housing (see illustration).
6 Disconnect the vacuum hoses from the front of the throttle housing, noting their connections.
7 Disconnect the injectors and hoses from the cylinder head, release them from the location clips and fold them back out of the way.
8 Unclip and detach the inlet ducting from the throttle housing.
9 Remove the bolts and disconnect the support bracket from the accelerator cable support/adjuster bracket and from the cam cover.

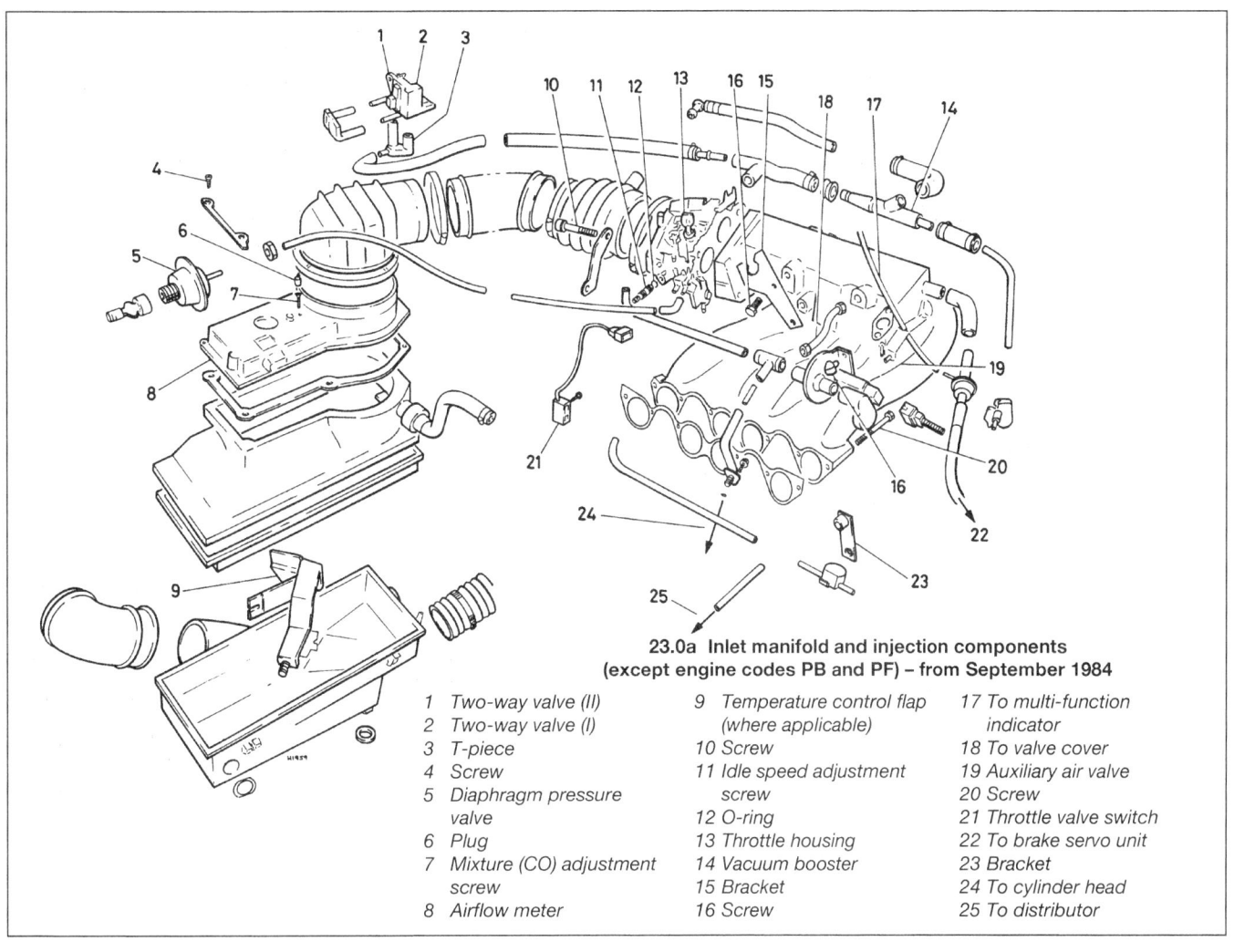

Fuel and exhaust systems - K-Jetronic fuel injection - 8 valve engines   4B•11

23.0a Inlet manifold and injection components (except engine codes PB and PF) – from September 1984

1 Two-way valve (II)
2 Two-way valve (I)
3 T-piece
4 Screw
5 Diaphragm pressure valve
6 Plug
7 Mixture (CO) adjustment screw
8 Airflow meter
9 Temperature control flap (where applicable)
10 Screw
11 Idle speed adjustment screw
12 O-ring
13 Throttle housing
14 Vacuum booster
15 Bracket
16 Screw
17 To multi-function indicator
18 To valve cover
19 Auxiliary air valve
20 Screw
21 Throttle valve switch
22 To brake servo unit
23 Bracket
24 To cylinder head
25 To distributor

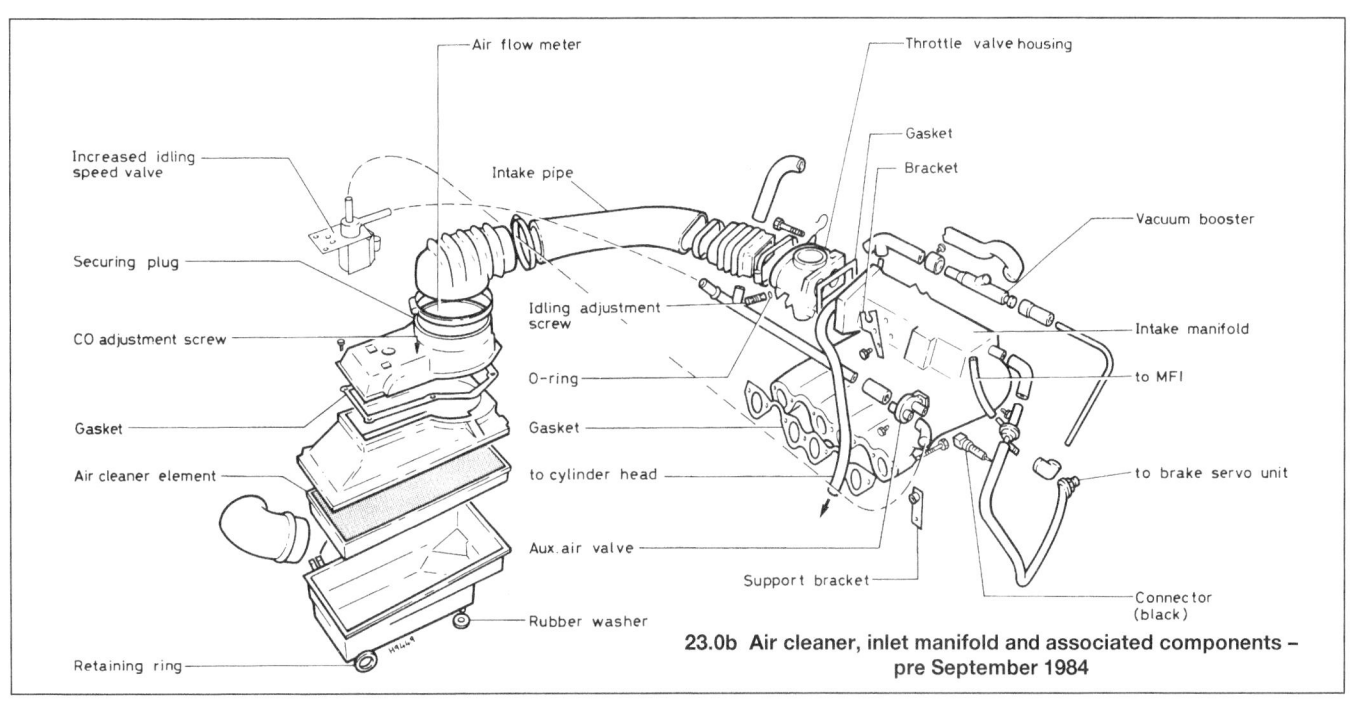

23.0b Air cleaner, inlet manifold and associated components – pre September 1984

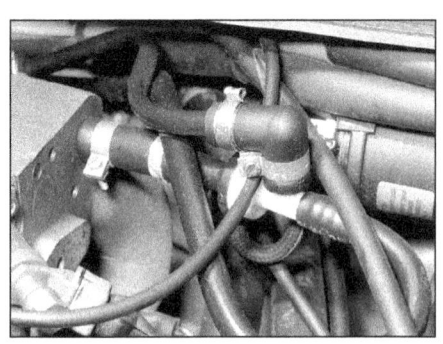

4B•12 Fuel and exhaust systems - K-Jetronic fuel injection - 8 valve engines

23.5 Vacuum hose-to-cylinder connector

10 Disconnect the cam cover-to-inlet manifold breather hose.
11 Undo and remove the inlet manifold retaining bolts then carefully lift the manifold, together with the throttle housing, away from the cylinder head. Disconnect any wiring or hose connections still attached as it is withdrawn.
12 The throttle housing can be unbolted from the manifold and then withdrawn from it.

Refitting

13 Refitting is a reversal of the removal procedure. Check that all mating faces are clean and use new gaskets. Tighten the securing bolts to the specified torque settings.
14 When reconnecting the accelerator cable, ensure it is correctly adjusted.
15 Check that all connections are secure and correctly made before restarting the vehicle.

24 Exhaust manifold - removal and refitting

Note: Before starting to remove the manifold, refer to Part A of this Chapter, Section 20, paragraph 1, which concerns details on the special tool required to release and subsequently reconnect the exhaust manifold-to-downpipe securing clips. Unless this tool is available, the manifold is best removed and refitted by your VW dealer

Remove the inlet manifold.
Removal and refitting of the exhaust manifold is now similar to that procedure described in Part A of this Chapter.

25 Exhaust system - inspection, removal and refitting

Without catalytic converter

1 Refer to Section 20 in Part A of this Chapter whilst noting that all models manufactured after August 1985 are fitted with a manifold/downpipe flange incorporating a gasket instead of spring clips.

With catalytic converter

2 The catalytic converter (where fitted) is positioned at the forward end of the exhaust system and comprises a steel casing over a ceramic body. It incorporates a longitudinal multi-passage honeycomb unit, which is coated with a layer of platinum or rhodium.
3 Removal is simply a matter of releasing the flange or socket type couplings and separating the components **(see illustration)**.
4 Note that the catalytic converter is fragile. Do not strike it with tools and take care not to allow it to contact jacks or lifting gear.
5 Always use new coupling seals and gaskets during reassembly.

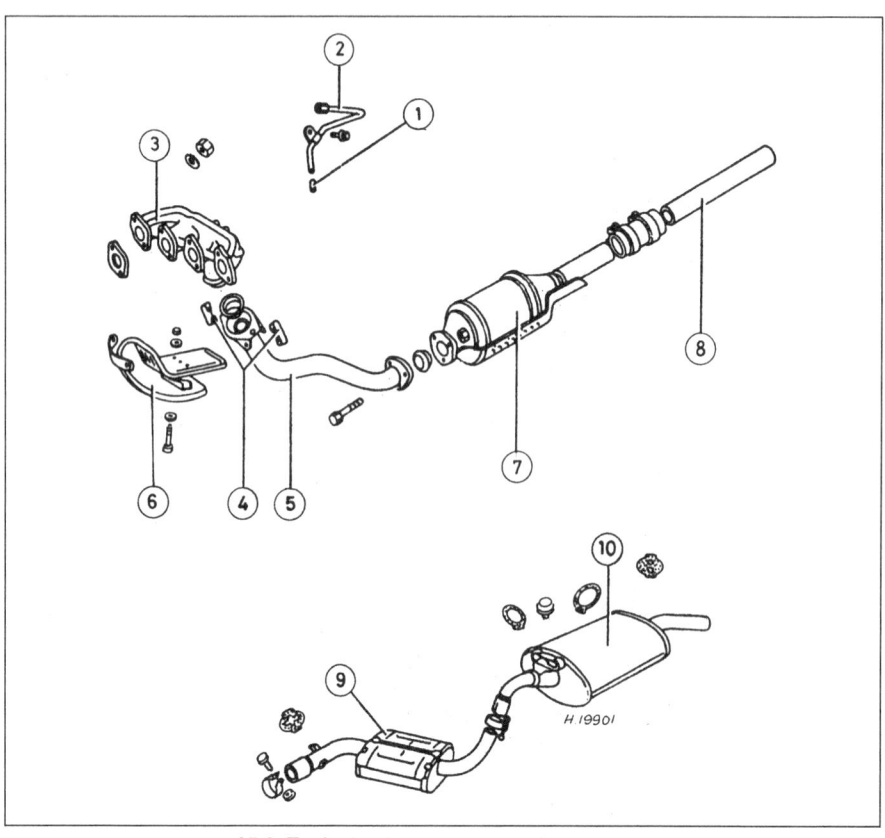

25.3 Typical exhaust system with catalyst

1 Cap
2 CO measuring pipe
3 Exhaust manifold
4 Spring clips
5 Exhaust front pipe
6 Heat shield
7 Catalytic converter
8 Intermediate pipe
9 Centre silencer
10 Rear silencer

Chapter 4 Part C:
Fuel and exhaust systems - K-Jetronic fuel injection - 16 valve engines

The following information is a revision of, or supplementary to, that contained in Part B of this Chapter

Contents

Diaphragm pressure switch - testing 5	Idle speed stabilisation system - testing 3
Exhaust system - inspection, removal and refitting 8	Inlet manifold - removal and refitting 7
General information 1	Overrun cut-off valve - testing 4
Idle speed - adjustment 2	Throttle valve switch - testing 6

Degrees of difficulty

Easy, suitable for novice with little experience	Fairly easy, suitable for beginner with some experience	Fairly difficult, suitable for competent DIY mechanic	Difficult, suitable for experienced DIY mechanic	Very difficult, suitable for expert DIY or professional

Specifications

Air cleaner
Type .... Automatic air temperature control

Injection system
Type .... K-Jetronic, continuous injection system (CIS)
Application .... 1.8 litre (code KR) engine
Idle speed .... 950 + 50 rpm

4C•2 Fuel and exhaust systems - K-Jetronic fuel injection - 16 valve engines

1 General information

The components of the K-Jetronic fuel injection system fitted to the 1.8 litre 16V engine are as shown **(see illustrations)**. All procedures are the same as described in Part B of this Chapter except for those given in the following Sections.

2 Idle speed - adjustment

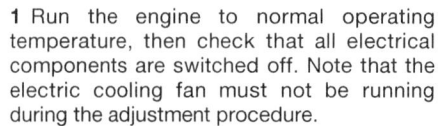

1 Run the engine to normal operating temperature, then check that all electrical components are switched off. Note that the electric cooling fan must not be running during the adjustment procedure.
2 Disconnect the crankcase ventilation hose **(see illustration)**.
3 Connect a tachometer and an exhaust gas analyser to the engine.
4 If the injector pipes have been removed and refitted just prior to adjustment, run the engine to 3000 rpm several times then allow it to idle for at least two minutes.
5 Check that when the ignition is switched on, the idling stabilisation control valve is heard to buzz. If not, check the system with reference to Section 3.
6 Disconnect the wiring plug for the idle stabilisation system. This is located near the ignition coil **(see illustration)**.
7 Allow the engine to idle, then check that the idle speed is 1000 ± 50 rpm. If necessary, remove the cap and turn the idle speed adjustment screw as required **(see illustration)**.

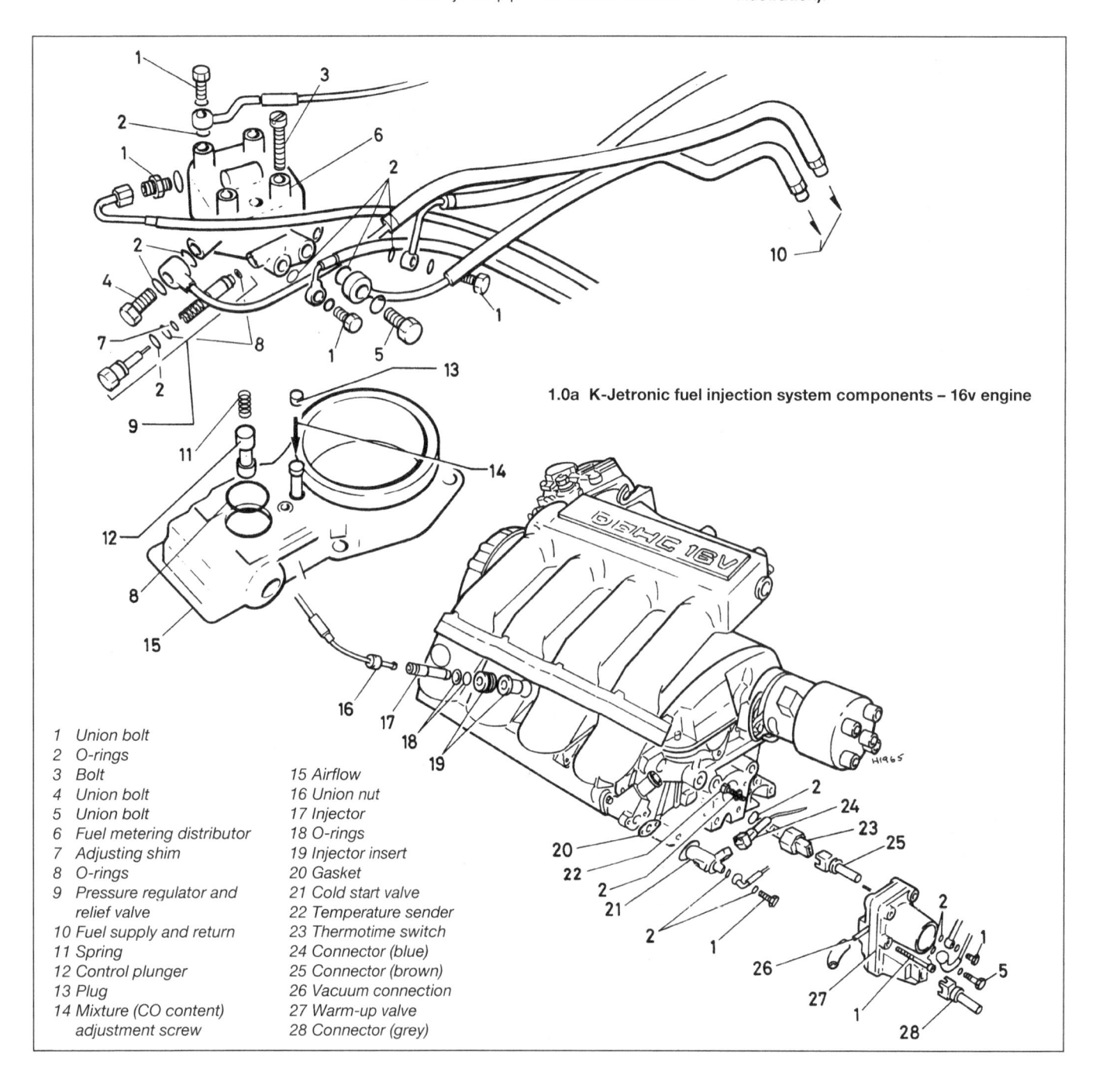

1.0a K-Jetronic fuel injection system components – 16v engine

1 Union bolt
2 O-rings
3 Bolt
4 Union bolt
5 Union bolt
6 Fuel metering distributor
7 Adjusting shim
8 O-rings
9 Pressure regulator and relief valve
10 Fuel supply and return
11 Spring
12 Control plunger
13 Plug
14 Mixture (CO content) adjustment screw
15 Airflow
16 Union nut
17 Injector
18 O-rings
19 Injector insert
20 Gasket
21 Cold start valve
22 Temperature sender
23 Thermotime switch
24 Connector (blue)
25 Connector (brown)
26 Vacuum connection
27 Warm-up valve
28 Connector (grey)

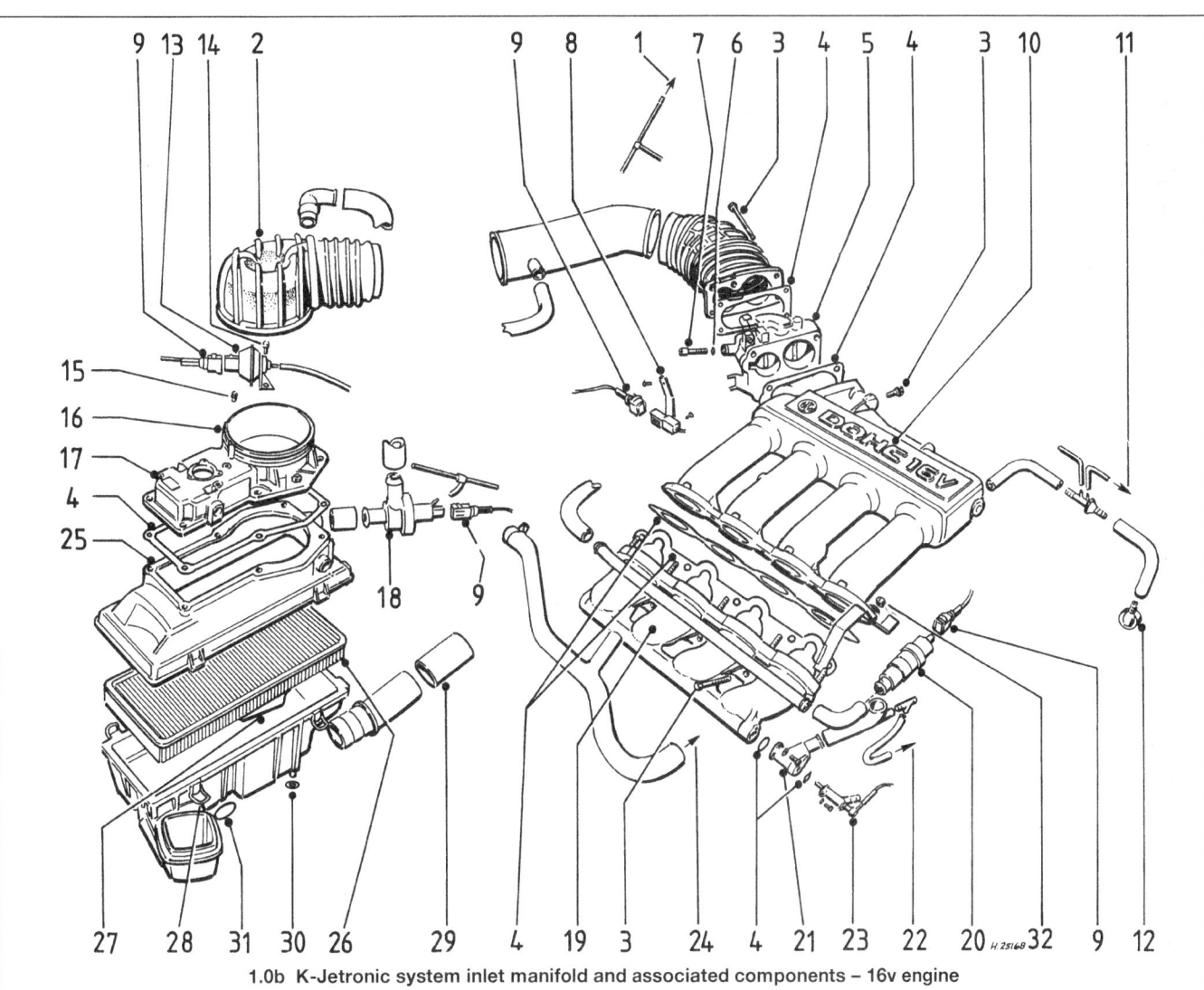

Fuel and exhaust systems - K-Jetronic fuel injection - 16 valve engines 4C•3

1.0b K-Jetronic system inlet manifold and associated components – 16v engine

1 To ignition control unit
2 Intake elbow
3 Screw
4 Gaskets
5 Throttle valve housing
6 O-ring
7 Idle speed adjustment screw
8 Throttle valve switch
9 Connector
10 Upper section of inlet manifold
11 To multi-function indicator
12 To brake servo unit
13 Diaphragm pressure valve
14 Screw
15 Plug
16 Mixture (CO) adjustment screw
17 Airflow meter
18 Overrun cut-off valve
19 Lower section of inlet manifold
20 Idle stabilisation control valve
21 Elbow
22 To warm-up valve
23 Cold start valve
24 To crankcase breather
25 Upper air cleaner
26 Air cleaner element
27 Temperature control flap
28 Lower air cleaner
29 Warm air hose
30 Washer
31 Retaining ring
32 Nut

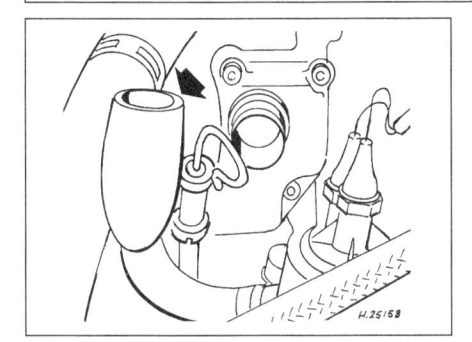

2.2 Disconnecting crankcase ventilation hose

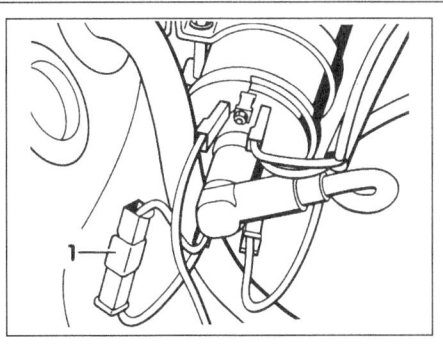

2.6 Idle stabilisation wiring plug (1)

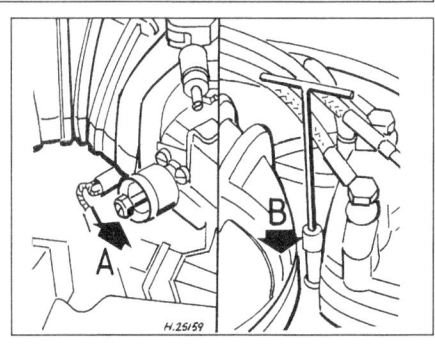

2.7 Idle speed (A) and mixture (B) screws

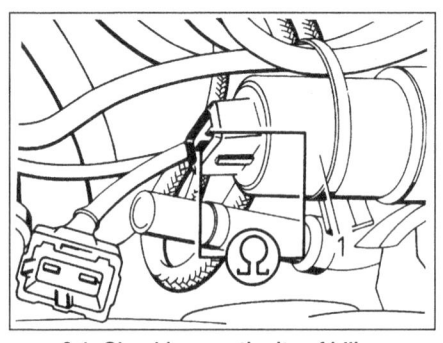

4C•4 Fuel and exhaust systems - K-Jetronic fuel injection - 16 valve engines

3.1 Checking continuity of idling stabilisation control valve wiring

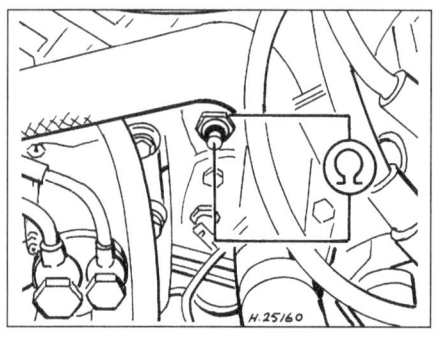

3.2 Checking temperature sender resistance

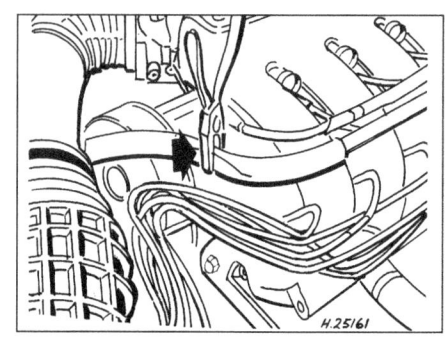

3.4 Checking idle stabilisation valve by pinching hose (arrowed)

8 Check that the mixture (CO reading) is as specified. Temporarily block off the exhaust tailpipe not fitted with the analyser probe while making the check. If necessary, turn the mixture screw as required after removing its cap. A special key is necessary in order to turn the screw but a suitable tool may be used as an alternative. Note that the screw must not be depressed or lifted and that the engine must not be revved with the tool in position.

9 Refit the crankcase ventilation hose. If the CO reading increases, the engine oil is diluted with fuel and should be renewed. Alternatively, if an oil change is not due, a long fast drive will reduce the amount of fuel in the oil.

10 Reconnect the wiring plug and remove the test instruments. Note that after reconnecting the wiring plug, the stabilisation system will return the idling to the specified speed.

3 Idle speed stabilisation system - testing

1 Check that the stabilisation control valve buzzes when the ignition is switched on. If not, use an ohmmeter to check the valve continuity after pulling off the connector **(see illustration)**.

2 Similarly, check the system temperature sender resistance at the following temperatures **(see illustration)**:
 a) At 20°C - approximately 1000 ohms
 b) At 60°C - approximately 250 ohms
 c) At 100°C - approximately 75 ohms

3 If the system fault cannot be traced using the previous test then check all associated wiring. If necessary, renew the control unit which is located behind the centre console.

4 The operations of the control valve may be checked by connecting a multi-meter to it. With a tachometer connected, run the engine (hot) at idle speed and note the control current. Now pinch the hose shown **(see illustration)** and check that the current rises. Release the hose, increase the engine speed to 1300 rpm and actuate the throttle valve switch. The control current should drop below 430 mA. With the wiring disconnected as described in paragraph 6, Section 2, the control current should be constant between 415 and 445 mA.

4 Overrun cut-off valve - testing

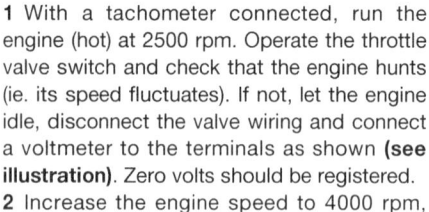

1 With a tachometer connected, run the engine (hot) at 2500 rpm. Operate the throttle valve switch and check that the engine hunts (ie. its speed fluctuates). If not, let the engine idle, disconnect the valve wiring and connect a voltmeter to the terminals as shown **(see illustration)**. Zero volts should be registered.

2 Increase the engine speed to 4000 rpm, then quickly close the throttle. At 1400 rpm, battery voltage should be indicated.

3 If necessary, renew the control unit which is located behind the centre console.

5 Diaphragm pressure switch - testing

Pull the wiring connector from the switch, then connect an ohmmeter to the switch terminals **(see illustration)**.

With the engine idling, the reading should be infinity. Quickly open and close the throttle and check that the resistance drops briefly then rises to infinity.

6 Throttle valve switch - testing

1 Pull the wiring connector from the throttle valve switch.

2 Using an ohmmeter, check that with the throttle closed there is zero resistance between terminals 1 and 2 but a reading of infinity between terminals 2 and 3. With the throttle open, the readings should be reversed **(see illustration)**.

3 To adjust the switch, insert a 0.10 mm feeler blade between the throttle lever and stop **(see illustration)**, then loosen the screws and move the switch towards the lever until the contacts are heard to click. Tighten the screws on completion and remove the feeler blade.

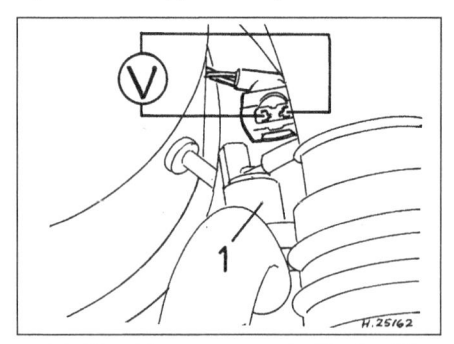

4.1 Checking overrun cut-off valve (1)

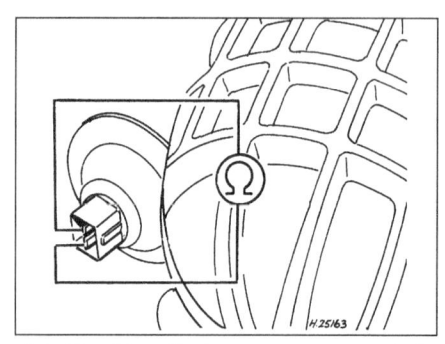

5.1 Checking diaphragm pressure switch

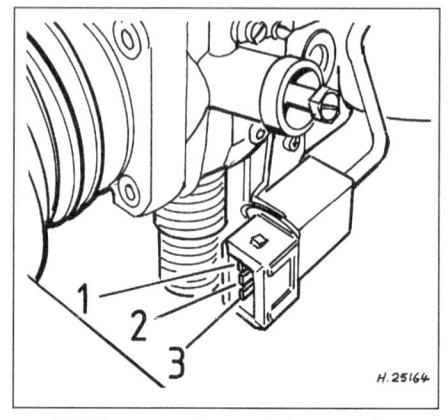

6.2 Throttle valve switch connector terminals

See text for terminal identification

Fuel and exhaust systems - K-Jetronic fuel injection - 16 valve engines 4C•5

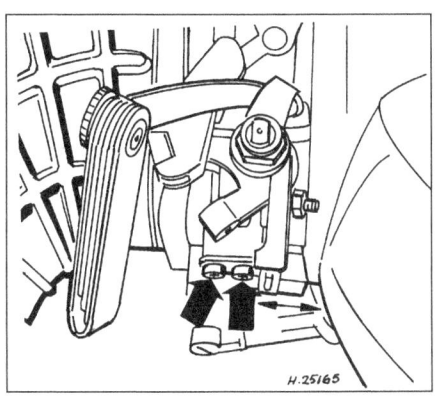

6.3 Throttle valve switch adjustment

7 Inlet manifold - removal and refitting

The inlet manifold is in two sections. When refitting the upper section, fully tighten the nuts securing it to the lower section first before attaching it to the rear support bracket.

8 Exhaust system - inspection, removal and refitting

The exhaust system incorporates four silencers together with twin downpipes and tailpipes **(see illustration)**.

The manifold/downpipe flange is of standard type with a gasket. Refer to Section 20 in Part A of this Chapter for the relevant procedures.

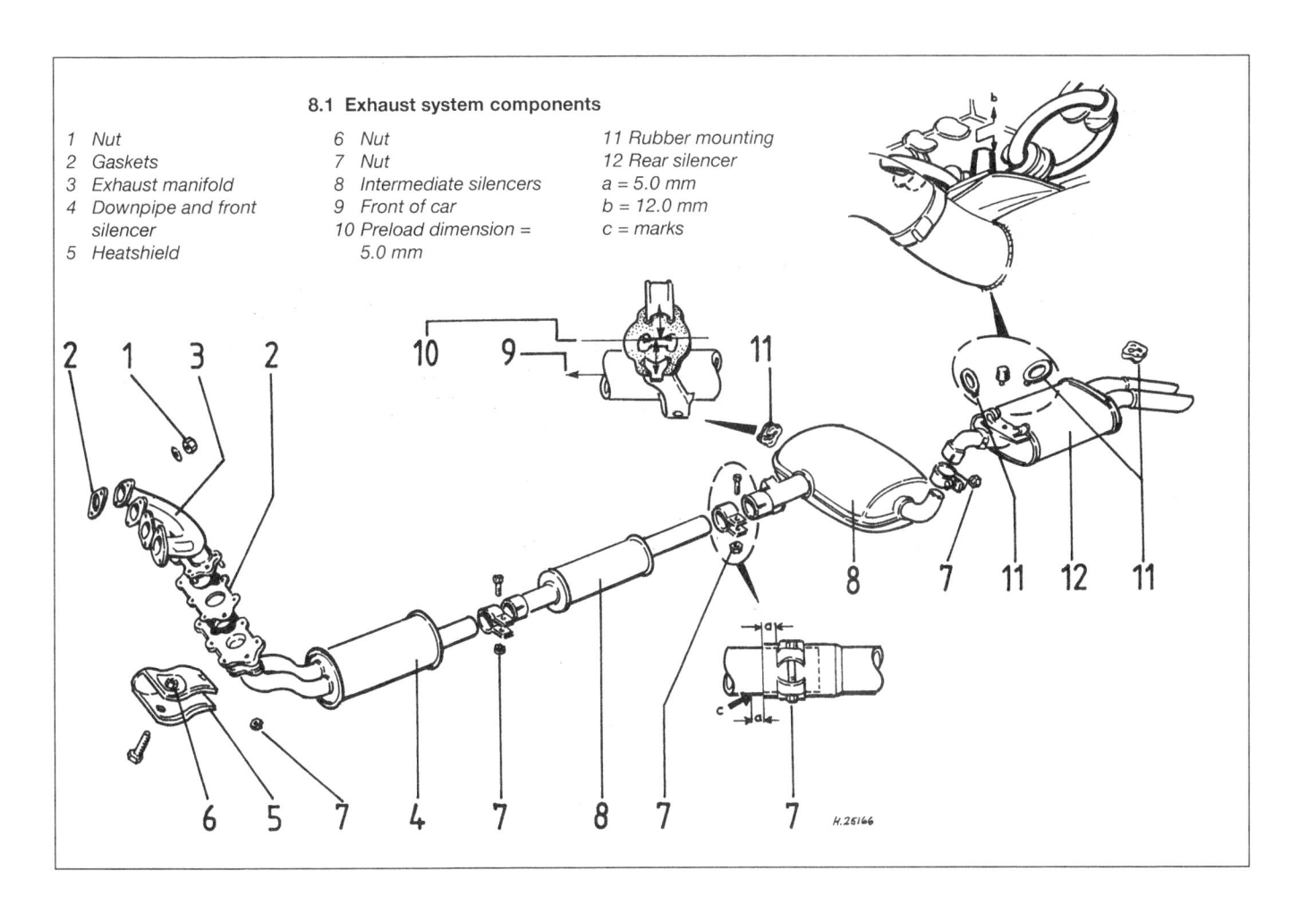

8.1 Exhaust system components

1 Nut
2 Gaskets
3 Exhaust manifold
4 Downpipe and front silencer
5 Heatshield
6 Nut
7 Nut
8 Intermediate silencers
9 Front of car
10 Preload dimension = 5.0 mm
11 Rubber mounting
12 Rear silencer
a = 5.0 mm
b = 12.0 mm
c = marks

… 4D•1

Chapter 4 Part D:
Fuel and exhaust systems - Mono Jetronic fuel injection

The following information is a revision of, or supplementary to, that contained in Part B of this Chapter

Contents

Air cleaner element - renewal	2	General information and precautions	1
Air inlet duct and manifold - removal and refitting	3	Idle speed and mixture (CO content) - testing	5
Air inlet pre-heater - testing	4	Idle switch control valve - testing	6
Fuel injector - testing, removal and refitting	7	Injector unit housing - removal and refitting	8
Fuel pump - testing, removal and refitting	10	Throttle damper - adjustment	9

Degrees of difficulty

Easy, suitable for novice with little experience	**Fairly easy**, suitable for beginner with some experience	**Fairly difficult**, suitable for competent DIY mechanic	**Difficult**, suitable for experienced DIY mechanic	**Very difficult**, suitable for expert DIY or professional

Specifications

Injection system
Type	Mono Jetronic, central injection system
Application	1.8 litre (code RP) engine
System pressure	0.8 to 1.2 bar
Idle speed	750 to 950 rpm (not adjustable)
CO content %	0.2 to 1.2
Holding pressure (system off for 5 minutes)	0.5 bar
Injector resistance	1.2 to 1.6 ohm

Torque wrench settings
	Nm	lbf ft
Air inlet manifold	10	7
Injector holder	5	3.7
Throttle valve positioner	6	4.4
Inlet manifold-to-injector unit flange	13	9
Inlet manifold	25	18
Inlet manifold pre-heater	10	7

4D•2 Fuel and exhaust systems - Mono Jetronic fuel injection

1 General information and precautions

General information

The Mono-Jetronic central fuel injection system is fitted to the 1.8 litre (code RP) engine. It is a simplified method of fuel injection **(see illustrations)**.

Fuel is injected into the inlet manifold by a single solenoid valve (fuel injector) mounted centrally in the top of the injector unit housing. The length of time for which the injector remains open determines the quantity of fuel reaching the cylinders for combustion. The electrical signals which determine the fuel injector opening duration are calculated by the Electronic Control Unit (ECU) from information supplied by its network of sensors. Fuel pressure is regulated mechanically.

The signals fed to the ECU include the following:

a) *The engine coolant temperature*
b) *The engine speed and crankshaft position - from the distributor*
c) *The position of the throttle valve plate - from the throttle position sensor*
d) *The oxygen content in the exhaust gases - via a sensor (Lambda probe) in the exhaust manifold*

Using the information gathered from the various sensors, the ECU sends out signals to control the system actuators as required.

The ECU also has a diagnostic function which can be used in conjunction with special VW test equipment for fault diagnosis. With the exception of basic checks to ensure that all relevant wiring and hoses are in good condition and securely connected, fault diagnosis should be entrusted to a VW dealer.

Basic testing can be carried out on the system components covered in the following text. More detailed testing can be carried out by using specialised equipment but this must be entrusted to a VW dealer.

Precautions

Refer to Sections 1 and 2 in Part B of this Chapter.

2 Air cleaner element - renewal

Refer to Chapter 1, Section 32

3 Air inlet duct and manifold - removal and refitting

1 Undo the retaining clips and release the duct from the manifold and air cleaner.
2 To remove the manifold from the top of the injector unit housing, detach the hoses from the temperature sensor unit on the manifold whilst noting their fitted positions.
3 Undo the retaining bolt and lift the manifold, together with its gasket, from the top face of the injector unit.
4 Refit in the reverse order of removal.

4 Air inlet pre-heater - testing

1 With the engine cold, detach and remove the upper section of the air cleaner followed by the filter element.
2 Check the air flap valve in the base of the lower section of the air cleaner for freedom of movement. Ensure that when closed, it shuts off the warm air passage.
3 Whilst running the engine at idle speed, check that the flap closes off the cold air passage.
4 To check that the temperature regulator is operating correctly, disconnect the two hoses from it **(see illustration)**, connect them together and then note if the warm air passage remains closed off. If this is the case, the vacuum unit is defective. Where the flap valve closes off the cold air passage, the temperature regulator is at fault and in need of replacement.
5 The position of the flap valve when the engine is running is dependent on the temperature of the regulator. When the temperature is below 35°C, the temperature regulator should be open and the cold air

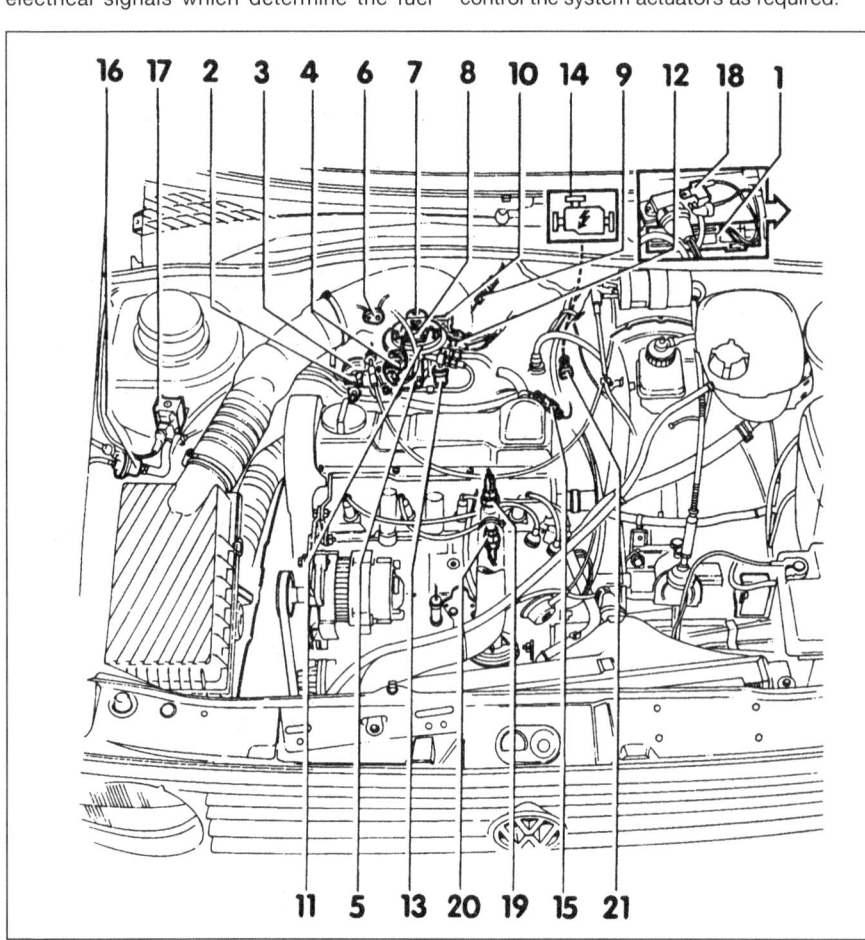

1.0a Mono-Jetronic system component location

1 *Electronic Control unit (ECU)*
2 *Connector (throttle valve positioner and idle switch)*
3 *Throttle damper*
4 *Connector (injector and air intake temperature sender)*
5 *Throttle valve positioner and idle switch*
6 *Intake air pre-heater temperature regulator*
7 *Injector and air temperature sender*
8 *Fuel pressure regulator*
9 *Inlet manifold pre-heater*
10 *Injection timing vacuum control valve*
11 *Injector*
12 *Throttle valve potentiometer*
13 *Water separator (throttle valve potentiometer)*
14 *Self diagnosis fault warning lamp*
15 *Lambda probe connector*
16 *Activated charcoal filter solenoid valve*
17 *Activated charcoal filter solenoid valve*
18 *Injector series resistor*
19 *Thermoswitch for manifold pre-heater*
20 *Coolant temperature sender*
21 *Self diagnosis plug*

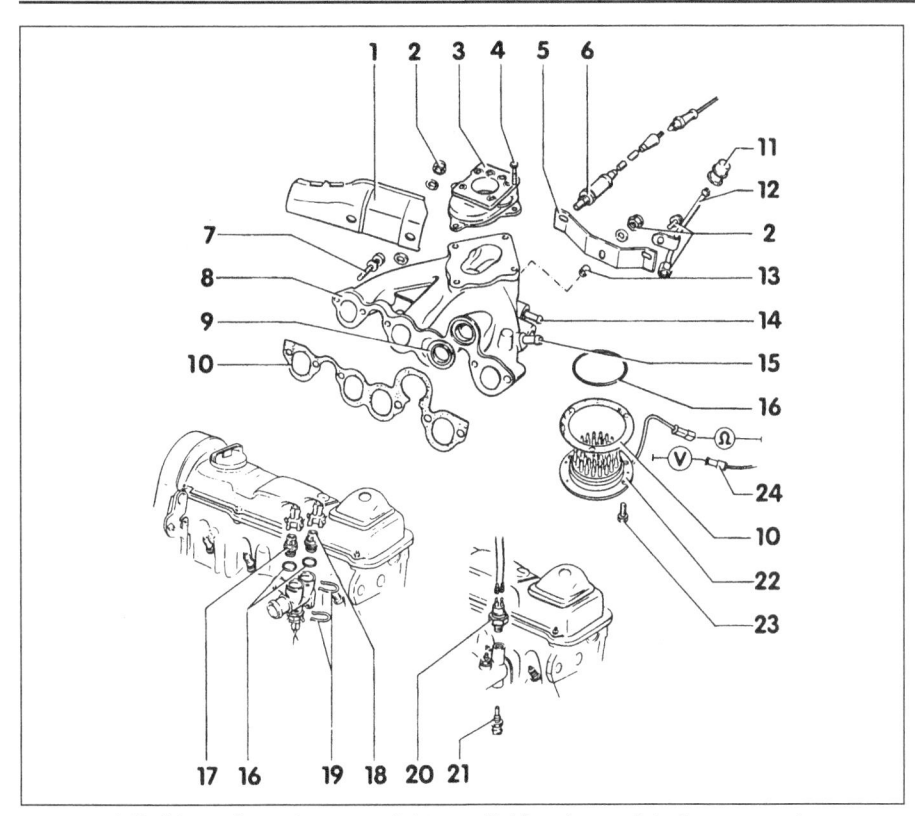

Fuel and exhaust systems - Mono Jetronic fuel injection 4D•3

1.0b Mono-Jetronic system inlet manifold and associated components

1 Warm air deflector
2 Nut
3 Flange
4 Bolt
5 Bracket
6 Lambda probe
7 Bolt
8 Inlet manifold
9 O-ring
10 Gasket
11 Cap
12 CO measuring pipe
13 Spacer
14 Coolant hose connection
15 Vacuum connection
16 O-ring
17 Thermoswitch (red) for manifold pre-heater – from 8/1988
18 Coolant temperature sender (blue)
19 Retainer spring
20 Thermoswitch (red) for manifold pre-heater – up to 7/1988
21 Coolant sender unit
22 Inlet manifold pre-heater
23 Screw
24 Connector

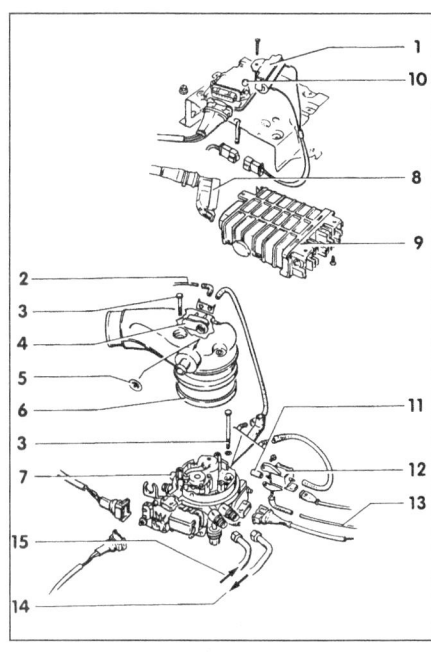

6.1 Injector, ECU and associated components

1 Series resistor
2 Vacuum hose
3 Fixing screw
4 Temperature regulator
5 Poppet valve
6 O-ring
7 Injector unit
8 Connector
9 Electronic Control Unit (ECU)
10 Spacer
11 Flap vent
12 Idle switch control valve
13 Vacuum pipe
14 Fuel return pipe
15 Fuel feed pipe

passage closed off. At temperatures above 45°C, the regulator should be closed and the warm air passage sealed off.

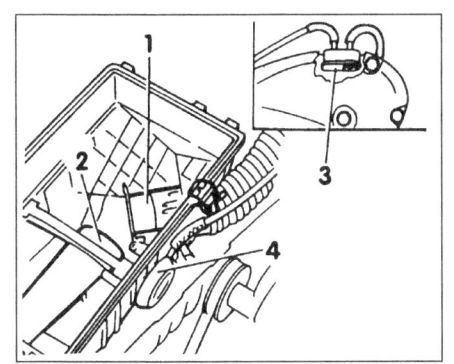

4.4 Air intake components in air cleaner housing

1 Warm air nozzle
2 Cold air nozzle
3 Temperature regulator
4 Vacuum unit

5 Idle speed and mixture (CO content) - testing

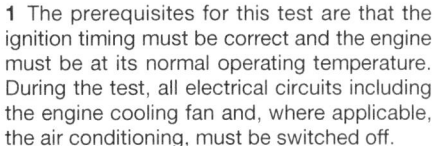

1 The prerequisites for this test are that the ignition timing must be correct and the engine must be at its normal operating temperature. During the test, all electrical circuits including the engine cooling fan and, where applicable, the air conditioning, must be switched off.

2 The ignition must be switched off before the test meter is attached to check engine speed. An exhaust gas analyser must be used to check the CO content from the exhaust.

3 The idle speed and mixture are not adjustable on this system and if they are not as specified, all that can be done is to inspect the various fuel system and associated vacuum electrical connections to ensure that they are in good condition and securely connected. If found to be in good condition, it will be necessary to have the system checked out by a VW dealer using specialised testing equipment to identify and rectify the fault.

6 Idle switch control valve - testing

This device is attached to the throttle position sensor (see illustration) and its function is to control the ignition timing vacuum advance. If defective, it can cause problems with the idle speed and/or the overrun cut-off.

A simple test can be made by switching on the ignition, then opening and closing the throttle valve. Listen to hear if the control valve clicks twice. If this is proved to be in order, start the engine, allow it to idle and then momentarily detach the wiring connector from the control valve and reconnect it. The idle speed should momentarily increase and then drop back to normal. If not, the control valve is faulty and should be renewed.

7 Fuel injector - testing, removal and refitting

Testing

1 Run the engine up to its normal operating temperature, then detach and remove the air inlet duct from the top of the injector unit.

4D•4 Fuel and exhaust systems - Mono Jetronic fuel injection

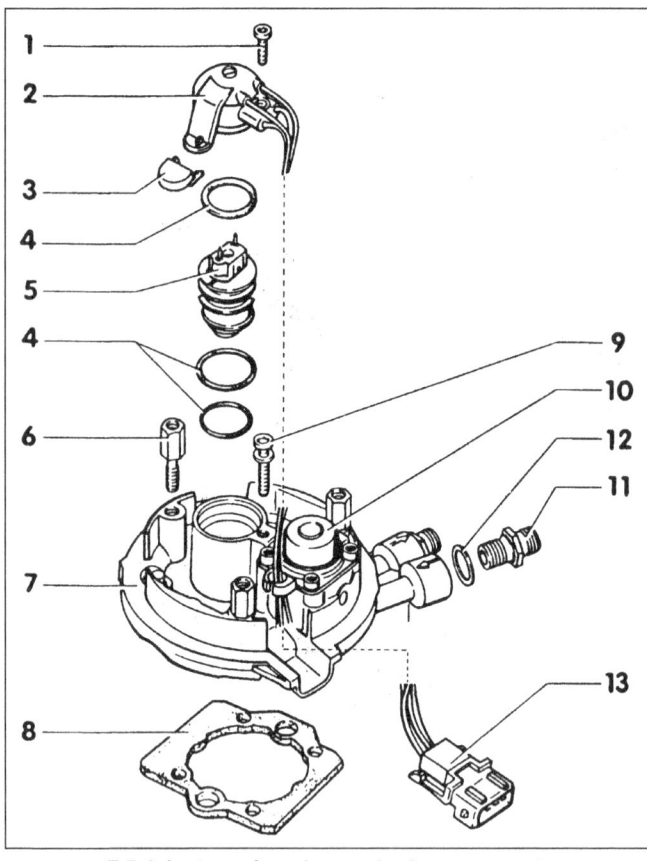

7.5 Injector unit and upper body components

1. Screw
2. Injector holder
3. Protector cap
4. O-ring
5. Injector
6. Stud
7. Injector upper body
8. Gasket
9. Screw
10. Pressure regulator
11. Fuel pipe adapter
12. Seal ring
13. Connector

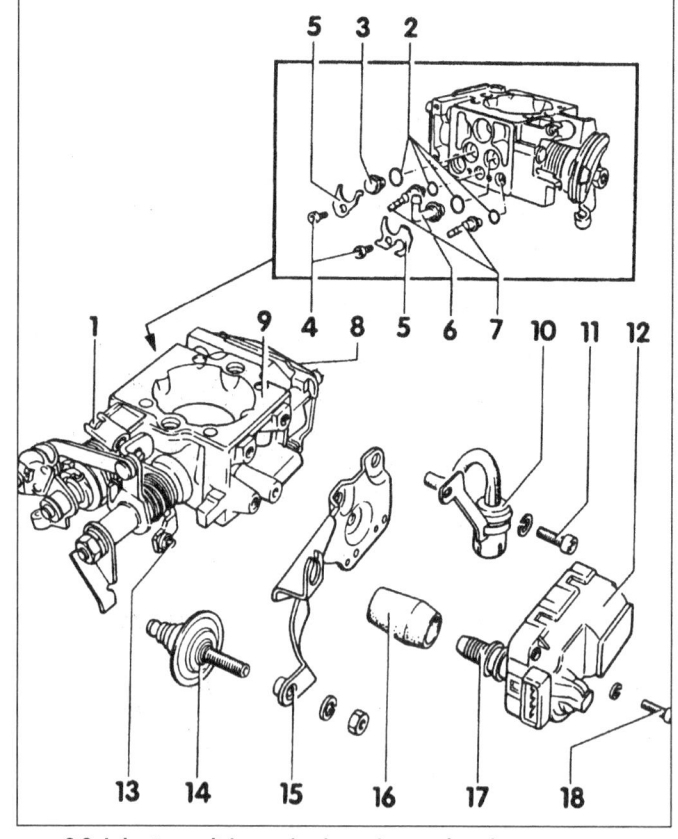

8.3 Injector unit lower body and associated components

1. Throttle valve stop screw
2. O-ring
3. Plug
4. Screw
5. Retainer
6. Connector
7. Connector
8. Throttle valve potentiometer
9. Injector lower body
10. Water separator
11. Screw
12. Throttle valve positioner
13. Throttle damper adjuster screw
14. Throttle damper
15. Bracket
16. Protector grommet (for idle switch)
17. Idle switch
18. Screw

2 With the engine running at idle speed, look into the top of the injector unit and check the fuel spray pattern which should be visible on the throttle valve.

3 Increase the engine speed to 3000 rpm then snap shut the throttle and check that the fuel spray from the injector is momentarily interrupted. Turn the ignition off and then check that no more than two drops of fuel per minute leak from the injector. This indicates that the overrun cut-off is functioning in a satisfactory manner.

Removal

4 Remove the inlet duct and manifold.

5 Undo the retaining screw and lift clear the injector holder and O-ring seal from the top of the injector. Note its orientation, then grip and pull the injector from its location in the housing. Remove the O-ring seals **(see illustration)**.

Refitting

6 Refit in the reverse order of removal. The O-ring seals must be renewed and lightly lubricated prior to fitting.

8 Injector unit housing - removal and refitting

Removal

1 Remove the air inlet duct and manifold.

2 Detach the fuel feed and return lines from their connections on the side of the injector unit. Allow for fuel spillage as they are detached and plug the hoses to prevent further leakage and the ingress of dirt.

3 Disconnect the wiring plugs from their connections on the injector unit **(see illustration)**.

4 Disconnect the accelerator cable from the throttle lever at the injector unit.

5 Undo the retaining screws and withdraw the injector unit housing from the inlet manifold. Remove the gasket and if damaged or in doubtful condition, renew it when refitting the injector unit.

Refitting

6 Refit in the reverse order of removal. Ensure that the mating faces of the housing and fuel lines are clean before reconnecting.

9 Throttle damper - adjustment

When the throttle valve is in the closed position, the throttle damper plunger should be pressed into the damper a minimum distance of 4.0 mm by the operating lever **(see illustration)**.

If adjustment is required, loosen off the adjuster locknut then rotate the damper screw to the point where the lever is just in contact with the plunger. Now turn the damper four and a half turns towards the lever, then retighten the locknut.

10 Fuel pump - testing, removal and refitting

From mid 1989, certain models fitted with the Mono Jetronic system were fitted with a single fuel pump in the fuel tank rather than the previous arrangement of one in the tank and a secondary pump outside the tank. The pump can be tested in the same manner as that for the "in-tank" dual pump referred to in Part F of this Chapter, Section 12.

The fuel pump can be removed in a similar manner to that described for the fuel gauge sender unit in Part A of this Chapter, Section 8.

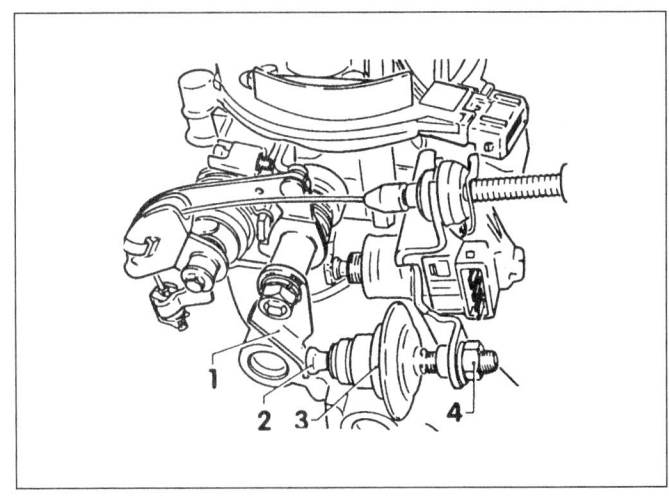

9.1 Throttle damper assembly

1 Throttle lever   3 Damper
2 Plunger   4 Locknut

Chapter 4 Part E:
Fuel and exhaust systems - Digijet fuel injection

Contents

Air cleaner element - renewal 2	Idle speed and mixture - adjustment 3
Airflow meter - testing 4	Inlet air pre-heater - testing 5
Evaporative fuel control system 10	Pre-throttle valve clearance - adjustment 8
Fuel injectors - testing 6	System components - removal and refitting 9
General information and precautions 1	Throttle valve switch - testing 7

Degrees of difficulty

Easy, suitable for novice with little experience	Fairly easy, suitable for beginner with some experience	Fairly difficult, suitable for competent DIY mechanic	Difficult, suitable for experienced DIY mechanic	Very difficult, suitable for expert DIY or professional

Specifications

Injection system

Type	Digijet
Application	1.3 litre (code NZ) engine
Control unit code colour:	
Up to July 1989	Copper-brown sticker
From July 1989	Blue sticker
System pressure (approx):	
Vacuum hose connected	2.5 bar
Vacuum hose disconnected	3.0 bar
Idle speed:	
Up to July 1989	750 to 850 rpm
July 1989	880 to 980 rpm
Speed limiter	6400 to 6500 rpm
CO content %:	
Up to July 1989	0.3 to 0.11
July 1989	0.3 to 1.5
Injectors:	
Resistance	15 to 20 ohms
Spray pattern	Conical

4E•2 Fuel and exhaust systems - Digijet fuel injection

1 General information and precautions

General information

The Digijet fuel injection system is fitted to the 1.3 litre (code NZ) engine (see illustrations).

The system is regulated in accordance with instructions received from a control unit, located in the bulkhead plenum chamber on the left-hand side. This unit was modified in July of 1989 and can be identified by a blue sticker on the unit, earlier units having a copper-brown sticker.

The fuel pump and its location is identical to that described in Part F of this Chapter for the Digifant fuel injection system.

The fuel tank and its associated components are identical to those shown in Part A of this Chapter, the only difference being the feed line attachment to the gravity valve from the charcoal filter.

Precautions

Refer to Sections 1 and 2 in Part B of this Chapter.

2 Air cleaner element - renewal

Refer to Chapter 1, Section 32

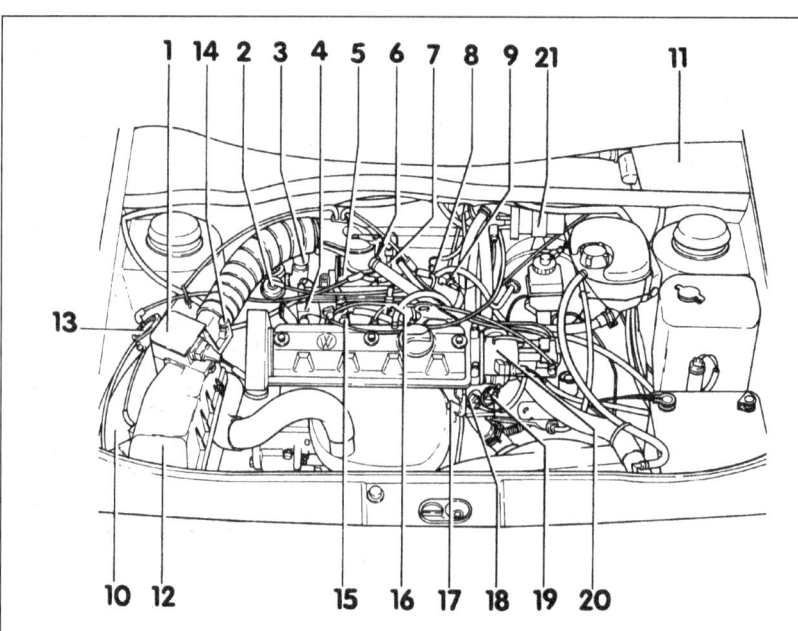

1.0a Digijet fuel injection system component location

1. Airflow meter
2. Fuel pressure regulator
3. Heater element
4. Injector
5. Throttle valve housing
6. Idle speed adjustment screw
7. Throttle valve switch
8. Auxiliary air valve connector
9. Lambda probe connector
10. Intake air preheating vacuum unit
11. Digijet control unit/TCI-H switch unit
12. Air cleaner
13. Cut-off valve
14. Mixture (CO) adjustment screw
15. Spark plug
16. Auxiliary air valve
17. CO measuring pipe
18. Temperature sender (blue) for Digijet system
19. Temperature sender (black) for coolant temperature gauge
20. Distributor (with Hall sender)
21. Ignition coil

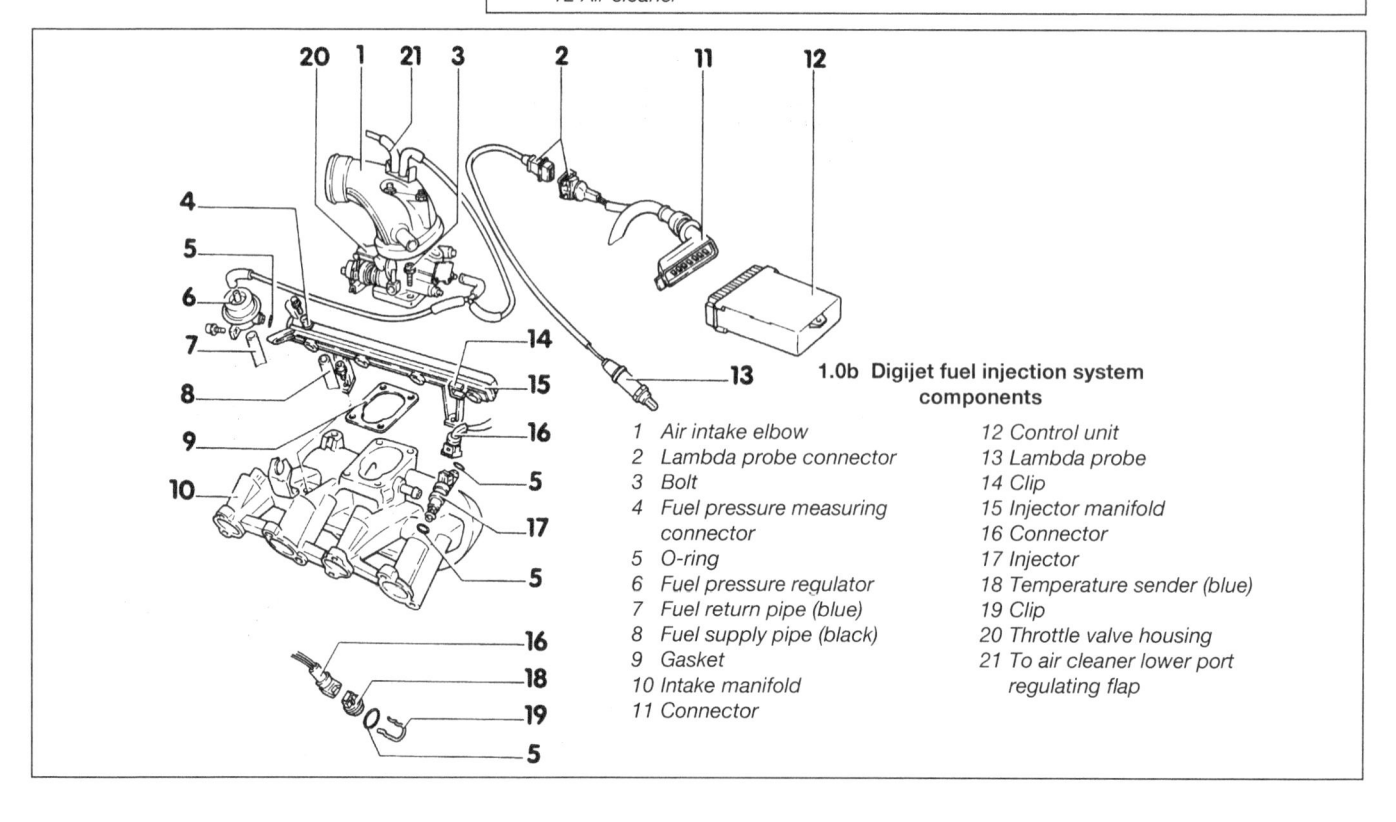

1.0b Digijet fuel injection system components

1. Air intake elbow
2. Lambda probe connector
3. Bolt
4. Fuel pressure measuring connector
5. O-ring
6. Fuel pressure regulator
7. Fuel return pipe (blue)
8. Fuel supply pipe (black)
9. Gasket
10. Intake manifold
11. Connector
12. Control unit
13. Lambda probe
14. Clip
15. Injector manifold
16. Connector
17. Injector
18. Temperature sender (blue)
19. Clip
20. Throttle valve housing
21. To air cleaner lower port regulating flap

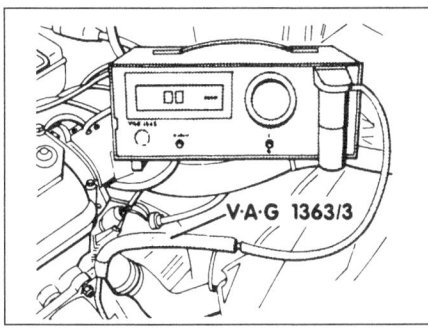

Fuel and exhaust systems - Digijet fuel injection   4E•3

3.4 CO analyser and connecting pipe

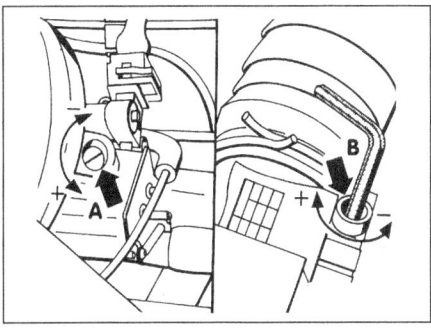

3.7 Idle speed (A) and mixture adjustment (B) screws

3 Idle speed and mixture - adjustment

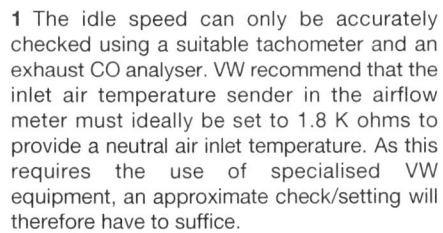

1 The idle speed can only be accurately checked using a suitable tachometer and an exhaust CO analyser. VW recommend that the inlet air temperature sender in the airflow meter must ideally be set to 1.8 K ohms to provide a neutral air inlet temperature. As this requires the use of specialised VW equipment, an approximate check/setting will therefore have to suffice.
2 When checking or making any adjustments to the idle speed, it is important to adhere to the following:
 a) *The engine must be at its normal operating temperature*
 b) *All electrical components must be switched off, including the cooling fan*
 c) *The ignition timing adjustment must be correct*
3 Pull free the crankcase ventilation hose from the pressure regulating valve and plug it.
4 With the ignition switched off, connect a tachometer in accordance with the manufacturer's instructions, then connect the CO analyser to the measuring pipe **(see illustration)**. An adapter will probably be needed to ensure a good seal between the analyser hose and measuring pipe.
5 Disconnect the Lambda probe wiring plug from its in-line connector.
6 Start the engine and check that the idle speed and CO content are as specified. If the idle speed is too high, check that the throttle valve is fully closing before making any adjustments to the idle speed.
7 If adjustment to the idle speed and/or the mixture (CO content) is required, turn the appropriate adjuster screw as necessary **(see illustration)**.
8 If the CO content is to be adjusted, the mixture screw's tamperproof cap will have to be carefully prised free and a suitable Allen key used to make the adjustment. On models produced from July 1989 on, the idle speed should initially be between 900 to 1000 rpm and the CO content between 1.0 and 1.4%. When the Lambda probe is reconnected, the idle speed and the CO content should settle down to the specified setting. Fit a new tamperproof cap over the mixture screw on completion.
9 With the idle speed/CO content correct, disconnect the analyser and reconnect the Lambda probe wiring plug.

4 Airflow meter - testing

The efficiency of the airflow meter in the inlet manifold is checked by measuring the resistance value between contacts 1 and 4 of the control unit plug **(see illustrations)**.
The potentiometer is measured in the same manner by connecting the probes to terminals 2 and 3 and simultaneously operating the airflow sensor plate. The resistance reading must be seen to fluctuate.

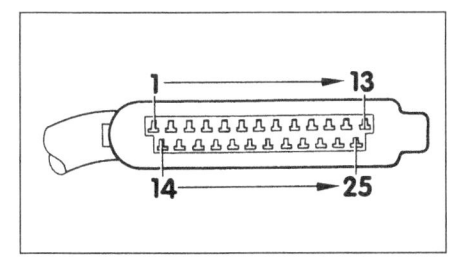

4.1a Control unit plug showing terminal connectors

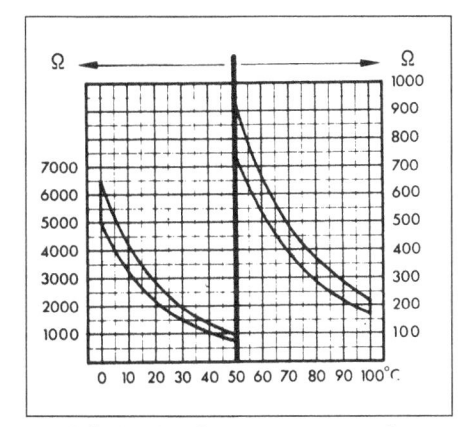

4.1b Intake air temperature sender resistance graph

5 Inlet air pre-heater - testing

1 The inlet air pre-heater is fitted to engines manufactured from September 1989.
2 A hot air blower such as a hair dryer can be used to test the pre-heater. First release the retaining clips, lift the lid from the air cleaner unit and remove the element - see illustration, Section 32, Chapter 1.
3 With the engine cold and with the air temperature around the pre-heater between 5 to 15° C, the warm air flap valve must be seen to be open. On heating up the air temperature in the area of the air inlet valve to over 20°C, the valve should be seen to close.

6 Fuel injectors - testing

Refer to Section 13 in Part B of this Chapter and proceed as described. Note however that the dribble test in paragraph 5 differs. Switch on the ignition for a period of 5 seconds and check that no more than 2 drips per minute leak from any of the injectors.

7 Throttle valve switch - testing

1 A multi-meter (set to the resistance scale) will be required to make this test.
2 Pull free the wiring connector from the throttle valve switch, connect up the meter probes between the switch contacts and check that the reading is zero ohms **(see illustration)**. Operate the throttle to fully open it (a high 'infinite' resistance reading will be shown on the meter), then slowly close the throttle to the point where 0.3 mm clearance exists between the throttle lever and the stop screw. Check that zero ohms is shown on the meter.

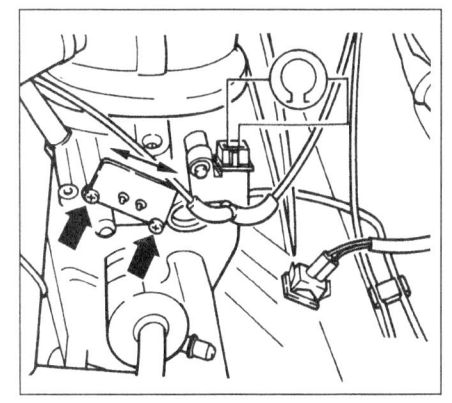

7.2 Throttle valve switch test meter connections and securing screws

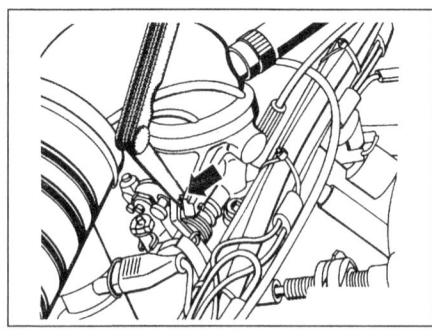

4E•4 Fuel and exhaust systems - Digijet fuel injection

7.3 Feeler blade location for throttle valve switch check

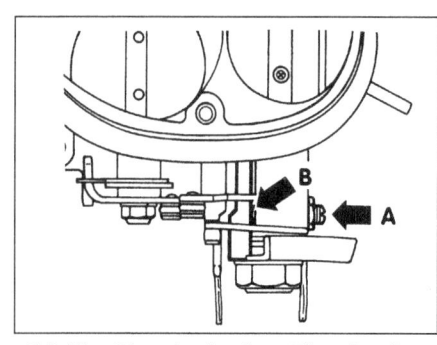

7.5 Throttle valve basic setting showing limiting screw (A) and stop (B)

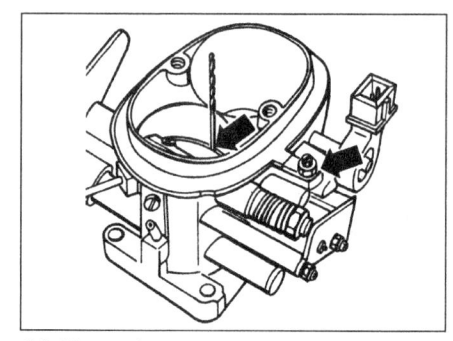

8.2 Measuring pre-throttle valve clearance using 0.5 mm twist drill

Adjustment screw and locknut also indicated

3 Insert a feeler blade of 0.3 mm thickness between the lever and the stop screw to ensure the correct clearance **(see illustration)**. If adjustment is required, loosen off the throttle valve switch screws then move the switch in the required direction to the point where the zero ohms reading is shown. Retighten the screws. Fully open the throttle valve and check that it is switched 'on' as described above. Reconnect the wiring connector to the switch on completion of the check.

4 It should be noted that the throttle valve basic setting is made during production and in normal circumstances, it should not require further adjustment.

5 If minor adjustment to the valve setting is necessary, it can be made by loosening off the limiting screw to provide a minimal clearance between the screw and the stop, then tightening the screw until it just comes into contact with the stop **(see illustration)**. This setting is critical and to judge when the contact point is made, a piece of thin paper should be positioned between the lever and stop screw. Move the paper and simultaneously tighten the screw to the point where the paper is just clamped by the screw. From this point, tighten the screw a further half turn.

6 If adjustment has been made, the idle speed and mixture should be checked, as should the throttle valve switch.

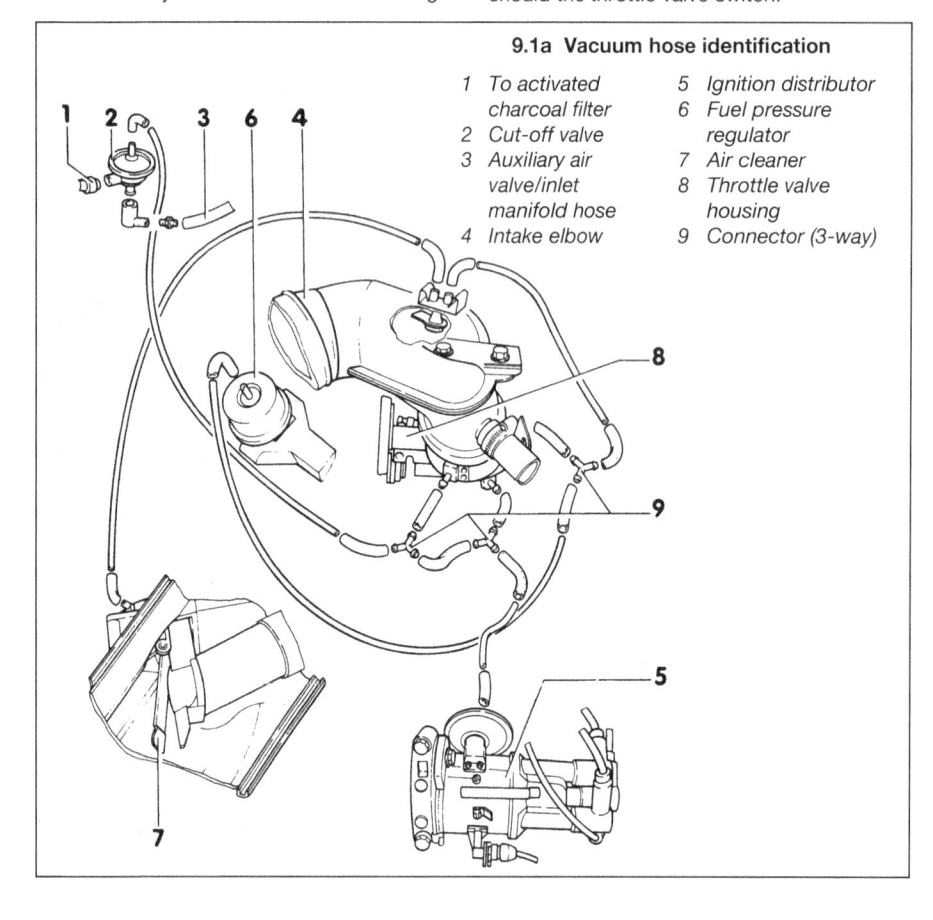

8 Pre-throttle valve clearance - adjustment

The pre-throttle valve clearance is set during production and under normal circumstances should not require checking and adjustment.

If the clearance is to be checked, first remove the air cleaner unit. Using a suitable 0.5 mm diameter twist drill, check the clearance at the point indicated **(see illustration)**. If adjustment is required, loosen off the locknut and turn the adjuster screw in the required direction to set the clearance, then retighten the locknut.

9 System components - removal and refitting

By reference to the illustrations accompanying this Chapter, removal and refitting of the various components of the system are self explanatory. However, the following special points should be noted:

a) Observe the precautions described in Sections 1 and 2, Part B of this Chapter, whenever any parts of the system are to be removed and refitted.
b) To ensure correct reassembly, ensure that the routings and connections of the system wiring, fuel and vacuum components are noted prior to disconnection **(see illustrations)**.
c) If the injector manifold is to be removed, it is first necessary to detach and remove the air inlet elbow complete with the throttle valve housing.
d) Any component O-rings and gaskets must be renewed.
e) The accelerator cable removal, refitting and adjustment procedures are as described in Part A of this Chapter.
f) The fuel tank and its associated components are removed in a similar manner to that described in Part A of this Chapter, the only difference being the

9.1a Vacuum hose identification

1 To activated charcoal filter
2 Cut-off valve
3 Auxiliary air valve/inlet manifold hose
4 Intake elbow
5 Ignition distributor
6 Fuel pressure regulator
7 Air cleaner
8 Throttle valve housing
9 Connector (3-way)

Fuel and exhaust systems - Digijet fuel injection 4E•5

feed line attachment to the gravity valve from the charcoal filter.
g) *The fuel pump and its location is identical to that described in Part F of this Chapter.*

10 Evaporative fuel control system

1 The function of this system is to aid evaporative fuel control by collecting and recirculating the fuel vapours in the fuel tank to prevent them from escaping to the atmosphere **(see illustration)**.
2 When the engine is stopped or idling, fuel vapour is collected by the charcoal canister where it is stored until the engine is started and run above idle speed. The vapour is then transferred from the canister, through a cut-off valve, into the air filter and inlet manifold to be burnt off during the normal combustion process.
3 The charcoal canister is secured to the base of the air cleaner unit and access to it for inspection or renewal is possible after first removing the air cleaner.

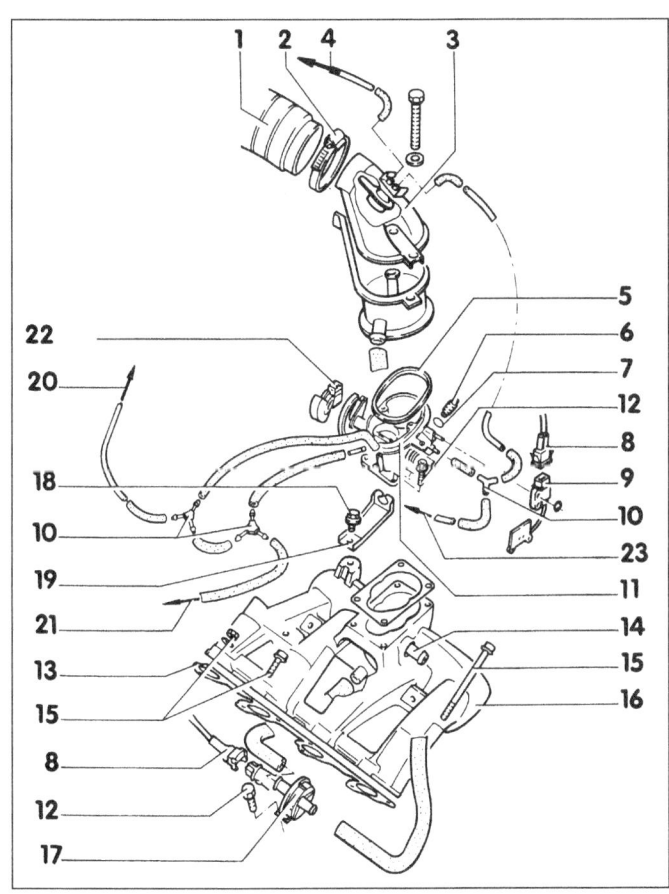

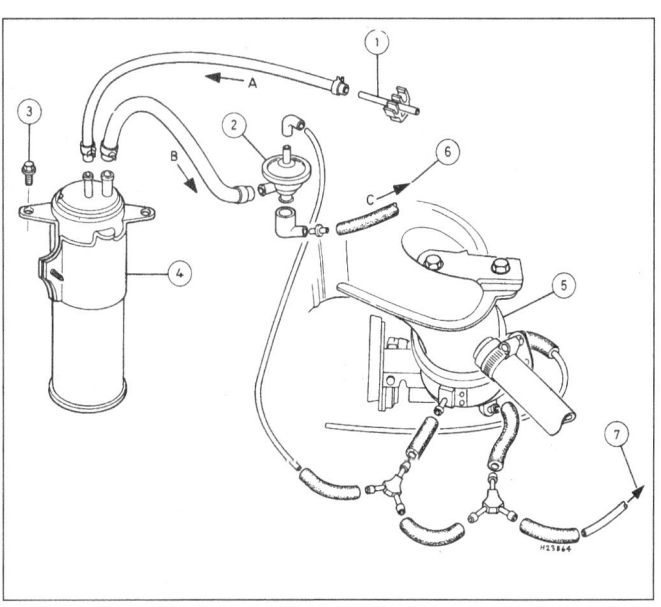

10.1 Activated charcoal filter system components

A	Fuel tank vapour route when engine is idling or stopped	3	Fixing screw
B/C	Fuel tank vapour route when engine is run above idle speed	4	Activated charcoal canister
		5	Throttle valve housing
1	Pipe (to fuel tank gravity valve in filler line)	6	Hose (auxiliary air valve/inlet manifold)
2	Cut-off valve	7	Hose (to ignition distributor)

9.1b Air intake manifold and associated components

1 Intake hose
2 Clip
3 Elbow
4 Hose to regulating flap
5 Gasket
6 Idle speed adjusting screw
7 O-ring
8 Connector
9 Throttle valve switch
10 Angled connector
11 Throttle valve housing
12 Screw
13 Gasket
14 Brake servo vacuum connection
15 Bolt
16 Intake manifold
17 Auxiliary air valve
18 Bolt
19 Bracket
20 Vacuum hose (to ignition distributor)
21 Vacuum hose (to non-return valve)
22 Fast idle cam
23 Fuel pressure regulator hose

Chapter 4 Part F:
Fuel and exhaust systems - Digifant fuel injection

The following information is a revision of, or supplementary to, that contained in Part B of this Chapter

Contents

Airflow meter - testing 9	General information and precautions 1
Automatic air cleaner temperature control - testing 4	Idle speed and mixture (CO content) - adjustment 2
Control unit - testing 10	Idle speed stabilisation system - testing 3
Fuel injectors - testing 8	Overrun cut-off and full throttle enrichment - testing 11
Fuel pressure regulator - testing 7	Throttle stop - adjustment 6
Fuel pumps - testing 12	Throttle valve switches - testing and adjustment 5

Degrees of difficulty

Easy, suitable for novice with little experience	Fairly easy, suitable for beginner with some experience	Fairly difficult, suitable for competent DIY mechanic	Difficult, suitable for experienced DIY mechanic	Very difficult, suitable for expert DIY or professional

Specifications

Injection system
Type	Digifant
Application	1.8 litre (codes PBX and PF) engine
System pressure at idle:	
On	Approximately 2.5 bar
Off	Approximately 3.0 bar
Idle speed	800 ± 50 rpm
CO content %	1.0 ± 0.5
Holding pressure (System off for 10 minutes)	2.0 bar minimum

Torque wrench settings
	Nm	lbf ft
Throttle valve housing	20	15
Inlet manifold	25	19
Fuel pressure regulator	15	11
Injector insert	20	15

1 General information and precautions

General information

The Digifant fuel injection system is fitted to the 1.8 litre (codes PB and PF) engine and is a fully electronic and computerised version of the K-Jetronic system described in Part B of this Chapter.

The main components include a computerised control unit, electronic injectors and various sensors to monitor engine temperature and speed, induction air flow and throttle position. The control unit determines the opening period of the injectors and also continuously adjusts ignition timing according to engine speed, load and temperature.

Precautions

Refer to Sections 1 and 2 in Part B of this Chapter whilst noting the following:

a) *Take extra care to prevent dust and dirt entering system components*
b) *Do not use compressed air or fluffy cloths for cleaning*
c) *Switch off the ignition before disconnecting any component wiring or when washing the engine*
d) *Boost-charging the battery is only permissible for one minute at 16.5 volts maximum*
e) *Disconnect both battery leads before carrying out any electric welding*

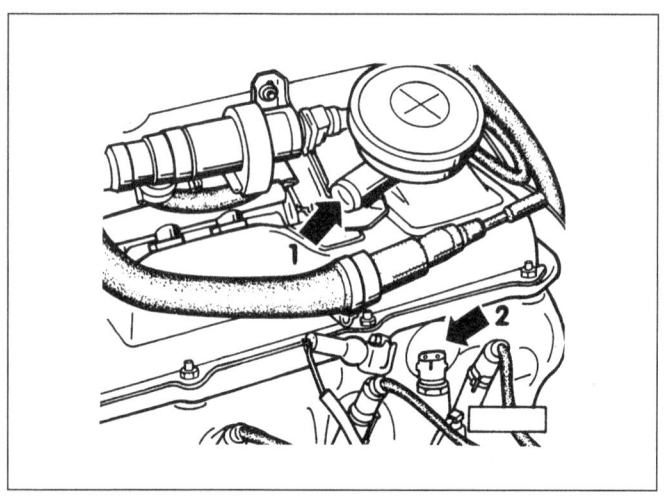

4F•2 Fuel and exhaust systems - Digifant fuel injection

2.6 Crankcase ventilation pressure regulating valve (1) and temperature sender (2)

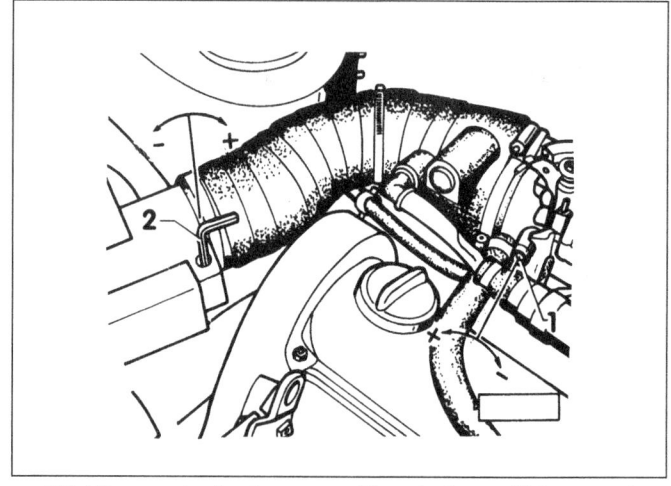

2.7 Idle speed adjusting screw (1) and mixture (CO content) adjusting screw (2)

2 Idle speed and mixture (CO content) - adjustment

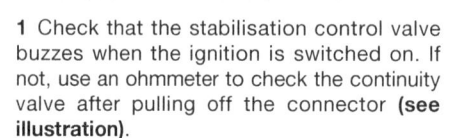

1 Run the engine until the oil temperature is at least 80°C. This should correspond to normal operating temperature.
2 Switch off all electrical components, including the air conditioning, where fitted. Note that the radiator fan must be stationary during adjustment.
3 For accurate adjustment, the throttle valve switch and idling stabilisation control valve must be functioning correctly and the ignition timing must be correct.
4 With the engine stopped, connect a tachometer to the engine. Plug one of the exhaust tailpipes and position the probe of an exhaust gas analyser in the remaining pipe.
5 Disconnect the crankcase ventilation hose from the pressure regulating valve on the valve cover and plug the hose.
6 Run the engine at idle speed. After approximately one minute, disconnect the wire from the temperature sender **(see illustration)** and quickly increase the engine speed to 3000 rpm three times.
7 With the engine idling, check the idle speed and CO content. If necessary, adjust the screws **(see illustration)**. The CO adjustment screw is fitted with a tamperproof plug at the factory. This plug should be prised out before making an adjustment.
8 Reconnect the temperature sender wire and again quickly increase the engine speed to 3000 rpm three times. With the engine idling, the idle speed and CO content should be as specified. If necessary, make any small corrections required.
9 Fit a new tamperproof plug.
10 Reconnect the crankcase ventilation hose. Note that if this increases the CO content, do not alter the adjustment. The cause is fuel dilution of the engine oil due to frequent stop/start use. A long fast drive should reduce the CO content to the correct level. Alternatively, an oil change will achieve the same objective.

3 Idle speed stabilisation system - testing

1 Check that the stabilisation control valve buzzes when the ignition is switched on. If not, use an ohmmeter to check the continuity valve after pulling off the connector **(see illustration)**.
2 Run the engine until the oil temperature is at least 80°C. This should correspond to normal operating temperature.
3 Connect a multi-meter to the stabilisation control valve in series with the existing wiring.
4 All electrical components must be switched off during the test and power steering (where fitted) centralised.
5 Run the engine at idle speed. After approximately one minute, quickly increase the engine speed to 3000 rpm three times. At idling speed, the control current should be approximately 420 ± 30 mA and fluctuating. With the temperature sender plug disconnected, the current should be approximately 420 ± 30 mA but constant.

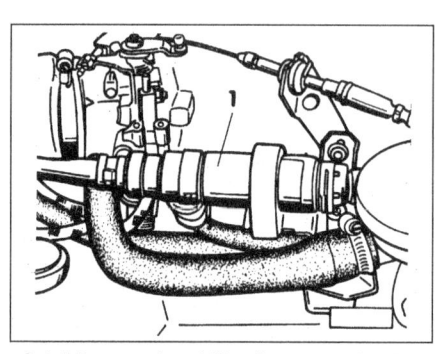

3.1 Idle speed stabilisation control valve (1)

4 Automatic air cleaner temperature control - testing

1 Disconnect the hose from the vacuum unit then remove the air cleaner cover and element.
2 Check that the flap in the lower body is closing the warm air inlet.
3 Suck on the vacuum hose and check that the flap moves freely to close the cold air inlet.
4 Flap operation may be checked with the engine idling by extending the vacuum hose and positioning a thermometer by the temperature regulator. Below 20°C, the cold air inlet must be closed. Above 30°C, the warm air inlet must be closed. Between 20°C and 30°C, the flap should be positioned midway so that both inlets are open.
5 Refit the air cleaner element and cover, then reconnect the hose.

5 Throttle valve switches - testing and adjustment

1 There are two throttle valve switches. Switch 1 monitors the throttle valve closed position and switch 2 monitors the throttle valve fully open position **(see illustration)**.
2 Disconnect the supply plug from switch 2 and check that approximately 5 volts is available across the two terminals with the ignition switched on. If not, check the wiring from the control unit.
3 Connect an ohmmeter across the terminals of switch 2, then slowly open the throttle valve until the switch points close. The gap at the throttle lever stop must be 0.20 to 0.60 mm when the points close. If necessary, adjust the position of switch 1.
4 A piece of card marked with 10° is required to check switch 2. Attach the card to the first stage throttle valve shaft.

Fuel and exhaust systems - Digifant fuel injection 4F•3

5 Fully open the throttle and align a datum with 0° on the card. Close the throttle by approximately 20°, then slowly open it until switch 2 points close. This should occur at 10° ± 2° before full throttle. If necessary, adjust the position of switch 2. Note that the throttle valve lever roller must contact the sloping part of switch 2.

6 Throttle stop - adjustment

1 Throttle stop adjustment is initially set at the factory and should not be tampered with. However, if it is accidentally disturbed, proceed as follows.
2 Back off the adjustment screw until a gap exists between the carrier lever and stop lever **(see illustration)**.
3 Turn the adjustment screw until the two levers just make contact, then continue to turn it a further half-turn. Tighten the locknut.
4 After making an adjustment, readjust the throttle valve switches, and the idle speed and mixture.

7 Fuel pressure regulator - testing

A pressure gauge and adapter is required for this test. As these will not normally be available to the home mechanic, it is recommended that a VW dealer carry out the test.

8 Fuel injectors - testing

1 Refer to Part B of this Chapter, Section 13, paragraphs 1 to 3, but in addition, carry out the following electrical tests **(see illustration)**.
2 Disconnect the wiring plug from the conduit next to the injectors and connect an ohmmeter across the terminals on the conduit. The resistance of all four injectors should be 3.7 to 5.0 ohms. If any number of injectors are open-circuited, then the resistance will be as follows:
One injector open-circuited - 5.0 to 6.7 ohms
Two injectors open-circuited - 7.5 to 10.0 ohms
Three injectors open-circuited - 15.0 to 20.0 ohms
3 If necessary, prise off the conduit and check that each individual injector has a resistance of 15.0 to 20.0 ohms.
4 Checking the injector spray patterns cannot be performed as described in Part B of this Chapter, due to the position of the fuel distributor. However, the injectors may be removed together with the fuel distributor and wiring conduit, and the engine turned on the starter for a few seconds. Use a suitable container to catch the fuel.

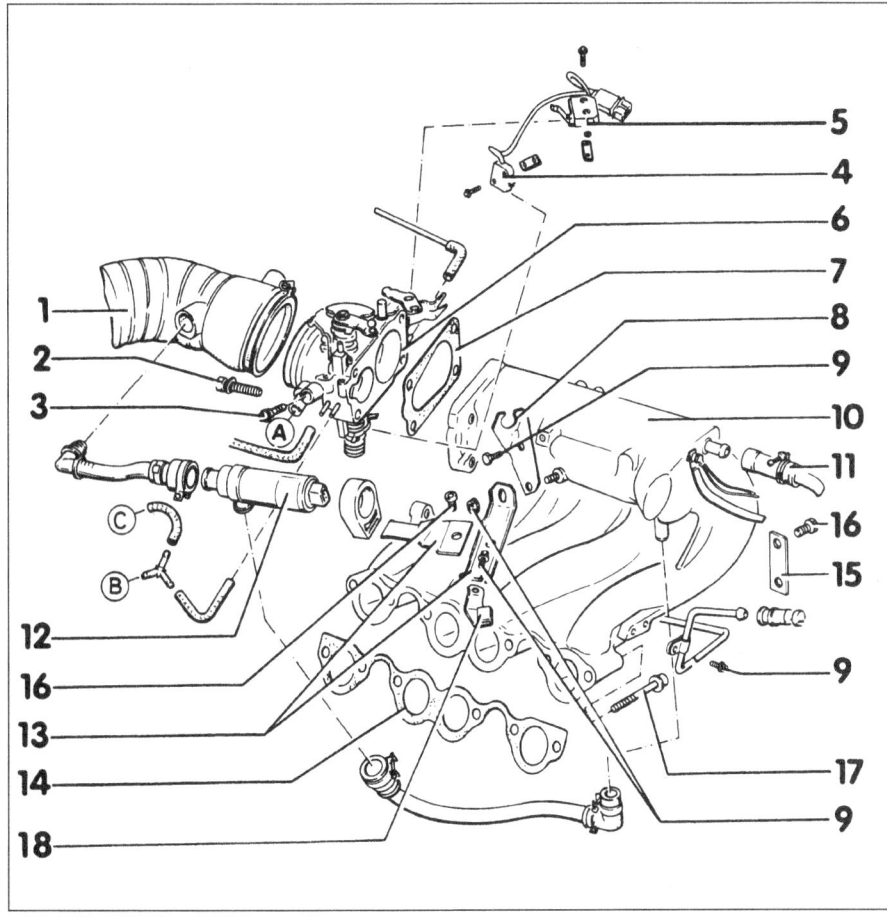

5.1 Throttle valve housing components

A Front crankcase ventilation valve
B Vacuum hose connection from fuel pressure regulator
C Vacuum hose from air cleaner temperature regulator

1 Air inlet hose
2 Bolt
3 Idle speed adjustment
4 Throttle valve switch 1
5 Throttle valve switch 2
6 Throttle valve housing
7 Gasket
8 Bracket
9 Bolt
10 Inlet manifold
11 Vacuum hose to brake servo unit
12 Idle speed stabilisation control valve
13 Support
14 Gasket
15 Support
16 Bolt
17 Bolt
18 Bracket

6.2 Throttle stop adjustment

1 Carrier lever   2 Stop lever
Arrow indicates adjustment screw

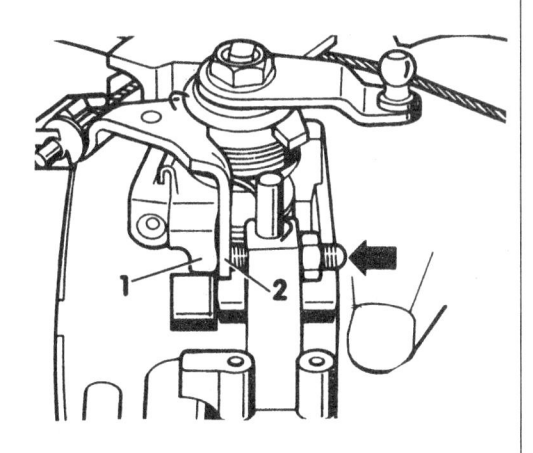

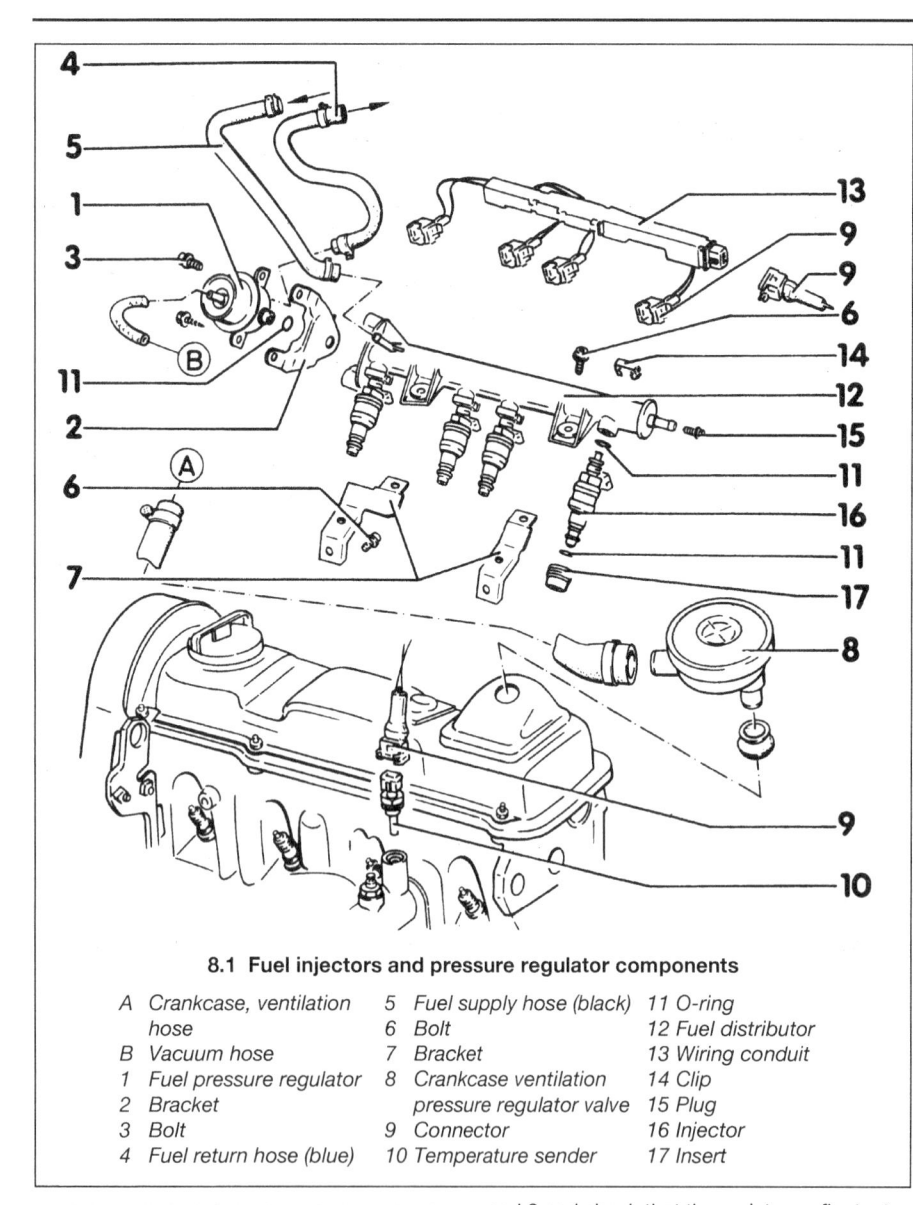

4F•4 Fuel and exhaust systems - Digifant fuel injection

8.1 Fuel injectors and pressure regulator components

- A Crankcase, ventilation hose
- B Vacuum hose
- 1 Fuel pressure regulator
- 2 Bracket
- 3 Bolt
- 4 Fuel return hose (blue)
- 5 Fuel supply hose (black)
- 6 Bolt
- 7 Bracket
- 8 Crankcase ventilation pressure regulator valve
- 9 Connector
- 10 Temperature sender
- 11 O-ring
- 12 Fuel distributor
- 13 Wiring conduit
- 14 Clip
- 15 Plug
- 16 Injector
- 17 Insert

9 Airflow meter - testing

1 Disconnect the wiring plug from the airflow meter **(see illustration)**.
2 Connect an ohmmeter between terminals 1 and 4 and check that the resistance of the inlet air temperature sender is as shown **(see illustration)** according to the ambient air temperature.
3 Connect the ohmmeter between terminals 3 and 4 and check that the resistance of the potentiometer is between 0.5 and 1.0 K ohms.
4 Connect the ohmmeter between terminals 2 and 3 and check that the resistance fluctuates as the airflow meter plate is moved.

10 Control unit - testing

The control unit is located on the left-hand side of the bulkhead. The ignition must always be switched off before disconnecting the plug.
It is not possible to test the control unit without using the VW test appliances. If a fault is suspected, the unit should be taken to a VW dealer.

11 Overrun cut-off and full throttle enrichment - testing

1 Run the engine until the oil temperature is at least 80°C (normal operating temperature) then let the engine idle.
2 Manually close the full throttle valve switch 2 and hold it closed.
3 Open the throttle until the engine speed is approximately 2000 rpm. Check that the engine speed surges, indicating that the overrun cut-off is functioning.
4 If the engine does not surge, disconnect the wiring from the temperature sender and connect a bridging wire between the two contacts on the plug.
5 Repeat the procedure in paragraphs 2 and 3. If the engine now surges, the temperature sender is proved faulty. However, if it still refuses to surge, check the associated wiring and throttle valve switch 2.
6 If no fault is found, renew the control unit.

12 Fuel pumps - testing

Pre mid 1989

1 The main fuel pump is located in the accumulator housing beneath the rear of the vehicle. An additional lift pump is located in the fuel tank, together with the fuel gauge sender **(see illustration)**.
2 With the engine stopped, have an assistant switch on the ignition. It should be possible to hear both pumps running for a short period. If not, check fuse 5 for continuity and also check all wiring connections.
3 With the ignition on, disconnect each wire connector from the pumps and check that there is a 12 volt supply by using a voltmeter.
4 Should there be no voltage at the pumps with the ignition switched on, the fuel pump relay (No 2 on fusebox) may be faulty. This is best checked by substituting a new relay.

From mid 1989

5 From mid 1989, certain models fitted with the Digifant system are fitted with a single fuel pump in the fuel tank rather than the previous arrangement described above. The pump can be tested in the same manner as that described for the previously fitted "in-tank" dual pump.
6 The fuel pump can be removed in a similar manner to that described for the fuel gauge sender unit in Part A of this Chapter, Section 8.

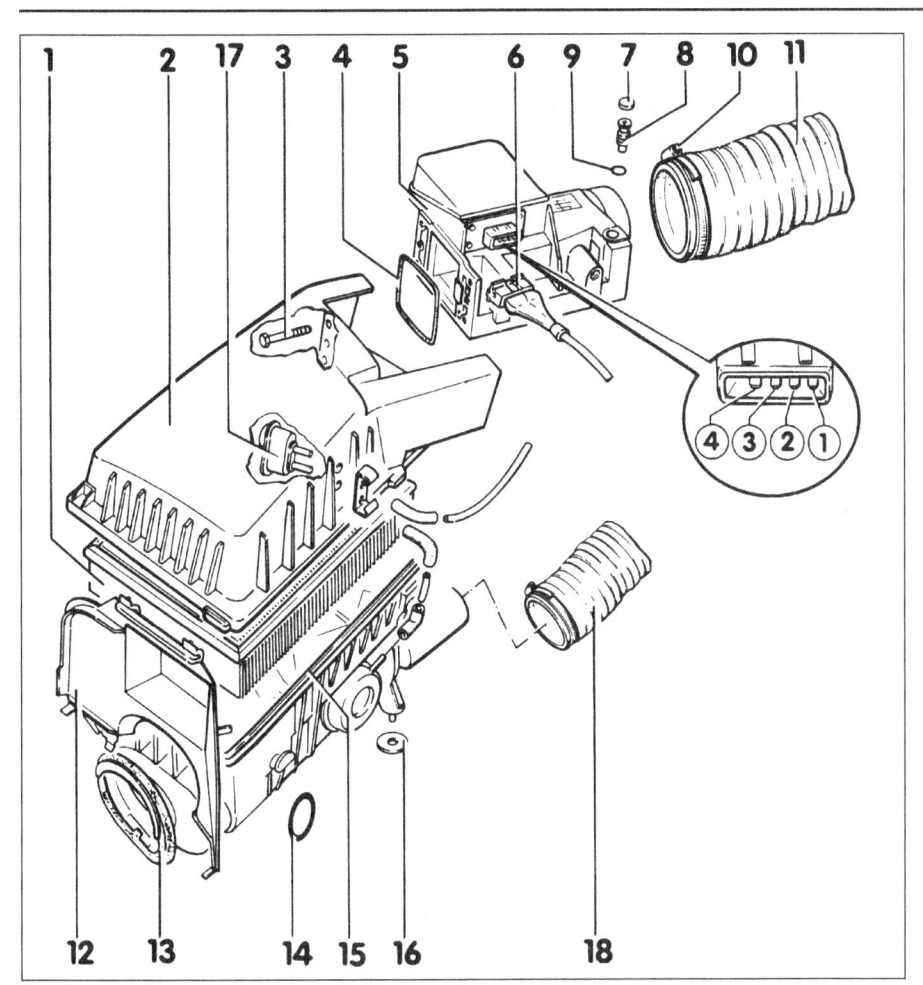

Fuel and exhaust systems - Digifant fuel injection 4F•5

9.1 Airflow meter components

1	Air cleaner element	9	O-ring
2	Cover	10	Clip
3	Bolt	11	Air inlet hose
4	Seal	12	Plate
5	Airflow meter	13	Seal
6	Connector	14	Retaining ring
7	Tamperproof plug	15	Air cleaner body
8	Mixture (CO content) adjustment screw	16	Rubber washer
		17	Temperature regulator
		18	Warm air hose

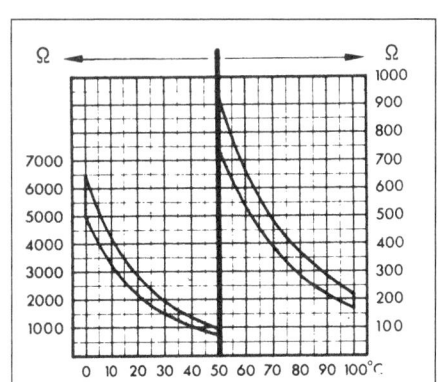

9.2 Inlet air temperature sender resistance graph

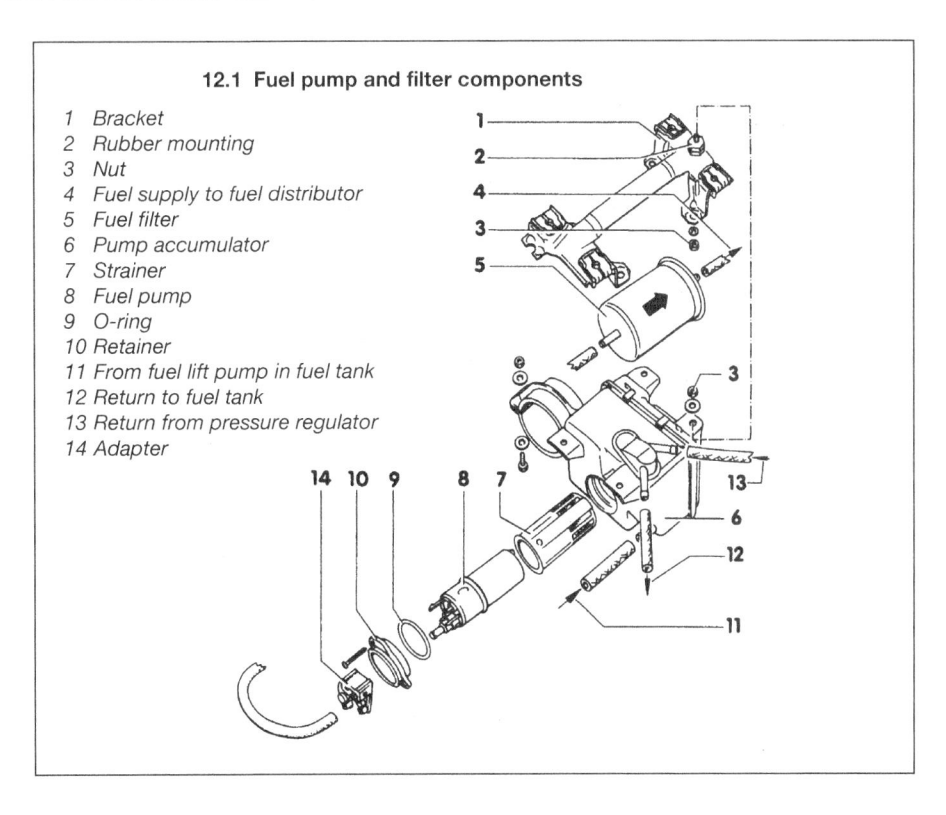

12.1 Fuel pump and filter components

1. Bracket
2. Rubber mounting
3. Nut
4. Fuel supply to fuel distributor
5. Fuel filter
6. Pump accumulator
7. Strainer
8. Fuel pump
9. O-ring
10. Retainer
11. From fuel lift pump in fuel tank
12. Return to fuel tank
13. Return from pressure regulator
14. Adapter

Notes

Chapter 5 Part A:
Ignition system - contact breaker type

Contents

Coil - testing 9
Condenser - testing, removal and refitting 6
Contact breaker points - inspection and adjustment 4
Contact breaker points - renewal 5
Distributor - removal, overhaul and refitting 7
General information and precautions 1
HT leads, distributor cap and rotor arm - inspection and renewal .. 3
Ignition timing - checking and adjustment 8
Spark plugs - renewal 2

Degrees of difficulty

Easy, suitable for novice with little experience	Fairly easy, suitable for beginner with some experience	Fairly difficult, suitable for competent DIY mechanic	Difficult, suitable for experienced DIY mechanic	Very difficult, suitable for expert DIY or professional

Specifications

General
System type .... 12 volt battery and coil with contact breaker points
Firing order .... 1-3-4-2 (No. 1 cylinder at crankshaft pulley end)

Spark plugs
Type .... Refer to Chapter 1 Specifications

Coil
Pre August 1987:
   Primary winding resistance .... 1.7 to 2.1 ohm
   Secondary winding resistance .... 7000 to 12 000 ohm
From August 1987:
   Primary winding resistance .... 0.6 to 0.8 ohm
   Secondary winding resistance .... 6900 to 8500 ohm

Distributor
Rotor rotation:
   1.05 and 1.3 litre .... Anti-clockwise
   1.6 and 1.8 litre .... Clockwise
Contact breaker gap (initial setting only) .... 0.4 mm
Dwell angle (1.05, 1.3 and 1.6 litre):
   Setting .... 44 to 50° (50 to 56%)
   Wear limit .... 42 to 58° (47 to 64%)
Rotor cut-out speed:
   1.05 and 1 3 litre (if applicable) .... 6300 to 6700 rpm
   1.6 and 1.8 litre (carburettor engine) .... No figures available
   1.8 litre (injection engine) .... 6500 to 6900 rpm
Centrifugal advance:
   1.05 litre .... Begins at 1100 to 1500 rpm
   1.3 litre .... Begins at 1500 to 1900 rpm
   1.6 litre .... Begins at 1100 to 1300 rpm
   1.8 litre (carburettor engine) .... Begins at 900 to 1100 rpm
   1.8 litre (fuel injection engine) .... Begins at 1150 to 1450 rpm
Ignition timing (at idle) .... Refer to Chapter 1 Specifications

5A•2 Ignition system - contact breaker type

Torque wrench settings	Nm	lbf ft
Spark plugs	20	15
Distributor clamp bolt:		
1.05 and 1.3 litre	10	7
1.6 and 1.8 litre	25	18

1 General information and precautions

General information

The ignition system covered in this Chapter is of the conventional contact breaker type. On 1.05 and 1.3 litre engines, the distributor is mounted on the left-hand (gearbox) end of the cylinder head and is driven direct from the camshaft **(see illustrations)**. On 1.6 and 1.8 litre engines, the distributor is mounted at the front (radiator) end of the engine and it is driven by a skew gear in mesh with the intermediate shaft of the engine **(see illustration)**.

To enable the engine to run correctly, it is necessary for an electrical spark to ignite the fuel/air mixture in the combustion chamber at exactly the right moment in relation to engine speed and load. The ignition system is based on feeding low tension voltage from the battery to the coil, where it is converted to high tension voltage. The high tension voltage is powerful enough to jump the spark plug gap in the cylinders many times a second under high compression, providing that the system is in good condition.

The ignition system is divided into two circuits, the low tension (LT) circuit and the high tension (HT) circuit.

The LT (primary) circuit comprises the battery, a lead to the ignition switch, a lead from the ignition switch to the LT coil windings (terminal +) and a lead from the LT coil windings (terminal -) to the contact breaker points and condenser in the distributor. The condenser is fitted in parallel with the contact points and its purpose is to reduce arcing between the points and also to accelerate the collapse of the coil low tension magnetic field.

The HT circuit comprises the HT (secondary) coil windings, the heavy ignition lead from the coil to the distributor cap, the rotor arm and the spark plug leads and spark plugs.

The system functions in the following manner. LT voltage is changed in the coil into HT voltage by the opening and closing of the contact breaker points. HT voltage is then fed via the carbon brush in the centre of the distributor cap to the rotor arm of the distributor and each time it comes in line with one of the four metal segments in the cap, which are connected to the spark plug leads, the opening and closing of the contact breaker points causes the HT voltage to build up, jump the gap from the rotor arm to the appropriate metal segment, and so via the spark plug lead to the spark plug, where it finally jumps the spark plug gap before going to earth.

Ignition timing is advanced and retarded automatically, to ensure that the spark occurs at just the right instant for the particular load at the prevailing engine speed.

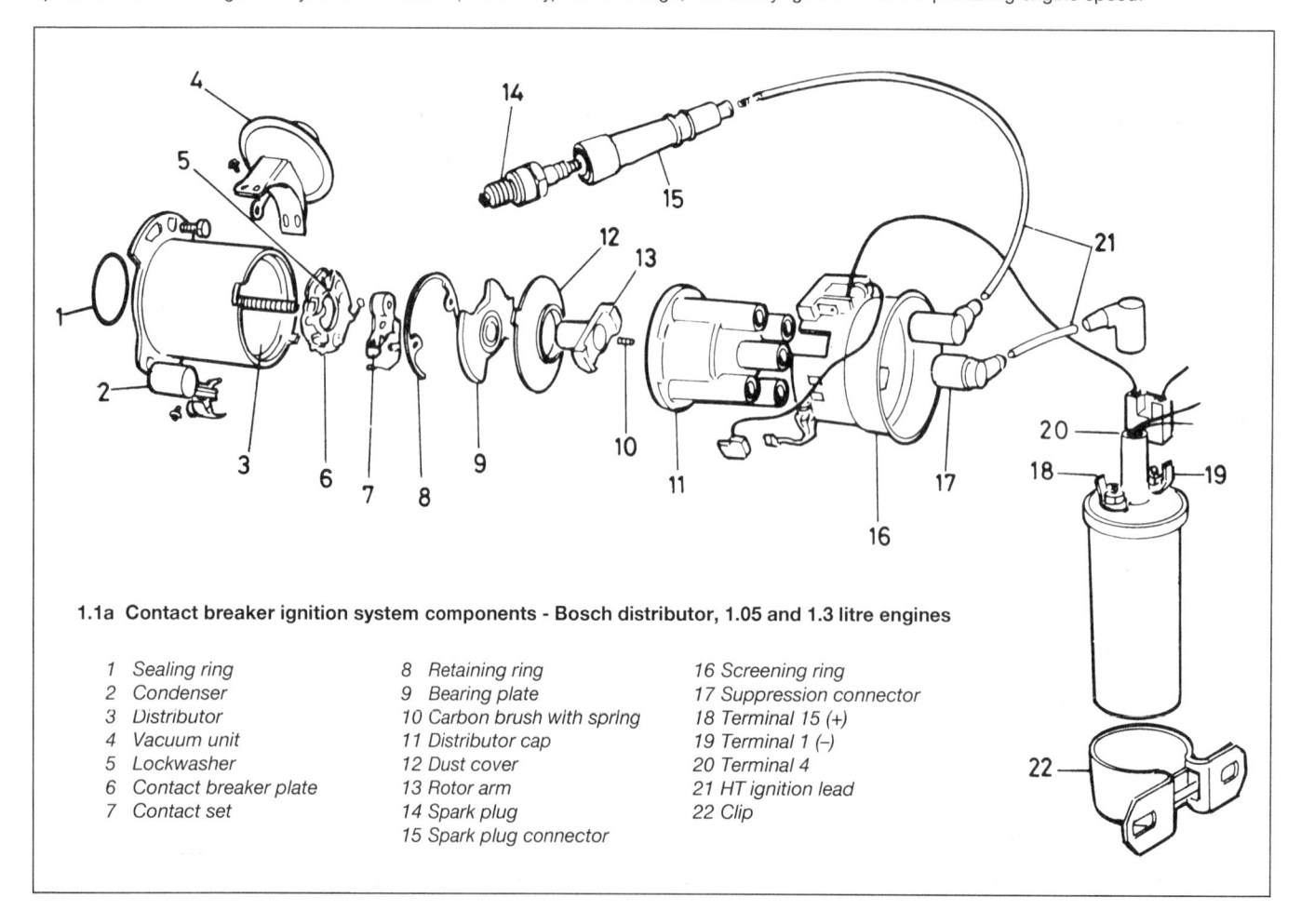

1.1a Contact breaker ignition system components - Bosch distributor, 1.05 and 1.3 litre engines

1 Sealing ring
2 Condenser
3 Distributor
4 Vacuum unit
5 Lockwasher
6 Contact breaker plate
7 Contact set
8 Retaining ring
9 Bearing plate
10 Carbon brush with spring
11 Distributor cap
12 Dust cover
13 Rotor arm
14 Spark plug
15 Spark plug connector
16 Screening ring
17 Suppression connector
18 Terminal 15 (+)
19 Terminal 1 (-)
20 Terminal 4
21 HT ignition lead
22 Clip

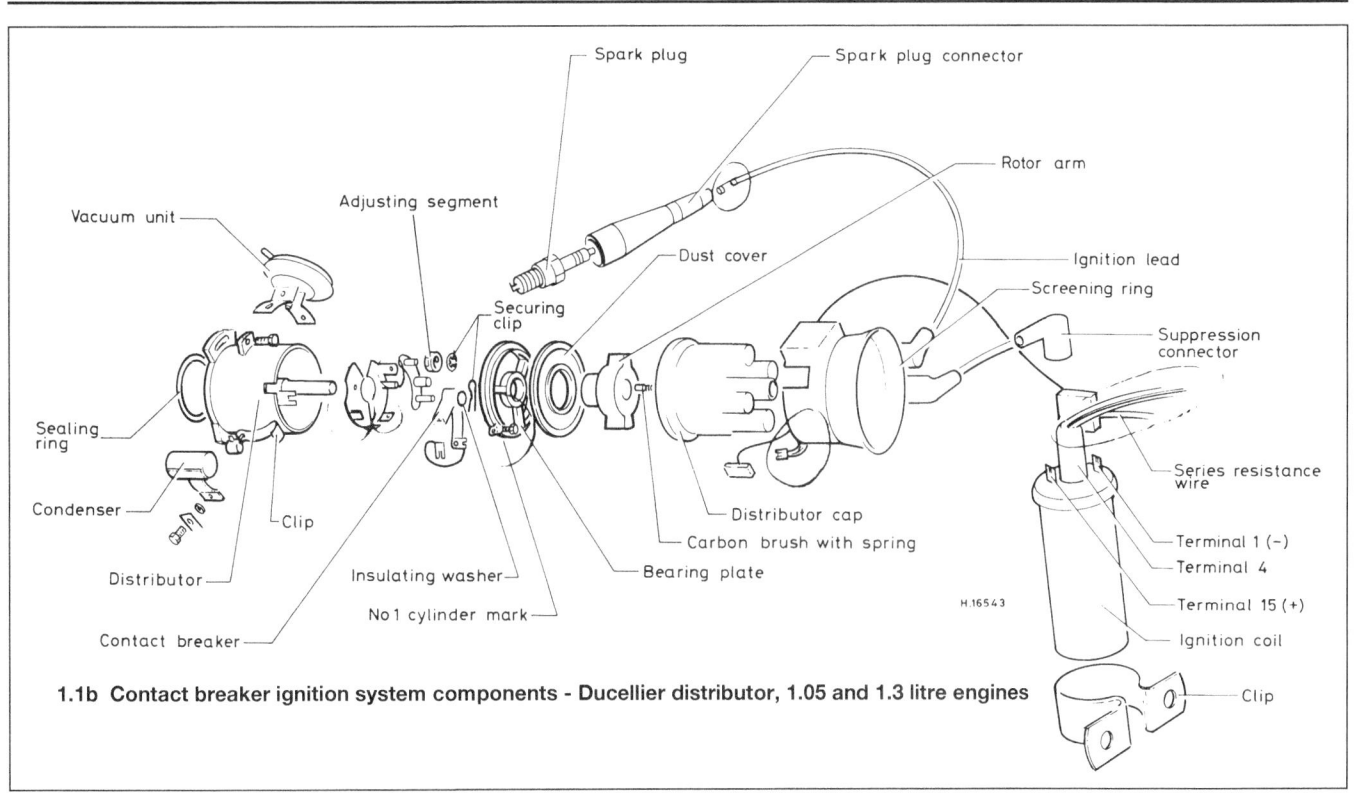

Ignition system - contact breaker type 5A•3

1.1b Contact breaker ignition system components - Ducellier distributor, 1.05 and 1.3 litre engines

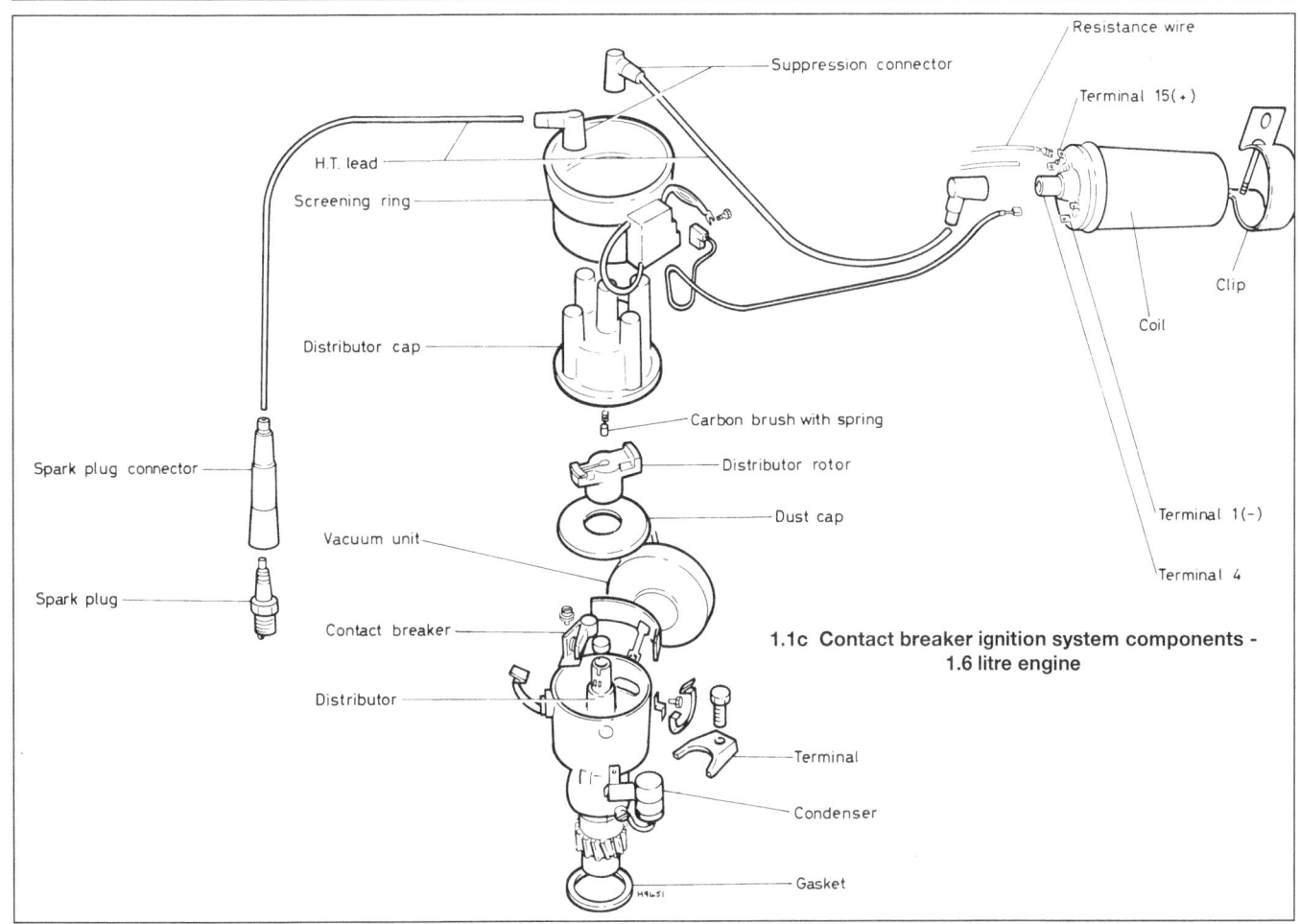

1.1c Contact breaker ignition system components - 1.6 litre engine

Ignition advance is controlled both mechanically and by a vacuum-operated system. The mechanical governor mechanism comprises two weights, which move out from the distributor shaft as the engine speed rises due to centrifugal force. As they move outwards, they rotate the cam relative to the distributor shaft and so advance the spark. The weights are held in position by two light springs and it is the tension of these springs which is largely responsible for correct spark advancement.

The vacuum control comprises a diaphragm, one side of which is connected via a small bore pipe to the inlet manifold and the other side to the contact breaker plate. Depression in the inlet manifold, which varies with engine speed and throttle opening, causes the diaphragm to move, so moving the contact breaker plate and advancing or retarding the spark. A fine degree of control is achieved by a spring in the vacuum assembly.

The system incorporates a ballast resistor or resistive wire in the low tension circuit, which is in circuit all the time that the engine is running. When the starter is operated, the resistance is bypassed to provide increased voltage at the spark plugs for easier starting.

Precautions

It is necessary to take extra care when working on the electrical system to avoid damage to semi-conductor devices (diodes and transistors) and to avoid the risk of personal injury. Take note of the following points:

a) Before disconnecting any wiring, or removing components, always ensure that the ignition is switched off.
b) Always remove rings, watches, etc. before working on the ignition system. Even with the battery disconnected, capacitive discharge could occur if a component live terminal is earthed through a metal object. This could cause a shock or nasty burn.
c) Do not reverse the battery connections. Components such as the alternator or any other having semi-conductor circuitry could be irreparably damaged.
d) If the engine is being started using jump leads and a slave battery, connect the batteries positive to positive and negative to negative. This also applies when connecting a battery charger.
e) Never disconnect the battery terminals, or alternator multi-plug connector, when the engine is running.
f) The battery leads and alternator multi-plug must be disconnected before carrying out any electric welding on the vehicle.
g) Never use an ohmmeter of the type incorporating a hand cranked generator for circuit or continuity testing.
h) The HT voltage generated by an electronic ignition system is extremely high and in certain circumstances, could prove fatal. Persons with surgically-implanted cardiac pacemaker devices should keep well clear of the ignition circuits, components and test equipment.
i) Do not handle HT leads, or touch the distributor or coil when the engine is running. If tracing faults in the HT circuit, use well insulated tools to manipulate live leads.

2 Spark plugs - renewal

Caution: When pulling the HT lead from a spark plug, grip the rubber end fitting not the lead, otherwise the lead connection may be fractured
Note: *To prevent dirt from dropping into the cylinders, remove dirt from the spark plug recesses before removing the plugs*
Refer to Chapter 1, Section 15

3 HT leads, distributor cap and rotor arm - inspection and renewal

1 Clean all HT and LT leads by wiping along their length with a fuel-moistened cloth. Inspect each lead for damage and renew if defective in any way.
2 Note the fitted position of each HT lead before disconnection. When removing a lead from a spark plug or the HT coil, pull the lead off by its rubber connector, not the lead itself.
3 The socket contacts on the distributor cap and HT coil should be cleaned if corroded. A smear of petroleum jelly (not grease) applied to the ferrule on the end of the HT lead will help to prevent corrosion.
4 Remove the distributor cap and rotor arm.
5 Examine the rotor arm and inside of the distributor cap . If the contacts are corroded or are excessively burnt, or if the carbon centre contact in the cap is worn away, renew the cap or rotor, as necessary. Check carefully for hairline cracks and signs of arcing.
6 Ensure that all HT leads are reinstalled in their correct firing order. Check that all leads are correctly routed and clear of moving or hot engine components. Ensure that all lead connections are secure and where applicable, protected.

4 Contact breaker points - inspection and adjustment

Inspection
Refer to Chapter 1, Section 11
Adjustment
Refer to Chapter 1, Section 16

5 Contact breaker points - renewal

Refer to Chapter 1, Section 16

6 Condenser - testing, removal and refitting

Testing

1 A faulty condenser can cause complete failure of the ignition system, as the points will be prevented from interrupting the low tension circuit.
2 To test the condenser, remove the distributor cap, rotor arm and dust cover and rotate the engine until the contact points are closed. Switch on the ignition and separate the points. If this is accompanied by a strong blue flash, the condenser is faulty. Note that a weak white spark is normal.
3 A further test can be made for short circuiting by removing the condenser and connecting a test lamp and leads to the supply lead and body (ie. connecting the condenser in series with a 12 volt supply). If the test lamp lights, the condenser is faulty.
4 If correct operation of the condenser is in doubt, substitute a new unit and check whether the fault persists.

Removal

5 To remove the condenser, unscrew its retaining screw and disconnect the LT supply lead (at the coil on some models) **(see illustration)**.
6 Withdraw the condenser far enough to disconnect the moving contact supply lead then withdraw the condenser. If the moving contact supply lead has insufficient length, it will be necessary to remove the distributor cap, rotor arm, dust cover and bearing plate (if applicable) first.

Refitting

7 Refitting is a reversal of removal.

6.5 Condenser location

Ignition system - contact breaker type 5A•5

7.4 Crankshaft pulley mark (A) timing mark (B) and TDC mark (C) with timing cover removed - 1.3 litre engine

7.5 Removing the distributor

7 Distributor - removal, overhaul and refitting

Removal

1 Disconnect the battery earth lead, then remove the distributor cap and screening ring.
2 Disconnect the vacuum hose.

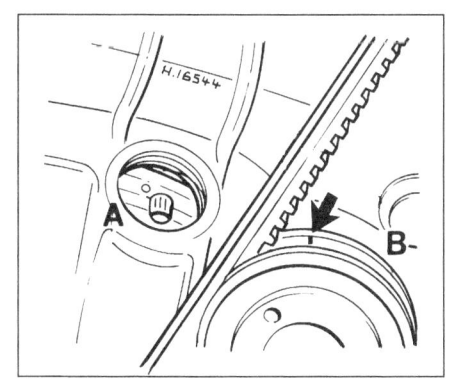

7.6a TDC timing marks - 1.6 and 1.8 litre engines

A Flywheel/driveplate
B Crankshaft pulley

1.05 and 1.3 litre engines

3 The distributor driveshaft is located in the end of the camshaft by an offset centre key and therefore the procedures described in paragraphs 4 and 5 are only necessary for checking purposes, such as when fitting a new distributor.
4 Turn the engine with a spanner on the crankshaft pulley bolt until the rotor arm points to the No. 1 spark plug lead position. On some models, a TDC groove is provided on the distributor body rim and the rotor arm must align with this. The mark on the crankshaft pulley should be aligned with the TDC pointer with No. 1 piston (timing belt end) at TDC compression (see illustration).
5 Mark the distributor flange and cylinder head in relation to each other, then unscrew the bolts and withdraw the distributor (see illustration).

1.6 and 1.8 litre engines

6 Unscrew and remove the TDC sensor or blanking plug from the top of the gearbox then turn the engine over so that the TDC "O" mark on the flywheel or driveplate is visible and aligned with the timing pointer. The crankshaft pulley timing notch should be aligned with the TDC arrow mark on the timing case (see illustration). The rotor arm should be pointing to the timing mark on the top rim of the distributor body (see illustration).
7 Mark the distributor body in line with the tip of the rotor arm and also mark the distributor body and cylinder block in relation to each other, then unscrew the clamp bolt and withdraw the clamp, followed by the distributor, from the cylinder block. Note by how much the rotor turns clockwise. Remove the distributor body sealing washer which must be renewed.

Overhaul

8 Overhauling of the distributor is similar for all models. The accompanying illustrations show the distributor fitted to 1.05 and 1.3 litre engines.
9 Remove the contact breaker points.
10 On the Bosch distributor, mark the position of the guide pin then remove the bearing plate retaining ring (see illustrations).
11 Before removing the vacuum unit on the Ducellier distributor, mark the adjustment segment position so that it can be correctly repositioned when reassembling.
12 Extract the circlip securing the vacuum unit arm to the contact breaker plate.
13 Remove the retaining screws, then unhook the arm and withdraw the vacuum

7.6b Rotor arm aligned with TDC mark on distributor body

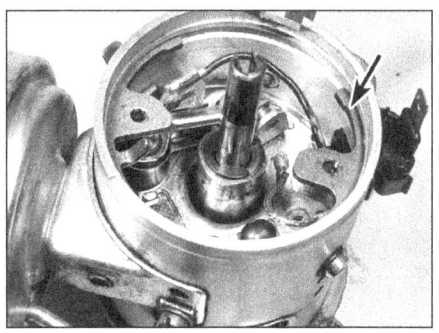

7.10a Correct fitted position of bearing plate retaining ring

7.10b Removing bearing plate retaining ring

5A•6 Ignition system - contact breaker type

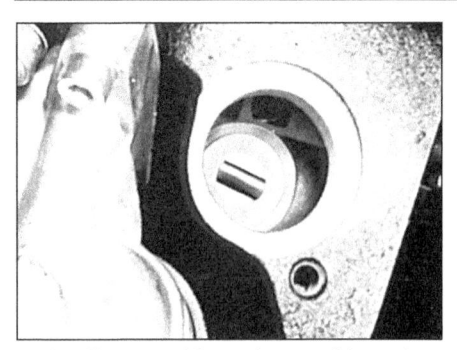

7.22 Oil pump drive spigot position prior to refitting distributor

unit. Note that the screws may also secure a suppression choke unit to the distributor body.

14 Remove the side screws, noting the location of the earth lead terminal, then remove the contact breaker plate by turning it anti-clockwise to align the lugs with the cut-outs (if applicable).

15 Wipe clean all electrical components. Clean the distributor body assembly with paraffin then wipe dry.

16 Check all components for wear and damage.

17 Reassembly is a reversal of the dismantling procedure.

18 On the Ducellier distributor, realign the vacuum unit adjuster segment with the mark made when removing it.

19 On the Bosch distributor, locate the retaining ring guide pin as previously marked.

20 Lubricate the centrifugal mechanism and the contact breaker plate with a little multi-purpose grease then adjust the contact breaker points.

Refitting

1.05 and 1.3 litre engines

21 To refit the distributor, reverse the removal procedure and align the timing marks made during removal before tightening the clamp bolts.

1.6 and 1.8 litre engines

22 To refit the distributor, first check that the oil pump drive spigot is correctly positioned with the spigot parallel to the crankshaft. This is visible through the distributor aperture **(see illustration)**. Check that the TDC "O" mark is still aligned. Set the rotor arm to the position noted, align the distributor body and cylinder block marks and insert the distributor. As the gears mesh, the rotor will turn anti-clockwise and point to the previously made mark. Refit the clamp and tighten the bolt. Reconnect the vacuum hose, and low tension lead or multi-plug (as applicable). Refit the TDC sensor or blanking plug.

All models

23 Refit the distributor cap, then reconnect the battery negative terminal.

24 Check and if necessary, adjust the ignition timing.

8 Ignition timing - checking and adjustment

Refer to Chapter 1, Section 17

9 Coil - testing

1 The coil is located on the bulkhead under the plenum chamber **(see illustration)**. It should be periodically wiped clean to prevent HT voltage loss through possible arcing.

2 To ensure that the correct HT polarity at the spark plugs, the coil LT leads must always be connected correctly. The ignition lead from the fusebox must be connected to the positive (+) terminal 15, and the distributor lead (usually green) must be connected to the negative (-) terminal 1. Incorrect connections can cause bad starting, misfiring, and short spark plug life.

3 Complete testing of the coil requires special equipment. However, if an ohmmeter is available, the primary and secondary winding resistances can be checked and compared with those specified. During testing, the LT and HT wires must be disconnected from the coil.

4 To test the primary winding, connect the ohmmeter between the two LT terminals. To test the secondary winding, connect the ohmmeter between the negative (-) terminal 1 and the HT terminal.

9.1 Ignition coil location

Chapter 5 Part B:
Ignition system - transistorised type

Contents

Coil - testing 9
Distributor - overhaul 7
Distributor - removal and refitting 6
General information and precautions 1
Hall sender - testing 5
HT leads, distributor cap and rotor arm - inspection and renewal .. 3
Ignition timing - checking and adjustment 8
Spark plugs - renewal 2
Switch unit - testing 4

Degrees of difficulty

Easy, suitable for novice with little experience	Fairly easy, suitable for beginner with some experience	Fairly difficult, suitable for competent DIY mechanic	Difficult, suitable for experienced DIY mechanic	Very difficult, suitable for expert DIY or professional

Specifications

General
System type .... Transistorised. 12 volt battery and coil
Firing order .... 1-3-4-2 (No 1 cylinder at crankshaft pulley end)

Spark plugs
Type and gap .... Refer to Chapter 1 *Servicing specifications*

Coil
Pre August 1987:
   Primary winding resistance .... 0.52 to 0.76 ohm
   Secondary winding resistance .... 2400 to 3500 ohm
From August 1987:
   Primary winding resistance .... 0.6 to 0.8 ohm
   Secondary winding resistance .... 6900 to 8500 ohm

Distributor
Rotor rotation:
   1.05 and 1.3 litre .... Anti-clockwise
   1.6 and 1.8 litre .... Clockwise
Dwell angle (1.05, 1.3 and 1.6 litre):
   Setting .... 44 to 50° (50 to 56%)
   Wear limit .... 42 to 58° (47 to 64%)
Rotor cut-out speed:
   1.05 and 1.3 litre * .... 6600 to 7000 rpm
   1.6 and 1.8 litre ** .... 6150 to 6460 rpm

* *Discontinued from 1986 models*
** *Only on engine without hydraulic tappets*

Torque wrench settings

	Nm	lbf ft
Spark plugs:		
1.05 and 1.3 litre	25	18
1.06 and 1.8 litre	20	15
Knock sensor (1.8 litre)	20	15

5B•2 Ignition system - transistorised type

1 General information and precautions

General information

TCI-H system

The transistorised (TIC-H) ignition system functions in a similar manner to that described in Part A of this Chapter for the contact breaker system, with the following exceptions. An electronic sender unit replaces the contact points and condenser in the distributor and a remotely-mounted electronic switch unit controls the coil primary circuit **(see illustrations)**.

Ignition timing is advanced and retarded automatically, to ensure that the spark occurs at just the right instant for the particular load at the prevailing engine speed.

Ignition advance is controlled both mechanically and by a vacuum-operated system. The mechanical governor mechanism comprises two weights, which move out from the distributor shaft as the engine speed rises due to centrifugal force. As they move outwards they rotate the cam relative to the distributor shaft, and so advance the spark. The weights are held in position by two light springs, and it is the tension of the springs which is largely responsible for correct spark advancement.

Vacuum control comprises a diaphragm, one side of which is connected via a small bore pipe to the inlet manifold, and the other side to the distributor baseplate. Depression in the inlet manifold, which varies with engine speed and throttle opening, causes the diaphragm to move, so moving the baseplate, and advancing or retarding the spark. A fine degree of control is achieved by a spring in the vacuum assembly.

Digifant system

Fitted to the 1.8 litre (code PB and PF) engine, the Digifant ignition system uses the TCI-H system described above but in addition, incorporates a knock sensor which senses the onset of pre-ignition and retards ignition timing accordingly. Normal ignition timing is automatically adjusted by the Digifant control unit which also controls the fuel injection system. Because of this, there are no centrifugal advance weights in the distributor **(see illustration)**.

Work procedures are basically as given for the TIC-H system, except for those described in the relevant Sections.

Precautions

In addition to the precautions listed in Part A of this Chapter, note the following:

a) *When turning the engine at starter speed without starting, the HT lead must be pulled from the centre of the distributor cap and kept earthed to a suitable part of the engine or bodywork*
b) *If the system develops a fault and it is necessary to tow the vehicle with the ignition on, the wiring must be disconnected from the TCI-H switch unit*
c) *Do not under any circumstances connect a condenser to the coil terminals*

2 Spark plugs - renewal

Refer to Chapter 1, Section 15

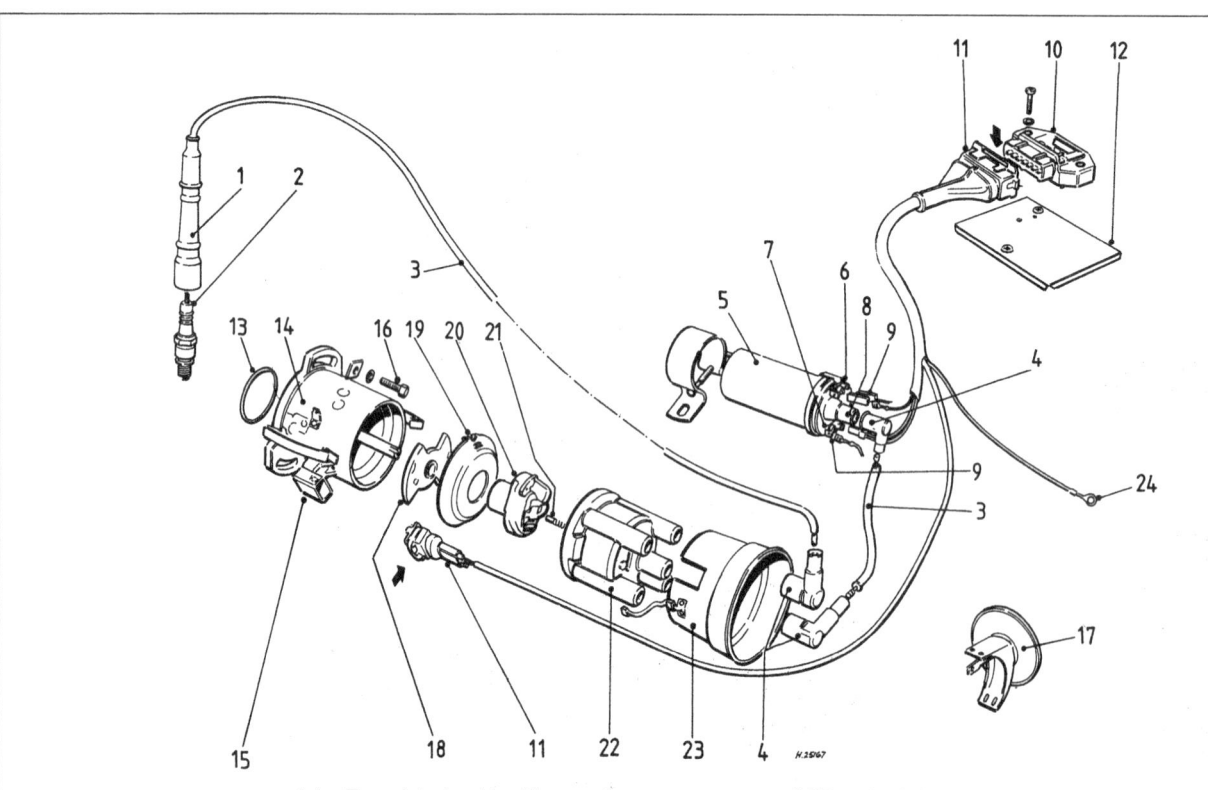

1.1a Transistorised ignition system components – 1.05 and 1.3 litre engines

1 Connector	6 Terminal (–)	11 Connector	16 Screw	21 Carbon brush with spring
2 Spark plug	7 Terminal 15 (+)	12 Heat sink	17 Vacuum unit	22 Distributor cap
3 HT lead	8 Terminal 4	13 O-ring	18 Bearing plate	23 Screening ring
4 Suppression connector	9 Connectors	14 Distributor	19 Dust cover	24 Earth lead
5 Ignition coil	10 TCI-H switch unit	15 Hall sender	20 Rotor arm	

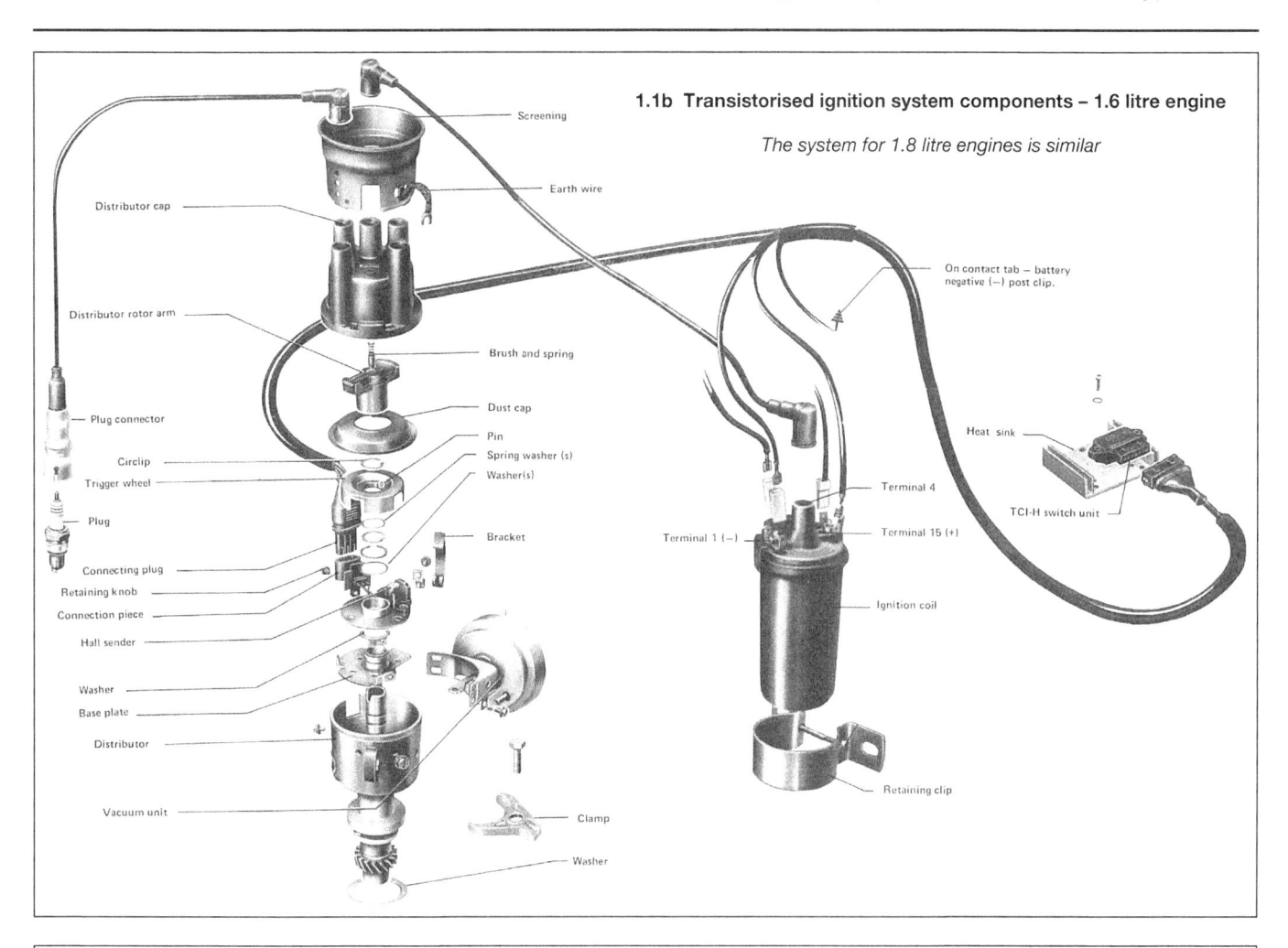

Ignition system - transistorised type 5B•3

1.1b Transistorised ignition system components – 1.6 litre engine

The system for 1.8 litre engines is similar

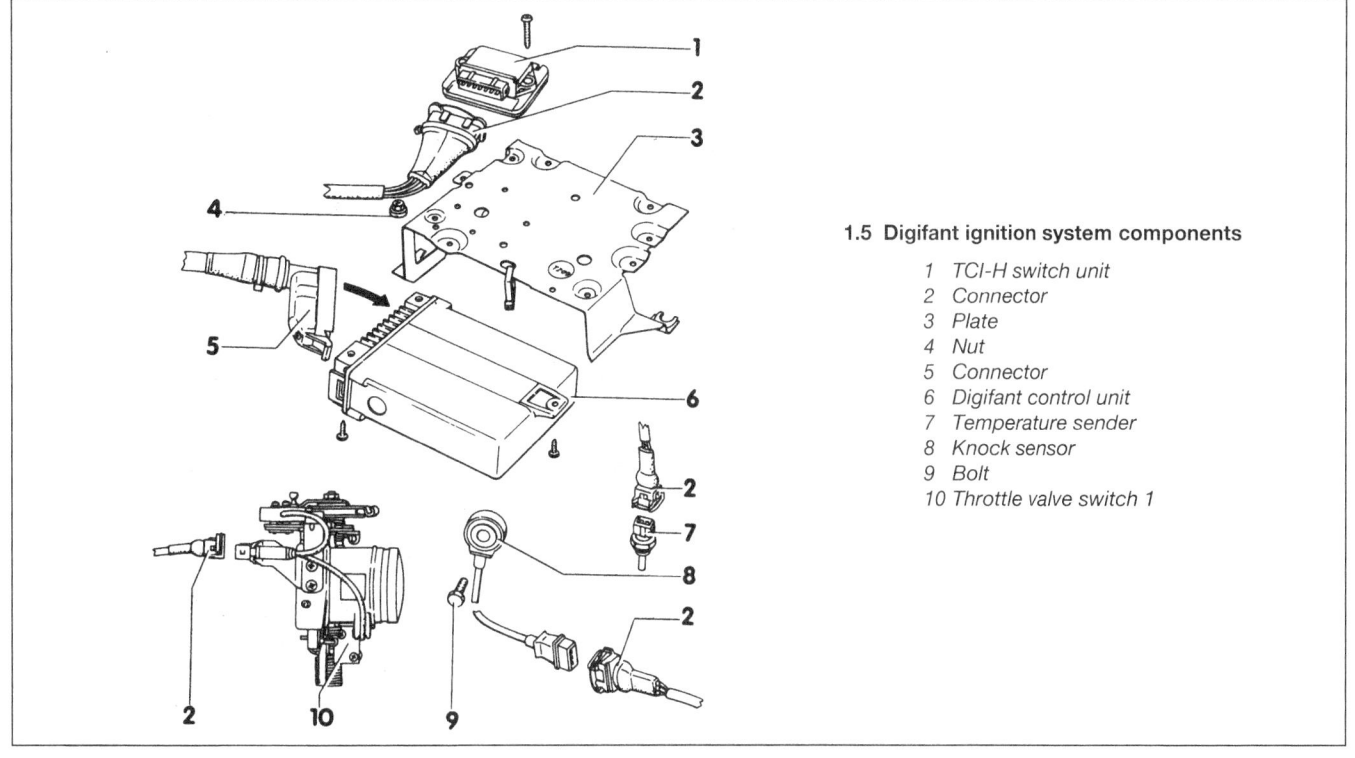

1.5 Digifant ignition system components

1. TCI-H switch unit
2. Connector
3. Plate
4. Nut
5. Connector
6. Digifant control unit
7. Temperature sender
8. Knock sensor
9. Bolt
10. Throttle valve switch 1

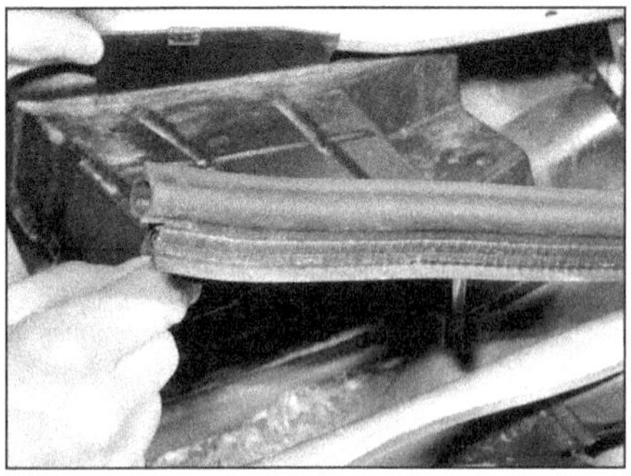

5B•4 Ignition system - transistorised type

4.2a Carefully prise free plastic cover ...

4.2b ... for access to ignition switch

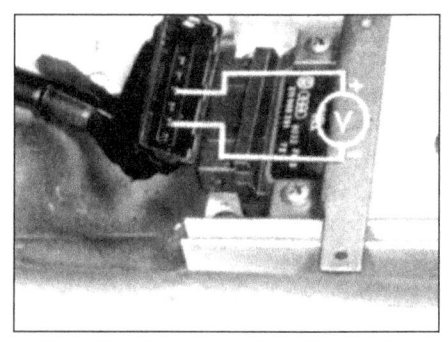

4.3 Voltmeter connection when testing ignition switch unit

3 HT leads, distributor cap and rotor arm - inspection and renewal

Refer to Section 3 in Part A of this Chapter

4 Switch unit - testing

1 When making this test, the coil must be in good condition.
2 Remove the plastic cover on the right-hand side of the plenum chamber for access to the switch unit **(see illustrations)**.
3 Disconnect the multi-plug from the switch unit and connect a voltmeter between terminals 4 and 2 **(see illustration)**.
4 Switch on the ignition and check that battery voltage, or slightly less, is available. If not, there is an open-circuit in the supply wires.
5 Switch off the ignition and reconnect the multi-plug to the switch unit.
6 Pull the multi-plug from the Hall sender on the side of the distributor **(see illustration)**, then connect a voltmeter across the low tension terminals on the coil **(see illustration)**.
7 Switch on the ignition and check that there is initially 2 volts, dropping to zero after 1 to 2 seconds. If this is not the case, renew the switch unit and coil.
8 Using a length of wire, earth the centre terminal of the distributor multi-plug briefly. The voltage should rise to at least 2 volts. If not, there is an open-circuit or the switch unit is faulty.
9 Switch off the ignition and connect the voltmeter across the outer terminals of the distributor multi-plug.
10 Switch on the ignition and check that 5 volts is registered on the voltmeter.
11 If a fault still exists, renew the switch unit.
12 Switch off the ignition, remove the voltmeter and reconnect the distributor multi-plug.

5 Hall sender - testing

1 Check that the ignition system wiring and plugs are fitted correctly.
2 The coil and TCI-H unit must both be in good condition.
3 Pull the HT lead from the centre of the distributor cap and earth it to the engine or bodywork.
4 Pull back the rubber boot from the switch unit and connect a voltmeter between terminals 6 and 3 **(see illustration)**.
5 Switch on the ignition and turn the engine by hand in its normal direction of rotation. The voltage should alternate from between 0 and a minimum of 2 volts. If not, the sender is faulty and must be renewed.

6 Distributor - removal and refitting

Note: *On 1.05 and 1.3 litre engines equipped with hydraulic tappets, distributor removal and refitting is basically the same as described in Part A of this Chapter for the contact breaker type*

TCI-H system

Removal

1 Pull the high tension connection from the centre of the ignition coil and remove the caps from the spark plugs.
2 Disconnect the screen (suppression) earth lead **(see illustration)** and withdraw the screen, then release the clips and lift off the distributor cap. Do not allow the cap retaining clips to fall inwards or the rotor or trigger wheel may be damaged.
3 Disconnect the control unit lead multi-plug by releasing the wire retaining clip.

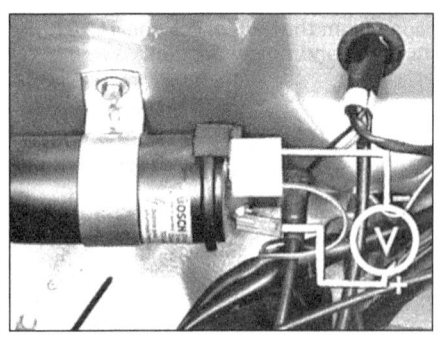

4.6a Multi-plug connection to Hall sender on side of distributor

4.6b Voltmeter connection to coil when testing ignition switch unit and coil

5.4 Voltmeter connection when testing Hall sender

6.2 Transistorised distributor earth lead connection to body (from screen)

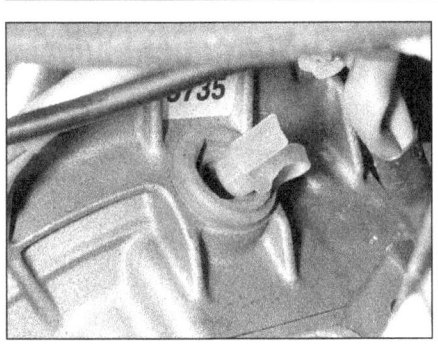

Ignition system - transistorised type 5B•5

6.4a TDC blanking plug – manual gearbox

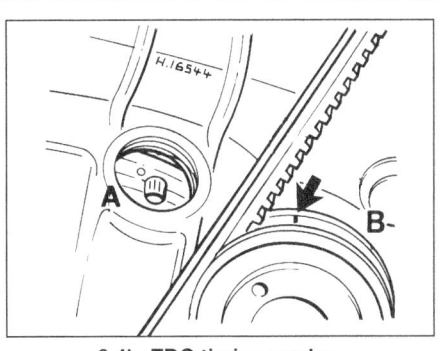

6.4b TDC timing marks - 1.6 and 1.8 litre engines

A Flywheel/driveplate
B Crankshaft pulley

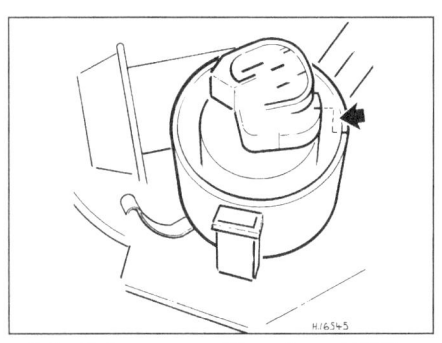

6.4c Rotor arm position when at TDC – 1.8 litre engine

4 Unscrew and remove the TDC sensor or blanking plug from the top of the gearbox **(see illustration)** then turn the engine over until the TDC "O" mark is aligned with the timing pointer **(see illustration)**. If not already marked, scribe an alignment mark on the distributor body in line with the tip of the rotor arm **(see illustration)**. Also mark the distributor body and cylinder block in relation to each other.
5 Pull the vacuum pipe(s) from the vacuum control unit, marking the position of the pipes if there is more than one.
6 Remove the bolt and washer from the distributor clamp plate and remove the clamp plate. Withdraw the distributor and remove the gasket, which must be renewed **(see illustrations)**.

Refitting

7 Refitting is a reversal of the removal procedure. When the distributor is in position, check that the rotor arm points to the No. 1 cylinder mark before tightening the clamp plate bolt.
8 On completion, check and if necessary adjust the ignition timing.

Digifant system

Removal

9 Release the distributor screen and cap. Place the cap to one side complete with HT leads **(see illustration)**.
10 Disconnect the wiring harness plug from the side of the distributor body.
11 Unscrew the clamp plate screw, remove the clamp plate and withdraw the distributor.

6.6a Distributor removal - 1.8 litre engine

6.6b The gasket must be removed

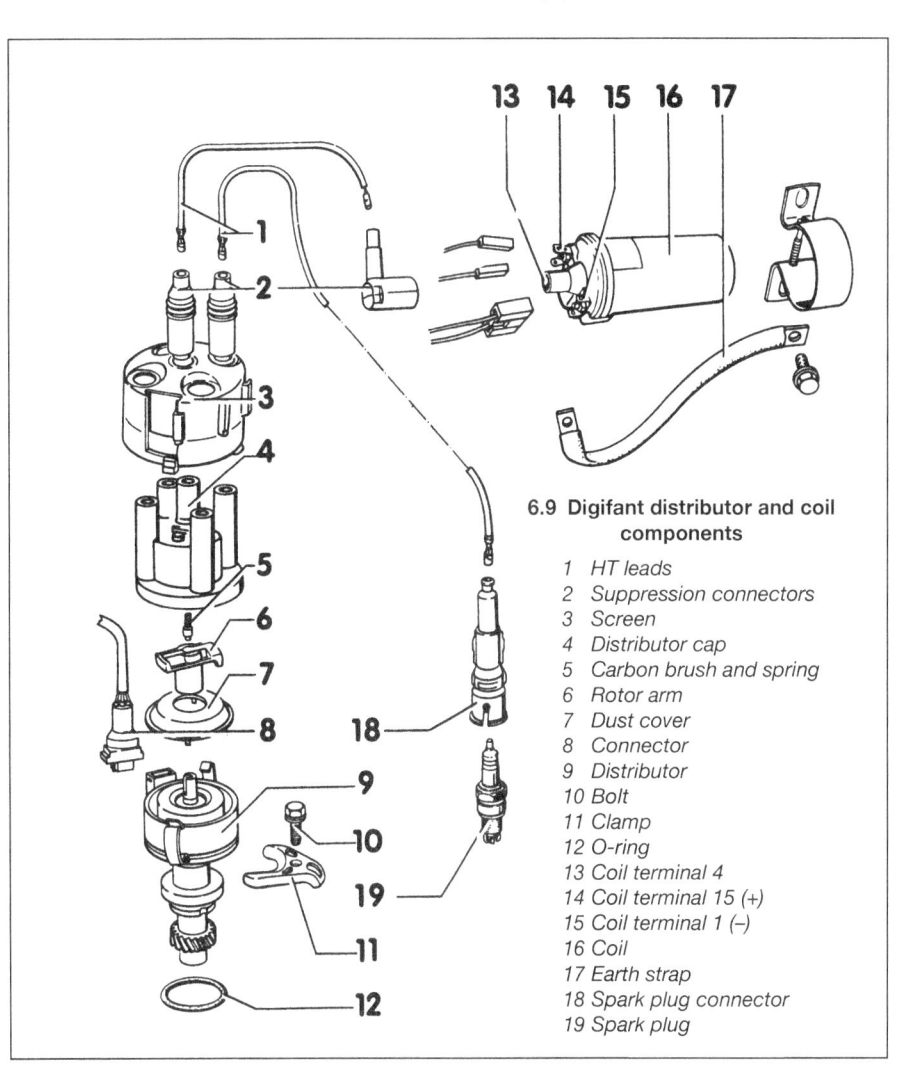

6.9 Digifant distributor and coil components

1 HT leads
2 Suppression connectors
3 Screen
4 Distributor cap
5 Carbon brush and spring
6 Rotor arm
7 Dust cover
8 Connector
9 Distributor
10 Bolt
11 Clamp
12 O-ring
13 Coil terminal 4
14 Coil terminal 15 (+)
15 Coil terminal 1 (–)
16 Coil
17 Earth strap
18 Spark plug connector
19 Spark plug

5B•6 Ignition system - transistorised type

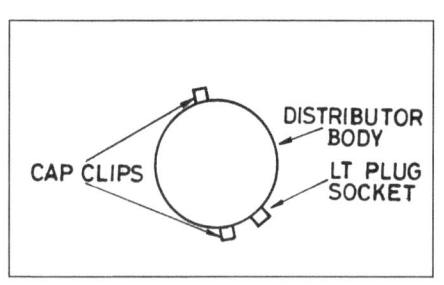

6.15 Distributor installation position – Digifant system

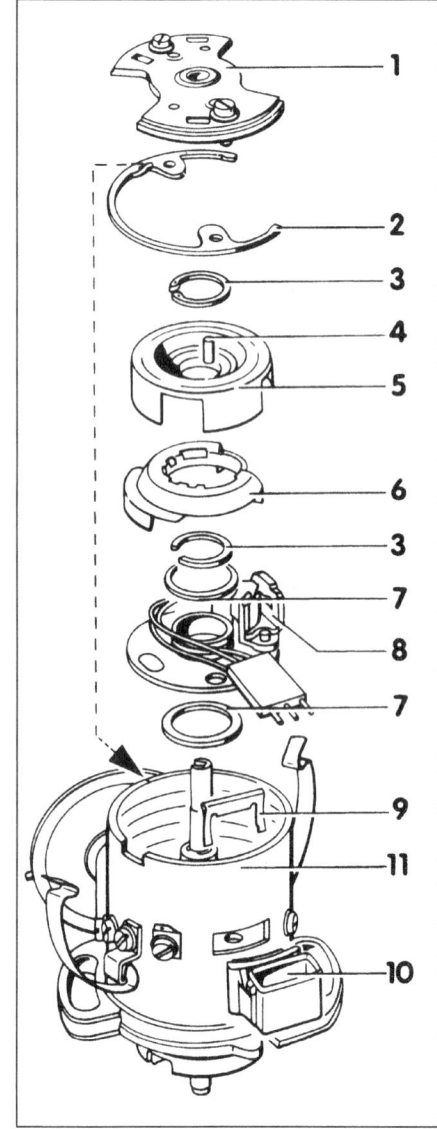

7.1 Transistorised ignition distributor components – 1.05 and 1.3 litre engines

1 Bearing plate
2 Tensioning ring
3 Circlip
4 Pin
5 Rotor
6 Cover
7 Shims
8 Hall sender
9 Clip
10 Connector
11 Main body

Refitting

12 Before fitting the distributor, set No. 1 piston to TDC. When correctly set, the flywheel mark or the crankshaft pulley vibration damper mark should align with the matching mark on the casing or belt cover. The mark on the camshaft sprocket must align with the joint of the camshaft cover.

13 Using a screwdriver, turn the slot in the end of the oil pump driveshaft so that it is parallel with the crankshaft centre-line.

14 Set the rotor arm so that it points to the mark (No. 1) on the distributor body rim.

15 Install the distributor so that the wiring harness LT plug socket is in the position shown **(see illustration)**. Check and if necessary adjust the ignition timing.

7 Distributor - overhaul

Note: *Before commencing work, check that spare parts are available.*

1.05 and 1.3 litre engines with hydraulic tappets

1 Distributor overhaul for these engine types is as described in paragraphs 2 to 14 but with reference to the accompanying illustration **(see illustration)** and the following:

a) *The distributor shaft is supported by a bearing plate which is removed by loosening the two screws securing it to the tensioning ring. Before removing the ring make a mark on the rim of the distributor body in line with the guide lug.*

b) *Shims are provided above and below the Hall sender and these should be selected to eliminate axial clearance and to provide for movement by the vacuum unit.*

All other engines

2 Wipe clean the exterior of the distributor.

3 Pull the rotor arm from the driveshaft then lift off the dust cover. Do not allow the cap retaining clips to touch the rotor during subsequent operations **(see illustrations)**.

4 Prise out the locking ring and withdraw the rotor up the shaft. Collect the locating pin **(see illustrations)**.

5 Undo the retaining screws securing the vacuum unit. Remove the vacuum unit, disengaging its operating arm **(see illustration)**.

6 Remove the locking ring and collect the washers from the shaft.

7 Undo the cap clip and baseplate retaining screws from the body and lift out the Hall sender unit and the baseplate **(see illustration)**.

8 Clean all the components and examine them for wear and damage.

9 Inspect the inside of the distributor cap for signs of burning or tracking. Make sure that the small carbon brush in the centre of the distributor cap is in good condition and can move up and down freely under the influence of its spring.

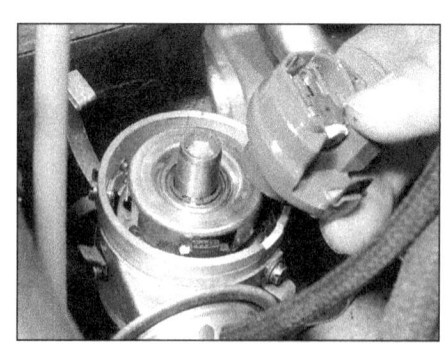

7.3a Pull free the rotor . . .

7.3b . . . and lift off the dust cap

7.4a Remove the locking ring and rotor . . .

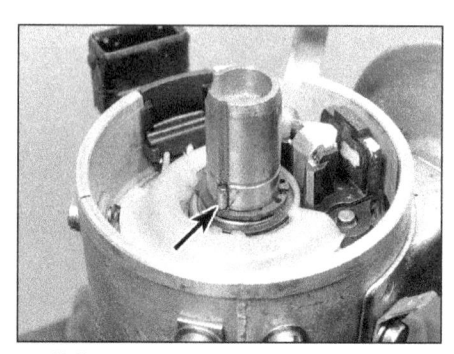

7.4b . . . and locating pin from shaft groove (arrowed)

Ignition system - transistorised type 5B•7

7.5 Vacuum unit removal

7.7 Hall sender unit, retaining ring and washers

7.13 Align rotor indent with groove in shaft when refitting

10 Check that the rotor arm is not damaged. Use an ohmmeter to measure the resistance between the brass contact in the centre of the rotor arm and the brass contact at the edge of the arm. The measured value of resistance should be between 600 and 1400 ohm.

11 Suck on the pipe connection to the vacuum diaphragm and check that the operating rod of the diaphragm unit moves. Retain the diaphragm under vacuum to check that the diaphragm is not perforated.

12 Reassemble the distributor in reverse order of dismantling. Smear a little grease on the bearing surface of the baseplate and the Hall sender bearing surfaces.

13 Before fitting the rotor (trigger wheel) back over the shaft, locate the small engagement pin in the groove in the shaft. Smear the pin with grease to retain it in position. Align the indent in the rotor inner bore with the groove in the shaft and slide it down into position over the pin **(see illustration)**.

14 On completion, rotate the distributor shaft by hand to ensure that it moves freely. If it does not, then the rotor is possibly distorted and will need renewal.

8 Ignition timing - checking and adjustment

Refer to Chapter 1, Section 17

9 Coil - testing

Refer to Section 9 in Part A of this Chapter

Notes

Chapter 5 Part C:
Ignition system - fully electronic type

The following information is a revision of, or supplementary to, that contained in Part B of this Chapter

Contents

Control unit - testing	5	HT leads, distributor cap and rotor arm - inspection and renewal	3
Distributor - overhaul	8	Ignition timing - checking and adjustment	9
Distributor - removal and refitting	7	Spark plugs - renewal	2
General information and precautions	1	Switch unit - testing	4
Hall sender - testing	6		

Degrees of difficulty

| Easy, suitable for novice with little experience | Fairly easy, suitable for beginner with some experience | Fairly difficult, suitable for competent DIY mechanic | Difficult, suitable for experienced DIY mechanic | Very difficult, suitable for expert DIY or professional |

Specifications

General
System type .... Fully Electronic Ignition (FEI)

Ignition timing
1.8 litre 16 valve engine .... 5 to 7° BTDC at 950 to 1050 rpm, with vacuum hose connected

1 General information and precautions

General information

The 1.8 litre 16 valve engine is fitted with a Fully Electronic Ignition (FEI) system **(see illustration)**.

This system functions in a similar manner to the transistorised system described in Part B of this Chapter. In addition, it incorporates an electronic control unit which adjusts the ignition timing electronically according to engine speed, load and temperature. The distributor is not fitted with centrifugal and vacuum advance mechanisms.

Precautions

The precautions listed in Parts A and B of this Chapter apply also to the FEI system. Note also the following:
a) *A digital multi-meter should be used for testing, otherwise readings may be inaccurate*
b) *When using a multi-meter, do not switch between ranges during testing as this may damage components*
c) *Do not under any circumstances use a test lamp, as this will damage the electronic components of the system*

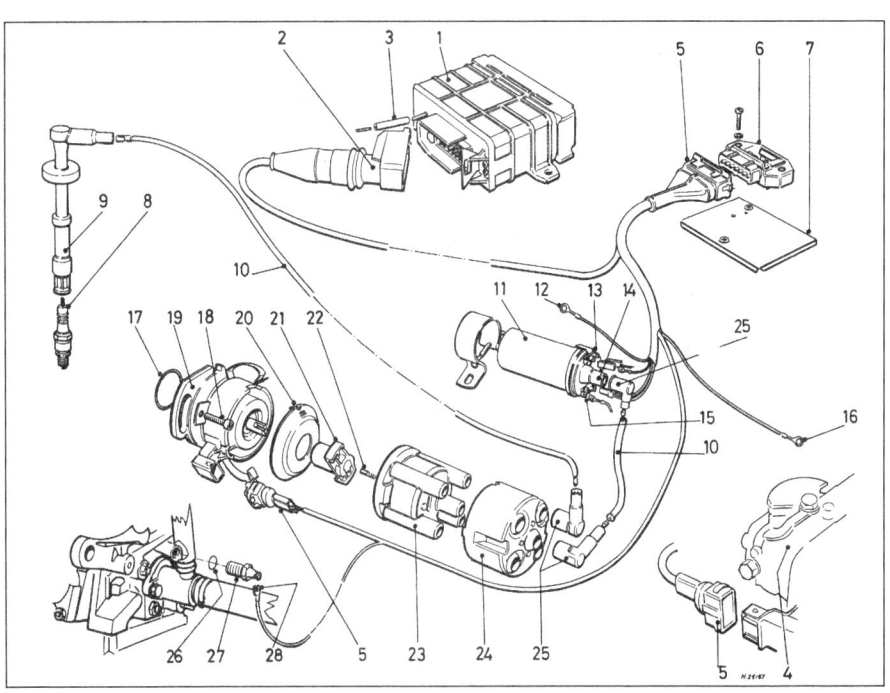

1.1 Fully Electronic Ignition system components

1 FEI control unit	8 Spark plug	16 Earth lead	23 Distributor cap
2 Connector	9 Connector	17 O-ring	24 Suppression cap
3 Vacuum line	10 HT lead	18 Screw	25 Suppression connectors
4 Throttle valve switch	11 Ignition coil	19 Distributor	26 Washer
5 Connector	12 Earth lead	20 Dust cover	27 Temperature sender
6 TCI-H switch unit	13 Terminal 1 (-)	21 Rotor arm	28 Connector
7 Heat sink	14 Terminal 4	22 Carbon brush and spring	
	15 Terminal 15 (+)		

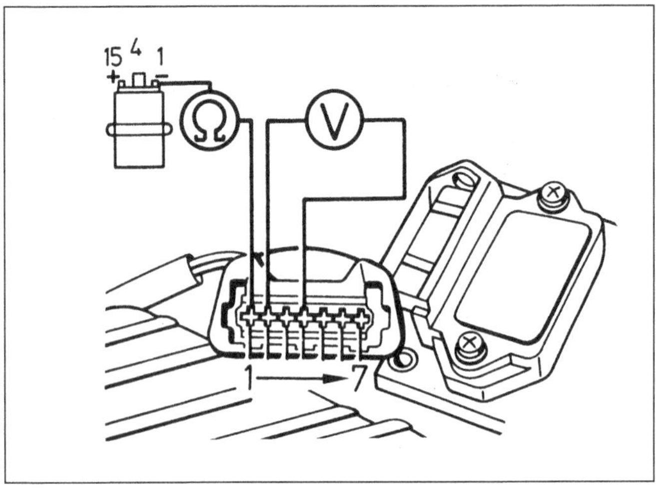

5C•2 Ignition system - fully electronic type

4.3 Testing FEI switch unit

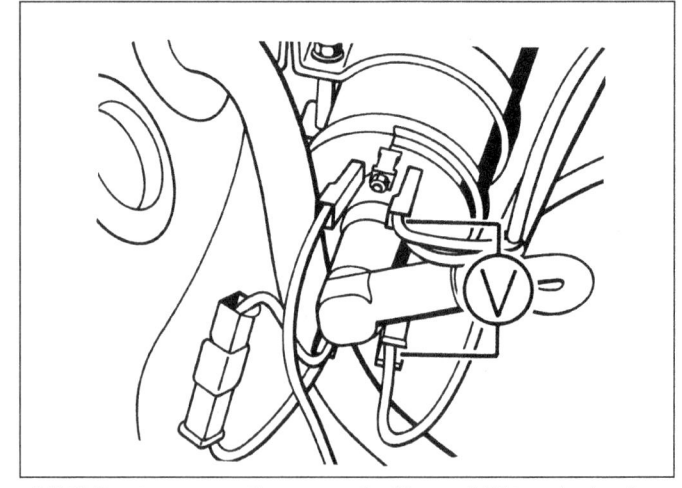

4.5 Voltmeter connection across ignition coil LT terminals when testing FEI switch unit

2 Spark plugs - renewal

Refer to Chapter 1, Section 15

3 HT leads, distributor cap and rotor arm - inspection and renewal

Refer to Section 3 in Part A of this Chapter

4 Switch unit - testing

1 The switch unit is located in the left-hand side of the plenum chamber beneath a plastic cover. The ignition coil should be in good condition before making this test.
2 Depress the wire clip and pull the connector from the switch unit.
3 Connect a voltmeter between terminals 4 and 2 on the connector (see illustration) then switch on the ignition and check that battery voltage is available. Switch off the ignition.
4 Using an ohmmeter, check that there is continuity between terminal 1 on the connector and terminal 1 on the coil.
5 Refit the connector to the switch unit, then connect a voltmeter across the low tension terminals on the coil (see illustration).
6 Release the spring and pull the connector from the control unit, then switch on the ignition. Check that initially a reading of 2 volts is registered on the voltmeter, dropping to zero after one to two seconds. If this is not the case, renew the switch unit and also if necessary, the ignition coil.
7 Using a temporary length of wire, briefly earth terminal 12 on the connector. The voltage should rise to at least 2 volts. If this is not the case, renew the switch unit.

5 Control unit - testing

1 Test the switch unit before checking the control unit.
2 Release the spring and pull the connector from the control unit located in the right-hand side of the plenum chamber.
3 Switch on the ignition, then use a voltmeter to check that battery voltage is available between terminals 3 and 5 on the connector (see illustration).
4 Check also that battery voltage is available between terminals 6 and 3, then operate the throttle valve switch and check that the voltage drops to zero. Switch off the ignition.
5 Using an ohmmeter, measure the resistance between the connector terminals 1 to 3. These are the temperature sender terminals and the resistance varies according to the coolant temperature.
6 Press the clip and pull the connector from the side of the distributor. Connect the voltmeter to the two outer terminals of the connector, then switch on the ignition. A reading of 5 volts should be registered. Switch off the ignition.

7 Connect a voltmeter across the low tension terminals of the ignition coil. Switch on the ignition.
8 Using a temporary length of wire, briefly earth the centre terminal of the distributor connector. The voltage should rise to at least 2 volts and the fuel pump should be heard to operate. If this is not the case, renew the control unit and if necessary check the fuel pump relay.

6 Hall sender - testing

Note: *A digital multi-meter should be used for testing. Do not use a test lamp*

Release the lead connector from the Hall sender unit. Check the voltage supply to the sender unit by connecting a multi-meter between the outer contacts of the plug, then switch on the ignition (see illustration). A minimum reading of 5 volts should be indicated, if not check the FEI control unit and wiring.
To check the signal from the Hall sender unit, slide the rubber grommet away from the sender plug and with the plug connected,

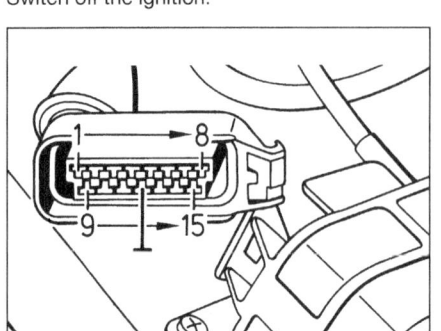

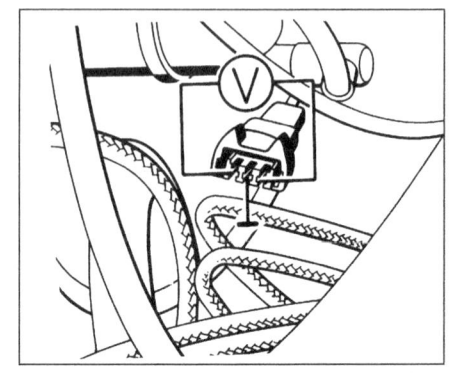

5.3 FEI control unit connector terminals

6.1 Testing Hall sender connector on side of distributor

Ignition system - fully electronic type 5C•3

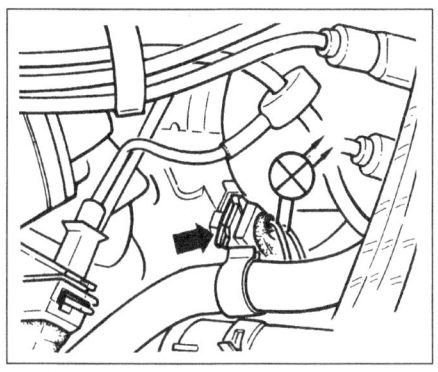

6.2 Signal check method from Hall sender unit

attach the diode test light to its centre and outer (brown/white) terminals **(see illustration)**. Operate the starter motor and check that the LED is seen to flicker. If it does not, the Hall sender unit is at fault and must be renewed.

7 Distributor - removal and refitting

Refer to Section 6 in Part B of this Chapter for the TCI-H system but ignore the reference to the vacuum pipe and renew the O-ring if necessary.

8 Distributor - overhaul

1 The only work likely to be necessary on the distributor is the renewal of the Hall sender which is available in kit form including a drive coupling, pin and circlip **(see illustration)**.
2 If the rotor arm is defective, it must be removed by crushing with pliers as it is permanently fixed to the shaft with strong adhesive. Clean the shaft and secure the new rotor arm with adhesive obtained from a VW dealer.
3 To renew the Hall sender, first note the position of the drive coupling offset in relation to the rotor arm.
4 Support the drive coupling in a vice, then drive out the roll pin after removing the circlip.
5 Remove the coupling followed by the shims and plastic washer.
6 Remove the shaft complete with rotor arm, followed by the plastic dust cover, shim and plastic washer.
7 Remove the screws and lift the Hall sender from inside the distributor body.
8 Clean all the components, then fit the new Hall sender using a reversal of the removal procedure, but lubricate the shaft with a little grease.

9 Ignition timing - checking and adjustment

1 This procedure is as described in Chapter 1, Section 17, for the TCI-H system. Operation of the control unit can also be checked as follows.
2 Run the engine at idling speed and note the basic ignition timing. Pull the vacuum hose from the control unit, then increase the engine speed to 4600 rpm and read off the ignition advance. Deduct the basic advance and the resultant value should be 18°, this being the advance attributable to engine speed.
3 Reconnect the vacuum hose, then run the engine to 4600 rpm. Note the ignition timing. Pull off the vacuum hose and again increase the engine speed to 4600 rpm. The ignition timing should be approximately 20° retarded from the previously-noted figure. This amount indicates the advance attributable to engine vacuum.

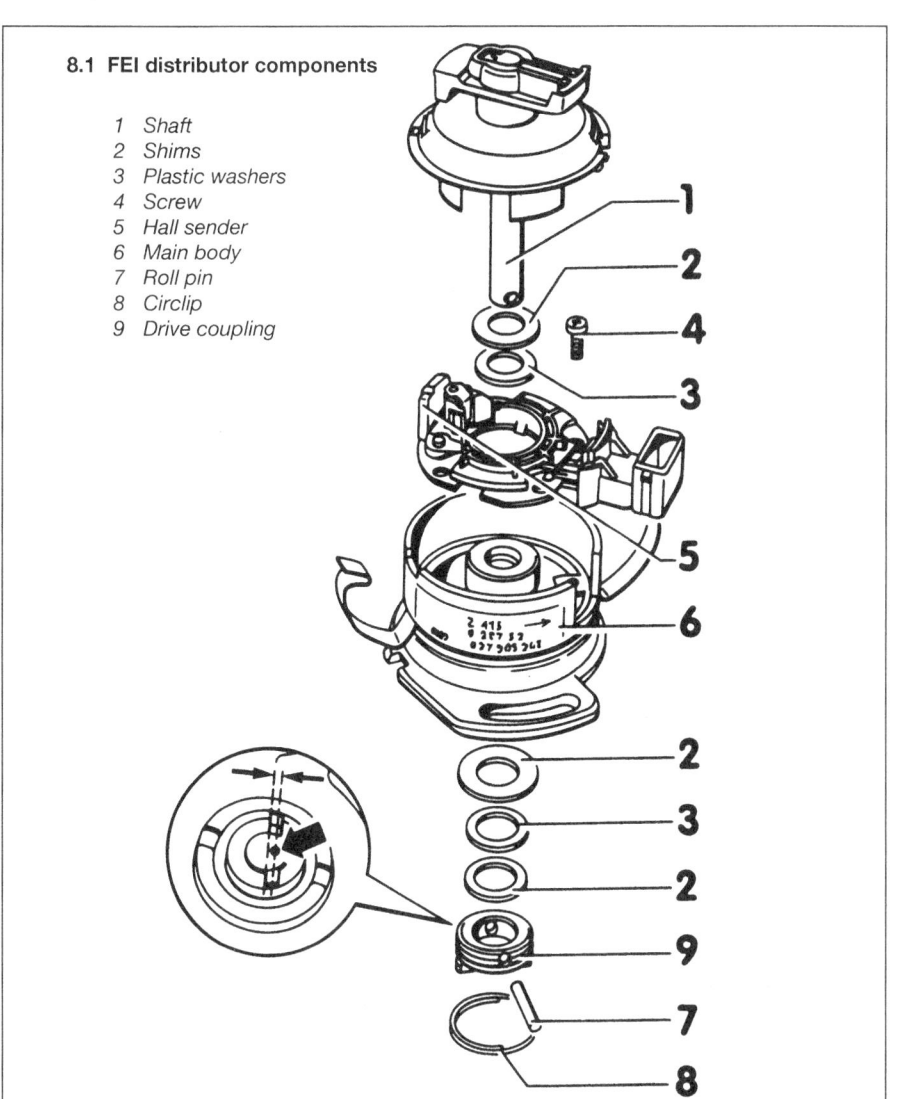

8.1 FEI distributor components

1 Shaft
2 Shims
3 Plastic washers
4 Screw
5 Hall sender
6 Main body
7 Roll pin
8 Circlip
9 Drive coupling

Chapter 5 Part D:
Starting and charging systems

Contents

Alternator - brush and voltage regulator renewal 8	Battery - charging 3
Alternator - removal and refitting 7	General information and precautions 1
Alternator - testing 6	Starting motor - brush renewal 11
Alternator drivebelt - inspection and adjustment 5	Starting motor - removal and refitting 10
Battery - removal and refitting 4	Starting motor - testing 9
Battery - maintenance 2	

Degrees of difficulty

Easy, suitable for novice with little experience	Fairly easy, suitable for beginner with some experience	Fairly difficult, suitable for competent DIY mechanic	Difficult, suitable for experienced DIY mechanic	Very difficult, suitable for expert DIY or professional

Specifications

System
Type . . . . 12 volt, negative earth

Battery
Rating . . . . 36 Ah or 45 Ah
Minimum voltage (under load) . . . . 9.6 volts at 110 amps

Alternator
Type	Bosch or Motorola	
Maximum output	55, 65 or 90 amp	
Minimum allowable brush length	5.0 mm	
Rotor winding resistance (ohms):	**Bosch**	**Motorola**
55 amp	2.9 to 3.2	3.1 to 3.3
65 amp	2.8 to 3.1	3.9 to 4.1
90 amp	3.0 to 4.0	-

Starter motor
Type . . . . Pre-engaged
Application/VW part No:
  1.05 and 1.3 litre . . . . 036 911 023 G
  1.3 litre . . . . 036 911 023 H
  1.6 litre:
    Manual gearbox . . . . 055 911 023 G
    Automatic transmission . . . . 055 911 023 A
  1.8 litre 027 911 023

Torque wrench settings
	Nm	lbf ft
Starter motor		
1.05 and 1.3 litre	20	15
1.6 and 1.8 litre (manual gearbox)	60	44
1.6 litre (automatic transmission)	20	15
Alternator		
Pulley nut	40	30
Mounting (to engine) bolts	45	33
Mounting/alternator pivot bolt	45	33
Adjuster strap bolts	25	18

5D•2 Starting and charging systems

1 General information and precautions

General information

The starting and charging system is of a 12 volt negative earth type. The battery is charged by a belt-driven alternator which incorporates a voltage regulator. The starter motor is of pre-engaged type, incorporating a solenoid which moves the drive pinion into engagement with the flywheel/driveplate ring gear before the motor is energised.

An automatic stop-start system is fitted as optional equipment to some models and is a fuel economy device. Activated by a control switch, the system automatically switches off the engine when the vehicle is stationary during traffic delays.

The system is switched on and off by means of a switch on the dash insert between the instrument panel and the heater/fresh air control panel. A warning light in the switch advises when the system is switched on.

The system should only be used when the vehicle has reached its normal operating temperature. When activated, the system will automatically stop the engine when the vehicle speed drops below 3.1 mph (5 kph) and has run at its normal idle speed for a period of at least 2 seconds. In addition the vehicle must previously have been driven at a speed in excess of 3.1 mph (5 kph).

When traffic conditions permit, the engine can be restarted by depressing the clutch pedal and moving the gear lever fully to the left in neutral. Once the engine has restarted, gear engagement can be made in the normal manner. If for any reason the engine stalls or stops after restarting, the restart procedure should be repeated but the gear lever must be moved back into neutral within 6 seconds.

Precautions

It is necessary to take extra care when working on the electrical system to avoid damage to semi-conductor devices (diodes and transistors) and to avoid the risk of personal injury. In addition to the precautions given in the *"Safety first!"* Section at the beginning of this Manual, take note of the following:

a) Before disconnecting any wiring or removing components, always ensure that the ignition is switched off.
b) Disconnect the battery leads before using a mains charger.
c) Do not reverse the battery connections. Components such as the alternator or any other having semi-conductor circuitry could be irreparably damaged.
d) If the engine is being started using jump leads and a slave battery, connect the batteries positive to positive and negative to negative. This also applies when connecting a battery charger.
e) Never disconnect the battery terminals or alternator multi-plug connector when the engine is running.
f) The battery leads and alternator multi-plug must be disconnected before carrying out any electric welding on the vehicle.
g) Never use an ohmmeter of the type incorporating a hand cranked generator for circuit or continuity testing.
h) When carrying out welding operations on the vehicle using electric welding equipment, disconnect the battery and alternator.

The following precautions should be taken when using the automatic stop-start system:

a) Do not use the system when the engine temperature is below 55°C or when the ambient temperature is very low as the engine will take longer to warm up
b) Do not allow the vehicle to roll when the engine is switched off, check that the handbrake is fully applied
c) During extended delays, switch the engine off in the normal manner with the ignition key as electrical accessories will otherwise be left on and the battery run down
d) If leaving the vehicle for any length of time, switch off the system and always take the ignition key with you

2 Battery - maintenance

Refer to *"Weekly Checks"*.

3 Battery - charging

Warning: The battery will be emitting significant quantities of (highly-inflammable) hydrogen gas during charging and for approximately 15 minutes afterwards. Do not allow sparks or naked flames near the battery or it may explode.

Caution: Specially rapid "boost" charges which are claimed to restore the power of a battery in 1 to 2 hours are not recommended as they can cause serious damage to the battery plates through overheating

Caution: If the battery is being charged from an external power source whilst the battery is fitted in the vehicle, both battery leads must be disconnected to prevent damage to the electrical circuits.

1 In winter when heavy demand is placed on the battery (starting from cold and using more electrical equipment), it is a good idea occasionally to have the battery fully charged from an external source. The charge rate will depend on battery type. For most owners however, the best method will be to use a trickle-charger overnight, charging at a rate of 1.5 amps.

2 Rapid 'boost' charges which are claimed to restore the power of the battery in 1 to 2 hours are not recommended, as they can cause serious damage to the battery plates through overheating and may cause a sealed battery to explode.

3 Ideally, the battery should be removed from the vehicle before charging and moved to a well-ventilated area.

4 Continue to charge the battery until all cells are gassing vigorously and no further rise in specific gravity or increase in no-load voltage is noted over a four-hour period. When charging is complete, turn the charger off before disconnecting its leads from the battery.

4 Battery - removal and refitting

Caution: When reconnecting the battery, always connect the positive lead first and the negative lead last.

Note: *If renewing the battery, a centralised ventilation type battery is recommended rather than one with ventilation plugs. If a battery with ventilated plugs is fitted, it will be necessary to fit a protective cover over the battery to prevent water spray entering and causing it to be over-filled, which would cause the acid level within the battery to overflow and damage surrounding components*

Removal

1 The battery is located in the engine compartment on the left-hand side.
2 Loosen the battery terminal clamp nuts and disconnect the negative lead followed by the positive lead **(see illustration)**.
3 Unscrew the bolt and remove the battery retaining clamp **(see illustration)**.
4 Lift the battery from its platform whilst taking care not to spill any electrolyte on the bodywork.

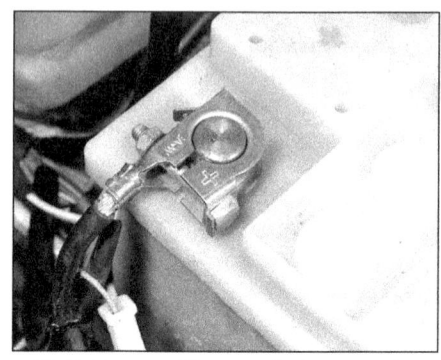

4.2 Battery positive terminal connection

Starting and charging systems 5D•3

4.3 Battery retaining clamp and bolt

Refitting

5 Refitting is a reversal of removal. Note the following:
a) Ensure that the leads are fitted to their correct terminals
b) Do not overtighten the lead clamp nuts or battery retaining clamp bolt
c) Smear a little petroleum jelly on the terminals and clamps

5 Alternator drivebelt - inspection and adjustment

Refer to Chapter 1, Section 13

6 Alternator - testing

1 Accurate testing of the alternator is only possible using specialised instruments and is therefore best left to a qualified electrician.
2 If the alternator is faulty, the condition of all brushes, soldered joints, etc., can be checked.
3 If no fault is found, refit the alternator and have it checked professionally.

7 Alternator - removal and refitting

Removal

1 Disconnect the battery negative lead.
2 Release the clip and pull the multi-plug from the rear of the alternator (see illustration).
3 Loosen the pivot and adjustment bolts (see illustration) then push the alternator in towards the engine and slip the drivebelt from the alternator.
4 Remove the adjustment link nut and washer.
5 Support the alternator then remove the pivot bolt and withdraw the unit from the engine.

Refitting

6 Refitting is a reversal of removal. Before fully tightening the pivot and adjustment bolts, tension the drivebelt.

8 Alternator - brush and voltage regulator renewal

Bosch

1 Disconnect the battery negative lead.
2 Wipe clean the exterior surfaces of the alternator around the voltage regulator.
3 Remove the two screws and withdraw the voltage regulator and brush assembly from the rear of the alternator (see illustration).
4 Check that the length of the carbon brushes is not less than the minimum amount specified (see illustration).
5 If the brushes are serviceable, clean them with a solvent-moistened cloth.
6 Check that brush spring pressure is equal for both brushes and holds the brushes securely against the slip rings. If in doubt about the condition of the brushes and springs, compare them with new items.
7 If the brushes are over worn, unsolder the brush leads and remove the brushes. Clean the housing, insert the new brushes and solder the new leads into position.
8 Clean the slip rings with a solvent-moistened cloth, then check for signs of scoring, burning or severe pitting. If worn or damaged, the slip rings should be attended to by an auto-electrician.
9 Reassembly is a reversal of the dismantling procedure.

Motorola

10 This procedure is similar to that described for the Bosch alternator. Identify the regulator wires for position before disconnecting them (see illustration).

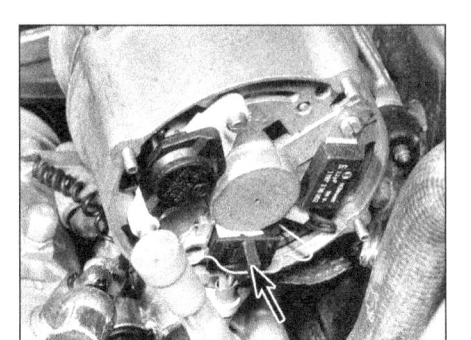

7.2 Lead multi-plug and retaining clip (arrowed) - Bosch alternator

7.3 Alternator pivot bolt and bracket – 1.3 litre

8.3 Removing voltage regulator and brush assembly

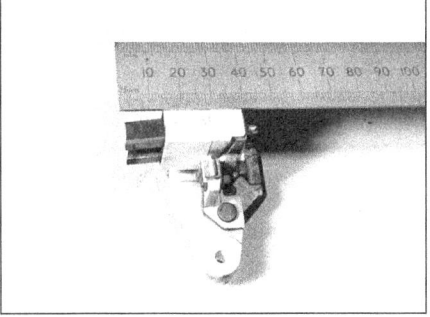

8.4 Checking alternator brush length

8.10 Voltage regulator/brush unit removal

5D•4 Starting and charging systems

10.4 Starting motor solenoid wiring connections – 1.3 litre

9 Starting motor - testing

Note: The following test was carried out with the starter motor in the vehicle

1 If the starter motor fails to operate, first check the condition of the battery by switching on the headlamps. If they glow brightly, then gradually dim after a few seconds, the battery is in an uncharged condition.
2 If the battery is in good condition, check the wiring connections on the starter for security and also check the earth wire between the gearbox and body.
3 If the starter still fails to turn, use a voltmeter or 12 volt test lamp and leads to check that current is reaching the main terminal (terminal 30) on the starter solenoid.
4 With the ignition switched on and the ignition key in the start position, check that current is reaching the remaining terminals on the solenoid. Also check that an audible click is heard as the solenoid operates indicating that the internal contacts are closed and that current is available at the field windings terminal.
5 Failure to obtain current at terminal 50 indicates a faulty ignition switch.
6 If current at the correct voltage is available at the starter motor, yet it does not operate, the unit is faulty and should be removed for further investigation.

10 Starting motor - removal and refitting

Removal

1 Disconnect the earth lead from the battery.
2 Jack up the front of the vehicle and support it on axle stands (see *"Jacking and vehicle support"*). Apply the handbrake.
3 Where a heat deflector plate is fitted, undo the retaining nuts and remove the plate.
4 Identify the wiring for position then disconnect it from the solenoid **(see illustration)**.
5 Where applicable, unbolt and detach the support bracket.
6 For 1.6 and 1.8 litre engines, move the steering fully to the right and if necessary detach the right-hand driveshaft at the gearbox drive flange to allow room for removal of the starter motor.
7 Undo the retaining bolts and withdraw the starter motor.

Refitting

8 Refitting is a reversal of removal. Tighten all bolts to the specified torque.
9 Where a support bracket is fitted, do not fully tighten the nuts and bolts until the bracket is correctly located and free of any tension.

11 Starting motor - brush renewal

1 With the starter motor removed from the vehicle, wipe clean its exterior around the end cover **(see illustration)**.
2 Remove the screws and lift off the end cap, then prise out the circlip and remove the shims whilst noting their fitted positions.
3 Unscrew the through-bolts and remove the end cover.
4 Lift the springs and remove the brushes from their holder.
5 Check each brush for excessive wear and if in doubt, renew the brushes as a set. Compare them with new items if necessary.
6 To renew each brush, crush it with a pair of pliers and then clean its lead. Insert the lead into the new brush and splay out its end. Solder the lead in position but grip the lead next to the brush with long-nosed pliers in order to prevent the solder penetrating the flexible section of the lead. File off any surplus solder.
7 Clean the commutator with a solvent-moistened cloth and, if necessary, use fine glass paper to remove any carbon deposits. If the commutator is worn excessively, it cannot be machined and renewal is necessary.
8 Reassembly is a reversal of the dismantling procedure. Note that the unit must be sealed with suitable sealant on the surfaces shown **(see illustration)**.

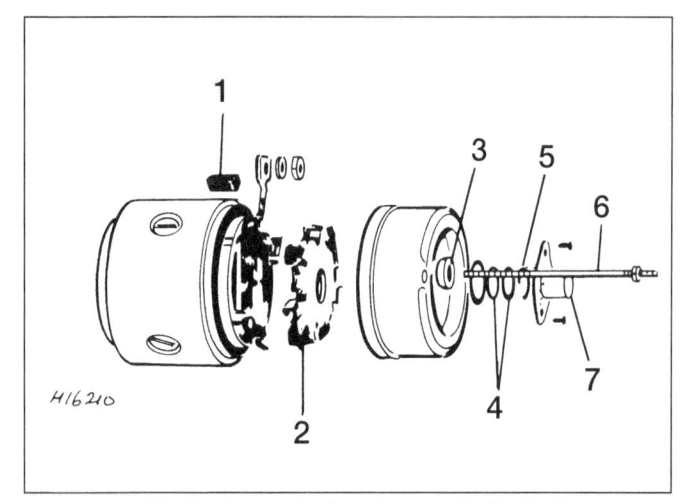

11.1 Starting motor brush assembly (typical)

1 Brushes
2 Brush holder
3 Bush
4 Shims
5 Circlip
6 Through-bolt
7 End cap

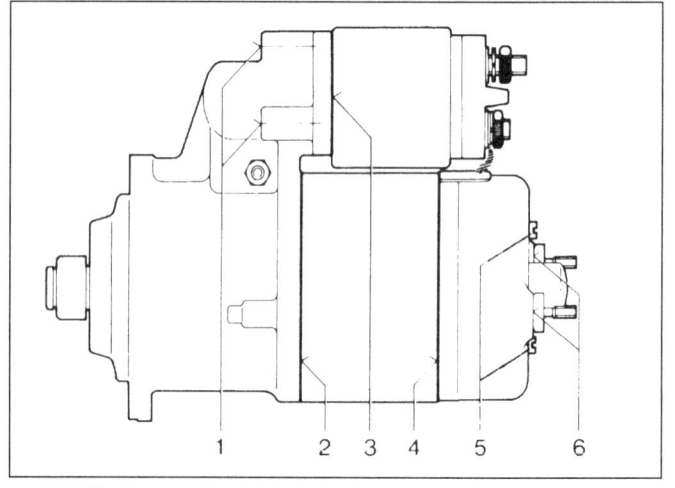

11.8 Surfaces to be sealed when reassembling starter motor

1 Solenoid securing screws
2 Starter/mounting surface
3 Solenoid joint
4 Starter/end cap joint
5 Through-bolts
6 Shaft cover joint and screws

Chapter 6
Clutch

Contents

Clutch - adjustment 2
Clutch - inspection 6
Clutch - removal and refitting 5
Clutch cable - renewal 3
Clutch pedal - removal and refitting 4
Clutch release mechanism - removal, checking and refitting 7
General information 1

Degrees of difficulty

Easy, suitable for novice with little experience	Fairly easy, suitable for beginner with some experience	Fairly difficult, suitable for competent DIY mechanic	Difficult, suitable for experienced DIY mechanic	Very difficult, suitable for expert DIY or professional

Specifications

Clutch
Type .... Single dry plate, diaphragm spring pressure plate, cable operation. Automatic adjustment on 1.8 litre models

Free play
At clutch pedal .... 15 to 20 mm

Friction disc diameter
084 gearbox .... 180 mm
085 gearbox .... 190 mm
020 4-speed gearbox .... 190 mm
020 5-speed gearbox (4+E) .... 200 mm
020 5-speed gearbox (Sports) .... 210 mm

Maximum inward taper
084 and 085 gearbox .... 0.3 mm
020, 4 and 5-speed gearbox .... 0 2 mm

Maximum run-out allowance *
084 and 085 gearbox .... 0.4 mm
020, 4 and 5-speed gearbox .... 0.3 mm
Measured 2.5 mm from outer edge

Diaphragm spring finger scoring depth
084 gearbox .... 0.3 mm maximum

Torque wrench settings

	Nm	lbf ft
084 gearbox		
Pressure plate	25	18
Flywheel	75	55
Guide sleeve	15	11
085 gearbox		
Flywheel:		
bolt with collar	100	74
bolt without collar	75	55
Guide sleeve	18	13
Pressure plate	25	18
020, 4 and 5-speed gearbox		
Flywheel	20	15
Pressure plate:		
Bolt without shoulder	75	55
Bolt with shoulder	100	74

6•2 Clutch

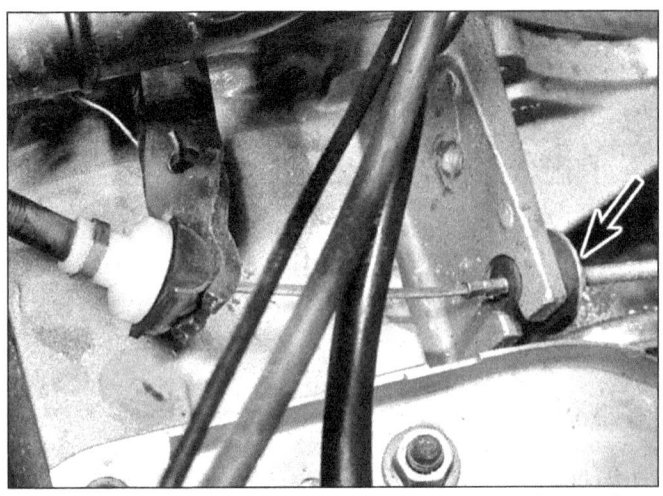

2.3 Clutch cable and release arm adjustment nut (arrowed)

2.5 Clutch cable adjuster

1 General information

084 and 085 gearboxes

With these gearbox types, the clutch is of a single dry plate type with a diaphragm spring pressure plate and cable actuation. The pressure plate assembly is bolted to the flywheel and transmits drive to the friction disc which is splined to the gearbox input shaft. Friction linings are riveted to each side of the disc and radial damper springs are incorporated in the hub in order to cushion rotational shocks.

With the clutch pedal depressed, the cable pulls the arm on the release shaft and the release bearing is pushed along the guide sleeve against the diaphragm spring fingers. Further movement causes the diaphragm spring to withdraw the pressure plate from the friction disc which also moves along the splined input shaft away from the flywheel. Drive then ceases to be transmitted to the gearbox.

With the clutch pedal released, the diaphragm spring forces the pressure plate back into contact with the friction disc which then moves along the input shaft into engagement with the flywheel. Drive is then transmitted directly through the clutch to the gearbox.

Wear of the friction disc linings causes the pressure plate to move closer to the flywheel and the cable free play to decrease. Cable adjustment must therefore be carried out as described in this Chapter.

020, 4 and 5-speed gearboxes

Unlike the more conventional clutch used with 084 and 085 gearboxes, this clutch pressure plate is bolted to the crankshaft flange. The flywheel, which is dish shaped, is bolted to the pressure plate with the friction disc being held between them. This is in effect the reverse of the more conventional arrangement where the flywheel is bolted to the crankshaft flange and the clutch pressure plate bolted to the flywheel.

The release mechanism comprises a metal disc (release plate) which is clamped in the centre of the pressure plate by a retaining ring. In the centre of the release plate is a boss into which the clutch pushrod is fitted. The pushrod passes through the centre of the gearbox input shaft and is actuated by a release bearing located in the gearbox end housing. A single finger lever presses on this bearing when the shaft to which it is spliced is turned by operation of the clutch pushrod, which in turn pushes the centre of the release plate inwards towards the crankshaft. The outer edge of the release plate presses on the pressure plate fingers, forcing them back towards the engine and removing the pressure plate friction face from the friction disc, thus disconnecting the drive. With the clutch pedal released, the pressure plate reasserts itself, clamping the friction disc firmly against the flywheel and restoring the drive.

As the friction linings on the disc wear, the pressure plate will gradually move closer to the flywheel and the cable free play will decrease. Periodic adjustment must therefore be carried out as described in this Chapter.

2 Clutch - adjustment

Automatic adjustment

1 On some 1.6 and 1.8 litre models the clutch is automatically adjusted by means of a segment and pawl at the pedal end of the clutch cable. The only adjustment necessary with this type is when the cable has been disconnected. Adjustment is made by depressing the clutch pedal several times once it is reconnected.

Manual adjustment

2 On all other models, clutch adjustment is made manually. Check for free play at the clutch pedal by measuring the distance it has to be moved in order to take up slack in the cable. If the distance is not as specified, adjust the cable as follows.

084 and 085 gearboxes

3 Locate the release arm on the gearbox clutch housing then turn the adjusting nut and half-round seating until adjustment is correct **(see illustration)**. Depress the arm if necessary to enable the nut to be turned more easily. If the nut is tight on its thread, hold the cable inner with a spanner.

4 Make sure that the adjusting nut is correctly seated in the release arm before finally checking adjustment.

020 gearbox

5 Loosen the cable outer locknut at the gearbox bracket, then turn the serrated disc while holding the outer cable stationary until pedal free play is correct **(see illustration)**.

6 Fully depress the pedal several times and recheck adjustment, then tighten the locknut. Lubricate the exposed part of the cable inner with a little multi-purpose grease.

3 Clutch cable - renewal

084 and 020 gearboxes

1 Loosen the cable at the gearbox end, then disconnect the inner and outer cable from the release lever and support bracket **(see illustrations)**.

2 On models with automatic cable adjustment, pivot the segment forwards and retain it with the pawl, then disengage the cable from it. Withdraw the cable.

3.1a Clutch pedal and cable components – 084 gearbox

3.1b Clutch pedal and cable components – 020 gearbox, early models

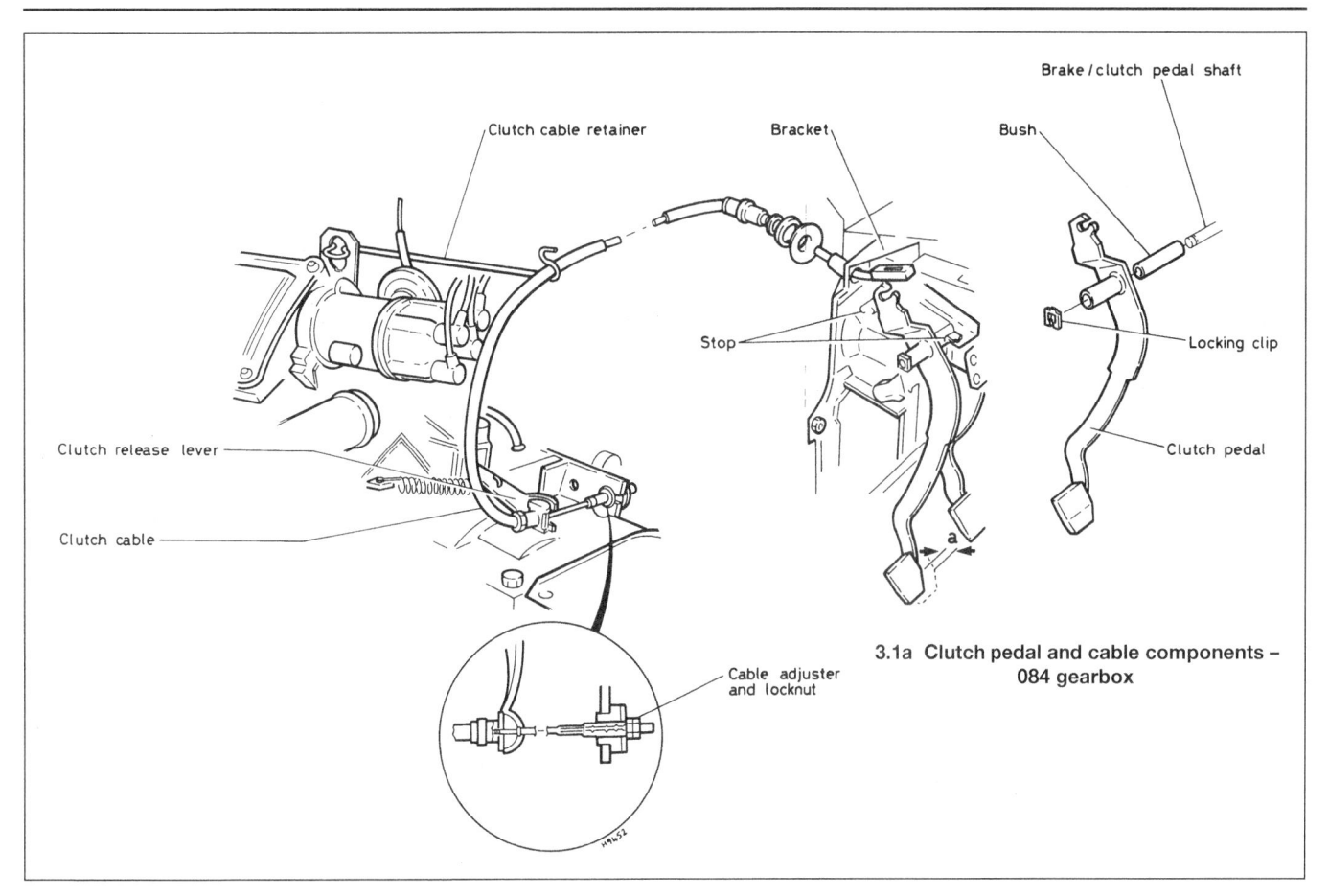

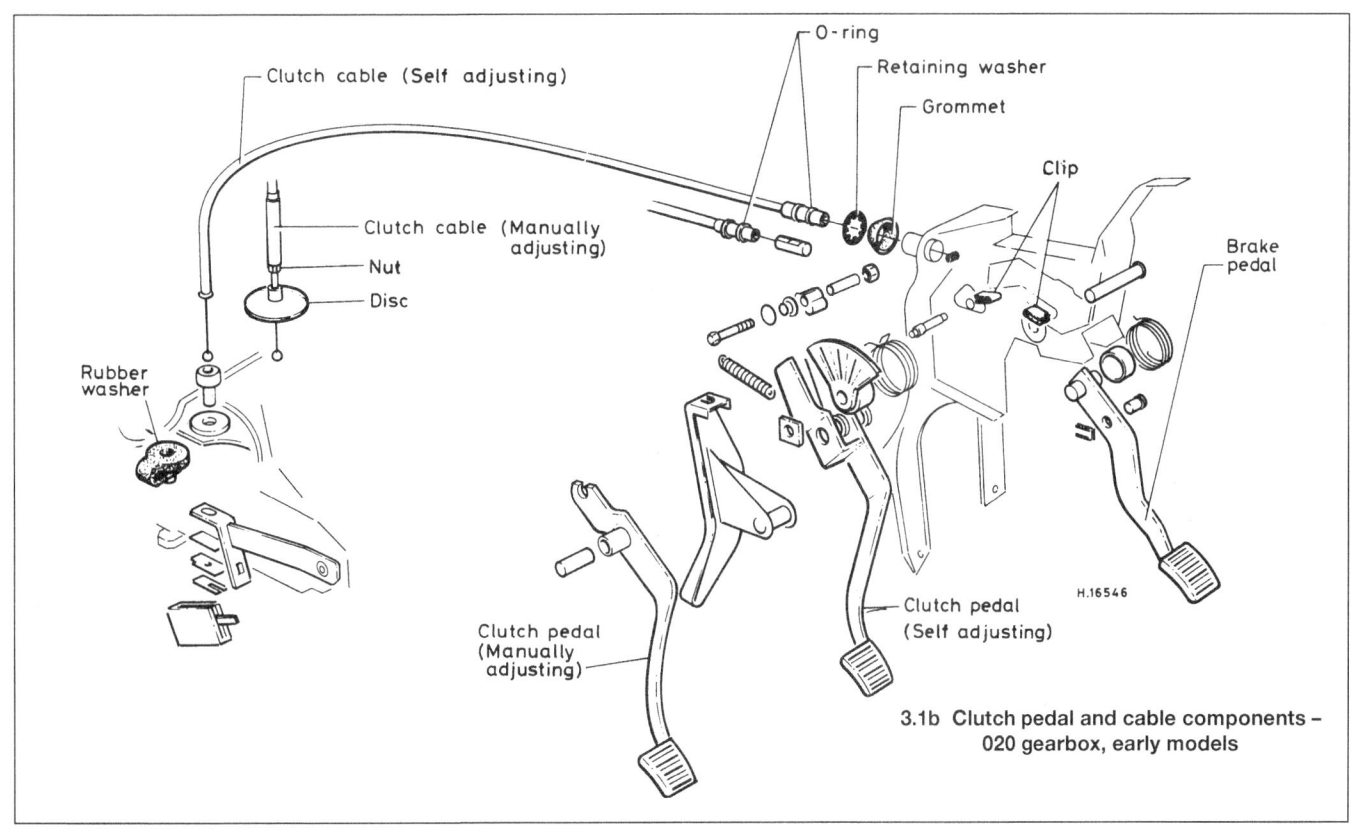

6•4 Clutch

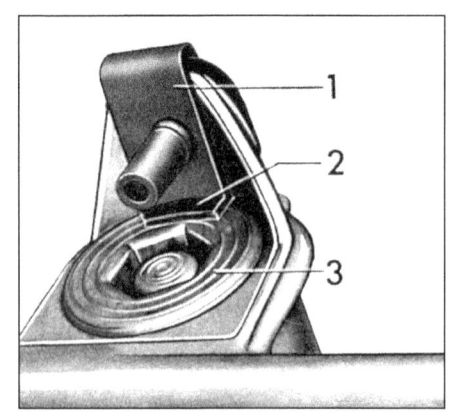

3.8 Clutch cable guide rubber washer (1) sealing lip (2) and selector shaft end cap (3) – 020 gearbox

3 On models with manual cable adjustment, unhook the cable inner from the clutch pedal, then withdraw the cable.

4 If necessary, prise the guide sleeve from the rubber washer on the gearbox bracket, then remove the washer.

5 Check that the cable locating grommet and washer are secure in the bulkhead.

6 Fit the new cable by using a reversal of the removal procedure.

7 Check that the sealing ring is correctly located on the bulkhead end of the outer cable and lightly lubricate the exposed parts of the cable inner with multi-purpose grease.

8 Ensure that the inner sealing lip of the rubber washer on the gearbox bracket is parallel to the end cap, otherwise the gearbox breather may become blocked with foreign matter **(see illustration)**.

9 Finally, adjust the cable.

085 and 020 gearboxes

10 A self-adjusting type of clutch cable is fitted to later models **(see illustration)**. Manual adjustment can be made for initial adjustment when a new cable is fitted. Also, in the event of full cable adjustment being taken up, a manual check of adjustment should be made to confirm this before renewing the cable. To do this, fully depress the clutch pedal five times then check to ensure that the clutch release lever cannot be pressed downwards, in which case the cable is in need of renewal.

11 To remove the cable, first disconnect the battery negative lead.

12 Depress the clutch pedal several times, then compress the adjusting mechanism within the dust excluding boot and retain it in this state. A special tool is available **(see illustration)** but wire or a ratchet-type cable strap can be used as an alternative.

13 Release the cable from the release lever and unhook the cable eye from the clutch pedal. Withdraw the cable through the bulkhead grommet.

14 Fit the new cable and connect it to the clutch pedal only.

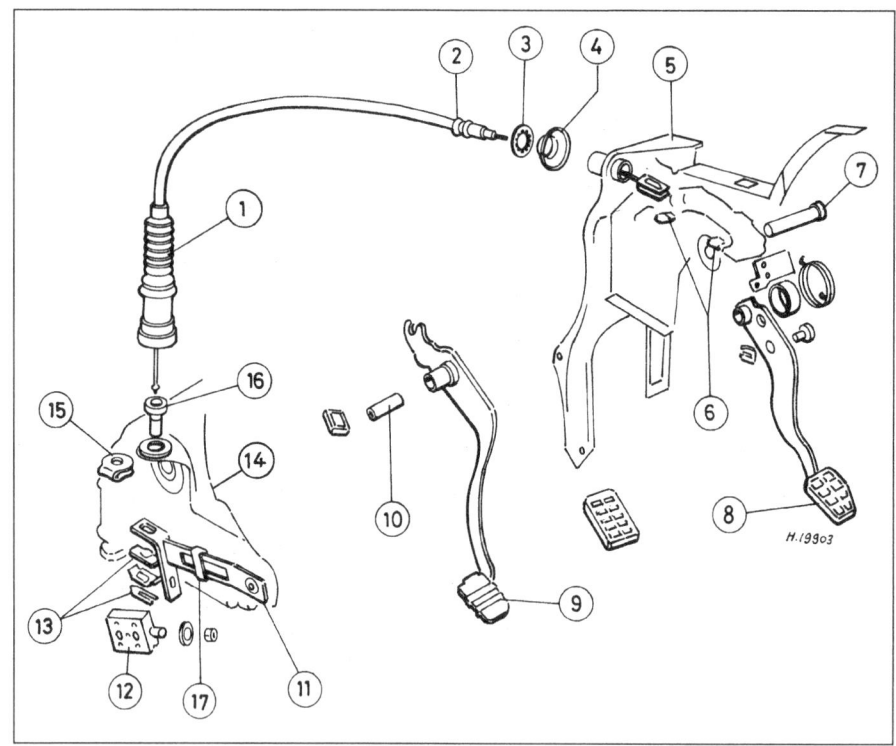

3.10 Clutch cable components - self-adjusting type, later models

1 Automatic adjustment mechanism	6 Stop clip	12 Balance weight
2 Seal	7 Pedal shaft	13 Cable fixings
3 Clamping washer	8 Brake pedal	14 Gearbox casing
4 Sleeve	9 Clutch pedal	15 Rubber washer
5 Mounting bracket	10 Bush	16 Rubber guide
	11 Release lever	17 Buffer

15 Depress the clutch pedal by hand while an assistant pulls the release lever end of the cable. Compress the adjusting mechanism within the dust excluding boot and retain it as previously described.

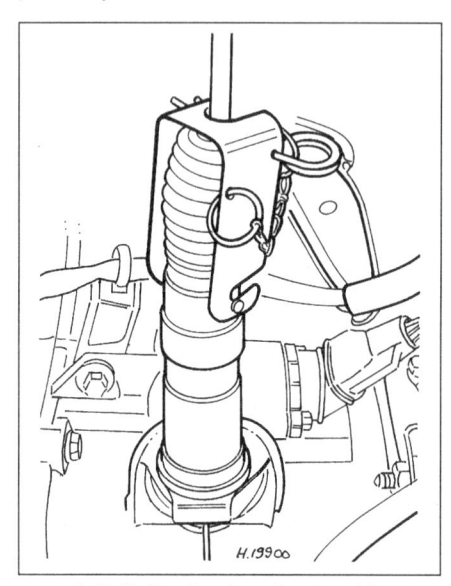

3.12 Self-adjusting clutch cable mechanism compressed by using VW tool 3151

16 Connect the cable to the release lever.

17 Depress the clutch pedal a minimum of five times. Grip the release lever and push it in the opposite direction to its normal direction of travel to a distance of about 10 mm. Check that the release lever moves freely.

18 On no account attempt to dismantle the automatic adjustment mechanism.

4 Clutch pedal - removal and refitting

Removal

1 Detach the clutch cable from the release arm on the gearbox clutch housing and then from the clutch pedal.

2 On models with a manually adjusted clutch, prise free the clip from the end of the pedal shaft then carefully slide the pedal free from the shaft.

3 On models with an automatic cable adjuster mechanism, disconnect the steering column and move it to the left to allow pedal removal. Tension the over-centre spring and hold it under tension during its removal. A suitable spring retainer will be required. If possible, use VW tool 3113 **(see illustration)**.

Clutch 6•5

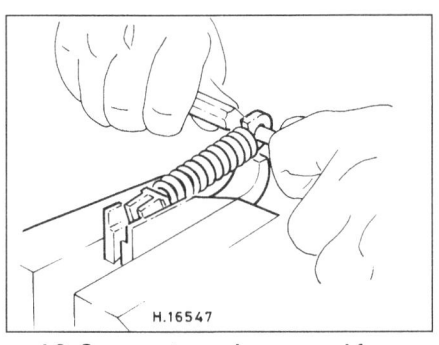

4.3 Over-centre spring removal from retainer using VW tool 3113

5.3 Removing pressure plate bolts

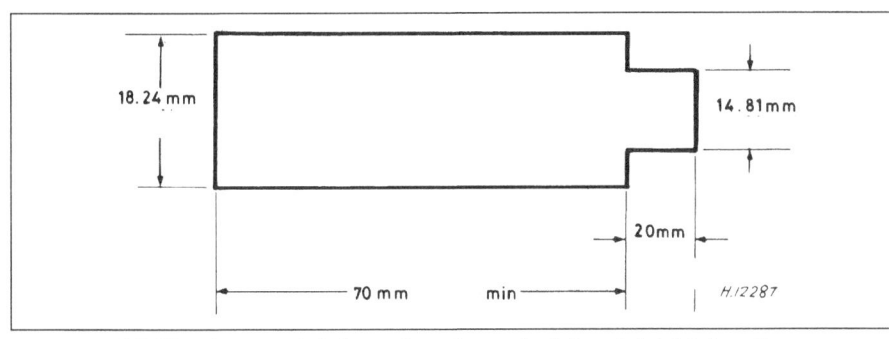

5.5 Wooden mandrel dimensions for centralising clutch friction disc

4 With the over-centre spring held under tension, remove the clip, the over-centre spring and retainer. Now remove the circlip securing the pedal unit and withdraw the pedal, together with the segment and pawl.

5 Examine the shaft and pedal bush for wear and renew if necessary. The bush is an interference fit in the pedal and can be removed or installed using a soft metal drift. Ensure that the ends of the bush are flush with the ends of the pedal tube.

6 If dismantling the segment and panel on the automatic adjuster clutch type, note the orientation of the segment and pawl spring prior to dismantling. Check the pawl bush for excessive wear and renew any parts as necessary.

Refitting

7 Refitting is a reversal of the removal procedure on both pedal types. Lubricate the pivot shaft with a little multi-purpose grease, also the pawl bush on the automatic adjuster.

8 On manual cable adjuster types, recheck and adjust the cable

9 On automatic adjuster types, depress the pedal a few times to take up adjustment.

5 Clutch - removal and refitting

Warning: Do not inhale asbestos dust when working on clutch components

Note: Both the friction disc and pressure plate are treated with anti-corrosion grease during manufacture in order to prolong the service life of the components. This grease must only be removed from the contact surface of the pressure plate and must be left intact on all remaining areas

084 and 085 gearboxes

Removal

1 Remove the gearbox.

2 Mark the pressure plate cover and flywheel in relation to each other.

3 Using an Allen key, unscrew the bolts securing the pressure plate cover to the flywheel in a diagonal sequence, one turn at a time **(see illustration)**. If the key handle is pressed towards the centre of the flywheel it should be possible to loosen the bolts while holding the cover stationary by hand. If necessary, hold the flywheel stationary using a screwdriver inserted in the starter ring gear teeth.

4 Withdraw the pressure plate assembly and the friction disc from the flywheel. Note that the friction disc hub extension containing the cushion springs faces the pressure plate.

Refitting

5 Before commencing refitting, a tool must be obtained for centralising the friction disc, otherwise difficulty will be experienced when refitting the gearbox. Unlike the normal arrangement, the gearbox input shaft does not enter a bush or bearing in the rear of the crankshaft. If the friction disc is not centralised, the gearbox dowels will not be aligned correctly. If no centralising tool is available, a wooden mandrel may be made to the dimensions shown **(see illustration)**.

6 Clean the friction faces of the flywheel and pressure plate, then fit the centralising tool to the crankshaft and locate the friction disc on it with the hub extension outwards **(see illustration)**.

7 Fit the pressure plate assembly to the flywheel (in its original position if not renewed), then insert the bolts and tighten them evenly in a diagonal sequence to the specified torque **(see illustrations)**. If working on a 085 gearbox, use thread locking compound on the bolt threads and note that the torque wrench setting differs according to bolt type (with or without a collar).

8 Check the release bearing before refitting the gearbox.

5.6 Friction disc and centralising tool

5.7a Fitting pressure plate assembly

5.7b Clutch unit reassembled

6•6 Clutch

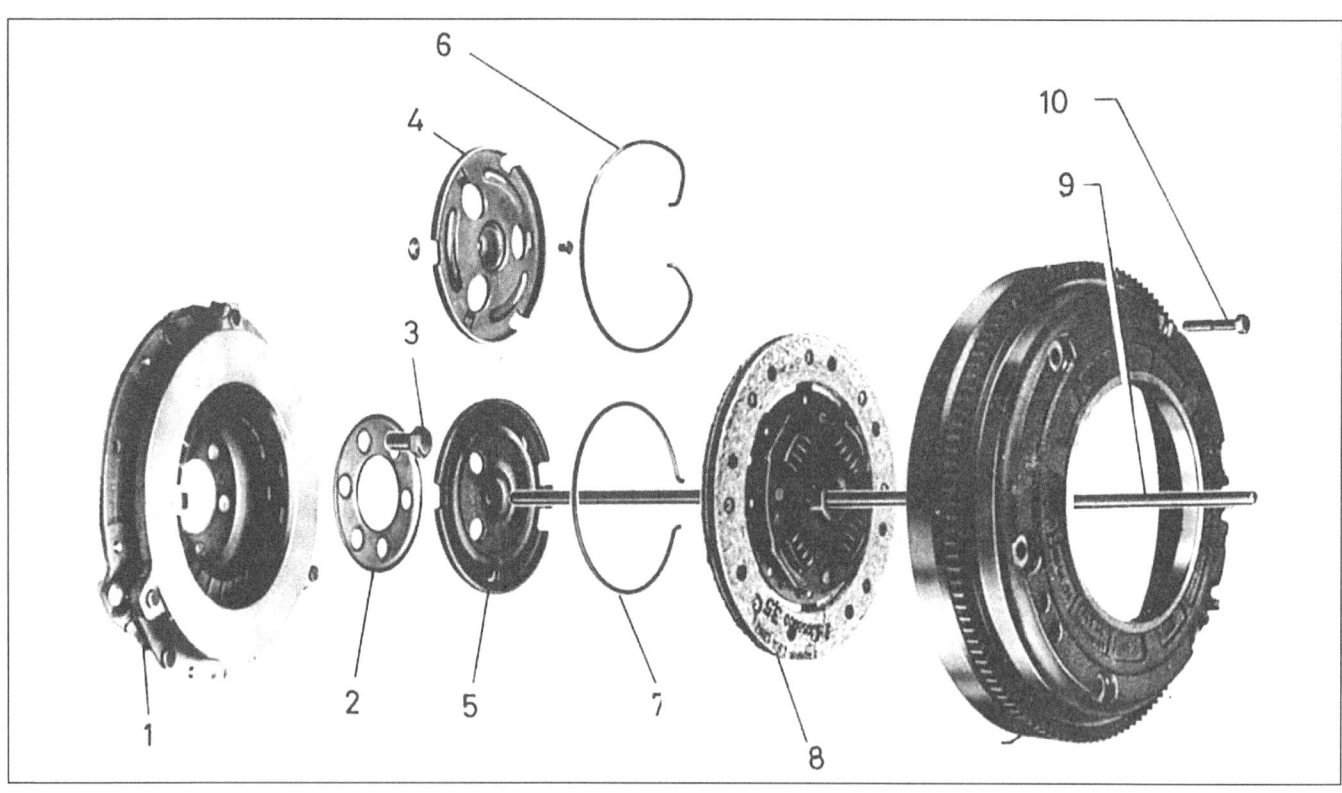

5.10a Clutch components – 020 gearbox

1 Pressure plate assembly
2 Packing plate
3 Bolt
4 Release plate (200 and 210 mm diameter clutch)
5 Release plate (190 mm diameter clutch)
6 Retaining ring (200 and 210 mm diameter clutch)
7 Retaining ring (190 mm diameter clutch)
8 Friction disc
9 Pushrod
10 Bolt

020 gearbox

Removal

9 Remove the gearbox.
10 Clamp the flywheel to prevent it turning, then undo the flywheel-to-pressure plate bolts in a progressive and diagonal sequence, releasing each one half a turn at a time until they are all slack before removing them. The flywheel and friction disc may now be removed. Note which way round the disc is fitted and also mark the flywheel and pressure plate in relation to each other, although centring pins are provided to ensure that the TDC mark on the flywheel is positioned correctly **(see illustrations)**.
11 Examine the pressure plate surface. If it is clean and free from scoring, then there is no reason to remove it unless the friction disc shows signs of oil contamination.
12 If the plate surface is defective then it must be removed. Note exactly where the ends of the retaining ring are located for reference when refitting and prise the ring out with a screwdriver. The release plate may now be removed **(see illustration)**.
13 The pressure plate is held to the crankshaft flange by six bolts coated with a thread locking compound. These will be difficult to remove as they were tightened to a high torque before the locking fluid set, so the plate must be held with a clamp similar to that shown **(see illustration)**. Once removed, these bolts must be renewed.

Refitting

14 Refitting is a reversal of removal. Use thread locking compound on the new bolts securing the pressure plate to the crankshaft flange (if removed) and tighten them to the specified torque **(see illustration)**. Note that the torque wrench setting differs according to bolt type (with or without a shoulder).

5.10b Flywheel expanding peg for centring pressure plate

5.12 Removing clutch release plate

5.13 Using VW tool to hold pressure plate stationary while unscrewing retaining bolts

Clutch 6•7

5.14 Tightening clutch pressure plate retaining bolts

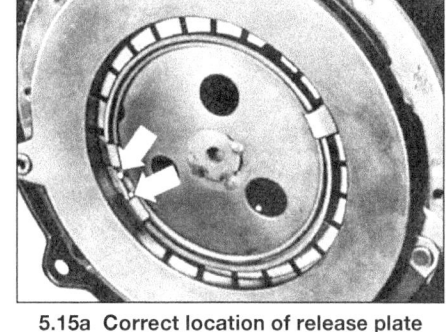

5.15a Correct location of release plate retaining ring ends (arrowed) on 190 mm clutch

5.15b Correct location of release plate retaining ring ends (arrowed) on 200 and 210 mm diameter clutch

5.18a Using VW tool 547 to centre clutch friction disc

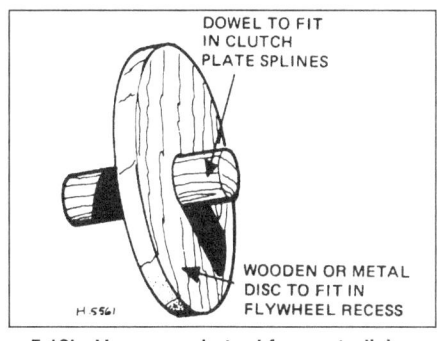

5.18b Home-made tool for centralising clutch friction disc

5.18c Using vernier calipers to check friction disc centralisation

15 Make sure that the retaining ring is correctly seated (see illustrations). Take care that no oil or grease is allowed to get onto the pressure plate or friction surfaces. Where a new pressure plate is being fitted, wipe the protective coating from the friction surfaces.

16 Lubricate the splines of the friction disc hub with a Moly paste or spray lubricant. Do not get any lubricant onto the linings.

17 When refitting the friction disc, ensure that the greater projecting boss which incorporates the cushion springs is furthest from the engine, then fit the flywheel over the pressure plate. Fit the securing bolts and tighten them finger tight only.

18 The next operation is to centre the friction disc. If this is not done accurately, the gearbox mainshaft will not be able to locate in the splines of the clutch disc hub and it will be impossible to fit the gearbox. The best centralising tool is VW 547 which fits in the flywheel and has a spigot which fits exactly in the centre of the clutch disc hub (see illustration). If you cannot borrow or hire this tool, then fabricate a tool as shown (see illustration). Alternatively, centre the disc using vernier calipers (see illustration). Once the friction disc is centred correctly, tighten the securing bolts in a diagonal sequence to the specified torque and check centralisation again.

19 When refitting the transmission, put a smear of lithium based grease on the end of the clutch pushrod at the release plate end.

6 Clutch - inspection

Caution: Do not use petrol or petroleum-based solvents to clean dust off clutch components

084 and 085 gearboxes

1 Examine the surfaces of the pressure plate and flywheel for signs of scoring. Light scoring is normal but if excessive, the pressure plate must be renewed and the flywheel either machined or renewed.

2 Check the pressure plate diaphragm spring fingers for wear caused by the release bearing. If the scoring exceeds the maximum depth specified, renew the assembly.

3 Using a straight-edge and feeler blade, check that the inward taper of the pressure plate does not exceed the maximum amount specified (see illustration). Also check for loose riveted joints and for any cracks in the pressure plate components.

4 Check the friction disc linings for wear and renew the disc if the linings are worn to within 1.0 mm of the rivets.

5 Check that the friction disc damper springs and all rivets are secure, and that the linings are not contaminated with oil. Temporarily fit the disc to the gearbox input shaft and check that the run-out does not exceed that specified.

6 If the clutch components are contaminated with oil, the leak should be found and rectified.

7 Having checked the clutch disc and pressure plate, it is always worthwhile to check the release bearing.

020 gearbox

8 The most probable part of the clutch to require attention is the friction disc. Normal wear will eventually reduce its thickness. The lining must stand proud of the rivets by not less than 0.6 mm. At this measurement, the lining is at the end of its life and a new friction disc is needed.

9 The friction disc should be checked for run-out if possible. Mount the disc between the centres of a lathe and measure the run-out at the specified dimension from the outer

6.3 Checking pressure plate for taper

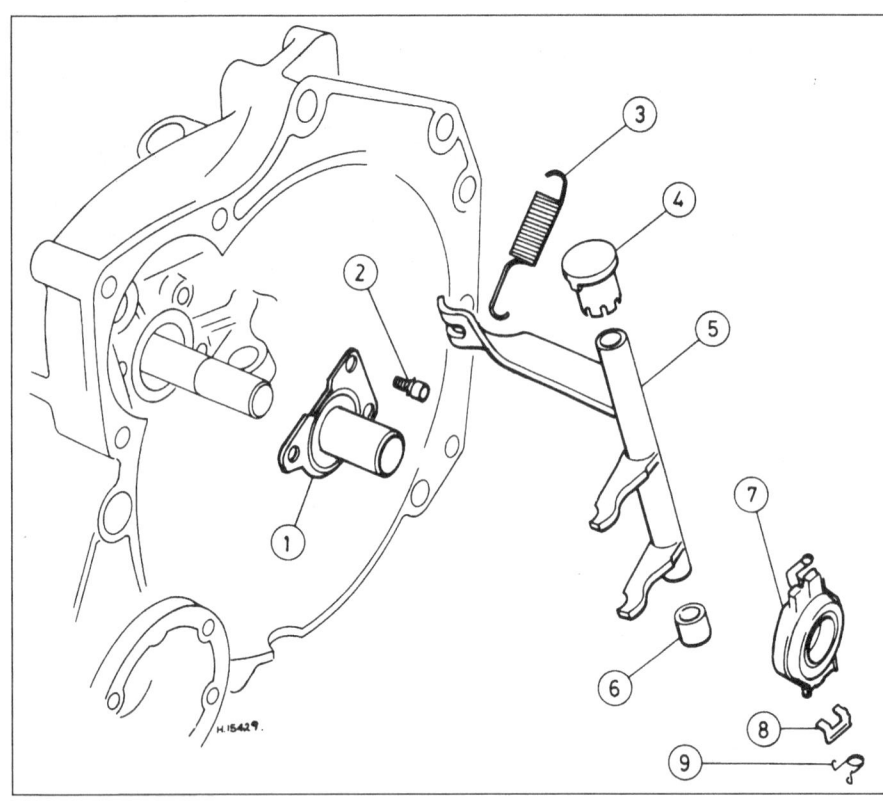

6•8 Clutch

7.1a Clutch release bearing and shaft components – 084 gearbox

1 Guide sleeve
2 Splined-head bolt
3 Return spring
4 Bush
5 Release shaft
6 Bush
7 Release bearing
8 Retaining clip
9 Retaining spring

7.1b Clutch release arm return spring

7.2a Release bearing fitted to arm

7.2b Release bearing and retaining clips

7.5 Withdrawing guide sleeve

wear and unless they can be removed by light application of emery paper, renew the plate

11 The flywheel friction surface must be similarly checked.

12 So far, the inspection has been for normal wear. Two other types of damage may be encountered.

13 The first is overheating due to clutch slip. In extreme cases, the pressure plate and flywheel may have radial cracks. Such faults mean that they require renewal.

14 The second problem is contamination by oil or grease. This will cause clutch slip but probably without the cracks. There will be shiny black patches on the friction disc which will have a glazed surface. There is no cure for this, a new friction disc is required. In addition, it is imperative that the source of contamination be located and rectified. It will be either the crankshaft oil seal or the gearbox input shaft oil seal (or both). Examine them and renew as necessary.

15 Whilst the gearbox is removed, check the release bearing for satisfactory condition.

7 Clutch release mechanism - removal, checking and refitting

084 gearbox

1 With the gearbox removed, unhook the return spring from the release arm **(see illustrations)**.

2 Turn the release arm to move the release bearing up the guide sleeve, then disengage the two spring clips from the release fork and withdraw the bearing **(see illustrations)**.

3 Note how the springs and clips are fitted, then prise the clips from the release bearing.

4 Spin the bearing by hand and check it for roughness, then attempt to move the outer race laterally against the inner race. If any excessive roughness or wear is evident, renew the bearing. Do not wash the bearing in solvent if it is to be re-used.

5 Using a splined key, unbolt and remove the guide sleeve from the clutch housing **(see illustration)**.

edge, then compare the result with that specified. However, this requires a dial gauge and a mandrel. If the clutch has not shown signs of dragging, then this test may be passed over but if it has, then we suggest that expert help be sought to test run-out.

10 Examine the pressure plate. There are three important things to check, as follows:

a) Put a straight-edge across the friction surface and measure any bow or taper with feeler blades
b) The rivets which hold the spring fingers in position must be tight. If any of them are loose then scrap the pressure plate
c) Inspect the condition of the friction surface. Ridges or scoring indicate undue

Clutch 6•9

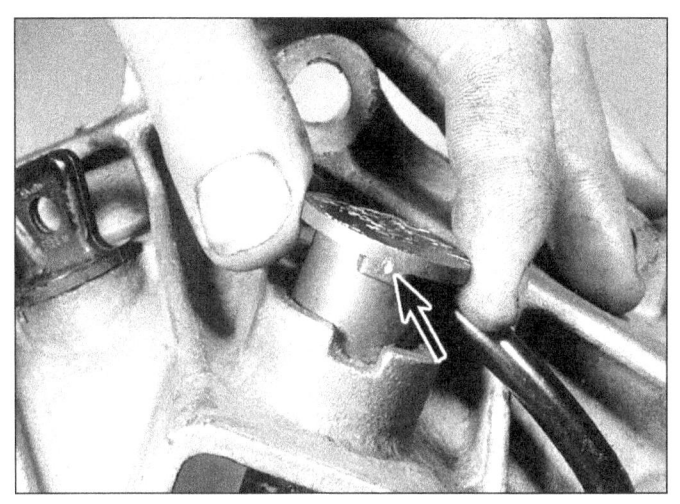

7.7 Removing release shaft

7.9 Location tab on release shaft outer bush

6 Using a narrow drift, drive the release shaft outer bush from the clutch housing. Alternatively, prise out the bush.
7 Pull the release shaft from the inner bearing then withdraw the shaft and arm from the housing **(see illustration)**.
8 Check the bushes and bearing surfaces of the shaft for wear and also check the guide sleeve for scoring. The inner bush may be removed by using a soft metal drift and the new bush driven in until flush.
9 Refitting is a reversal of removal. Lubricate all bearing surfaces with a little high melting-point grease. Ensure that the release shaft outer bush is correctly sealed with the tab located in the cut-out in the clutch housing **(see illustration)**.

085 gearbox

10 The clutch release mechanism on this gearbox differs from the 084 version by having a release lever splined to the release shaft **(see illustration)**. This enables the shaft to be removed without first removing the guide sleeve.
11 To remove the release shaft, prise out the two locking clips then slide out the shaft and withdraw the release lever.
12 The bushes may be driven from the clutch housing with a suitable drift, although VW tools may be required for the removal and fitting of the inner bush (consult a VW dealer if in doubt). The outer bush should be installed to allow flush fitting of the seal.
13 Refit the release shaft using a reversal of the removal procedure. A master spline is incorporated on the shaft and release lever to ensure correct assembly. Lubricate the bearing surfaces with a molybdenum disulphide grease.

020 gearbox

14 The clutch release mechanism is located in the gearbox end housing and is accessible after removal of the end cover or plate (as applicable) **(see illustration)**.

15 On 4-speed gearboxes, unbolt the end cover from the gearbox and remove the gasket **(see illustration)**.
16 On 5-speed gearboxes, first support the engine/gearbox unit with a trolley jack, then disconnect the unit front mounting and gearbox rear mounting. Lower the jack a few inches to gain access to the end plate in the gearbox housing cover. Using a sharp instrument, pierce the endplate and lever it out from the gearbox. A new plate must be obtained.

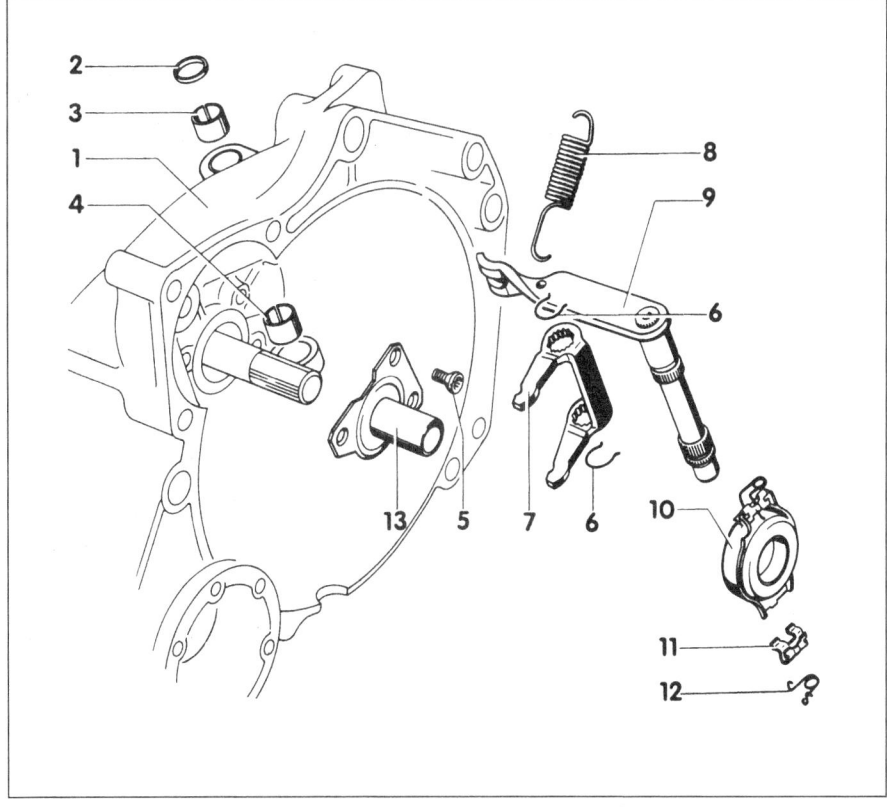

7.10 Clutch release mechanism components - 085 gearbox

1 Clutch housing	5 Screw	10 Release bearing
2 Seal	6 Locking clips	11 Retaining clip
3 Outer bush	7 Release lever	12 Retaining spring
4 Inner bush	8 Return spring	13 Guide sleeve
	9 Release shaft	

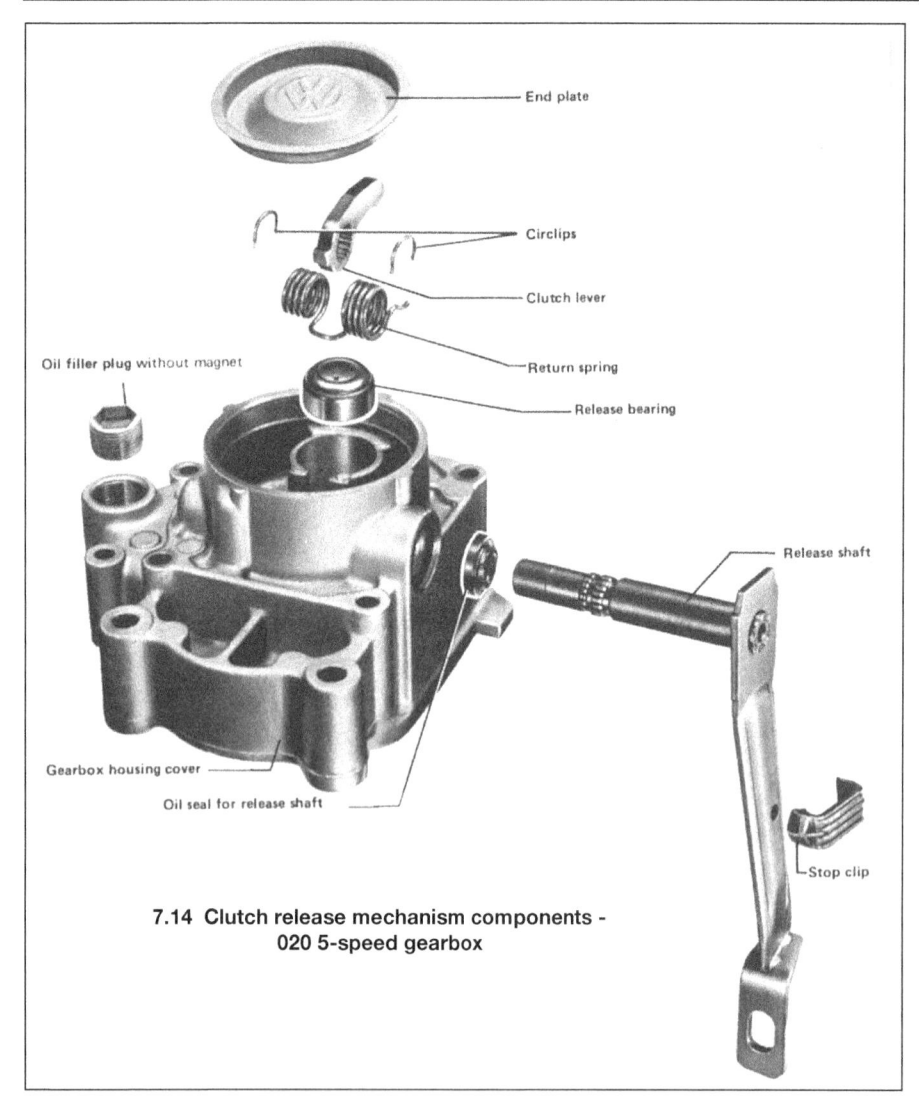

6•10 Clutch

7.14 Clutch release mechanism components - 020 5-speed gearbox

7.15 Removing gearbox end cover

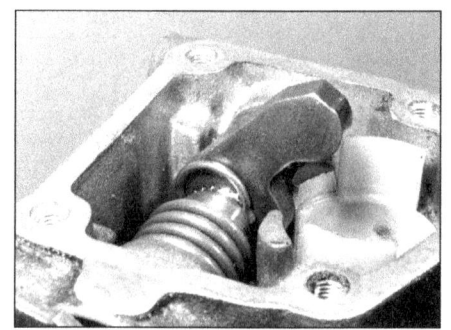

7.17 Extracting clutch release lever location circlips

7.18 Withdrawing clutch release arm and shaft

7.19 Removing clutch release bearing

17 On both 4 and 5-speed gearboxes, the release lever is located on the shaft by two circlips. Extract the circlips **(see illustration)**.
18 With the clutch cable disconnected, withdraw the release arm and shaft from the gearbox and remove the lever and spring **(see illustration)**.
19 Remove the release bearing **(see illustration)** and on 4-speed models only, extract the guide sleeve. Removal of the pushrod on 4-speed gearboxes is not possible unless the unit is lowered.
20 Rotate the release bearing and check it for wear and roughness. Renew if necessary. Check the shaft oil seal for wear or deterioration and if necessary, prise it out and drive in a new seal squarely using a suitable length of metal tubing. Fill the space between the seal lips with multi-purpose grease.
21 Refitting is a reversal of removal. Note that the release lever and shaft have a master spline. When fitting the return spring, ensure that the bent ends bear against the casing with the centre part hooked over the release lever.
22 On 4-speed gearboxes, always fit a new gasket to the end cover.
23 On 5-speed gearboxes, use a suitable length of metal tubing to drive the new endplate into the housing.

Chapter 7 Part A:
Manual gearbox

Contents

Gearbox - removal and refitting 3
Gearbox - overhaul 4
Gearshift mechanism - removal, refitting and adjustment 2
General information 1

Degrees of difficulty

| Easy, suitable for novice with little experience | Fairly easy, suitable for beginner with some experience | Fairly difficult, suitable for competent DIY mechanic | Difficult, suitable for experienced DIY mechanic | Very difficult, suitable for expert DIY or professional |

Specifications

Gearbox
Type .... 4 or 5-speed (all synchromesh) and reverse

Identification codes
4-speed:
   1.05 litre 084 (6F)
   1.3 litre .... 084 (4F or 5F)
   1.6 litre 020 (4R)
5-speed:
   1.3 litre 085 (8N)
   1.6 litre .... 085 (AEN)
   1.6 litre .... 020 (4T or 9A)
   1.8 litre .... 085 (ACD, AEN, 2Y, AUG, ATH or AVZ)
   1.8 litre 020 (9A)

Wear limits
084 gearbox:
   Synchro ring gap clearance .... 0.5 mm
   Input and output shaft maximum endfloat .... 0.5 mm
020, 4 and 5-speed gearbox:
   Synchro-ring gap clearance .... 0.5 mm
   3rd gear axial play circlip thickness:
     Brown .... 2.5 mm
     Black .... 2.6 mm
     Bright .... 2.7 mm
     Copper .... 2.8 mm
     Brass .... 2.9 mm
     Blue .... 3.0 mm

7A•2 Manual gearbox

Torque wrench settings

	Nm	lbf ft
084 gearbox		
Clutch guide sleeve to gearbox	15	11
Gear lever stop plate nuts	10	7
Shift rod mounting coupling screw (new)	20	15
Shift rod clip nut	20	15
Gearshift housing bolts	15	11
Gearbox to engine:		
M12	75	55
M10	45	33
Driveshaft to gearbox	45	33
Bracket to engine	45	33
Gearbox mountings	60	44
Drive flange bolt	25	18
Clutch housing-to-gearbox bolts	25	18
Gearbox nousing cover bolts	25	18
Relay lever bolt	35	26
Oil filler plug	25	18
Oil drain plug	25	18
Selector finger (to inner shift lever)	25	18
085 gearbox		
End cover bolt	8	6
Gear lever bracket (inside gearbox)	16	12
Selector arm pinch-bolt	25	19
020 4-speed gearbox		
Gearbox to engine (M12)	75	55
Starter motor to gearbox/engine	60	44
Driveshafts to flange	45	33
Left console to gearbox	35	26
Left console to subframe	60	44
Rear right console to engine	25	18
Gearbox to clutch housing	25	18
Peg bolt for selector shaft	20	15
Reverse shaft set screw:		
Hex head type	20	15
Torx head type	30	22
Selector shaft end cap	50	37
Output shaft bearing plate bolts	40	30
Input shaft bearing clamp screw nut	15	11
020 5-speed gearbox		
Gear lever retaining plate nuts	10	7
Selector shaft lever nut	15	11
Gearbox housing cover bolts	25	18
Gearbox-to-clutch housing bolts	25	18
Selector shaft end cap	50	37
Reverse shaft securing bolt	20	15
Selector shaft securing bolt	20	15
First gear synchroniser screw	150	111
Bearing plate bolts	40	30
Oil filler plug	25	18
Selector shaft location screw* (from 1989)	20	15

Smear threads with sealant prior to fitting screw

1 General information

The 084 and 020 gearboxes incorporate 4 or 5 forward speeds and one reverse speed, with synchromesh engagement on all forward speeds.

The 085 gearbox is a 5-speed version of the 084 gearbox. Although its construction appears similar to that of the 084 type, there are major differences which make most servicing procedures different.

The clutch withdrawal mechanism comprises a release arm and lever located at the outer end of the gearbox and a pushrod located in the input shaft.

Gearshift is by means of a floor-mounted lever connected by a remote control housing and shift rod to the gearbox selector shaft and relay lever.

The differential (final drive) unit is integral with the gearbox and is located between the main casing and bearing housing.

2 Gearshift mechanism - removal, refitting and adjustment

084 and 085 gearboxes - pre January 1991

Removal

1 Jack up the front of the vehicle and support on axle stands (see "*Jacking and vehicle support*"). Apply the handbrake.

Manual gearbox 7A•3

2 With neutral selected, mark the shift rod and coupling in relation to each other, then unscrew the coupling clamp and pull out the shift rod (see illustration).

3 Working inside the vehicle, unscrew the gear knob and remove the gaiter.

4 Unscrew the nuts from the ballhousing stop plate and withdraw the complete gearchange mechanism upwards into the vehicle (see illustration). Recover the spacers.

5 Dismantle the mechanism as necessary and examine the components for wear and damage. Renew as necessary.

Refitting

6 Refitting is a reversal of the removal procedure.

7 Lubricate all joints and bearing surfaces with high melting-point grease.

8 When refitting the gear lever gaiter, it is essential to fit it in the correct manner to avoid possible damage. Manipulate the gaiter so that it is inside-out then slide it down the lever so that it locates against the collar flange (55 mm down the shaft). Now pull the frame down so that it turns the gaiter back the correct way and engage its locating lugs with the central console. Ensure that the gaiter is not twisted (see illustration).

Adjustment

9 If a new coupling has been fitted, it will be necessary to adjust the coupling position. This is best carried out by a VW garage using tool 3069 but if necessary, the following method can be used in an emergency.

10 With the coupling disconnected and the gearbox in neutral, have an assistant hold the gear lever in neutral position between 3rd and 4th gear positions (ie. halfway between front and rear movement and to the right). Engage the shift rod and coupling fully and, with the gear lever in the same position, tighten the clamp bolt.

020, 4 and 5-speed gearboxes – pre January 1991

Relay linkage assembly

11 The most likely items to require inspection and attention are those of the relay linkage assembly (see illustration). The shift rod bushes, relay links and lever pivots will wear and cause a progressive deterioration in the positive action of the gearchange.

12 If removing any parts of the linkage mechanism, first take note of its orientation to avoid possible confusion when refitting.

13 The selector rods (long and short) have balljoint linkages. These can be detached by pressing back the clips on the plastic ends using a screwdriver.

14 When reassembling, lubricate the linkage pivot joints.

Gear lever and shift rod

15 Remove the gear lever knob and withdraw the rubber gaiter.

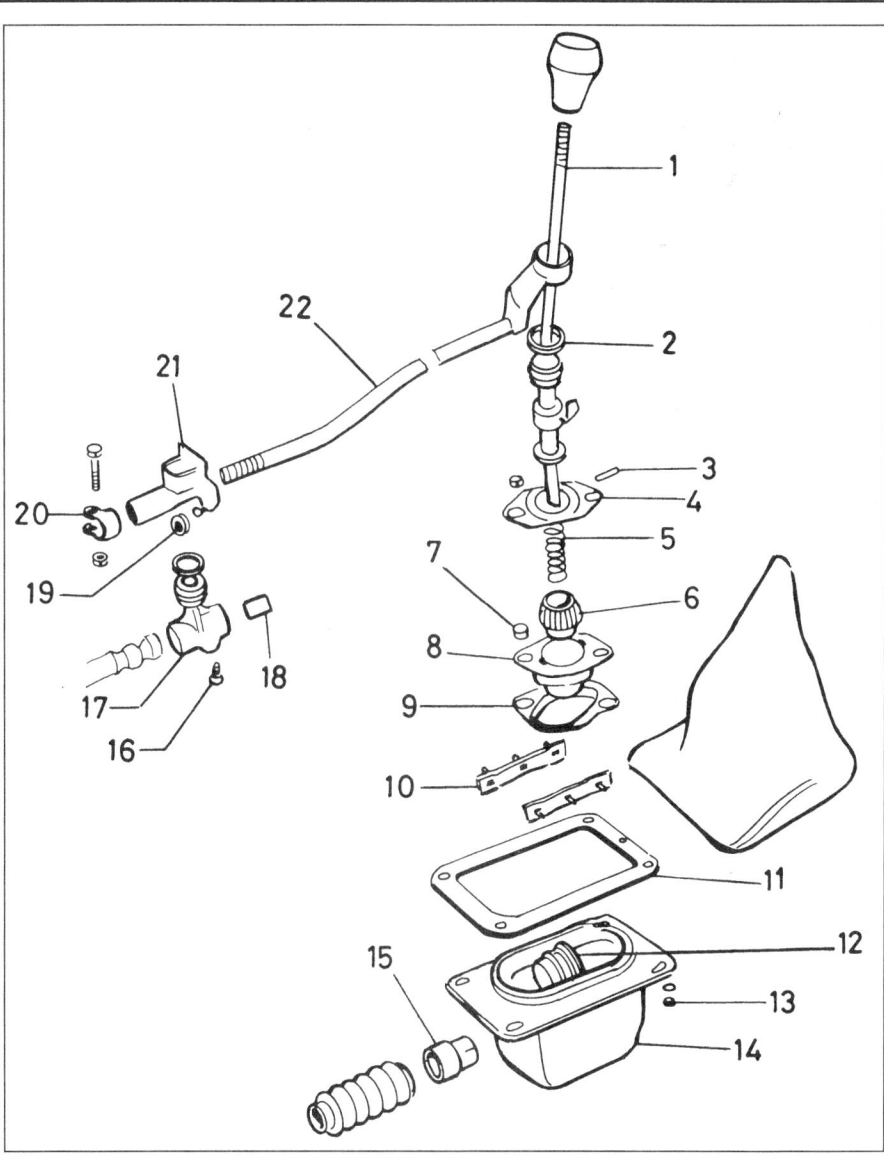

2.2 Gearchange mechanism components – 084 gearbox

1 Gear lever	6 Ball	12 Bearing race	18 Bush
2 Plastic ring	7 Spacer	13 Self-locking nut	19 Foam plastic washer
3 Pin	8 Ballhousing	14 Housing	20 Clip
4 Stop plate	9 Seal	15 Bush	21 Shift finger
5 Spring	10 Stop	16 Mounting screw	22 Shift rod
	11 Seal	17 Coupling	

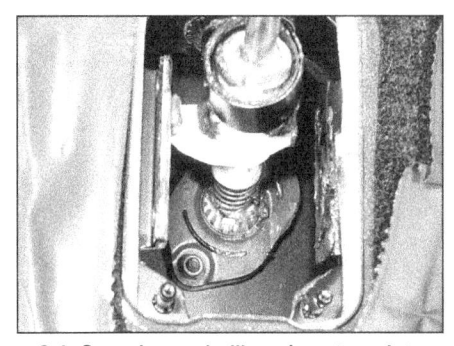

2.4 Gearchange ballhousing stop plate

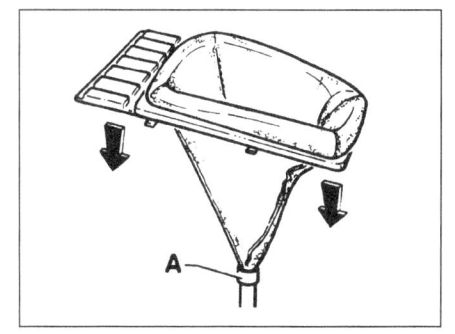

2.8 Gear lever boot fitting method showing collar (A)

7A•4 Manual gearbox

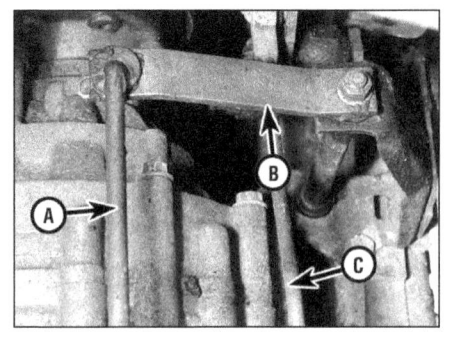

2.11 Shift linkage connecting link (A) lever (B) and selector rod (C)

16 Undo the console retaining screw and withdraw the console.
17 Unbolt and remove the exhaust downpipe from the manifold and intermediate pipe section. Disconnect the deflector plate and remove it by pulling it forwards.
18 Mark the relative positions of the shift rod and front clips, then loosen the clip bolt **(see illustration)**.
19 Undo the three retaining screws and detach the mounting from the steering and remove from the shift rod.
20 Disconnect the lever housing from the body, pull the housing forwards and, pressing it downwards, remove it.
21 Disconnect the retaining plate then press out the shift rod bush (inwards) and withdraw the rod from the housing.
22 Refitting is a reversal of the removal procedure.
23 When refitting the gear lever gaiter, it is essential to fit it in the correct manner to avoid possible damage. Manipulate the gaiter so that it is inside-out then slide it down the lever so that it locates against the collar flange (55 mm down the shaft). Now pull the frame down so that it turns the gaiter back the correct way and engage its locating lugs with the central console. Ensure that the gaiter is not twisted.
24 Align the shift rod and clip alignment marks to initially set the shift linkage adjustment. If, on completion, the respective gears cannot be positively engaged and further adjustment is necessary, try readjustment by loosening the shift rod clip and with the gears in neutral, centralise the gear lever in neutral and retighten the clip bolt. Accurate adjustment of the gear lever/shift linkage mechanism can only be made using a special VW tool and as this is not generally available, have the adjustment checked and set by your VW dealer.

All 4 and 5-speed gearboxes - from January 1991

25 From January 1991, the gearshift mechanism is modified and now has an eccentric adjuster in place of the ball used on earlier models.
26 As with earlier models, the gearshift adjustment should always be checked (and where necessary an approximate adjustment made) whenever the gearbox and/or the gearshift mechanism has been removed and refitted. The adjustment procedure for the eccentric type is as described for earlier models but the following additional check should also be made.
27 Check that with 1st gear engaged, dimension 'a' is as specified **(see illustration)**. If required, fine adjustment can be made by pressing the lever knob down and to the left to take up any minor play in the shift mechanism, then loosening off the eccentric securing screw and turning the eccentric as required to provide the specified clearance. Retighten the screw to set the fine adjustment. Ensure that the lever remains in the 1st gear selected position as the adjustment is made.

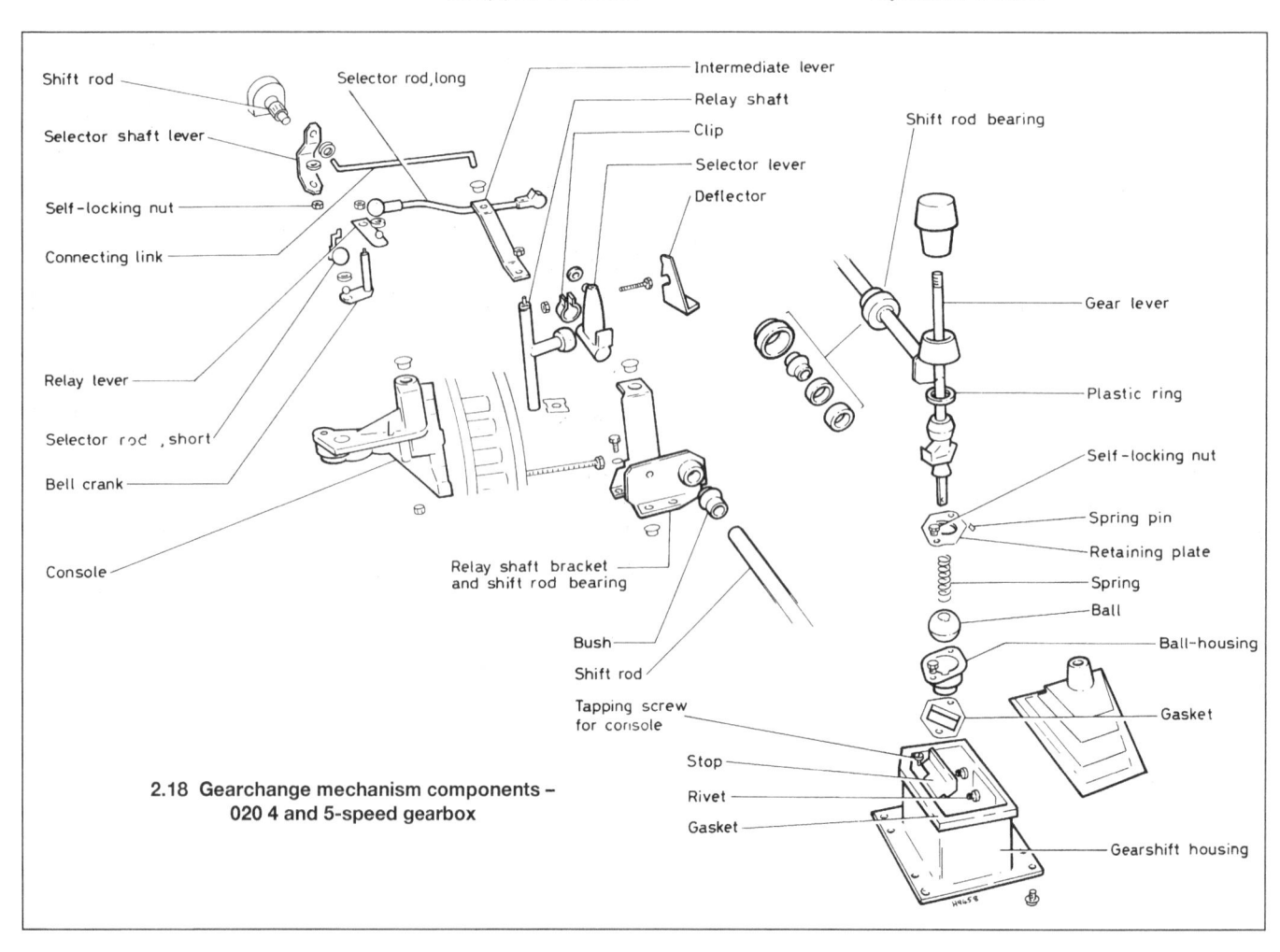

2.18 Gearchange mechanism components – 020 4 and 5-speed gearbox

Manual gearbox 7A•5

28 Unlike the gear lever balljoint on earlier models, the eccentric can if required be removed by simply loosening off the retaining screw and levering the eccentric up from the lever. Refit in the reverse order of removal and adjust the position of the eccentric as described in the previous paragraph.

3 Gearbox - removal and refitting

Note: *The following paragraphs describe how to remove the gearbox with the engine in situ. However, if work is necessary on the engine as well, the engine/gearbox unit should be removed then separated on the bench*

084 and 085 gearboxes

Removal

1 The gearbox is removed downwards, so the vehicle must be raised from the ground sufficiently to withdraw the box from underneath. The ideal is to work over a pit but axle stands or similar support under the body can be arranged (see "*Jacking and vehicle support*"). Note that you must be able to turn the wheels to disconnect the driveshafts.
2 Since the engine will be left unsupported at the rear, it is necessary to make provision to take its weight. If you have a block and tackle or a crane this will be simple but if not, it is possible to make a support similar to that used by VW **(see illustration)**. Alternatively, the engine can be supported from underneath with blocks placed under the sump but this method means that the vehicle cannot be moved while the gearbox is out of the vehicle.
3 Remove the bonnet and place it safely out of the way.
4 Having supported the engine, disconnect the battery negative lead.
5 For the purposes of this Section, the front is the engine end of the gearbox, left and right are as if you are standing at the side of the vehicle behind the gearbox looking towards the engine.
6 Remove the left gearbox mounting complete. Unscrew the drain plug from the differential housing, drain the oil into a suitable container, then refit the plug **(see illustration)**.
7 Disconnect the clutch cable from the gearbox.
8 Disconnect the earth strap at the gearbox support.
9 Unbolt and remove the starter motor.
10 Disconnect the reversing light lead from the gearbox **(see illustration)**.
11 Disconnect the speedometer drive cable from the gearbox by undoing its retaining collar.
12 Unscrew and remove the upper engine-to-gearbox securing bolts.
13 Disconnect the inner ends of the drive shafts from the gearbox flanges and tie them out of the way.
14 Unbolt and remove the cover plate from the clutch housing **(see illustration)**.
15 Unscrew and remove the remaining engine-to-gearbox bolts, noting the location of the rear mounting bracket.
16 Unscrew the rear mounting nut and remove the bracket, or leave the mounting on the bracket and remove the mounting bolts **(see illustration)**.

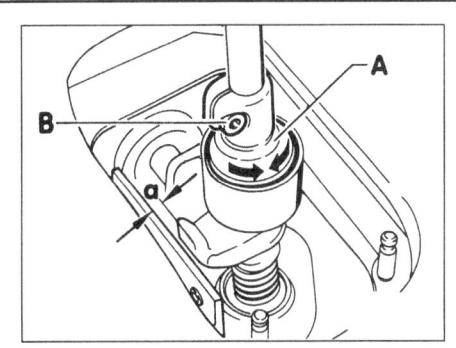

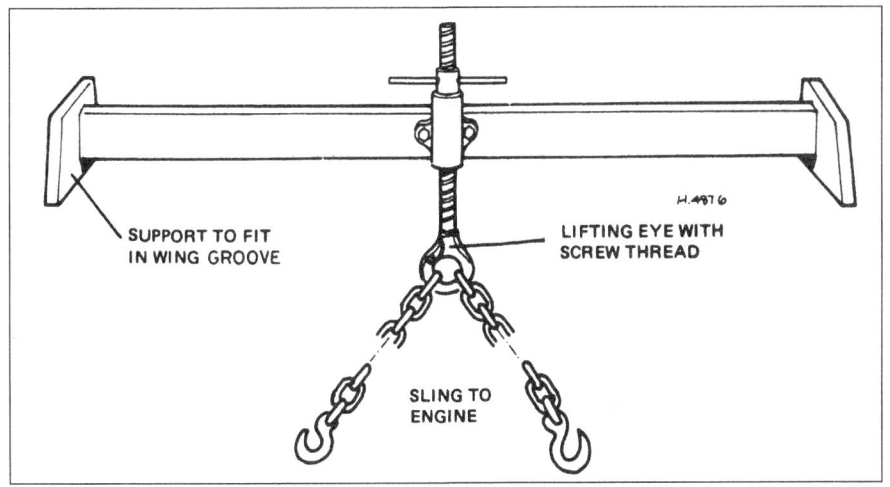

2.27 Eccentric adjuster (A) and securing screw (B)

Clearance 'a' must be set at 1.0 to 1.5 mm

3.2 Lifting bar arrangement to support engine

3.6 Differential housing drain plug location

3.10 Disconnecting reversing light switch wiring

3.14 Clutch housing cover plate

3.16 Gearbox rear mounting and securing bolt

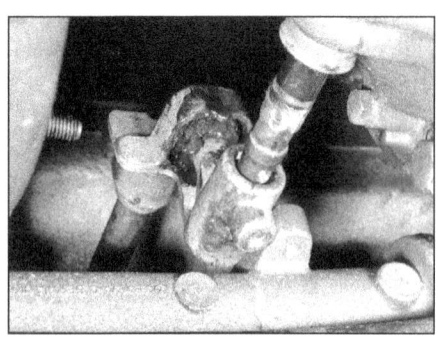

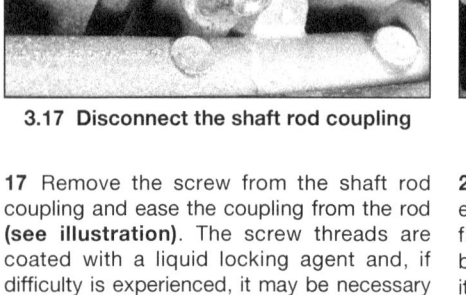

7A•6 Manual gearbox

3.17 Disconnect the shaft rod coupling

3.25 Gearbox drain plug location

3.27 Speedometer cable and retaining bolt

17 Remove the screw from the shaft rod coupling and ease the coupling from the rod **(see illustration)**. The screw threads are coated with a liquid locking agent and, if difficulty is experienced, it may be necessary to heat up the coupling with a blowlamp whilst observing the necessary fire precautions. If required, remove the coupling ball from the adapter.

18 Support the gearbox on a trolley jack (if available).

19 Check that nothing else is holding the gearbox then assess just how it is to be lowered. Apart from the dowels, the gearbox driveshaft splines are engaged in the friction disc of the clutch and the box must be pulled back to withdraw the shaft from the boss of the disc. This must be done carefully or there will be damage to the friction disc. In fact, if the box is not kept level the shaft will jam in the splines.

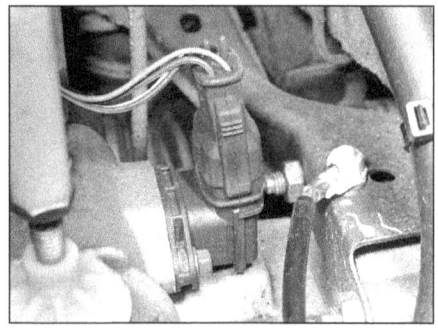

20 Do not try to separate the box from the engine by driving a wedge between the flanges, this will damage the castings. This box can be pulled backwards easily enough if it is kept level. The dowels are a tight fit and when they come out of the dowel holes the weight of the box will be felt suddenly. Do not let the box drop at all or you will damage the gear driveshaft splines. Move it away from the engine until you can see the shaft clear and then lower the box to the ground and remove it from under the vehicle.

Refitting

21 Refitting is a reversal of removal. Smear a little molybdenum disulphide based grease on the splines of the input shaft and make sure that the engine rear plate is correctly located on the dowels.

22 On the 085 gearbox, ensure that the location dowels are correctly inserted in the cylinder block.

23 Delay fully tightening the mounting nuts and bolts until the gearbox is in its normal position. Adjust the gearchange if necessary.

24 Adjust the clutch and check that the gearshift mechanism operates correctly. Refill the gearbox with oil.

020, 4 and 5-speed gearboxes

Removal

25 Proceed as described in paragraphs 1 to 5 inclusive. Drain the oil from the gearbox **(see illustration)**.

26 Disconnect the clutch cable from the release arm.

27 Disconnect the speedometer cable from the gearbox by undoing the retaining bolt and withdrawing the cable **(see illustration)**. Tie the clutch and speedometer cables back out of the way.

28 Disconnect the multi-function switch connector from the gearbox **(see illustration)**.

29 Undo the retaining nut and detach the gearbox mounting support arm. Undo the nut and detach the earth strap.

30 Detach the gearchange selector rod by pressing back the clips on the plastic balljoint connectors **(see illustration)**.

31 Detach the gearchange connecting link. If removing completely, note that the link ends differ in angle and the end with the notched mark is at the selector shaft lever end.

32 Detach the heater hose support bracket (inboard of the starter motor).

33 Unbolt and remove the starter motor, leaving the leads attached. Position the starter motor out of the way.

34 Undo the single retaining bolt and withdraw it from the mounting to the rear of the left-hand driveshaft (right rear of gearbox looking from left side of vehicle).

35 Unbolt and remove the engine/gearbox mounting on the left-hand side (front of vehicle) **(see illustration)**.

36 Unscrew and remove the engine-to-gearbox attachment bolts at the top.

37 Working underneath the vehicle, detach the right and left-hand driveshafts at their driveshaft flanges. Tie up the driveshafts to support them.

38 Detach and remove the wheel arch cover on the left-hand side.

3.28 Multi-function switch location

3.30 Gearchange connecting rod links and plastic balljoint

3.35 Front engine/gearbox mounting viewed from underneath - 1.8 litre

3.39 Clutch housing cover plate

Manual gearbox 7A•7

39 Unbolt and remove the clutch housing cover plate bolts **(see illustration)**.
40 Unscrew and remove the lower engine-to-gearbox attachment bolt (under the right-hand drive flange) and the cover plate bolts **(see illustration)**.
41 Disconnect the exhaust downpipe from the manifold flange.
42 Unbolt and detach (but do not remove) the engine mounting unit (between the engine and the bulkhead) **(see illustration)**. This will allow the engine to be pivoted to allow gearbox removal.
43 Lower the engine/gearbox unit a little and pull the gearbox to the front. Take care not to strain any of the engine ancillary attachments. An assistant will be useful here to check on this and to hold the engine at the angle required so that the gearbox will clear the wheel arch when being separated from the engine.
44 Pull the gearbox free and separate it from the engine, as described in paragraphs 18, 19 and 20.

Refitting

45 Refitting is a reversal of the removal procedure. Ensure that all joint surfaces are clean and smear a small amount of graphite powder, Moly paste or spray onto the input shaft splines. Line up the gearbox so that the input shaft will enter the clutch friction disc.
46 When the engine and gearbox are re-engaged, refit the attachment bolts and tighten them to the specified torque. Do not allow the weight of the gearbox to rest on the input shaft at any time.
47 With the engine/gearbox unit located on its mountings, check that the mountings are not under any strain prior to tightening their retaining bolts.
48 Adjust the clutch and check that the gearshift mechanism operates correctly. Refill the gearbox with oil.

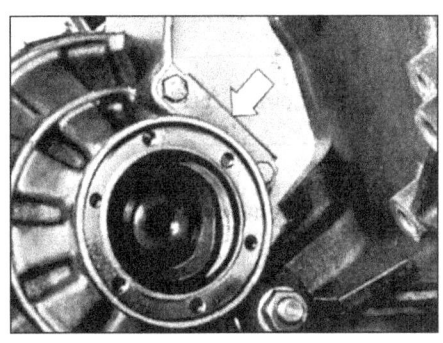

3.40 Remove cover plate from driveshaft flange (arrowed)

4 Gearbox - overhaul

1 Overhauling a gearbox is a difficult and involved job for the DIY home mechanic. In addition to dismantling and reassembling many small components, clearances must be precisely measured and if necessary, changed by selecting shims and spacers. Internal components are also often difficult to obtain and in many instances, are extremely expensive. Because of this, if the gearbox develops a fault or becomes noisy, the best course of action is to have the unit overhauled by a specialist repairer, or to obtain an exchange reconditioned unit.
2 Nevertheless, it is not impossible for the more experienced mechanic to overhaul a gearbox, provided the special tools are available and that the job is done in a deliberate step-by-step manner so that nothing is overlooked.
3 The tools necessary for an overhaul may include the following:
  a) Internal and external circlip pliers

3.42 Right-hand rear engine mounting viewed from underneath - 1.8 litre

  b) Bearing pullers
  c) Slide hammer
  d) Set of pin punches
  e) Dial test indicator
  f) Hydraulic press

4 In addition, a large, sturdy workbench and a vice will be required.
5 Before dismantling, it will help if you have some idea which area is malfunctioning. Certain problems can be closely related to specific areas in the gearbox, which can make component examination and replacement easier.
6 During dismantling, make careful notes of how each component is fitted to make reassembly easier and accurate.

Notes

Chapter 7 Part B:
Automatic transmission

Contents

General information and precautions 1	Transmission - removal and refitting 5
Selector cable - removal, refitting and adjustment 3	Transmission - stall test 4
Throttle and accelerator pedal cables (2E2 carburettor) - adjustment 2	

Degrees of difficulty

Easy, suitable for novice with little experience	Fairly easy, suitable for beginner with some experience	Fairly difficult, suitable for competent DIY mechanic	Difficult, suitable for experienced DIY mechanic	Very difficult, suitable for expert DIY or professional

Specifications

Transmission
Type .... 3-speed epicyclic geartrain, incorporating multi-plate clutches and brake and one brake band. Drive from engine transmission by torque converter

Identification codes
Code number 010
Transmission code:
   1.6 litre .... TKA
   1.8 litre .... TJA
Torque converter code:
   1.6 litre .... M
   1.8 litre .... K

Torque wrench settings
	Nm	lbf ft
Selector lever cable clamp nut	8	6
Driveshaft to flange	45	33
Converter to driveplate	35	26
Gearbox to engine	75	55
Left-hand gearbox mounting to gearbox	60	44
Left-hand gearbox mounting to console	35	26
Console (rear right) to engine	25	18
Oil pan bolts	20	15
Oil strainer (filter) cover bolts	3	2
Driveplate-to-crankshaft bolts:		
Stage 1	30	22
Stage 2	Further tighten 90°	

1 General information and precautions

General information

The automatic transmission is of the 3-speed epicyclic geartrain type and incorporates two multi-plate clutches, one multi-plate brake and one brake band. A fluid-filled torque converter transmits drive from the engine.

Three forward gears and one reverse are provided, with a kickdown facility for rapid acceleration during overtaking when an immediate change to a lower gear is required.

Due to the complex design of the automatic transmission, only the procedures described in the following Sections should be contemplated by the home mechanic. If the unit develops a fault, then it should be tested by a VW agent while still in the vehicle.

Precautions

Observe the following precautions to avoid damage to the transmission:
a) *Do not attempt to start the engine by pushing or towing the vehicle.*
b) *If the vehicle has to be towed for recovery, only tow the vehicle with the front wheels clear of the ground.*
c) *Only engage 'P' when the vehicle is stationary.*

7B•2 Automatic transmission

2 Throttle and accelerator pedal cables (2E2 carburettor) - adjustment

1 Start the engine and run it until its normal operating temperature and idle speed is reached. This ensures that the throttle valve is in the overrun position essential for this adjustment.
2 With the selector lever at P, loosen the accelerator pedal adjustment nut and detach the cable **(see illustration)**.
3 Remove the air cleaner unit.
4 Loosen the throttle cable nut at the support bracket on the carburettor **(see illustration)**.
5 Rotate the warm-up lever so that the throttle control pin is not touching it, then retain the lever in this position by moving lever C with a screwdriver **(see illustration)**.
6 Pull free and detach the respective vacuum hoses from the three/four point unit.
7 You will now need a vacuum pump with a connecting hose suitable for connecting to the lower vacuum hose connection (E) on the three/four point unit. Blank off connections F and G **(see illustration)**.
8 Apply vacuum with the pump so that the diaphragm pushrod holds in the overrun position and a clearance exists between the cold idle adjustment screw and the diaphragm pushrod. Pull the throttle cable sleeve away from the carburettor to take up the play whilst ensuring that the throttle valve remains closed and the operating lever at the transmission remains against the overrun stop. Tighten the throttle cable adjuster so that it contacts the support bracket and is stress-free, then retighten the locknut to secure **(see illustration)**.
9 Reconnect the accelerator pedal cable then get an assistant to press the accelerator pedal down to the kickdown stop position. Rotate the accelerator pedal adjustment nut so that the gearbox operating lever is in contact with the kickdown stop, then tighten the locknut.
10 To check adjustment is correct, the throttle must be in the overrun position and the gearbox operating lever must be in contact with the overrun stop. Get an assistant to depress the accelerator pedal until the full throttle pressure point is reached (not kickdown), then check that the throttle lever is resting against the full throttle stop and that the over-centre spring is not compressed.

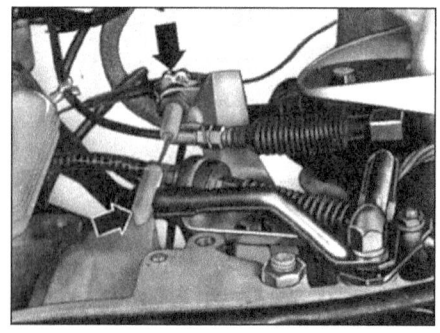

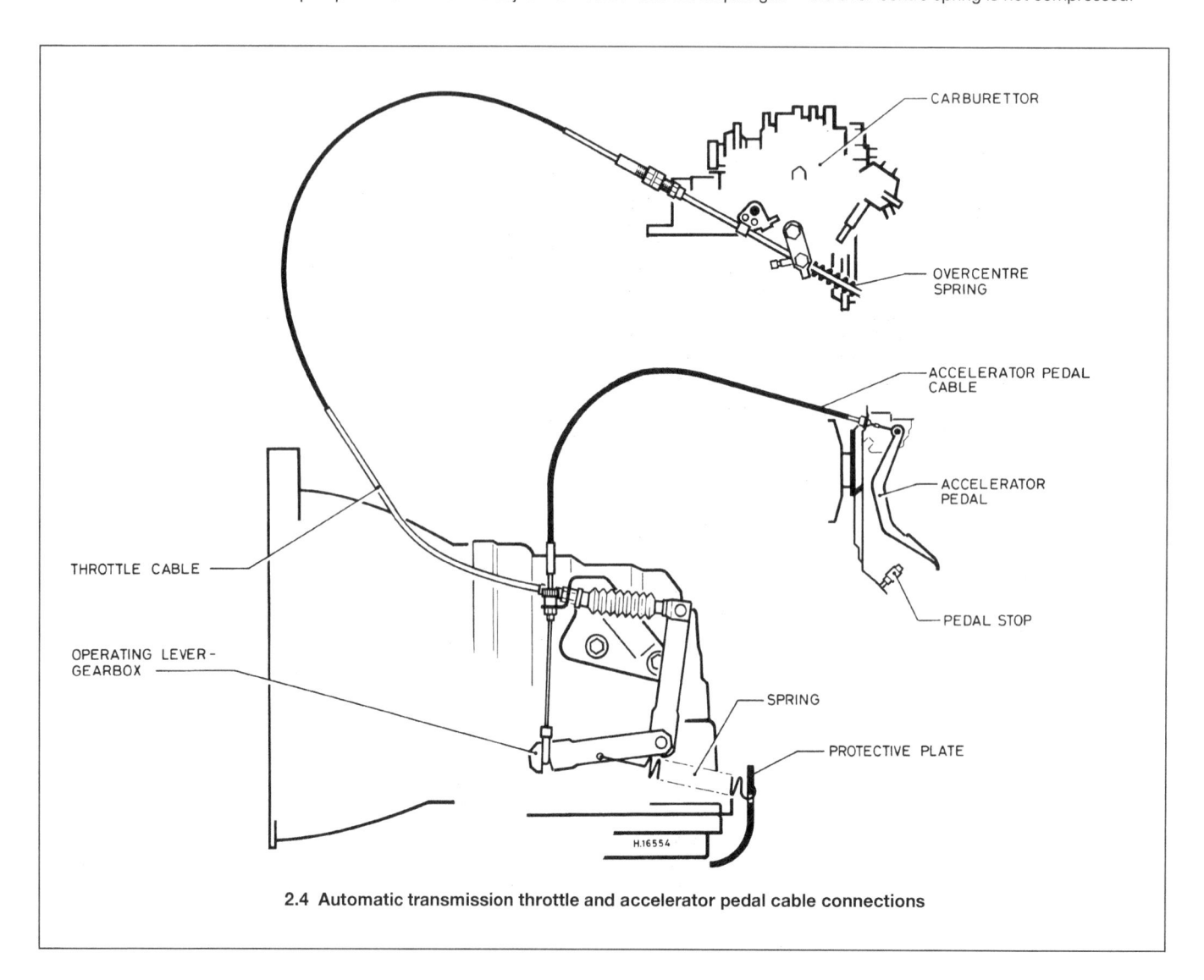

2.2 Accelerator pedal cable adjusting nut and operating lever connection (arrowed)

2.4 Automatic transmission throttle and accelerator pedal cable connections

Automatic transmission 7B•3

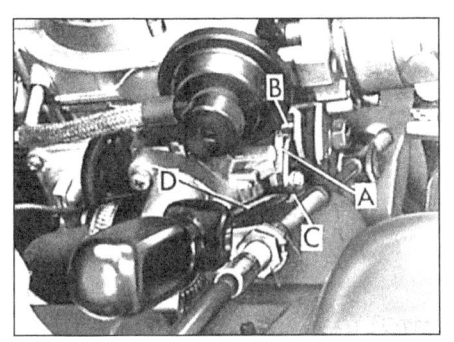

2.5 Warm-up lever (A) throttle valve control pin (B) lever (C) and screwdriver location (D)

2.7 Vacuum pump connections to three/four-point vacuum unit

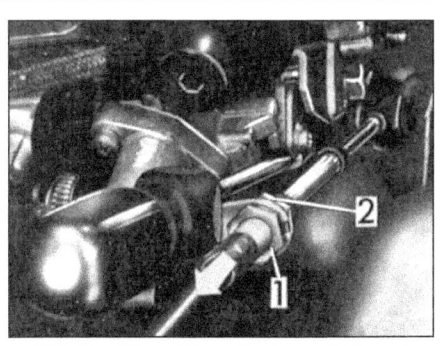

2.8 Throttle cable adjuster nut (1) and locknut (2)

2.11 Throttle cable over-centre spring compression point (a)

11 Next depress the accelerator pedal past the full throttle position to the kickdown position and then check that the gearbox operating lever rests against the kickdown stop and the over-centre spring is compressed approximately 8 mm (see illustration).
12 On completion refit the air cleaner to the carburettor.

3 Selector cable - removal, refitting and adjustment

Removal

1 At the transmission end of the cable, undo the cable clamp nut and detach the cable from the selector lever cable bracket (see illustration).
2 Working inside the vehicle, remove the retaining screws securing the selector lever cover to the console, lift the cover up the lever and turn it to one side.
3 Prise free the retaining clip (locking washer) securing the selector cable to the shift mechanism and detach the cable.
4 The cable can now be withdrawn and removed.

Refitting

5 Refit the selector cable reversing the removal procedure.
6 Lubricate the cable at each end with some light grease before connecting. Use a new locking washer to secure it to the selector mechanism.
7 Before tightening the cable clamp nut at the transmission, operating lever adjustment must be made.

Adjustment

8 To adjust the selector cable, push the selector lever to the P position and move the selector lever at the gearbox rearwards against the stop to the corresponding P position. Check that the cable is not kinked or bent at any point through its run then tighten the clamp nut.

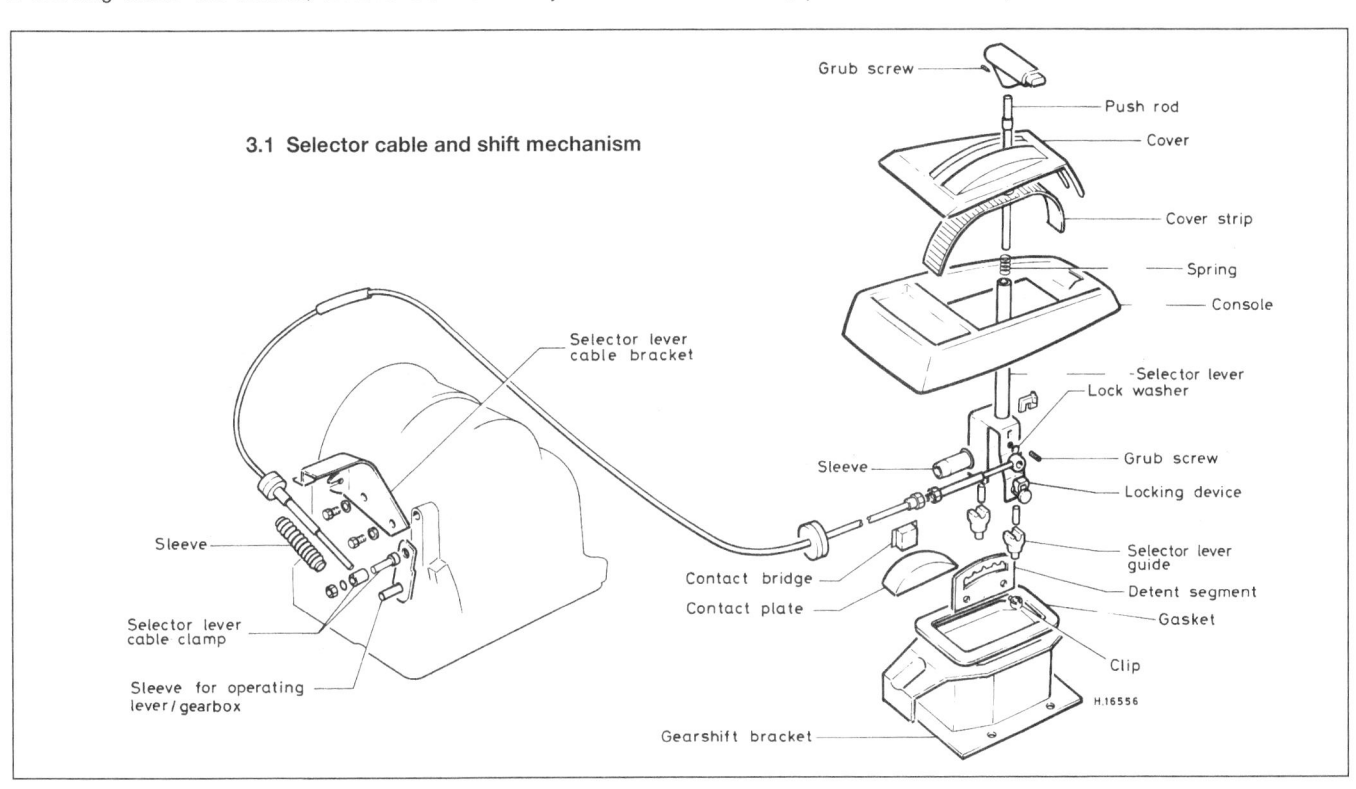

3.1 Selector cable and shift mechanism

4 Transmission - stall test

1 This stall test is used to check the performance of the torque converter. The results can also indicate certain faults in the transmission.
2 Connect a tachometer to the engine, then run the engine until warm.
3 Apply the handbrake and footbrake, then select position D.
4 Fully depress the accelerator pedal and record the engine speed, then release the pedal. Do not depress the pedal for any period longer than five seconds otherwise the torque converter will overheat. After a period of twenty seconds repeat the test. According to transmission type, the stall speeds should be as follows. Deduct 125 rpm per 1000 m altitude.

Transmission type	Stall speed
TJA	2390 to 2640 rpm
TKA	2340 to 2590 rpm

5 If the stall speed is higher than that specified, then the forward clutch or 1st gear one-way clutch may be slipping. Repeat the test in position 1. If the stall speed is now correct, then the 1st gear one-way clutch is faulty. If the speed is still too high, the forward clutch is faulty.
6 A stall speed up to 200 rpm below the specified amount indicates poor engine performance. The engine should therefore be tuned as necessary.
7 If the stall speed is more than 200 rpm below the specified amount, the torque converter stator one-way clutch is faulty and the torque converter should be renewed. First ensure that the engine is tuned correctly and, if adjustments are necessary, recheck the stall speed.
8 Switch off the engine and disconnect the tachometer.

5 Transmission - removal and refitting

Removal

1 Disconnect the battery earth lead.
2 Detach the speedometer drive cable connection from the transmission.
3 Unscrew and remove the upper engine-to-transmission securing bolts and the upper starter motor retaining bolt.
4 Referring to Section 3 in Part A of this Chapter, use one of the methods suggested in paragraphs 1 and 2 to support the engine/transmission.
5 With the engine supported, undo the three engine mounting retaining bolts at the right-hand rear side of the engine.
6 Unbolt and remove the left rear engine/transmission mounting, complete with support.
7 Unbolt and remove the front engine/transmission mounting. Push the engine rearwards to withdraw the mounting.
8 Unbolt and detach the left-hand driveshaft from the transmission drive flange.
9 Undo the starter motor lower retaining bolts and withdraw the starter motor.
10 Unbolt and withdraw the engine sump protector plate.
11 Check that the selector lever is in the P position then detach the drive range selector cable.
12 Detach the cable support bracket from the transmission.
13 Disconnect the throttle and accelerator pedal cables but do not alter their settings.
14 Working through the hole left by the starter, locate and undo the three bolts holding the torque converter to the driveplate. These can be seen also in the gap left when the bottom cover plate is removed.
15 Unbolt and detach the right-hand driveshaft.
16 Detach the lower balljoint from the track control arm (wishbone) then support it at the outboard end. Take care not to damage the driveshaft gaiter.
17 Now push the engine/transmission to the right as far as the stop, then lift and tie the left-hand driveshaft out of the way.
18 Locate a trolley jack under the transmission for support.
19 The transmission is too heavy for one person to lift so a sling and tackle must be used to support and lower the transmission if a suitable trolley jack is not available.
20 Undo and remove the remaining engine-to-transmission bolts at the bottom then check that all other transmission attachments are disconnected.
21 The transmission may now be removed. Lift a little and push the driveshaft up and out of the way. Pull the transmission off the dowels and lower it gently, at the same time supporting the torque converter which will fall out if not held in place in the transmission. There are two shafts and two sets of splines, be careful not to bend either of them or you will have a leaking torque converter.
22 When the transmission is separated from the engine, it can be lowered and manoeuvred from beneath the vehicle.
23 Position a suitable support plate across the torque converter housing to retain the torque converter in position whilst the transmission is removed.

Refitting

24 Refitting is the reversal of removal. Ensure that the torque converter remains fully engaged when attaching the engine and transmission.
25 Semi-tighten the respective mountings as they are attached then, when fully located, remove the engine/transmission supports and fully tighten the mounting bolts to the specified torque wrench settings.
26 If a new transmission has been fitted, then it will be necessary to readjust the throttle cable.
27 Check selector cable adjustment.
28 Refill the transmission with the correct quantity of fluid and check the fluid level.
29 Remove the final drive filler/level plug and check that the oil level is to the bottom of the hole. If necessary, top-up the level with the specified oil then refit the plug.

Chapter 8
Driveshafts

Contents

Drive flange oil seals - renewal 4
Driveshaft - dismantling and reassembly 3
Driveshaft - removal and refitting 2
General information 1

Degrees of difficulty

| Easy, suitable for novice with little experience | Fairly easy, suitable for beginner with some experience | Fairly difficult, suitable for competent DIY mechanic | Difficult, suitable for experienced DIY mechanic | Very difficult, suitable for expert DIY or professional |

Specifications

Driveshafts

Type .... Solid (left) and tubular (right) with constant velocity (CV) joints at each end. Vibration damper fitted to right-hand shaft on 55 and 66 kW engine types

Length: | Left-hand | Right-hand
084 and 085 gearboxes .... 465 mm | 677.2 mm
020 gearbox:
  Not GTi models .... 443 mm | 677.2 mm
  GTi models .... 447 mm | 681.2 mm
010 automatic transmission .... 443 mm | 677.2 mm

Torque wrench settings | Nm | lbf ft
Driveshaft to flange .... 45 | 33
Driveshaft/hub nut .... 265 | 195
Drive flange retaining bolt (1.05 and 1.3 litre) .... 25 | 18

1 General information

Drive from the differential unit to the roadwheels is provided by two driveshafts. Each shaft has a constant velocity (CV) joint at each end, the inner end being flanged and secured to the final drive flange by bolts and the outer end being splined to the hub **(see illustration)**.

The left-hand driveshaft is of solid construction and is shorter than the tubular right-hand shaft.

The driveshaft joints are sealed and require no maintenance apart from that listed in Chapter 1.

2 Driveshaft - removal and refitting

Removal

1 Each driveshaft is secured to the drive flange at the gearbox end by socket-head bolts, the removal of which will require the use of a special splined key.

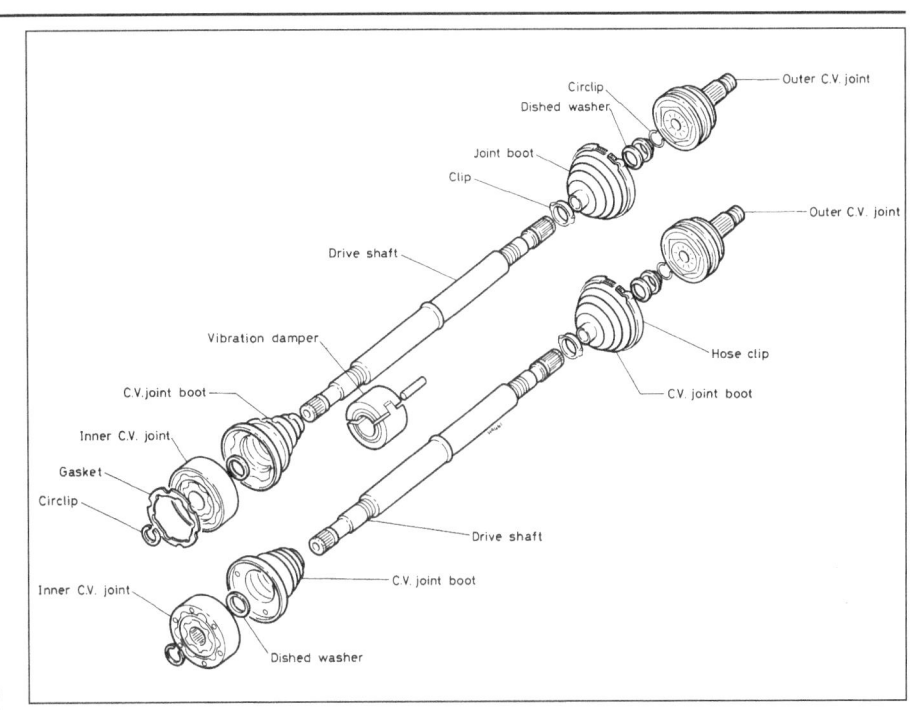

1.1 Driveshaft components

Upper - GTi models   *Lower - all other models*

8•2 Driveshafts

2.4 Removal of socket-head bolts and spacer plates

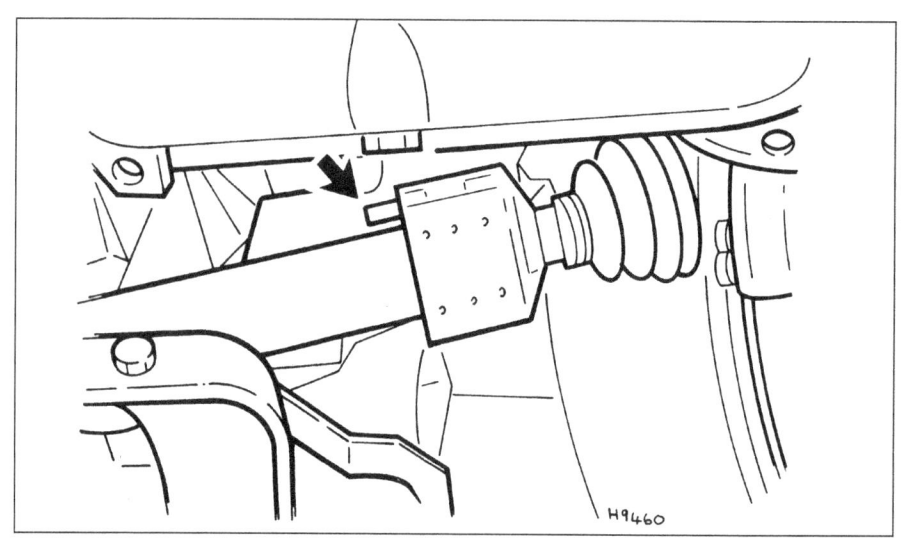

2 Remove the wheel trim from the relevant wheel. With the handbrake applied, loosen the driveshaft nut. The nut is tightened to a high torque and a socket extension may be required.

3 Jack up the front of the vehicle and support it on axle stands (see "*Jacking and vehicle support*"). Remove the roadwheel.

4 Using a splined tool, remove the socket-head bolts holding the inner CV joint to the final drive flange. Be careful to use a proper key to avoid damaging the bolts. These bolts are quite tight **(see illustration)**.

5 Once all the bolts are removed, the CV joint may be pulled away from the final drive and the shaft removed from the hub joint. If difficulty is experienced, separate the track control arm (wishbone) from the wheel bearing housing and pivot the arm downwards. The suspension strut can then be pulled outwards and the driveshaft removed. Do not move the vehicle on its wheels with either driveshaft removed, otherwise damage may occur to the wheel bearings.

6 If the driveshaft(s) are to be renewed complete, the vibration damper fitted to the right-hand driveshaft on 1.6 and 1.8 litre carburettor models will have to be transferred to the new shaft. To remove the damper, use a pin punch and drive out one of the retaining spring pins **(see illustration)**. The damper can then be pivoted open and removed from the driveshaft. Note the position of the damper unit on the shaft as it must be refitted in the same position.

7 Before fitting the vibration damper, check that the adhesive tape on its inner diameter is still sticky. Renew the tape if necessary. It is also advisable to renew the spring pin when refitting the damper. When the damper is in position check it for security.

Refitting

8 Refitting of a driveshaft is a reversal of the removal procedure. The hub and driveshaft splines must be clean and lubricated with a little molybdenum disulphide based grease.

9 Check that the inner flange/CV joint mating faces are clean and, where applicable, renew the joint gasket on the joint face of the inner CV unit.

10 A new driveshaft/hub nut must be fitted, initially hand tightened, then fully tightened to

2.6 Vibration damper and retaining pin (arrowed) – 1.6 and 1.8 litre carburettor models

the specified torque when the vehicle is lowered to the ground. Also tighten the inner bolts to the specified torque setting.

3 Driveshaft - dismantling and reassembly

1 Having removed the shaft from the vehicle, it may be dismantled for the individual parts to be checked for wear.

2 The rubber boots, clips and thrustwashers should be renewed as necessary. The CV joints may only be renewed as complete assemblies. It is not possible to fit new hubs, outer cases, ball cages or balls separately, for they are mated to a tolerance on manufacture. A replacement CV joint assembly kit will include the rubber boot and a tube of special grease. You will need to specify the vehicle model as CV joints differ.

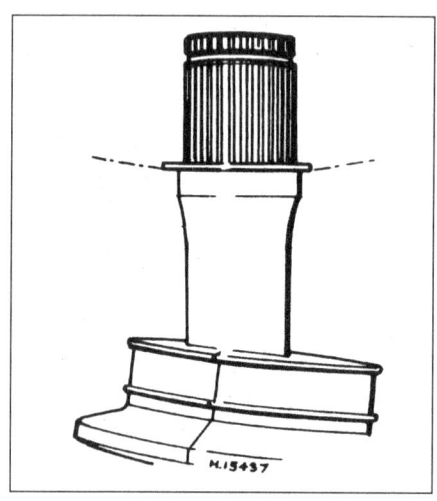

3.5 Correct fitment of dished washer

Outer joint

Dismantling

3 Loosen the rubber boot retaining clips and release the large diameter end of the boot from the joint.

4 Using a soft-faced mallet, drive the outer joint from the driveshaft.

5 Extract the circlip from the driveshaft and remove the spacer (if fitted) and dished washer. Note that the concave side of the dished washer faces the outboard end of the driveshaft **(see illustration)**.

6 Slide the rubber boot and clips from the driveshaft.

7 Mark the hub in relation to the cage and joint housing.

8 Swivel the hub and cage until the rectangular apertures are aligned with the housing then withdraw the cage and hub **(see illustration)**.

9 Turn the cage until the rectangular apertures are aligned with the housing then withdraw the cage and hub **(see illustration)**.

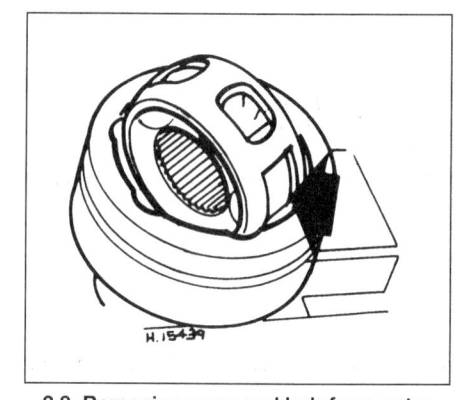

3.8 Removing cage and hub from outer joint housing

Arrow shows rectangular aperture

Driveshafts 8•3

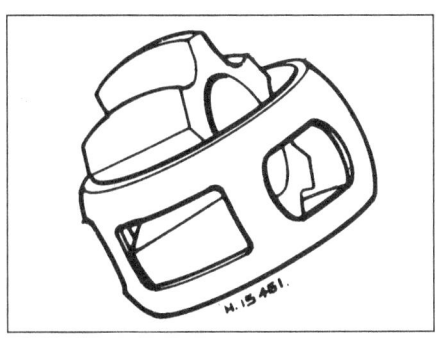

3.9 Removing outer joint hub from cage

3.21 Driveshaft inner joint retaining clip (arrowed) – 1.3 litre

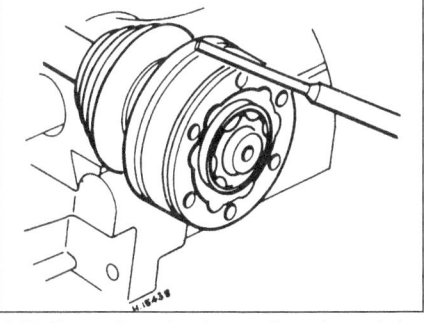

3.22 Removing plastic cap from inner joint housing

10 Turn the hub and insert one of the segments into one of the rectangular apertures, then swivel the hub from the cage.

11 Note that the joint components including the balls form a matched set and must only be fitted to the correct side.

12 Clean the components in paraffin and examine them for wear and damage. Excessive wear will have been evident when driving the vehicle, especially when changing from acceleration to overrun. Renew the components as necessary.

Reassembly

13 Commence reassembly by inserting half the amount of special grease (ie. 45g) into the joint housing.

14 Fit the hub to the cage by inserting one of the segments into the rectangular aperture.

15 With the rectangular apertures aligned with the housing, fit the hub and cage to the housing in its original position.

16 Swivel the hub and cage and insert the balls from alternate sides.

17 Fit the rubber boot and clips on the driveshaft.

18 Fit the dished washer and spacer (if applicable) to the driveshaft and insert the circlip in the groove.

19 Locate the outer joint on the driveshaft and, using a soft-faced mallet, drive it fully into position until the circlip is engaged.

20 Insert the remaining grease in the joint then locate the boot and tighten the clips. On models fitted with the 90 mm diameter CV joint, ventilate the joint briefly prior to tightening the small hose clip, to balance the pressure in the joint.

Inner joint - except GTi

Dismantling

21 Extract the retaining clip **(see illustration)**.

22 Where applicable, use a small drift to drive the plastic cap from the joint housing **(see illustration)**.

23 Mark the exact location of the rubber boot end face relative to the driveshaft for reference when refitting. A length of insulation tape or quick-drying paint applied to the shaft will suffice.

24 Loosen the clip and slide the rubber boot away from the joint.

25 Support the joint over the jaws of a vice and, using a soft metal drift, drive out the driveshaft.

26 Remove the dished washer from the driveshaft, noting that the concave side faces the end of the driveshaft.

27 Slide the rubber boot and clip from the driveshaft.

28 Mark the hub in relation to the cage and joint housing.

29 Turn the hub and cage 90° to the housing and press out the hub and cage.

30 Extract the balls then turn the hub so that one of the track grooves is located on the rim of the cage. Withdraw the hub **(see illustration)**.

31 Note that the joint components, including the balls, form a matched set and must only be fitted in the correct side.

32 Clean the components in paraffin and examine them for wear and damage. Excessive wear will have been evident when driving the vehicle, especially when changing from acceleration to overrun. Renew the components as necessary.

Reassembly

33 Commence reassembly by fitting the hub to the cage.

34 Insert the balls into position using the special grease to hold them in place.

35 Press the hub and cage into the housing, making sure that the wide track spacing on

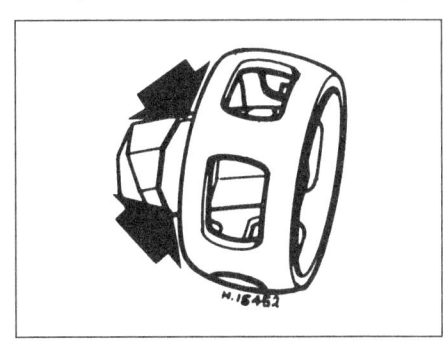

3.30 Removing inner joint hub from cage

Align grooves arrowed

the housing is adjacent to the narrow spacing on the hub **(see illustration)** when fully assembled. Note also that the chamfer on the hub splines must face the large diameter side of the housing.

36 Swivel the cage ahead of the hub so that the balls enter their respective tracks then align the hub and cage with the housing.

37 Check that the hub can be moved freely through its operating arc.

38 Fit the rubber boot and clip to the driveshaft, followed by the dished washer.

39 Mount the driveshaft in a vice then drive the joint onto the driveshaft using a suitable metal tube on the hub.

40 Fit the retaining circlip in its groove.

41 Insert the remaining grease in the joint then tap the plastic cap into position (where applicable).

42 Reposition the driveshaft boot, ensuring that when fitted it is not twisted or distorted abnormally and that the outer end aligns with the mark made during removal.

Inner joint - GTi

43 Proceed as described for other models but note that a gasket is located on the drive flange end face of the inner joint. This gasket must be renewed. Wipe dry the mating face on the joint, peel the protective foil from the

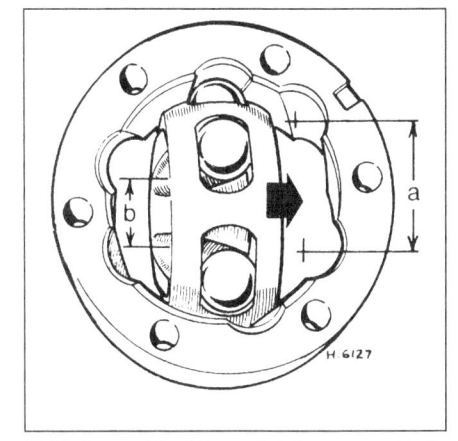

3.35 Assembly of inner joint cage and hub to housing

"a" must be aligned with "b"

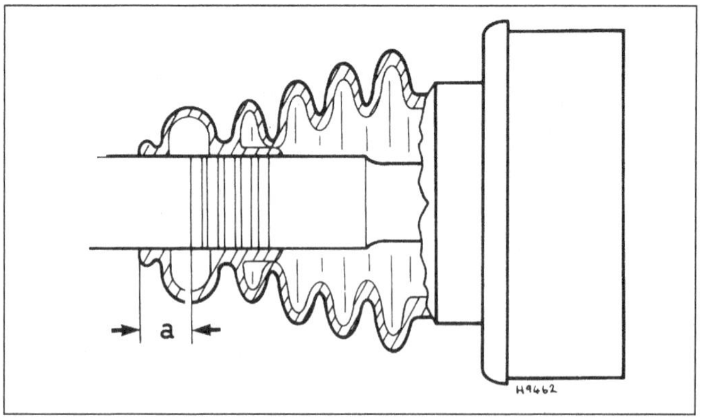

8•4 Driveshafts

3.44a Inner CV joint boot installation position – GTi models

a = 17.0 mm on left-hand shaft

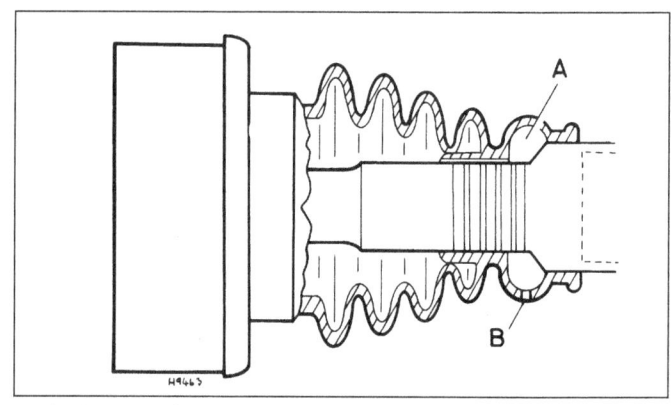

3.44b Inner CV joint boot installation position on right-hand driveshaft – GTi models

A Ventilation chamber   B Ventilation hole

gasket and carefully locate it onto the inner face of the joint.

44 When refitting the driveshaft boot, note that its fitted position is critical **(see illustrations)**.

4 Drive flange oil seals - renewal

1 Jack up the front of the vehicle and support on axle stands (see "*Jacking and vehicle support*"). Apply the handbrake.
2 Detach the inner ends of the driveshafts from the drive flange whilst noting the following:

a) *On 1.05 and 1.3 litre models, detachment of the right-hand driveshaft will necessitate unbolting the anti-roll bar from its body mounting and disconnecting the track control arm from the suspension strut on that side. Pivot the track control arm downwards.*
b) *On automatic transmission models, detachment of the left-hand driveshaft will necessitate disconnecting the track control arm from the suspension strut on that side. Pivot the track control arm downwards.*

3 With the driveshaft disconnected from the drive flange, tie it out of the way.
4 On 1.05 and 1.3 litre models, unscrew the bolt from the centre of the drive flange using a bar and two temporarily inserted bolts to hold the flange stationary **(see illustration)**.
5 On other models, prise off the cap (where fitted) and extract the circlip and dished washer from the drive flange. Note which way round the dished washer is fitted.
6 Place a container beneath the gearbox then remove the drive flanges and lever out the old oil seals **(see illustration)**. Identify the flanges side for side.
7 Clean and inspect the oil seal recesses. Where applicable, renew the sleeve in the recess if it is damaged.

8 Fill the space between the lips of the new seal with multi-purpose grease, then drive it fully into the housing using a suitable length of metal tube.
9 Refit the drive flange, taking care not to damage the oil seal lips. If available, use VW special tool to fit the flange **(see illustrations)**.
10 With the drive flange in position, proceed as follows according to model type:
11 On 1.05 and 1.3 litre models, refit and tighten the securing bolt to the specified torque wrench setting.
12 On other models, locate the dished washer (ensuring correct orientation noted when removing) and the circlip.
13 Refit the cap (where applicable) and the driveshaft.
14 Reconnect the track control arm to the suspension strut and the anti-roll bar to the body mounting, where applicable.
15 With the vehicle lowered to the ground, remove the final drive filler/level plug and check that the oil level is to the bottom of the hole. If necessary, top-up the level with the specified oil then refit the plug.

4.4 Drive flange removal using VW tool on 020 gearbox

4.6 Prising out drive flange oil seal from gearbox housing

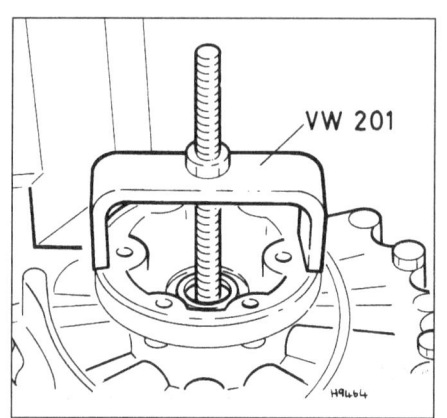

4.9a Drive flange refitting using VW tool on 020 gearbox

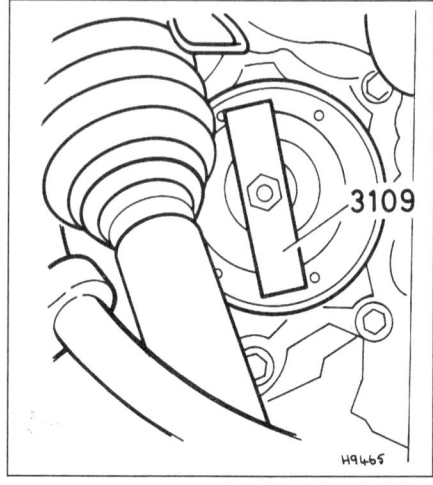

4.9b Drive flange refitting using VW tool on automatic transmission

Chapter 9
Braking system

Contents

Brake calipers - removal, overhaul and refitting 3
Brake discs - examination, removal and refitting 4
Brake pads - inspection and renewal 2
Brake pressure regulator - testing, removal and refitting 10
Footbrake pedal - removal and refitting 15
General information and precautions 1
Handbrake cables - removal, refitting and adjustment 14
Handbrake lever - removal and refitting 13
Hydraulic pipes and hoses - renewal 11
Hydraulic system - bleeding 12
Master cylinder - removal and refitting 9
Rear brake cylinder - removal, overhaul and refitting 7
Rear brake drum - examination and renovation 8
Rear brake shoes - inspection and renewal 6
Rear hub bearings - renewal 5
Vacuum servo unit - removal and refitting 17
Vacuum servo unit - testing 16

Degrees of difficulty

Easy, suitable for novice with little experience	**Fairly easy,** suitable for beginner with some experience	**Fairly difficult,** suitable for competent DIY mechanic	**Difficult,** suitable for experienced DIY mechanic	**Very difficult,** suitable for expert DIY or professional

Specifications

Brake system
Type .... Hydraulic, dual circuit, split diagonally, pressure regulator on some models. Disc front brakes. Drum or disc rear brakes. Cable-operated handbrake on rear wheels.

Front brakes
Disc thickness:
New:
    1.05 and 1.3 litre .... 10.0 mm
    1.6 and 1.8 litre .... 12.0 mm
    1.8 litre with ventilated discs .... 20.0 mm
Minimum:
    1.05 and 1.3 litre .... 8.0 mm
    1.6 and 1.8 litre .... 10.0 mm
    1.8 litre with ventilated discs .... 18.0 mm
Pad thickness:
New - excluding backplate:
    1.05 and 1.3 litre .... 12.0 mm
    1.6 and 1.8 litre .... 14.0 mm
    1.8 litre with ventilated discs .... 10.0 mm
Minimum - including backplate:
    All models .... 7.0 mm

Rear drum brakes
Drum internal diameter:
    New .... 180.0 mm
    Maximum .... 181.0 mm
Drum maximum run-out:
    Radial - at friction surface .... 0.05 mm
    Lateral - wheel contact surface .... 0.2 mm
Lining thickness:
    Minimum - including shoe .... 5.0 mm
    Minimum - excluding shoe .... 2.5 mm

Rear disc brakes

Disc thickness:
- New . . . . 10.0 mm
- Minimum . . . . 8.0 mm

Disc maximum run-out . . . . 0.06 mm

Pad thickness:
- New - including backplate . . . . 12.0 mm
- Minimum - including backplate . . . . 7.0 mm

Master cylinder

Diameter . . . . 20.65 mm

Wheel cylinder

Diameter . . . . 14.29 mm

Servo unit

Diameter:
- Manual gearbox . . . . 178.0 mm
- Automatic transmission . . . . 228.0 mm

Torque wrench settings

	Nm	lbf ft
Caliper upper securing bolt	25	19
Caliper lower securing bolt	25	19
Master cylinder securing nuts	20	15
Servo unit securing nuts	20	15
Splash guard to strut	10	7
Backplate to rear axle	60	44
Rear disc brake guide pin (self-locking)	35	26
Rear disc brake carrier bolts	65	48
Rear disc brake cover plate-to-axle bolts	60	44
Roadwheel bolt	110	81

1 General information and precautions

General information

The braking system is of hydraulic, dual circuit type with discs at the front and drum or discs at the rear. The hydraulic circuit is split diagonally so that with the failure of one circuit, one front and one rear brake remain operative.

A load-sensitive pressure regulator is incorporated in the rear hydraulic circuits on some models to prevent the rear wheels locking in advance of the front wheels during heavy application of the brakes. The regulator proportions the hydraulic pressure between the front and rear brakes according to the load being carried and is located on the under-body, in front of the left-hand rear wheel.

A vacuum servo unit is located between the brake pedal and master cylinder. It provides assistance to the driver when the brake pedal is depressed. The unit operates by vacuum from the inlet manifold and comprises a diaphragm and non-return valve. With the brake pedal released, vacuum is channelled to both sides of the diaphragm. With the pedal depressed, one side is opened to atmosphere. The resultant unequal pressures are harnessed to assist in depressing the master cylinder pistons.

The handbrake operates on the rear wheels only, its lever incorporating a switch which illuminates a warning light on the instrument panel when the handbrake is applied. The same warning light is wired into the low hydraulic fluid switch circuit.

Precautions

Hydraulic fluid is poisonous. Wash off immediately and thoroughly in the case of skin contact and seek immediate medical advice if any fluid is swallowed or gets into the eyes.

Certain types of hydraulic fluid are inflammable and may ignite when allowed into contact with hot components. When servicing any hydraulic system, it is safest to assume that the fluid is inflammable and to take precautions against the risk of fire as though it is petrol that is being handled.

Hydraulic fluid is an effective paint stripper and will attack plastics. If any is spilt, it should be washed off immediately using copious quantities of fresh water. Finally, it is hygroscopic, that is it absorbs moisture from the air. Old fluid may be contaminated and unfit for further use.

When topping-up or renewing fluid, always use the recommended type and ensure that it comes from a freshly-opened sealed container.

When working on the brake components, take care not to disperse brake dust into the air, or to inhale it, since it may contain asbestos which is injurious to health

When servicing any part of the system, work carefully and methodically. Observe scrupulous cleanliness when overhauling any part of the system. Always renew components (in axle sets, where applicable) if in doubt about their condition and use only genuine VW replacement parts, or at least those of known good quality.

2 Brake pads - inspection and renewal

Warning: When working on brake components, take care not to disperse brake dust into the air or to inhale it, since it may contain asbestos which is injurious to health.

Warning: Always support the vehicle on axle stands before removing the roadwheel to service brake assemblies.

Front pads

Inspection

1 Refer to Chapter 1, Section 26.

Removal

2 To remove the pads, first jack up the front of the vehicle and support it on axle stands (see "*Jacking and vehicle support*"). Apply the handbrake and remove both front wheels.

Braking system 9•3

2.3a Caliper securing bolt removal

2.3b Removing the caliper

2.5 Removing a pad retaining spring

3 Use an Allen key and unscrew the upper and lower caliper securing bolts **(see illustration)**. Withdraw the caliper and tie it up out of the way. Do not allow the weight of the caliper to stretch or distort the brake hose **(see illustration)**.
4 Withdraw each pad by sliding it sideways from the wheel bearing housing. Note that the pads differ, the pad with the larger friction area being fitted to the outside.
5 The retaining spring can be detached from the wheel bearing housing whilst noting its orientation **(see illustration)**. Renew the spring when renewing the pads.
6 Brush the dust and dirt from the caliper, piston, disc and pads whilst taking care not to inhale it. Scrape any scale or rust from the disc and pad backing plates.
7 If the pads are to be renewed, they must be replaced as a set on both sides at the front. If the original pads are to be re-used they must be refitted to their original positions each side.

Fitting

8 Using a piece of wood, push the piston back into the caliper. While doing this, check the level of the fluid in the reservoir and if necessary draw off some with a pipette or release some from the caliper bleed screw. Tighten the screw immediately afterwards.
9 Relocate the retaining spring **(see illustration)**.
10 Refit the inner pad (smaller friction area), followed by the outer pad. Locate the pad backing plate notches as shown **(see illustration)**.
11 Refit the brake caliper, locating it at the top end first. Pivot the bottom end into position, align the upper and lower retaining bolt holes, then insert the bolts. Take care not to press the caliper in more than is necessary when fitting the bolts or the retainer springs may be distorted which, in turn, will give noisy braking. Tighten the bolts to the specified torque.
12 On completion, the brake pedal should be depressed firmly several times with the vehicle stationary so that the brake pads take up their normal running positions. Check the fluid level in the reservoir and top-up if necessary.

Rear pads

Inspection

13 Refer to Chapter 1, Section 26.

Removal

14 To remove the pads, chock the front wheels, jack up the rear of the vehicle and support it on axle stands (see *"Jacking and vehicle support"*). Remove both rear wheels.
15 Release the handbrake then detach the handbrake cable from the caliper **(see illustration)**.
16 If the brake hydraulic hose connects to the underside of the caliper, undo the caliper upper retaining bolt **(see illustration)**. If the hydraulic hose connects to the top of the caliper, undo both caliper retaining bolts. Note that these self-locking bolts must be renewed on reassembly.
17 If the upper retaining bolt was removed, pivot the caliper downwards **(see illustration)**.

2.9 Pad retaining spring is located as shown

2.10 Refitting front brake pads

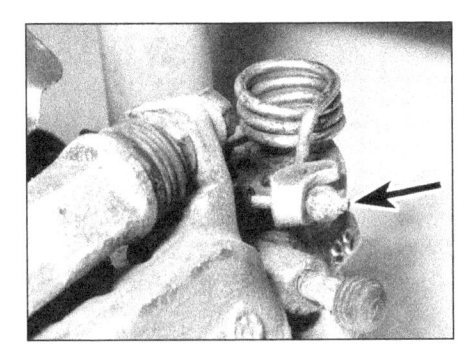

2.15 Release handbrake cable (arrowed) from caliper

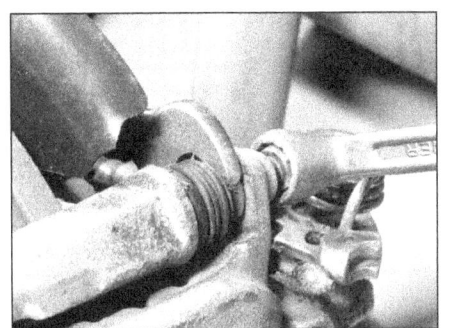

2.16 Rear caliper bolt removal
Prevent guide pin from turning with open-ended spanner

2.17 Rear brake caliper removal

9•4 Braking system

2.18 Removing rear brake pads

2.20a Retracting caliper piston using an Allen key

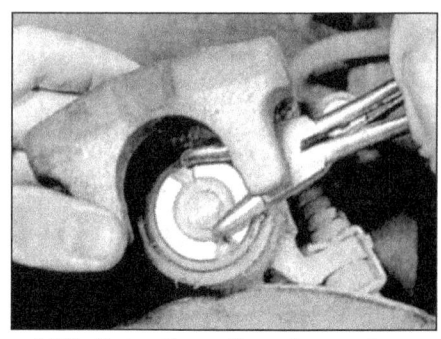

2.20b Retracting caliper piston using a pair of angled circlip pliers

If both bolts were removed, carefully lift off and support the caliper.

18 If the pads are to be re-used, mark them for identification to ensure that they are refitted to their original location. Their positions must not be changed **(see illustration)**.

19 Brush all dust and dirt from the caliper, piston, disc and pads whilst taking care not to inhale it. Scrape any scale or rust from the disc and pad backing plates.

Fitting

20 Move the piston back into the caliper by turning it clockwise using either an Allen key or a pair of angled circlip pliers according to caliper type **(see illustrations)**. As the piston moves back into the caliper, check the fluid level in the reservoir and if necessary draw some off with a pipette or release some from the caliper bleed screw. Tighten the screw immediately afterwards.

21 Locate the respective brake pads in position.

22 Before refitting the caliper, piston position must be set to provide a 1.0 mm clearance between the outer pad and the caliper. Check the adjustment by temporarily refitting the caliper and retaining bolts (use the old ones) and check the clearance with a feeler blade as shown **(see illustration)**. If adjustment is necessary, remove the caliper and rotate the piston clockwise or anti-clockwise until the correct clearance is achieved.

23 Refit the caliper and insert the new self-locking bolts when adjustment is correct. Tighten the bolts to the specified torque setting.

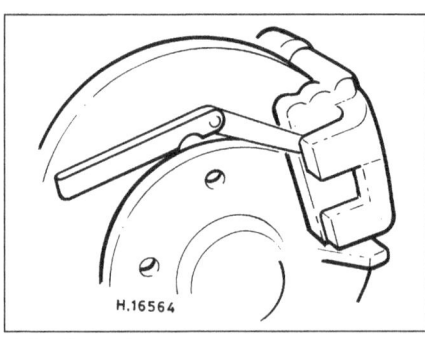

24 If new brake pads and/or discs have been fitted, it is necessary to carry out a basic rear brake adjustment before reconnecting the handbrake cable. To do this, apply a medium pressure to the brake pedal and depress it a total of 40 times (vehicle stationary).

25 Reconnect the handbrake cable to the caliper.

26 On completion, check handbrake adjustment.

3 Brake calipers - removal, overhaul and refitting

> **Warning: Brake hydraulic fluid may be under considerable pressure in a pipeline, take care not to allow hydraulic fluid to spray into the face or eyes when loosening a connection.**

> **Warning: Never refit old seals when reassembling brake system components**

Front calipers

1 Jack up the front of the vehicle and support it on axle stands (see "*Jacking and vehicle support*"). Apply the handbrake and remove both front wheels. Unbolt and remove the caliper from the wheel bearing housing.

2 If available, fit a hose clamp to the caliper flexible brake hose. Alternatively, remove the fluid reservoir filler cap and tighten it down onto a piece of polythene sheet in order to reduce any loss of hydraulic fluid.

3 Loosen and detach the brake hose union at the caliper, allowing for a certain amount of fluid spillage. Plug the hose union to prevent ingress of dirt.

4 Clean the external surfaces of the caliper with paraffin and wipe dry. Plug the fluid inlet during this operation.

5 Prise free and remove the dust seal from the piston **(see illustration)**.

6 Using air pressure from a foot pump in the fluid inlet, blow the piston from the cylinder whilst taking care not to drop the piston. Prise the sealing ring from the cylinder bore. Take care not to scratch the cylinder bore.

7 Clean all components with methylated spirit and allow to dry. Inspect the surfaces of the piston, cylinder and frames for wear, damage and corrosion. If necessary, renew the caliper. If all components are in good condition then obtain a repair kit of seals.

8 Dip the new sealing ring in brake fluid and locate it in the cylinder bore groove using the fingers only to manipulate it.

9 Manipulate the new dust cap into position on the piston, engaging the inner seal lip in the piston groove. Use a suitable screwdriver to ease it into position whilst taking care not to damage the seal or scratch the piston **(see illustration)**.

10 Smear the piston with brake fluid and press it into position in the caliper bore.

11 Check that the brake hose union is clean, then unplug it and refit it to the caliper. Do not fully tighten it at this stage.

12 Refit the caliper to the wheel bearing housing.

2.22 Checking outer brake pad-to-caliper clearance

3.5 Removing the dust seal

3.9 Dust seal location on caliper piston

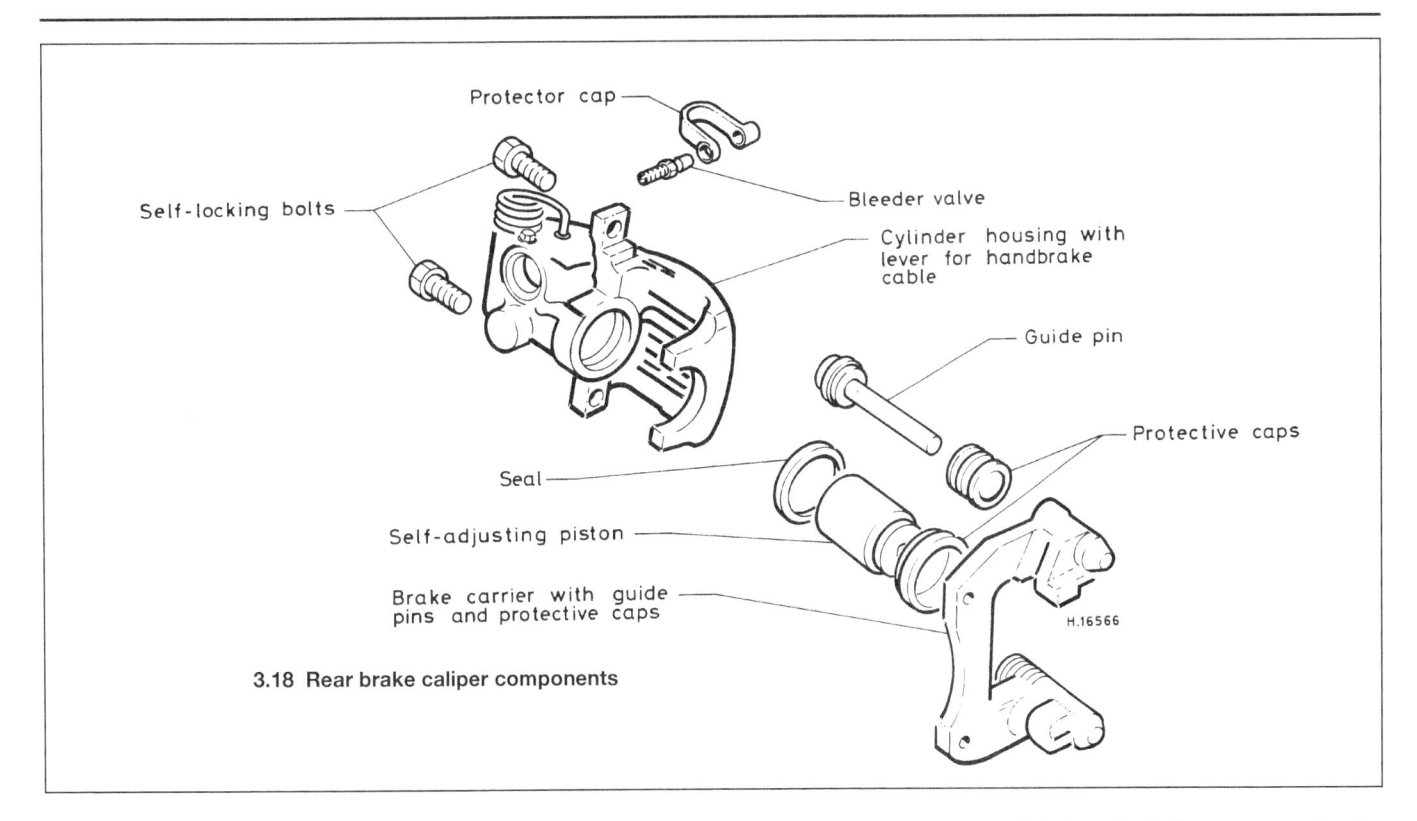

Braking system 9•5

3.18 Rear brake caliper components

13 Tighten the brake hose union so that the hose is not twisted or in a position where it will chafe against surrounding components.
14 Remove the hose clamp or polythene sheet from the reservoir. Top-up the brake fluid and bleed the brakes.

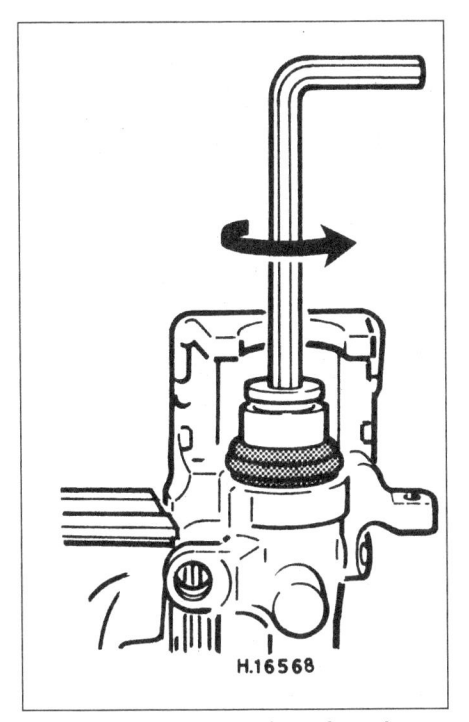

Rear calipers

15 Chock the front wheels, jack up the rear of the vehicle and support it on axle stands (see "*Jacking and vehicle support*"). Remove both rear wheels and remove the brake pads.
16 If available, fit a hose clamp to the caliper flexible brake hose. Alternatively, remove the fluid reservoir filler cap and tighten it down onto a piece of polythene sheet in order to reduce any loss of hydraulic fluid.
17 Loosen and detach the brake hose union at the caliper. Allow for a certain amount of fluid spillage and plug the hose union to prevent the ingress of dirt.
18 Unscrew and remove the lower caliper retaining bolt (where applicable) and remove the caliper **(see illustration)**. This self-locking bolt must be removed.
19 Clean the external surfaces of the caliper with paraffin and wipe dry. Plug the fluid inlet during this operation.
20 Secure the caliper in a soft-jawed vice. Using an Allen key or angled circlip pliers, unscrew the piston from the cylinder **(see illustration)**.
21 Using a screwdriver, carefully ease out the O-ring from the cylinder bore **(see illustration)**.
22 Prise free the protective cap from the piston.
23 Clean the components with methylated spirit and allow to dry. Inspect the surfaces of the piston, cylinder and frames for wear, damage and corrosion. If necessary, renew the caliper. If the components are in good condition then obtain a repair kit of seals.
24 Dip the new O-ring in brake fluid and locate it in the cylinder bore groove using the fingers only to manipulate it.
25 Smear the piston with brake fluid then manipulate the new protective cap into position on the inner end of the piston with the outer seal lip on the piston **(see illustration)**.
26 Hold the piston at the entrance to the cylinder housing and carefully manipulate the inner seal lip of the protective cap into the groove in the cylinder bore using a suitable screwdriver **(see illustration)**.

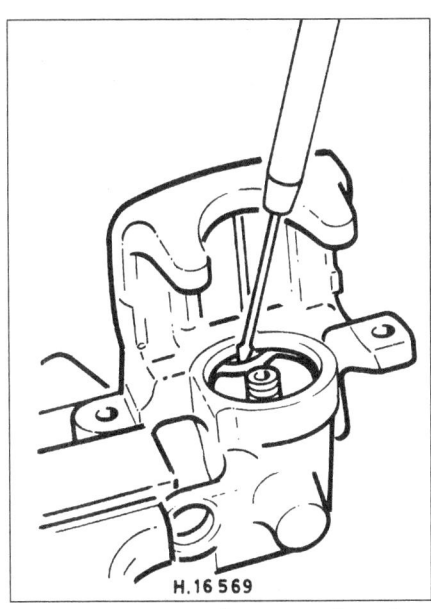

3.20 Removing the piston from the cylinder

3.21 Removing the O-ring seal from the cylinder

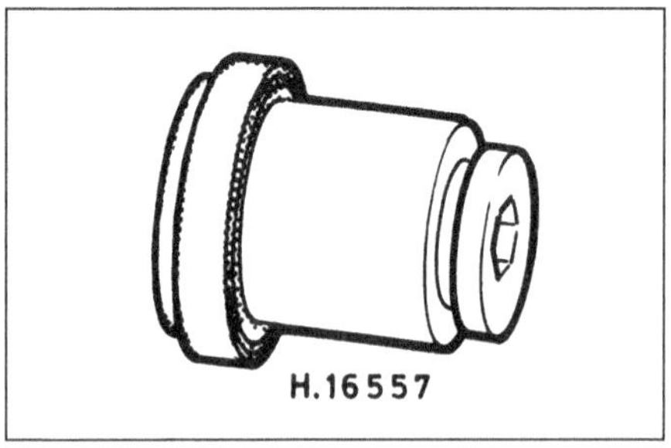

9•6 Braking system

3.25 Protective cap on piston

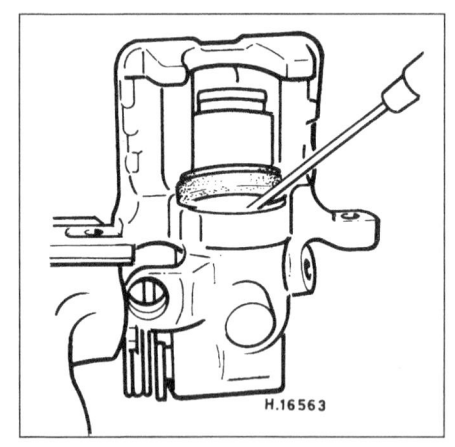

3.26 Manipulating inner seal lip of protective cap into cylinder bore groove

27 Locate the Allen key or angled circlip pliers into the piston and pressing firmly down, screw the piston fully home into the cylinder so that the outer seal lip of the protective cap springs into the location groove in the piston **(see illustration)**.
28 Caliper reassembly is now complete but before refitting it to the vehicle, it must be topped up with brake fluid and bled. To do this, unscrew the bleeder valve then support the caliper in the upright position. Connect a suitable union, hose and fluid supply applicator to the bleed valve connection in the caliper. Apply fluid and top-up the caliper until fluid is seen to emerge from the brake hose connection without air bubbles. Tighten the bleed valve and plug the brake hose connection aperture **(see illustration)**.
29 The caliper can now be refitted to the vehicle.

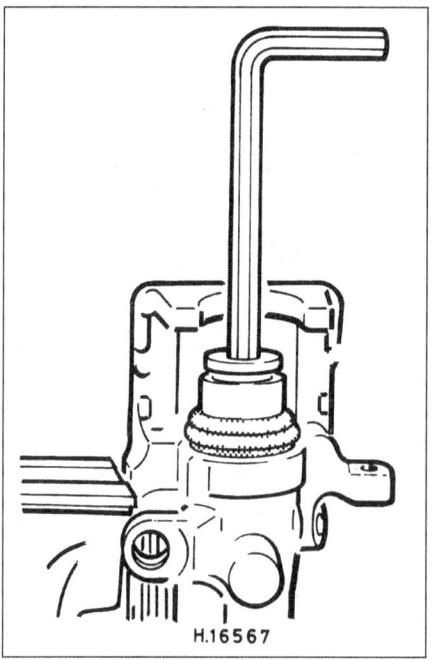

3.27 Screwing piston downwards through protective cap and into position in cylinder

4 Brake discs - examination, removal and refitting

Front discs

1 Jack up the front of the vehicle and support it on axle stands (see "*Jacking and vehicle support*"). Apply the handbrake and remove both front wheels.
2 Using an Allen key, unscrew the upper and lower caliper securing bolts. Withdraw the caliper and tie it clear of the disc. Do not allow the weight of the caliper to stretch or distort the brake hose.
3 Rotate the disc and examine it for deep scoring or grooving.
4 Using a micrometer, check that the disc thickness is not less than the minimum amount specified.
5 Remove the cross-head screw and withdraw the brake disc from the hub **(see illustration)**.

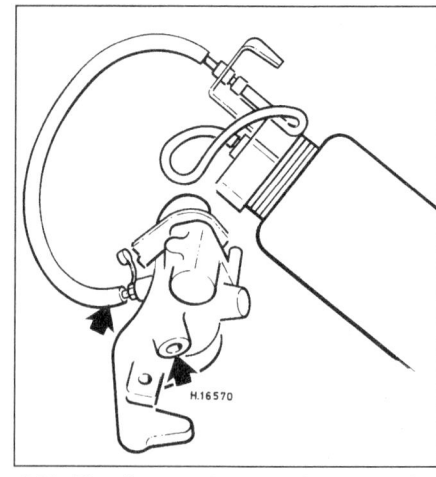

3.28 Bleeding rear brake caliper unit prior to refitting

Arrows indicate brake bleed valve and brake hose connection point

6 If necessary, the splash guard can be removed from the wheel bearing housing by unscrewing the three bolts.
7 Refitting is a reversal of removal. Ensure that the mating faces of the disc and hub are clean.

Rear discs

8 Chock the front wheels, jack up the rear of the vehicle and support it on axle stands. Remove both rear wheels.
9 Remove the caliper and tie it clear of the disc. Do not allow the weight of the caliper to stretch or distort the brake hose.
10 Rotate the disc and examine it for deep scoring or grooving.
11 Using a micrometer, check that the disc thickness is not less than the minimum amount specified.
12 Using a dial gauge or metal block and feeler blades, check that the disc run-out measured on the friction surface does not exceed the maximum amount specified.
13 Unbolt and remove the rear brake carrier. Use a screwdriver and prise free the hub cap **(see illustration)**.
14 Straighten and extract the split pin, then withdraw the locking ring **(see illustration)**.

4.5 Front brake disc retaining screw (arrowed)

4.13 Prise free the hub cap . . .

4.14 . . . remove the split pin and lock ring . . .

Braking system 9•7

4.15 . . . followed by the outer washer and bearing

15 Undo the hub nut and then withdraw the thrustwasher and outer taper bearing race **(see illustration)**.
16 Withdraw the disc from the stub axle.
17 Unless a disc is being renewed after a low mileage due to damage or other defect, both discs must be renewed at the same time.
18 Refer to the following Section for hub bearing replacement.
19 Lubricate the stub axle with grease then fit the disc over it, taking care not to damage the inner oil seal lips.
20 Lubricate the outer taper roller bearing with grease and locate it onto the stub axle against its bearing outer race.
21 Refit the thrustwasher, engaging the inner lug with the groove in the stub axle. Hand tighten the securing nut to the point where the thrustwasher can just be moved with a screwdriver and finger pressure but without levering it. Check that the disc rotates freely without binding or excessive endfloat, then locate the locking ring over the nut and insert a new split pin to secure.
22 Half fill the hub cap with bearing grease and tap it carefully into position .
23 Before refitting the brake carrier, check that the protective caps and guide pins are not damaged. If they are, then the carrier must be renewed. Locate and fit the carrier retaining bolts, tightening to the specified torque setting.
24 The caliper can now be refitted.

5 Rear hub bearings - renewal

1 Remove the rear brake disc.
2 Remove the inner bearing from the disc by levering free the dust cap, prising out the oil seal and extracting the bearing.
3 The bearing outer races can be removed from the disc by drifting them out with a soft drift whilst supporting the disc.
4 Check that the bearing recesses in the disc are clean, support the disc and drive the new bearing outer races into position by using a suitable tube drift. Ensure that they are fully home.
5 Lubricate the inner bearing with grease and locate it onto its outer race. The oil seal can now be driven into position. Lubricate its seal lip when fitted.
6 Drive the dust cap into position using a suitable tube drift.
7 Refit the rear brake disc.

6 Rear brake shoes - inspection and renewal

Inspection
1 Jack up the rear of the vehicle and support it on axle stands (see "Jacking and vehicle support"). Chock the front wheels.
2 Working beneath the vehicle, remove the rubber plugs from the front of the backplates and check with a torch that the linings are not worn below the minimum thickness specified. On completion, refit the plugs.

Removal
3 Remove the rear wheels.
4 Prise off the hub cap then extract the split pin and remove the locking ring **(see illustrations)**.
5 Unscrew the hub nut and remove the thrustwasher and outer wheel bearing **(see illustrations)**.
6 Check that the handbrake is fully released, then withdraw the brake drum. If difficulty is experienced, the brake shoes must be backed away from the drum first. To do this, insert a screwdriver through one of the bolt holes and push the automatic adjuster wedge upwards against the spring tension. This will release the shoes from the drum.
7 Brush all dust from the brake drum, shoes and backplate whilst taking care not inhale it. Scrape any scale or rust from the drum. Note that the shoes should be renewed as a set of four.
8 Using a pair of pliers, depress the steady spring cups, turn them through 90° and remove the cups, springs and pins **(see illustration)**.
9 Note the location of the return springs and strut on the brake shoes, then lever the shoes from the bottom anchor. Unhook and remove the lower return spring **(see illustration)**.
10 Disengage the handbrake cable from the lever on the trailing brake shoe **(see illustration)**.
11 Release the brake shoes from the wheel cylinder, unhook the wedge spring and upper return spring and withdraw the shoes **(see illustration)**.

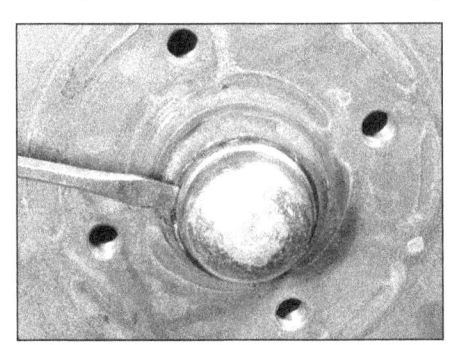

6.4a Remove the hub cap . . .

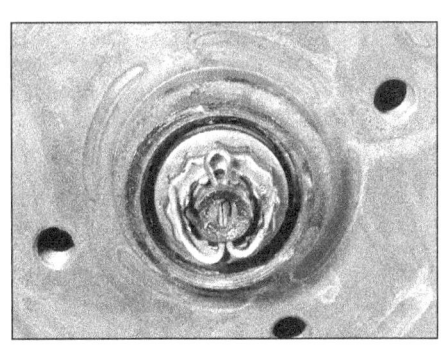

6.4b . . . the split pin and lock ring

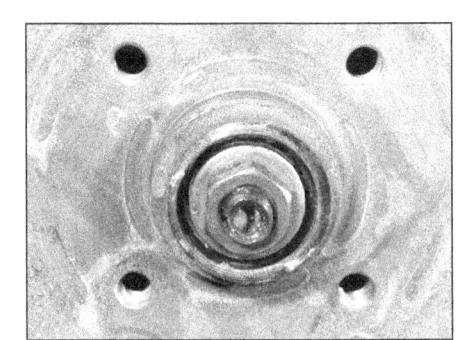

6.5a Undo the hub nut . . .

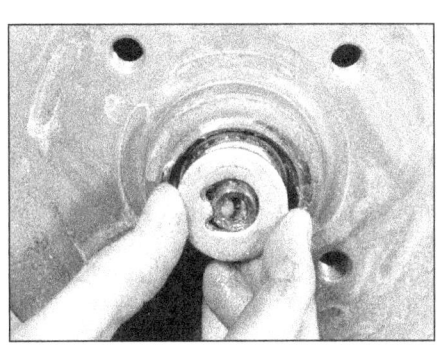

6.5b . . . remove the thrustwasher . . .

6.5c . . . and outer bearing

9•8 Braking system

6.8 Brake shoe steady spring and cup (arrowed)

6.9 Lower return spring fixing points to brake shoes

6.10 Handbrake cable attachment point to trailing brake shoe (arrowed)

12 Grip the strut in a vice and release the shoe, then remove the wedge and spring. The backplate and stub axle may be removed if necessary, by unscrewing the four bolts after removing the wheel cylinder. Note the location of the handbrake cable bracket. If the wheel cylinder is being left in position, retain the pistons with an elastic band. Check that there are no signs of fluid leakage and, if necessary, repair or renew the wheel cylinder.

Fitting

13 Fit the new brake shoes using a reversal of the removal procedure. Note that the lug on the wedge faces the backplate.
14 Check the brake drum for wear and damage.
15 Before refitting the brake drum, smear the lips of the oil seal with a little grease.
16 Refit the drum onto the stub axle whilst taking care not to damage the oil seal, then lubricate the outer taper roller bearing and fit it onto the stub axle.
17 Fit the thrustwasher and hub nut then tighten the nut, hand tight only.
18 Refit the wheel.
19 With the hub cap, split pin and locking ring removed, tighten the hub nut firmly while turning the wheel in order to settle the bearings.
20 Back off the nut then tighten it until it is just possible to move the thrustwasher laterally with a screwdriver under finger pressure. Do not twist the screwdriver or lever it.
21 Fit the locking ring, together with a new split pin, then tap the hub cap into the drum with a mallet.
22 Check that the brake drum rotates freely then refit the roadwheel(s) and lower the vehicle to the ground. Finally, fully depress the brake pedal several times in order to set the shoes in their correct position.

7 Rear brake cylinder - removal, overhaul and refitting

Removal

1 Remove the rear brake shoes.
2 If available, fit a hose clamp to the flexible brake hose. Alternatively, remove the fluid reservoir filler cap and tighten it down onto a piece of polythene sheet in order to reduce any loss of hydraulic fluid.

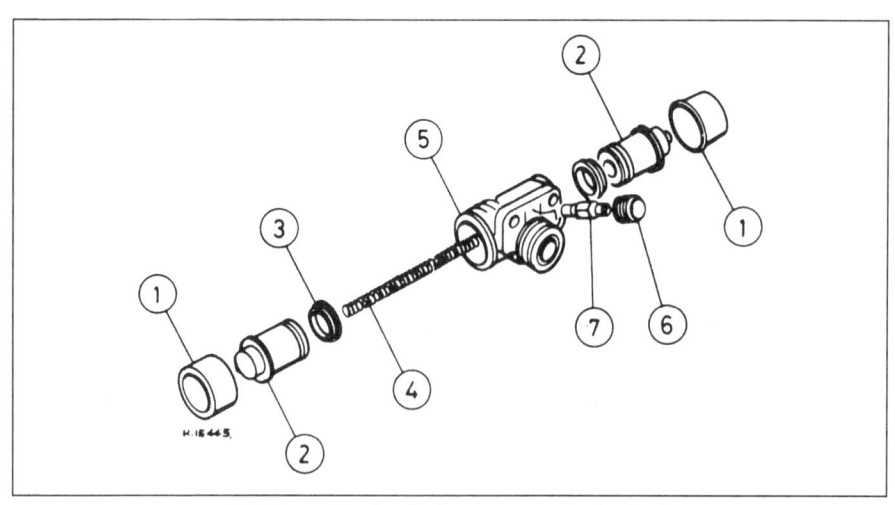

6.11 Wheel cylinder, upper return spring and pushrod assembly

3 Unscrew the hydraulic pipe union from the rear of the cylinder and plug the end of the pipe.
4 Remove the two screws and withdraw the wheel cylinder from the backplate.

Overhaul

5 Prise off the dust caps then remove the pistons, keeping them identified for location. If necessary, use air pressure from a foot pump in the fluid inlet (see illustration).
6 Remove the internal spring and, if necessary, unscrew the bleed valve.
7 Clean all components in methylated spirit and allow to dry. Examine the surfaces of the piston and cylinder bore for wear, scoring and corrosion. If evident, renew the complete wheel cylinder. If the components are in good condition, discard the seals and obtain a repair kit.
8 Dip the inner seals in clean brake fluid then fit them to the piston grooves using the fingers only to manipulate them. Ensure that the larger diameter ends face the inner ends of the pistons.
9 Smear brake fluid on the pistons then insert the spring and press the pistons into the cylinder, taking care not to damage the seal lips.
10 Locate the dust caps on the pistons and in the grooves on the outside of the cylinder.
11 Insert and tighten the bleed valve.

Refitting

12 Clean the mating faces then fit the wheel cylinder to the backplate and tighten the screws.

7.5 Rear wheel cylinder components (typical)

1 Boot
2 Piston
3 Cap
4 Spring
5 Brake cylinder housing
6 Dust cap
7 Bleed valve

Braking system 9•9

13 Refit the hydraulic pipe and tighten the union. Remove the hose clamp or polythene sheet.
14 Refit the brake shoes.
15 Top-up the brake fluid reservoir and bleed the valves.

8 Rear brake drum - examination and renovation

1 Whenever the brake drums are removed, they should be checked for wear and damage. Light scoring of the friction surface is normal but if excessive, the drums must either be renewed as a pair or reground provided that the maximum internal diameter specified is not exceeded.
2 After a high mileage, the drums may become warped and oval. Run-out can be checked with a dial gauge and, if in excess of the maximum amount specified, the drums should be renewed as a pair.
3 The inner oil seal should be checked for condition and if necessary, renewed. Prise out the old seal using a screwdriver (see illustration). Drive the new seal into position so that it is flush with the boss face.

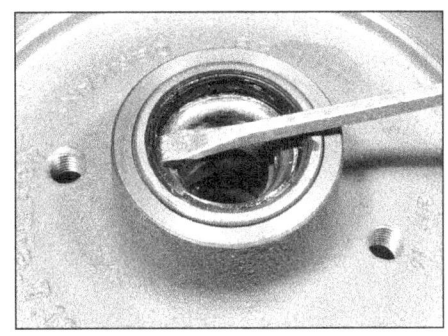

8.3 Prising out brake drum oil seal

9 Master cylinder - removal and refitting

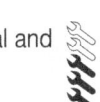

Removal

1 Disconnect the battery negative lead.
2 Disconnect the wiring from the fluid level switches on the master cylinder and fluid reservoir filler cap.
3 On carburettor models, remove the air cleaner.
4 On fuel injection models, detach the injection hoses from the retaining clips on the inlet ducting, then unclip and detach the inlet duct between the fuel distributor unit and the throttle housing.
5 Place a suitable container beneath the master cylinder and place some cloth on the surrounding body to protect it from any spilled brake fluid.
6 Unscrew the unions and disconnect the hydraulic fluid pipes from the master cylinder.
7 Unscrew the mounting nuts and withdraw the master cylinder from the servo unit. Remove the spacer and seal where applicable (see illustration).
8 Remove the master cylinder from the engine compartment, taking care not to spill any hydraulic fluid on the body paintwork.
9 Clean the exterior of the master cylinder with paraffin and wipe dry.
10 If the master cylinder is defective it cannot be overhauled and must be renewed as a unit. This being the case, remove the reservoir by pulling it free from the rubber grommets, then prise free the grommets from the cylinder.
11 Commence reassembly by smearing the rubber grommets in brake fluid and pressing them into the cylinder, then press the reservoir into the grommets.

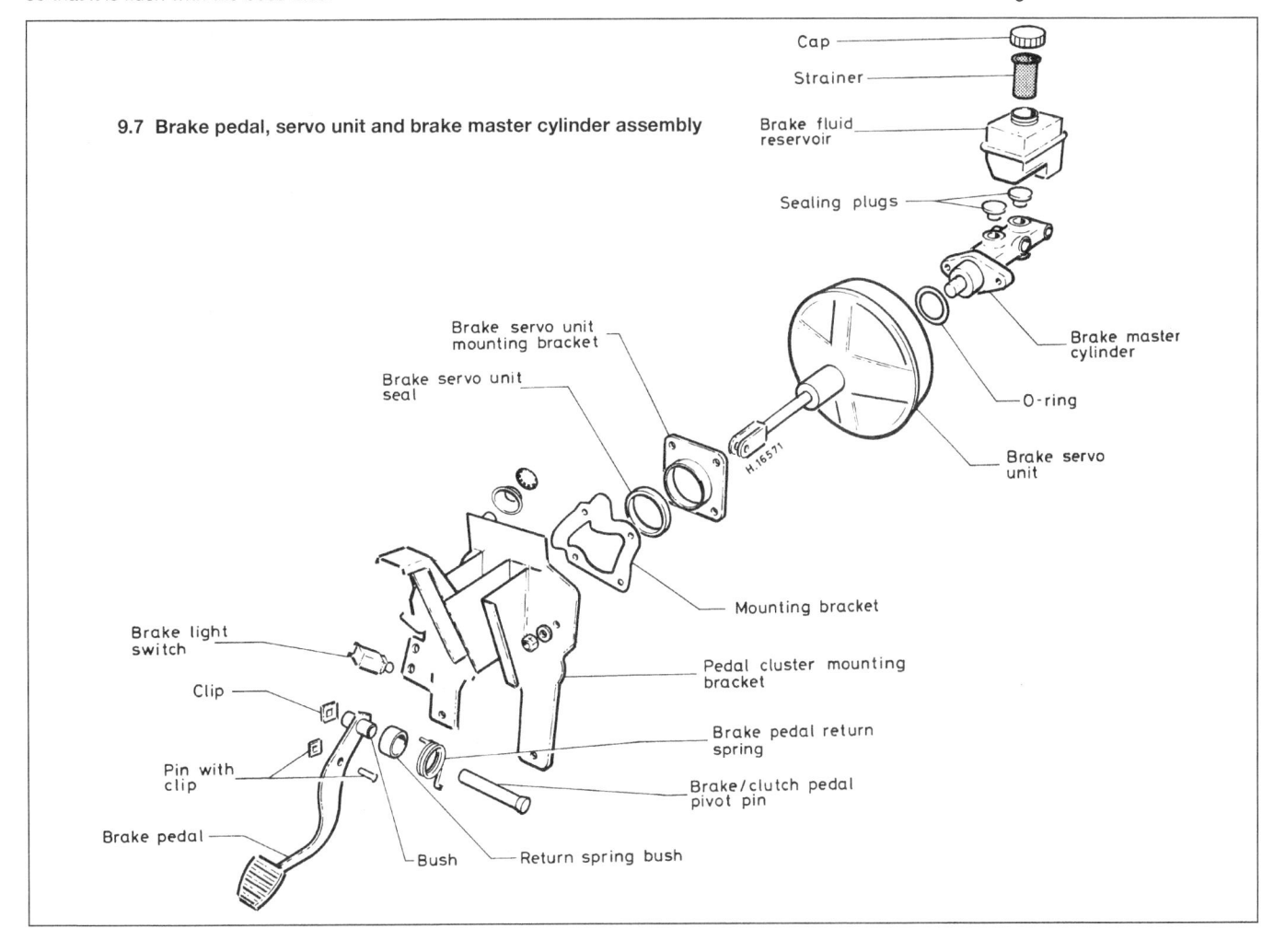

9.7 Brake pedal, servo unit and brake master cylinder assembly

9•10 Braking system

Refitting

12 Refitting the master cylinder is a reversal of the removal procedure. Fit a new mounting seal between the cylinder and servo unit.
13 On completion, bleed the brake hydraulic system.

10 Brake pressure regulator - testing, removal and refitting

1 The regulator is located on the under-body, in front of the left-hand rear wheel (see illustration).
2 Checking of the regulator is best left to a VW garage, as special pressure gauges and spring tensioning tools are required.
3 Adjustment is made by varying the spring tension. Again, this must be carried out by a VW garage.
4 Removal and refitting are straightforward. After fitting, bleed the hydraulic system and have the regulator adjusted by a VW garage.
5 When bleeding the hydraulic system of vehicles fitted with a pressure regulator, the lever of the regulator should be pressed toward the rear axle.

11 Hydraulic pipes and hoses - renewal

1 To remove a rigid brake pipe, unscrew the union nuts at each end and where necessary, remove the line from its retaining clips. Refitting is a reversal of removal.
2 To remove a flexible brake hose, unscrew the union nut securing the rigid brake pipe to the end of the flexible hose and remove the spring clip and hose end fitting from the bracket (see illustration). Unscrew the remaining end from the component or rigid pipe according to position. Refitting is a reversal of removal.
3 Bleed the complete hydraulic system after fitting a brake pipe or hose.

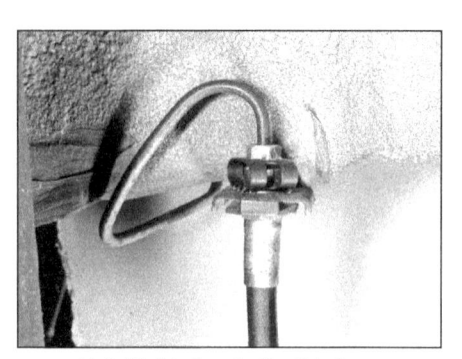

10.1 Brake pressure regulator unit

12 Hydraulic system - bleeding

Caution: Take great care not to spill brake fluid onto paintwork as it will act as a paint stripper. If spilled, wash it off at once with cold water.

1 Bleeding of the hydraulic system will be required after any component in the system has been disturbed or any part of the system "broken". When an operation has only affected one circuit of the system, then bleeding will normally only be required to that circuit (front and rear diagonally opposite).
2 If the master cylinder or pressure regulating valve have been disturbed, then the complete system must be bled. Note that where a brake pressure regulator is fitted, the regulator lever should be pressed toward the rear axle during the bleeding of the rear brakes.
3 One of three methods can be used to bleed the system.

Two-man method

4 Obtain a clean jar and length of tube which will fit the bleed valve tightly. The help of an assistant will be required.
5 Clean around the bleed valve on the rear brake and attach the bleed tube to the valve (see illustration)
6 Check that the master cylinder reservoir is topped up and then destroy the vacuum in the brake servo (where fitted) by giving several applications of the brake foot pedal.

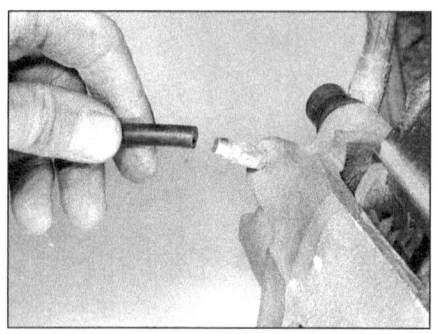

7 Immerse the open end of the bleed tube in the jar, which should contain 50 to 76 mm depth of hydraulic fluid. The jar should be positioned about 300 mm above the bleed valve to prevent any possibility of air entering the system down the threads of the bleed valve when it is slackened.
8 Open the bleed valve half a turn and have your assistant depress the brake pedal slowly to the floor and then quickly remove his foot to allow the pedal to return unimpeded. Tighten the bleed valve at the end of each downstroke to prevent expelled air and fluid being drawn back into the system.
9 Observe the submerged end of the tube in the jar. When air bubbles cease to appear, fully tighten the bleed valve when the pedal is being held down by your assistant
10 Top-up the fluid reservoir. It must be kept topped up throughout the bleeding operations. If the connecting holes in the master cylinder are exposed at any time due to low fluid level, then air will be drawn into the system and work will have to start all over again.
11 Repeat the operation on the diagonally opposite front brake.
12 On completion, remove the bleed tube. Discard the fluid which has been bled from the system unless it is required for bleed jar purposes. Never use it for filling the system.

With one-way valve

13 There are a number of one-man brake bleeding kits currently available from motor accessory shops. It is recommended that one of these kits should be used whenever possible as they greatly simplify the bleeding operation and also reduce risk of expelled air or fluid being drawn back into the system.
14 Connect the outlet tube of the bleeder device to the bleed valve and then open the valve half a turn. Depress the brake pedal to the floor and slowly release it. The one-way valve in the device will prevent expelled air from returning to the system at the completion of each stroke. Repeat this operation until clean hydraulic fluid, free from air bubbles, can be seen coming through the tube. Tighten the bleed screw and remove the tube.
15 Repeat the procedure on the on the diagonally opposite brake whilst remembering to keep the master cylinder reservoir full.

With pressure bleeding kits

16 These are available from motor accessory shops and are usually operated by air pressure from the spare tyre.
17 By connecting a pressurised container to the master cylinder fluid reservoir, bleeding is then carried out by simply opening each bleed valve in turn and allowing the fluid to run out until no air bubbles are visible in the fluid being expelled.
18 Using this system, the large reserve of fluid provides a safeguard against air being drawn into the master cylinder during the bleeding operations.

11.2 Rigid pipe-to-flexible hose connection

12.5 Connect bleed tube to bleed valve

Braking system 9•11

19 This method is particularly effective when bleeding "difficult" systems or when bleeding the entire system at routine fluid renewal.

All methods

20 If the entire system is being bled, the procedures described above should now be repeated at each wheel. The correct sequence is as follows. Do not forget to recheck the fluid level in the master cylinder at regular intervals and top-up as necessary.
Right-hand rear wheel
Left-hand rear wheel
Right-hand front wheel
Left-hand front wheel

21 When completed, recheck the fluid level in the master cylinder, top-up if necessary and refit the cap. Check the feel of the brake pedal which should be firm and free from any sponginess which would indicate air still present in the system.

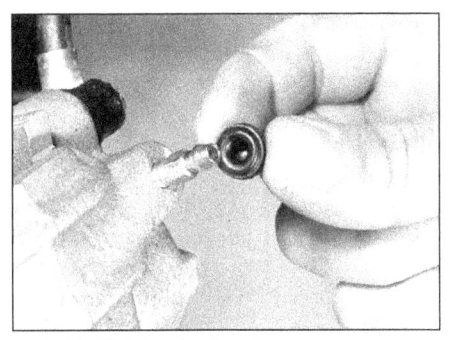

12.23 Fit bleed valve the protector cap

22 Discard any expelled hydraulic fluid as it is likely to be contaminated with moisture, air and dirt, which makes it unsuitable for further use.

23 On completion, refit the rubber protector caps over each bleed valve **(see illustration)**.

13 Handbrake lever - removal and refitting

Removal

1 Position a chock each side of the front wheels. Pull the cover from the lever by prising open its bottom edges, then fully release the handbrake.

2 Undo each cable locknut and adjuster nut then disconnect the cables from the compensating lever **(see illustration)**.

3 Prise free the lever retaining clamp on the right-hand side, then withdraw the pivot pin and remove the lever.

4 If required, remove the screw from the lever switch, disconnect the wiring and remove the switch.

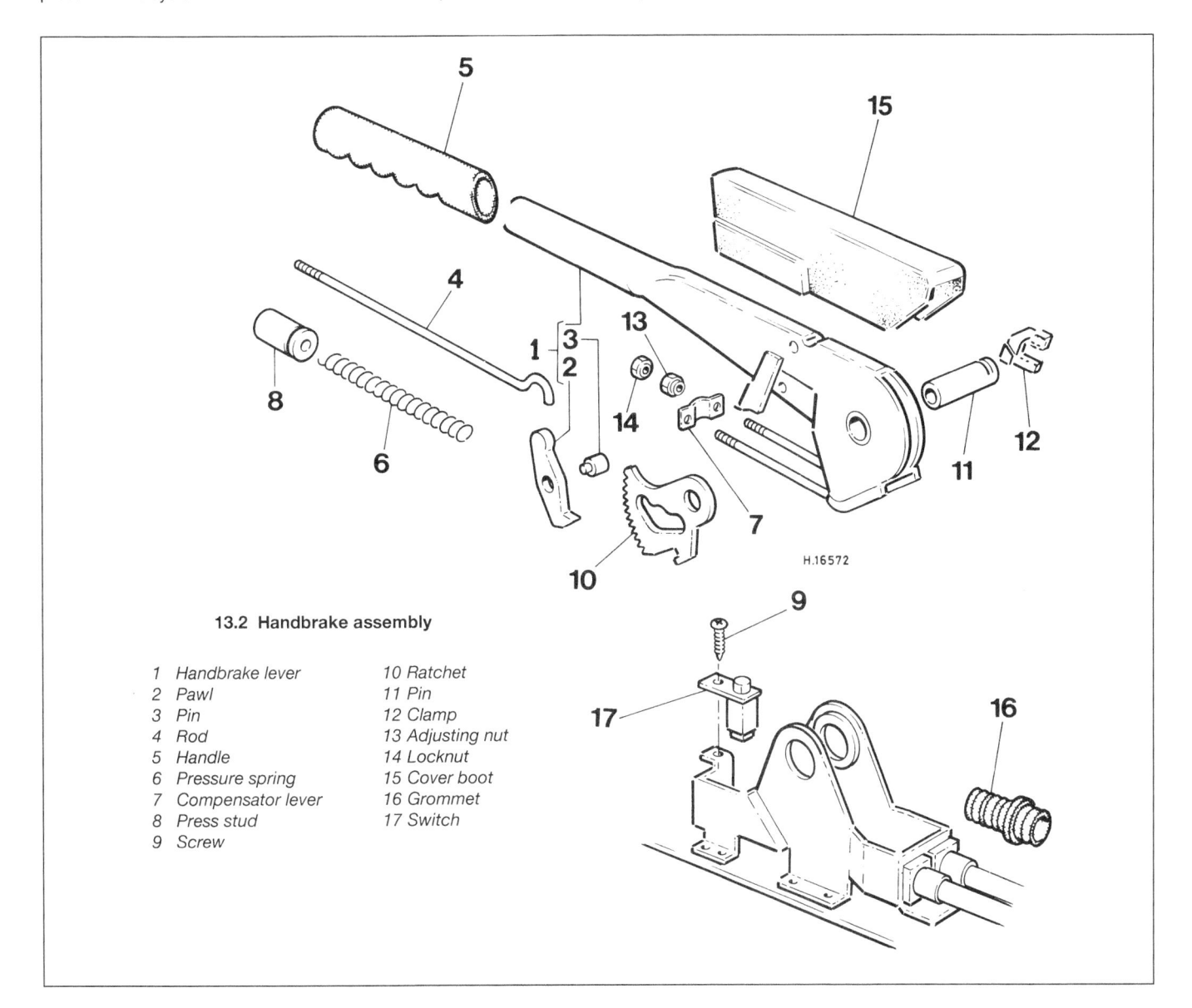

13.2 Handbrake assembly

1 Handbrake lever
2 Pawl
3 Pin
4 Rod
5 Handle
6 Pressure spring
7 Compensator lever
8 Press stud
9 Screw
10 Ratchet
11 Pin
12 Clamp
13 Adjusting nut
14 Locknut
15 Cover boot
16 Grommet
17 Switch

9•12 Braking system

Refitting

5 Refitting is a reversal of removal. Lubricate the pivot pin and on completion, adjust the handbrake cables.

14 Handbrake cables - removal, refitting and adjustment

Removal

1 Chock the front wheels, then jack up the rear of the vehicle and support it on axle stands (see "*Jacking and vehicle support*"). Release the handbrake.
2 Remove the cover from the handbrake lever then undo the locknut and adjuster nut from the cable concerned.
3 Remove the rear roadwheel(s).
4 On drum brake models, remove the brake drum and disconnect the cable from the shoe operating lever. Detach the cable from the backplate.
5 On models fitted with rear disc brakes, disengage the cable from the caliper lever then prise free the outer cable retaining clip from the caliper. Note how the clip is located.
6 Release the cable from its retaining clips and then carefully withdraw it from under the vehicle **(see illustration)**.

Refitting

7 Refitting is a reversal of removal, but adjust the cable as follows before lowering the vehicle.

Adjustment

Drum brakes

8 With the handbrake lever fully released, depress the footbrake applying firm pressure, once only. Now pull the handbrake up onto its second notch position.
9 Tighten the adjuster nut on the cable concerned so that the rear roadwheel is just felt to bind when rotated. Fully release the handbrake lever then check that the roadwheel spins freely without binding. Tighten the locknut against the adjuster nut then apply the handbrake and check that the wheel is locked. Repeat the procedure with the other cable.

Disc brakes

10 Before checking and adjusting the handbrake cables, first check the outer brake pad to caliper clearance.
11 Fully release the handbrake lever then tighten the cable adjuster nut to the point where the caliper lever just separates from its stop **(see illustration)**. An assistant is useful here to ensure that as the nut is tightened, the lever-to-stop clearance does not exceed 1.0 mm. Tighten the locknut then fully release the handbrake and check that the roadwheel rotates freely, then apply the handbrake and check that the roadwheel is locked.
12 Repeat the procedure on the other side.

15 Footbrake pedal - removal and refitting

Removal

1 The brake and clutch pedals share a common bracket assembly and pivot shaft.
2 Remove the clutch pedal.
3 Extract the clip and withdraw the clevis pin securing the servo pushrod.
4 Extract the clip from the pivot shaft, unhook the return spring, withdraw the pivot shaft and remove the pedal.
5 Check the pedal bushes for wear. If necessary, drive them out from each side and press in new bushes using a soft-jawed vice.

Refitting

6 Refitting is a reversal of removal, but lubricate the pivot shaft with a little multi-purpose grease.

16 Vacuum servo unit - testing

1 The vacuum servo unit is located between the brake pedal and the master cylinder.
2 Normally, the unit is very reliable but if it becomes faulty, it should be renewed. In the event of a failure, the hydraulic system is in no way affected, except that higher pedal pressures will be necessary.
3 To test the servo unit, depress the brake pedal several times with the engine switched off to dissipate the vacuum. Apply moderate pressure to the brake pedal then start the engine. The pedal should move down slightly if the servo unit is operating correctly.
4 To test the check valve in the vacuum hose, disconnect it from the hose then blow through the valve in the direction of the arrow marking. Air should pass through the valve. If air is blown in the reverse direction, it should not pass through the valve. Renew the valve if defective.

17 Vacuum servo unit - removal and refitting

Removal

1 Remove the brake master cylinder.
2 Pull the vacuum hose free from the servo unit connector and, where applicable, the non-return valve.
3 Working inside the vehicle, detach the lower trim panel on the driver's side.
4 Disconnect the pushrod clevis from the brake pedal by releasing the clip and withdrawing the clevis pin.
5 Unscrew the mounting nuts and withdraw the servo unit from the bulkhead into the engine compartment.

Refitting

6 Refitting is a reversal of removal. Lubricate the clevis pin with a little molybdenum disulphide based grease. The mounting nuts are self-locking and should always be renewed.

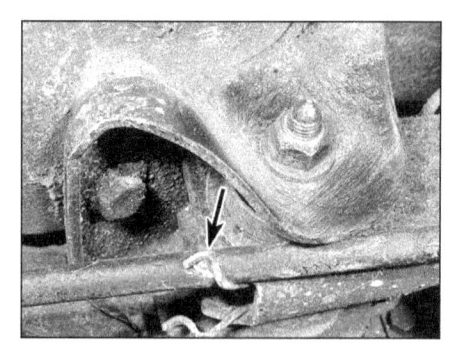

14.6 Handbrake cable retaining clip (arrowed) at rear axle beam pivot

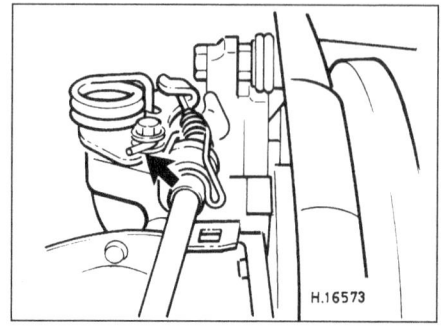

14.11 Handbrake adjustment on rear disc brakes

Lever on caliper (arrowed) should be just clear of stop

Chapter 10
Suspension and steering

Contents

Front anti-roll bar - removal and refitting	4
Front suspension - camber adjustment	3
Front suspension strut - removal, overhaul and refitting	2
Front wheel bearing housing - removal and refitting	5
Front wheel bearing - renewal	6
General information	1
Power steering fluid - draining and refilling	18
Power steering pump - removal, refitting and drivebelt adjustment	19
Rear axle beam - removal and refitting	9
Rear suspension strut and coil spring - removal and refitting	8
Rear wheel hub bearings - renewal	10
Steering column - removal, overhaul and refitting	12
Steering gear - adjustment	16
Steering gear bellows - renewal	14
Steering gear unit - removal and refitting	17
Steering lock - removal and refitting	13
Steering wheel - removal and refitting	11
Tie-rods and balljoints - removal and refitting	15
Track control arm - removal, overhaul and refitting	7
Wheel alignment - checking and adjustment	20

Degrees of difficulty

Easy, suitable for novice with little experience	**Fairly easy,** suitable for beginner with some experience	**Fairly difficult,** suitable for competent DIY mechanic	**Difficult,** suitable for experienced DIY mechanic	**Very difficult,** suitable for expert DIY or professional

Specifications

Front suspension
Type .... Independent with spring struts, lower track control arms and anti-roll bar (some models). Telescopic shock absorbers incorporated in struts

Rear suspension
Type .... Semi-independent. Incorporating torsion axle beam, trailing arms and spring struts/shock absorbers. Anti-roll bar on some models

Steering
Type .... Rack and pinion with safety column. Power steering optional on Golf GL models
Turning circle .... 10.5 m
Steering roll radius .... Negative 8.2 mm
Steering wheel turns lock to lock:
   Standard 3.83
   Power-assisted 3.17
Steering ratio:
   Standard 20.8
   Power-assisted 17.5

Front wheel alignment
Total toe .... 0° ± 10'
Camber (straight-ahead position):
   Golf GTi and Jetta GT .... - 35' ± 20'
   All other models .... - 30' ± 20'
   Maximum difference - side-to-side .... 30'
Castor:
   Golf GTI and Jetta GT .... 1°35' ± 30'
   All other models .... 1°30' ± 30'
   Maximum difference - side to side .... 1°

Note: *Camber and castor settings may differ on some variants - check with VW dealer*

Rear wheel alignment
Total toe .... 25' ± 15'
Maximum deviation in adjustment .... 25'
Camber .... -1° 40' ± 20'
Maximum difference - side-to-side .... 30'

10•2 Suspension and steering

Roadwheels
Golf base, C, CL and C Formel E	5J x 13
Golf GL	5½J x 13
Golf GTI	5½ or 6J x 14
Jetta	5½J x 13

Tyres
Type	Radial ply
Size:	
Golf base, C, GL and C Formel E	155 SR 13
Golf GL	175/70 SR 13
Golf GTI	185/60 HR 14
Jetta	175/70 SR 13

Torque wrench settings

	Nm	lbf ft
Front suspension		
Strut to body	60	44
Strut to wheel bearing housing:		
19 mm nut	80	59
18 mm nut	95	70
Lower track control arm:		
Pivot bolt to subframe	130	96
Lower balljoint bolts	35	26
Track control arm/subframe bolts	130	96
Subframe rear mounting strut to body	80	59
Shock absorber slotted nut	40	30
Anti-roll bar eye bolt nut	25	18
Hub nut	265	195
Rear suspension		
Mounting bracket shouldered bolt:		
Pre 1988	85	63
From 1988	70	52
Shock absorber lower mounting nut	70	52
Stub axle	60	44
Axle beam/mounting bracket pivot bolt nut	60	44
Brake pressure regulator spring bracket	35	26
Shock absorber top cover nut	15	11
Shock absorber spacer retaining nut	15	11
Steering		
Steering wheel	40	30
Column tube mounting bracket	20	15
Tie-rod inner	35	26
Tie-rod balljoint	35	26
Tie-rod balljoint locknut	50	37
Rack mounting clip	30	22
Steering column joint	30	22
Power steering pressure and return hose unions	20	15
Power steering pump and swivel bracket bolts	20	15
Power steering pump tensioner/bracket	20	15
Power steering pump pulley	20	15
Power steering tie-rod to rack	70	52
Roadwheels	110	81

1 General information

The front suspension is of independent type, incorporating coil struts and lower track control arms (wishbones). The struts are fitted with telescopic shock absorbers and both suspension units are mounted on a subframe. An anti-roll bar is fitted to the track control arm on some models (see illustration).

The rear suspension comprises a transverse torsion axle with trailing arms rubber-bushed to the body. The axle is attached to the lower ends of the shock absorbers, which act as struts since they incorporate mountings for the coil springs (see illustration).

The steering is of rack and pinion type mounted on the front subframe. The tie-rods are attached to a single coupling which is itself bolted to the steering rack. Power assistance is fitted to some models.

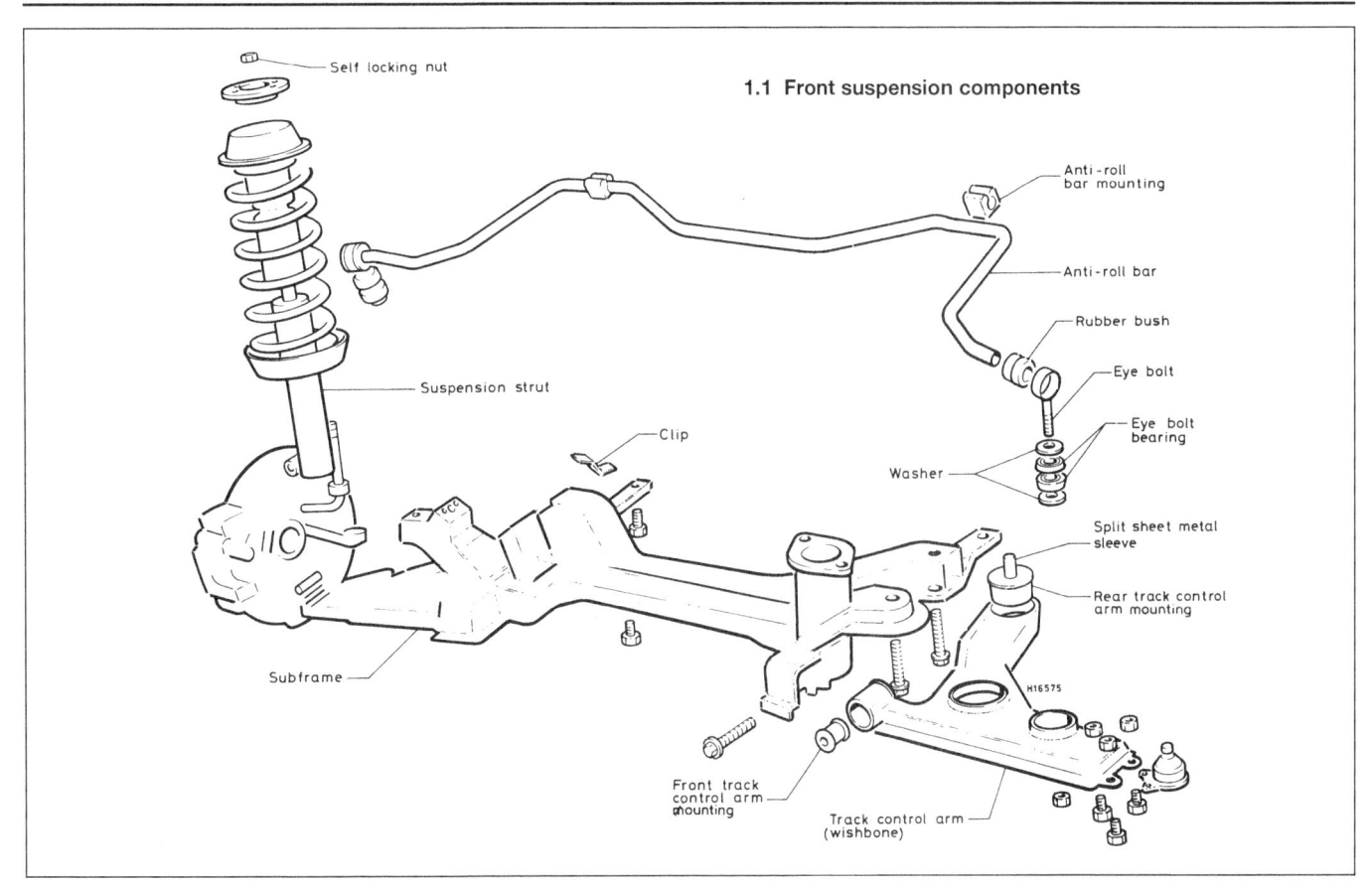

Suspension and steering 10•3

1.1 Front suspension components

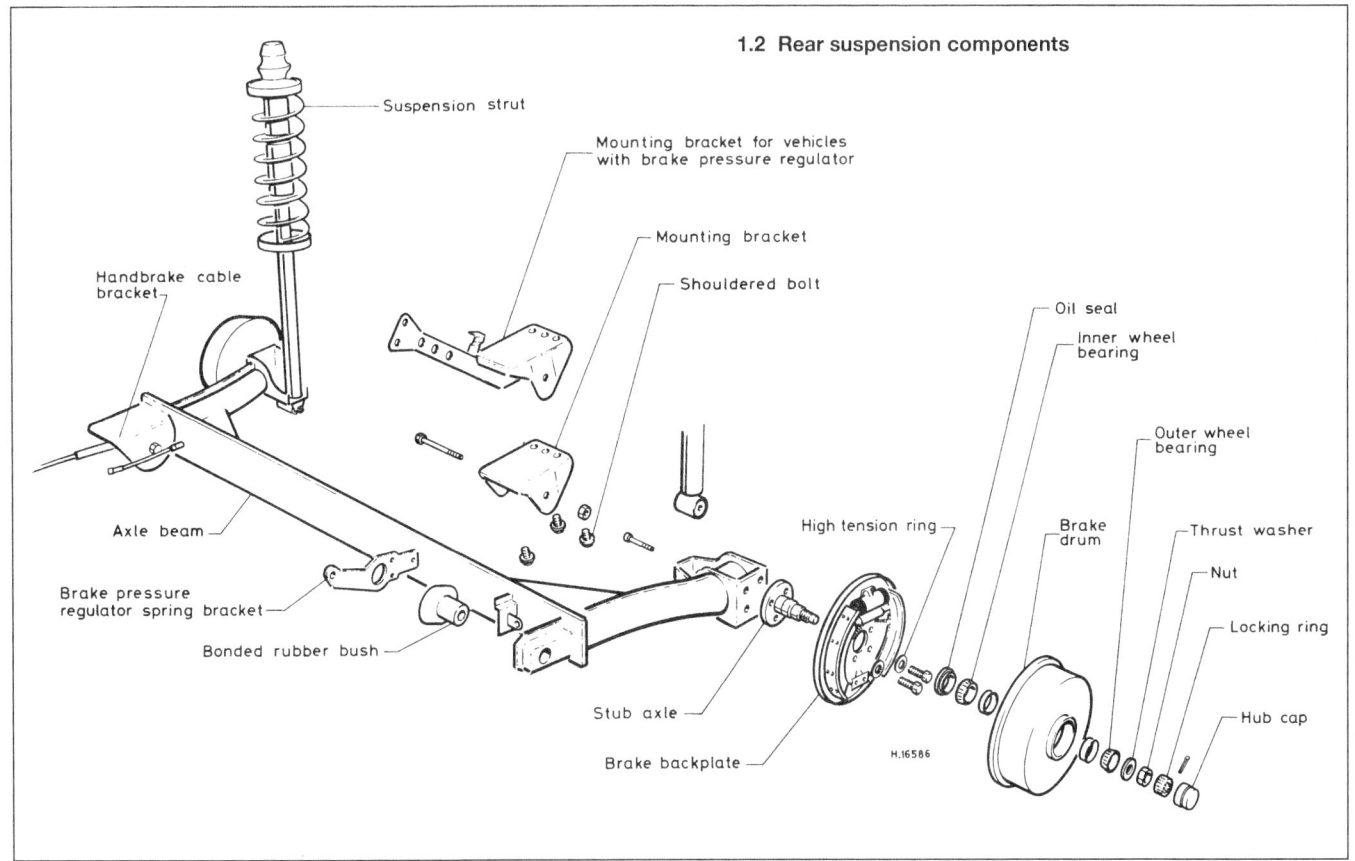

1.2 Rear suspension components

10•4 Suspension and steering

2 Front suspension strut – removal, overhaul and refitting

Removal

1 Apply the handbrake then jack up and support the front of the vehicle on axle stands (see "*Jacking and vehicle support*"). Remove the roadwheel on the side concerned.
2 Position a jack under the outer end of the track control arm for support.
3 In the engine compartment, prise the cap from the top of the strut **(see illustration)** and unscrew the self-locking nut whilst holding the piston rod stationary with an Allen key. Renew the self-locking nut.
4 Undo and remove the anti-roll bar eye bolt nut.
5 Detach the steering tie-rod balljoint.
6 Remove the brake caliper and hang it up to one side. Detach the brake line from the strut.
7 Scribe an alignment mark around the periphery of the suspension strut-to-wheel bearing housing location lugs to ensure accurate positioning when refitting, then undo the two retaining nuts and withdraw the two bolts securing the strut at its bottom end to the wheel bearing housing **(see illustration)**. Renew the self-locking nuts and washers.
8 Lower the track control arm to disengage the strut from its top mounting, then prise it free from the wheel bearing housing.

2.3 Removing front suspension strut top cap

Overhaul

9 Do not attempt to remove the coil spring from the strut unless a spring compressor is available. If a suitable compressor is not available, take the strut to a garage for dismantling and assembly.
10 Support the lower end of the strut in a vice, then fit the coil spring compressor into position and check that it is securely located.
11 Compress the spring until the upper spring retainer is free of tension, then remove the slotted nut from the top of the piston rod. To do this, a special tool is available **(see illustration)**. However, it is possible to hold the piston rod stationary with an Allen key or spanner on the flats (as applicable) and use a peg spanner to unscrew the slotted nut.
12 Remove the strut bearing, followed by the spring retainer **(see illustration)**.
13 Lift the coil spring from the strut with the compressor still in position. Mark the top of the spring for reference.
14 Withdraw the bump stop components from the piston rod, noting their order of removal.
15 Move the shock absorber piston rod up and down through its complete stroke and check that the resistance is even and smooth. If there are signs of seizing or lack of resistance, or if fluid has been leaking excessively, the shock absorber/strut unit should be renewed.
16 The coil springs are normally colour-coded. If the springs are to be renewed (it is advisable to renew the springs as an axle set), be sure to get the correct replacement type with an identical colour code.
17 Reassembly is a reversal of removal. Tighten the slotted nut to the specified torque before releasing the spring compressor.

Refitting

18 Refitting is a reversal of the removal procedure. Tighten all retaining nuts to the specified torque and use only new self-locking nuts with special washers to secure the strut-to-wheel bearing housing bolts.

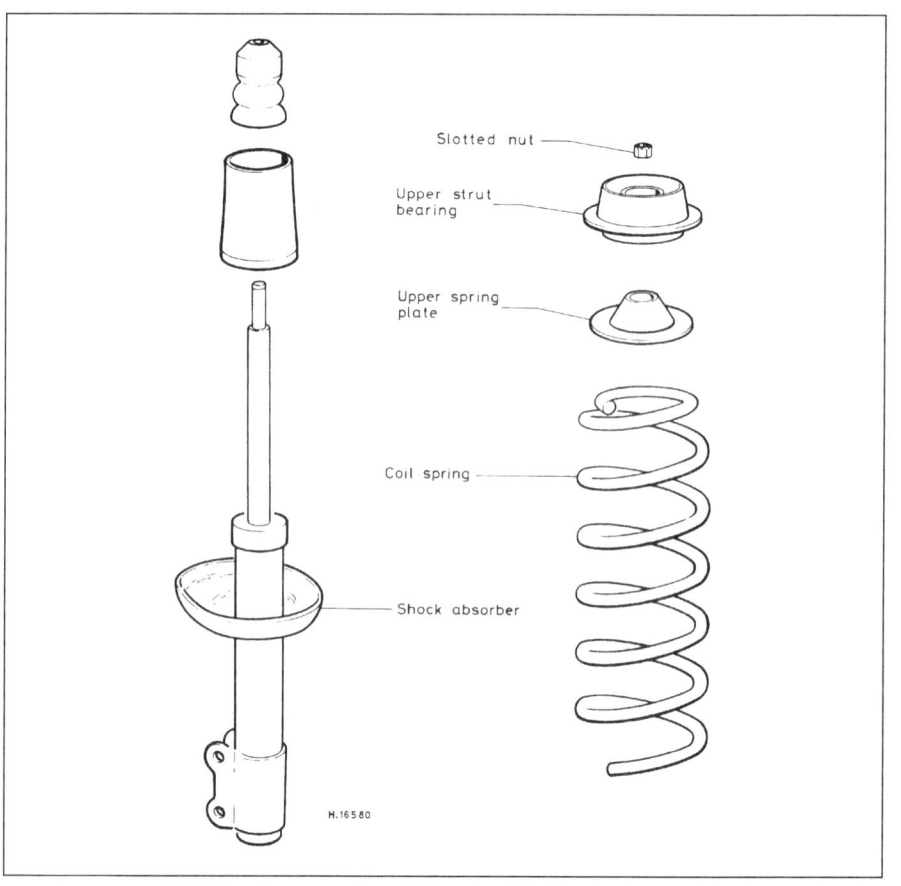

2.7 Strut-to-front wheel bearing housing retaining nuts/bolts

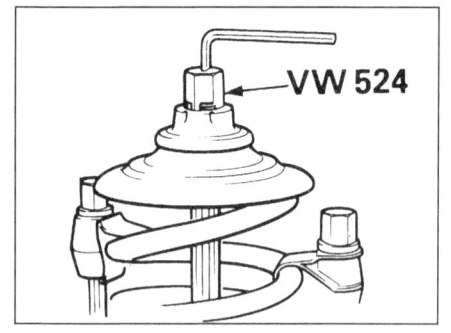

2.11 Using special tool to unscrew slotted nut from front suspension
Peg spanner and Allen key or suitable spanner will suffice

2.12 Front suspension strut and coil spring components

Suspension and steering 10•5

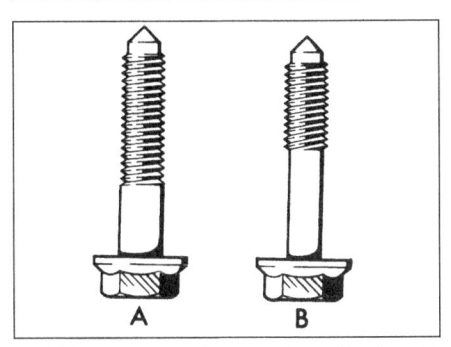

3.2 Front suspension camber adjustment bolts for later models

A Standard 12.0 mm diameter bolt
B Special 11.0 mm diameter bolt

3 Front suspension - camber adjustment

Early models

1 On early models, front suspension camber adjustment is possible by loosening the two bolts securing the strut to the wheel bearing housing, then turning the eccentric top bolt as required. The position of the eccentric bolt must be accurately marked before removing it, otherwise the camber adjustment will have to be reset.

Later models

2 On later models no adjustment is possible as assembly tolerances have been reduced sufficiently to make any adjustment unnecessary. However, in isolated instances, it may be found that slight correction of the camber angle within 1° or 2° is required. In this case, a special bolt (part no. N 903-334-01) can be obtained from a VW dealer. The bolt shank is of 11 mm diameter instead of the standard 12 mm diameter and allows a small amount of adjustment to be made **(see illustration)**.
3 This special bolt should first be fitted in the top bolt position. If this does not provide sufficient adjustment, the lower bolt should also be changed for the special type. No attempt should be made to reduce the diameter of the original bolts.

4 Front anti-roll bar - removal and refitting

Removal

1 Apply the handbrake then jack up the front of the vehicle and support it on axle stands (see "*Jacking and vehicle support*").
2 Undo and remove the anti-roll bar eye bolt nuts from the underside of the track control arm each side **(see illustration)**.
3 Position a jack under the subframe to support it.

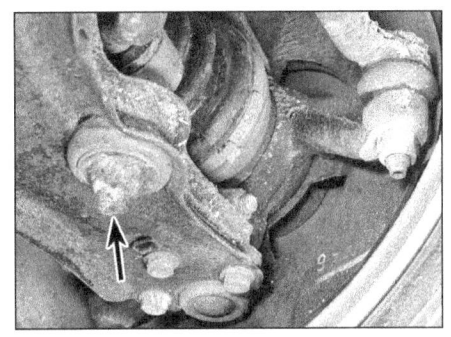

4.2 Anti-roll bar eye bolt nut (arrowed)

4 Undo the subframe-to-body strut retaining bolt at the rear end. Loosen the front bolt and swing the strut round to provide clearance for anti-roll bar and bush removal. Repeat on the other side.
5 Lift the anti-roll bar eye bolts and disengage them from the anti-roll bar **(see illustration)**. Note the location and orientation of the eye bolt bushes and washers. Remove the anti-roll bar.
6 Renew the anti-roll bar if damaged or distorted. Renew the bushes if perished or worn.

Refitting

7 Refitting is a reversal of the removal procedure. Check that the eye bolt bushes are fitted with their conical face towards the washers, the cover faces of which must face away from the bush mountings.
8 Do not fully tighten the retaining nuts and bolts until the vehicle is free standing and has been bounced a few times to settle the mountings.

4.5 Anti-roll bar location in eye bolt

5 Front wheel bearing housing - removal and refitting

Removal

1 Remove the driveshaft on the side concerned.
2 Disconnect the tie-rod balljoint from the wheel bearing housing **(see illustration)**.
3 Remove the brake caliper. Leave the brake hydraulic line connected to the caliper and hang up the caliper to support it. Disconnect the hydraulic line location bracket from the strut.
4 Undo the retaining screw and remove the brake disc.
5 Scribe an alignment mark around the periphery of the suspension strut-to-wheel bearing housing location lugs, to ensure accurate positioning when refitting.

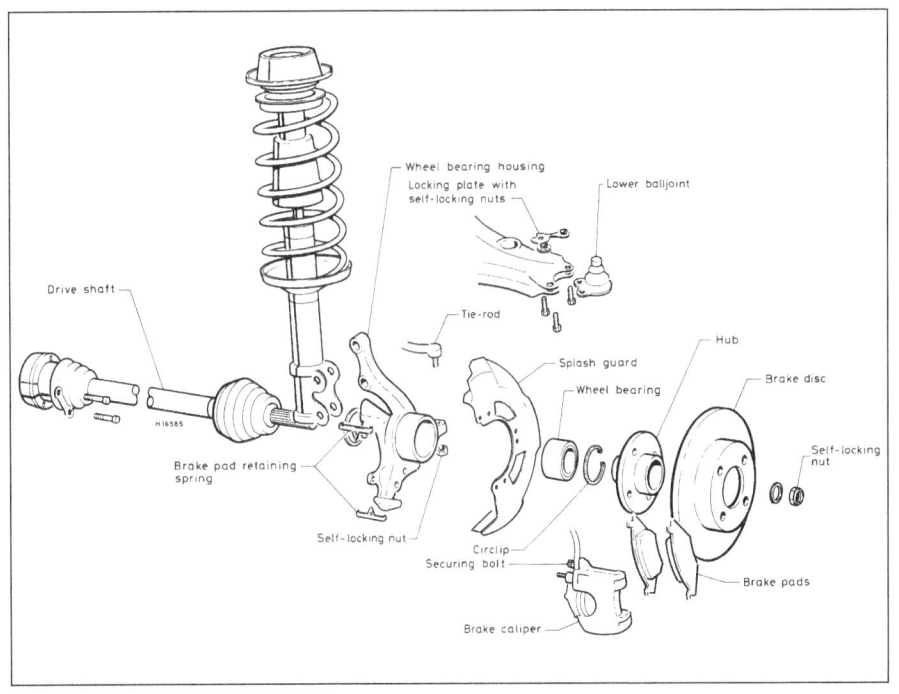

5.2 Wheel bearing housing and associated components

10•6 Suspension and steering

6 Undo the two suspension arm-to-wheel bearing retaining bolt nuts and remove them, together with their special washers. These nuts must be renewed when refitting. Withdraw the bolts and separate the wheel bearing housing from the suspension strut.
7 If the wheel bearing housing is to be renewed, remove the wheel bearing then fit the bearing and hub to the new housing.

Refitting

8 Refitting is a reversal of the removal procedure. Renew all self-locking nuts.
9 When refitting the suspension strut to the wheel bearing housing, check that they are correctly positioned according to the alignment scribe marks made during dismantling before tightening the securing bolts and nuts to the specified torque setting.
10 Refit the driveshaft.
11 Reconnect the tie-rod balljoint and anti-roll bar (where applicable) to the track control arm.
12 Refit the brake disc and caliper.
13 On completion, lower the vehicle to the ground and tighten the hub nut to the specified torque wrench setting.

6 Front wheel bearing - renewal

Removal

1 Remove the wheel bearing housing.
2 If still fitted, undo the cross-head screw and remove the brake disc.
3 Remove the screws and withdraw the splash guard.
4 Support the wheel bearing housing with the hub facing downward and press or drive out the hub by using a suitable mandrel. The bearing inner race will remain on the hub and once removed, it is not possible to re-use the bearing. Use a puller to remove the inner race from the hub.
5 Extract the circlips then, while supporting the wheel bearing housing, press or drive out the bearing by using a mandrel on the outer race.

Fitting

6 Clean the recess in the housing, then smear it with a little general purpose grease. Where a new wheel bearing kit has been obtained, the kit will contain a sachet of Molypaste. Smear some Molypaste onto the bearing seat (not the bearing).
7 Fit the outer circlip, then support the wheel bearing housing and press or drive in the new bearing by using a metal tube on the outer race only.
8 Fit the inner circlip, ensuring that it is correctly seated.
9 Position the hub with its bearing shoulder facing upward, then press or drive on the bearing and housing by using a metal tube on the inner race only.

10 Refit the splash guard and brake disc, then refit the wheel bearing housing.
11 On completion, lower the vehicle to the ground and tighten the hub nut to the specified torque setting.
12 If the bearings have been renewed, it is advisable to raise the vehicle at the front again after the hub nut has been tightened and check that the front roadwheel and hub can be spun freely without excessive binding or lateral play.

7 Track control arm - removal, overhaul and refitting

Removal

1 Loosen the front roadwheel bolts, jack up the front of the vehicle and support on axle stands (see "*Jacking and vehicle support*"). Remove the roadwheel(s).
2 Where applicable, remove the anti-roll bar.
3 Unscrew and remove the track control arm balljoint clamp bolt at the wheel bearing housing **(see illustration)**. Note that the bolt head faces forwards. Tap the control arm downwards to release the balljoint from the wheel bearing housing.
4 Unscrew and remove the pivot bolt from the front inboard end of the track control arm (to subframe) **(see illustration)**.
5 Undo and remove the track control arm rear mounting bolt and remove the bolt, together with the strut. Withdraw the split sleeve from the bolt hole using suitable pliers.
6 Pivot the track control arm downwards at the front and withdraw it from the subframe at the rear mounting, levering if necessary.

Overhaul

7 With the track control arm removed, clean it for inspection.
8 Check the balljoint for excessive wear and the pivot bushes for deterioration. Also examine the track control arm for damage and distortion. If necessary, the balljoint and bushes should be renewed.
9 To renew the balljoint, first outline its exact position on the track control arm. This is important as the relative positions of the track control arm and the balljoint are set during

7.4 Track control arm pivot bolt

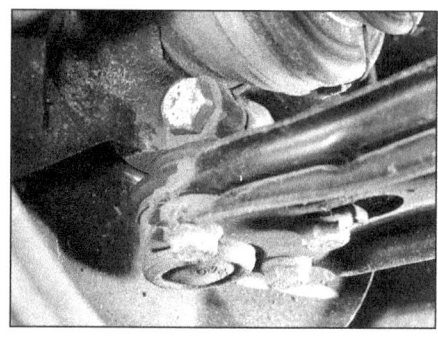

7.3 Track control arm balljoint and clamp bolt

production and the new balljoint must be accurately positioned when fitting. Unscrew the nuts and remove the balljoint and clamp plate. Fit the new balljoint in the exact outline and tighten the nuts. If fitting a new track control arm, locate the balljoint centrally in the elongated hole.
10 To renew the front pivot bush, use a long bolt, together with a metal tube and washers, to pull the bush from the track control arm. Fit the new bush using the same method but to ease insertion, dip the bush into soapy water first.
11 The rear mounting bonded rubber bush can be removed by prising it free. Failing this, you will need to carefully cut through its rubber and steel sections to split and release it by driving it out. The latter course of action should only be necessary if it is badly corroded into position.
12 Press or drive the new mounting bush into position from the top end of the control arm whilst ensuring that it is positioned correctly **(see illustration)**.

Refitting

13 Refitting the track control arm is a reverse of removal.

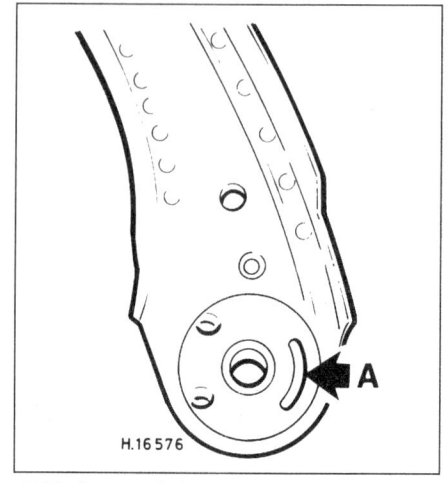

7.12 Correct fitting position for mounting bush in control arm

Opening A to be located on inboard side of vehicle

Suspension and steering 10•7

8.4 Removing rear suspension strut top cap

8.6 Rear suspension strut bottom mounting

8.7 Remove rear suspension strut and coil spring downwards

14 Delay tightening the pivot bolts until the weight of the vehicle is on the suspension.
15 Have the front wheel camber angle checked and if necessary, adjusted by a VW dealer.

8 Rear suspension strut and coil spring - removal and refitting

Removal

1 Detach the trim panel from the top of the rear suspension strut within the luggage compartment.
2 Chock the front roadwheels and then jack up the rear of the vehicle and support on axle stands (see "*Jacking and vehicle support*"). Remove the rear roadwheel(s).
3 Support the weight of the trailing arm with a trolley jack.
4 Remove the cap from the top of the strut **(see illustration)**. Unscrew the upper securing nut from the top of the strut, if necessary holding the rod stationary with a spanner.
5 Withdraw the dished washer then undo the second retaining nut and withdraw the thrustwasher and upper bearing ring.
6 At the bottom end of the strut, engage a spanner on the self-locking nut retaining the mounting bolt. Access is through the trailing arm tube **(see illustration)**. Undo the bolt and withdraw it.
7 Lower the trailing arm as far as possible and withdraw the strut assembly **(see illustration)**.
8 To remove the coil spring from the strut, undo the retaining nut then withdraw the spacer sleeve, lower bearing ring, upper spring seat and packing. Note how the packing is fitted for reference on reassembly **(see illustration)**.
9 Withdraw the coil spring, rubber stop and ring with protective tube, bottom cap, packing piece and lower spring seat.
10 If the shock absorber is faulty, it will normally make a knocking noise as the vehicle is driven over rough surfaces. With the unit removed, uneven resistance tight spots will be evident as the central rod is operated. Check the condition of the buffers, bump stop and associated components and renew them as necessary.
11 Coil springs should only be renewed as an axle set and it is important to fit correct replacements only. The springs are colour-coded for identification.

Refitting

12 Refitting is a reversal of removal. Ensure that the coil spring is correctly located in the seats. Delay tightening the lower mounting bolt until the full weight of the vehicle is on the roadwheels.
13 If new coil springs have been fitted, it is advisable to have a rear wheel alignment check made by your VW dealer after an initial distance of 1000 miles (1500 km) has been covered and the springs have settled.

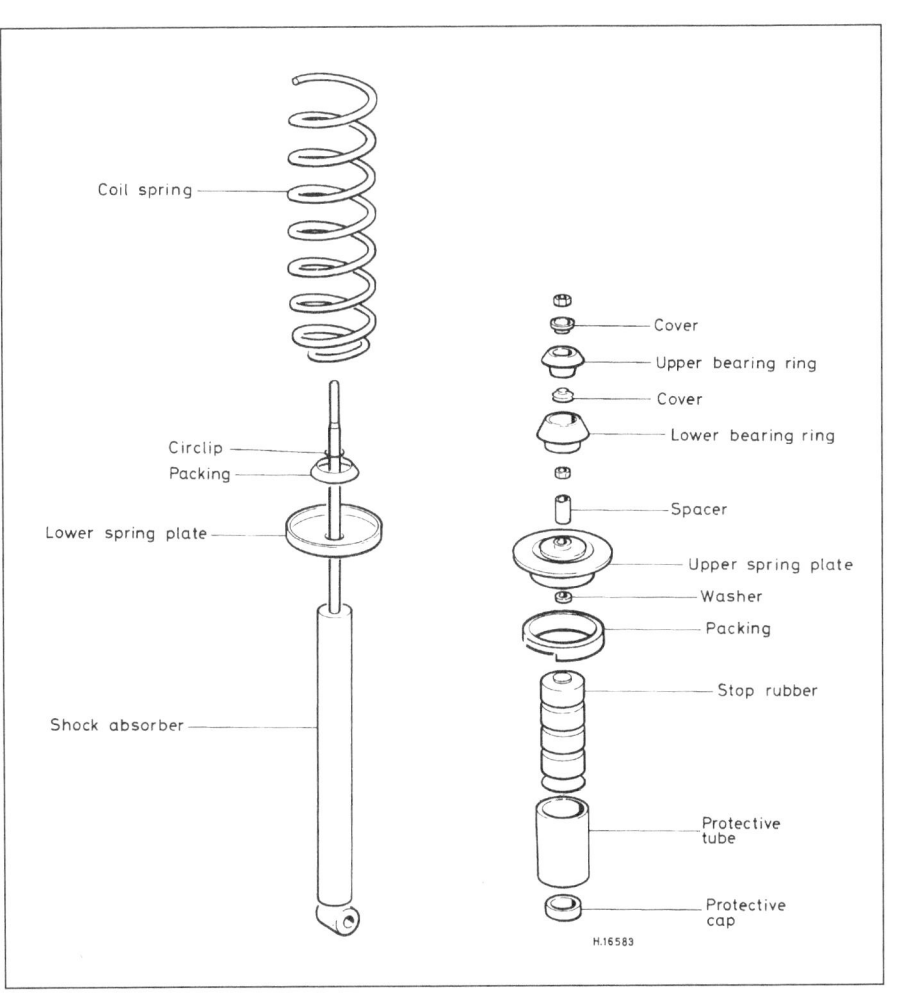

8.8 Rear suspension strut and coil spring components

10•8 Suspension and steering

9.3 Brake pressure regulator unit showing spring bracket

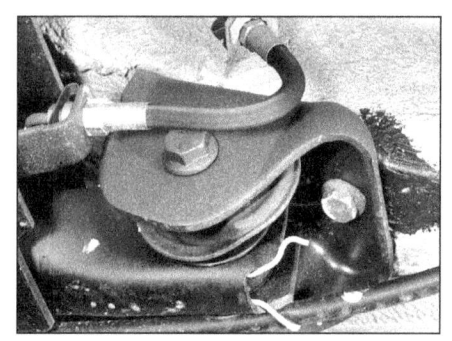

9.7 Axle beam pivot bolt head fitting position

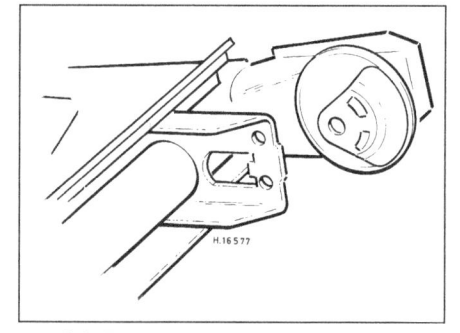

9.8 Rear axle bonded rubber bush orientation

Protruding segments to face forwards

9 Rear axle beam - removal and refitting

Note: *If the axle beam is suspected of being distorted, then it should be checked in position by a VW garage using optical alignment equipment*
Modification: *On 1988 models, the rear suspension mounting bracket bolts incorporate a modified shoulder. Their tightening torque is reduced to that specified.*

Removal

1 Remove the rear stub axles.
2 Support the weight of the trailing arms with axle stands (see "*Jacking and vehicle support*") then disconnect the struts/shock absorbers by removing the lower mounting bolts.
3 On models fitted with a brake pressure regulator unit, unbolt the spring bracket from the axle beam **(see illustration)**.
4 Disconnect the handbrake cables from the axle beam and from the left-hand side and underbody bracket.
5 Remove the brake fluid reservoir filler cap and tighten it down onto a piece of polythene sheet in order to reduce the loss of hydraulic fluid.
6 Lower the axle beam and disconnect the brake hydraulic hoses. Plug the hoses to prevent the ingress of dirt.
7 Support the weight of the axle beam with axle stands then unscrew and remove the pivot bolts and lower the axle beam to the ground. Note that the pivot bolt heads face as shown **(see illustration)**.
8 If the bushes are worn renew them. Using a two-arm puller, force the bushes from the axle beam. Dip the new bushes in soapy water before pressing them in from the outside with the puller. Locate the bush so that the segments which protrude point in the direction of travel **(see illustration)**. When fitted, the cylindrical bush section should protrude by 8 mm.
9 If the mounting bracket is removed, note its fitted position relative to the axle. If the bolts shear during removal, the stud will have to be accurately drilled out and the resultant hole tapped for a 12 mm x 1.5 thread. Be careful to drill in the centre of the broken stud since misalignment of the hole will in turn mean misalignment of the axle. Unless you have experience in this type of work it is best entrusted to a trained mechanic.
10 When the mounting bracket is refitted, its inclination angle to the axle beam should be 12° ± 2°.

Refitting

11 Refitting is a reversal of removal whilst noting the following.
12 When the axle is fitted into position with the mountings under tension, locate the securing bolts then align the right side mounting so that the bolts are centralised in the slotted holes. Now on the left-hand side, use a couple of suitable levers and press the mounting to the rubber bush so that a minimal gap exists on the inside **(see illustration)**. The respective retaining bolts can now be tightened to the specified torque wrench setting.
13 On completion, bleed the brake hydraulic system.

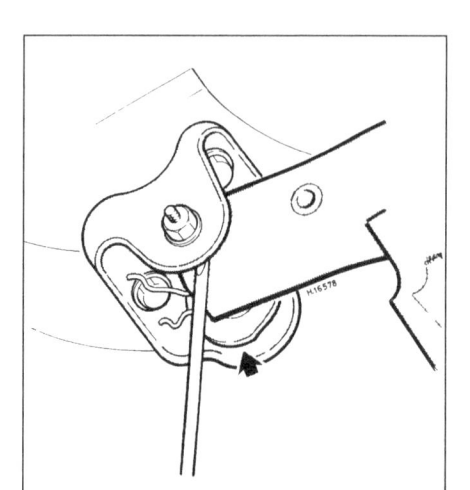

9.12 Rear axle refitting

Check that clearance (arrowed) is minimal on left-hand mounting inner side

10 Rear wheel hub bearings - renewal

1 On models fitted with rear disc brakes, refer to Chapter 9.
2 On models fitted with rear drum brakes, remove the brake drum. The bearings and oil seal can be removed in the same manner as that given for the corresponding components in the rear brake disc.
3 Refit the brake disc or drum, as applicable, and adjust the bearing as described in Chapter 9.

11 Steering wheel - removal and refitting

Removal

1 Disconnect the battery earth lead.
2 Set the front roadwheels in the straight-ahead position.
3 Prise free the cover from the centre of the steering wheel. Where the cover is the horn push button, note the location of the wires and disconnect them from the terminals on the cover **(see illustrations)**.
4 Mark the steering wheel and inner column in relation to each other, then unscrew the nut and withdraw the steering wheel **(see illustration)**. Remove the washer.

11.3a Removing steering wheel centre cover – 1.3 litre

Suspension and steering 10•9

11.3b Removing steering wheel centre cover – GTi

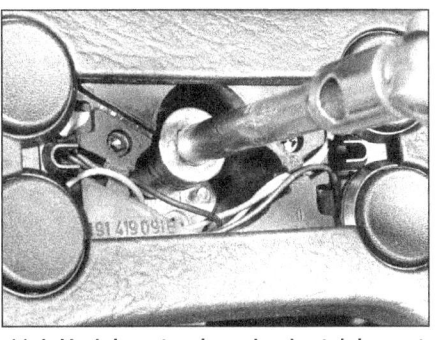

11.4 Undoing steering wheel retaining nut – GTi

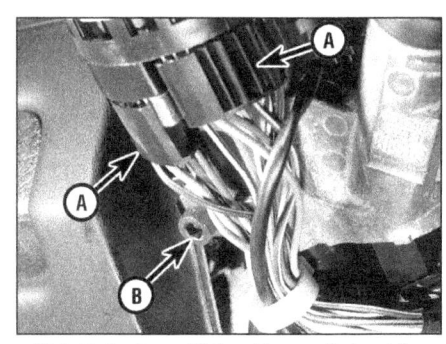

12.4 Detach multi-function switch wiring connectors (A)

Steering column mounting bolt also shown (B)

Refitting

5 Refitting is a reversal of removal. Ensure that the turn signal lever is in its neutral position, otherwise damage may occur in the cancelling arm. The cancelling ring tongue points to the left. Tighten the retaining nut to the specified torque.
6 On completion, reconnect the battery and check that the horn and column switches operate satisfactorily.

12 Steering column - removal, overhaul and refitting

Removal

1 Disconnect the battery negative lead.
2 Remove the steering wheel.
3 Remove the screws and withdraw the steering column lower shroud.
4 Remove the three screws and withdraw the combination switch. Disconnect the wiring multi-connectors **(see illustration)**.
5 Remove the screws and withdraw the lower facia trim panel.
6 Remove the column mounting bolts. Where shear-head bolts have been fitted, it will be necessary to drill off the heads and unscrew the threaded portions or use a centre punch to unscrew them. On some models, one of the mounting bolts may be a socket-head type, in which case use an Allen key to unscrew it.
7 Undo and withdraw the universal joint-to-column clamp bolt **(see illustration)**. Undo the lower mounting-to-column transverse bolt then withdraw the column from the universal joint and collect the coil spring.
8 On pre-July 1984 models, a two section column is fitted **(see illustration)**. With this type, push the two sections together to

12.7 Steering column universal joint (upper). Clamp bolt arrowed

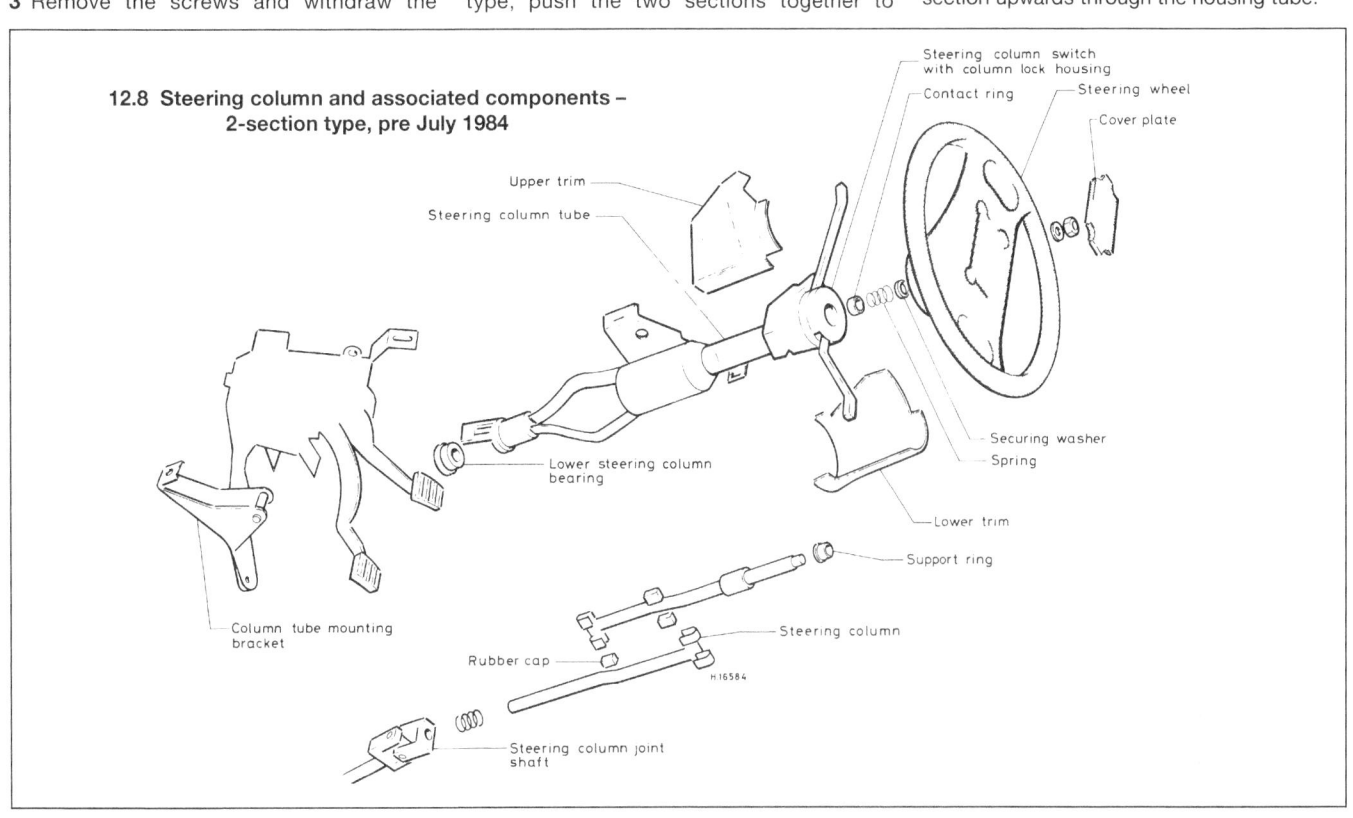

disengage the rectangular engagement pins within the housing, collect the rubber insulation caps and withdraw the lower section upwards through the housing tube.

12.8 Steering column and associated components – 2-section type, pre July 1984

- Upper trim
- Steering column tube
- Lower steering column bearing
- Column tube mounting bracket
- Rubber cap
- Steering column joint shaft
- Steering column switch with column lock housing
- Contact ring
- Steering wheel
- Cover plate
- Securing washer
- Spring
- Lower trim
- Support ring
- Steering column

10•10 Suspension and steering

12.16 Steering column - from July 1984
Reassembly alignment hole arrowed

Overhaul

9 Check the various components for excessive wear. If the column has been damaged in any way then it must be renewed as a unit. If renewing the earlier type column as a unit, then the later telescopic type column unit may be fitted, in which case a new lower mounting must also be fitted as the earlier type is not compatible with the later type.

10 To dismantle the top housing (both types), prise free the lockwasher from the inner column and withdraw the spring and contact ring. Renew the lockwasher.

11 Check the condition of the flange tube bushes and if necessary renew them. Lever the old bushes out with a screwdriver then press in the new bushes after dipping them in soapy water. Unscrew the old shear bolt(s) and obtain new bolts.

12 Using an Allen key, unscrew the clamp bolt securing the steering lock and withdraw the lock. Note that the ignition key must be inserted and the lock released.

13 Withdraw the inner column from the outer columns and remove the support ring.

14 Clean the components and examine them for wear. Renew them as necessary.

Refitting

15 Reassembly is a reversal of dismantling. Lubricate bearing surfaces with multi-purpose grease and renew the inner column lockwasher.

16 On later models with the telescopic single section column, reassembly differs. Secure the lower end of the column in a soft-jawed vice so that the upper section rests on the jaws and the two halves of the column cannot be slid together. The small lug in the lower part must be visible through the hole in the upper part **(see illustration)**. Assemble the support ring with the column switch and lock housing, the contact ring, spring and locking washer.

17 On both steering column types, the locking washer is fitted by driving it down the shaft until it is completely pressed on. On the earlier two section type column, compress the two columns together using a suitable pair of pliers as the washer is driven into position.

18 Check that column alignment is correct when connecting it to the universal joint. Tighten the retaining nuts and bolts to the specified torque setting. Tighten each shear bolt until its head breaks off.

19 On completion, check that operation of the steering, the various steering column switches and the horn are satisfactory.

13 Steering lock - removal and refitting

Removal

1 Disconnect the battery negative lead.
2 Remove the steering wheel.
3 Remove the screws and withdraw the steering column lower shroud.
4 Remove the three screws and withdraw the combination switch. Disconnect the wiring plug.
5 Using an Allen key, unscrew the clamp bolt securing the steering lock.
6 Prise the lockwasher from the inner column and remove the spring and contact ring.
7 Disconnect the wiring plug and withdraw the steering lock from the top of the column, together with the upper shroud. Note that the ignition key must be inserted to ensure that the lock is in its released position.
8 Remove the screw and withdraw the switch from the lock housing.
9 To remove the lock cylinder, drill a 3.0 mm diameter hole in the location shown **(see illustration)**. Depress the spring pin and extract the cylinder.

Refitting

10 Refitting is a reversal of removal. Renew the inner column lockwasher and press it fully onto the stop while supporting the lower end of the column.

14 Steering gear bellows - renewal

1 The steering gear bellows can be removed and refitted with the steering gear unit in situ or removed from the vehicle.
2 Remove the tie-rod outer balljoint or the tie-rod, as applicable. On power steering models, the outer balljoint can be removed from the left and right-hand side tie-rods and there is therefore no need to remove the tie-rod.
3 Unscrew and remove the outer balljoint locknut nut from the tie-rod.

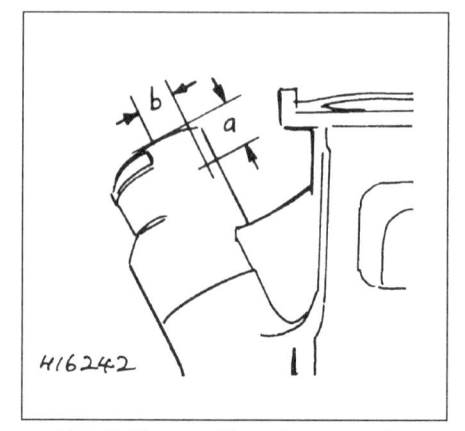

13.9 Drilling position when removing steering lock cylinder

a = 12.0 mm   b = 10.0 mm

Suspension and steering 10•11

14.4 Steering tie-rod bellows and retaining clip

15.1 Right-hand adjustable balljoint

15.4 Balljoint separator tool in position on left-hand balljoint

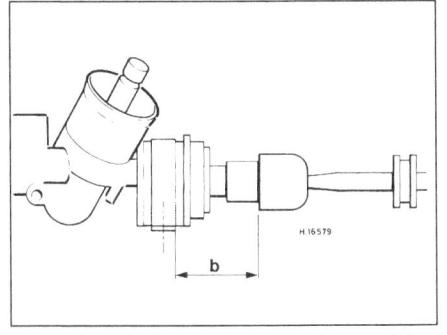

15.10a Tie-rod-to-rack dimensions (b)

All models: b = 70.5 mm

15.10b Steering rack centralised when dimension (a) is equal on each side

4 Release the retaining clips and withdraw the bellows from the steering gear and tie-rod **(see illustration)**.
5 Refit in the reverse order of removal. Smear the inner bore of the bellows with lubricant prior to fitting to ease its assembly. Renew the balljoint locknuts.
6 On completion, check front wheel alignment.

15 Tie-rods and balljoints - removal and refitting

Manual steering

Removal

1 If the steering tie-rod and balljoints are worn, play will be evident as the roadwheel is rocked from side to side. In this case, the balljoint must be renewed. On RHD models, the right-hand tie-rod is adjustable **(see illustration)** and the balljoint on this tie-rod can be renewed separately, however the left-hand tie-rod must be renewed complete. On LHD models, the tie-rods are vice versa.
2 Jack up the front of the vehicle and support on axle stands (see "*Jacking and vehicle support*"). Apply the handbrake and remove the front wheel(s).
3 If removing the tie-rod end balljoint, measure the distance of the exposed thread inboard of the locknut. Make a note of the distance then loosen the locknut.

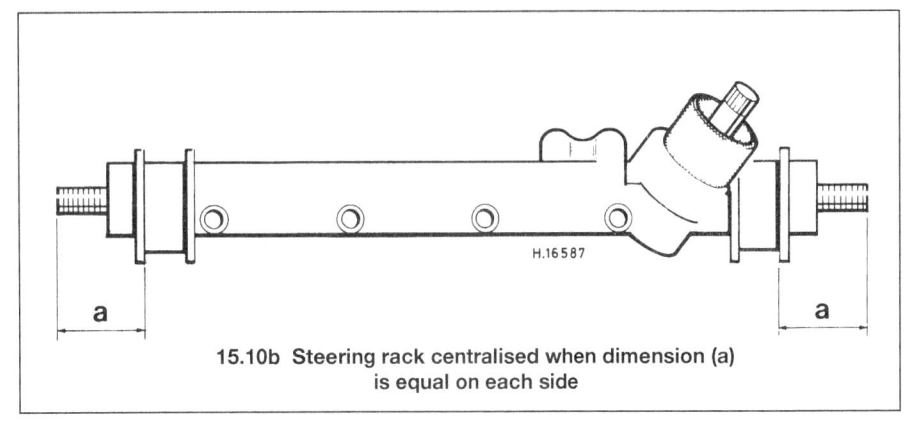

4 Unscrew the balljoint nut on the side concerned then use a balljoint nut separator tool to release the joint from the wheel bearing housing **(see illustration)**. With the tie-rod outer joint separated from the wheel bearing housing, the outer balljoint can be unscrewed from the tie-rod (where applicable).
5 To remove the tie-rod, release the retaining clips from the steering gear bellows then slide the bellows outwards along the tie-rod to expose the inner balljoint.
6 Loosen the inner joint locknut then unscrew the tie-rod from the steering rack. The steering gear bellows can then be withdrawn from the inboard end of the tie-rod. Renew the bellows if they are damaged or perished.

Refitting

7 Refitting is a reversal of the removal procedure but note the following.
8 Clean the old locking fluid from the steering rack and from the old tie-rod if it is being refitted. Smear both threads with a locking solution prior to assembly.
9 Lubricate the inner bore of the gaiter ends before sliding it onto the tie-rod.
10 When reconnecting the tie-rod to the rack, screw it in to give the specified dimension "b" **(see illustration)**. Where both tie-rods (left and right) are being refitted to the rack, centralise the rack so that dimension "a" **(see illustration)** is equal on each side.
11 Centralise the steering, then set the length of the left-hand tie-rod at a distance "a" **(see illustration)**, measured between the centre of the outer balljoint and the steering gear stop face on the inboard end of the driveshaft, When the distance is correct, tighten the locknut against the tie-rod end to set it at the specified fixed length. Set the right-hand tie-rod to the original length measured on dismantling, This will provide an approximate initial setting only, On completion, it will be necessary to check the toe-in setting. If further minor adjustment is required, adjust the right-hand tie-rod to provide the specified front wheel toe-in alignment. Any subsequent adjustments to the track setting must only be made by altering the length of the right-hand tie-rod.
12 Alternatively, screw on the balljoint to give the exposed thread dimension noted during removal, then tighten the locknut. Check that the steering gear-to-inner balljoint distance is as previously specified, then lock the inner locknut. Refit the steering gear bellows and ensure that they are not distorted.

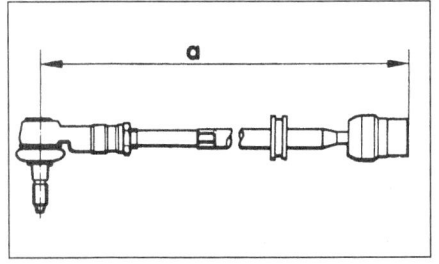

15.11 Check that fixed length of left-hand driveshaft is as specified between points indicated

Distance 'a' = 410 mm

10•12 Suspension and steering

16.1 Manual steering gear adjustment screw (arrowed)

13 Reconnect the outer balljoints to the wheel bearing housing and tighten the locknuts to the specified torque wrench settings. Always fit new locknuts if refitting the old balljoints/tie-rod.
14 On completion, check front wheel alignment.

Power steering

Removal

15 Remove the steering gear unit together with the tie-rods from the vehicle. This is necessary to avoid damaging the rack and pinion.
16 With the steering gear removed, clean it externally then release the clips and slide the bellows outwards along the tie-rods away from the inner joints.
17 Support the steering gear in a soft jaw vice with the steering rack in the jaws. Do not clamp the rack into a vice not fitted with protective jaws.
18 Each tie-rod and outer balljoint can be removed in a similar manner to that described for the manual steering gear unit.

Refitting

19 Refit the steering tie-rods to the rack and adjust the fitted lengths, as given. Tighten the tie-rods to the specified torque when the settings are correct.
20 Refit the steering gear and tie-rods.
21 On completion, check front wheel alignment.

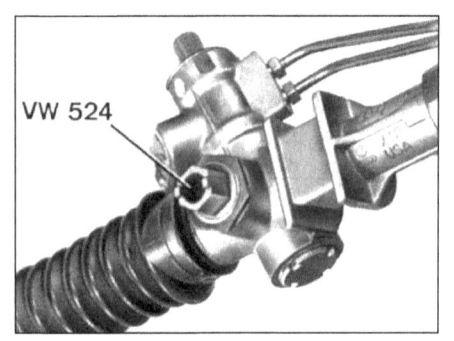

16.8 Power steering gear adjustment – use VW tool

16 Steering gear - adjustment

Manual

1 If there is any undue slackness in the steering gear which results in noise or rattles, then the steering gear should be adjusted as follows **(see illustration)**.
2 Raise and support the vehicle at the front end on axle stands (see "*Jacking and vehicle support*").
3 With the wheels in the straight-ahead position, tighten the self-locking adjustment screw by approximately 20°.
4 Lower the vehicle to the ground then road test the vehicle. If the steering fails to self-centre after cornering, loosen the adjustment screw a fraction at a time until it does.
5 If, when the correct self-centring point is reached, there is still excessive wear in the steering, retighten the adjuster nut a fraction to take up the play.
6 If the above adjustment procedure does not provide satisfactory steering adjustment, then it is probable that the steering gear is worn beyond an acceptable level and it must be removed and overhauled.

Power-assisted

7 Remove the steering gear unit.
8 Loosen the adjuster screw locknut then turn the adjustment screw in to the point where the rack can just be moved by hand without binding or sticking **(see illustration)**. Retighten the locknut.
9 Refit the steering gear to the vehicle.

17 Steering gear unit - removal and refitting

Modification - power steering gear pinion: *From May 1985, the pinch-bolt clamping the intermediate shaft to the steering gear pinion is located approximately 1.0 mm nearer the centre line of the pinion. To identify the modified pinion, a flat is cut opposite the pinch-bolt location. When renewing either of the components separately, it may be necessary to increase the depth of the pinch-bolt recess in the pinion by 1.0 mm so that the two components match. Do not alter the hole in the intermediate shaft* **(see illustration)**.

Removal

1 Apply the handbrake, jack up the front of the vehicle and support it on axle stands (see "*Jacking and vehicle support*"). Remove the roadwheels.
2 Disconnect the inner ends of the tie-rods.
3 On power steering models, detach the fluid suction hose at the pump unit end by

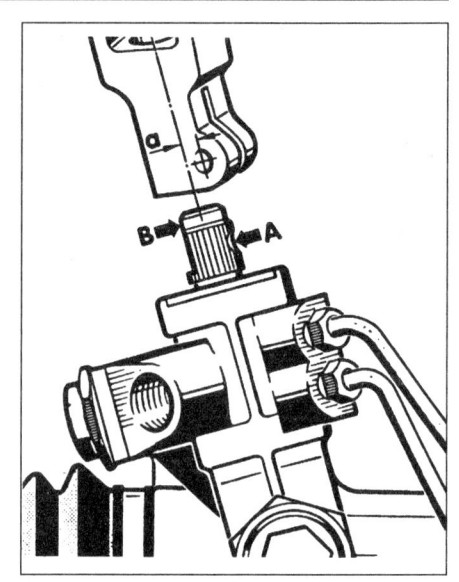

17.0 Power steering gear pinion modification

- a Dimension reduced from 12.1 mm to 11.0 mm
- A Notch depth increased
- B Flat for identification

loosening the hose clip, withdrawing the hose from the pump and draining the fluid into a suitable container **(see illustration)**.
4 Disconnect the steering tie-rod outer balljoints.
5 Where applicable, disconnect the gearshift securing bracket from the steering gear.
6 Undo and remove the steering gear pinion-to-lower column joint clamp bolt **(see illustration)**. Prise free the joint shaft bellows and pull the bellows up the shaft for access to the clamp bolt.
7 Undo and remove the steering gear unit retaining clamp nuts and withdraw the clamps. Note that the retaining bolts remain in the subframe **(see illustration)**. If necessary the bolts can be removed by driving them out downwards using a soft metal drift.
8 On power steering models, disconnect the pressure and return flow fluid hoses at the union connections to the steering gear unit.
9 To enable the steering unit to be withdrawn, it may be necessary to detach and withdraw

17.6 Steering gear pinion-to-lower column joint

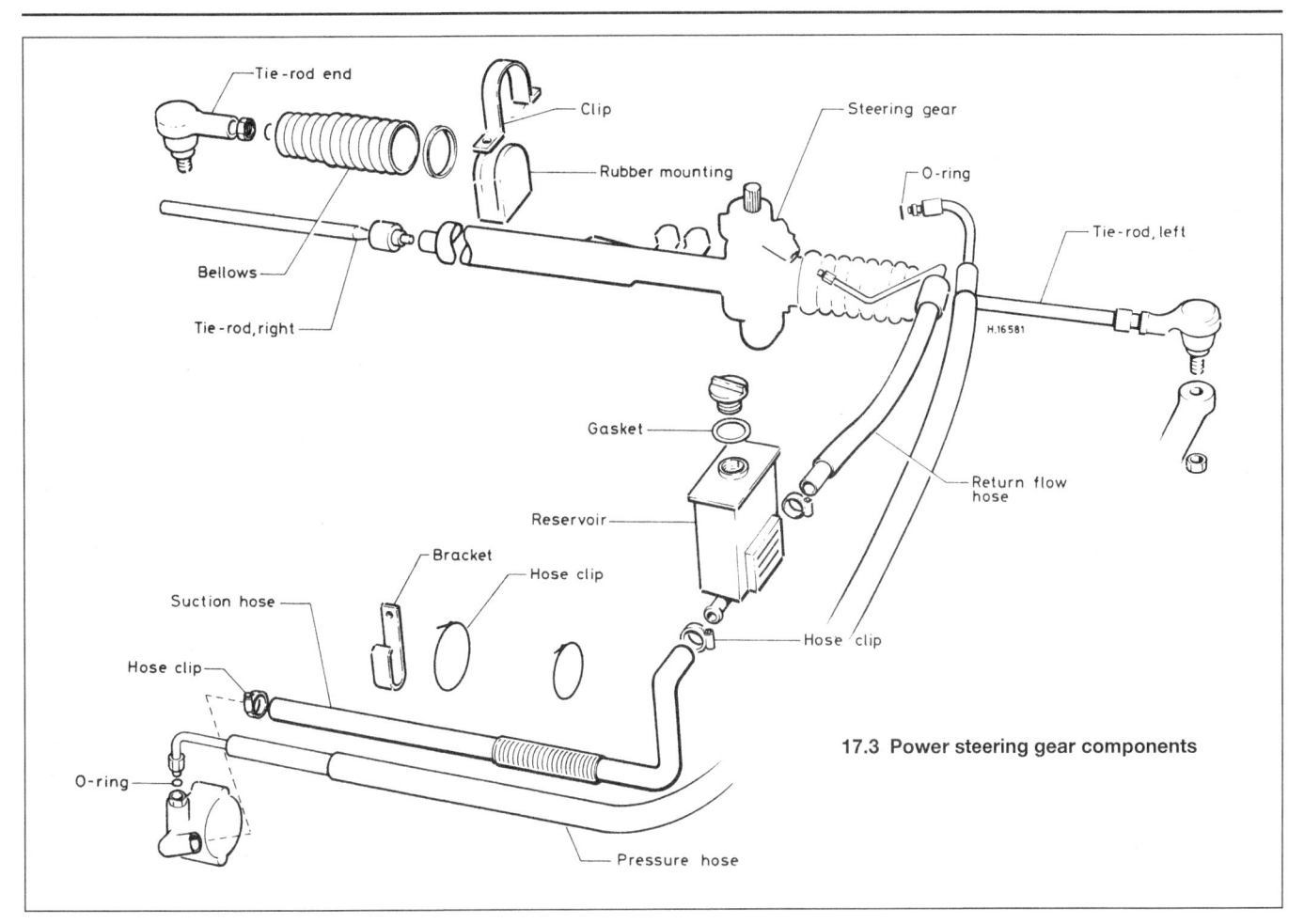

Suspension and steering 10•13

17.3 Power steering gear components

17.7 Manual steering gear components

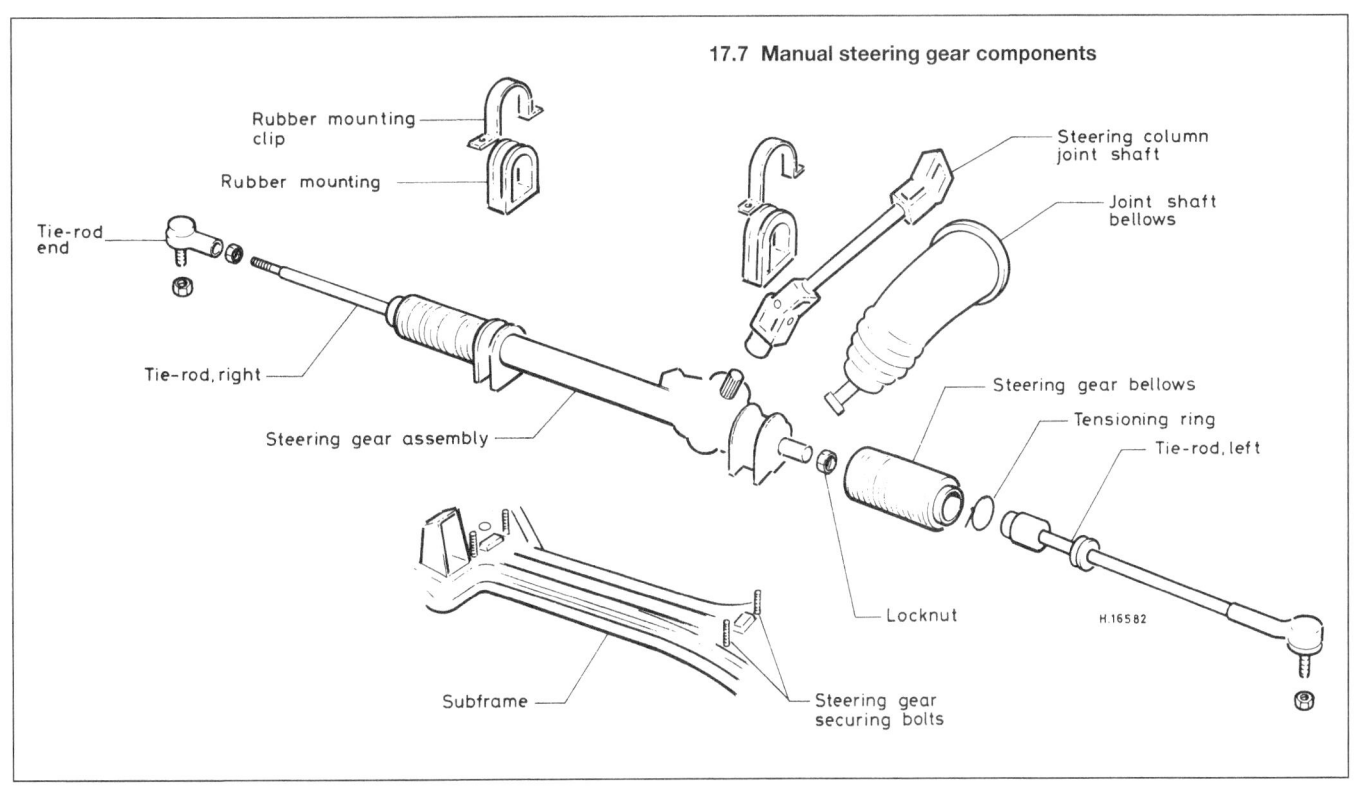

10•14 Suspension and steering

the steering column a sufficient amount to enable the pinion shaft to disengage from the lower column joint. Before disengaging the pinion from the lower column joint, it is advisable to make an index mark between the two to ensure correct alignment when refitting.
10 On power steering models, support the weight of the engine/gearbox unit by using a hoist then unscrew and remove the left-hand subframe bolt. Loosen but do not remove the right-hand subframe retaining bolt.
11 On manual steering models, withdraw the steering gear unit through the aperture in the left-hand side wheel arch.
12 On power steering models, remove the steering gear unit from the left side, guiding it past the partially lowered subframe. Plug the power steering fluid hoses whilst the steering gear is removed to prevent the ingress of dirt.
13 Remove the tie-rods from the steering gear.

Refitting

14 Refitting is a reversal of the removal procedure. All self-locking nuts must be renewed.
15 Lubricate the steering gear rack with steering gear grease before refitting the tie-rods. Adjust the tie-rods when fitting them to the rack.
16 Establish that pinion shaft-to-lower column alignment is correct to ensure that correct steering centralisation is made. If a new steering gear unit is being fitted, centralise the rack and steering column before assembly.
17 Delay tightening all nuts and bolts until the weight of the vehicle is on its suspension. Check and if necessary, adjust front wheel alignment.
18 On power steering models, unplug the hoses and reservoir cap ventilation hole. Connect the hoses whilst taking care not to let dirt enter the system. Top-up the system fluid and check for any signs of leakage on completion.

18 Power steering fluid - draining and refilling

Draining

1 To drain fluid from the system, detach the fluid suction hose at the pump unit and drain the fluid into a container for disposal. When draining, turn the steering wheel from lock to lock to expel as much fluid as possible.

Refilling

2 After draining off the fluid, reconnect the suction hose to the pump unit then fill the reservoir to the top with new fluid from a sealed container. Restart the engine and switch off as soon as it fires. Repeat the starting and stopping sequence several times, this will cause fluid to be drawn into the system quickly.
3 Watch the level of fluid and keep adding fluid so that the reservoir is never sucked dry. When the fluid ceases to drop as a result of the start/stop sequence, start the engine and allow it to run at idling speed.
4 Turn the steering from lock to lock several times, being careful not to leave the wheels on full lock because this will cause pressure in the system to build up.
5 Watch the level of the fluid in the reservoir and add fluid if necessary to keep the level at the MAX mark.
6 When the level stops falling and no more air bubbles appear in the reservoir, switch the engine off and fit the reservoir cap. The level of fluid will rise slightly when the engine is switched off.

19 Power steering pump - removal, refitting and drivebelt adjustment

1 If the power steering is suspected of malfunction, have the supply and system pressure checked by your VW dealer. The pump unit cannot be overhauled or repaired and if defective, must be renewed as a unit.

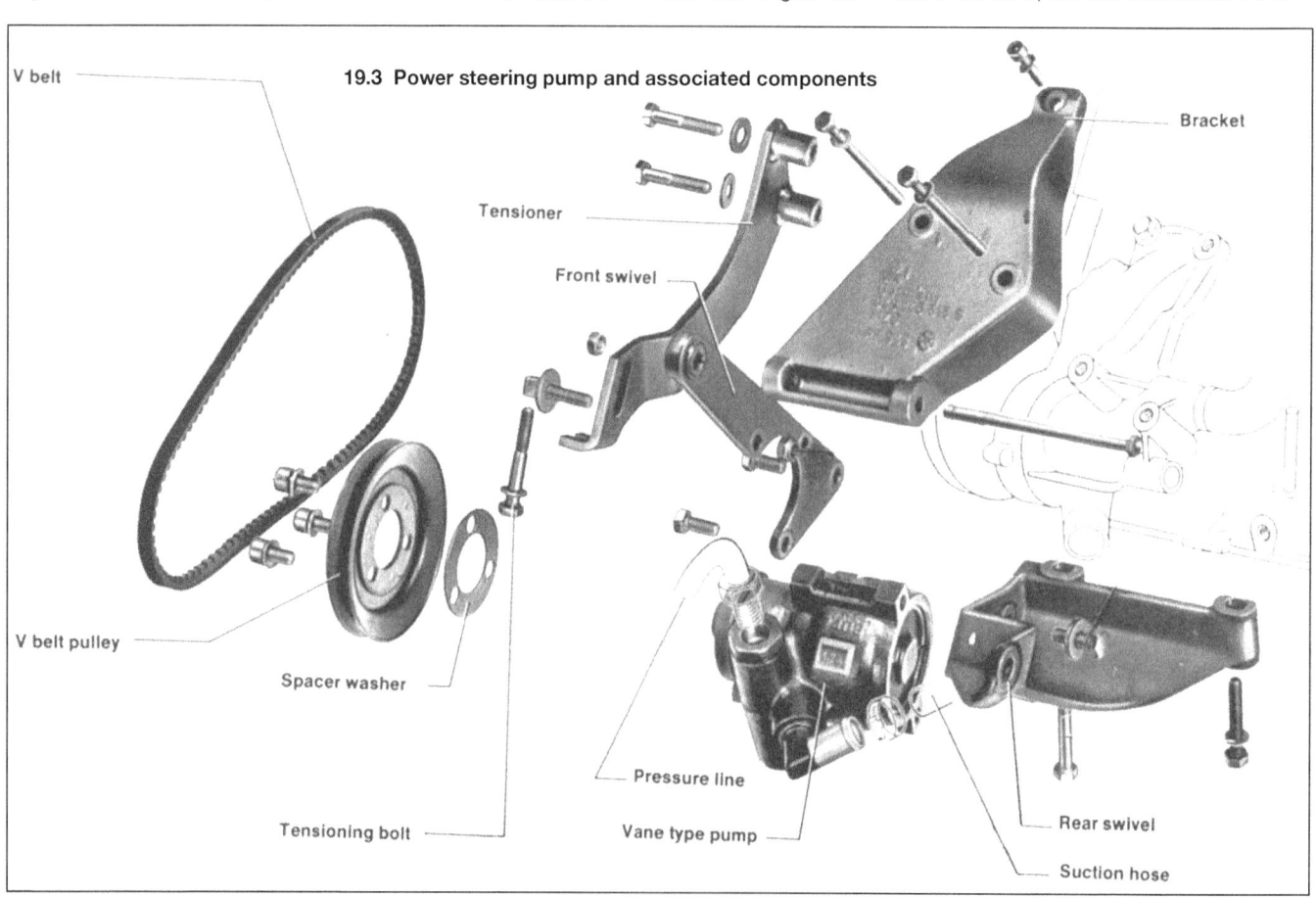

19.3 Power steering pump and associated components

V belt — Tensioner — Front swivel — Bracket — V belt pulley — Spacer washer — Tensioning bolt — Pressure line — Vane type pump — Rear swivel — Suction hose

Removal

2 To remove the pump unit, first drain the system fluid.
3 Disconnect the pressure hose from the pump unit **(see illustration)**.
4 Loosen the pump unit retaining bolts and pivot the pump so that the drivebelt can be disconnected from the pulley.
5 Support the pump, withdraw the retaining bolts and withdraw the pump unit.

Refitting

6 Refitting is a reversal of removal. Tension the drivebelt, top-up with new fluid and bleed the system.

Drivebelt adjustment

7 Refer to Chapter 1, Section 13.

20 Wheel alignment - checking and adjustment

1 Accurate wheel alignment is essential for good steering and slow tyre wear. Alignment details are given in *Specifications* and can be accurately checked by a suitably equipped garage. However, front wheel alignment gauges can be obtained from most motor accessory stores and used as follows.
2 Check that the vehicle is only loaded to kerbside weight, with a full fuel tank and the tyres correctly inflated.
3 Position the vehicle on level ground with the wheels straight-ahead, then roll the vehicle backwards 4.0 m and forwards again.
4 Using a wheel alignment gauge in accordance with the manufacturer's instructions, check that the front wheel toe dimension is as specified. If adjustment is necessary, loosen the balljoint-to-tie-rod locknut on the right-hand side and turn the tie-rod as required, then retighten the locknut. Note that the left-hand tie-rod is set at the specified length - **see illustration 15.11**. Its setting should not be changed.
5 Although the camber angle of the front wheels can be adjusted, this is a task best entrusted to your VW dealer.
6 The castor angle is not adjustable. As with the camber angle, is best checked by your VW dealer.

Chapter 11
Bodywork and fittings

Contents

Body protective and decorative trim fittings - removal and refitting . 27	Front seats - removal and refitting 31
Bonnet - removal, refitting and adjustment 6	Front wheel housing liner - removal and refitting 25
Bonnet lock and release cable - removal and refitting 7	Front wing - removal and refitting 26
Boot lid - removal, refitting and adjustment 12	General information 1
Boot lid lock and lock cylinder - removal and refitting 13	Major body damage - repair 4
Bumper trim covering - removal and renewal 23	Minor body damage - repair 3
Bumpers - removal and refitting 22	Radiator grille - removal and refitting 8
Central locking system - component removal and refitting 19	Rear seat - removal and refitting 32
Centre console - removal and refitting 29	Seat belts- renewal 33
Door - removal and refitting 16	Sunroof - removal, refitting and adjustment 28
Door handles - removal and refitting 15	Tailgate - removal and refitting 10
Door lock - removal and refitting 18	Tailgate lock, grip and lock cylinder - removal, refitting and
Door rattles - tracing and rectification 5	adjustment 11
Door striker - adjustment 17	Tailgate support strut - removal and refitting 9
Door trim panel - removal and refitting 14	Vehicle exterior and interior - maintenance and inspection 2
Dust and pollen filter - renewal 34	Window regulator - removal and refitting 20
Exterior mirrors - removal and refitting 24	Windows - removal and refitting 21
Facia panel - removal and refitting 30	

Degrees of difficulty

Easy, suitable for novice with little experience	Fairly easy, suitable for beginner with some experience	Fairly difficult, suitable for competent DIY mechanic	Difficult, suitable for experienced DIY mechanic	Very difficult, suitable for expert DIY or professional

Specifications

Torque wrench settings	Nm	lbf ft
Bumper bracket bolts:		
Front	82	61
Rear	70	52
Tailgate spider nut	6	4
Front seat cap nut	1.5	1.1
Seat belt anchor bolts	40	30

1 General information

The vehicle bodyshell is of all-steel unit construction with impact-absorbing front and rear crumple zones which take the brunt of any accident thereby leaving the passenger compartment with minimum distortion. The front crumple zones take the form of two corrugated box sections in the scuttle and firewall.

The Golf is available in two or four-door hatchback versions, all models having a large tailgate which is propped open with a steel rod or gas-filled telescopic strut.

The Jetta is available only as a four-door notchback, incorporating a conventional boot and lid.

On all models, the front wings are bolted to the body and can easily be renewed in the event of damage.

2 Vehicle exterior and interior - maintenance and inspection

Vehicle exterior

The general condition of a vehicle's bodywork is the one thing that significantly affects its value. Maintenance is easy but needs to be regular. Neglect, particularly after minor damage, can lead quickly to further deterioration and costly repair bills. It is important also to keep watch on those parts of the vehicle not immediately visible, for instance the underbody, inside all the wheel arches and the lower part of the engine compartment.

The basic maintenance routine for the bodywork is washing - preferably with a lot of water, from a hose. This will remove all the loose solids which may have stuck to the vehicle. It is important to flush these off in such a way as to prevent grit from scratching the finish. The wheel arches and underbody need washing in the same way to remove any accumulated mud which will retain moisture and tend to encourage rust, particularly in winter when it is essential that any salt (from that put down on the roads) is washed off. Oddly enough, the best time to clean the underbody and wheel arches is in wet weather when the mud is thoroughly wet and soft. In very wet weather the underbody is usually cleaned automatically of large accumulations; this is therefore a good time for inspection.

11•2 Bodywork and fittings

If the vehicle is very dirty, especially underneath or in the engine compartment, it is tempting to use one of the pressure washers or steam cleaners available on garage forecourts. Whilst these are quick and effective, especially for the removal of the accumulation of oily grime which sometimes is allowed to become thick in certain areas, their usage does have some disadvantages. If caked-on dirt is simply blasted off the paintwork, its finish soon becomes scratched and dull and the pressure can allow water to penetrate door and window seals and the lock mechanisms. If the full force of such a jet is directed at the vehicle's underbody, the wax-based protective coating can easily be damaged and water (with whatever cleaning solvent is used) could be forced into crevices or components that it would not normally reach. Similarly, if such equipment is used to clean the engine compartment, water can be forced into the components of the fuel and electrical systems and the protective coating can be removed that is applied to many small components during manufacture; this may therefore actually promote corrosion (especially inside electrical connectors) and initiate engine problems or other electrical faults. Also, if the jet is pointed directly at any of the oil seals, water can be forced past the seal lips and into the engine or transmission. Great care is required, therefore, if such equipment is used and, in general, regular cleaning by such methods should be avoided.

A much better solution in the long term is just to flush away as much loose dirt as possible using a hose alone, even if this leaves the engine compartment looking dirty. If an oil leak has developed, or if any other accumulation of oil or grease is to be removed, there are one or two excellent grease solvents available, which can be brush applied. The dirt can then be simply hosed off. Take care to replace the wax-based protective coat, if this was affected by the solvent.

Normal washing of the bodywork is best carried out using cold or warm water with a proprietary car shampoo. Remove dead insects with a proprietary cleaning product; tar spots can be removed either by using white spirit, followed by soapy water to remove all traces of spirit, or by using a tar remover. Try to keep water out of the bonnet air inlets and check afterwards that the heater air inlet box drain tube is clear so that any water has drained out of the box.

After washing the paintwork, wipe off with a chamois leather to give an unspotted clear finish. A coat of clear protective wax polish, will give added protection against chemical pollutants in the air. If the paintwork sheen has dulled or oxidised, use a cleaner/polisher combination to restore the brilliance of the shine. This requires a little effort, but such dulling is usually caused because regular washing has been neglected. Care needs to be taken with metallic paintwork, as special non-abrasive cleaner/polisher is required to avoid damage to the finish.

Brightwork should be treated in the same way as paintwork.

Windscreens and windows can be kept clear of the smeary film which often appears, by the use of a proprietary glass cleaner. Never use any form of wax or chromium polish on glass.

Vehicle interior

Mats and carpets should be brushed or vacuum cleaned regularly to keep them free of grit. If they are badly stained remove them from the vehicle for scrubbing or sponging and make quite sure they are dry before refitting.

Where leather upholstery is fitted it should be cleaned only if necessary, using either a mild soap (such as saddle soap) or a proprietary leather cleaner; do not use strong soaps, detergents or chemical cleaners. If the leather is very stained, seek the advice of a VW dealer. Fabric-trimmed seats and interior trim panels can be kept clean by wiping with a damp cloth and a proprietary cleaner. If they do become stained (which can be more apparent on light coloured upholstery) use a little liquid detergent and a soft nail brush to scour the grime out of the grain of the material. Do not forget to keep the headlining clean in the same way as the (fabric) upholstery.

When using liquid cleaners of any sort inside the vehicle, do not over-wet the surfaces being cleaned. Excessive damp could get into the seams and padded interior causing stains, offensive odours or even rot. If the inside of the vehicle gets wet accidentally it is worthwhile taking some trouble to dry it out properly, particularly where carpets are involved. *Do not leave oil or electric heaters inside the vehicle for this purpose.*

3 Minor body damage - repair

Repair of minor scratches in bodywork

If the scratch is very superficial and does not penetrate to the metal of the bodywork, repair is very simple. Lightly rub the area of the scratch with a paintwork renovator, or a very fine cutting paste to remove loose paint from the scratch and to clear the surrounding bodywork of wax polish. Rinse the area with clean water.

Apply touch-up paint or a paint film, to the scratch using a fine paint brush. Continue to apply fine layers of paint until the surface of the paint in the scratch is level with the surrounding paintwork. Allow the new paint at least two weeks to harden, then blend it into the surrounding paintwork by rubbing the scratch area with a paintwork renovator, or a very fine cutting paste. Finally apply wax polish.

Where the scratch has penetrated right through to the metal of the bodywork, causing the metal to rust, a different repair technique is required. Remove any loose rust from the bottom of the scratch with a penknife, then apply rust inhibiting paint, to prevent the formation of rust in the future. Using a rubber or nylon applicator fill the scratch with bodystopper paste. If required, this paste can be mixed with cellulose thinners, to provide a very thin paste which is ideal for filling narrow scratches. Before the stopper-paste in the scratch hardens, wrap a piece of smooth cotton rag around the top of a finger. Dip the finger in cellulose thinners, and quickly sweep it across the surface of the stopper-paste in the scratch; this will ensure that the surface of the stopper-paste is slightly hollowed. The scratch can now be painted over as described earlier in this Section.

Repair of dents in bodywork

When deep denting of the vehicle's bodywork has taken place, the first task is to pull the dent out, until the affected bodywork almost attains its original shape. There is little point in trying to restore the original shape completely, as the metal in the damaged area will have stretched on impact and cannot be reshaped fully to its original contour. It is better to bring the level of the dent up to a point which is about 3 mm below the level of the surrounding bodywork. In cases where the dent is very shallow anyway, it is not worth trying to pull it out at all. If the underside of the dent is accessible, it can be hammered out gently from behind, using a mallet with a wooden or plastic head. Whilst doing this, hold a suitable block of wood firmly against the outside of the panel to absorb the impact from the hammer blows and thus prevent a large area of the bodywork from being "belled-out".

Should the dent be in a section of the bodywork which has a double skin or some other factor making it inaccessible from behind, a different technique is called for. Drill several small holes through the metal inside the area - particularly in the deeper section. Then screw long self-tapping screws into the holes just sufficiently for them to gain a good purchase in the metal. Now the dent can be pulled out by pulling on the protruding heads of the screws with a pair of pliers.

The next stage of the repair is the removal of the paint from the damaged area and from an inch or so of the surrounding sound bodywork. This is accomplished most easily by using a wire brush or abrasive pad on a power drill, although it can be done just as effectively by hand using sheets of abrasive paper. To complete the preparation for filling, score the surface of the bare metal with a screwdriver or the tang of a file, or alternatively, drill small holes in the affected area. This will provide a really good key for the filler paste. To complete the repair see the Section on filling and respraying.

Repair of rust holes or gashes in bodywork

Remove all paint from the affected area and from an inch or so of the surrounding sound bodywork, using an abrasive pad or a wire brush on a power drill. If these are not available a few sheets of abrasive paper will do the job most effectively. With the paint removed you will be able to judge the severity of the corrosion and therefore decide whether to renew the whole panel (if this is possible) or to repair the affected area. New body panels are not as expensive as most people think and it is often quicker and more satisfactory to fit a new panel than to attempt to repair large areas of corrosion.

Remove all fittings from the affected area except those which will act as a guide to the original shape of the damaged bodywork (eg headlamp shells etc). Then, using tin snips or a hacksaw blade, remove all loose metal and any other metal badly affected by corrosion. Hammer the edges of the hole inwards in order to create a slight depression for the filler paste.

Wire brush the affected area to remove the powdery rust from the surface of the remaining metal. Paint the affected area with rust inhibiting paint, if the back of the rusted area is accessible treat this also.

Before filling can take place it will be necessary to block the hole in some way. This can be achieved by the use of aluminium or plastic mesh, or aluminium tape.

Aluminium or plastic mesh or glass-fibre matting, is probably the best material to use for a large hole. Cut a piece to the approximate size and shape of the hole to be filled, then position it in the hole so that its edges are below the level of the surrounding bodywork. It can be retained in position by several blobs of filler paste around its periphery.

Aluminium tape should be used for small or very narrow holes. Pull a piece off the roll and trim it to the approximate size and shape required, then pull off the backing paper (if used) and stick the tape over the hole; it can be overlapped if the thickness of one piece is insufficient. Burnish down the edges of the tape with the handle of a screwdriver or similar, to ensure that the tape is securely attached to the metal underneath.

Bodywork repairs - filling and respraying

Before using this Section, see the Sections on dent, deep scratch, rust holes and gash repairs.

Many types of bodyfiller are available, but generally speaking those proprietary kits are best for this type of repair which contain a tin of filler paste and a tube of resin hardener, or a 'no mix' which can be used directly from the tube. A wide, flexible plastic or nylon applicator will be found invaluable for imparting a smooth and well contoured finish to the surface of the filler.

Mix up a little filler on a clean piece of card or board - measure the hardener carefully (follow the maker's instructions on the pack) otherwise the filler will set too rapidly or too slowly. Alternatively, a 'no mix 'can be used straight from the tube without mixing, but daylight is required to cure it. Using the applicator apply the filler paste to the prepared area; draw the applicator across the surface of the filler to achieve the correct contour and to level the surface. As soon as a contour that approximates to the correct one is achieved, stop working the paste - if you carry on too long the paste will become sticky and begin to pick-up on the applicator. Continue to add thin layers of filler paste at twenty minute intervals until the level of the filler is just proud of the surrounding bodywork.

Once the filler has hardened, excess can be removed using a metal plane or file. From then on, progressively finer grades of abrasive paper should be used, starting with a 40 grade production paper and finishing with a 400 grade wet-and-dry paper. Always wrap the abrasive paper around a flat rubber, cork, or wooden block - otherwise the surface of the filler will not be completely flat. During the smoothing of the filler surface the wet-and-dry paper should be periodically rinsed in water. This will ensure that a very smooth finish is imparted to the filler at the final stage.

At this stage, the dent should be surrounded by a ring of bare metal, which in turn should be encircled by the finely feathered edge of the good paintwork. Rinse the repair area with clean water, until all of the dust produced by the rubbing-down operation has gone.

Spray the whole area with a light coat of primer, - this will show up any imperfections in the surface of the filler. Repair these imperfections with fresh filler paste or bodystopper and once more smooth the surface with abrasive paper. If bodystopper is used, it can be mixed with cellulose thinners to form a really thin paste which is ideal for filling small holes. Repeat this spray and repair procedure until you are satisfied that the surface of the filler and the feathered edge of the paintwork are perfect. Clean the repair area with clean water and allow to dry fully.

The repair area is now ready for final spraying. Paint spraying must be carried out in a warm, dry, windless and dust free atmosphere. This condition can be created artificially if you have access to a large indoor working area, but if you are forced to work in the open, you will have to pick your day very carefully. If you are working indoors, dousing the floor in the work area with water will help to settle the dust which would otherwise be in the atmosphere. If the repair area is confined to one body panel, mask off the surrounding panels; this will help to minimise the effects of a slight mis-match in paint colours. Bodywork fittings (eg chrome strips, door handles etc) will also need to be masked off. Use genuine masking tape and several thicknesses of newspaper for the masking operations.

Before commencing to spray, agitate the aerosol can thoroughly, then spray a test area (an old tin, or similar) until the technique is mastered. Cover the repair area with a thick coat of primer; the thickness should be built up using several thin layers of paint rather than one thick one. Using 400 grade wet-and-dry paper, rub down the surface of the primer until it is really smooth. While doing this, the work area should be thoroughly doused with water and the wet-and-dry paper periodically rinsed in water. Allow to dry before spraying on more paint.

Spray on the top coat, again building up the thickness by using several thin layers of paint. Start spraying in the centre of the repair area and then, with a side-to-side motion, work outwards until the whole repair area and about 50 mm of the surrounding original paintwork is covered. Remove all masking material 10 to 15 minutes after spraying on the final coat of paint.

Allow the new paint at least two weeks to harden, then, using a paintwork renovator, or a very fine cutting paste, blend the edges of the paint into the existing paintwork. Finally, apply wax polish.

Plastic components

With the use of more and more plastic body components by the vehicle manufacturers (eg bumpers, spoilers and in some cases major body panels), rectification of more serious damage to such items has become a matter of either entrusting repair work to a specialist in this field, or renewing complete components. Repair of such damage by the DIY owner is not really feasible owing to the cost of the equipment and materials required for effecting such repairs. The basic technique involves making a groove along the line of the crack in the plastic using a rotary burr in a power drill. The damaged part is then welded back together by using a hot air gun to heat up and fuse a plastic filler rod into the groove. Any excess plastic is then removed and the area rubbed down to a smooth finish. It is important that a filler rod of the correct plastic is used, as body components can be made of a variety of different types (eg polycarbonate, ABS, polypropylene).

Damage of a less serious nature (abrasions, minor cracks etc) can be repaired by the DIY owner using a two-part epoxy filler repair material or a 'no mix' which can be used directly from the tube. Once mixed in equal proportions (or applied direct from the tube in the case of a 'no mix'), this is used in similar fashion to the bodywork filler used on metal panels. The filler is usually cured in twenty to thirty minutes, ready for sanding and painting.

If the owner is renewing a complete component himself, or if he has repaired it with epoxy filler, he will be left with the problem of finding a suitable paint for finishing which is compatible with the type of plastic

11•4 Bodywork and fittings

6.2 Bonnet hinge

6.3 Disconnecting windscreen washer tubes from bonnet

6.6 Bonnet rubber buffer

used. At one time the use of a universal paint was not possible owing to the complex range of plastics encountered in body component applications. Standard paints, generally speaking, will not bond satisfactorily to plastic or rubber, but a proprietary paint to match any plastic or rubber finish can be obtained from dealers. However, it is now possible to obtain a plastic body parts finishing kit which consists of a pre-primer treatment, a primer and coloured top coat. Full instructions are normally supplied with a kit, but basically the method of use is to first apply the pre-primer to the component concerned and allow it to dry for up to 30 minutes. Then the primer is applied and left to dry for about an hour before finally applying the special coloured top coat. The result is a correctly-coloured component where the paint will flex with the plastic or rubber, a property that standard paint does not normally possess.

4 Major body damage - repair

Where serious damage has occurred, or large areas need renewal due to neglect, it means that complete new panels will need welding in. This is best left to professionals. If the damage is due to impact, it will also be necessary to check completely the alignment of the bodyshell. This can only be carried out accurately by a VW dealer using special jigs. If the body is left misaligned, it is primarily dangerous as the vehicle will not handle properly and secondly, uneven stresses will be imposed on the steering, suspension and possibly transmission, causing abnormal wear or complete failure, particularly to items such as the tyres.

5 Door rattles - tracing and rectification

1 Check first that each door is not loose at its hinges and that the latch is holding the door firmly in position.

2 Check that each door lines up with the aperture in the vehicle body. Adjust the door if out of alignment.
3 If a latch is holding its door in the correct position but the latch still rattles, then the lock mechanism is worn and should be renewed.
4 Other rattles from the door could be caused by loose glass channels or wear in the window operating or interior lock mechanisms.

6 Bonnet - removal, refitting and adjustment

1 Support the bonnet in its open position and place some cardboard or rags beneath the corners by the hinges.
2 Mark the location of the hinges with a pencil then loosen the four retaining bolts (see illustration).
3 Where applicable, disconnect the windscreen washer tubes from the jets on the bonnet (see illustration).
4 With the help of an assistant, release the stay, remove the bolts and withdraw the bonnet from the vehicle.
5 Refitting is a reversal of removal. Adjust the hinges to their original positions and check that the bonnet is level with the surrounding bodywork.
6 If necessary, adjust the height of the bonnet front edge by screwing the rubber buffers in or out (see illustration).
7 Check that the bonnet lock operates in a satisfactory manner.

7.1 Bonnet lock and securing rivets

7 Bonnet lock and release cable - removal and refitting

Bonnet lock

1 The bonnet lock is not adjustable for position and is secured to the front cross panel by four pop-rivets (see illustration). To remove the lock, disconnect the lock release cable then carefully drill down through the rivets and withdraw the lock.
2 Refit the lock by reversing the removal procedure. Ensure that the new pop-rivets secure the lock firmly.

Release cable

3 To remove the bonnet lock release cable, raise and support the bonnet then remove the radiator grille.
4 Reaching through the aperture in the front, press the release to one side and disconnect the cable from it (see illustration). Release the cable from the retaining clip on the underside of the front panel.
5 Unclip the cable from the retainers in the engine compartment.
6 Detach the cable from the release handle inside the vehicle and pull the cable through the bulkhead grommet and remove it.
7 Refit the cable in the reverse order to removal. Check for satisfactory operation of the catch before closing the bonnet.
8 If the cable should break with the bonnet shut, it is possible to release the catch by

7.4 Bonnet release cable-to-lock attachment

Bodywork and fittings 11•5

hand. A largish screwdriver will just reach the lock release when inserted through the grille centre badge. By pushing the screwdriver or carefully using the badge as a pivot, the bonnet can be unlocked.

8 Radiator grille - removal and refitting

1 Raise and support the bonnet.
2 Undo and remove the two grille retaining screws on the top front edge (see illustration).
3 Release the clips from the top of the grille (see illustration). Withdraw the grille lifting it upwards from the front valance.
4 Refit in the reverse order of removal.

9 Tailgate support strut - removal and refitting

1 Open and support the tailgate.
2 Unhook the spring clip from the end of the strut attached to the body, pull up the ball-head and disconnect the strut from the ball-pin (see illustrations).
3 Lever the spring clip from the other end of the strut, remove the washer and withdraw the strut from the pivot pin.
4 Refit in the reverse order of removal.

10 Tailgate - removal and refitting

Removal

1 Open and support the tailgate. Disconnect the straps supporting the rear shelf.
2 Remove the trim panel using a wide-bladed screwdriver and disconnect the wiring from the heated rear window and wiper motor. Disconnect the washer tube and pull the wiring and tube from the tailgate.
3 Pull the weatherseal from the body aperture by the hinge positions.

8.2 Undoing front grille retaining screws

4 Carefully pull the headlining down to reveal the hinge bolts.
5 Lever the spring clips from the struts, remove the washers and disconnect the struts from the tailgate.
6 Unscrew the hinge bolts and withdraw the tailgate from the vehicle.

Refitting

7 Refitting is a reversal of removal. Before tightening the hinge bolts, ensure that the tailgate closes centrally within the body aperture.
8 On completion, adjust the lock if necessary.

8.3 Front grille securing clips

11 Tailgate lock, grip and lock cylinder - removal, refitting and adjustment

1 Open the tailgate and unscrew the two lock retaining screws with an Allen key. Withdraw the lock (see illustrations).
2 The striker plate can be removed by undoing the two retaining screws.
3 To remove the tailgate grip and lock cylinder, undo the cross-head screws on the outside. Move to the inside and compress the

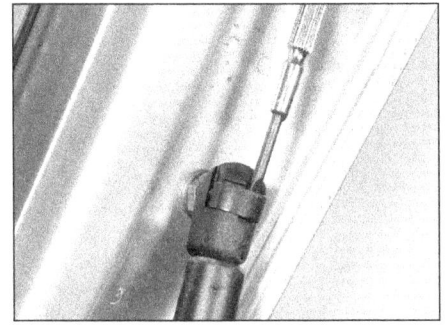

9.2a Releasing tailgate strut balljoint clip

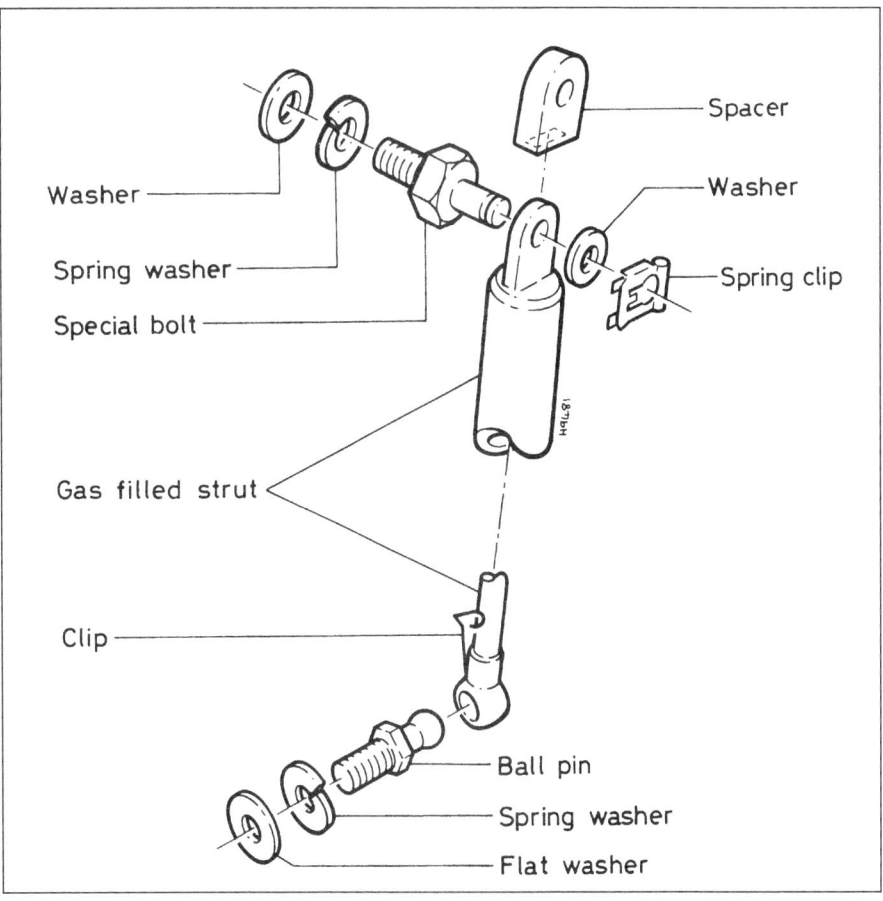

9.2b Tailgate support strut end fittings

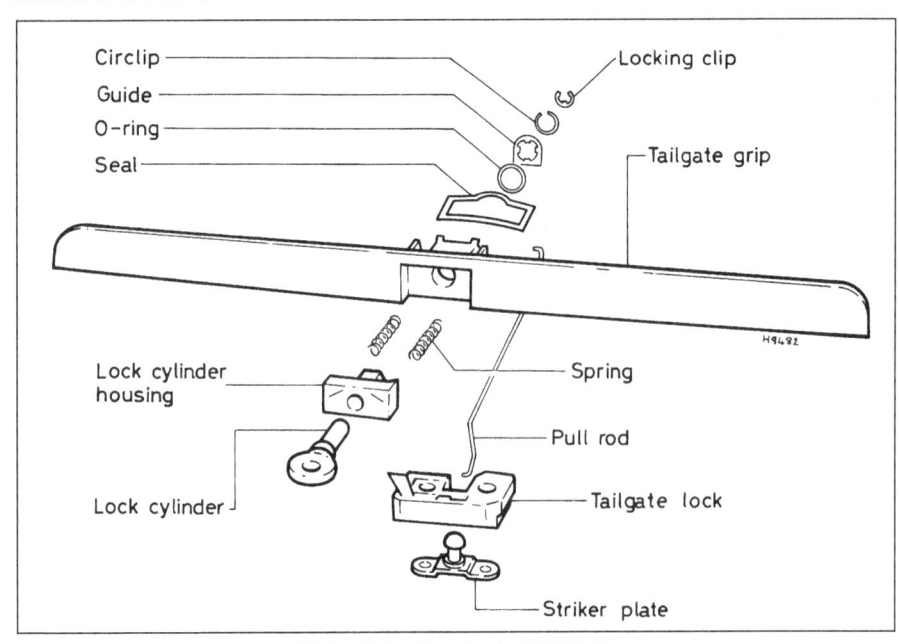

11•6 Bodywork and fittings

11.1a Tailgate lock components

11.1b Tailgate lock

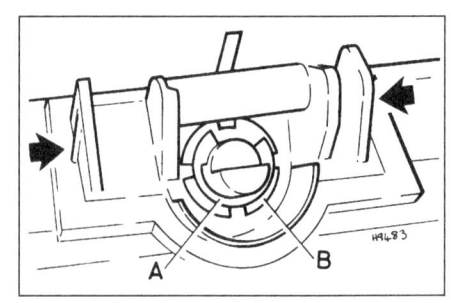

11.3 Tailgate grip/lock cylinder retaining clip (A) and securing ring (B)

Compress lugs (arrowed) in direction indicated

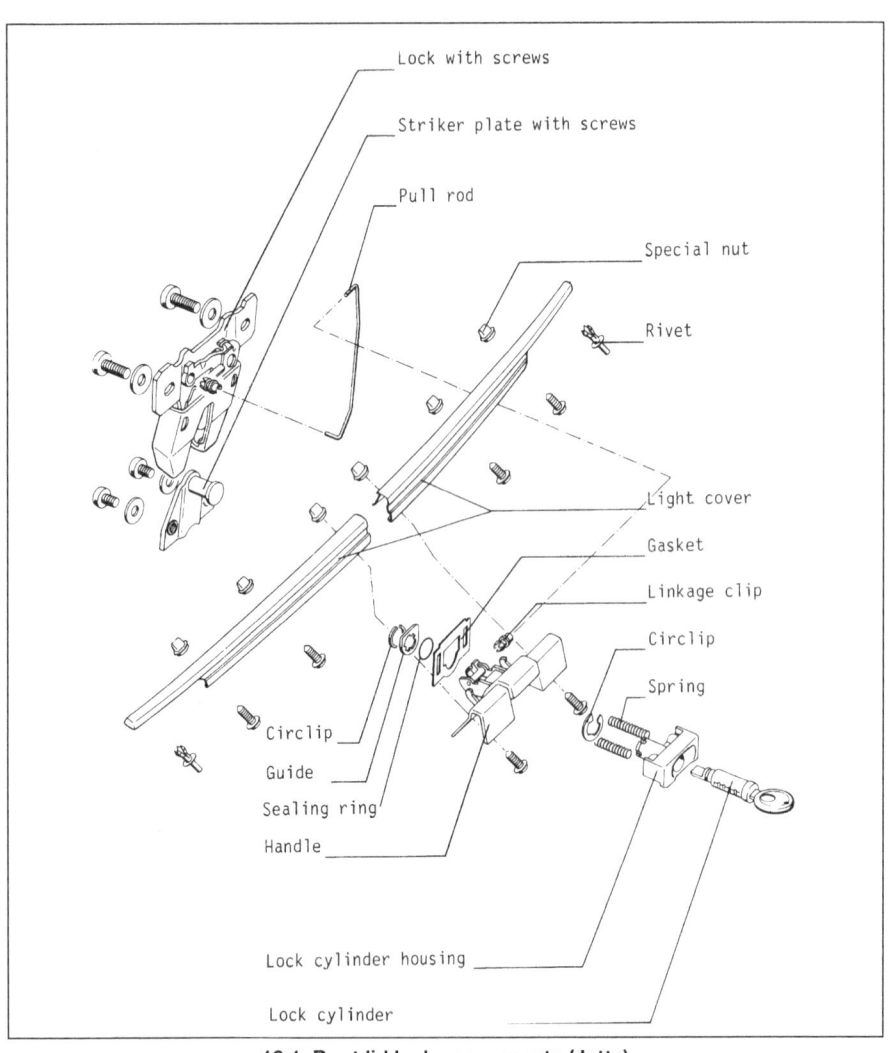

retaining lugs each side of the lock cylinder together then pull free the grip **(see illustration)**.

4 Fit the key to the lock cylinder, prise free the retaining clip and withdraw the lock cylinder by pulling on the key.

5 To remove the cylinder housing, prise free the retaining ring and withdraw the housing from the grip.

6 Refitting is a reversal of removal. Before fully tightening the striker, close and open the tailgate two or three times to centralise it.

12 Boot lid - removal, refitting and adjustment

1 Support the boot lid in the open position then place some cardboard or rags beneath the corners by the hinges.
2 Disconnect the wiring loom and mark the location of each hinge.
3 With the help of an assistant, unscrew the nuts and withdraw the boot lid from the vehicle.
4 Refitting is a reversal of removal. Adjust the hinges to their original positions so that the boot lid is level with the surrounding bodywork.

13 Boot lid lock and lock cylinder - removal and refitting

The boot lid lock and lock cylinder are of similar design to the equivalent items on the tailgate fitted to Golf models **(see illustration)**. Refer to Section 11 for removal and refitting details.

13.1 Boot lid lock components (Jetta)

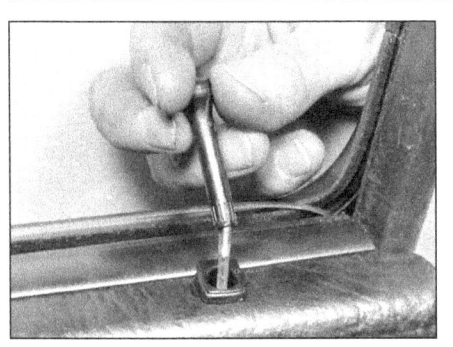

Bodywork and fittings 11•7

14.1 Unscrewing door locking knob

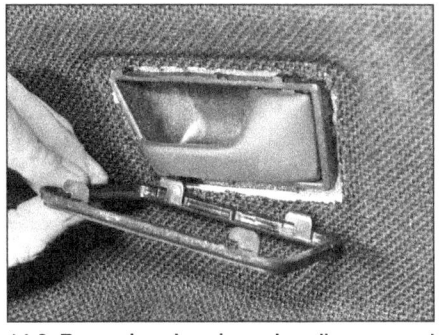

14.2 Removing door inner handle surround

14.3a Removing door pull cover

14 Door trim panel - removal and refitting

Removal

1 Unscrew and remove the door locking knob (see illustration).
2 Remove the inner handle surround by sliding it to the rear (see illustration).
3 Prise the cover from the door pull with a small screwdriver, remove the cross-head screws and withdraw the door pull (see illustrations).
4 Note the position of the window regulator handle with the window shut then prise off the cover, remove the cross-head screw and withdraw the handle and washer (see illustrations).
5 Where applicable, prise free the door mirror adjuster knob and remove the gaiter (see illustration).
6 Remove the self-tapping screws and withdraw the storage compartment panel (where applicable).
7 Prise out the stoppers and remove the cross-head screws from the trim panel (see illustrations).
8 Using a wide-bladed screwdriver, prise the trim panel clips from the door whilst taking care not to damage the panel. Remove the panel.
9 Remove the window regulator handle packing (where applicable).
10 Carefully prise free the plastic cover for access to the inner door components (see illustration).

Refitting

11 Refitting is a reversal of removal. It is recommended that the window regulator handle retaining screw is locked by coating its threads with a liquid locking agent.

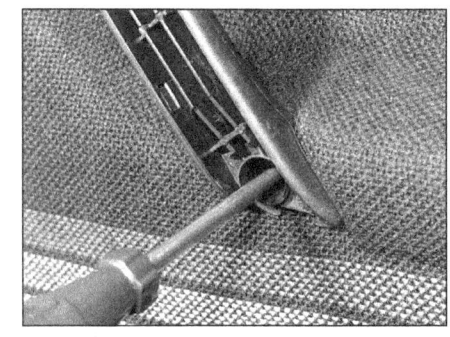

14.3b Removing door pull retaining screws

14.4a Remove window regulator handle cover . . .

14.4b . . . and handle retaining screw

14.5 Removing door mirror adjuster knob

14.7a Remove stoppers (where necessary) for access to trim panel screws

14.7b Trim panel retaining screw removal (rear edge)

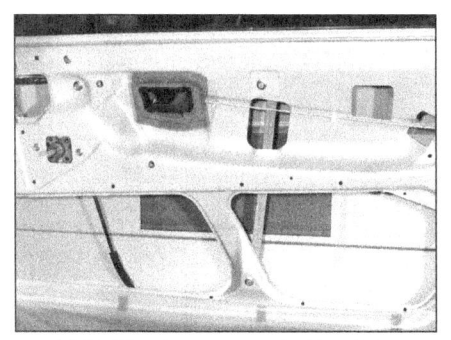

14.10 Plastic cover peeled back for access to door components

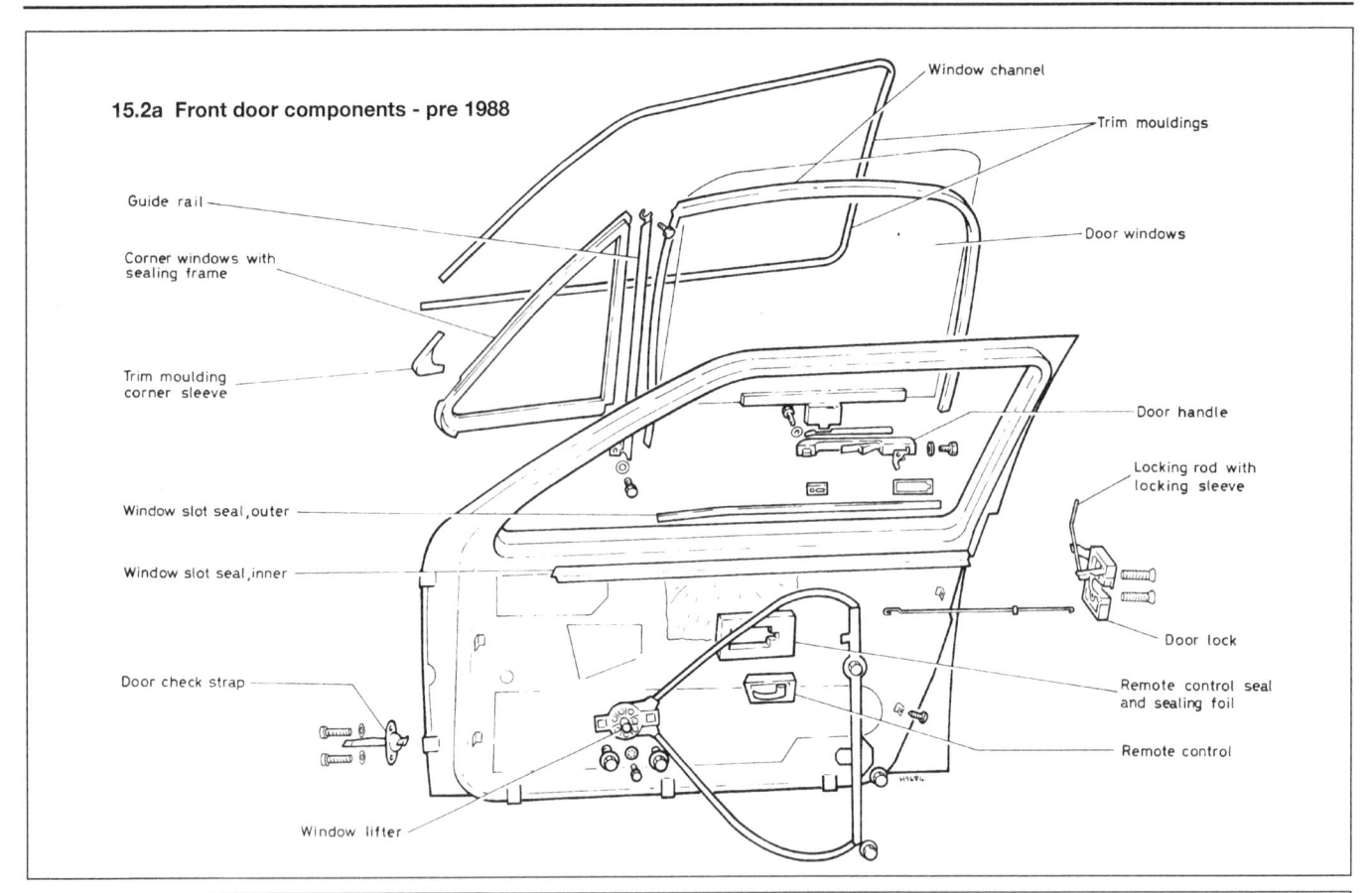

11•8 Bodywork and fittings

15.2a Front door components - pre 1988

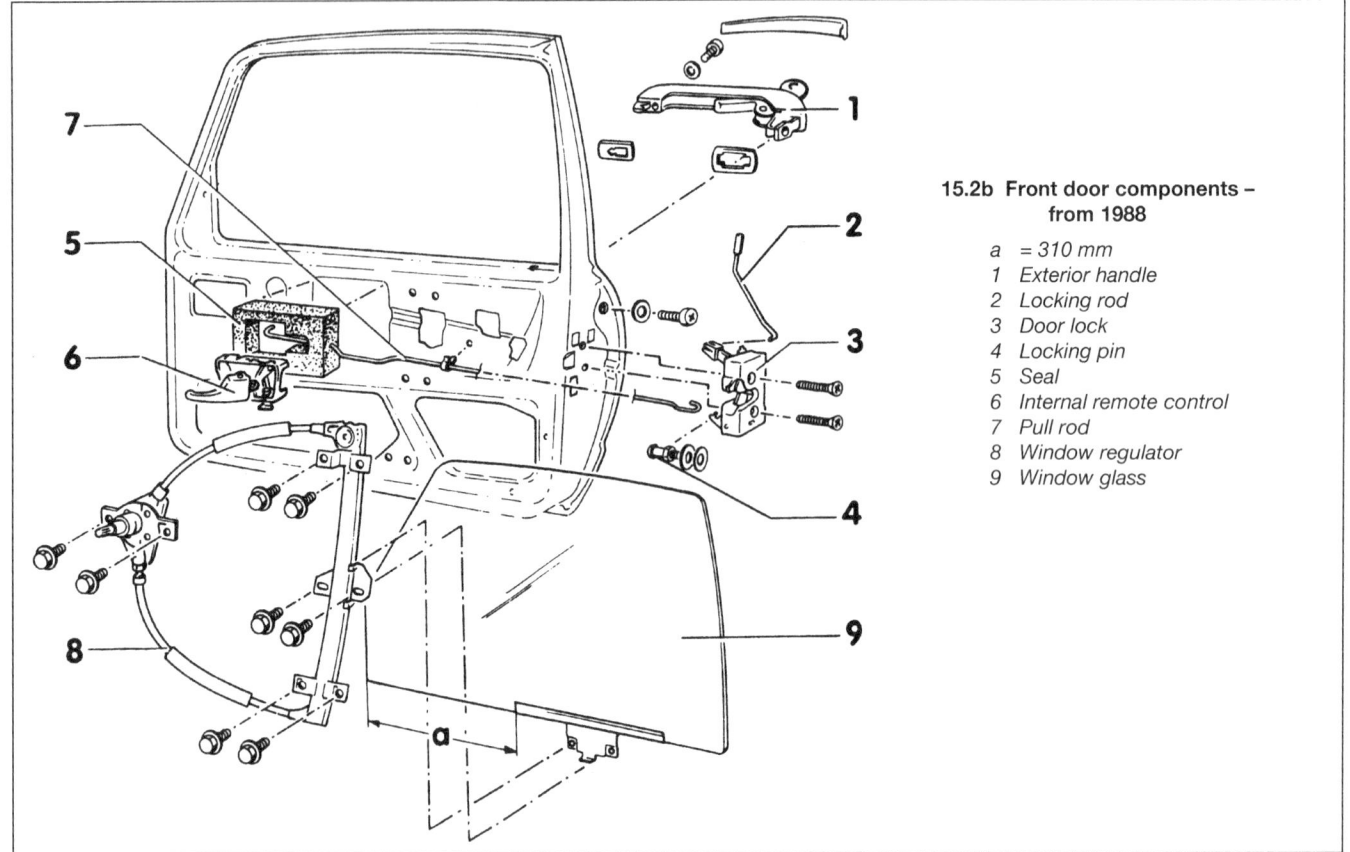

- Window channel
- Trim mouldings
- Guide rail
- Corner windows with sealing frame
- Door windows
- Trim moulding corner sleeve
- Door handle
- Window slot seal, outer
- Locking rod with locking sleeve
- Window slot seal, inner
- Door lock
- Door check strap
- Remote control seal and sealing foil
- Remote control
- Window lifter

15.2b Front door components – from 1988

- a = 310 mm
- 1 Exterior handle
- 2 Locking rod
- 3 Door lock
- 4 Locking pin
- 5 Seal
- 6 Internal remote control
- 7 Pull rod
- 8 Window regulator
- 9 Window glass

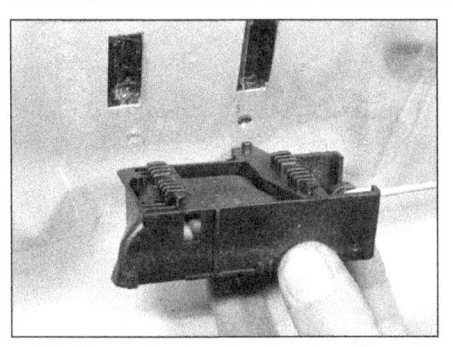

Bodywork and fittings 11•9

15.3 Removing interior door handle and finger plate

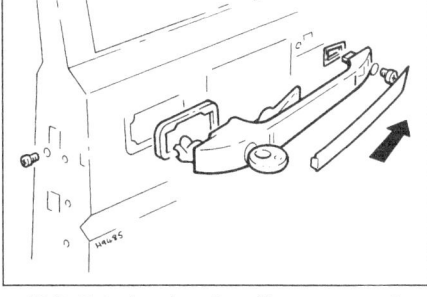

15.8 Exterior door handle components
Remove handle in direction of arrow

16.1 Door check strap and hinge

15 Door handles - removal and refitting

Interior

1 Remove the door trim panel.
2 Pull the foam seal away then prise the retainer from the bottom of the handle **(see illustrations)**.
3 Press the finger plate forwards out of the door and unhook it from the rod **(see illustration)**.
4 Refitting is a reversal of removal.

Exterior

5 Remove the door trim panel.
6 Using a small screwdriver, lever the plastic strip from the exterior door handle.
7 Remove the cross-head screws from the handle grip and the end of the door.
8 Withdraw the handle and release it from the lock **(see illustration)**. Remove the gaskets.
9 Refitting is a reversal of removal. Fit new gaskets if necessary.

16 Door - removal and refitting

Removal

1 Open the door and use a punch to drive the pivot pin up from the check strap **(see illustration)**.

2 Mark the position of the door on its hinges.
3 Support the door then unscrew and remove the lower hinge bolt followed by the upper hinge bolt. Withdraw the door from the vehicle.

Refitting

4 Refitting is a reversal of removal.
5 If necessary, adjust the position of the door on the hinges so that when closed, it is level with the surrounding bodywork and central within the body aperture.
6 Lubricate the hinges with a little oil and the check strap with grease.
7 If necessary, adjust the door striker position.

17 Door striker - adjustment

1 Mark round the door striker with a pencil or fine ballpoint pen **(see illustration)**.
2 Fit a spanner to the hexagon on the striker and unscrew the striker about one turn so that it moves when tapped with a soft-headed hammer.
3 If the door has been rattling, tap the striker towards the inside of the vehicle.
4 If the door fits too tightly, tap the striker towards the outside of the vehicle.
5 At all times, be careful to keep the striker in the same horizontal line unless it also requires vertical adjustment. Only move the striker a small amount at a time. The actual amount moved can be checked by reference to the marks made before the striker was loosened.
6 When a position has been found in which the door closes firmly but without difficulty, then tighten the striker.

18 Door lock - removal and refitting

Removal

1 It is not necessary to remove the trim panel to carry out this task.
2 Open the door and set the lock in the locked position, either by moving the interior knob or by turning the exterior key.
3 Using an Allen key, unscrew the retaining screws and withdraw the lock approximately 12 mm to expose the operating lever **(see illustration)**.
4 Retain the operating lever in the extended position by inserting a screwdriver through the hole in the bottom of the lock **(see illustration)**.
5 Unhook the remote control rod from the operating lever and pull the upper lever from the sleeve. Withdraw the lock from the door.

Refitting

6 Refitting is a reversal of removal. Set the lock in the locked position first and ensure that the lugs on the plastic sleeve are correctly seated.

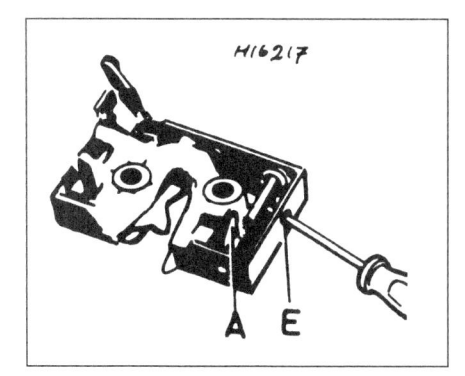

17.1 Door striker

18.3 Door lock

18.4 Using a screwdriver through the door lock hole (E) to retain operating lever (A) in extended position

11•10 Bodywork and fittings

19 Central locking system – component removal and refitting

1 The central locking system fitted to some models comprises the following **(see illustration)**:
 a) Pressure/vacuum pump
 b) Control element - on driver's door
 c) Shift elements - on remaining doors and fuel tank flap
 d) Interconnecting tubing.

2 To remove the pressure/vacuum pump, release the rubber strap in the luggage compartment, remove the cover, then withdraw the pump and disconnect the wiring and tube.

3 To remove a control or shift element, first remove the door, tailgate, or luggage compartment trim panel (as appropriate). On door elements, carefully peel back the protective foil. Remove the element mounting screws and disconnect the tubing. On the driver's door only, disconnect the wiring. Disconnect the operating rod (except on the fuel tank flap) and withdraw the element.

4 Refitting is a reversal of removal. Ensure that the door protective foil is firmly stuck to prevent water penetration and use double-sided tape to secure it if necessary.

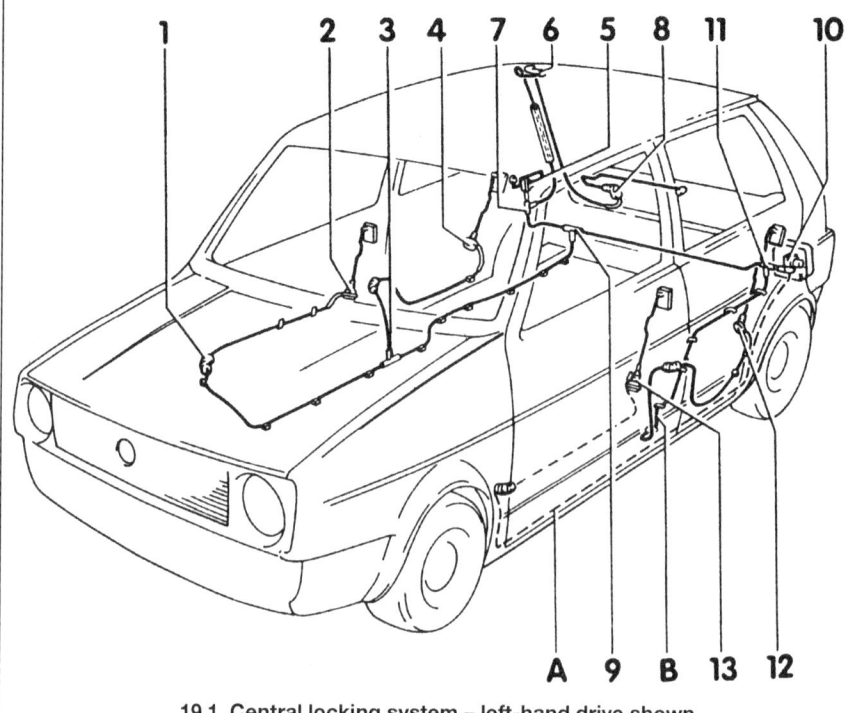

20 Window regulator – removal and refitting

Manual

1 Remove the door trim panel.
2 Temporarily refit the window regulator handle and lower the window until the lifting plate is visible.
3 Remove the bolts securing the regulator to the door and the bolts securing the lifting plate to the window channel **(see illustrations)**.
4 Release the regulator from the door and remove it through the aperture.
5 Refitting is a reversal of removal. Ensure that the inner cable is adequately lubricated with grease and if necessary, adjust the position of the regulator so that the window moves smoothly.

Electric

6 Disconnect the battery earth lead.
7 Remove the door trim panel.
8 Lower the window to enable the bolts securing the lifting plate to the window channel to be unscrewed.
9 Disconnect the wiring connector.
10 Unscrew and remove the window regulator motor securing bolts and the three bolts securing the guide rail **(see illustration)**.
11 Withdraw the window regulator assembly (ie. the motor, cables and guide rails) from the aperture at the bottom end of the door.
12 Refit in the reverse order of removal. Ensure that the upper cable is located underneath the guide rail securing bracket and, when refitting the door trim panel, the plastic cover is crease free.

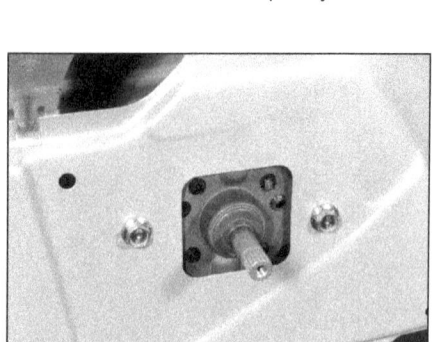

19.1 Central locking system – left-hand drive shown

A Wiring
B Tubing
1 Bellows
2 Front door shift element (or control element on RHD)
3 Connector
4 Rear door shift element
5 Fuel tank flap shift element
6 Grommet
7 Connector
8 Tailgate shift element
9 Connector
10 Pressure/vacuum pump
11 Connector
12 Rear door shift element
13 Front door control element (or shift element on RHD)

20.3a Window regulator securing bolts

20.3b Lifting plate-to-window channel bolts

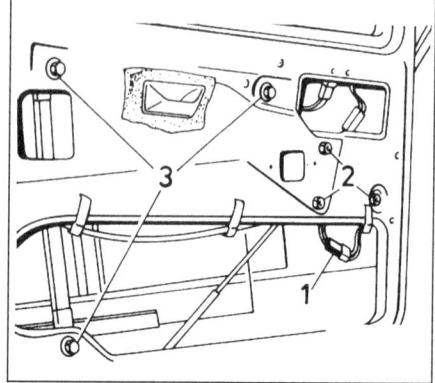

20.10 Window regulator (electric)

1 Wiring connector
2 Motor securing bolts
3 Guide rail bolts

Bodywork and fittings 11•11

22.4 Front bumper bracket securing points to longitudinal member (arrowed)

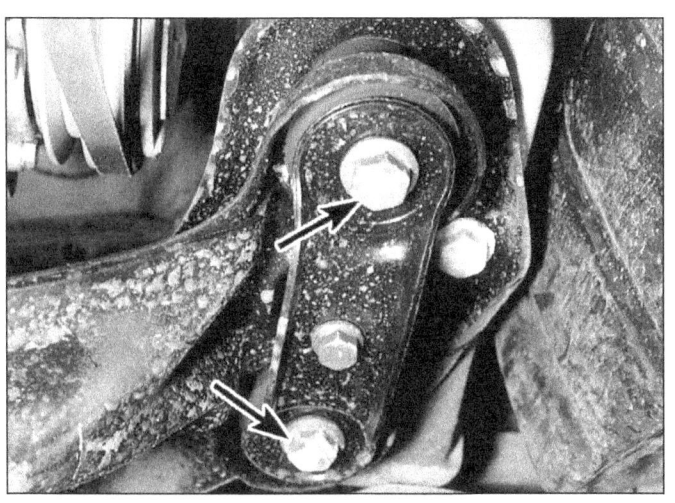

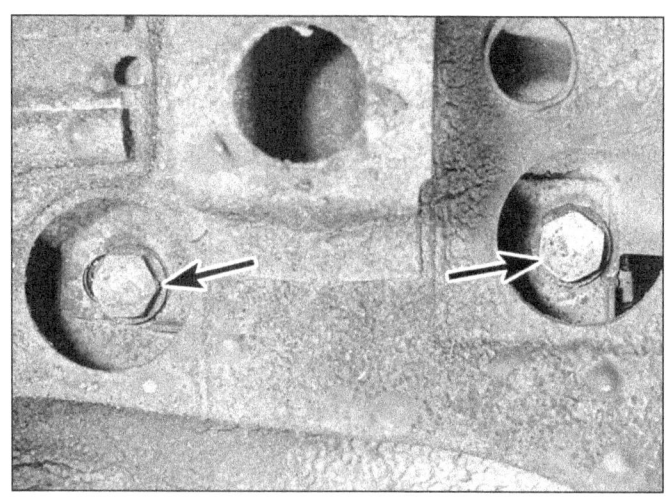

22.7 Rear bumper bracket bolts (arrowed)

21 Windows - removal and refitting

Doors

1 Remove the window regulator.
2 With the window fully lowered, unclip the inner and outer mouldings from the window aperture.
3 Remove the bolt and screw and pull out the front window channel abutting the corner window.
4 Withdraw the corner window and seal.
5 Lift the glass from the door.
6 Refitting is a reversal of removal. If the glass is being renewed, make sure that the lift channel is located in the same position as in the old glass.

Windscreen and fixed glass

7 Removal and refitting of the windscreen and fixed glass windows is best left to a VW garage or windscreen specialist who will have the necessary equipment and expertise to complete the work properly.

22 Bumpers - removal and refitting

Warning: Under no circumstances should the vehicle be driven with the front bumper and bumper brackets not securely fitted, as in this condition the front crossmember which supports the engine is no longer properly secured.

Front

1 Disconnect the battery negative lead and the wiring to the direction indicator lights.
2 Raise the front of the vehicle and support securely on axle stands (see "*Jacking and vehicle support*").
3 Place a jack (with interposed block of wood) under the engine front mounting and raise the jack head until it is just taking the weight of the engine.
4 Working underneath the front of the vehicle, undo and remove the bumper brackets from the longitudinal member on each side then withdraw the bumper **(see illustration)**.
5 Refitting is a reversal of removal Check that the indicators operate in a satisfactory manner on completion.

Rear

6 Raise and support the vehicle securely at the rear.
7 Working underneath the rear of the vehicle, undo and remove the two bumper support bracket retaining bolts on each side **(see illustration)**.
8 Withdraw the bumper by pulling it rearwards and disengaging it from the guide on each side quarter panel **(see illustration)**.
9 Refitting is a reversal of removal.

22.8 Bumper side quarter panel location guide

23 Bumper trim covering - removal and renewal

1 Remove the bumper concerned.
2 Use a suitable lever to carefully prise free the old covering from the bumper.
3 To fit the new covering, locate the covering on the bumper then support the covering and bumper with the covering underneath (bumper inverted). Use a firmly padded support if possible to protect the new covering.
4 Press or tap the bumper down onto the covering so that the securing clips engage in the bumper. Start from the centre and work progressively outwards, alternating from side to side.
5 Refit the bumper on completion.

24 Exterior mirrors - removal and refitting

Pre 1988

Non remote control

1 Prise the plastic cover from inside the door.
2 Unscrew the cross-head screws and remove the clips.
3 Withdraw the outer cover and mirror.
4 Refitting is a reversal of removal.

Remote control

5 Pull off the adjusting knob and bellows from the inside of the door **(see illustration)**.
6 Remove the door trim panel.
7 Unscrew the locknut and remove the adjusting knob from the bracket.
8 Prise off the plastic cover then unscrew the cross-head screws and remove the clips.
9 Withdraw the mirror, together with the adjusting knob and gasket.
10 Refitting is a reversal of removal. If necessary, fit a new gasket.

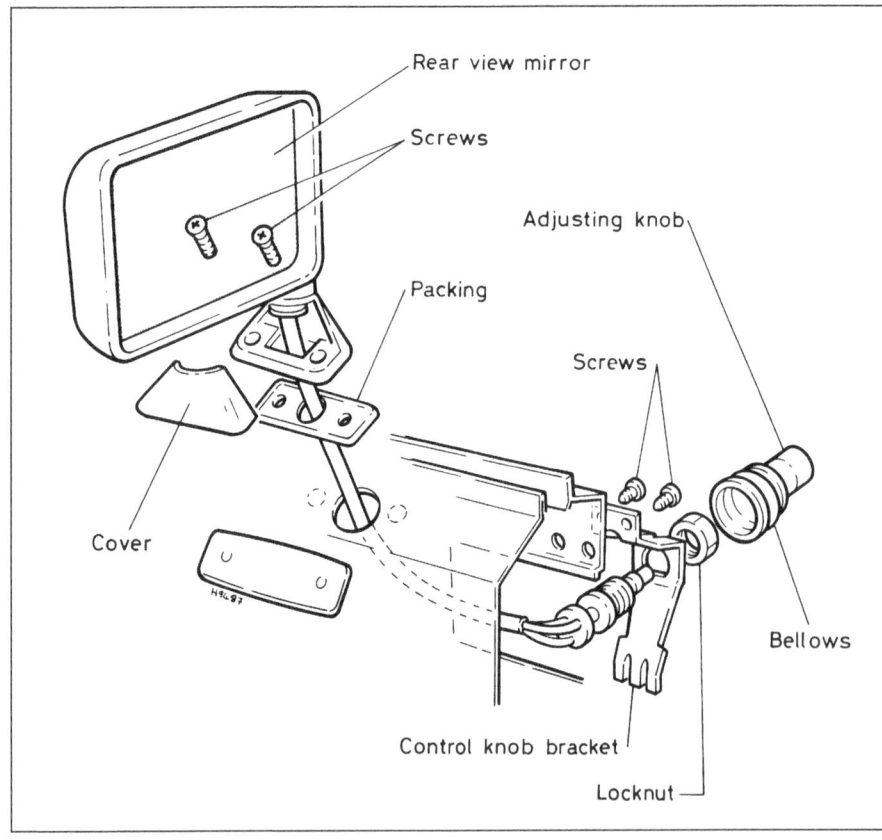

11•12 Bodywork and fittings

1988-on

11 From 1988, the exterior mirrors are mounted in the triangular area in front of the window glass **(see illustration)**.
12 The removal and refitting procedures are basically the same as for earlier models.
13 The mirror glass is clipped in position and may be removed by carefully levering out the bottom edge, then the top edge, using a plastic or wooden tool.
14 When refitting the glass, align the guide pins and use a wad of cloth, pressing only on the middle of the glass.

25 Front wheel housing liner - removal and refitting

1 Raise the front of the vehicle and support it on axle stands (see "*Jacking and vehicle support*").
2 Remove the roadwheel from the side concerned.
3 Remove the two cross-head screws from the positions indicated **(see illustration)**.
4 Swivel the liner 90° downwards and pull it free from the elongated hole.
5 Undo and remove the cross-head screws (with washers) from the points indicated **(see illustration)** then withdraw the liner after disengaging its location peg "A" from the leading lower edge.

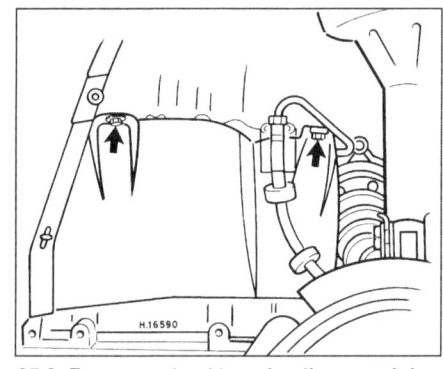

24.5 Exploded view of remote control exterior mirror - pre 1988

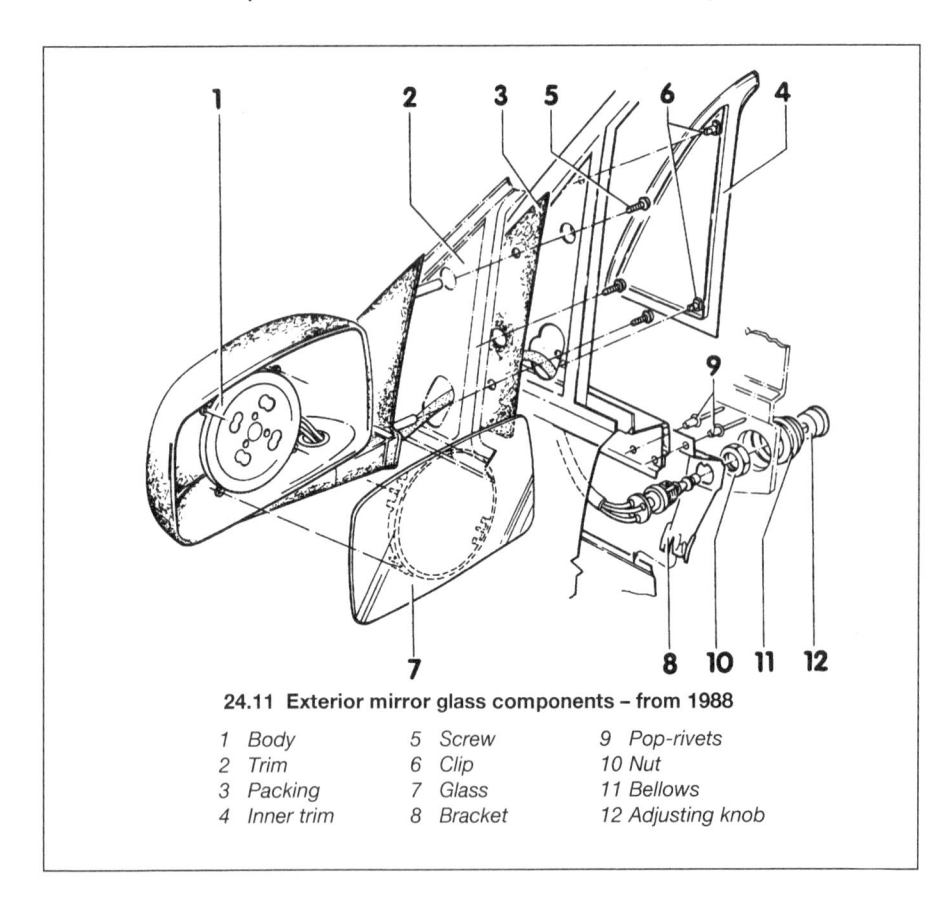

24.11 Exterior mirror glass components – from 1988

1 Body
2 Trim
3 Packing
4 Inner trim
5 Screw
6 Clip
7 Glass
8 Bracket
9 Pop-rivets
10 Nut
11 Bellows
12 Adjusting knob

25.3 Remove wheel housing liner retaining screws (arrowed)

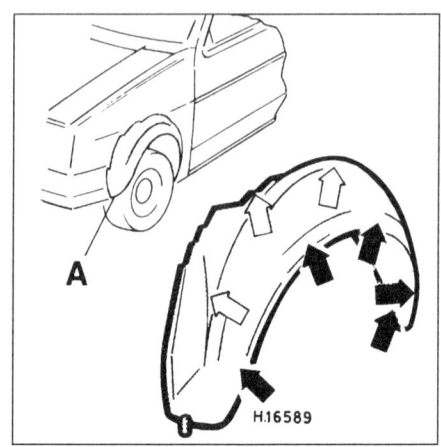

25.5 Wheel housing liner securing screw locations (arrowed)

Bodywork and fittings 11•13

6 Renew any retaining screw location rivets which are damaged.
7 Refit in the reverse order of removal.

26 Front wing - removal and refitting

1 A damaged front wing may be renewed complete. First, remove the front bumper.
2 Remove the screws and withdraw the liner from inside the wing.
3 Where applicable, disconnect/remove the wing-mounted radio aerial.
4 Remove all the screws and lever the wing from the guides (see illustration). If necessary, warm the sealing joints with a blowlamp to melt the adhesive underseal whilst observing the necessary fire precautions.
5 Clean the mating faces and treat with rust inhibitor if necessary.
6 Apply sealant along the line of the screws before fitting the wing. Once in place, apply underseal as necessary.
7 Paint the wing then fit the liner and front bumper.

27 Body protective and decorative trim fittings - removal and refitting

Tailgate spoiler and foils - GTi

1 The spoiler is secured by a nut, grommet and spacer sleeve. Access to the retaining nuts is gained by removing the inner trim panel and prising free the nut cap (see illustration).
2 When refitting the spoiler, ensure that the body surface is clean.
3 The foils are stuck in position with adhesive and are best removed and refitted by a VW dealer. If refitting them yourself, the working temperature must be between 15 and 25°C and it is essential that the body surface to which the foil is to be fitted is thoroughly cleaned and prepared.

Rear spoiler - Jetta GT

4 Open the boot lid and unscrew the nuts which secure the spoiler retaining clips.
5 Lift the spoiler from the boot lid.

Wheel arch extensions

6 These are secured to the wing panels by pop-rivets. Drill out the rivet heads and remove the arch extensions (see illustration).
7 Refit in the reverse order, ensuring that the adjacent body sections are cleaned off and prepared. Start riveting at the centre and work alternately down from it (side to side).

Protective rubbing strips

Adhered type

8 To remove a rubbing strip, you will need to heat the strip using a suitable hot air blower.

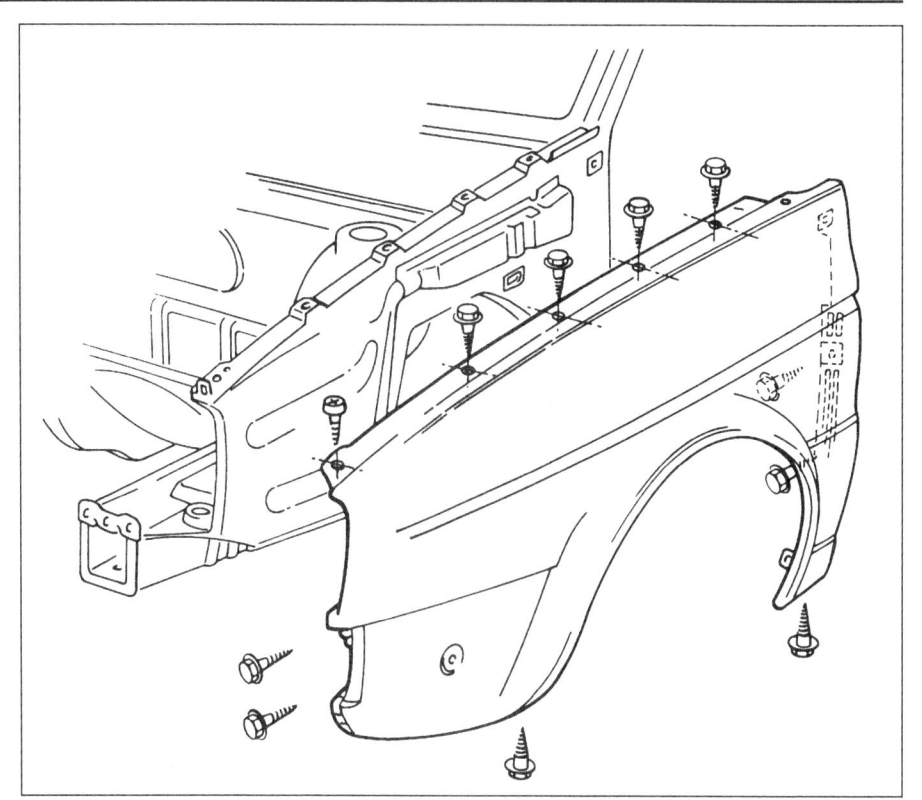

26.4 Front wing retaining screw positions (Jetta)

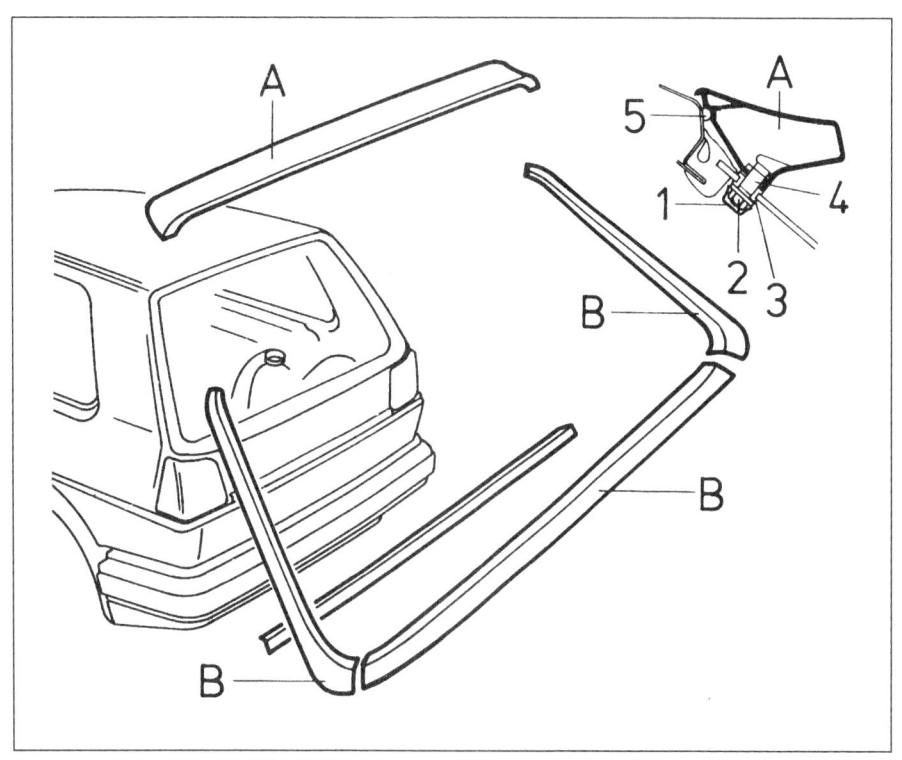

27.1 Tailgate spoiler (A) and foils (B) – GTi

1 Protective cap
2 Nut
3 Rubber grommet
4 Spacer sleeve
5 Butyl cord (5.0 mm dia.)

11•14 Bodywork and fittings

27.6 Wheel arch extensions showing retaining rivet positions at trailing lower edge

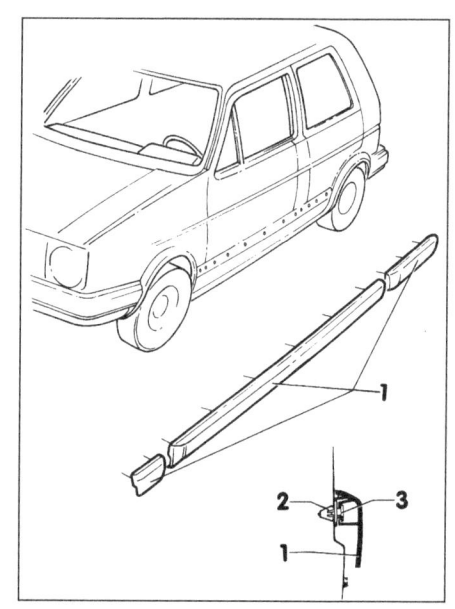

27.11 Side rubbing strip components

1 Rubbing strip   3 Clip
2 Retainer

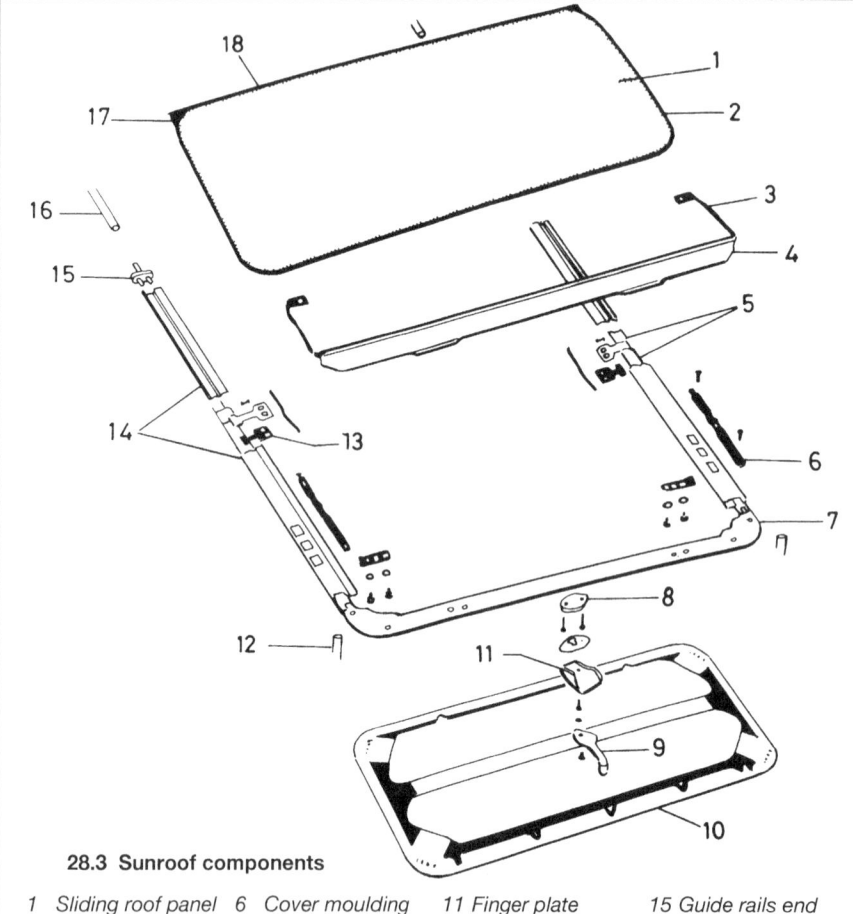

Care must be taken to protect the paintwork.
9 Clean off any adhesive and polish using white spirit and a suitable silicone remover.
10 Before fitting the new strip into position, check that the contact area on the body is dry and heat it to a temperature of 35°C. Peel back the foil from the new strip and carefully locate it into position by pressing firmly home, particularly at each end.

Clipped type

11 The side rubbing strips may be removed using a lever to prise them from their fixing clips (see illustration). Protect the paintwork by taping the end of the lever.
12 When fitting a strip, engage the lower edge under the clip and give a sharp blow with the hand to force the upper edge into engagement.

28 Sunroof - removal, refitting and adjustment

Removal

1 Half open the sunroof then prise off the five steel trim clips.
2 Close the sunroof and push the trim to the rear.
3 Unscrew the guide screws from the front of the sunroof and remove the guides (see illustration).
4 Disengage the leaf springs from the rear guides by pulling them inwards.
5 Remove the screws and withdraw the rear support plates.
6 Lift the sunroof from the vehicle.

28.3 Sunroof components

1 Sliding roof panel
2 Moulded seal
3 Deflector arm
4 Wind deflector
5 Rear guide with cable (one part)
6 Cover moulding
7 Cable guide
8 Cable drive mechanism
9 Crank
10 Panel headlining
11 Finger plate
12 Front water drain hose
13 Support plate
14 Guide rail
15 Guide rails end section
16 Rear water drain hose
17 Water trap plate
18 Panel seat

Bodywork and fittings 11•15

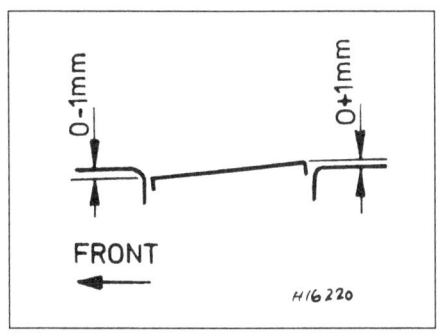

28.9 Sunroof adjustment dimensions

Refitting

7 To refit the sunroof, locate it in the aperture and fit the front guides.
8 With the sunroof closed and correctly aligned, fit the rear guides and leaf springs.

Adjustment

9 For correct adjustment, the front edge of the sunroof must be level with, or a maximum of 1.0 mm below, the roof panel. The rear edge must be level with, or a maximum of 1.0 mm above, the roof panel (see illustration).
10 To adjust the front edge of the sunroof, loosen the front guide screws and turn the adjustment screws as necessary, then tighten the guide screws.
11 To adjust the rear edge, detach the leaf springs, loosen the slotted screws and move the sunroof as necessary in the serrations. Tighten the screws and refit the leaf springs after making the adjustment.
12 Refit the trim with the clips.

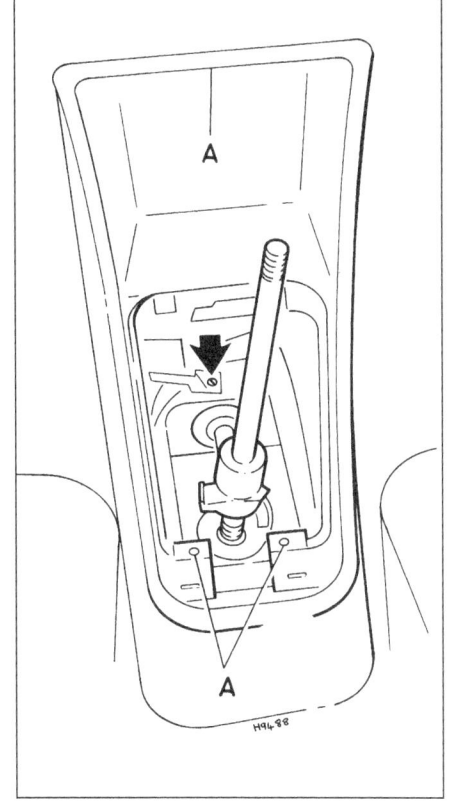

29.3 Centre console retaining screw (arrowed) and guide locations (A)

29 Centre console - removal and refitting

1 Disconnect the battery earth lead.
2 Unscrew and remove the gear lever knob then unclip and withdraw the gaiter.
3 Undo the retaining screws and pull free the console from its guides at the rear. Disconnect any console switch lead connectors (see illustration).
4 Refit in the reverse order of removal. Check the operation of the console switches (where fitted) on completion.

30 Facia panel - removal and refitting

Removal

1 Remove the steering wheel.
2 On certain models, a protective knee-bar is fitted across the lower edge of the facia panel. To remove the bar, first peel back the weatherstrip from the edge of the door aperture and the trim in the vicinity of the knee-bar end brackets. Extract the bracket fixing screws and withdraw the bar (see illustration).
3 Undo the retaining screws and withdraw the undertray on the driver and passenger sides (see illustrations).

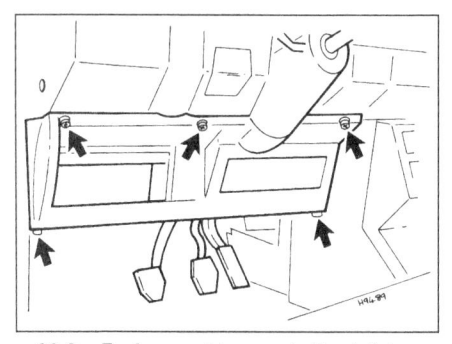

30.3a Facia panel lower shelf retaining screw locations – driver's side (left-hand drive) shown

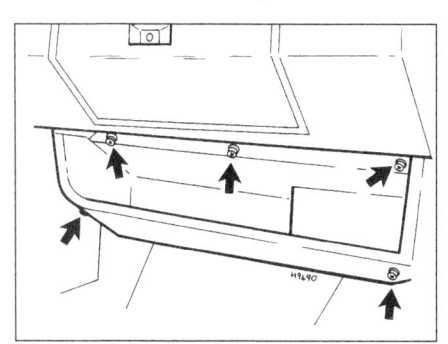

30.3b Facia panel lower shelf retaining screw locations – passenger side (left-hand drive) shown

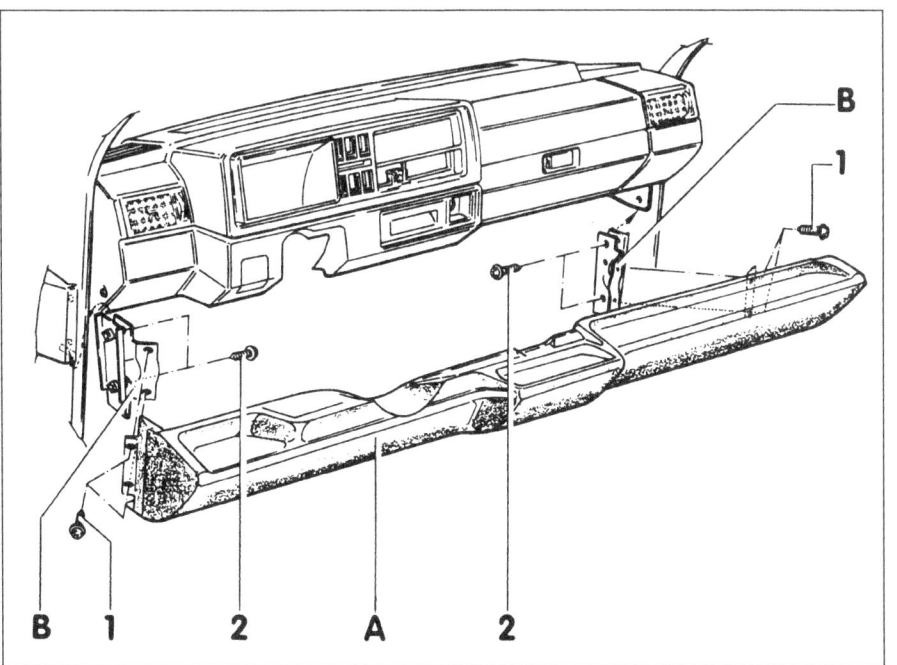

30.2 Knee-bar attachments

A Knee-bar   B Retaining bracket   1 Screw   2 Screw

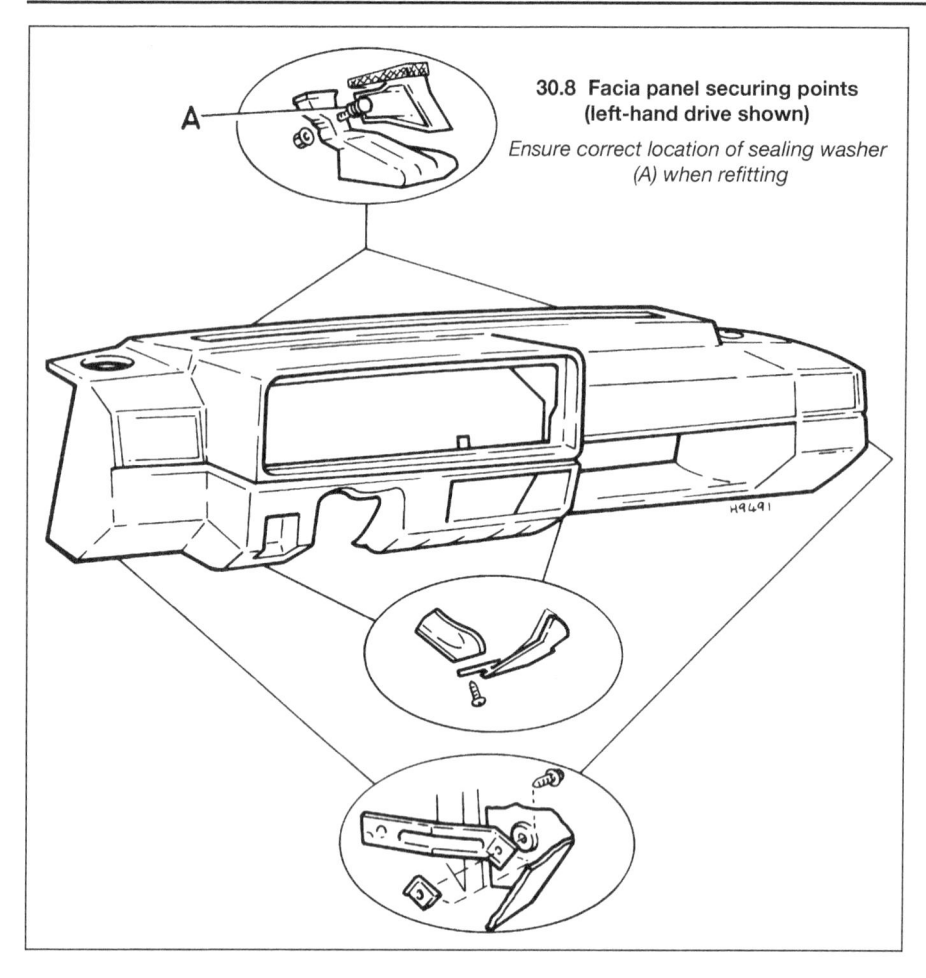

11•16 Bodywork and fittings

30.8 Facia panel securing points (left-hand drive shown)
Ensure correct location of sealing washer (A) when refitting

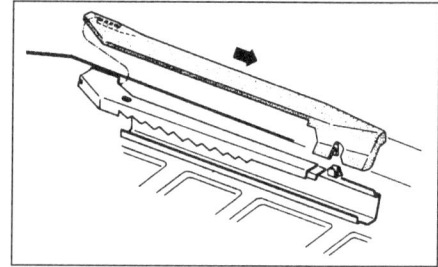

31.1 Front seat runner cover removal - pre 1986
Unclip cover and remove in direction arrowed

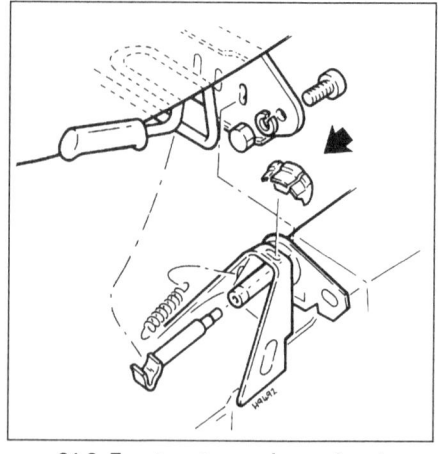

31.3 Front seat securing rod and associated components - pre 1986
Front slide arrowed

4 Remove the centre console.
5 Pull free the heater/fresh air control knobs then carefully unclip the control panel trim and detach the electrical connectors.
6 Remove the radio/cassette unit or cubby hole, the instrument panel cluster and the loudspeaker and grille.
7 Remove the air vent pivot grilles by carefully levering them free. Undo the screws securing the air vent housing and lever out the housing.
8 Remove the facia panel retaining screws from the points indicated **(see illustration)**. To remove the nuts/bolts at the front, access is from the plenum chamber in the engine compartment.
9 Check that the facia panel is fully disconnected then carefully withdraw it from the vehicle.

Refitting

10 Refit in the reverse order of removal. When fitting the securing nuts in the plenum chamber use the correct type of sealing washers.
11 On completion, check the operation of the various instruments, switches and controls.

31 Front seats - removal and refitting

Pre 1986

1 Prise free the runner cover and clip towards the rear of the seat **(see illustration)**.
2 Pull the cover from the runner and then pull the seat forwards.
3 Unscrew the cap nut then remove the washer and cheesehead screw **(see illustration)**.

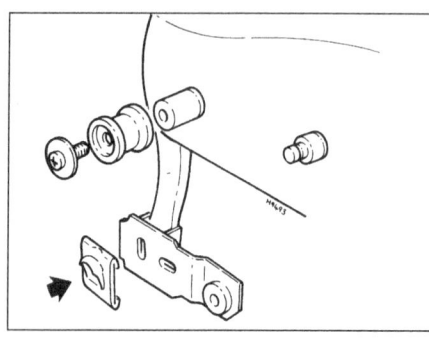

4 After releasing the securing rod, remove the seat rearwards.
5 Difficulty in seat position adjustment longitudinally is probably due to worn front and rear slides, in which case they must be renewed **(see illustration)**.
6 Refitting is a reversal of the removal procedure. Tighten the cap nut to the specified torque setting.

1986 on

7 Remove the screw (1) and slide off the cover (2) from the runner **(see illustration)**.

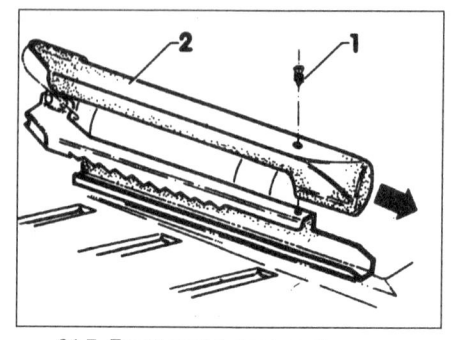

31.5 Front seat rear slide (arrowed) - pre 1986

31.7 Front seat runner and cover – from 1986

1 Screw   2 Cover

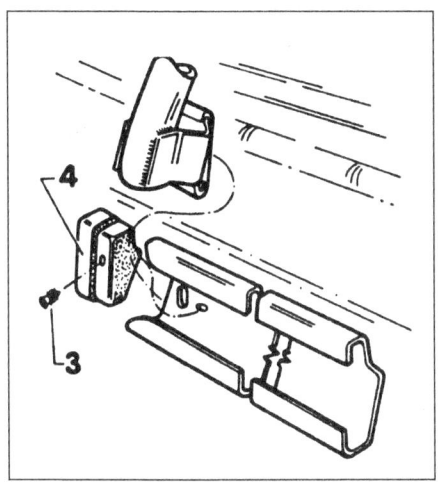

Bodywork and fittings 11•17

31.8 Front seat guide fixing – from 1986

3 Screw   4 Cap

8 Remove the cross-head screw (3) and pull the cap (4) from the seat guide **(see illustration)**.
9 Slide the seat fully forward and then unscrew the cap nut. Extract the circlip and fillister head screw.
10 Release the locking bar and slide the seat rearwards out of the guide rails.
11 Refitting is a reversal of removal.

32.1 Rear seat cushion pressure points for removal (arrowed)

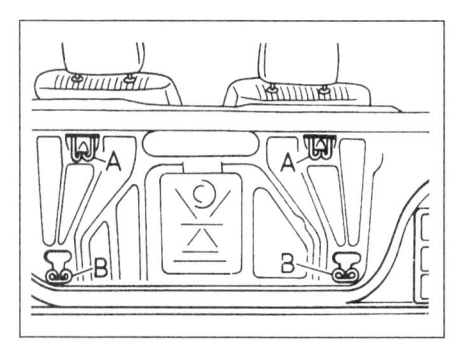

32 Rear seat - removal and refitting

1 Remove the seat cushion by pressing on the pressure points each side at the front lower edge of the cushion, then lifting the cushion **(see illustration)**.
2 On the luggage compartment side, release the backrest retaining hooks whilst an assistant pushes the backrest downwards **(see illustration)**.
3 Refitting is a reversal of the removal procedure. Ensure that the backrest retaining hooks fully engage.

32.2 Rear seat backrest retaining hook locations in luggage compartment – A and B (Jetta and Golf convertible)

33 Seat belts - renewal

1 When removing each seat belt anchor bolt, note carefully the fitted order of the washers, bushes and anchor plate for reference during reassembly **(see illustrations)**.
2 Note that from early 1986, some models are fitted with front seat belts incorporating height adjustment of the B pillar attachment point **(see illustration)**.

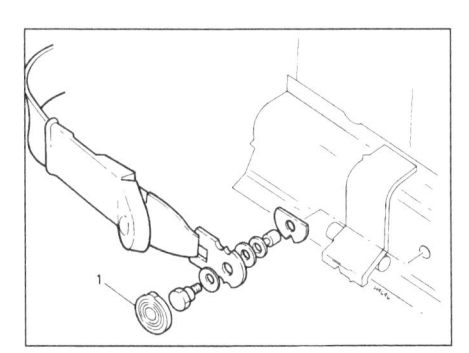

33.1a Front seat belt anchorage to side-member

Spring end (1) points to upper recess of belt link and is then tensioned 270° and hooked onto link pin

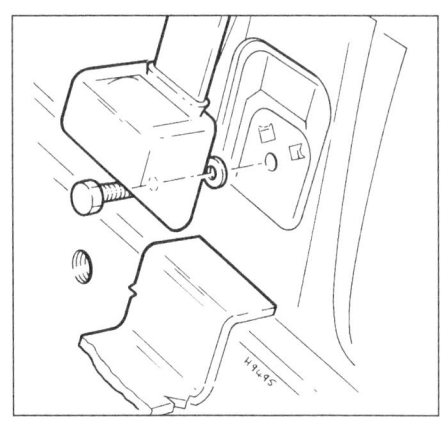

33.1b Front seat belt anchorage to B pillar (lower)

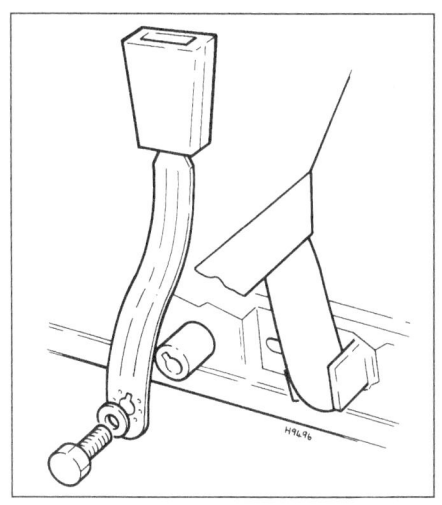

33.1c Front seat frame anchorage

33.1d Front seat belt anchorage to B pillar (upper)

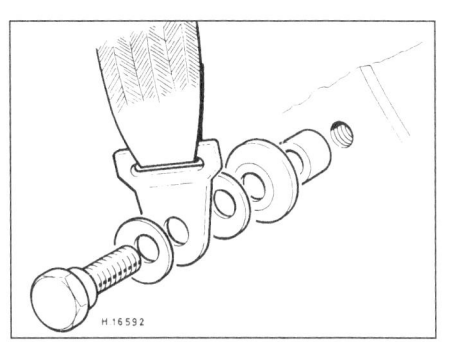

33.1e Rear seat belt anchorage to floor

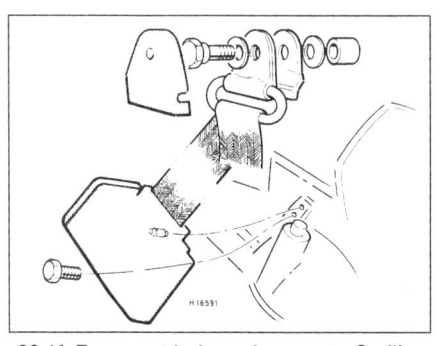

33.1f Rear seat belt anchorage to C pillar

11•18 Bodywork and fittings

3 These adjustable seat belts can be fitted to any model having a chassis number later than 16/19 G 054 900, but a new B pillar trim must also be fitted.

4 Never modify a seat belt or alter its attachment point to the body.

34 Dust and pollen filter - renewal

This filter is fitted (or can be fitted) to all models covered by this Manual.

The filter is located in the air inlet within the plenum chamber at the right-hand side of the underbonnet area **(see illustration)**. Access to the filter is gained after removing the anti-leaf mesh and the water deflector.

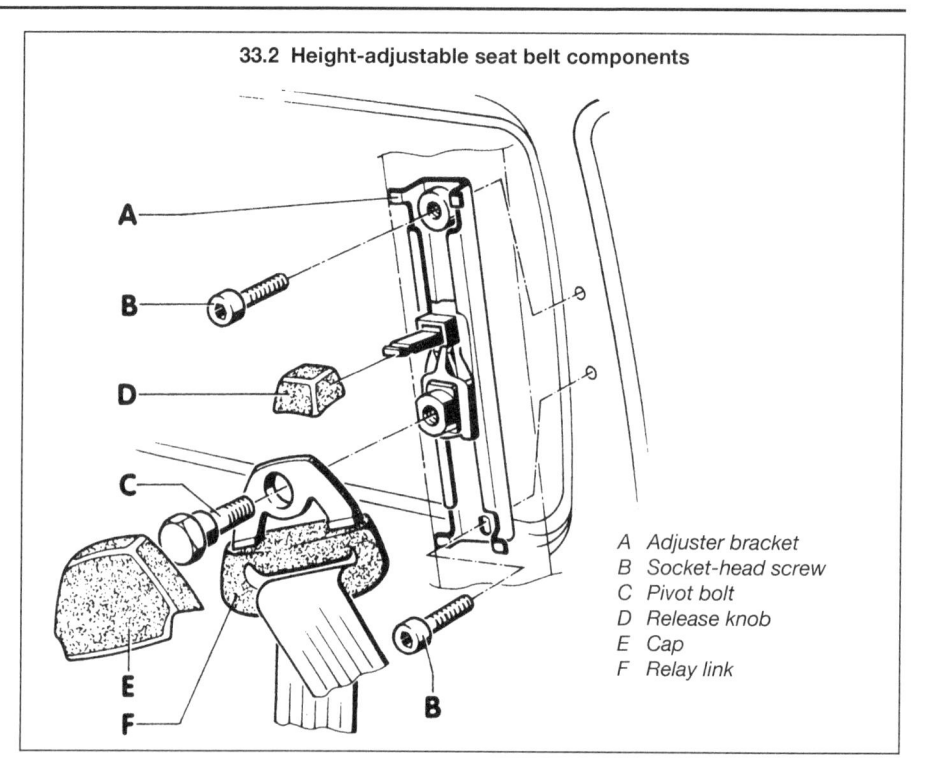

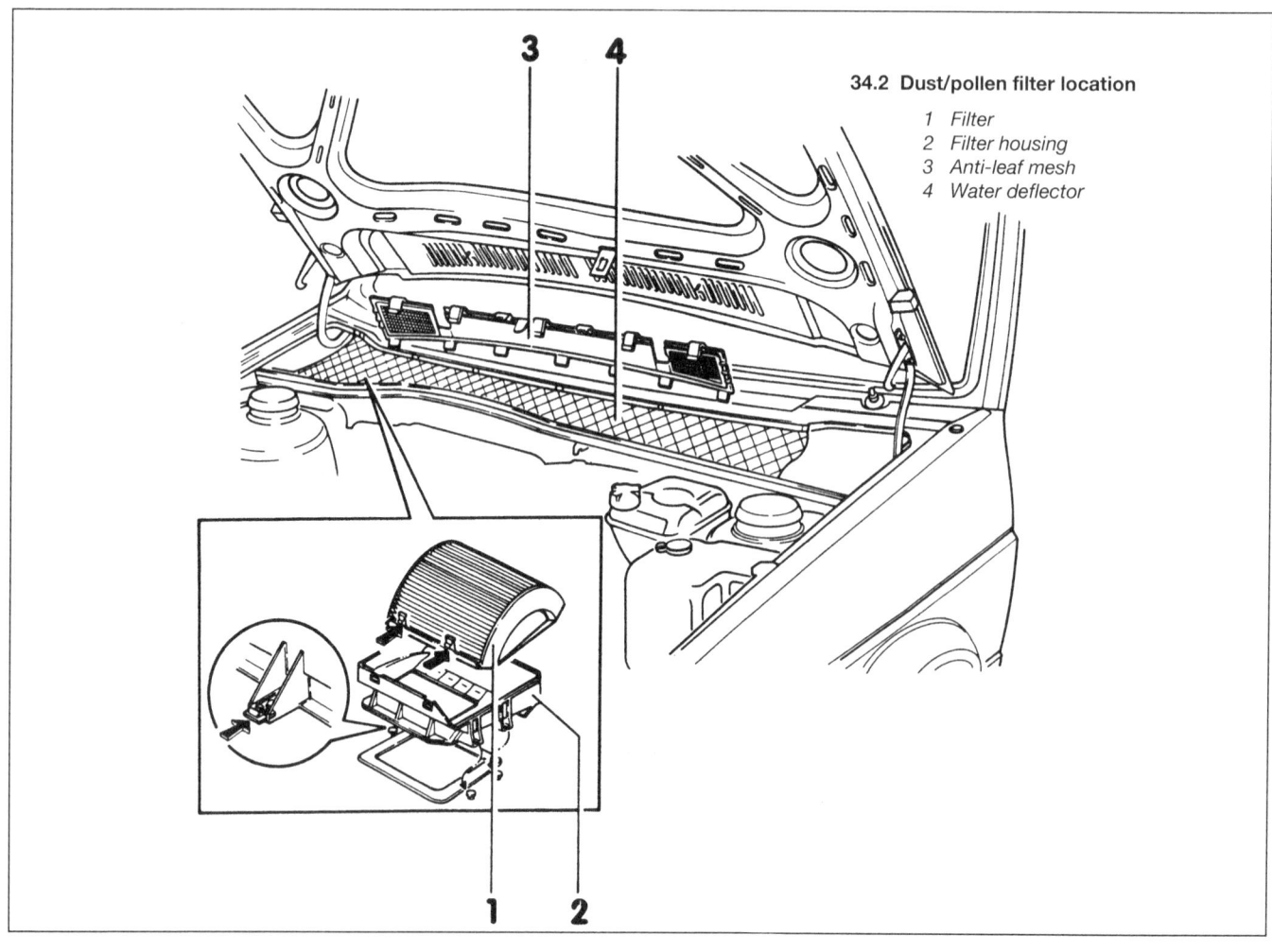

33.2 Height-adjustable seat belt components

A Adjuster bracket
B Socket-head screw
C Pivot bolt
D Release knob
E Cap
F Relay link

34.2 Dust/pollen filter location

1 Filter
2 Filter housing
3 Anti-leaf mesh
4 Water deflector

Chapter 12
Body electrical systems

Contents

Cigarette lighter - removal and refitting	21
Combination switches - removal and refitting	12
Courtesy and luggage compartment light switches - removal and refitting	14
Direction indicators and hazard flasher system - operation and testing	9
Electrical fault-finding - general information	2
Electrically-operated door mirror motor - removal and refitting	23
Facia switches - removal and refitting	13
Facia trim panel - removal and refitting	18
Front foglight bulb and unit - removal and refitting	7
Fuses and relays - location and renewal	3
Gearchange and consumption gauge - operation	20
General information and precautions	1
Headlamp bulbs and headlamps - removal and refitting	4
Headlamp range control - removal and refitting	6
Headlamps - alignment	5
Horn - removal and refitting	24
Ignition switch/steering column lock - removal and refitting	11
Instrument panel - dismantling, testing and reassembly	17
Instrument panel cluster - removal and refitting	16
Lamp bulbs - renewal	8
Loudspeakers - removal and refitting	32
Multi-function indicator - operation and testing	19
Oil pressure warning switches - testing	15
Radio/cassette player - removal and refitting	31
Rear window wiper motor - removal and refitting	28
Speedometer cable - removal and refitting	22
Warning lamp cluster - removal and refitting	10
Windscreen and headlamp washer system - pump renewal	30
Windscreen wiper linkage - removal and refitting	29
Windscreen wiper motor - removal and refitting	27
Wiper arms - removal and refitting	26
Wiper blades - renewal	25
Wiring diagrams - general information	33

Degrees of difficulty

Easy, suitable for novice with little experience	Fairly easy, suitable for beginner with some experience	Fairly difficult, suitable for competent DIY mechanic	Difficult, suitable for experienced DIY mechanic	Very difficult, suitable for expert DIY or professional

Specifications

System
Type .... 12 volt, negative earth

Fuses - pre August 1989

Fuse	Component	Rating (amps)
1	Radiator fan	30
2	Brake light	10
3	Cigarette lighter, radio, clock, interior light, central locking, boot light (Jetta)	15
4	Emergency light system	15
5	Fuel pump	15
6	Foglights (main current)	15
7	Tail and sidelights, left	10
8	Tail and sidelights, right	10
9	High beam right, high beam warning lamp	10
10	High beam, left	10
11	Windscreen wipers and washer, headlight washer	15
12	Rear wiper and washer, seat heater control, electric mirror control	15
13	Rear window heating, mirror heating	15
14	Blower, glovebox light	20
15	Reversing lights, shift pattern illumination (automatic transmission)	10
16	Horn	15
17	Carburettor	10
18	Horn (dual tone), coolant level warning lamp	15
19	Turn signals, stop-start system, brake warning lamp	10
20	Number plate light, foglights (switch current)	10
21	Low beam, left, headlight range control, left	10
22	Low beam right, headlight range control, right	10

Fuses - pre August 1989 (continued)

Additional fuses (In separate holders above fusebox)	Rating (amps)
Rear foglight	10
Electric windows	30
Air conditioner	30

Fuses - from August 1989

Fuse	Component	Rating (amps)
1	Low beam, left	10
2	Low beam, right	10
3	Instrument and number plate lights	10
4	Glovebox light	15
5	Windscreen wash/wipe system	15
6	Fresh air blower	20
7	Side/tail lights, right	10
8	Side/tail lights, left	10
9	Heated rear window	20
10	Foglights	10
11	High beam, left	10
12	High beam, right	10
13	Horn	10
14	Reversing lights, heated washer jets	10
15	Electromagnetic cut-off, fuel pump run-on	10
16	Dash panel insert	15
17	Emergency light system	10
18	Fuel pump Lambda probe heating	20
19	Radiator fan, A/C relay	30
20	Brake stoplights	30
21	Interior light, digital clock	15
22	Radio system/cigarette lighter	10

Relays

Type .... See wiring diagrams at the end of this Chapter

Bulbs

	Wattage
Headlamps	60/55
Sidelights	4
Tail lights	5
Stop-lights	21
Direction indicators	21
Foglight (rear)	21
Reversing light	21
Instrument lights	1.2

1 General information and precautions

General information

The electrical system is of a 12-volt negative earth type and comprises a battery, an alternator with integral voltage regulator, a starter motor and related electrical accessories, components and wiring.

Further details of the various systems are given in the relevant Sections of this Chapter. While some repair procedures are given, the usual course of action is to renew the component concerned. The owner whose interest extends beyond mere component renewal should obtain a copy of the "*Automobile Electrical & Electronic Systems Manual*" which is available from the publishers of this Manual.

Precautions

It is necessary to take extra care when working on the electrical system to avoid damage to semi-conductor devices (diodes and transistors) and to avoid the risk of personal injury. In addition to the precautions given in *Safety first!* at the beginning of this Manual, observe the following when working on the system:

a) *Always remove rings, watches, etc. before working on the electrical system. Even with the battery disconnected, capacitive discharge could occur if a component's live terminal is earthed through a metal object. This could cause a shock or nasty burn.*

b) *Always disconnect the battery negative lead before working on the electrical system.*

c) *Before disconnecting any wiring or removing components, always ensure that the ignition is switched off.*

d) *Disconnect the battery leads before using a mains charger.*

e) *Do not reverse the battery connections. Components such as the alternator or any other having semi-conductor circuitry could be irreparably damaged.*

f) *If the engine is being started using jump leads and a slave battery, connect the batteries positive to positive and negative to negative. This also applies when connecting a battery charger.*

g) *Never disconnect the battery terminals or alternator multi-plug connector when the engine is running.*

h) *Do not allow the engine to turn the alternator when the alternator is not connected.*

I) *Never test for alternator output by "flashing" the output lead to earth.*

j) *The battery leads and alternator multi-plug must be disconnected before carrying out any electric welding on the vehicle.*

Body electrical systems 12•3

k) Never use an ohmmeter of the type incorporating a hand cranked generator for circuit or continuity testing.
l) When carrying out welding operations on the vehicle using electric welding equipment, disconnect the battery and alternator.
m) When fitting electrical accessories it is important that they are connected correctly, otherwise serious damage may result to the components concerned. Items such as radios, tape recorders, electronic ignition systems, electronic tachometers, automatic dipping etc, should all be checked for correct polarity.

2 Electrical fault-finding - general information

1 A typical electrical circuit consists of an electrical component, any switches, relays, motors, fuses, fusible links or circuit breakers related to that component and the wiring and connectors that link the component to both the battery and the chassis. To help you pinpoint an electrical circuit problem, wiring diagrams are included at the end of this Chapter.

2 Before tackling any troublesome electrical circuit, first study the appropriate wiring diagram to get a complete understanding of what components are included in that individual circuit. Trouble spots, for instance, can be narrowed down by noting if other components related to the circuit are operating properly. If several components or circuits fail at one time, the problem is probably in a shared fuse or earth connection, as more than one circuit can be routed through the same connections.

3 Electrical problems usually stem from simple causes, such as loose or corroded connections, a faulty earth, a blown fuse, a melted fusible link or a faulty relay. Visually inspect the condition of all fuses, wires and connections in a problem circuit before testing the components. Use the diagrams to note which terminal connections will need to be checked in order to pinpoint the trouble spot.

4 The basic tools needed for electrical fault-finding include a circuit tester or voltmeter (a 12-volt bulb with a set of test leads can also be used), a continuity tester, a battery and set of test leads, and a jumper wire, preferably with a circuit breaker incorporated, which can be used to bypass electrical components. Before attempting to locate a problem with test instruments, use the wiring diagram to decide where to make the connections.

Voltage checks

5 Voltage checks should be performed if a circuit is not functioning properly. Connect one lead of a circuit tester to either the negative battery terminal or a known good earth. Connect the other lead to a connector in the circuit being tested, preferably nearest to the battery or fuse. If the tester bulb lights, voltage is present, this means that the part of the circuit between the connector and the battery is problem-free. Continue checking the rest of the circuit in the same fashion. When you reach a point at which no voltage is present the problem lies between that point and the last test point with voltage. Most problems can be traced to a loose connection. Bear in mind that some circuits are live only when the ignition switch is switched to a particular position.

Finding a short circuit

6 One method of finding a short circuit is to remove the fuse and connect a test lamp or voltmeter to the fuse terminals with all the relevant electrical components switched off. There should be no voltage present in the circuit. Move the wiring from side to side while watching the test lamp. If the bulb lights there is a short to earth somewhere in that area, probably where the insulation has rubbed through. The same test can be performed on each component in the circuit, even a switch.

Earth check

7 To check whether a component is properly earthed, disconnect the battery and connect one lead of a self-powered test lamp (sometimes known as a continuity tester) to a known good earth point. Connect the other lead to the wire or earth connection being tested. If the lamp lights, the earth is sound; if not, it must be rectified.

8 The battery negative terminal is connected to earth (the metal of the vehicle body) and most systems are wired so that they only receive a positive feed, the current returning via the metal of the vehicle's body. This means that the component mounting and the body form part of that circuit and loose or corroded mountings, therefore, can cause a range of electrical faults. Note that these may range from total failure of a circuit to a puzzling partial fault. In particular, lamps may shine dimly (especially when another circuit sharing the same earth point is in operation), motors (eg. wiper motors or the radiator cooling fan motor) may run slowly and the operation of one circuit may have an apparently unrelated effect on another. Note that a poor earth may not cause the circuit's fuse to blow; in fact it may reduce the load on the fuse.

9 If an earth connection is thought to be faulty, dismantle the connection and clean back to bare metal both the bodyshell and the wire terminal or the component's earth connection mating surface. Be careful to remove all traces of dirt and corrosion, then use a knife to trim away any paint, so that a clean metal-to-metal joint is made. On reassembly, tighten the joint fasteners securely; if a wire terminal is being refitted, use serrated washers between the terminal and the bodyshell to ensure a clean and secure connection. When the connection is remade, prevent the onset of corrosion in the future by applying a coat of petroleum jelly or silicone-based grease or by spraying on (at regular intervals) a proprietary ignition sealer or a water dispersant lubricant.

Continuity check

10 A continuity check is necessary to determine if there are any breaks in a circuit. With the circuit switched off (ie no power in the circuit), a self-powered test lamp (sometimes known as a continuity tester) can be used to check the circuit. Connect the test leads to both ends of the circuit (or to the positive end and a good earth); if the test lamp lights, the circuit is passing current properly. If the lamp does not light, there is a break somewhere in the circuit.

11 The same procedure can be used to test a switch, by connecting the continuity tester to the switch terminals. With the switch in the relevant position, the test lamp should light.

Finding an open circuit

12 When checking for possible open circuits, it is often difficult to locate them by sight because oxidation or terminal misalignment are hidden by the connectors; merely moving a connector on a sensor or in the wiring harness may correct the fault. Remember this if an open circuit is indicated when fault-finding in a circuit. Intermittent problems may also be caused by oxidised or loose connections.

General

13 Electrical fault-finding is simple if you keep in mind that all electrical circuits are basically electricity flowing from the battery, through the wires, switches, relays, fuses and fusible links to each electrical component (light bulb, motor, etc.) and to earth, from where it is passed back to the battery. Any electrical problem is an interruption in the flow of electricity from the battery.

3 Fuses and relays - location and renewal

1 The fuses and relays are located under the facia panel on the right-hand side (see illustration).

3.1 Removing fuse/relay unit cover

12•4 Body electrical systems

3.2 Removing a fuse

3.3 Removing a relay

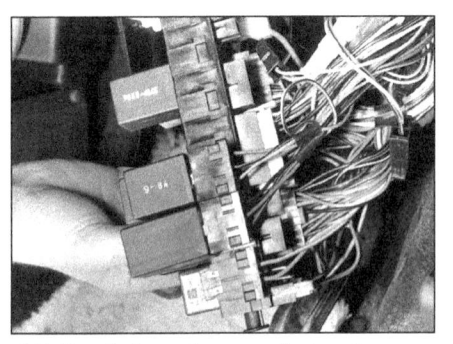

3.5 Fuse/relay unit removal, showing rear connections

3.6 Typical relay installation in engine compartment

2 The fuses are numbered consecutively for identification. Always renew a fuse with one of identical rating and never renew it more than once without finding out the source of the problem **(see illustration)**.
3 All relays are of the plug-in type and are numbered for identification, though not consecutively **(see illustration)**.
4 Relays cannot be repaired and if at all suspect, should be removed and taken to an auto-electrician for testing.
5 The fuse/relay unit holder complete can be removed by twisting the securing knob on the lower right-hand side and removing the knob.

Twist the slotted retainer on the left-hand side and withdraw the fuse/relay box. The various connectors on the rear face of the unit are then accessible for detachment as required **(see illustration)**.
6 In addition to those fuses and relays located at the main fuse/relay unit, some models will have in-line fuses and relays fitted to some circuits, these being shown in the wiring diagrams at the end of this Chapter **(see illustration)**.

4 Headlamp bulbs and headlamps - removal and refitting

1 To remove a headlamp bulb, first open the bonnet and pull the connector from the rear of the headlamp **(see illustration)**.
2 Prise off the rubber cap.
3 Squeeze the bulb retaining spring clips together and release the clip from the bulb **(see illustration)**.
4 Withdraw the bulb but do not touch its glass with your fingers if it is to be re-used **(see illustration)**.
5 To remove the headlamp unit, first remove the radiator grille.
6 With the headlamp bulb removed, release the screws securing the carrier plate to the front panel and withdraw the unit.
7 Refitting is a reversal of removal. Check and, if necessary, adjust headlamp beam alignment.

5 Headlamps - alignment

Refer to Chapter 1, Section 27

4.1 Detaching headlamp bulb connector

4.3 Squeeze bulb retaining clips . . .

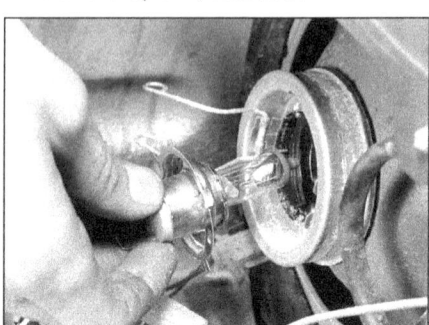

4.4 . . . and withdraw headlamp bulb

Body electrical systems 12•5

6 Headlamp range control - removal and refitting

1 Where fitted, this system is designed to provide the driver with in-car headlamp adjustment to counteract the effects of heavy loading at the rear. The system operates on dipped headlamps only and the light units are raised or lowered by means of an electrically-operated motor mounted at the rear of each unit. For safety reasons an integral height adjustment limit control is fitted.
2 The range control switch can be removed in the manner described for facia switches.
3 To remove a range control motor from the rear of a headlamp unit first disconnect the battery earth lead.
4 Pull free the plug connector from the rear of the motor unit.
5 On round headlamp units, detach the motor from the frame by twisting it to the right (clockwise) (see illustration).
6 On rectangular headlamp units, the adjuster motor on the right-hand side is disconnected by turning it to the left, whilst on the left-hand unit it must be turned to the right.
7 Undo the headlamp adjustment screw from the front (see illustration) then pull the motor from the frame to the rear for removal.
8 Refit in the reverse order of removal. Check the range control operation on completion.

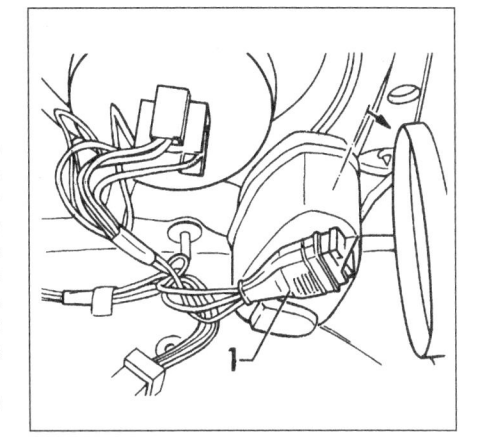

6.5 Range control motor and terminal multi-connector (1) – round headlamp
Detach motor by rotating clockwise (arrowed)

7 Front foglight bulb and unit - removal and refitting

1 To remove the bulb, pull back the rubber cover from the rear of the lamp unit, compress the bulb retaining spring clip and release it.
2 The bulb can now be withdrawn whilst taking care not handle its glass with the fingers (see illustration).
3 The foglight unit can be removed in a similar manner to that described for the headlamps.

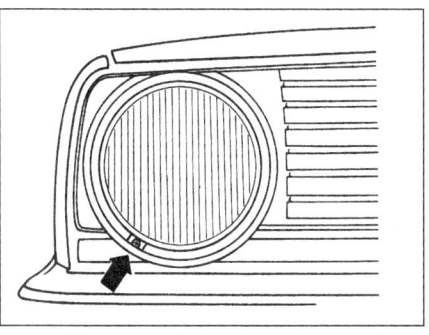

6.7 Remove headlamp adjuster screw (arrowed)

4 Refit in the reverse order of removal and check lamp operation on completion. If necessary, adjust beam alignment by means of the adjustment screws (see illustration).
5 Foglight alignment should be carried out by a VW dealer with the proper beam setting equipment. In an emergency, follow the procedure given for the headlamps.

8 Lamp bulbs - renewal

Note: *Lamp bulbs should always be renewed with ones of similar type and rating, as specified*

Sidelights

1 Open the bonnet and pull the connector from the sidelight bulbholder located beneath the headlamp bulb.
2 Turn the bulbholder anti-clockwise and remove it from the reflector (see illustration).
3 Depress and twist the bulb to remove it.

Front indicator lights

4 Remove the cross-head screws and withdraw the lens (see illustration).
5 Depress and twist the bulb to remove it (see illustration).
6 If necessary, the lamp unit can be withdrawn from the bumper and the wiring disconnected (see illustration).
7 When refitting the lens, ensure that the gasket is correctly located.

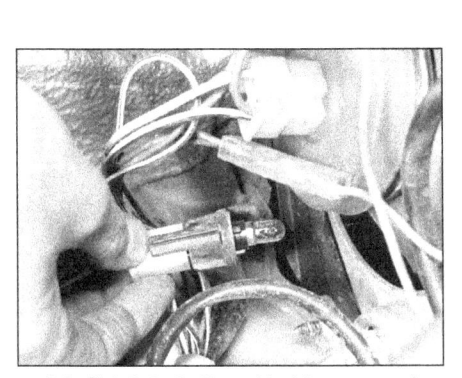

7.2 Bulb and holder removal from foglight

7.4 Foglight beam alignment adjuster screws (arrowed)

8.2 Sidelight bulb and holder removal

8.4 Front indicator lens removal

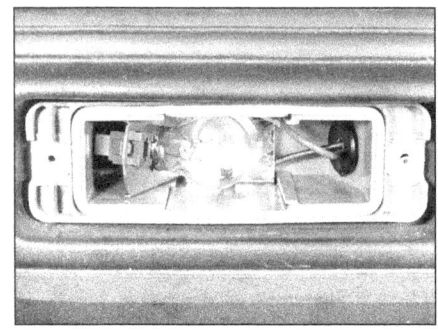

8.5 Front indicator lamp bulb

12•6 Body electrical systems

8.6 Front indicator lamp unit removal

Rear lights

8 Open the tailgate or bootlid, as applicable. Compress the bulb carrier securing tabs to release the bulb carrier and withdraw it for bulb inspection/renewal (see illustration).
9 Depress and twist the relevant bulb to remove it.

Number plate light

10 Remove the cross-head screws and withdraw the lens and cover (see illustration).
11 Depress and twist the bulb to remove it.
12 When refitting the lens and cover, ensure that the lug is correctly located.

Interior light

13 Using a screwdriver, depress the spring clip then withdraw the light from the roof (see illustrations).
14 Release the festoon type bulb from the spring terminals.

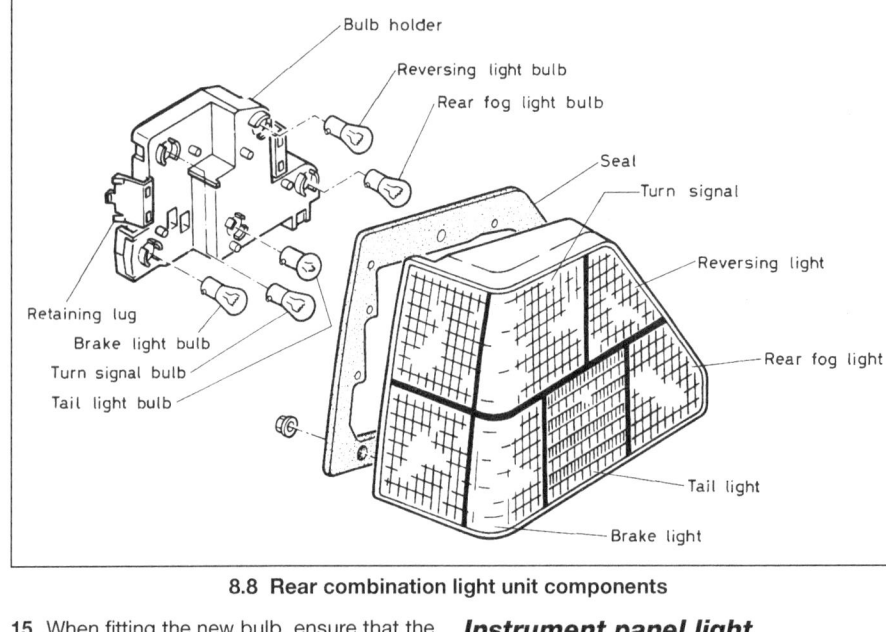

8.8 Rear combination light unit components

15 When fitting the new bulb, ensure that the terminals are tensioned sufficiently to retain the bulb. The switch end of the light should be inserted into the roof first.

Luggage compartment light and glovebox light

16 Prise free and withdraw the lens. The bulb is retained in the lens and can be pulled free for renewal (see illustration).
17 If renewing the lens, detach the wiring spade connectors from the lens.

Instrument panel light

18 Remove the instrument panel.
19 Twist the bulbholder through 90° to withdraw it (see illustration) then pull out the bulb.

Facia switch lights

20 Remove the relevant facia switch.
21 Remove the bulb from the switch or connector as applicable.

9 Direction indicators and hazard flasher system - operation and testing

1 The direction indicators are controlled by the left-hand column switch.
2 A switch on the facia board operates all four flashers simultaneously. Although the direction indicators will not work when the ignition is switched off, the emergency switch overrides this and the flasher signals continue to operate.
3 All circuits are routed through the relay on the console and its fuse.

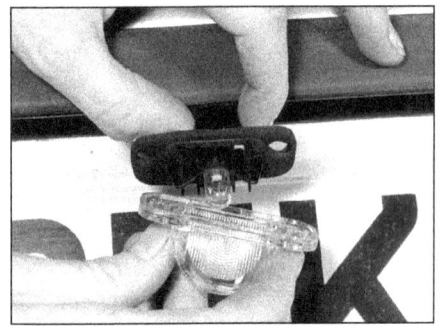

8.10 Number plate lens removal

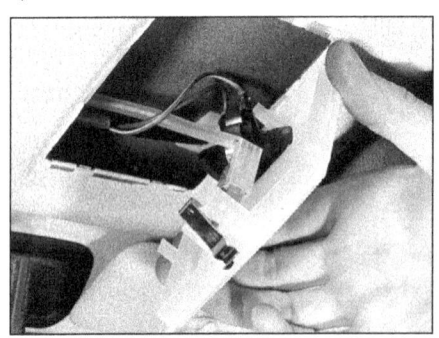

8.13a Interior light removal – 1.3 litre

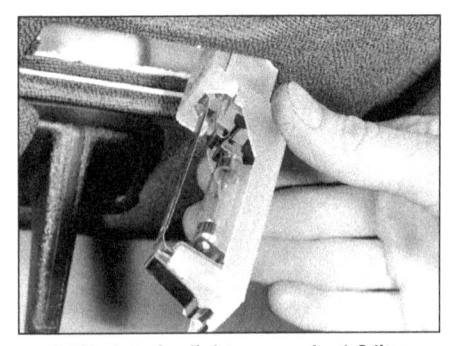

8.13b Interior light removal – 1.8 litre

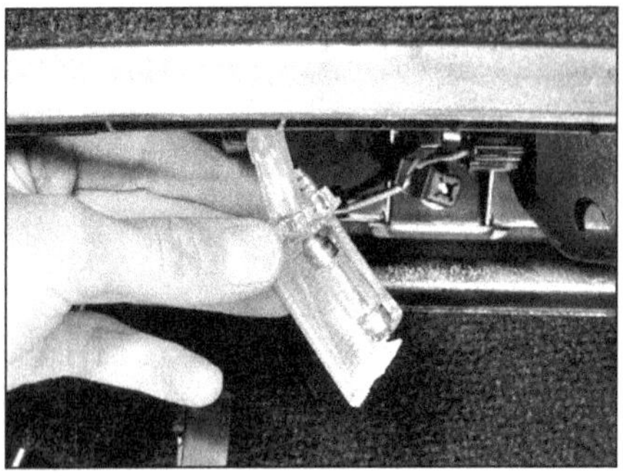

8.16 Luggage compartment lamp lens removal

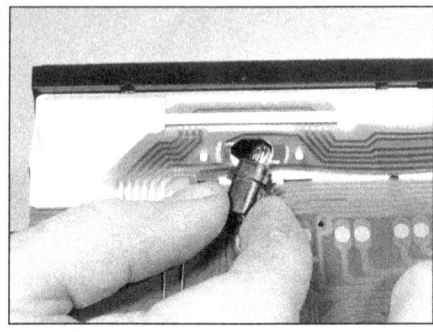

8.19 Instrument panel light bulb and holder removal

Body electrical systems 12•7

4 If the indicators do not function correctly, a series of tests may be done to find which part of the circuit is at fault.
5 The most common fault is in the flasher lamps, defective bulbs and dirty or corroded contacts or mountings. Check these first, then test the emergency switch. Remove it from the circuit and check its operation.
6 If the switch is in good order, refit it and again turn on the emergency lights. If nothing happens, then the relay is not functioning properly and it should be renewed.
7 If the lights function on emergency but not on operation of the column switch, then the wiring and column switch are suspect.

10 Warning lamp cluster - removal and refitting

1 Disconnect the battery earth lead.
2 Remove the facia control switches then, reaching through the vacant switch apertures in the facia, compress the retainers and push out the warning lamp cluster unit (see illustration).
3 Disconnect the multi-plug for full cluster removal.
4 Withdraw the warning light bulbholder from the cluster and pull free the bulb for inspection and, if necessary, renewal (see illustration).
5 Where two or more warning lamp bulbs are contained in a single mounting plate, the plate unit complete must be renewed as it is not possible to renew a single bulb in this instance.
6 Refit in the reverse order of removal. On completion, check the operation of the switches and warning light bulb(s).

11 Ignition switch/steering column lock - removal and refitting

This procedure is described in Chapter 10 for removal and refitting of the steering lock.

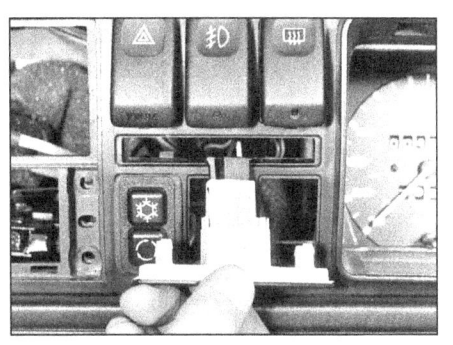

10.2 Warning lamp cluster removal

12 Combination switches - removal and refitting

1 Remove the steering wheel.
2 Disconnect the battery negative lead.
3 Remove the screws and withdraw the steering column lower shroud.
4 Remove the three screws securing the combination switch (see illustration).
5 Disconnect the multi-plugs (see illustration).
6 Rotate the indicator switch clockwise and withdraw it, noting location of the plastic retaining arms (see illustration).
7 Withdraw the wiper control switch from the column. Full removal of the switch of GTi models will necessitate detaching the additional wire from its connector under the dash panel (see illustrations).

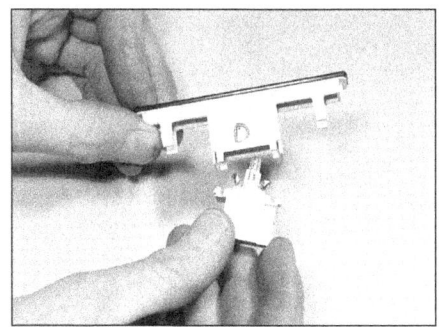

10.4 Warning lamp cluster bulbholder removal

8 Refitting is a reversal of the removal procedure. Check that the indicator switch is centralised before fitting the steering wheel otherwise the cancelling cams could be damaged.
9 Refit the steering wheel.
10 On completion, check the operation of the switches.

13 Facia switches - removal and refitting

1 Disconnect the battery earth lead.
2 To remove a rocker type switch such as the lighting switch, press the switch to the ON position then insert a suitable screwdriver blade into the notch at the base of the switch, and prise the switch free from the facia (see illustration).

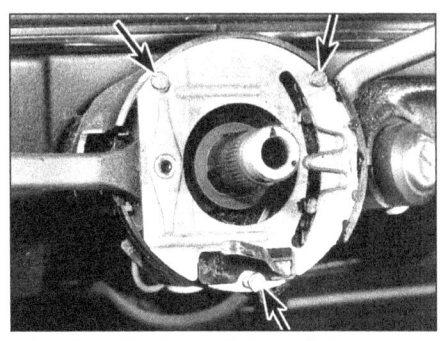

12.4 Combination switch retaining screws (arrowed)

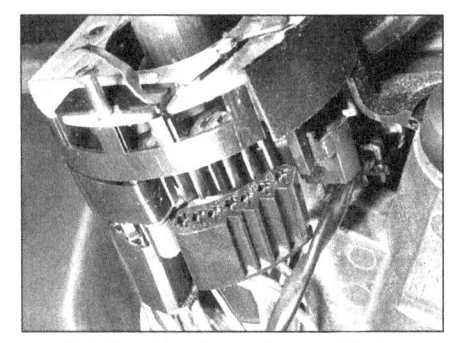

12.5 Combination switch multi-plug connections

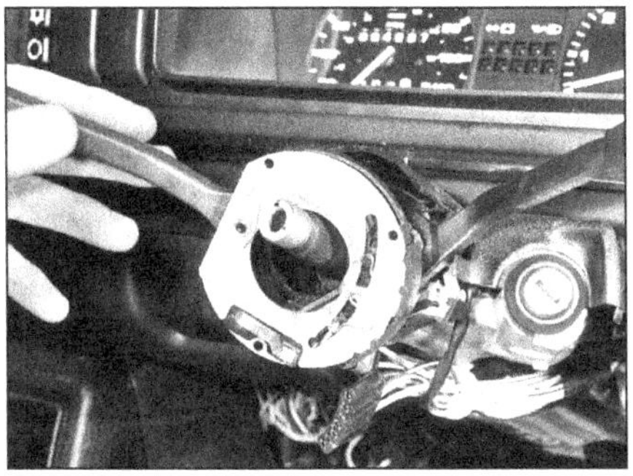

12.6 Removing indicator switch . . .

12.7a . . . and wiper control switch

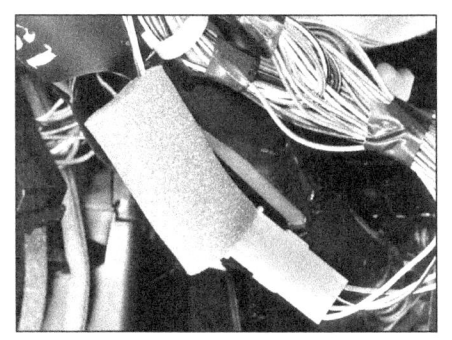

12.7b Additional under dash wiring connection and insulator – GTi

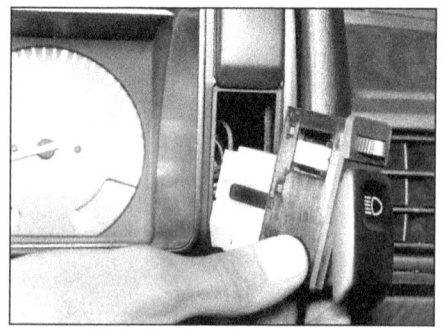

12•8 Body electrical systems

13.2 Facia switch removal

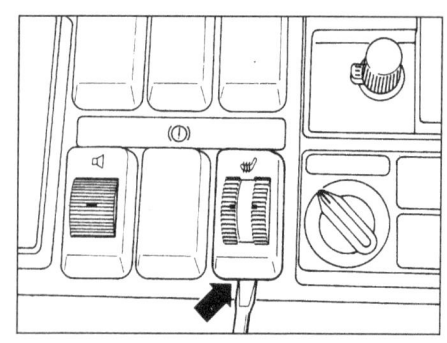

13.3 Prise free switch from bottom edge

14.2 Tailgate actuated luggage compartment light switch

3 On other switch types such as the heated rear seat switch, simply lever the switch free from the bottom edge **(see illustration)**.
4 With the switch withdrawn, detach the wiring connector. Where applicable, warning light bulb holders can be withdrawn from the switch and the bulb removed.
5 Refitting is a reversal of the removal procedure. Check the switch for satisfactory operation on completion.

14 Courtesy and luggage compartment light switches - removal and refitting

1 Disconnect the battery negative lead.
2 Open the door, boot lid or tailgate (as applicable) and unscrew the cross-head screw from the switch **(see illustration)**.
3 Withdraw the switch and disconnect the wiring. Tie a loose knot in the wire to prevent it from dropping into the door pillar **(see illustration)**.
4 Check the switch seal for condition and renew it, if necessary.
5 Refitting is a reversal of removal.

15 Oil pressure warning switches - testing

1 Some models are equipped with an optical and acoustic oil pressure warning system. This system incorporates two oil pressure switches, a 0.3 bar switch with brown insulation on the cylinder head and a 1.8 bar switch with white insulation on the oil filter head.
2 On starting the engine, as soon as the oil pressure rises above 0.3 bar, the oil pressure warning light will go out. At engine speeds above 2000 rpm, the high pressure switch comes into operation and should the oil pressure drop below 1.8 bar, the oil warning light will come on and the buzzer will sound.
3 Testing each switch should be done by substitution. Little can be done by way of maintenance and your VW dealer should be consulted if the system malfunctions.

16 Instrument panel cluster - removal and refitting

1 Disconnect the battery earth lead.
2 Remove the facia panel.
3 Remove the instrument panel retaining screws (one each side at the top) **(see illustration)**.
4 Prise the panel away, tilting from the top edge. Reach behind the panel and disconnect the speedometer cable **(see illustration)** and, where applicable, the vacuum hose from the vacuum sender. Detach the wiring multi-connectors from the rear lower edge then lift the instrument panel out whilst taking care not to damage the printed circuit on its rear face.
5 The individual circuits of the printed circuit foil can be checked for continuity using an ohmmeter. For circuit identification, refer to the appropriate wiring diagram.
6 Refitting is a reversal of the removal sequence. Ensure that all connections are securely made and check instruments for satisfactory operation on completion.

17 Instrument panel - dismantling, testing and reassembly

Dismantling

1 Remove the instrument panel cluster.
2 Remove the relevant instrument **(see illustrations)** whilst taking particular care not to damage the printed circuit foil.

Gearchange/consumption indicator

3 If renewing the gearchange/consumption indicator, avoid touching the back of the gauge. Removal necessitates detaching the printed circuit and the vacuum sender unit then undoing the three securing screws **(see illustration)**. Renew the diode (LED) or consumption indicator unit, as necessary.

Clock - normal type

4 When renewing the normal type clock (which incorporates the fuel gauge), it is important to ensure that the correct printed circuit connections are made when refitting **(see illustration)**.

Clock - digital type

5 The digital type clock is secured by two retaining screws. When removing the clock, take care not to allow the adjuster pins for the hours and minutes to fall out.

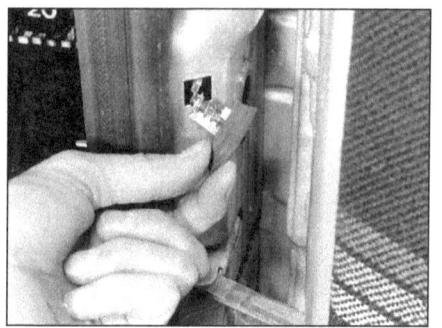

14.3 Door courtesy light switch removal

16.3 Instrument panel screw removal

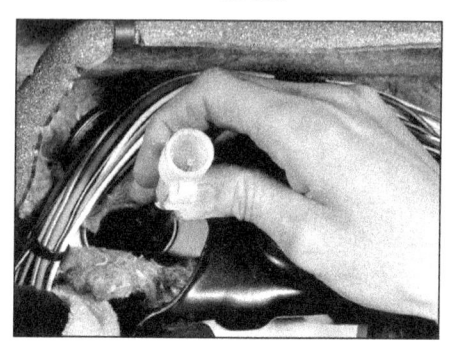

16.4 Disconnect speedometer cable

17.2a Instrument panel unit components – type A

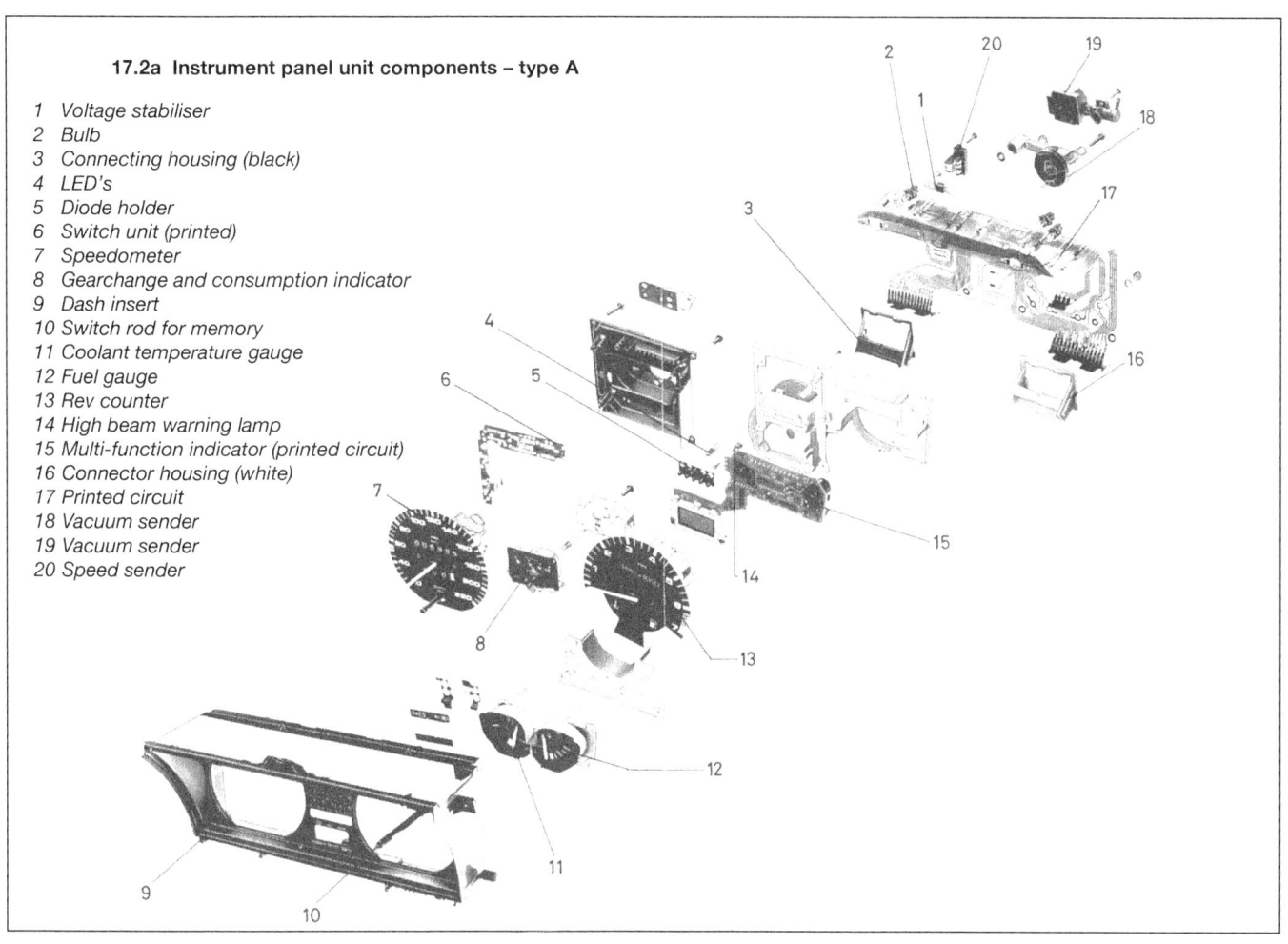

1 Voltage stabiliser
2 Bulb
3 Connecting housing (black)
4 LED's
5 Diode holder
6 Switch unit (printed)
7 Speedometer
8 Gearchange and consumption indicator
9 Dash insert
10 Switch rod for memory
11 Coolant temperature gauge
12 Fuel gauge
13 Rev counter
14 High beam warning lamp
15 Multi-function indicator (printed circuit)
16 Connector housing (white)
17 Printed circuit
18 Vacuum sender
19 Vacuum sender
20 Speed sender

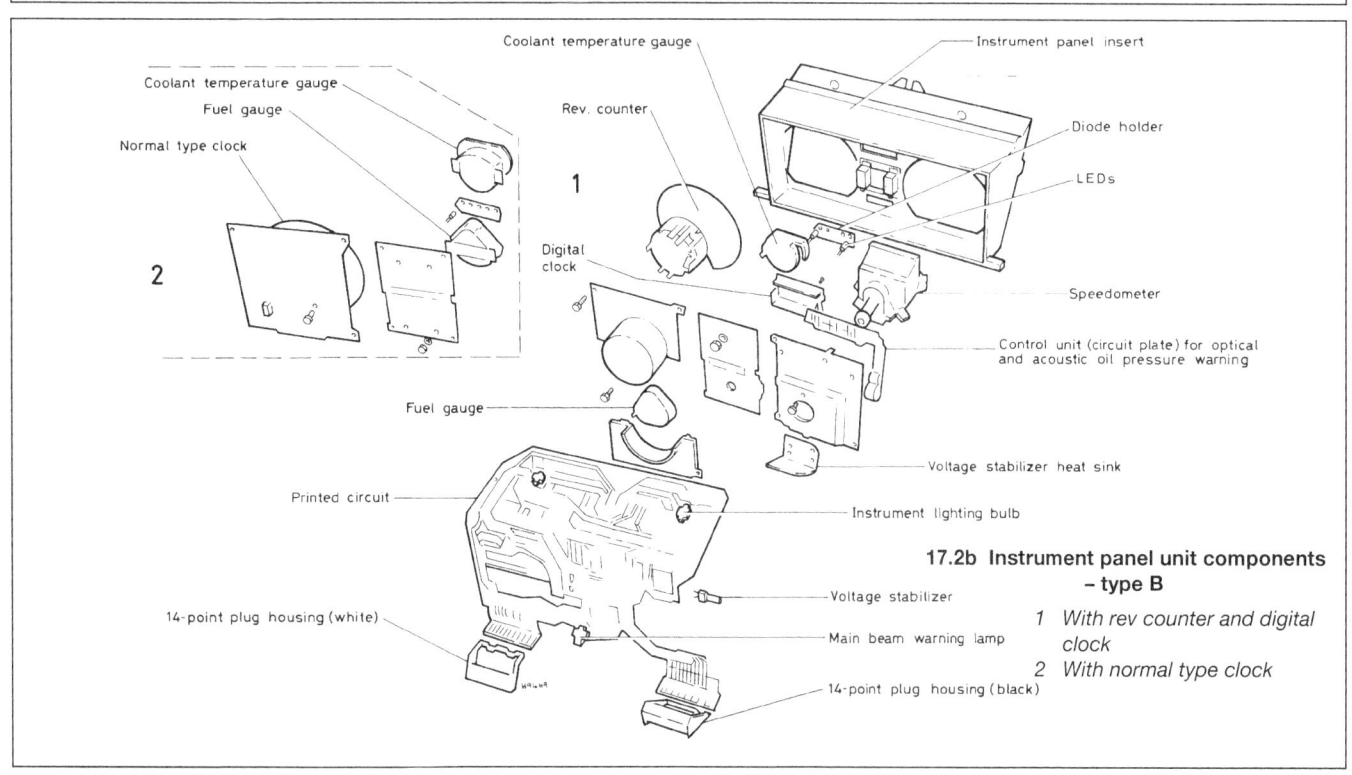

17.2b Instrument panel unit components – type B

1 With rev counter and digital clock
2 With normal type clock

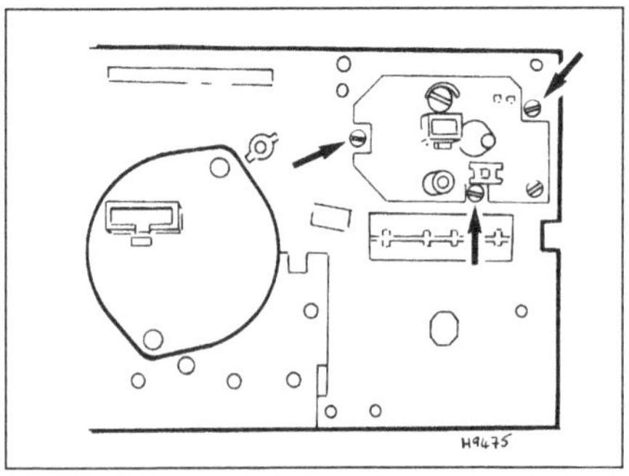

17.3 Gearchange and fuel indicator unit retaining screws (arrowed)

17.4 Normal type clock connections
1 Earth connection
2 Plus (+) live connection

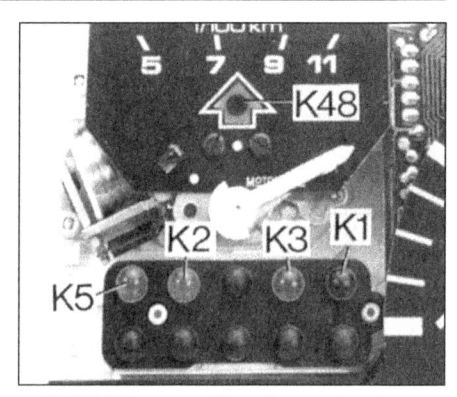

17.6 LED connections in warning lamp housing

K1 Main beam (blue)
K2 Alternator (red)
K3 Oil pressure (red)
K5 Indicators (green)
K48 Gearchange indicator (yellow)

LED indicators

6 The warning lamp LED indicators in the lamp housing are positioned as shown **(see illustration)**. When renewing the LEDs, each diode can be pulled free from the retainer plate. Note that one of the connector prongs is wider. This is the negative connection and it is important that it is correctly refitted. If necessary, the diode holder unit can be removed by carefully levering it free from the warning lamp housing.

Printed circuit foil

7 If renewing the printed circuit foil, it should be noted that a common type may be supplied for all models. If fitting a new printed circuit foil to the dash insert on models with a normal type clock, it may be necessary to cut off the connector pins used for the digital clock and vice versa for models with the digital clock. Check this with your supplier.

Plug housing

8 To remove the plug housing from the instrument panel insert, use a screwdriver to press the plastic rib on the housing over the engagement lugs and pull the housing with printed circuit in the direction of the arrow **(see illustration)**. The plug housing can be removed from the printed circuit by pressing free the engagement lugs and pulling the housing away from the printed circuit in the direction of the arrow shown **(see illustration)**.

Tachometer/VDO multi-function indicator

9 If removing the tachometer, first remove the gearshift and fuel consumption indicator then undo the two retaining screws **(see illustration)** and remove the tachometer, together with the multi-function indicator (printed circuit). The VDO type multi-function indicator can then be removed by undoing the retaining screws, pressing the retaining lugs from the printed circuit and withdrawing the indicator unit **(see illustration)**.

Motometer multi-function indicator

10 The Motometer type multi-function indicator is removed in a similar manner to that given for the VDO type indicator **(see illustration)**.

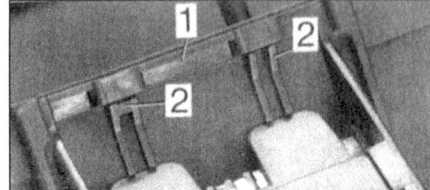

17.8a Plug housing detachment from instrument panel insert
1 Plastic rib
2 Engagement lugs
Pull housing in direction of arrow

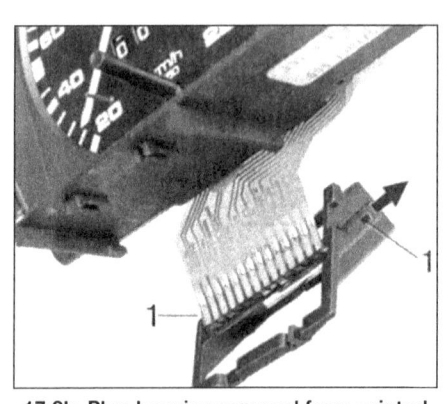

17.8b Plug housing removal from printed circuit
1 Engagement lugs
Pull housing in direction of arrow

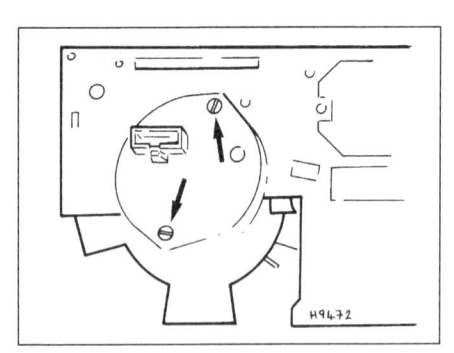

17.9a Tachometer retaining screws (arrowed)

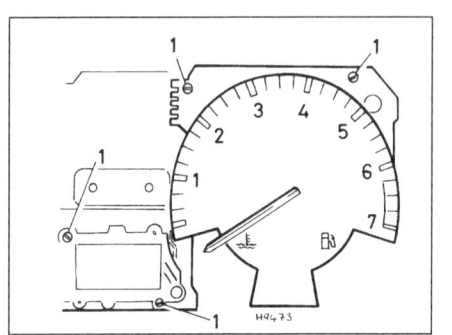

17.9b Multi-function indicator (VDO type) and retaining screws (1)

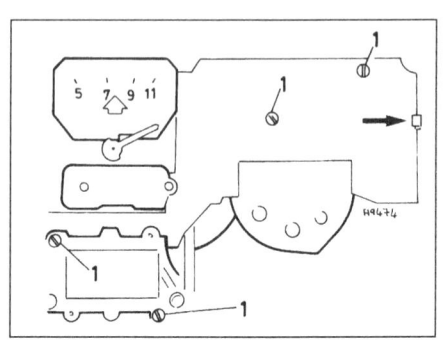

17.10 Multi-function indicator (Motometer type) and retaining screws (1)

Body electrical systems 12•11

Component testing

Voltage stabiliser

11 To test the voltage stabiliser, connect a voltmeter between the terminals shown **(see illustration)** with a 12 volt supply to the remaining terminal. A constant voltage of 10 volts must be registered. If the voltage is above 10.5 volts or below 9.5 volts renew the voltage stabiliser.

Fuel gauge

12 The accuracy of the fuel gauge can be checked by draining the fuel tank and then adding exactly 5 litres of fuel. After leaving the ignition switched on for at least two minutes the fuel gauge needle should be level with the upper edge of the red reserve zone. If not, either the fuel gauge or tank unit is faulty.

Printed circuits

13 The individual circuits of the printed circuit foil can be checked for continuity using an ohmmeter and referring to the appropriate wiring diagram.

Reassembly

14 Reassembly of the instrument panel is a reversal of the dismantling procedure.

18 Facia trim panel - removal and refitting

1 Disconnect the battery earth lead.
2 To improve accessibility, remove the steering wheel.

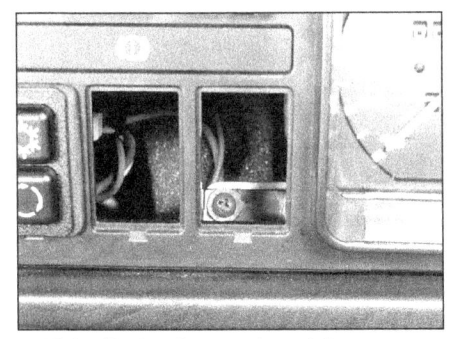

18.6a Facia trim panel retaining screw through fader control aperture

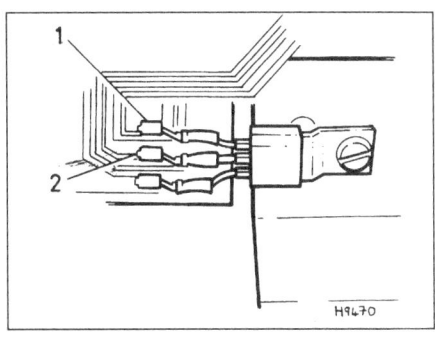

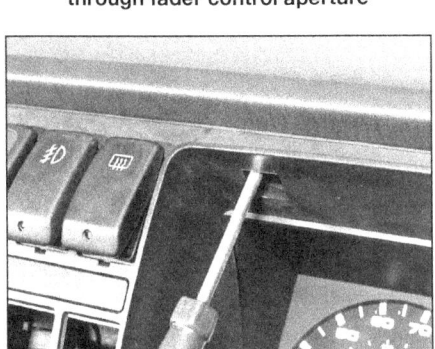

18.6b Remove instrument panel retaining screws at top

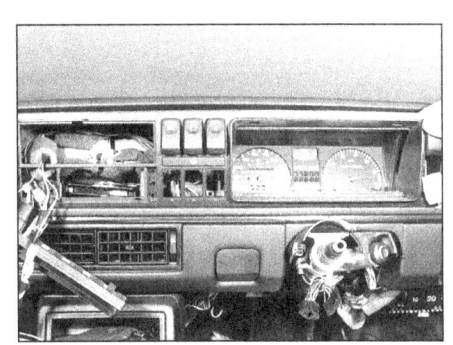

17.11 Voltage stabiliser test terminals

Connect a voltmeter between 1 and 2

3 Remove the radio.
4 Pull free the heater/fresh air control lever knobs, then release the control panel retaining clips around the outer edge and pull out the panel. Detach the wiring multi-connectors.
5 Remove the lower switches from the facia panel and where applicable, remove the blank pads by prising them free.
6 Unscrew the facia trim panel retaining screws from the following locations:
a) Light switch aperture
b) Top inner edge of radio aperture
c) Fader control (or blank) aperture **(see illustration)**
d) Heater control panel aperture
e) Top of the instrument panel **(see illustration)**
f) Top left side of panel
7 Partially withdraw the panel and detach any remaining switch lead multi-connectors. Remove the facia panel **(see illustration)**.
8 Refit in the reverse order of removal, ensuring that all wiring connections are securely made.
9 On completion, check for correct operation of the various switches and controls.

19 Multi-function indicator - operation and testing

Some models are equipped with a multi-function indicator consisting of an electronic processor and digital display unit.

18.7 Facia trim panel removal

With the ignition switched on, the following information can be accessed by repeatedly pressing the MFA recall button on the end of the windscreen wiper control stalk.
  Current time
  Driving time
  Distance driven
  Average speed
  Average fuel consumption
  Engine oil temperature
  Ambient temperature

Should a fault occur in the system, the associated wiring should be checked for security and damage, particularly where it connects to the various sensors. Further checks should be made by a VW dealer using the special test instruments necessary.

20 Gearchange and consumption gauge - operation

1 When fitted, the gearchange and consumption gauge is fitted in the instrument panel in place of the coolant temperature gauge.
2 The gearchange indicator lights up in all gears except top gear when better economy without loss of power can be obtained by changing up to a higher gear. The indicator does not operate during acceleration or deceleration, or on carburettor engines when the engine is cold.
3 The gearchange indicator light goes out when a higher gear is engaged .
4 On automatic transmission models, the gearchange indicator is non-operational since all forward gears are automatically changed in accordance with engine speed/output and vehicle speed.
5 The fuel consumption indicator operates only in top gear (D in automatic transmission models) and indicates the actual fuel consumption in mpg.
6 The gearchange and consumption gauge is operated by a switch on the gearbox and a sender in the vacuum line to the distributor **(see illustration)**.

20.6 Fuel consumption gauge sender unit

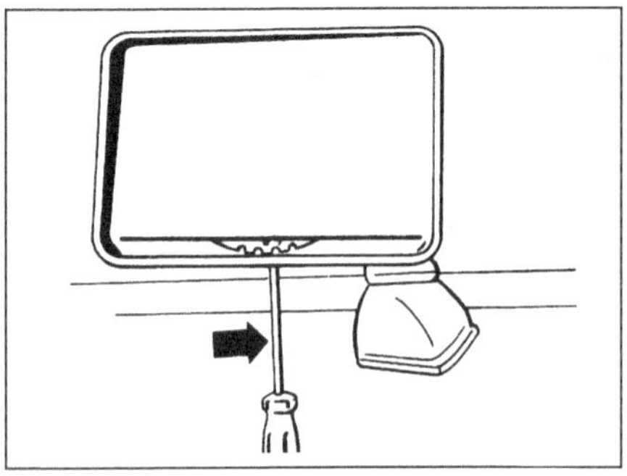

12•12 Body electrical systems

23.2 Turn retainer anti-clockwise for electrically-operated door mirror removal

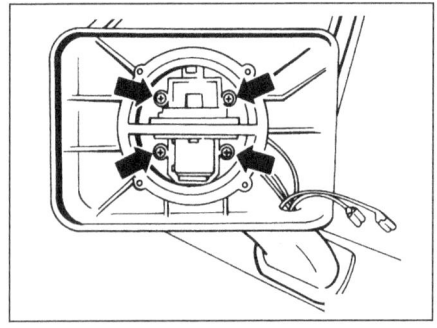

23.4 Mirror motor retaining screws (arrowed)

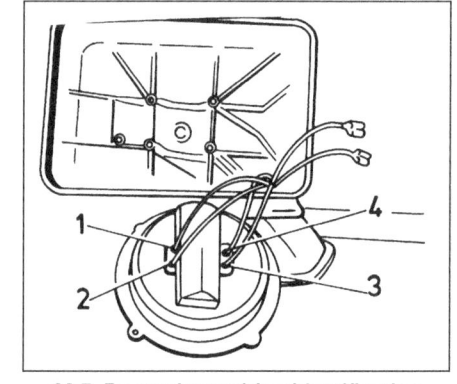

23.7 Door mirror wiring identification
1 Blue   3 White
2 Brown   4 Black

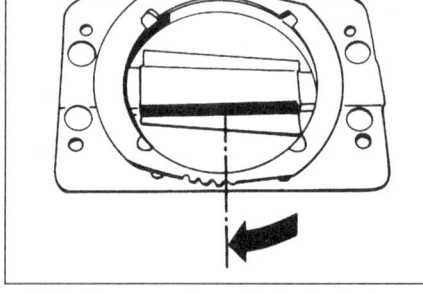

23.8 Rotate retainer clockwise before fitting glass

21 Cigarette lighter - removal and refitting

1 Disconnect the battery negative lead.
2 Remove the lower facia panel then reach up and disconnect the wiring from the cigarette lighter.
3 Remove the retaining ring and withdraw the cigarette lighter from the facia.
4 Refitting is a reversal of removal.

22 Speedometer cable - removal and refitting

1 Open the bonnet, then either unscrew the cable retaining collar, or the retaining plate bolt, and withdraw the cable from the transmission.
2 Withdraw the instrument panel far enough to disconnect the cable.
3 Remove the air cleaner.
4 Carefully unclip and detach the plastic cover from the top edge of the bulkhead. Pull the speedometer cable through the bulkhead and withdraw it from the engine compartment side.
5 Refitting is a reversal of removal. Ensure that the grommet is correctly fitted in the bulkhead and that there are no sharp bends in the cable. Do not grease the cable ends.

23 Electrically-operated door mirror motor - removal and refitting

1 Disconnect the battery earth lead.
2 Release the mirror glass by rotating the retainer anti-clockwise with a suitable screwdriver **(see illustration)**.
3 Remove the mirror and disconnect the wiring.
4 Undo the four retaining screws and withdraw the mirror motor **(see illustration)**. Detach the wiring from the motor.
5 Carefully lever free the door mirror adjuster switch from the trim panel and withdraw it

so that the multi-connector plug can be detached.
6 Further removal of the wiring will necessitate door trim removal.
7 Refitting is a reversal of the removal procedure. Note that the mirror motor wires are colour-coded for correct reconnection **(see illustration)**.
8 When refitting the mirror glass, rotate the retainer in a clockwise direction to its full extent then carefully insert the glass into its housing **(see illustration)**.

24 Horn - removal and refitting

1 If a single horn is fitted it will be located behind the radiator grille. On models with two horns the additional high tone horn is located under the forward section of the front left-hand wheel arch **(see illustrations)**.
2 To remove the horn, first disconnect the battery negative lead.
3 For access to the low tone horn, remove the radiator grille.
4 Unscrew the mounting bolt, disconnect the wires and withdraw the horn.
5 If the horn emits an unsatisfactory sound, it may be possible to adjust it by removing the sealant from the adjusting screw and turning it one way or the other.
6 Refitting is a reversal of removal. Check that the horn(s) operate in a satisfactory manner.

25 Wiper blades - renewal

Refer to "Weekly Checks"

26 Wiper arms - removal and refitting

1 Ensure that the wiper arms are in their parked position then remove the wiper blade.
2 Lift the hinged cover and unscrew the nut **(see illustration)**.

24.1a Single horn location behind front grille

24.1b High tone horn location – twin horn installation

Body electrical systems 12•13

26.2 Undo wiper arm nut . . .

26.3 . . . and withdraw arm from spindle

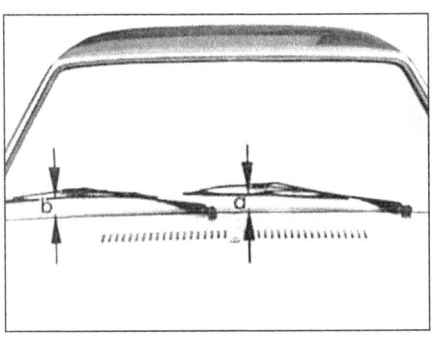

26.5 Windscreen wiper blade setting positions

$a = 55.0$ mm $\qquad b = 59.0$ mm

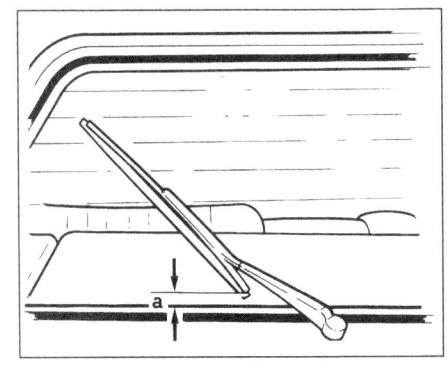

3 Ease the wiper arm from the spindle, taking care not to damage the paintwork (see illustration).
4 Refitting is a reversal of removal.
5 In the parked position, the end of the wiper arm (ie. middle of the blade), should be positioned as shown (see illustration).
6 On the rear window, the dimension should be measured at the points shown (see illustration).

3 Unscrew the nut and remove the crank from the motor spindle.
4 Disconnect the wiring multi-plug (see illustration).
5 Unscrew the bolts and withdraw the wiper motor from the frame.
6 Refitting is a reversal of removal. When fitting the crank to the spindle (motor in parked position), ensure that the marks are aligned (see illustration).

26.6 Rear window wiper adjustment position

$a = 15.0$ mm

27 Windscreen wiper motor - removal and refitting

28 Rear window wiper motor - removal and refitting

1 Open the bonnet and disconnect the battery negative lead.
2 Pull the weatherstrip from the front of the plenum chamber and remove the plastic cover.

1 Disconnect the battery negative lead.
2 Open the tailgate and prise off the inner trim panel.
3 Remove the wiper arm and unscrew the outer nut. Remove the spacers.

4 Undo the bearing retaining bolts and the motor mounting bolts. Withdraw the motor and disconnect the wiring plug (see illustrations).
5 If detaching the crank and connecting rod from the wiper motor pivot, mark a corresponding alignment position across the crank arm and pivot end face. Undo the nut to detach the crank arm.
6 The wiper motor is secured to the mounting by three bolts.
7 Refitting is a reversal of the removal procedure. Correctly align the crank arm when refitting so that the wiper arm will park correctly (see illustration).

27.4 Windscreen wiper motor showing multi-plug connection and retaining bolts

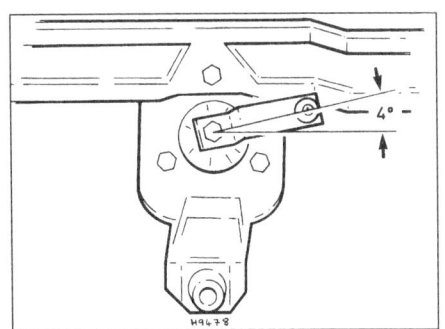

27.6 Windscreen wiper motor bellcrank angle (motor at rest)

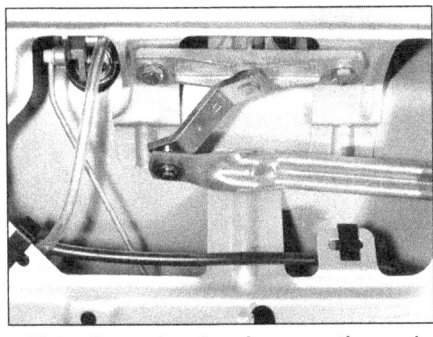

28.4a Rear wiper bearing mounting and connecting rod

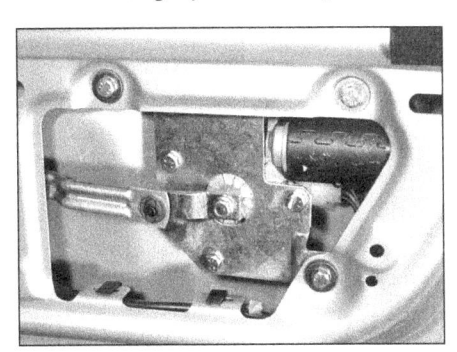

28.4b Rear wiper motor mounting in tailgate

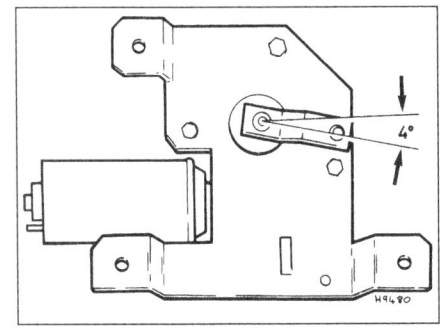

28.7 Rear wiper motor bellcrank angle

12•14 Body electrical systems

29.2a Windscreen wiper components

- Wiper arm
- Wiper rubber
- Protective cap
- Connection rods
- Wiper frame
- Wiper bearing
- Windscreen wiper motor
- Crank

29.2b Rear window wiper components

- Wiper rubber
- Wiper arm
- Protection cap
- Jets
- Wiper bearing
- Connecting rod
- Rear wiper motor
- Crank
- Pump
- Fluid container

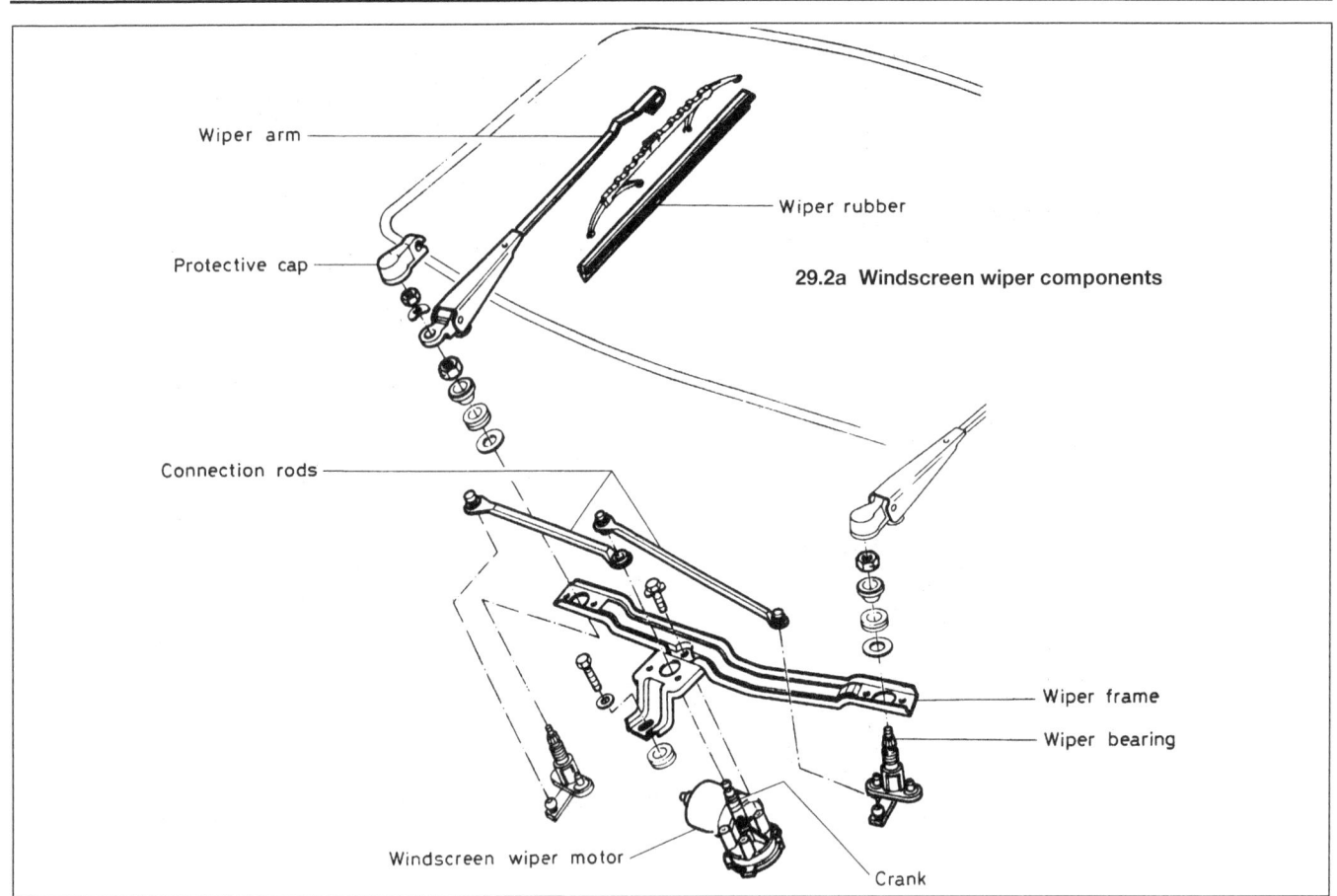

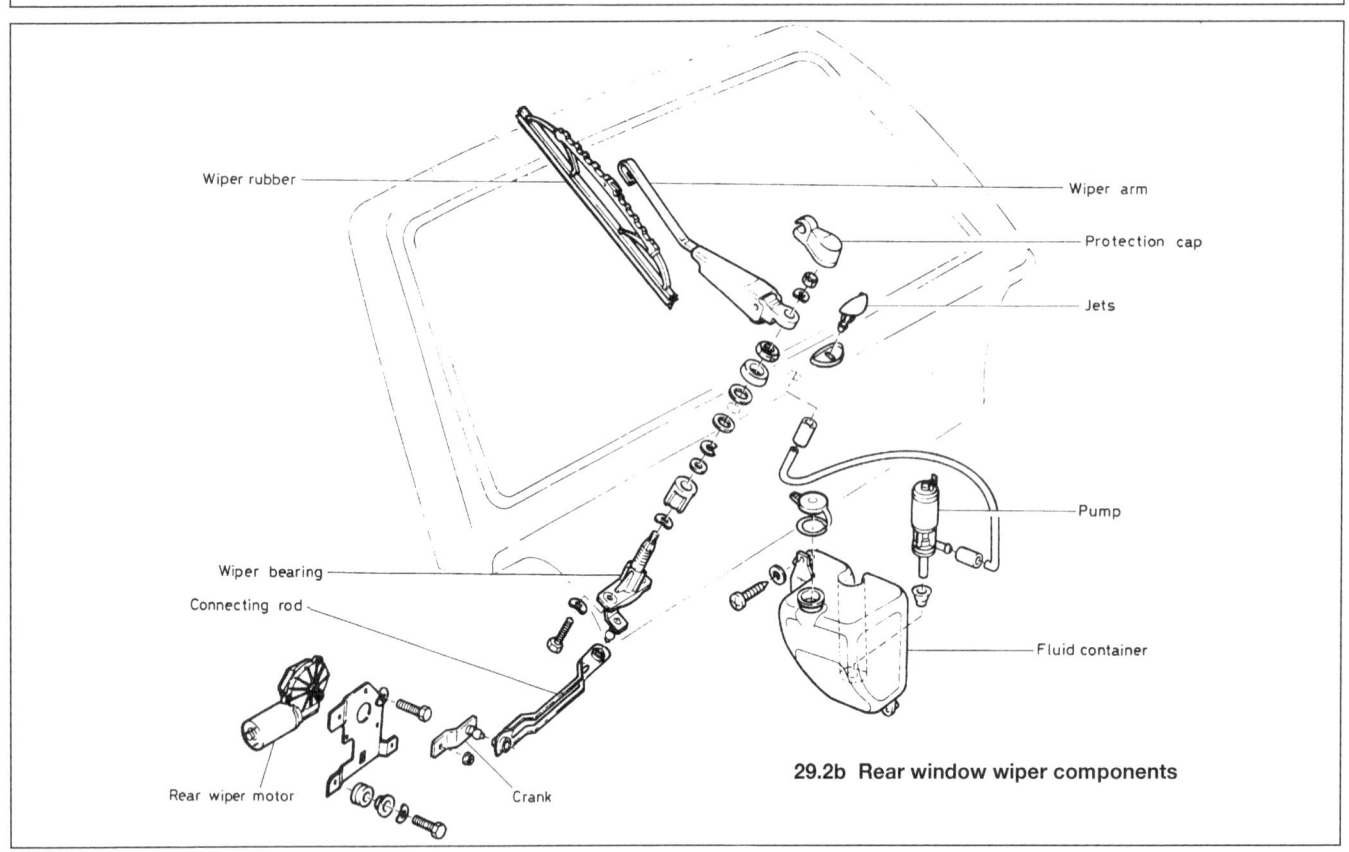

Body electrical systems 12•15

30.1 Windscreen washer pump and wire connector

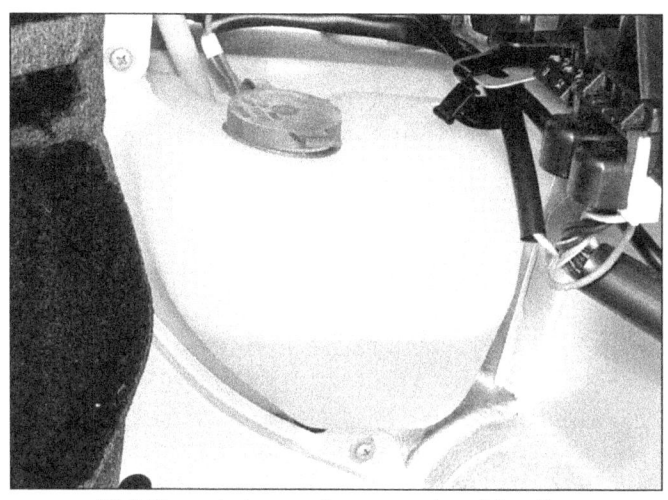

30.2 Rear window washer reservoir unit location

29 Windscreen wiper linkage - removal and refitting

1 Disconnect the battery negative lead.
2 Remove the wiper arms, then unscrew the bearing nuts and remove the spacers **(see illustrations)**.
3 Pull the weatherstrips from the front of the plenum chamber and remove the plastic cover.
4 Disconnect the wiring multi-plug.
5 Unscrew the frame mounting bolt, then withdraw the assembly from the bulkhead.
6 Prise the pullrods from the motor crank and bearing levers.
7 Unbolt the wiper motor from the frame.
8 Refitting is a reversal of removal. Lubricate the bearing units and pullrod joints with molybdenum disulphide grease.

30 Windscreen and headlamp washer system - pump renewal

Pre 1986

1 The windscreen washer fluid reservoir is located on the left-hand side of the engine compartment. The pump is fitted to the side of the reservoir **(see illustration)**.
2 The rear window washer reservoir is located on the right-hand side rear corner of the luggage compartment. The pump is attached to the side of the reservoir **(see illustration)**.
3 In either case, remove the pump by disconnecting its electrical connection and pulling the pump upwards out of the reservoir orifice. Be prepared for loss of water from the reservoir.
4 To fit the pump, locate a new seal in the reservoir orifice and push the pump into it so that it is firmly home. Reconnect the electrical connection.

From 1986

5 From early 1986, the washer system is modified and now has a single reservoir and pump located in the engine compartment, with a plastic tube to the rear window incorporated in the rear wiring loom. The wiper motor switch incorporates two sets of contacts which energise the pump with opposite polarities, causing rotation of the pump vane in two alternative directions. Using in-line non-return valves, water is directed either to the windscreen or rear window according to which direction the pump is rotating.

31 Radio/cassette player - removal and refitting

1 Disconnect the battery earth lead.
2 To withdraw the radio/cassette unit from its aperture, you will need to fabricate a pair of U-shaped extractors from wire rod of suitable gauge to insert into the withdrawal slots on each side of the unit **(see illustration)**.
3 Insert the withdrawal tools then, pushing each outwards simultaneously, pull them evenly to withdraw the radio/cassette unit. It is important that an equal pressure is applied to each tool as the unit is withdrawn.
4 Once withdrawn from its aperture, disconnect the aerial cable, the power lead, the aerial feed, the speaker plugs, the earth lead and the light and memory feed (where applicable).
5 Push the retaining clips inwards to remove the removal tool from each side **(see illustration)**.
6 The radio/cassette container box is secured by locking tabs. To remove the container box, bend back the tabs and withdraw the box **(see illustration)**.
7 Refit in the reverse order of removal. The withdrawal tools do not have to be used, simply push the unit into its aperture until the securing clips engage in their slots.

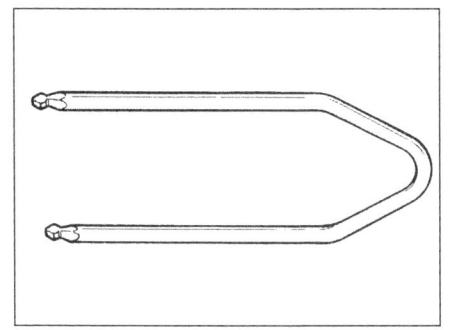

31.2 Radio/cassette extractor tool

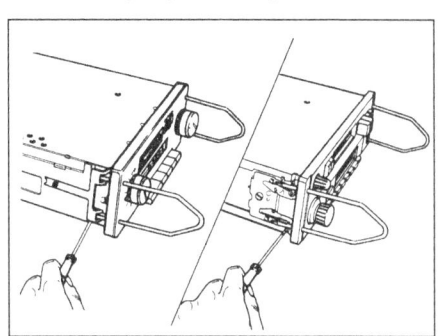

31.5 Releasing radio extractor tool

31.6 Radio/cassette container removal

12•16 Body electrical systems

32.3 Facia-mounted loudspeaker retaining screws (arrowed)

32.5 Luggage compartment loudspeaker retaining nuts (arrowed)

32 Loudspeakers - removal and refitting

1 Disconnect the battery earth lead.

Facia-mounted speakers

2 Carefully prise free the small square plastic cap covering the screw head in the speaker grille then undo and remove the screw. Lift the speaker grille clear.
3 Undo the two screws securing the speaker unit and lift the speaker out far enough to enable the leads to be disconnected **(see illustration)**.
4 Refit in the reverse order of removal.

Luggage compartment speakers

5 Undo the retaining nuts from underneath, withdraw the loudspeaker unit and detach the wiring connector **(see illustration)**.
6 Refit in reverse order of removal.

33 Wiring diagrams - general information

Each wiring diagram covers a particular system of the appropriate vehicle, as indicated in its caption. Carefully read the Key to each diagram before commencing work.

Wiring diagrams

Key for all wiring diagrams

No	Description
A	Battery
B	Starter
C	Alternator
C1	Voltage regulator
D	Ignition switch
E1	Lighting switch
E2	Indicator switch
E3	Hazard warning light switch
E4	Headlight dip and flasher switch
E9	Fresh air blower switch
E15	Heated rear window switch
E17	Starter/inhibitor and reversing light switch
E19	Parking light switch
E20	Instrument/dash insert lighting control
E22	Intermittent wiper switch
E23	Foglight and rear foglight switch
E39	Electric window switch
E40	Electric window switch, left
E41	Electric window switch, right
E43	Mirror adjustment switch
E48	Mirror adjustment changeover switch
E52	Electric window switch, rear left, in door
E53	Electric window switch, rear left, in console
E54	Electric window switch, rear right, in door
E55	Electric window switch, rear right, in console
E86	Call-up button for multi-function indicator
E102	Headlight beam adjuster
E109	Memory switch for multi-function indicator
F	Brake light switch
F1	Oil pressure switch (1.8 bar)
F2	Door contact switch, front left
F3	Door contact switch, front right
F4	Reversing light switch
F5	Boot light
F9	Handbrake warning switch
F10	Thermo-switch for radiator fan
F18	Radiator fan thermal switch
F22	Oil pressure switch (0.3 bar)
F25	Throttle valve switch
F26	Thermo-switch for choke
F34	Brake fluid level warning contact
F35	Thermo-switch for intake preheating
F59	Central locking system switch
F60	Idle switch
F62	Gearchange indicator vacuum switch
F66	Low level coolant switch
F68	Switch for gearchange and consumption indicator
F69	Central locking switch (driver's door)
F80	Thermo-switch for N52
F81	Full-throttle switch
F87	Thermo-switch for radiator from run-on
F89	Switch for accelerator enrichment
F93	Vacuum timeswitch
G	Fuel gauge sender
G1	Fuel gauge
G2	Coolant temperature sender
G3	Coolant temperature gauge
G5	Rev counter
G6	Fuel pump
G8	Oil temperature sender

No	Description
G17	Feeler for outside temperature
G18	Temperature sensor
G19	Potentiometer for airflow meter
G23	Electric fuel pump II
G32	Low coolant level indicator sender unit
G39	Lambda probe with heater
G40	Hall sender
G42	Intake air temperature sender
G51	Consumption indicator
G54	Speed sensor for multi-function indicator
G55	Vacuum sensor for multi-function indicator
G61	Knock sensor
G62	Coolant temperature sender unit
G114	Switch unit for oil pressure warning
H	Horn control
H1	Dual tone horn
J2	Indicators flasher relay
J4	Dual tone horn relay
J5	Foglight relay
J6	Voltage stabiliser
J17	Fuel pump relay
J20	Emergency lamp – trailer towing
J26	Radiator fan relay
J30	Rear wash/wipe relay
J31	Intermittent wash/wipe relay
J39	Headlamp wash system relay
J51	Electric window relay
J59	Relief valve (for X contact)
J81	Intake preheating relay
J86	Electronic ignition control unit
J88	Electronic ignition control unit (in plenum chamber, LH side)
J98	Gearchange indicator switch unit
J114	Oil pressure monitor switch unit
J119	Multi-function indicator
J120	Switch unit for low coolant indicator
J130	Switch unit for overrun cut-off valve
J134	Diode
J138	Control unit for radiator fan run-on
J143	Switch unit for speed increase
J147	Digijet control unit
J159	Control unit for idle speed stabiliser and overrun cut-off
J167	Digijet relay and idle speed stabilization unit
J169	Control unit for Digifant
J176	Digifant current supply and idle speed stabilization
K	Dash insert
K1	High beam warning lamp
K2	Alternator warning lamp
K3	Oil pressure warning lamp
K5	Indicators warning lamp
K6	Warning lamp for hazard lights
K7	Dual circuit and handbrake warning lamp
K10	Heated rear window warning lamp
K13	Rear foglight warning lamp
K17	Foglight warning lamp
K18	Trailer operation warning lamp
K28	Coolant temperature warning lamp (too hot, red)
K48	Gearchange indicator warning lamp
L1	Twin filament headlight bulb, left
L2	Twin filament headlight bulb, right

No	Description
L8	Clock light bulb
L9	Lighting switch bulb
L10	Dash insert bulb
L16	Fresh air control bulb
L19	Gear selector bulb
L20	Rear foglight bulb
L22	Foglight bulb
L23	Foglight bulb, right
L28	Cigarette lighter bulb
L39	Heated rear window switch bulb
L40	Foglight switch bulb
L52	Connection for fader control unit
L53	Electric window switch light
L54	Headlight beam adjuster bulb
L66	Cassette storage illumination
M1	Parking light bulb, left
M2	Tail light bulb, right
M3	Parking light bulb, right
M4	Tail light bulb, left
M5	Indicator bulb, front left
M6	Indicator bulb, rear left
M7	Indicator bulb, front right
M8	Indicator bulb, rear right
M9	Brake light bulb, left
M10	Brake light bulb, right
M16	Reversing light bulb, left
M17	Reversing light bulb, right
M18	Side indicator bulb, left
M19	Side indicator bulb, right
N	Ignition coil
N1	Automatic choke
N3	Bypass cut-off valve
N6	Resistance wire
N9	Warm-up valve
N10	Temperature sensor (NTC resistance)
N17	Cold start valve
N21	Auxiliary air valve
N23	Series resistance for fresh air blower
N30	Fuel injector, cylinder No 1
N31	Fuel injector, cylinder No 2
N32	Fuel injector, cylinder No 3
N33	Fuel injector, cylinder No 4
N35	Mirror adjustment solenoid (driver's side)
N39	Radiator fan series resistance
N41	TCI control unit
N42	Mirror adjustment solenoid, passenger's
N51	Heater element for manifold preheating
N52	Heater element for carburettor throttle passage
N60	Solenoid valve for consumption indicator
N62	Idling speed – acceleration valve
N65	Overrun cut-off valve
N68	Idling – overrun cut-off valve
N69	Thermotime valve for overrun cut-off
N71	Control valve for idling stabilisation
N98	Series resistance, headlamp dim-dip system (front right of engine compartment)
N113	Heater resistance for washer jets
O	Distributor
P	Spark plug connector
Q	Spark plug
R	Connection for radio
R9	Loudspeaker, front left
R10	Loudspeaker, front right

Key for all wiring diagrams (continued)

No	Description
S24	Overheating fuse
S27	Separate fuse for rear foglight
S37	Fuse for electric windows
T	Connector, behind relay plate
T1	Single connector, various locations
T1a	Single connector, various locations
T1b	Single connector, left of engine compartment or behind relay plate
T1c	Single connector, various locations
T1d	Single connector, various locations
T1e	Single connector, right of engine compartment or behind relay plate
T1f	Single connector, near carburettor or coil
T1g	Single connector, various locations
T1h	Single connector, behind relay plate
T1i	Single connector, behind relay plate
T1k	Single connector, behind relay plate or on radiator cowl
T11	Single connector, behind relay plate
T1m	Single connector, behind dash
T1n	Single connector, behind relay plate or near carburettor
T1p	Single connector, on radiator cowl
T1q	Single connector behind relay plate
Tr	Single connector – luggage boot
T1s	Single connector behind relay plate
T1v	Single connector behind steering wheel switch trim
T1x	Single connector, near coil
T1y	Single connector, near carburettor or behind relay
T2	2-pin connector, various locations
T2a	2-pin connector, various locations
T2b	2-pin connector, various locations
T2c	2-pin connector, left of boot or behind dash
T2d	2-pin connector, left of boot or behind dash (near inlet manifold on Digifant system)
T2e	2-pin connector, left of engine compartment
T2f	2-pin connector. various locations
T2g	2-pin connector, right of engine compartment
T2h	2-pin connector, left of engine compartment
T2i	2-pin connector, behind door trim
T2k	2-pin connector, various locations
T21	2-pin connector, behind dash or front of engine compartment
T2m	2-pin connector, behind dash
T2n	2-pin connector, behind dash
T20	2-pin connector, right of engine compartment
T2p	2-pin connector, various locations
T2q	2-pin connector, right of engine compartment
T2r	2-pin connector, behind door trim
T2s	2-pin connector, behind door trim
T2t	2-pin connector, behind door trim
T2u	2-pin connector, left of boot
T2v	2-pin connector, behind right A-pillar trim or in engine compartment
T2w	2-pin connector, behind dash
T2x	2-pin connector, front of engine compartment or behind dash

No	Description
T2y	2-pin connector, front of engine compartment
T2z	2-pin connector, behind left A-pillar trim
T3	3-pin connector, on throttle valve housing or behind relay plate
T3a	3-pin connector, behind relay plate (in plenum chamber on Digijet system)
T3b	3-pin connector, behind door trim (in rear of engine compartment on Digifant system)
T3c	3-pin connector, behind door trim
T3d	3-pin connector, behind door trim
T3e	3-pin connector, behind door trim
T3f	3-pin connector, behind right B-pillar trim
T3g	3-pin connector, behind left B-pillar trim (near starter on Digifant system)
T3h	3-pin connector, behind relay plate
T4	4-pin connector, behind dash (in plenum chamber on Digijet system)
T4a	4-pin connector, behind steering column trim (near inlet manifold on Digijet system)
T4c	4-pin connector, behind steering column trim
T5	5-pin connector on left of bulkhead
T5b	5-pin connector, behind steering column switch trim
T5c	5-pin connector, behind steering column switch trim
T5e	5-pin connector, on series resistance N23
T6	6-pin connector, behind relay plate
T6a	6-pin connector, rear left-hand tail lamp
T6b	6-pin connector, rear right-hand tail lamp
T7	7-pin connector, on dash insert or behind steering column trim
T7a	7-pin connector, on dash insert
T7b	7-pin connector, on dash insert
T7c	7-pin connector, on dash insert
T8	8-pin connector, on gearbox or behind dash
T16	16-pin connector, on multi-function indicator
T28	28-pin connector, on instrument panel
T32	32-pin connector, behind facia panel
U	Socket
U1	Cigarette lighter
V	Windscreen wiper motor
V2	Fresh air blower
V5	Windscreen washer pump
V7	Radiator fan
V11	Headlight washer pump
V12	Wiper motor
V13	Washer pump motor
V14	Window motor, left
V15	Window motor, right
V17	Mirror adjustment motor, driver's
V25	Mirror adjustment motor, passenger's
V26	Window motor, rear left
V27	Window motor, rear right
V37	Central locking motor
V48	Headlight motor, left
V49	Headlight motor, right
V59	Washer pump
W	Interior light, front

No	Description
W3	Boot light
W6	Glovebox light
W15	Delayed interior light
X	Number plate light
Y2	Digital clock
Z1	Heated rear window
Z4	Heated mirror, driver's
Z5	Heated mirror, passenger's
Z20	Heater resistance, LH washer jet
Z21	Heater resistance, RH washer jet

Earth connections

No	Description
1	Battery earth strap
10	Near relay plate
12	On cylinder head cover or distributor
14	Near steering column or in tailgate
15	In front loom or on cylinder head
16	In instrument loom
17	In instrument loom
17	On intake manifold (1989 on)
18	On cylinder block
19	In boot on right
20	On front seat crossmember, in tailgate or in instrument loom
21	In electric window loom
22	In electric window loom
23	In electric window loom
30	In front loom or next to relay plate
42	Next to steering column
44	Base of LH A-pillar
46	Next to relay plate
50	In boot on left
51	In boot on right
54	On rear cross panel
63	Bulbholder, left-hand tail lamp
64	Bulbholder, right-hand tail lamp
80	In instrument loom
81	In instrument loom
82	In front loom
84	Engine block wiring loom
85	In engine compartment wiring loom
89	In electric window loom
94	In Digifant wiring loom
107	In exterior mirror wiring loom
108	In front loom
116	In Digijet wiring loom
119	In headlamp wiring loom
120	In headlamp wiring loom
A11	In instrument loom
C3	Positive (+) connector (30) in headlamp wiring loom
C10	Positive connector (30) in headlamp wiring loom
E1	Positive (+) connector in Digijet wiring loom
G3	Positive (+) connector in cable sleeve – injector
G4	Connector in cable sleeve – injector
Q1	In electric window loom
Q9	In window lift wiring loom
X1	Positive connector (15) in carburettor wiring loom

Wiring diagrams 12•19

Wiring diagrams – layout explanation

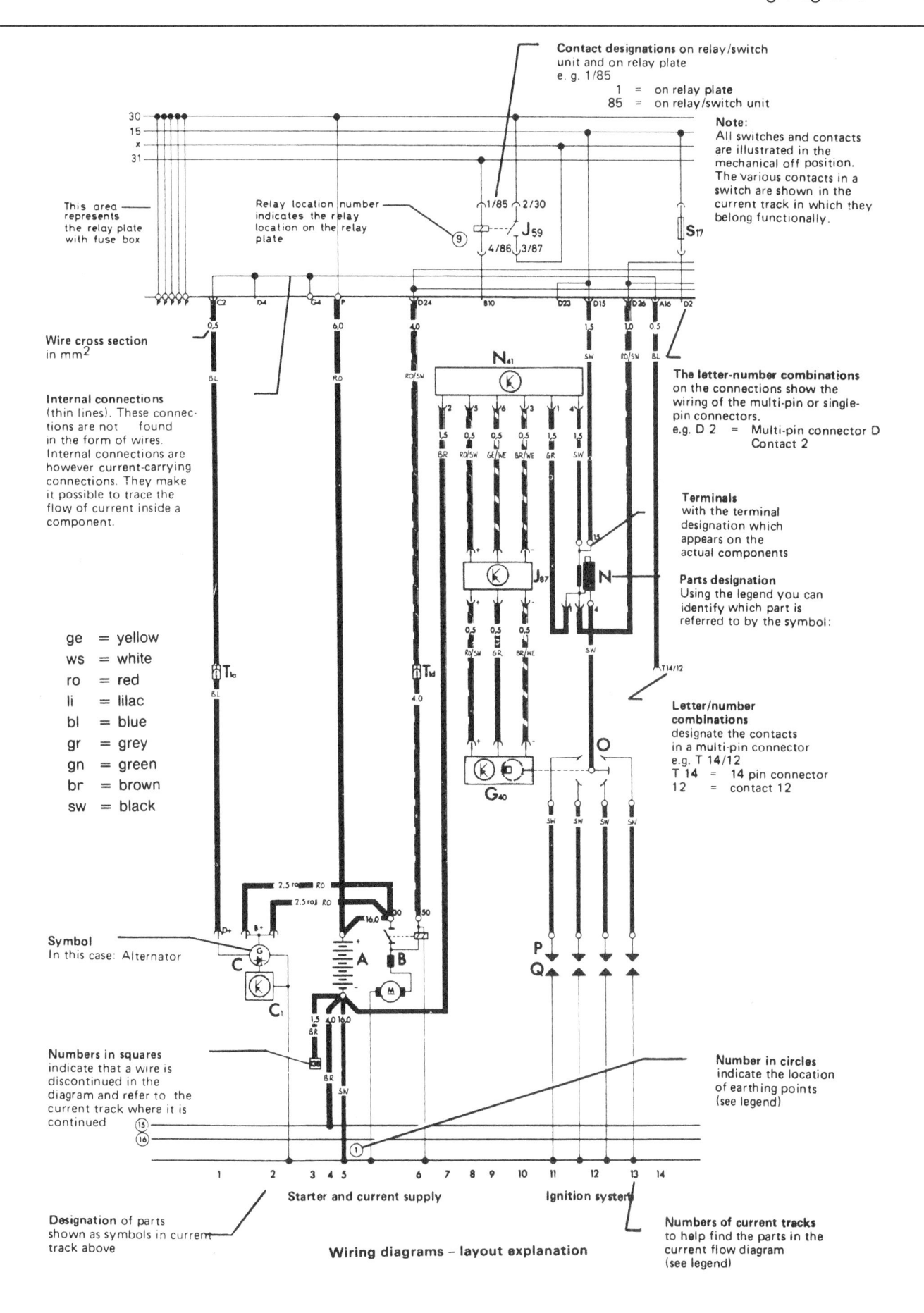

12•20 Wiring diagrams

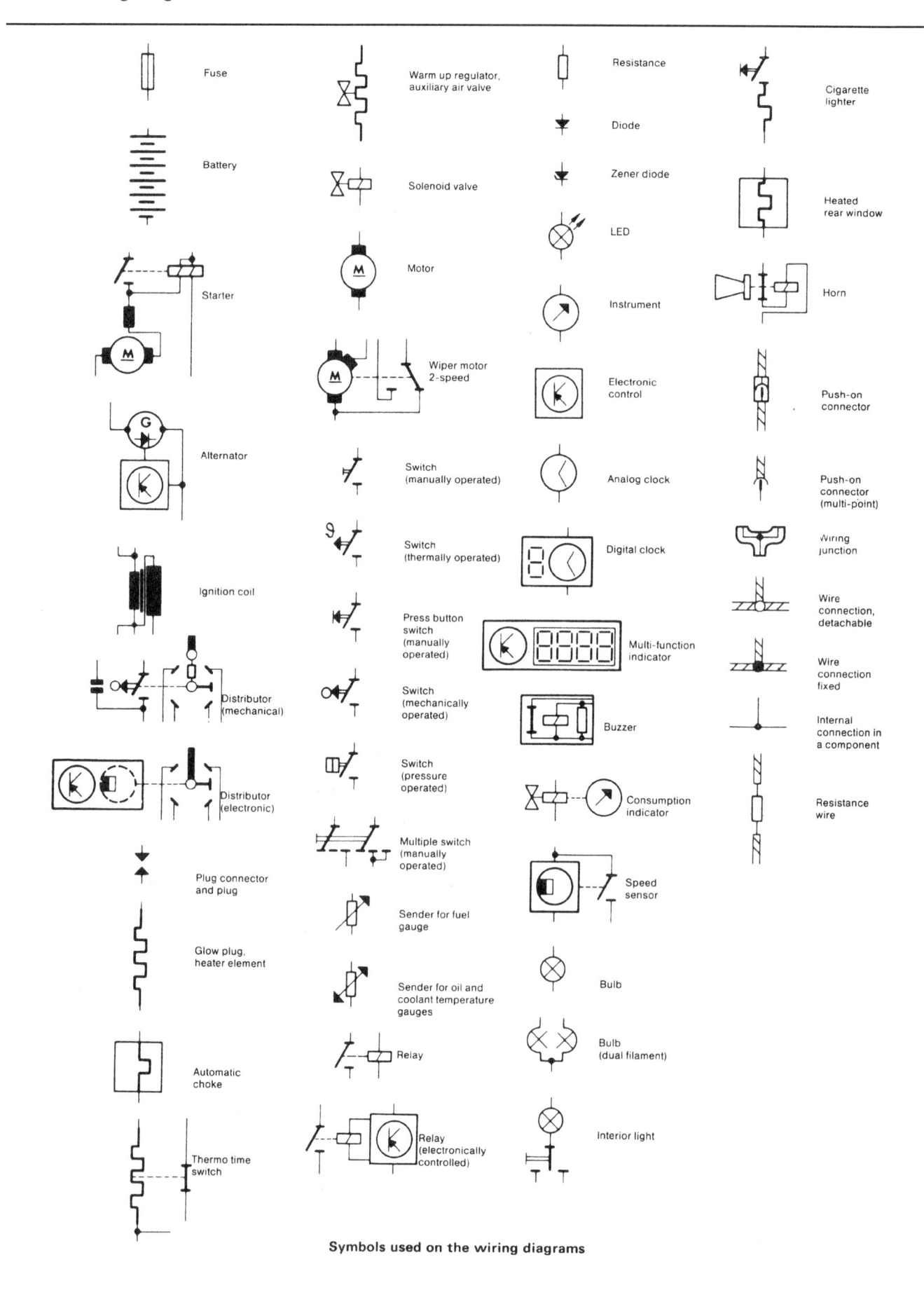

Symbol	Description
	Fuse
	Battery
	Starter
	Alternator
	Ignition coil
	Distributor (mechanical)
	Distributor (electronic)
	Plug connector and plug
	Glow plug, heater element
	Automatic choke
	Thermo time switch
	Warm up regulator, auxiliary air valve
	Solenoid valve
	Motor
	Wiper motor 2-speed
	Switch (manually operated)
	Switch (thermally operated)
	Press button switch (manually operated)
	Switch (mechanically operated)
	Switch (pressure operated)
	Multiple switch (manually operated)
	Sender for fuel gauge
	Sender for oil and coolant temperature gauges
	Relay
	Relay (electronically controlled)
	Resistance
	Diode
	Zener diode
	LED
	Instrument
	Electronic control
	Analog clock
	Digital clock
	Multi-function indicator
	Buzzer
	Consumption indicator
	Speed sensor
	Bulb
	Bulb (dual filament)
	Interior light
	Cigarette lighter
	Heated rear window
	Horn
	Push-on connector
	Push-on connector (multi-point)
	Wiring junction
	Wire connection, detachable
	Wire connection fixed
	Internal connection in a component
	Resistance wire

Symbols used on the wiring diagrams

Wiring diagrams 12•21

Relay locations

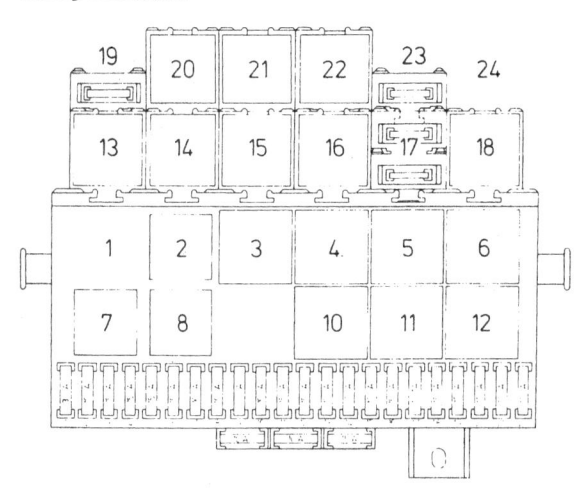

Connections

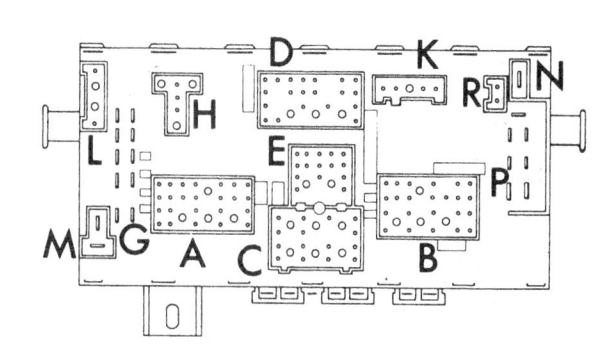

Wiring relays and connections – all models

Relays (typical)

1. Vacant
2. Intake manifold preheating relay (carburettor models) or fuel pump relay (injection models)
3. Seat belt warning system relay
4. Gearshift indicator control unit
5. Air conditioner relay
6. Dual tone horn relay
7. Relay for foglights and rear foglight
8. Relief relay for X contact
10. Intermittent wash/wipe relay
11. Rear window wiper relay
12. Turn signal flasher or trailer towing warning relay
13. Seat belt warning system (interlock) or rear window, driving lights and oil pressure warning relay
14. Window lift or seat belt warning system relay
15. Headlight washer relay
16. Control unit for idling speed increase
17. Fuse for rear foglight
18. Control unit for coolant shortage indicator
19. Thermo fuse for window lifters
20. Switch unit for heated driver's seat
21. Switch unit for heated passenger's seat
22. Switch unit for overrun cut-off
23. Vacant
24. Vacant

Relays are symbolised as a number in a black box

Not all relays are fitted to all models

Connections

A Multi-pin connector (blue) for dash panel loom
B Multi-pin connector (red) for dash panel loom
C Multi-pin connector (yellow) for engine compartment loom left
D Multi-pin connector (white) for engine compartment loom right
E Multi-pin connector (black) for rear wiring loom
G Single connector
H Multi-pin connector (brown) for air conditioner or wiring loom
K Multi-pin connector (transparent) for seat belt warning system loom
L Multi-pin connector (black) for lighting switch terminal 56 and dip and flasher switch terminal 56b (carburettor models) or multi-pin connector (grey) for dual tone horn (injection models)
M Multi-pin connector (black) for lighting switch terminal 56 and dip and flasher switch terminal 56b (injection models)
N Single connector for separate fuse (manifold heater element)
P Single connector (terminal 30)
R Not in use

Fuse colours

Blue	5A
Green	30A
Red	10A
Yellow	20A

12•22 Wiring diagrams

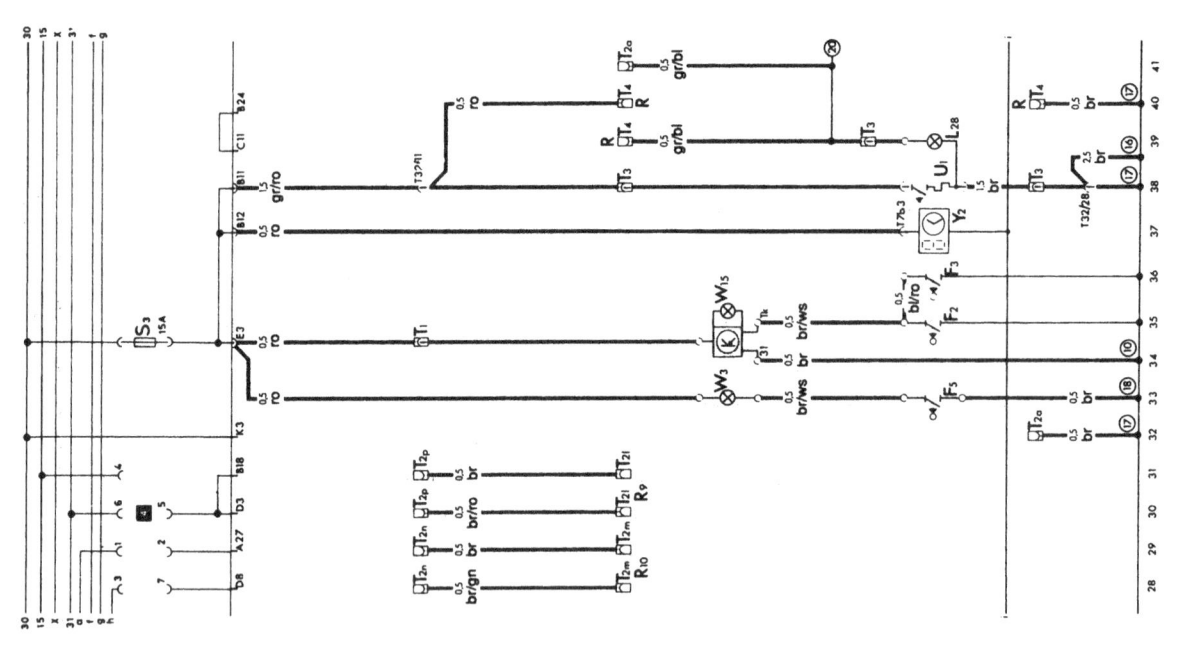

Diagram 2 Interior light, boot light, radio and cigarette lighter - 1.05, 1.3 and 1.6 models, pre July 1987

Diagram 1 Starter, alternator, battery and ignition system - 1.05, 1.3 and 1.6 models, pre July 1987

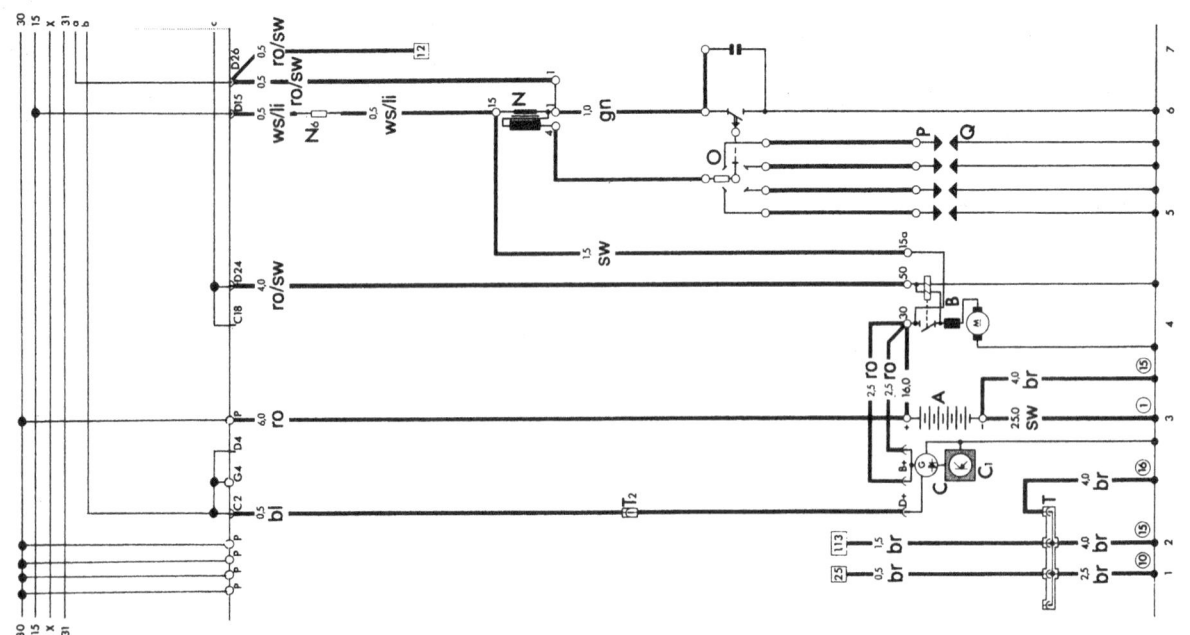

Wiring diagrams 12•23

Diagram 4 Headlights, tail lights and dip/flasher headlight switch - 1.05, 1.3 and 1.6 models, pre July 1987

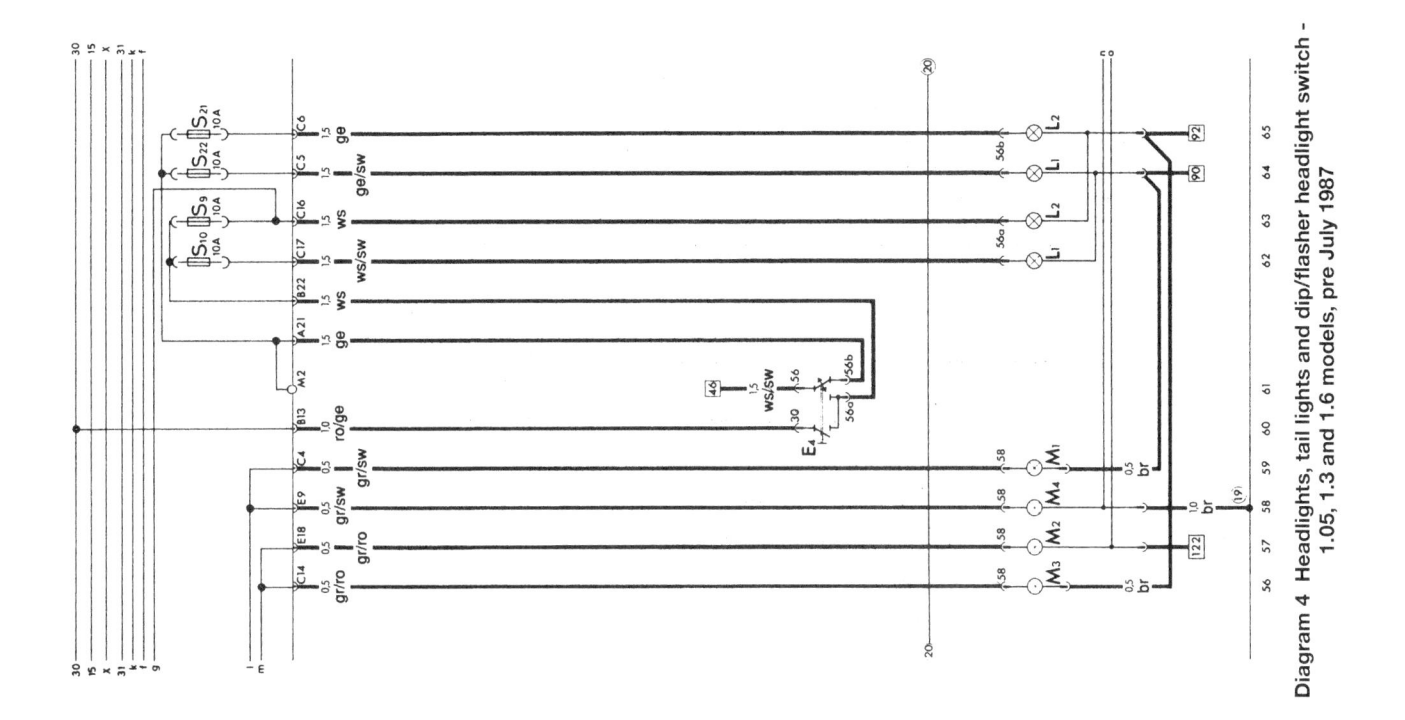

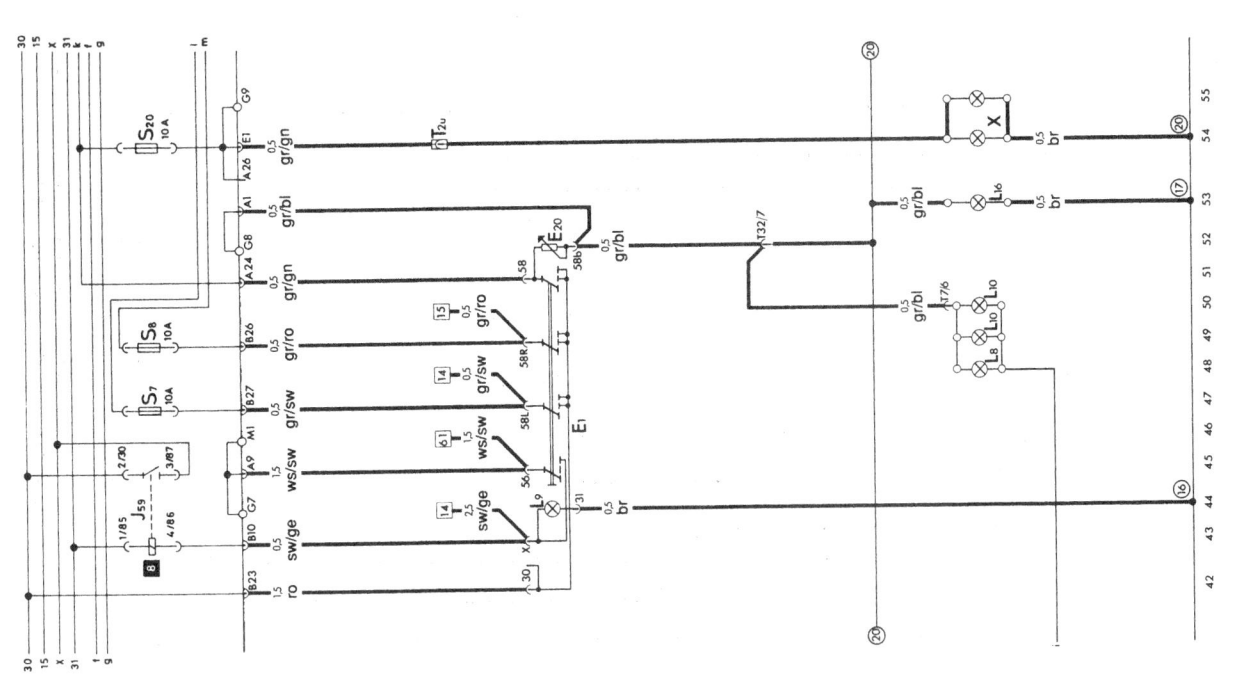

Diagram 3 Lighting switch, instrument and dash insert lights - 1.05, 1.3 and 1.5 models, pre July 1987

12•24 Wiring diagrams

Diagram 6 Indicators and hazard warning lights - 1.05, 1.3 and 1.6 models, pre July 1987

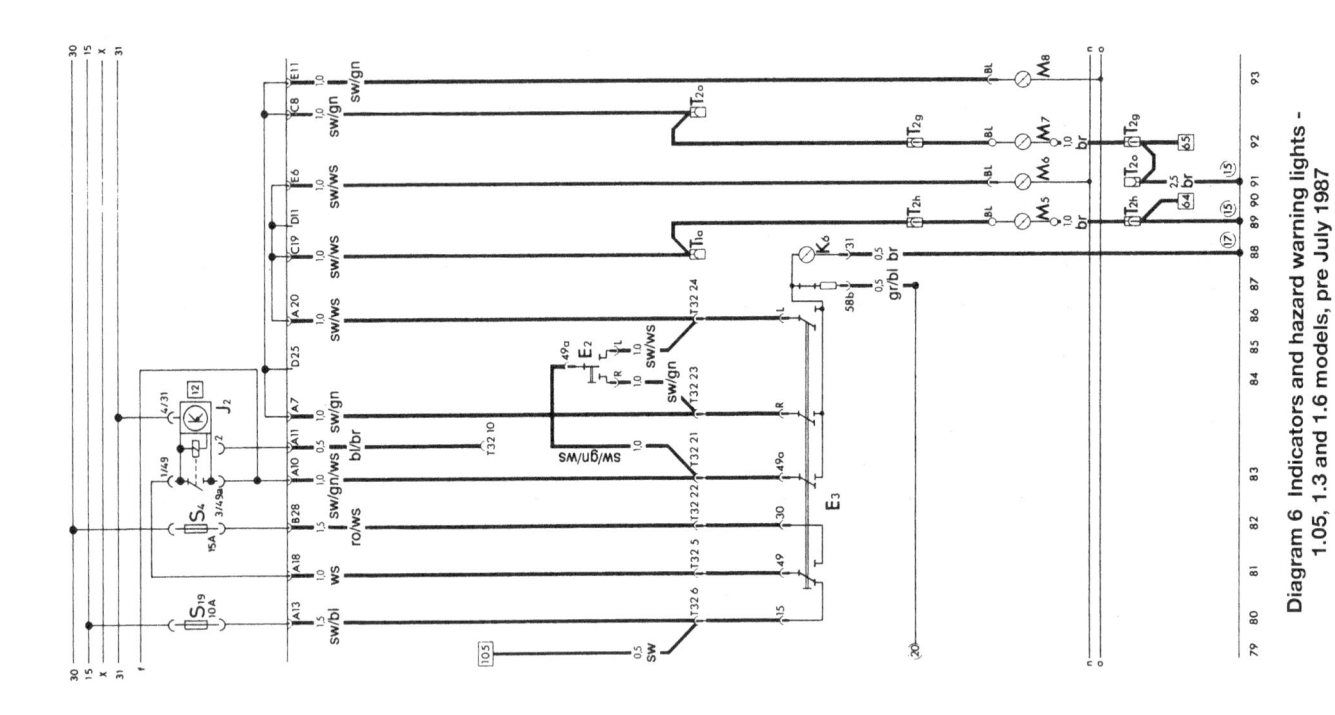

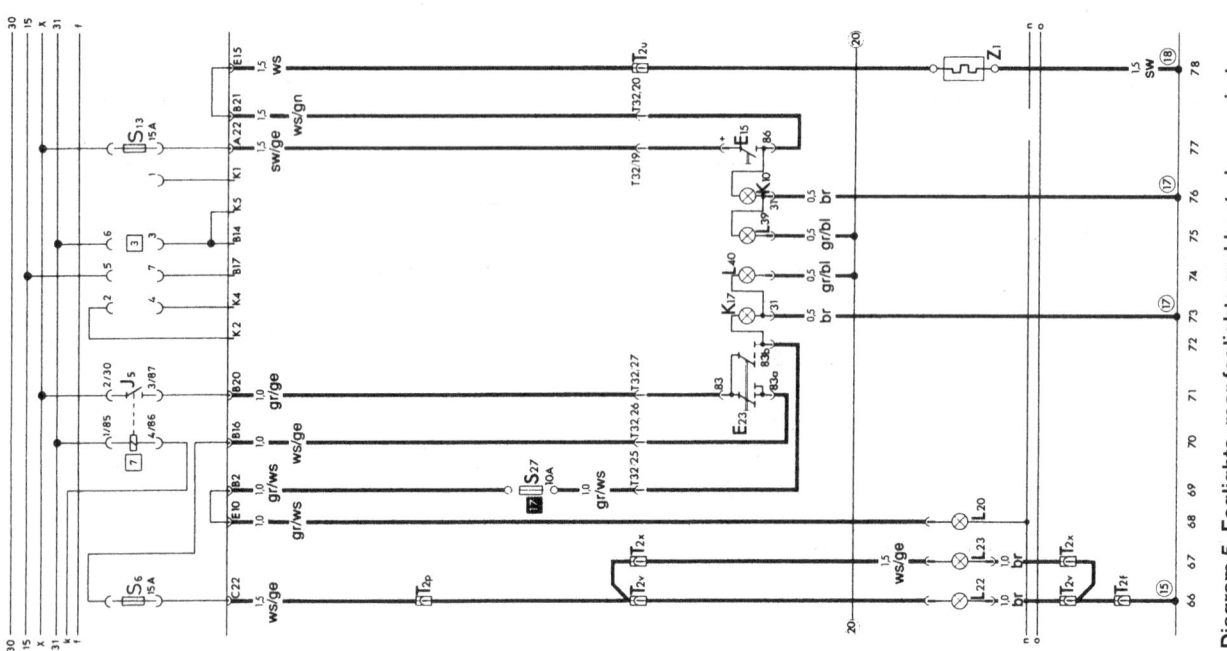

Diagram 5 Foglights, rear foglights and heated rear window - 1.05, 1.3 and 1.6 models, pre July 1987

Wiring diagrams 12•25

Diagram 8 Dual tone horn, handbrake and brake fluid level warning - 1.05, 1.3 and 1.6 models, pre July 1987

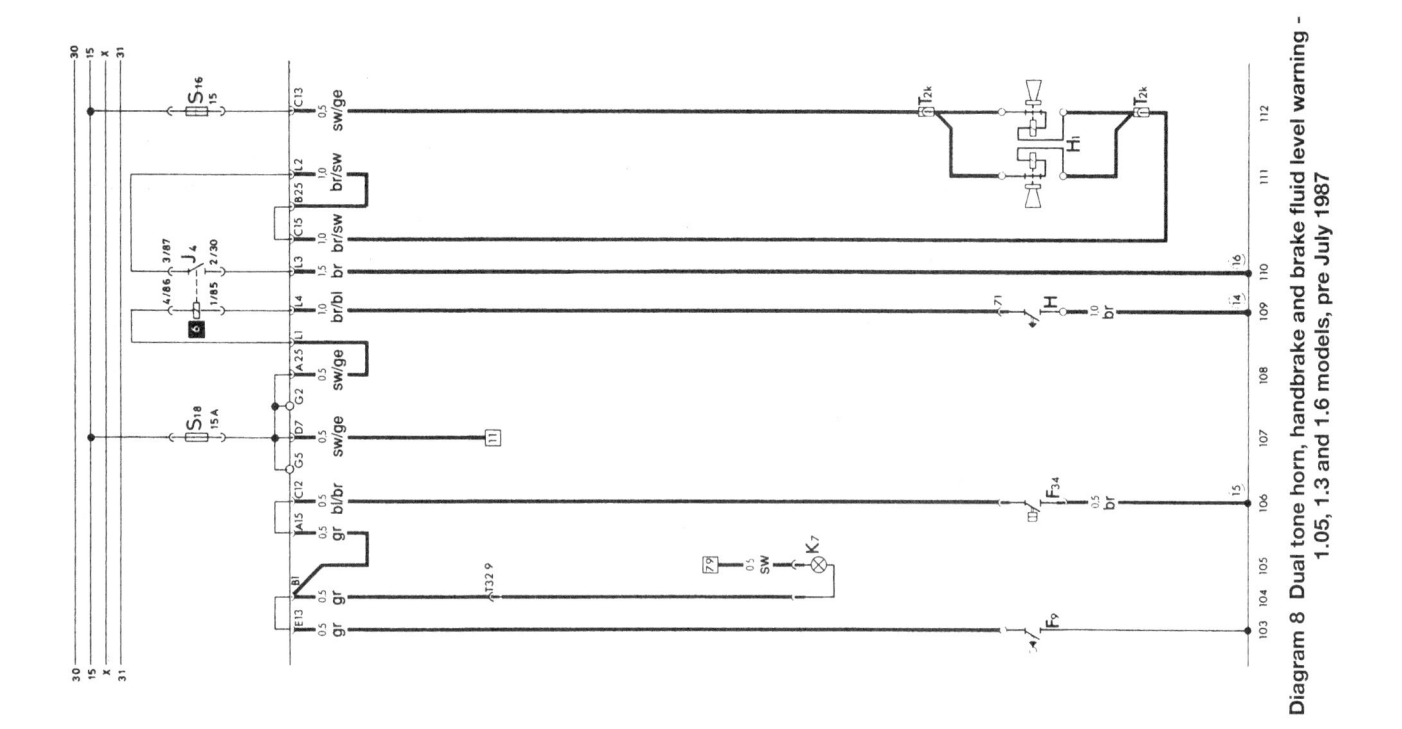

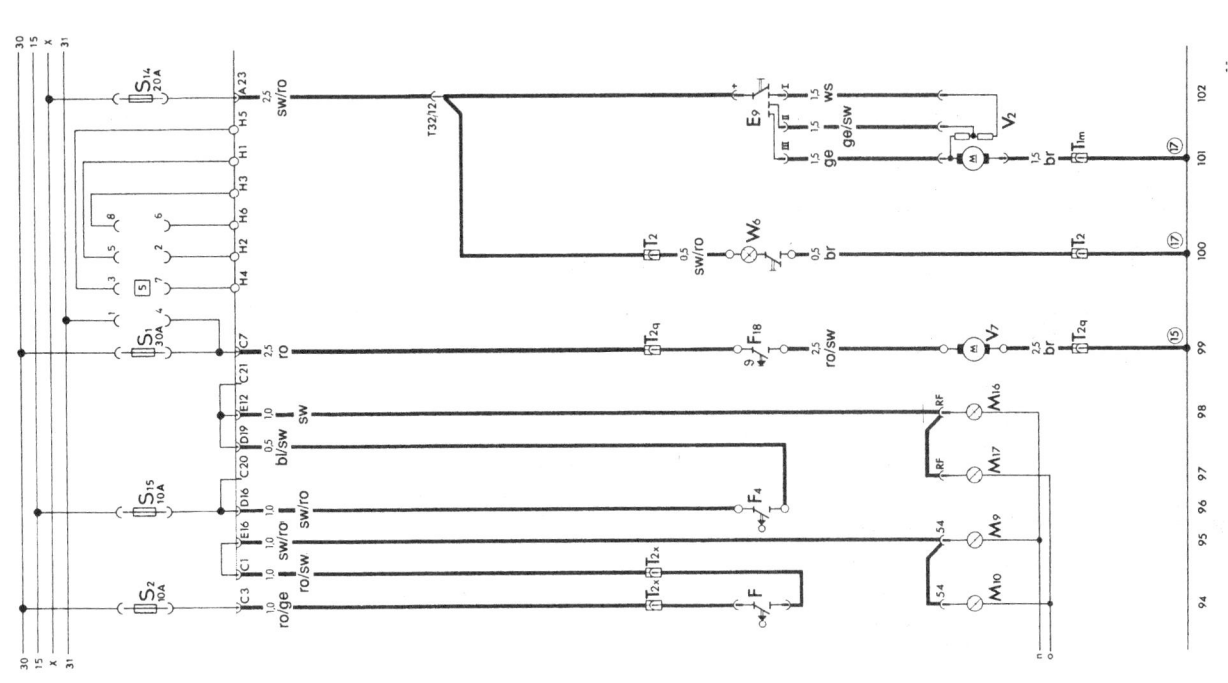

Diagram 7 Brake lights, fresh air blower, reversing lights and radiator fan - 1.05, 1.3 and 1.6 models, pre July 1987

12•26 Wiring diagrams

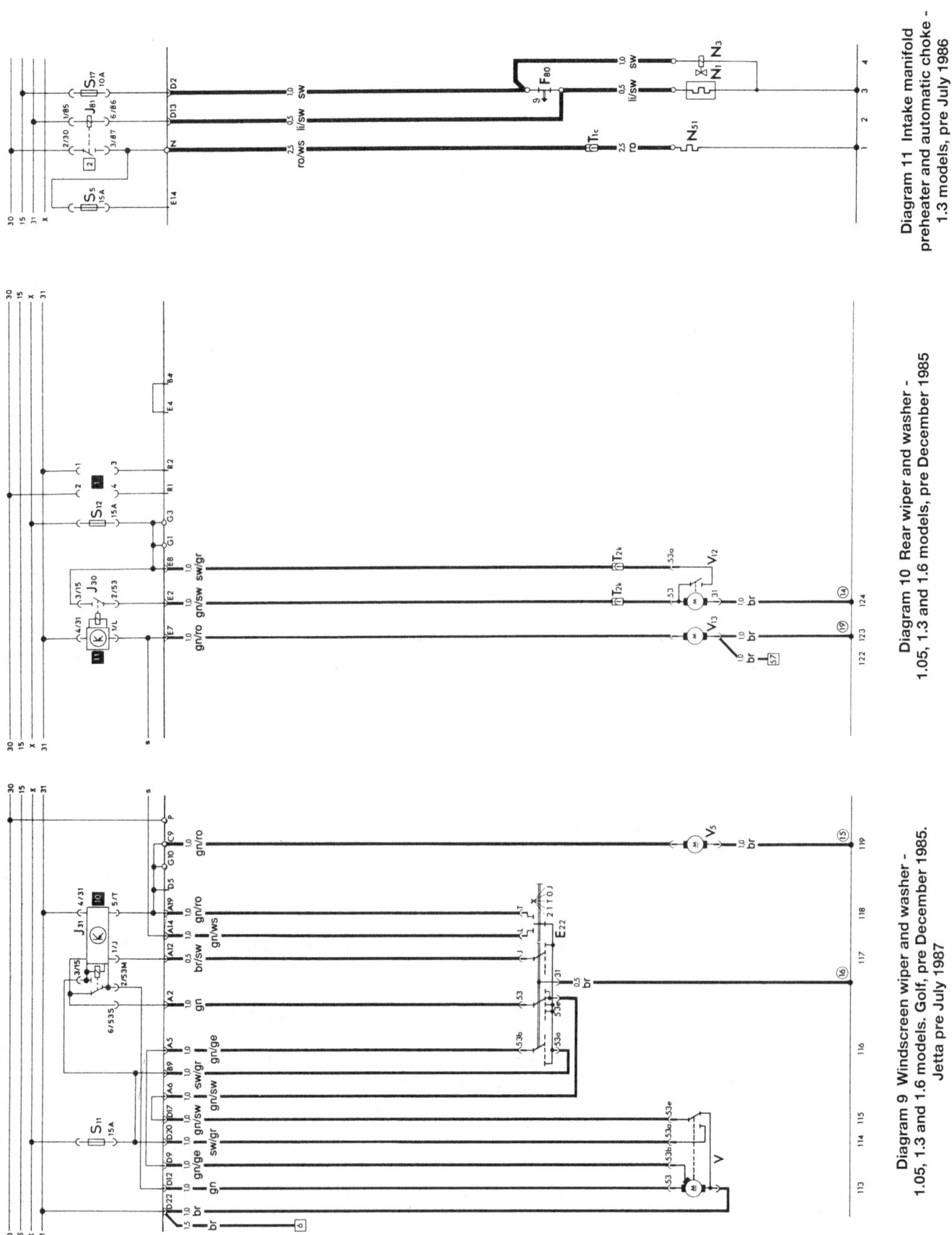

Diagram 11 Intake manifold preheater and automatic choke - 1.3 models, pre July 1986

Diagram 10 Rear wiper and washer - 1.05, 1.3 and 1.6 models, pre December 1985

Diagram 9 Windscreen wiper and washer - 1.05, 1.3 and 1.6 models. Golf, pre December 1985. Jetta pre July 1987

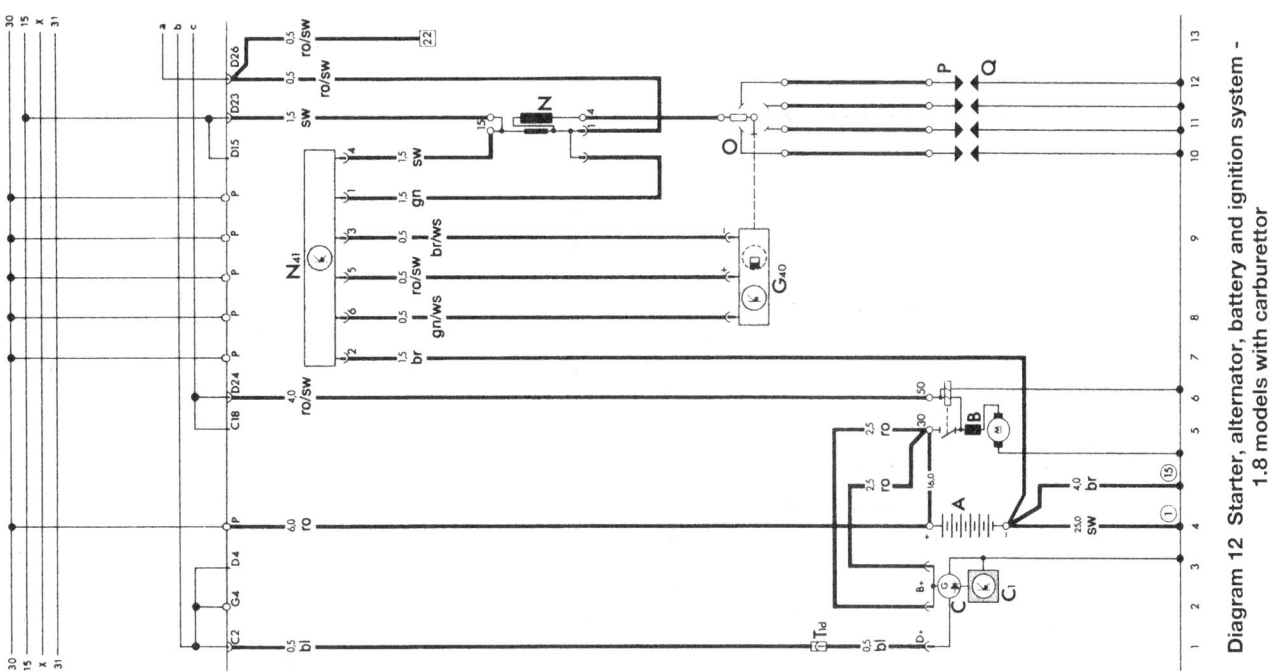

Wiring diagrams 12•27

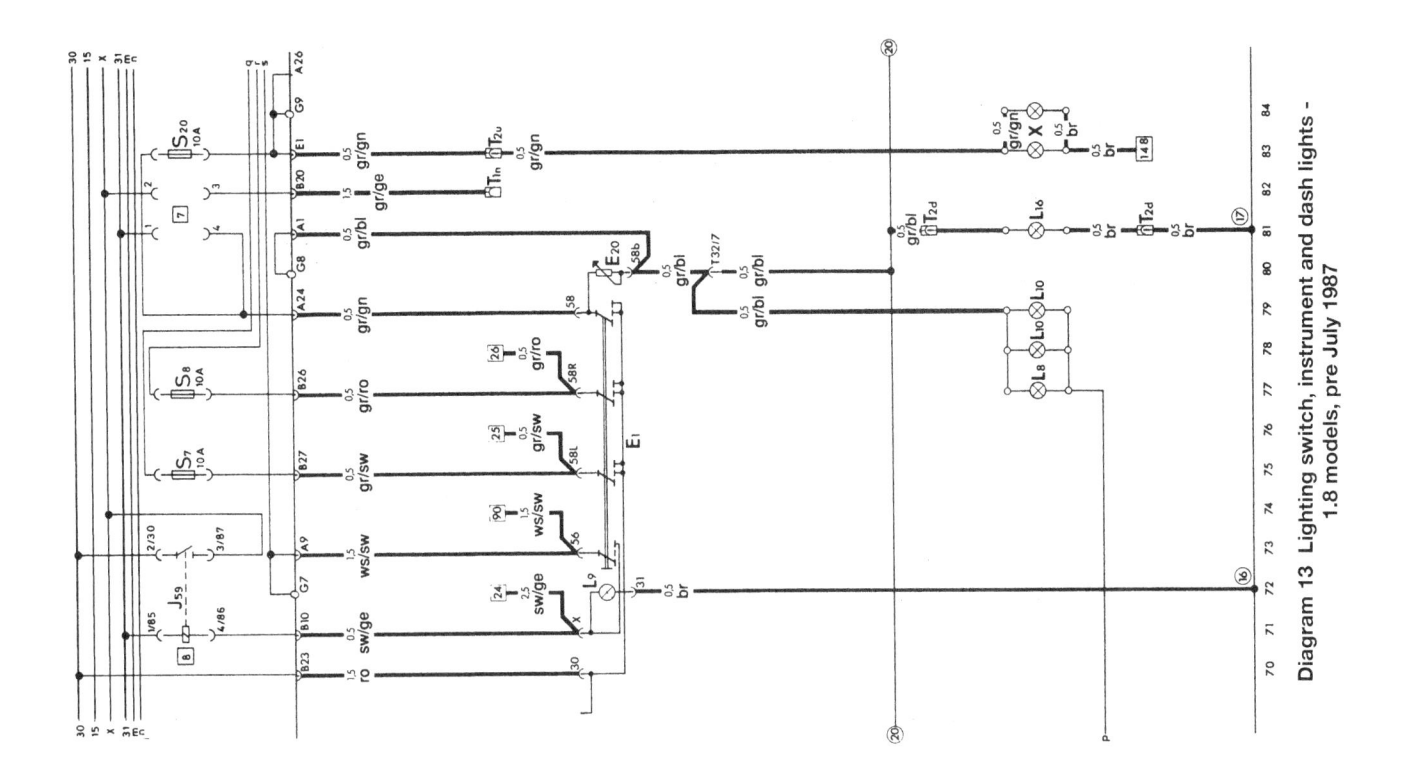

Diagram 13 Lighting switch, instrument and dash lights - 1.8 models, pre July 1987

Diagram 12 Starter, alternator, battery and ignition system - 1.8 models with carburettor

12•28 Wiring diagrams

Diagram 15 Rear foglight and heated rear window - 1.8 models, pre July 1987

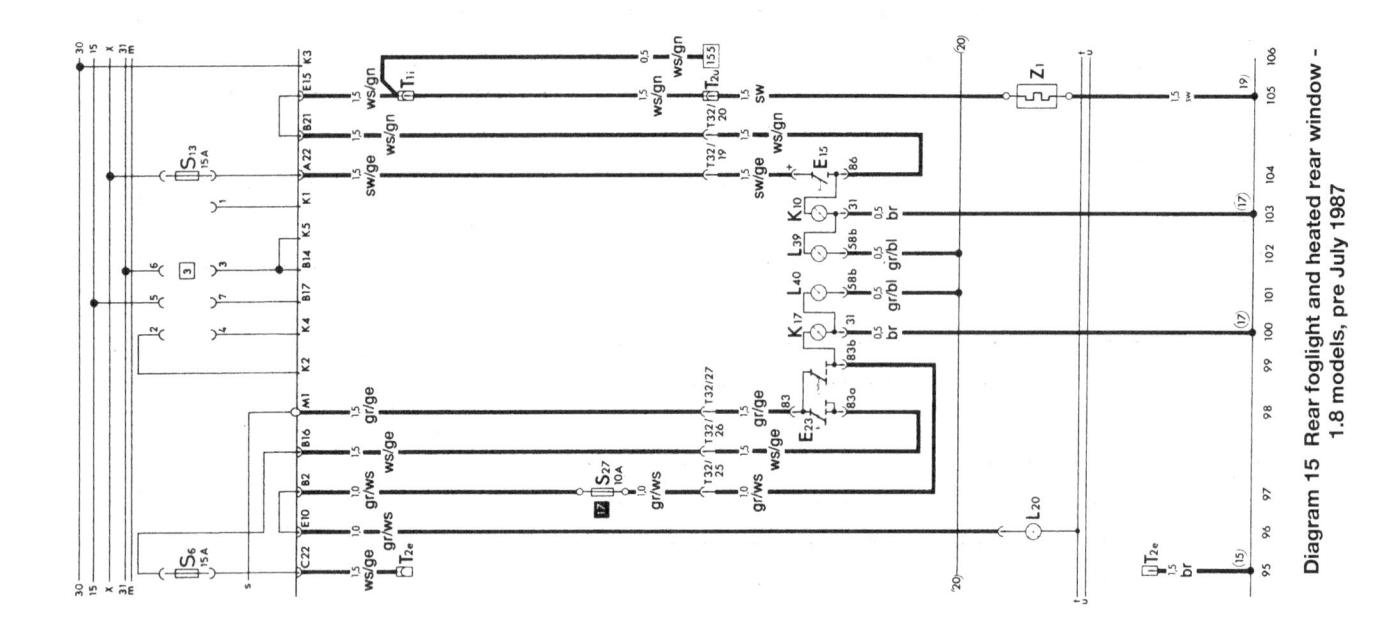

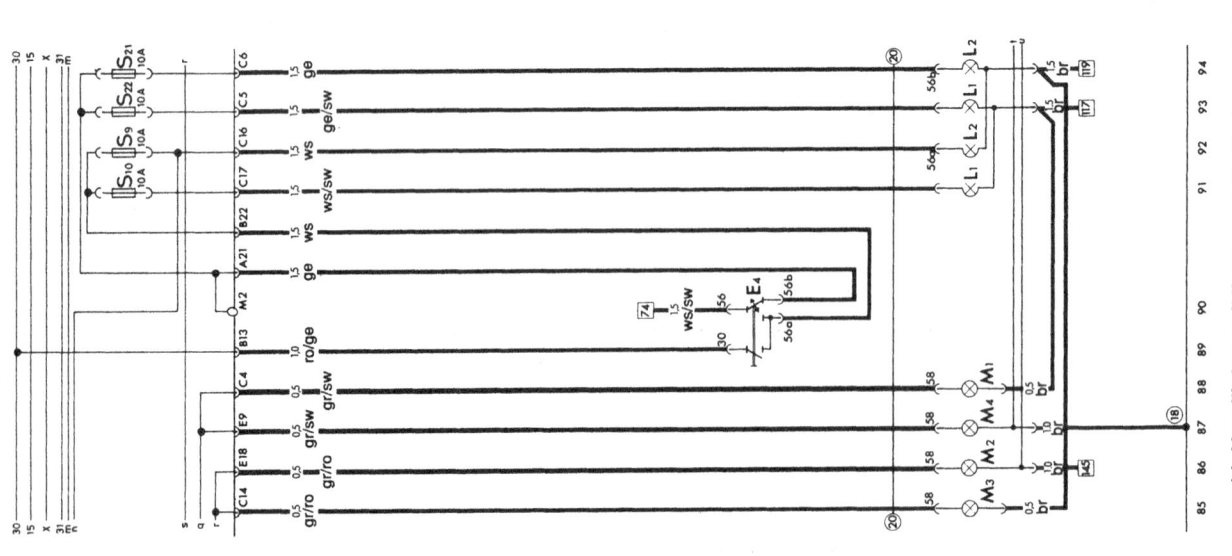

Diagram 14 Headlights, tail lights and dip flasher switch - 1.8 models, pre July 1987

Wiring diagrams 12•29

Diagram 17 Brake lights, fresh air blower, reversing lights and radiator fan - 1.8 models, pre July 1987

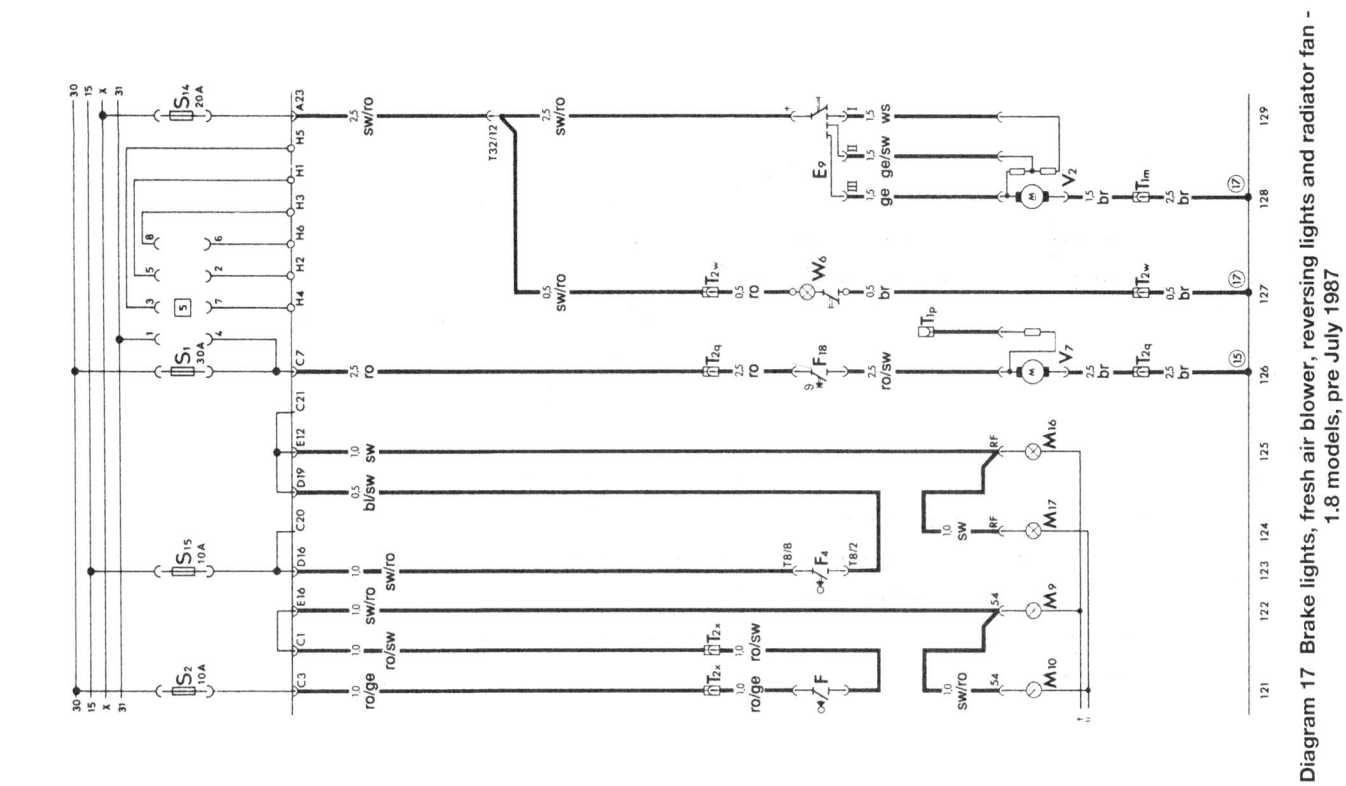

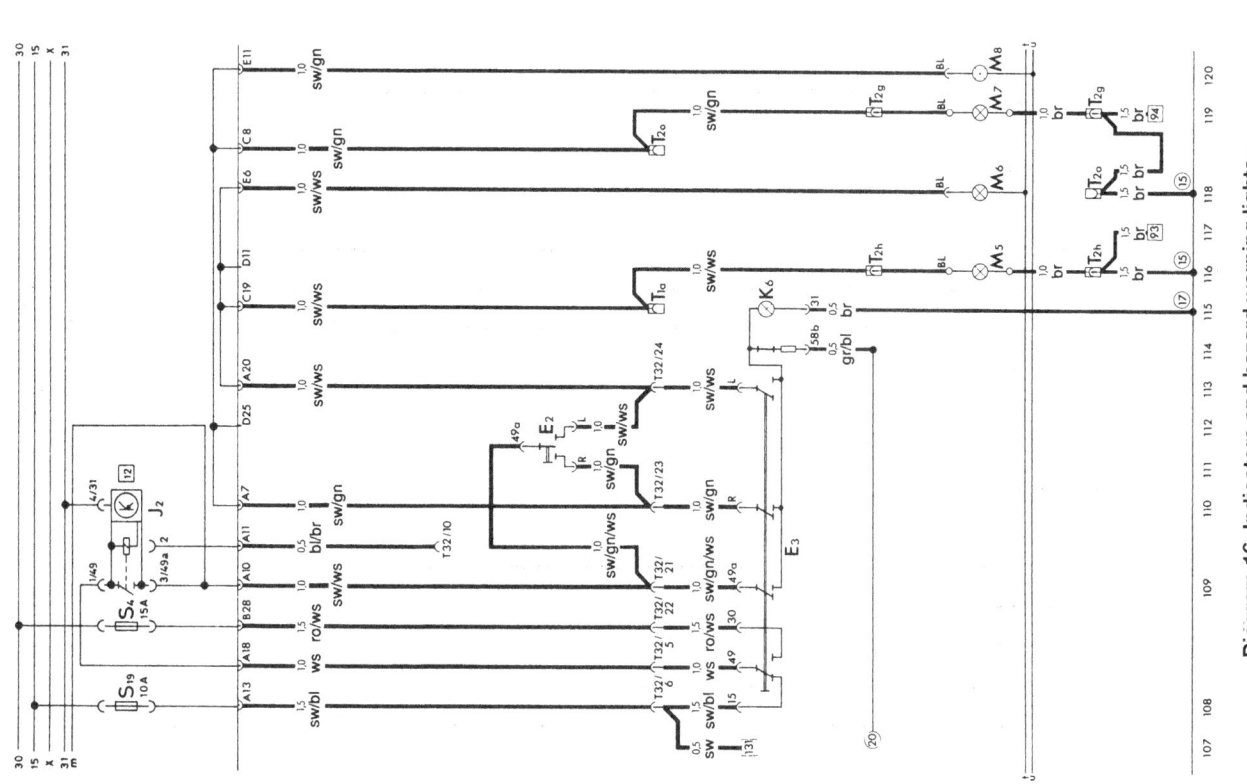

Diagram 16 Indicators and hazard warning lights - 1.8 models, pre July 1987

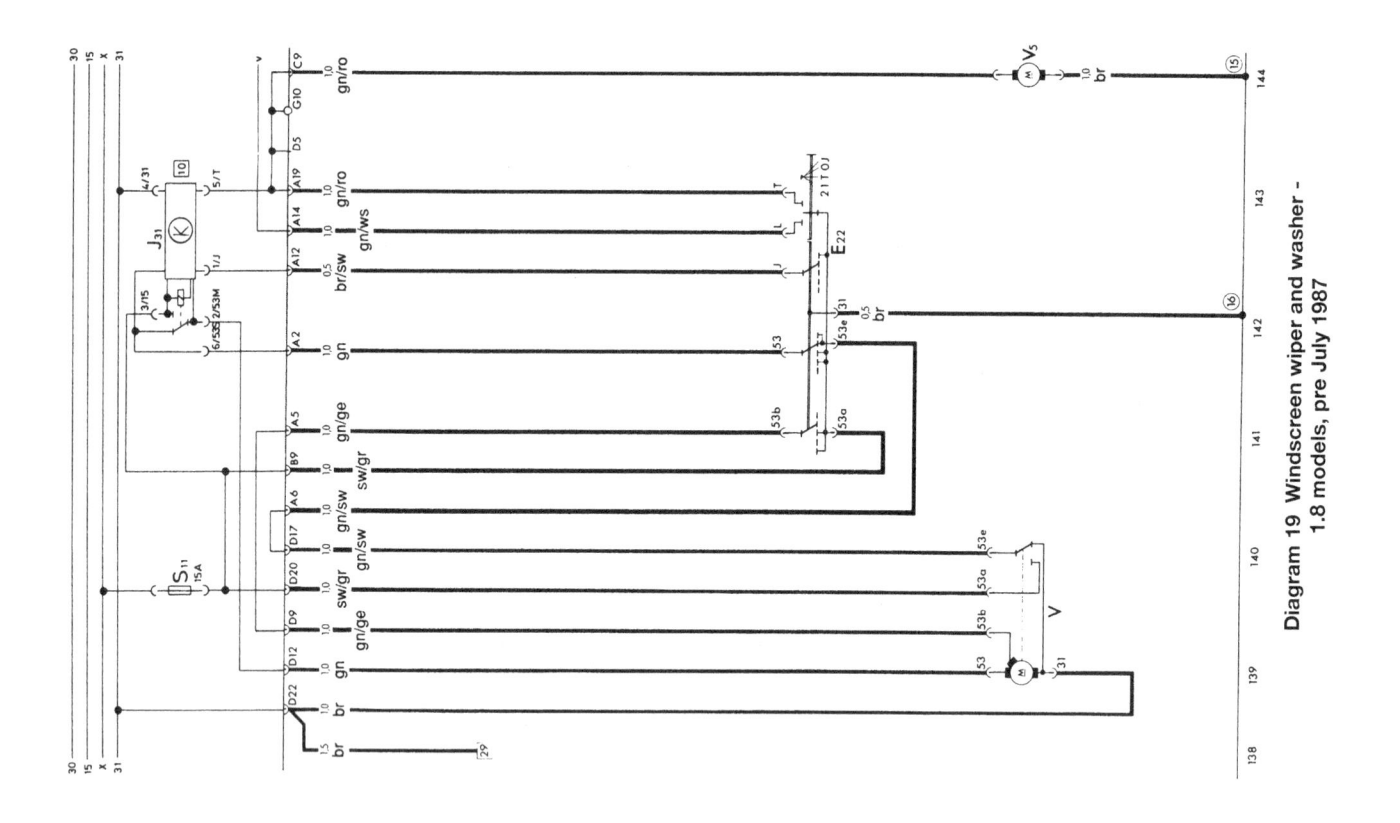

12•30 Wiring diagrams

Diagram 19 Windscreen wiper and washer – 1.8 models, pre July 1987

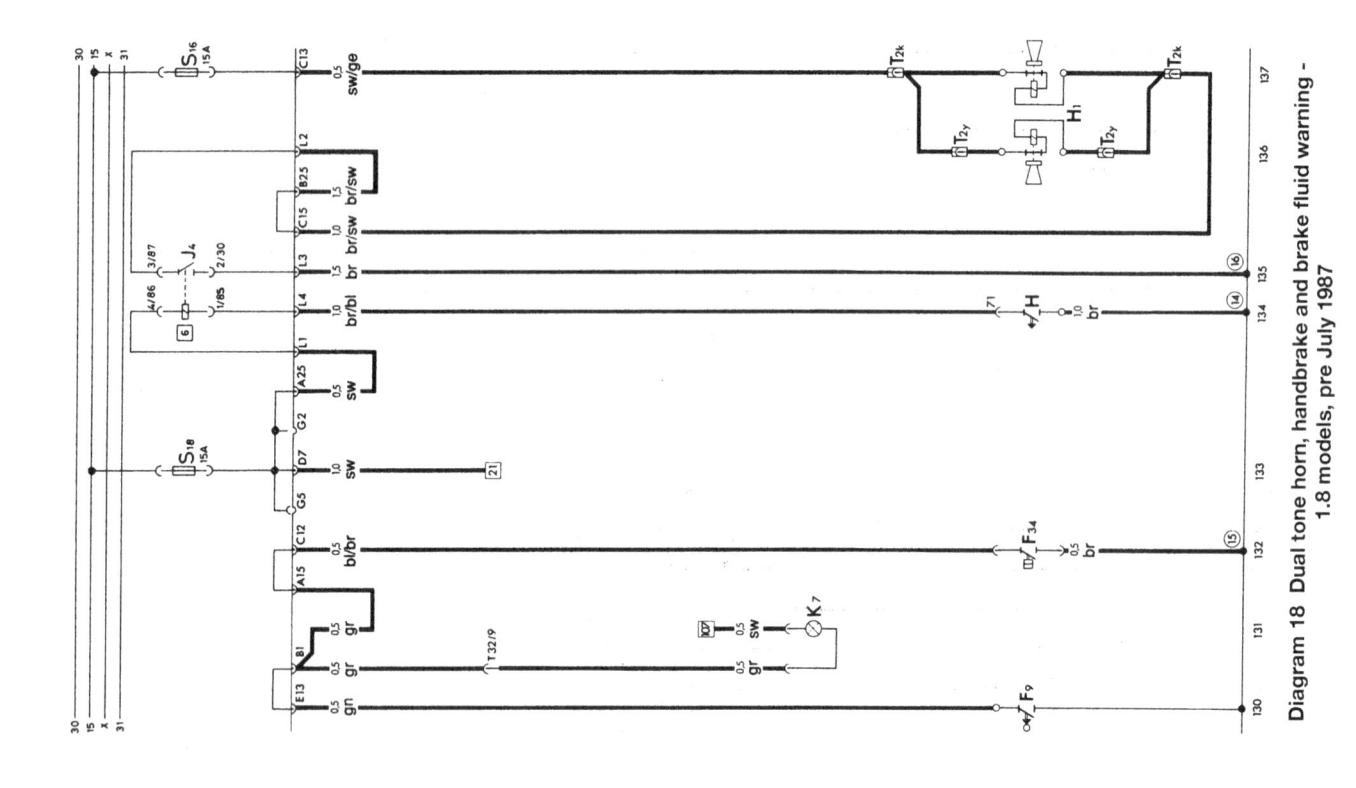

Diagram 18 Dual tone horn, handbrake and brake fluid warning – 1.8 models, pre July 1987

Wiring diagrams 12•31

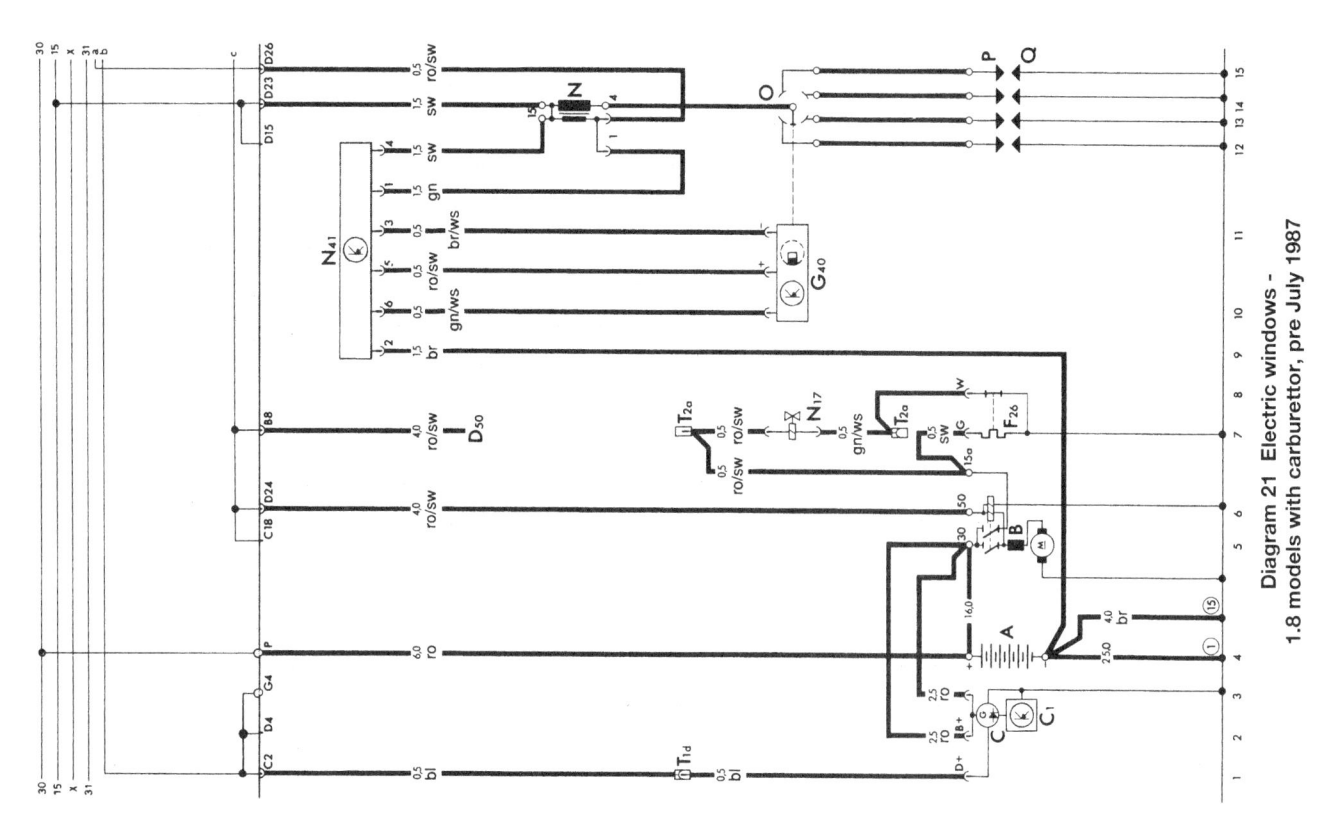

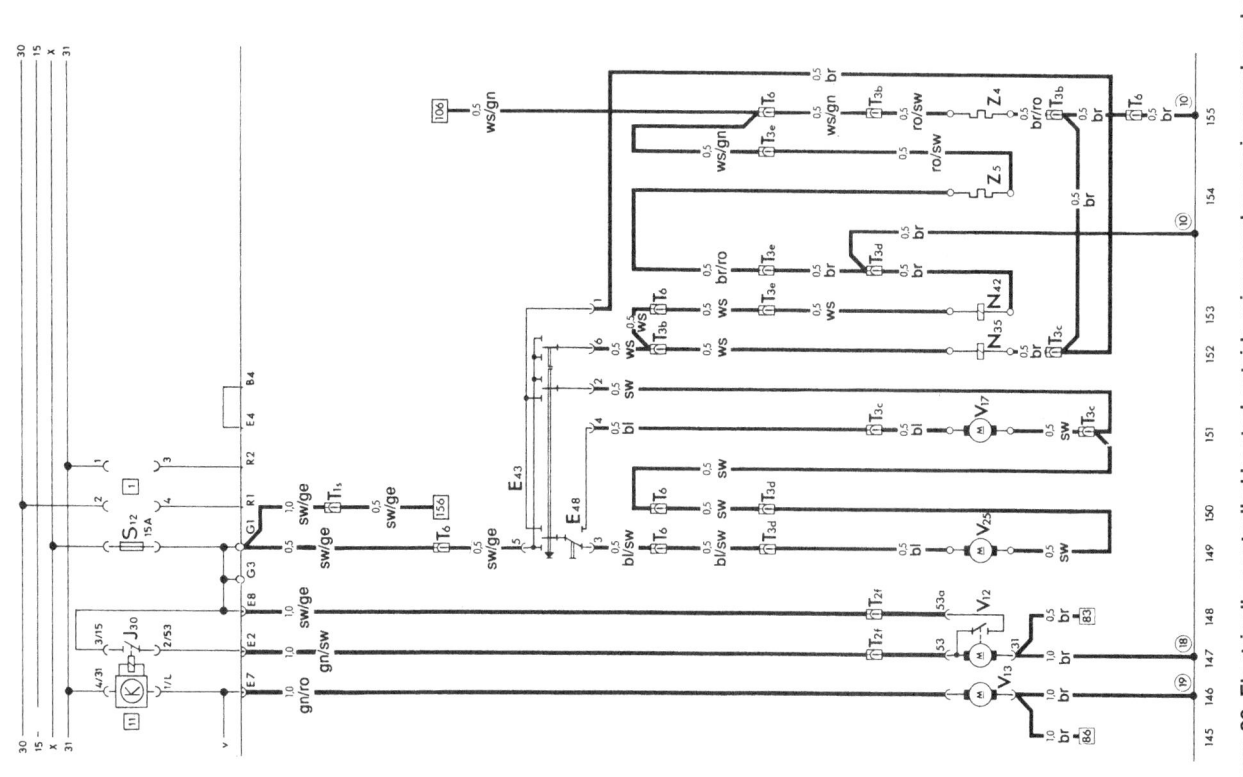

Diagram 21 Electric windows – 1.8 models with carburettor, pre July 1987

Diagram 20 Electrically-controlled heated outside mirror and rear wiper and washer – 1.8 models, pre December 1985

12•32 Wiring diagrams

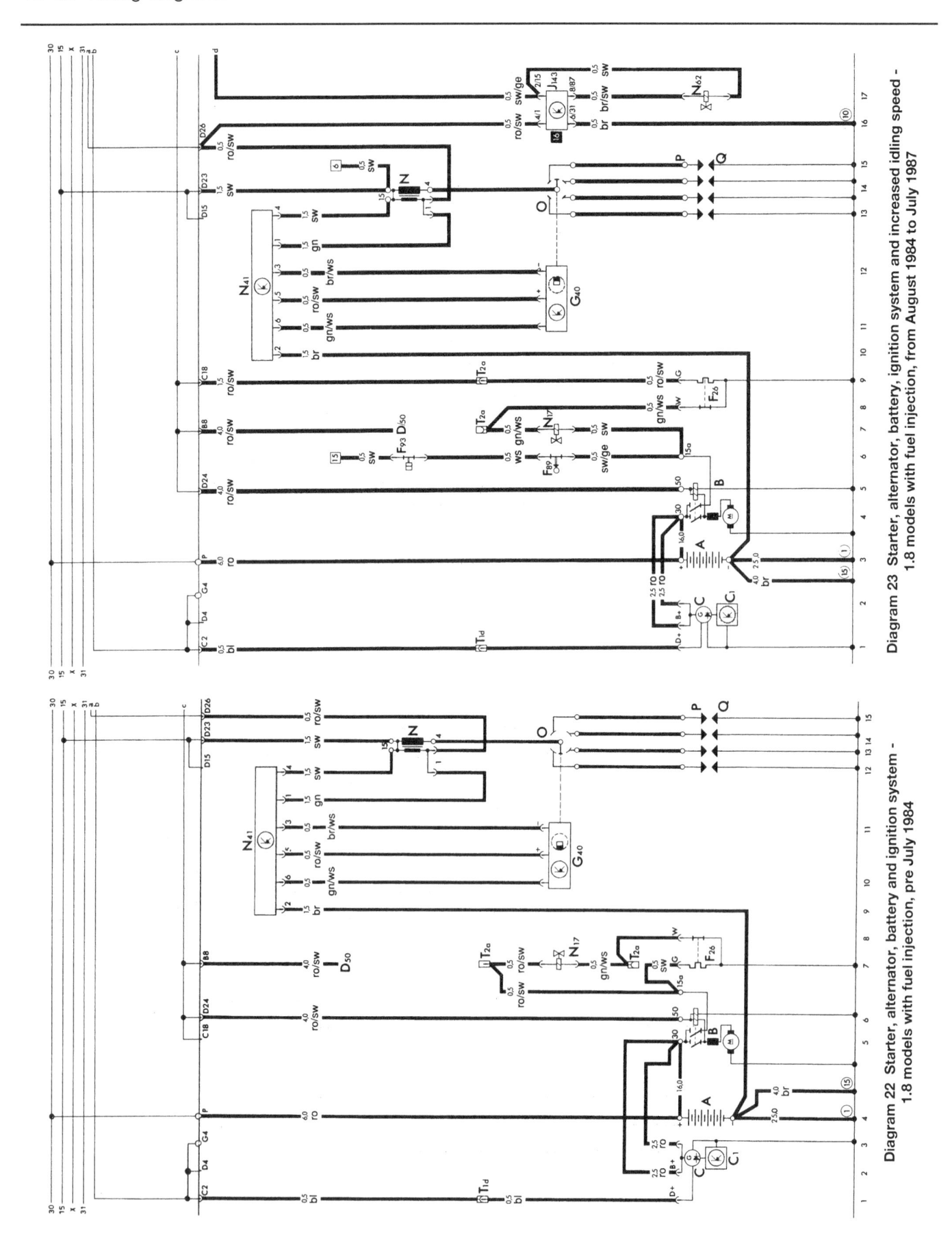

Diagram 23 Starter, alternator, battery, ignition system and increased idling speed - 1.8 models with fuel injection, from August 1984 to July 1987

Diagram 22 Starter, alternator, battery and ignition system - 1.8 models with fuel injection, pre July 1984

Wiring diagrams 12•33

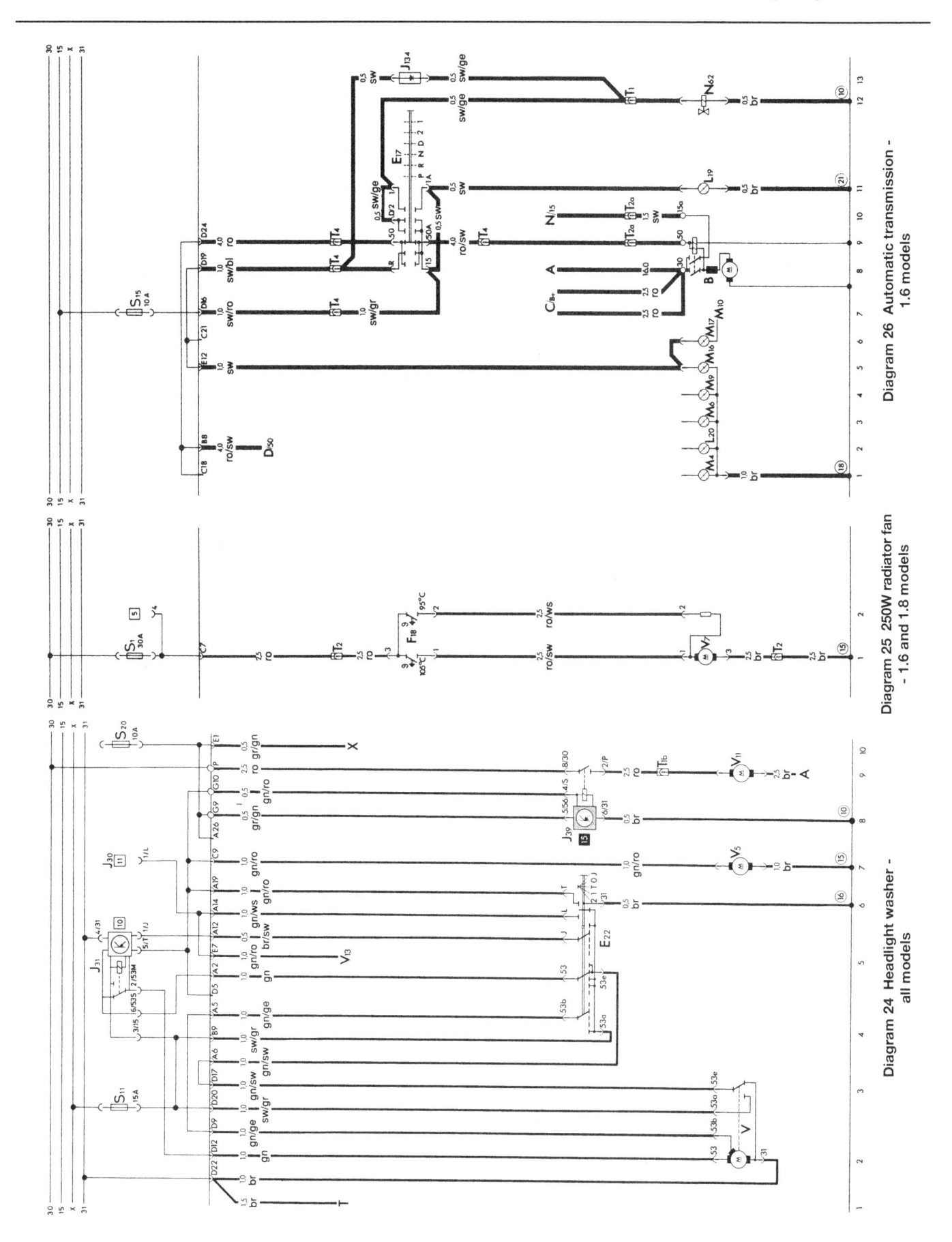

Diagram 26 Automatic transmission – 1.6 models

Diagram 25 250W radiator fan – 1.6 and 1.8 models

Diagram 24 Headlight washer – all models

12•34 Wiring diagrams

Diagram 28 Starter, alternator and battery - 1.8 16v models

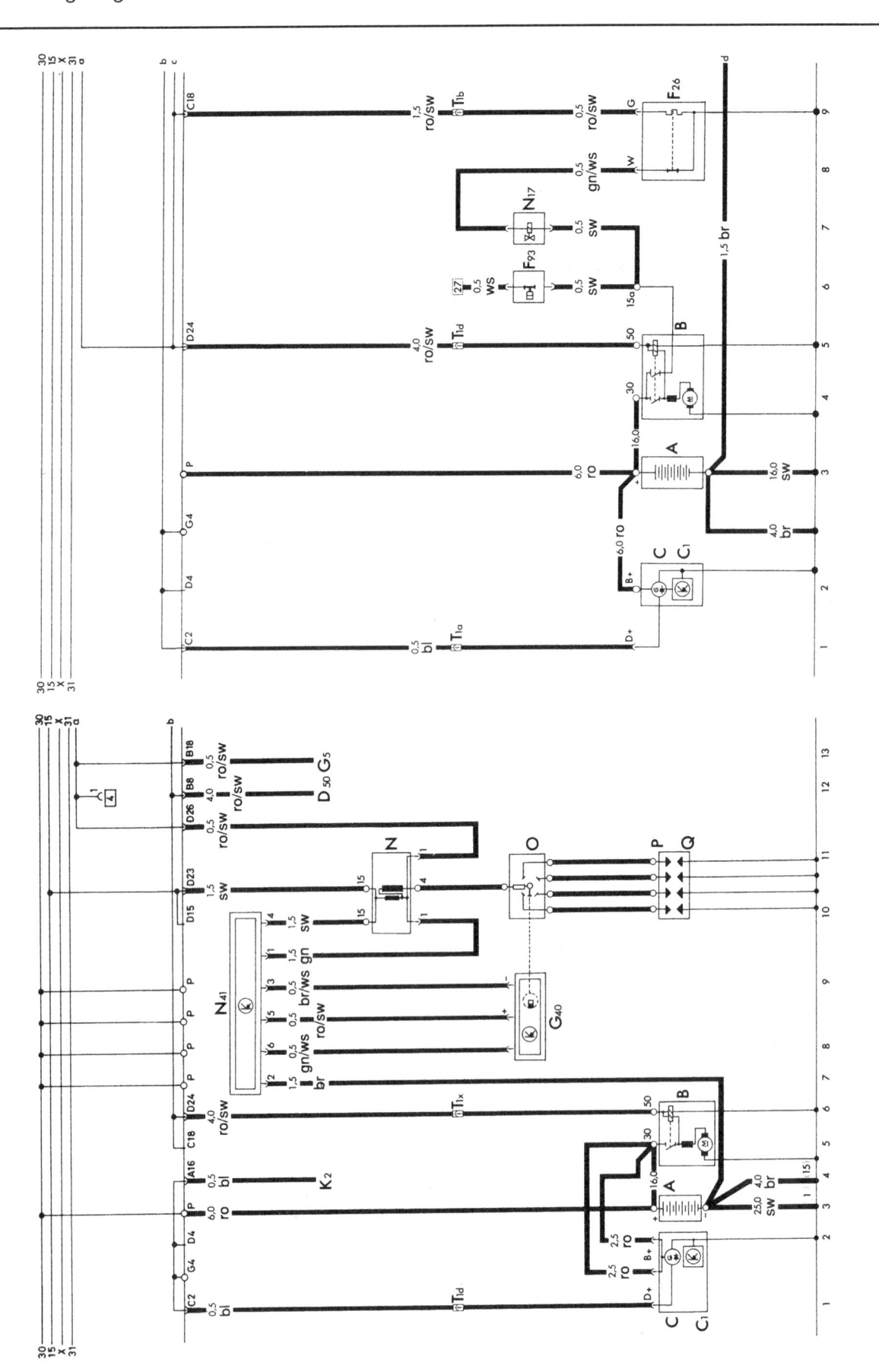

Diagram 27 Starter, alternator, battery and ignition system - 1.3 models, from August 1985

Wiring diagrams 12•35

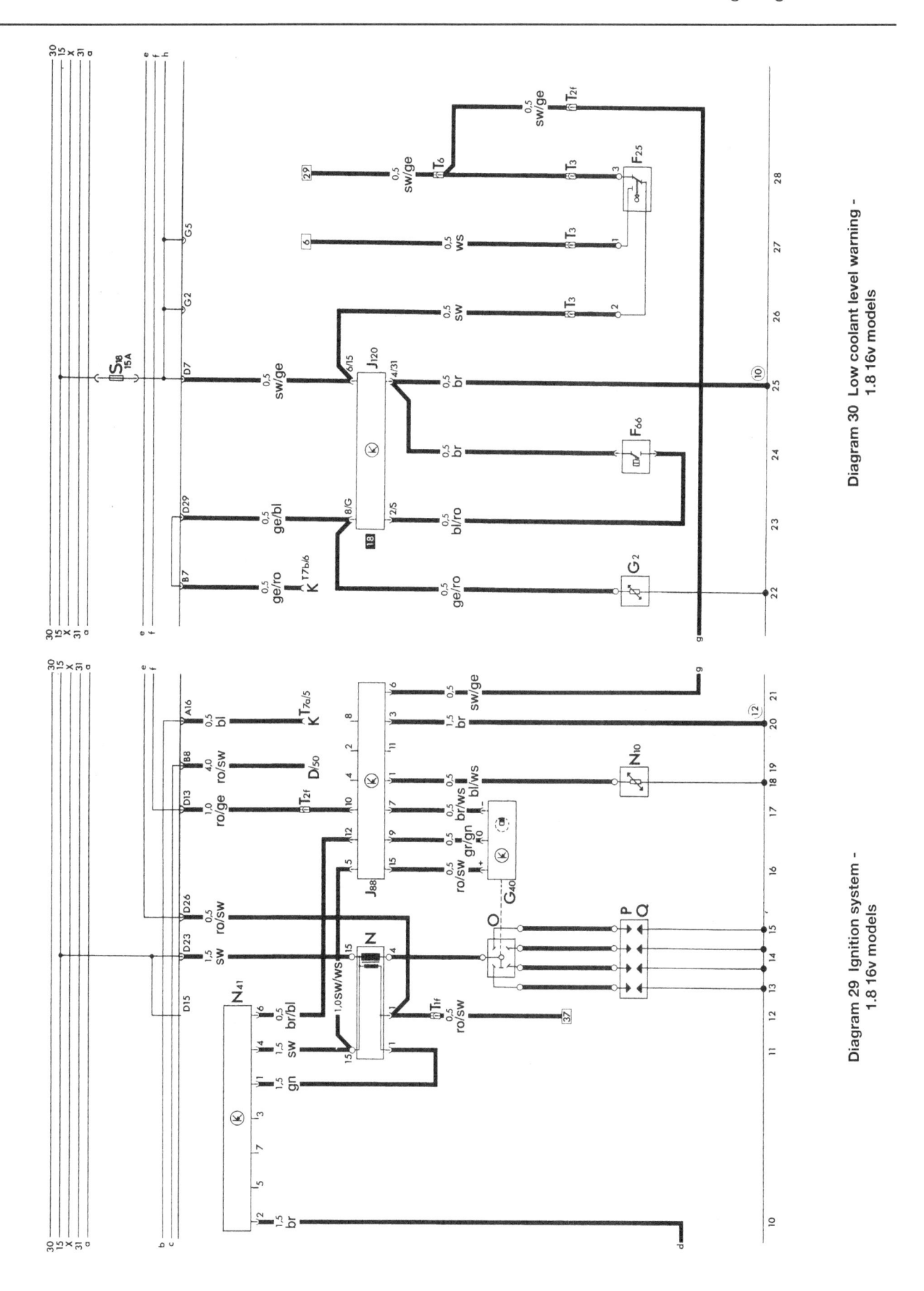

Diagram 30 Low coolant level warning – 1.8 16v models

Diagram 29 Ignition system – 1.8 16v models

12•36 Wiring diagrams

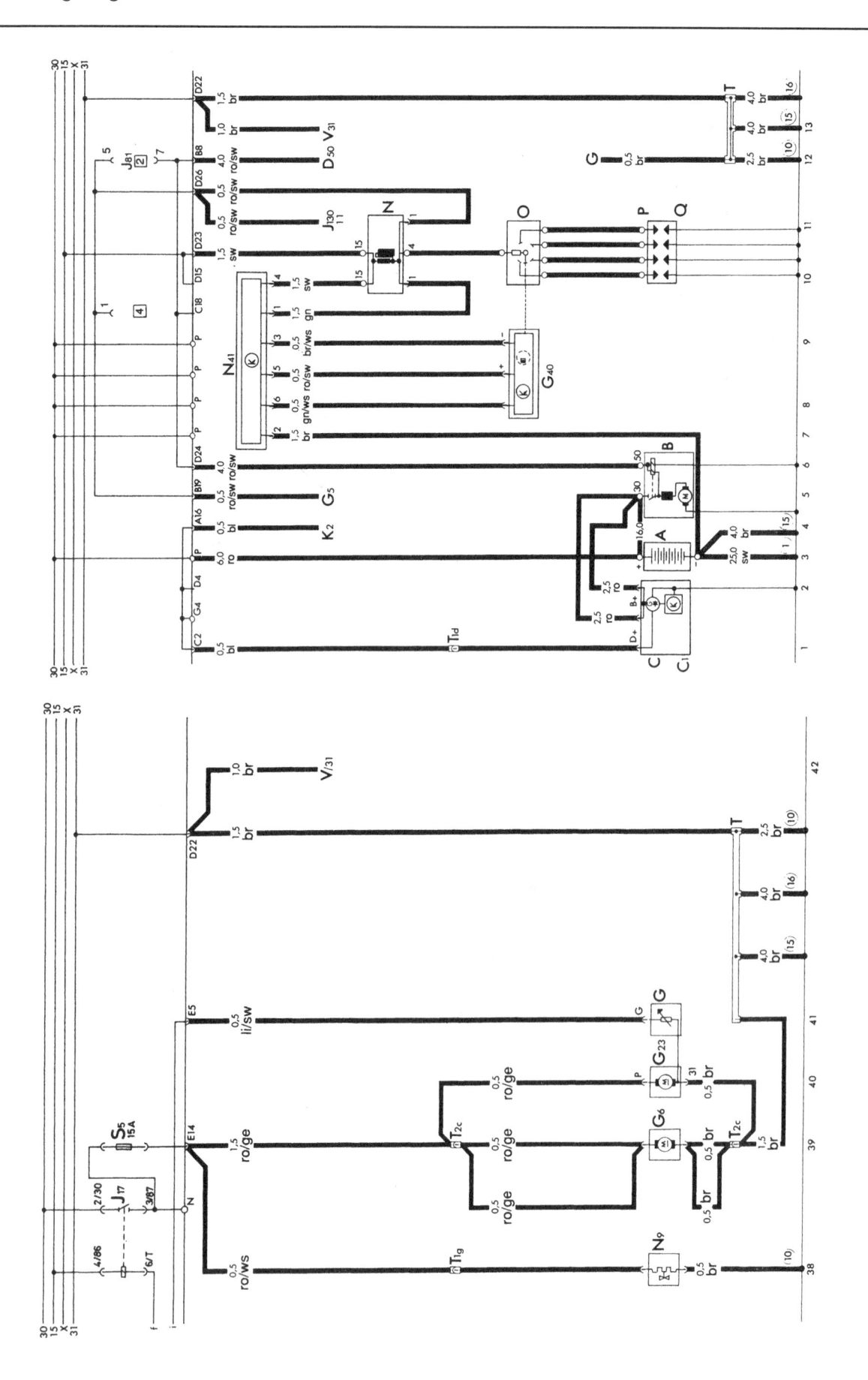

Diagram 32 Starter, alternator, battery and ignition system - 1.6 models from August 1985 to July 1987

Diagram 31 Fuel supply - 1.8 16v models

Diagram 34 Windscreen wiper – all Golf models from January 1986 to July 1987

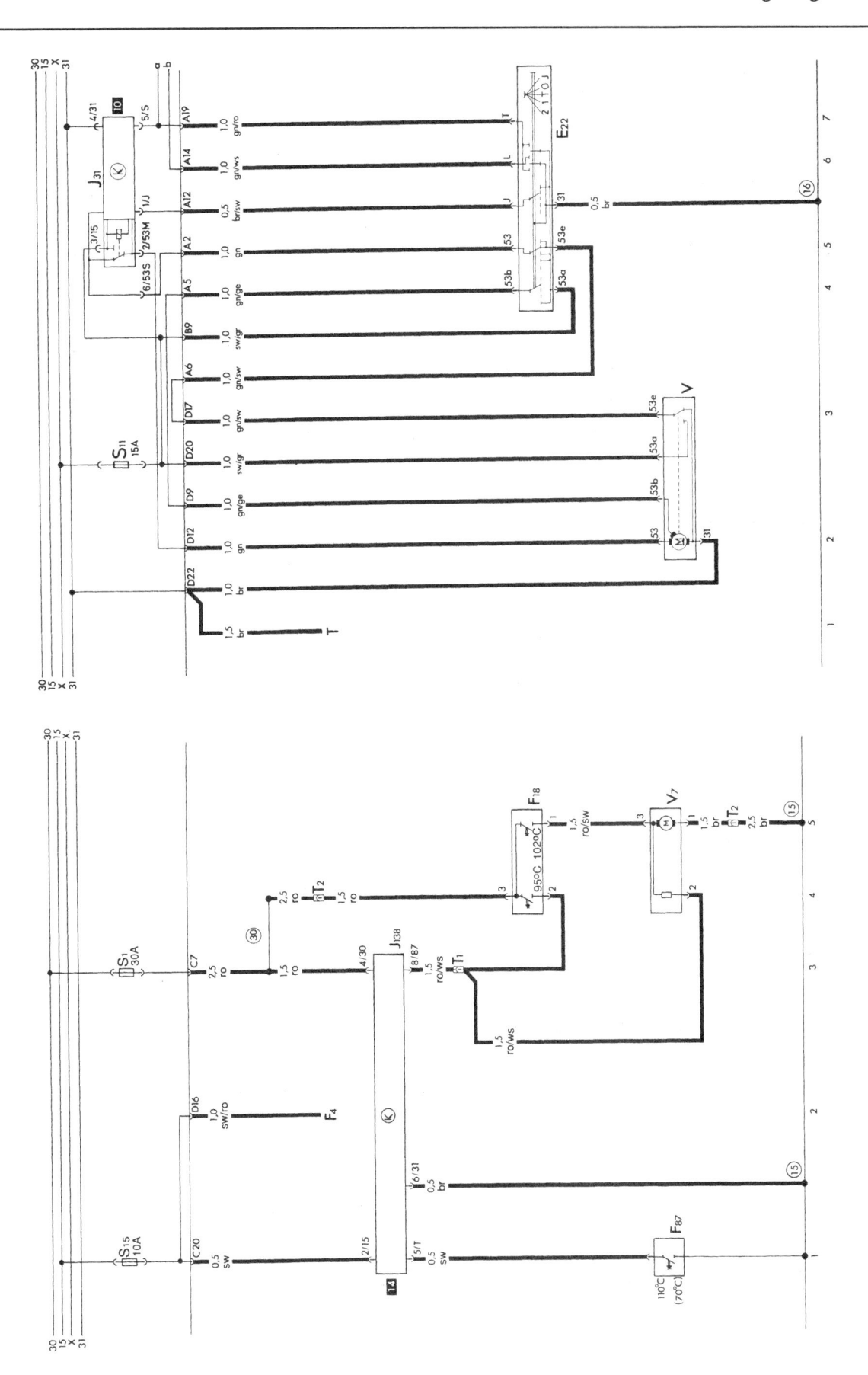

Diagram 33 Radiator fan run-on – 1.6 and 1.8 models from March 1986 to July 1987

12•38 Wiring diagrams

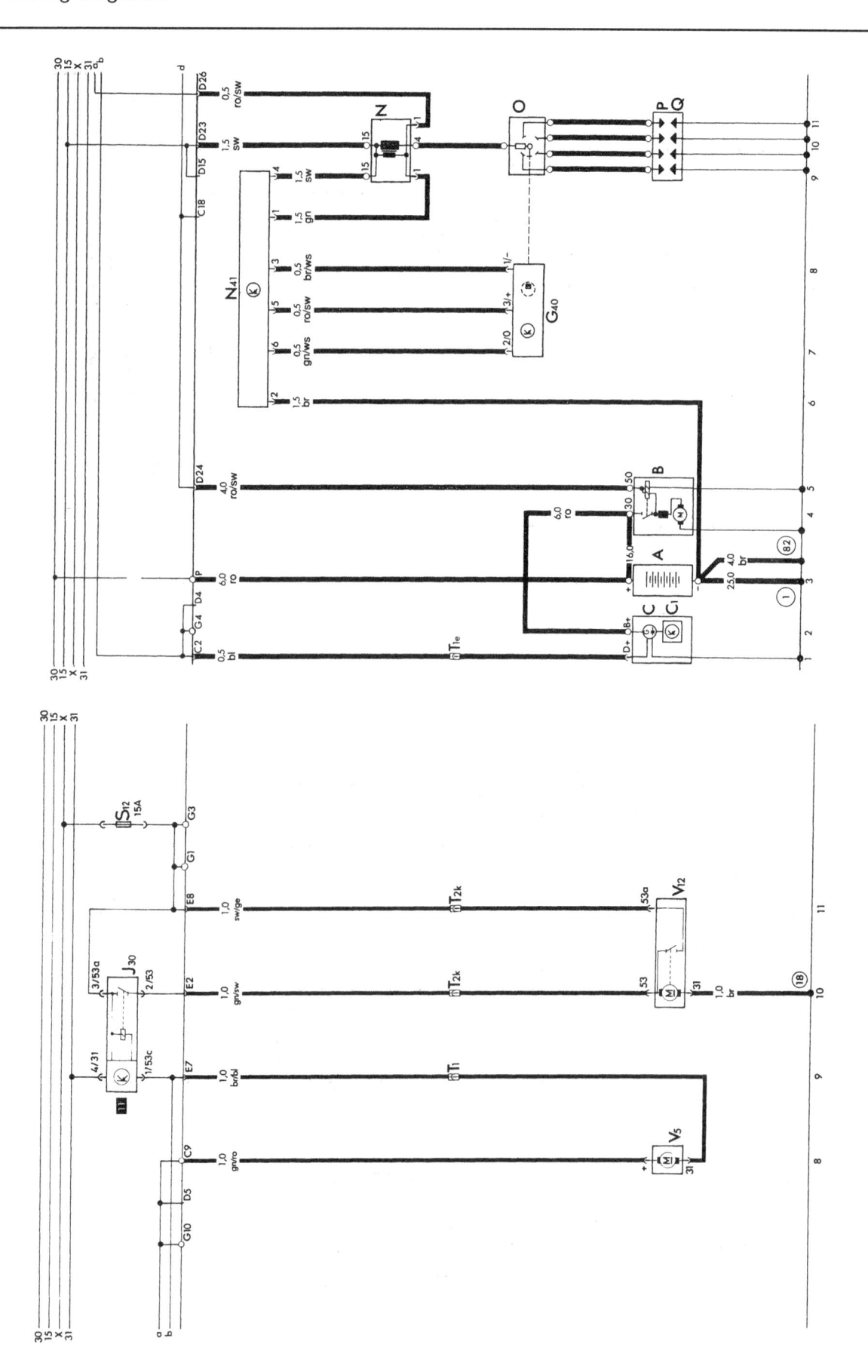

Diagram 36 Starter, alternator, battery and ignition system – 1.6 models, from August 1987

Diagram 35 Windscreen washer, rear wiper and washer – all Golf models from January 1986 to July 1987

Wiring diagrams 12•39

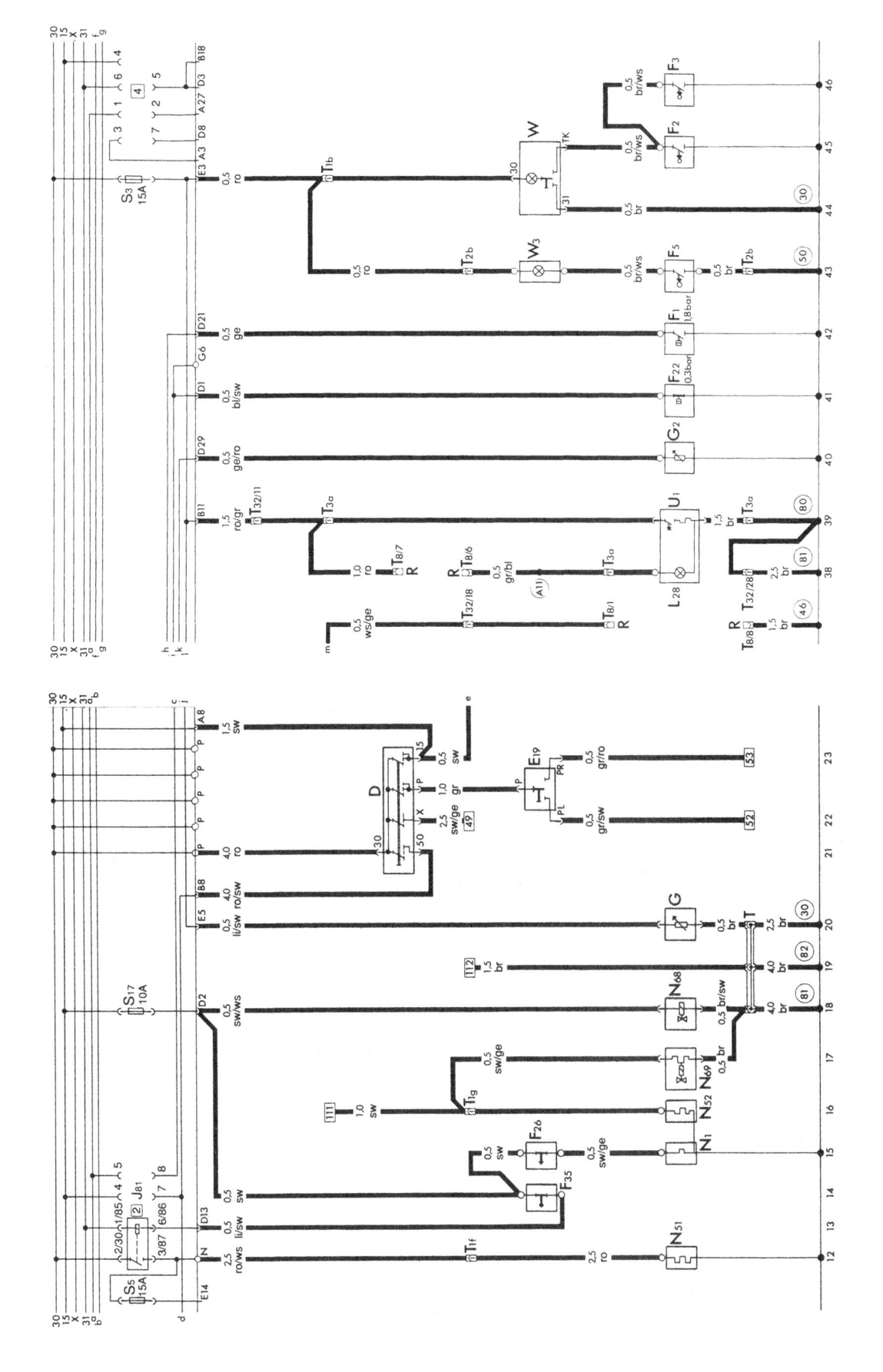

Diagram 38 Interior lights, boot light and radio - all models, from August 1987

Diagram 37 Inlet manifold preheating and automatic choke - 1.6 models, from August 1987

12•40 Wiring diagrams

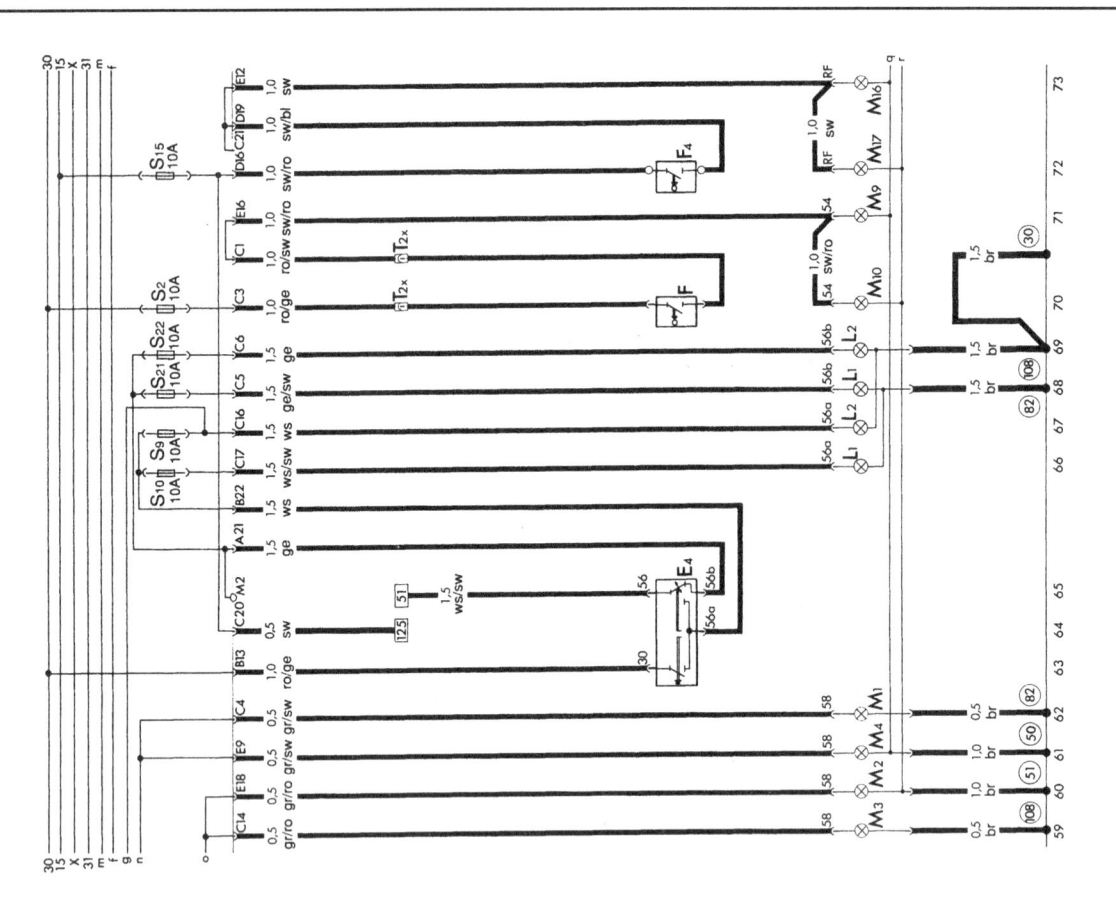

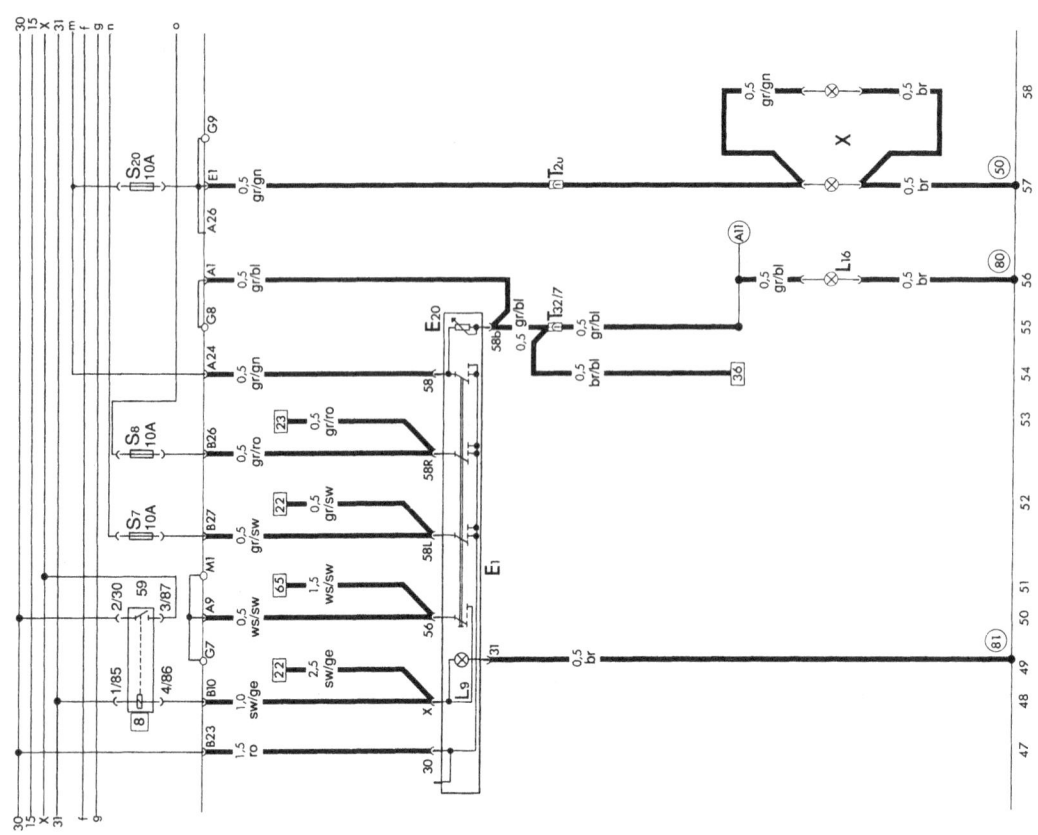

Diagram 40 Headlights, tail lights, dip/flasher headlight switch, brake light switch and reversing light switch - all models, from August 1987

Diagram 39 Light switch and number plate lights - all models, from August 1987

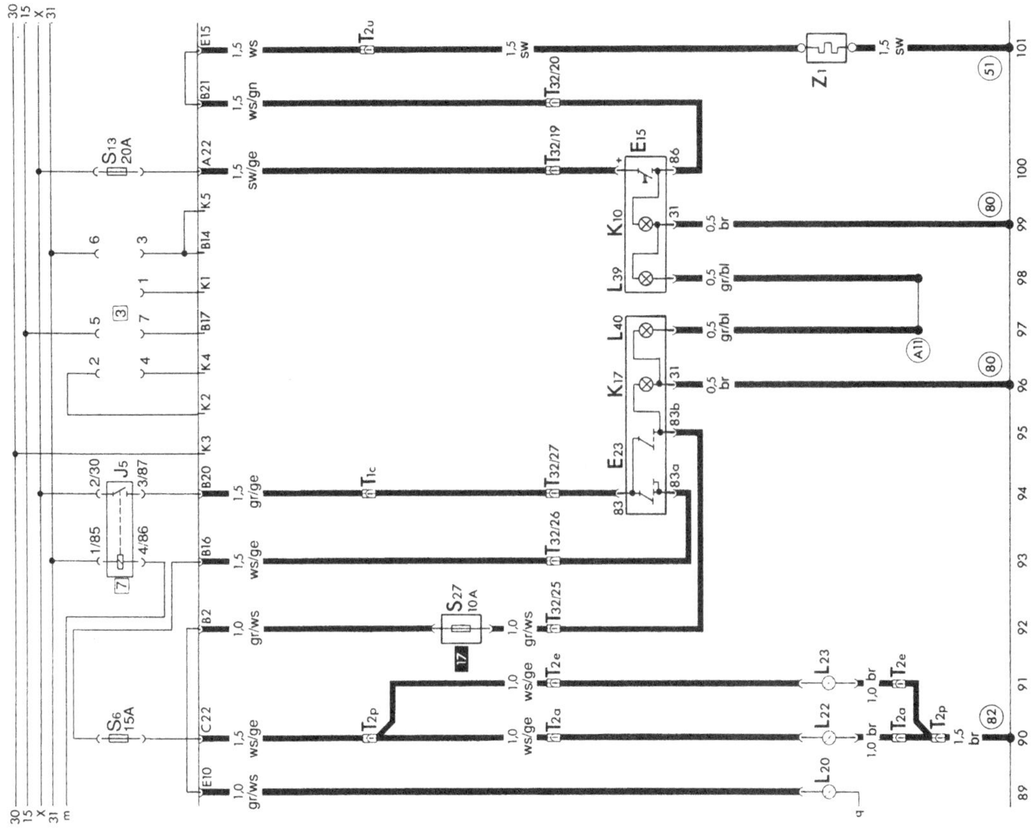

Wiring diagrams 12•41

Diagram 42 Foglights, rear foglights and heated rear window - all models, from August 1987

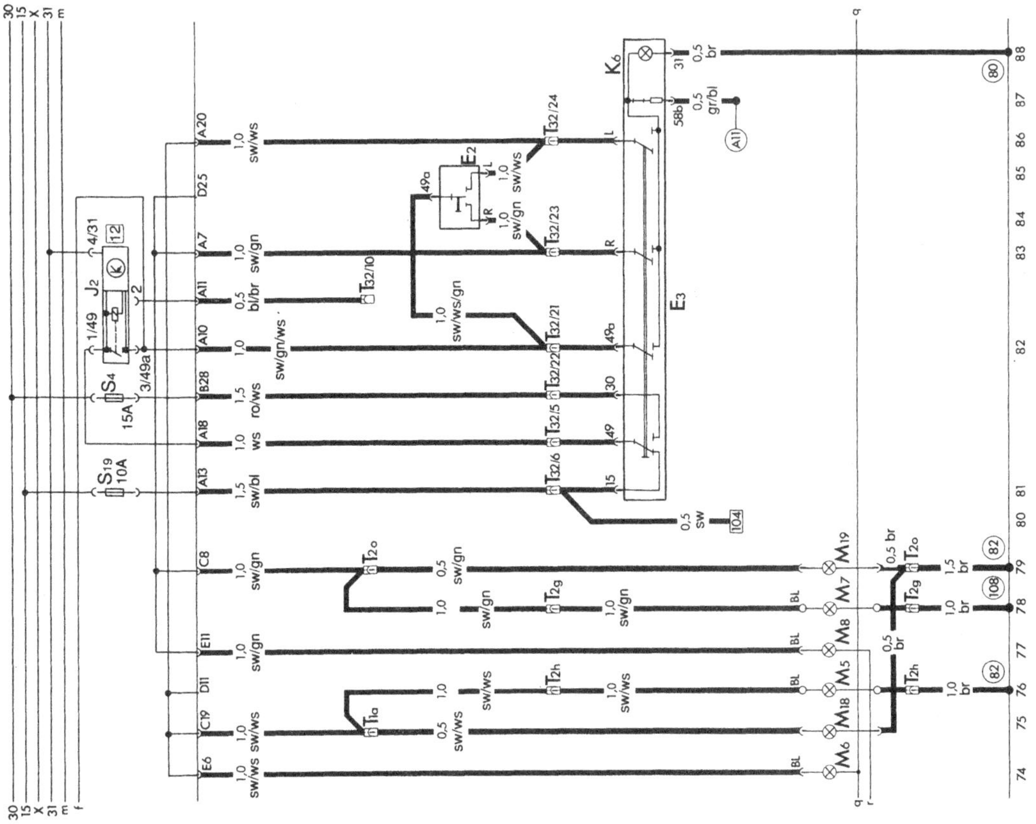

Diagram 41 Indicators and hazard warning lights - all models, from August 1987

12•42 Wiring diagrams

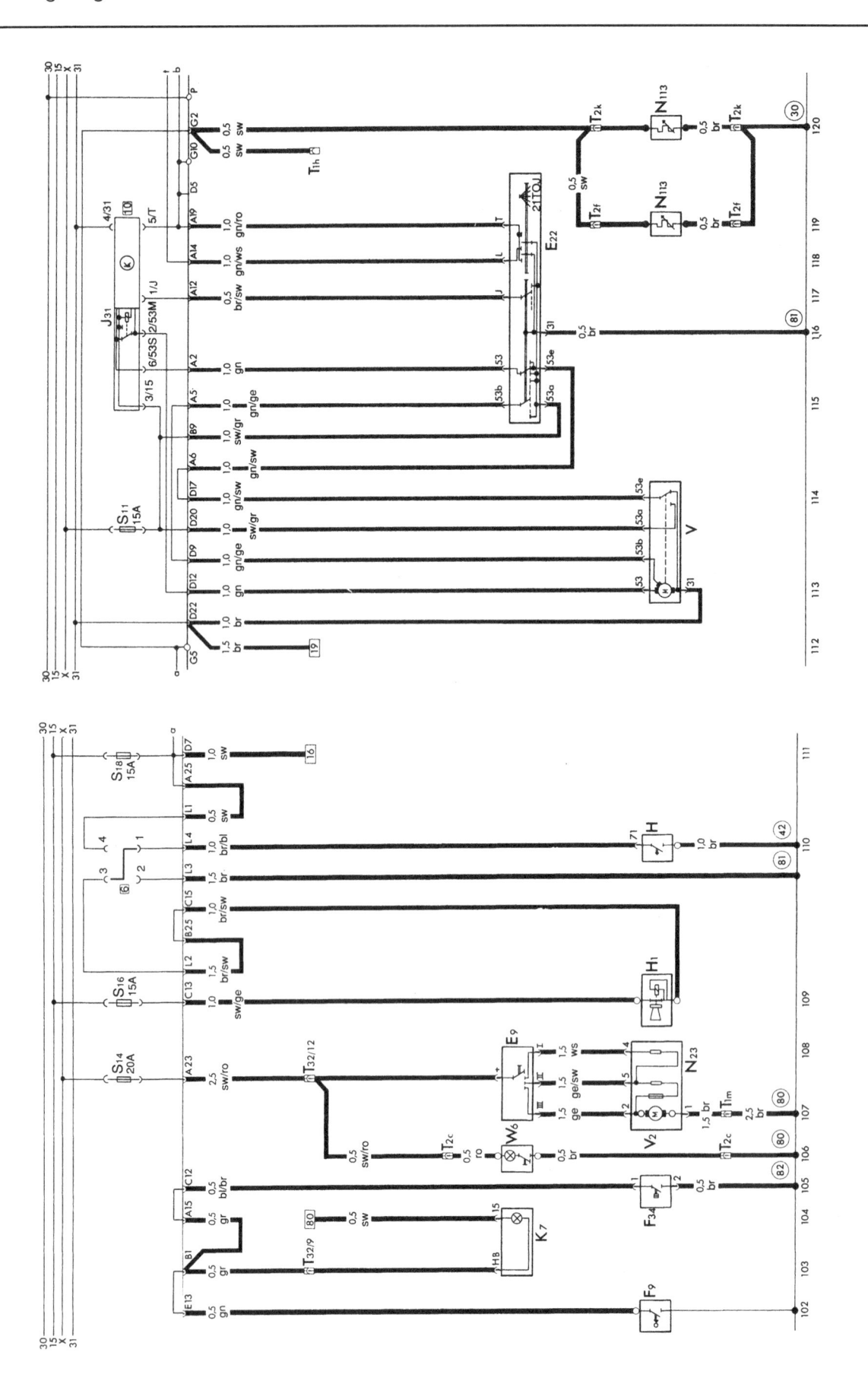

Diagram 44 Windscreen wiper and washers (with heated jets) - all models, from August 1987

Diagram 43 Handbrake and brake fluid level warning, fresh air blower, glovebox light and horn - all models, from August 1987

Wiring diagrams 12•43

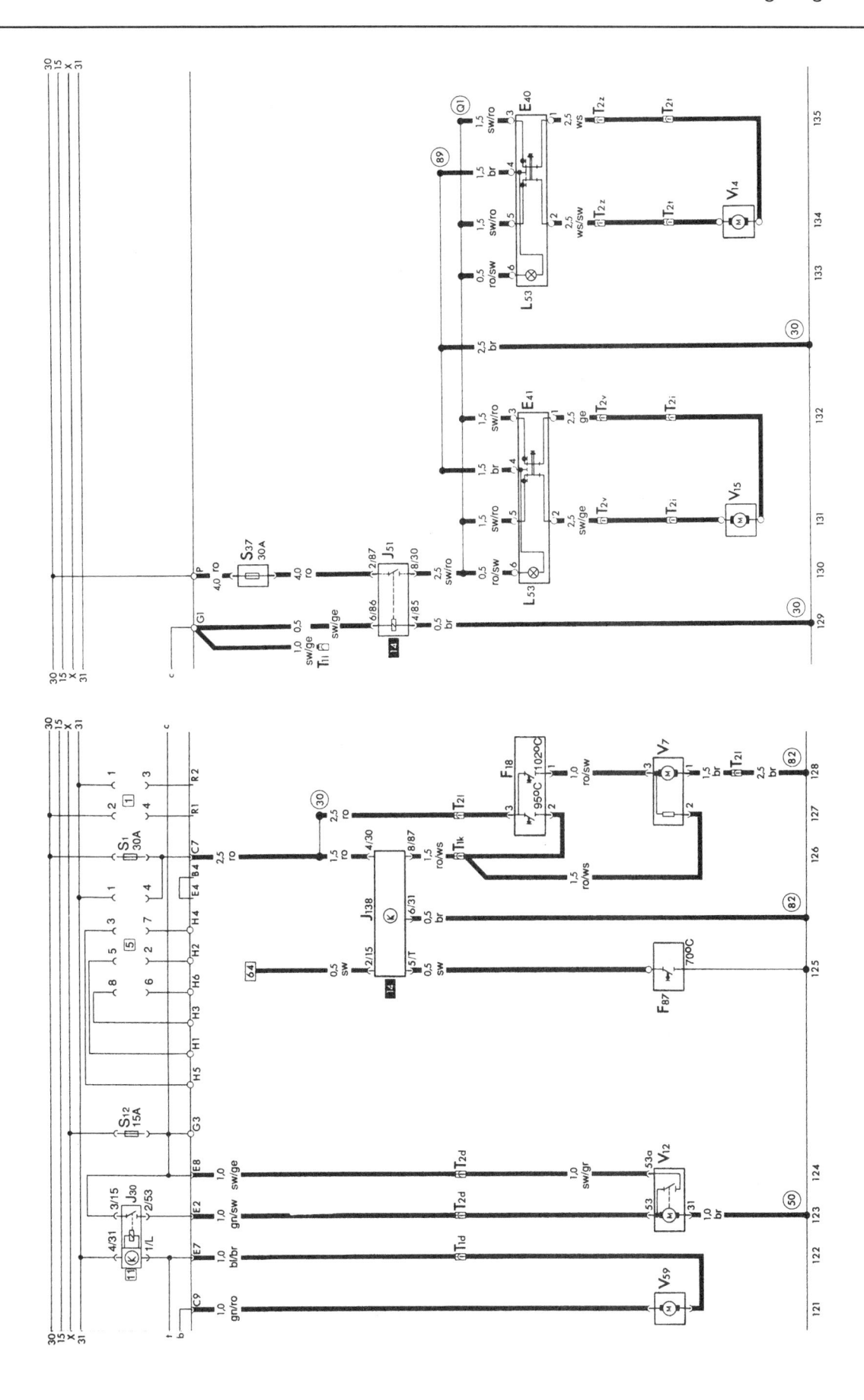

Diagram 46 Electric windows – 1.6 models, from August 1987

Diagram 45 Rear window wiper and radiator fan run-on – 1.6 and 1.8 carburettor models, from August 1987

12•44 Wiring diagrams

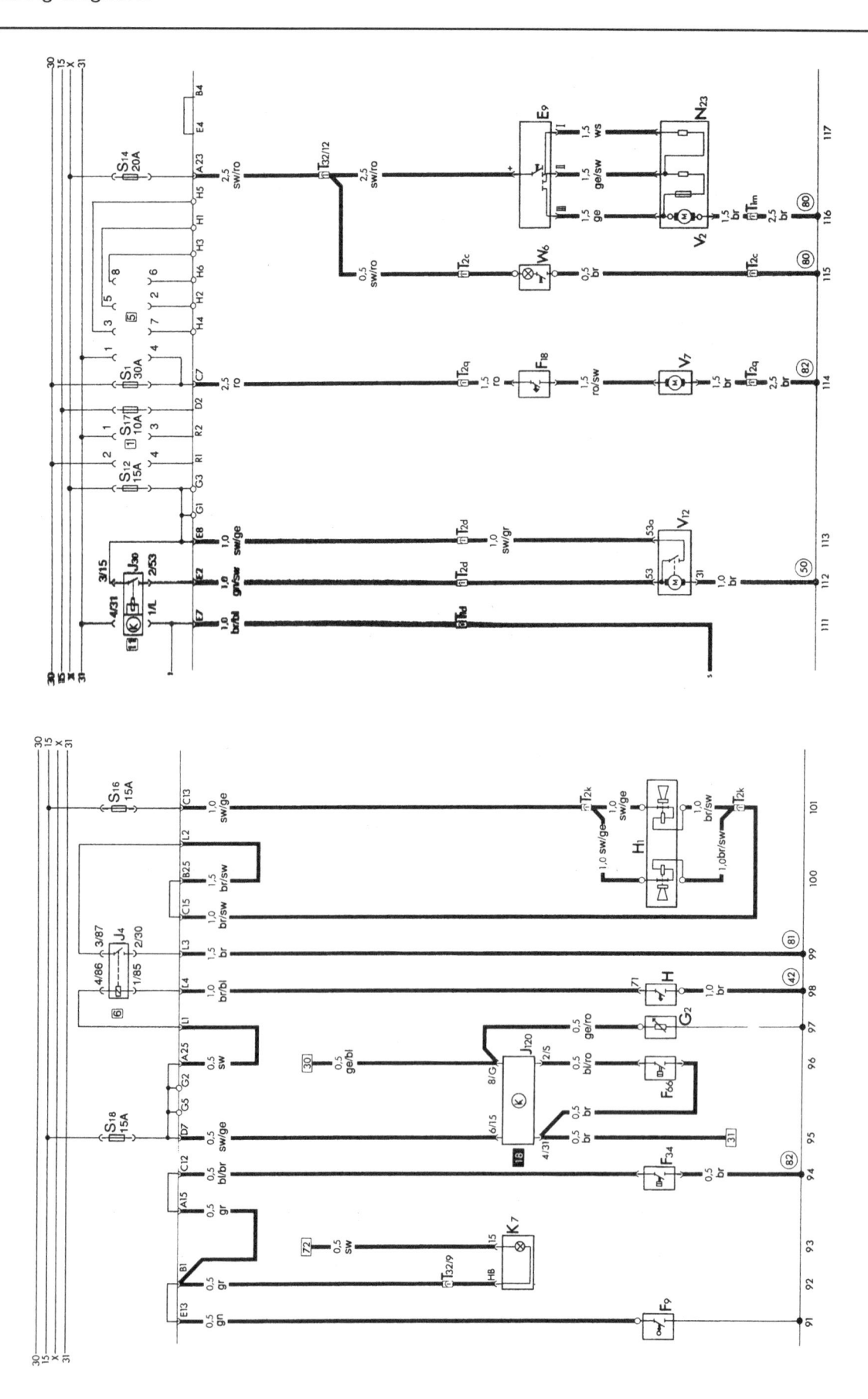

Diagram 48 Rear window wiper and radiator fan – 1.05, 1.3 and 1.8 fuel injection models, from August 1987

Diagram 47 Handbrake, brake fluid warning, low coolant level indicator and dual tone horn – all models from 1987

Wiring diagrams 12•45

Diagram 50 Alternator, battery, starter motor and ignition switch - 1.6 and 1.8 carburettor models, from January 1989

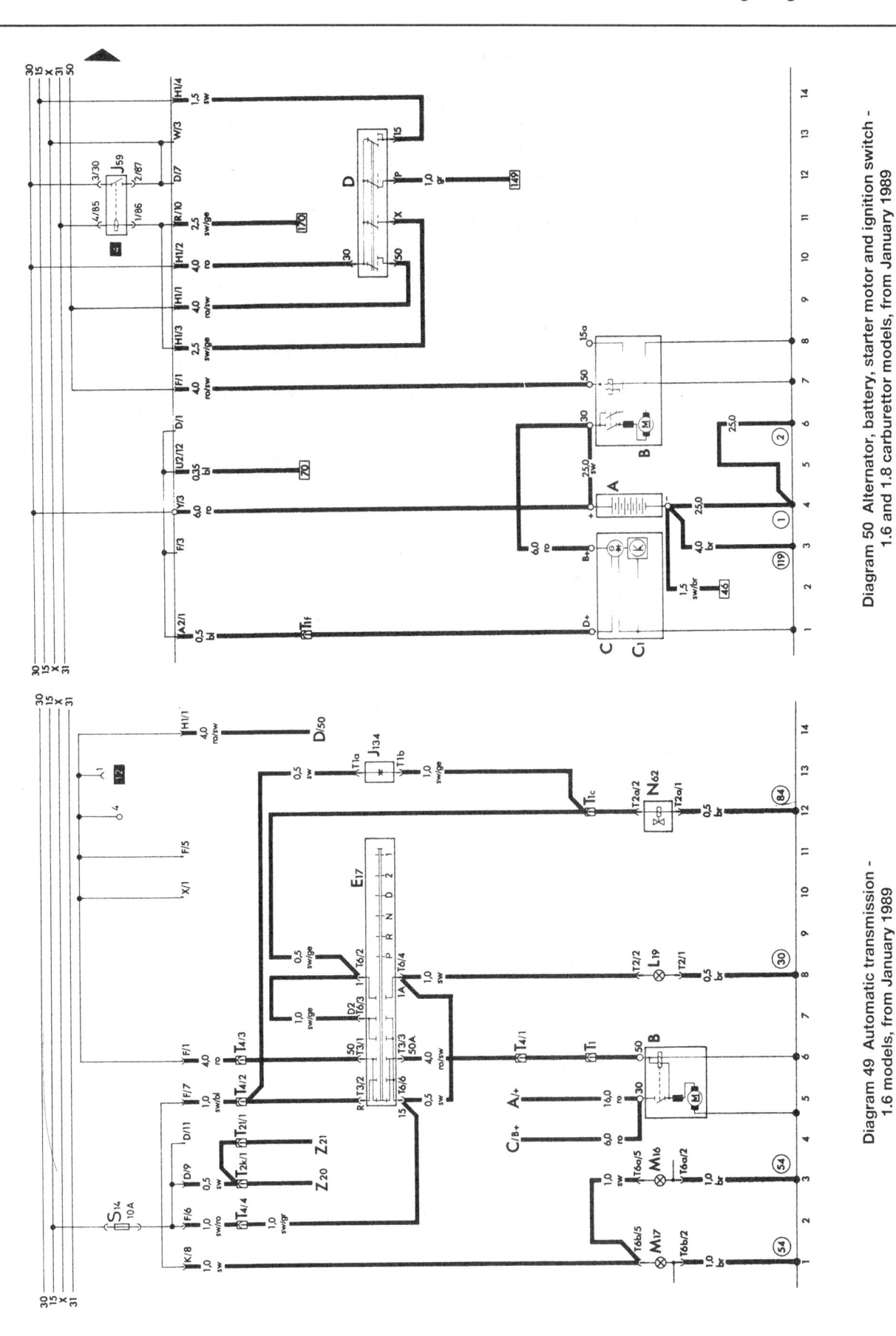

Diagram 49 Automatic transmission - 1.6 models, from January 1989

12•46 Wiring diagrams

Diagram 52 Automatic choke and inlet manifold preheating – 1.6 and 1.8 carburettor models, from January 1989

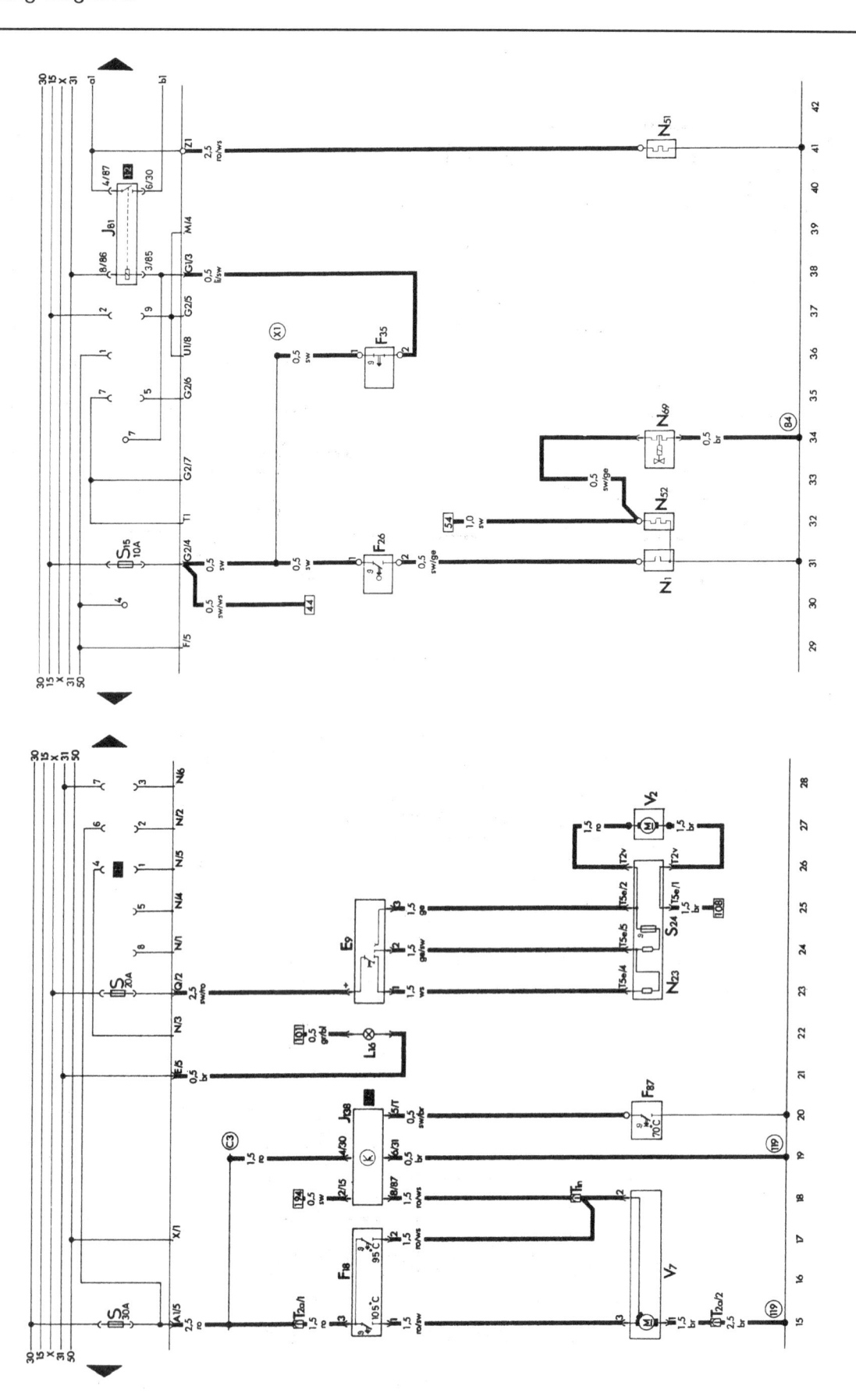

Diagram 51 Radiator fan and fresh air blower – 1.6 and 1.8 carburettor models, from January 1989

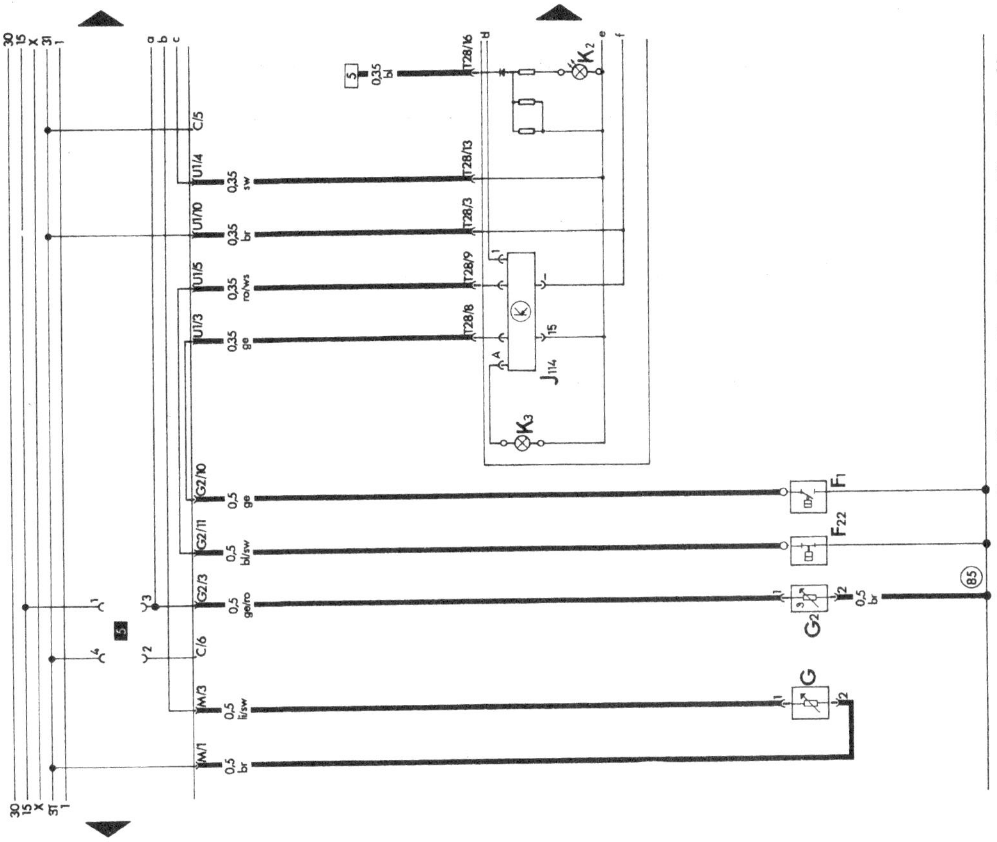

Diagram 54 Instrument panel and oil pressure warning system – 1.6 and 1.8 carburettor models, from January 1989

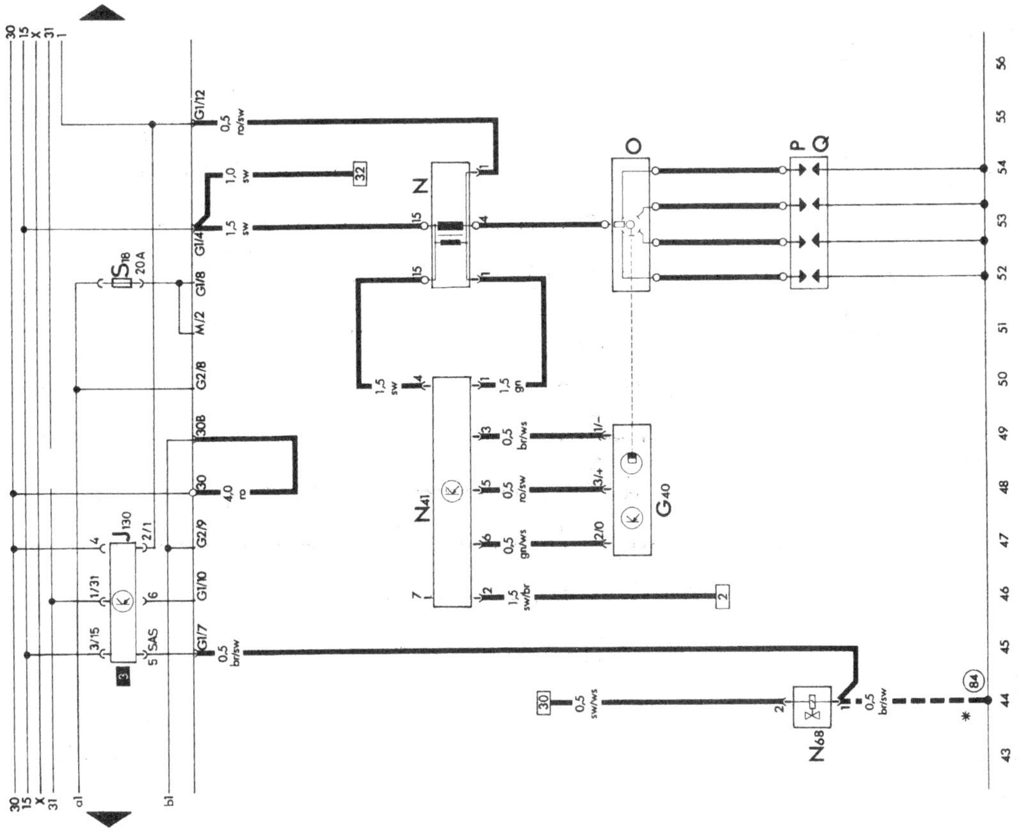

Diagram 53 Ignition system and overrun cut-off – 1.6 and 1.8 carburettor models, from January 1989

12•48 Wiring diagrams

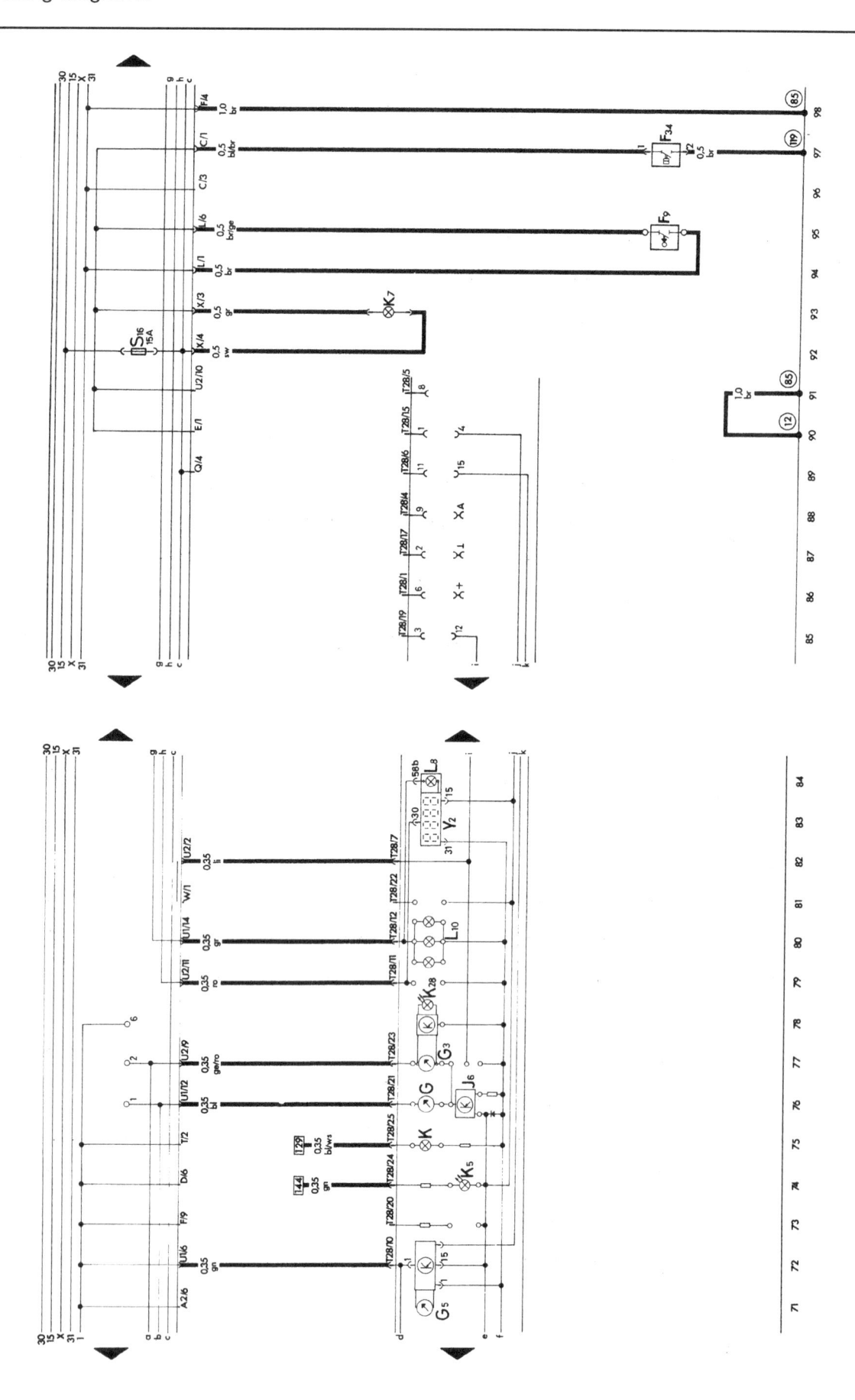

Diagram 56 Handbrake 'on' and brake fluid level warning – 1.6 and 1.8 carburettor models, from January 1989

Diagram 55 Instrument panel (tachometer clock, fuel and temperature gauges) – 1.6 and 1.8 carburettor models, from January 1989

Wiring diagrams 12•49

Diagram 58 Interior light, boot light and number plate light - 1.6 and 1.8 carburettor models, from January 1989

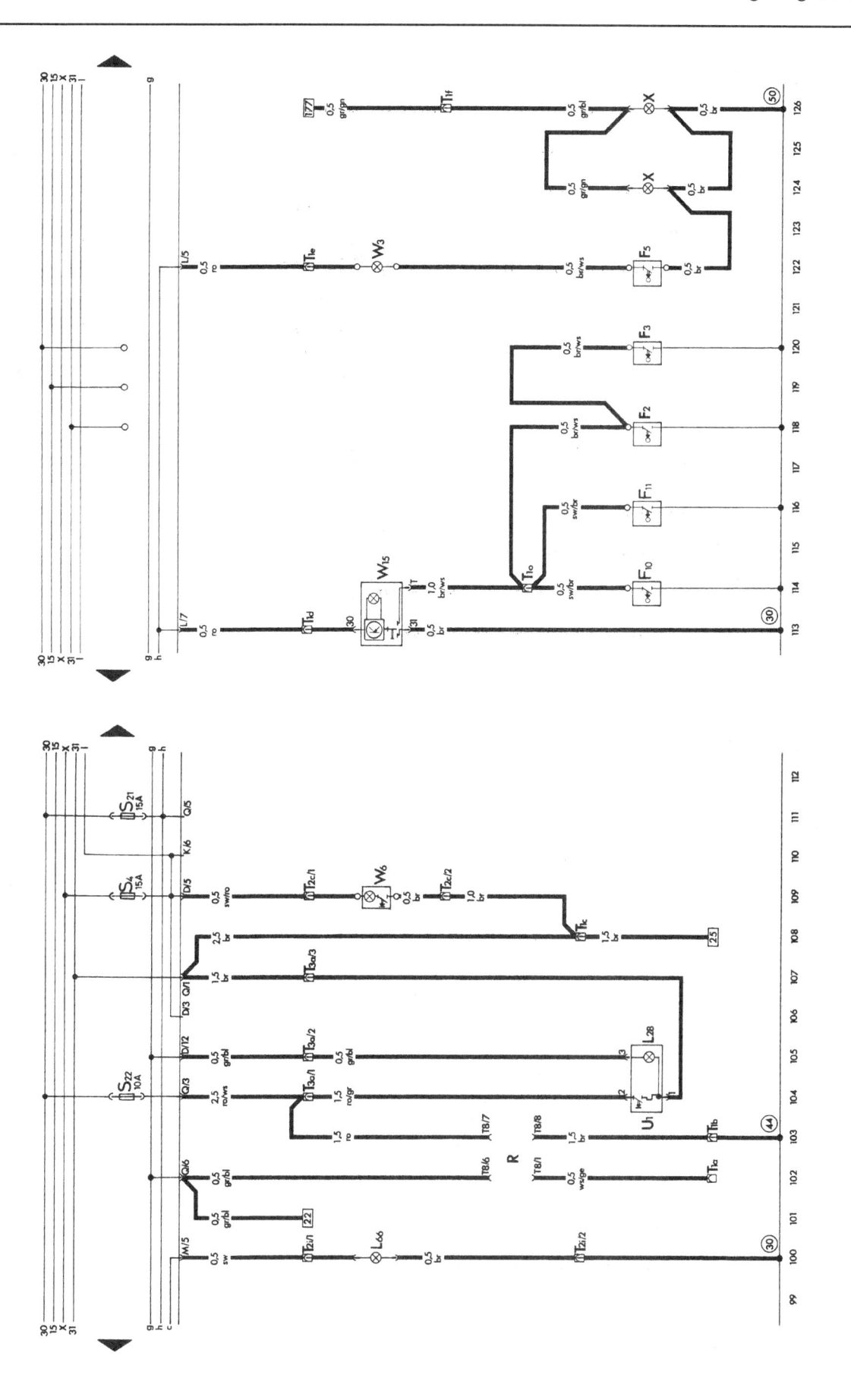

Diagram 57 Glovebox light, cigarette lighter, radio connection and cassette storage light - 1.6 and 1.8 carburettor models, from January 1989

12•50 Wiring diagrams

Diagram 60 Direction indicators, hazard warning lights and parking light switch – 1.6 and 1.8 carburettor models, from January 1989

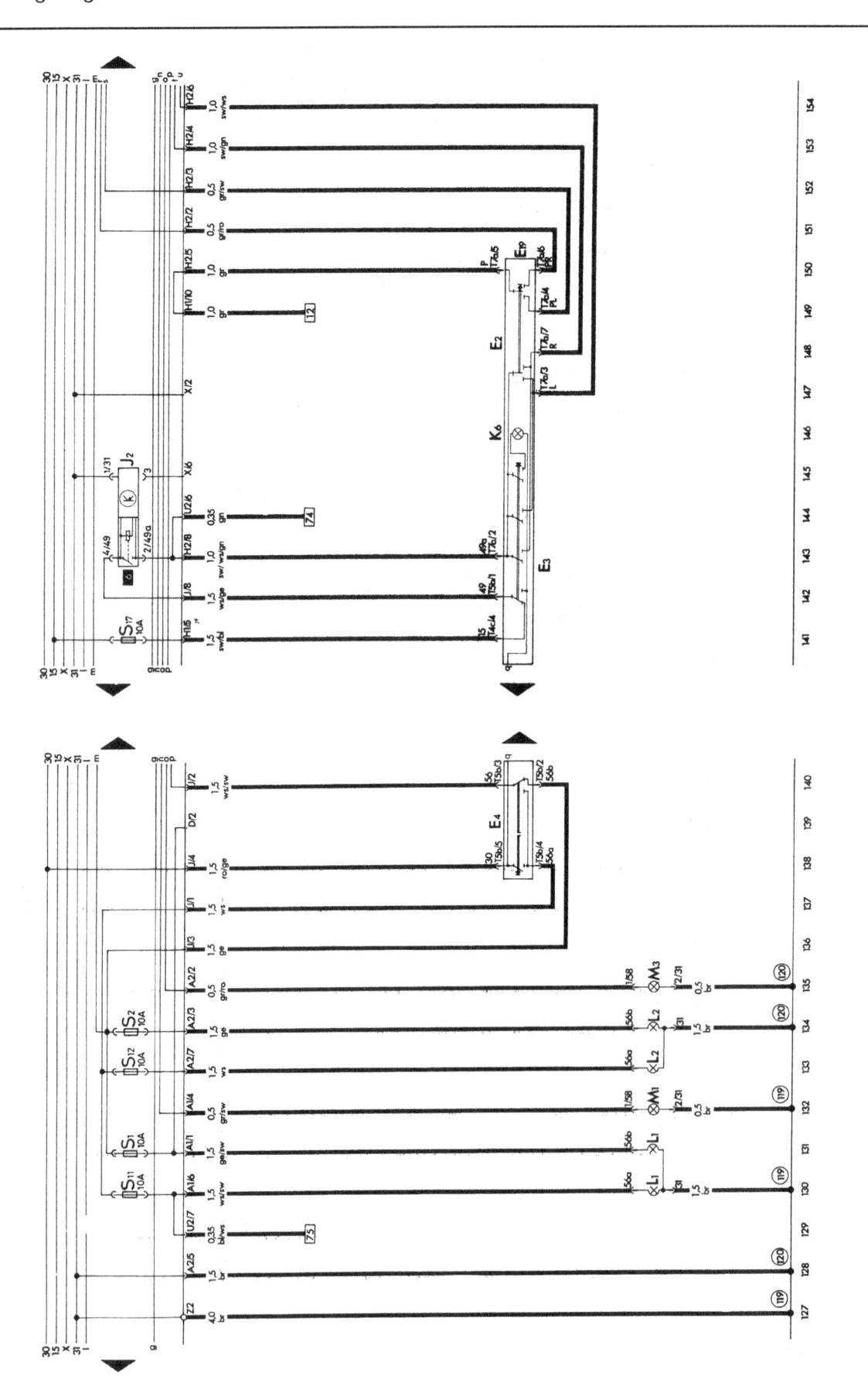

Diagram 59 Headlights, sidelights and headlight dip/flash switch – 1.6 and 1.8 carburettor models, from January 1989

Wiring diagrams 12•51

Diagram 62 Lighting switch and brake lights - 1.6 and 1.8 carburettor models, from January 1989

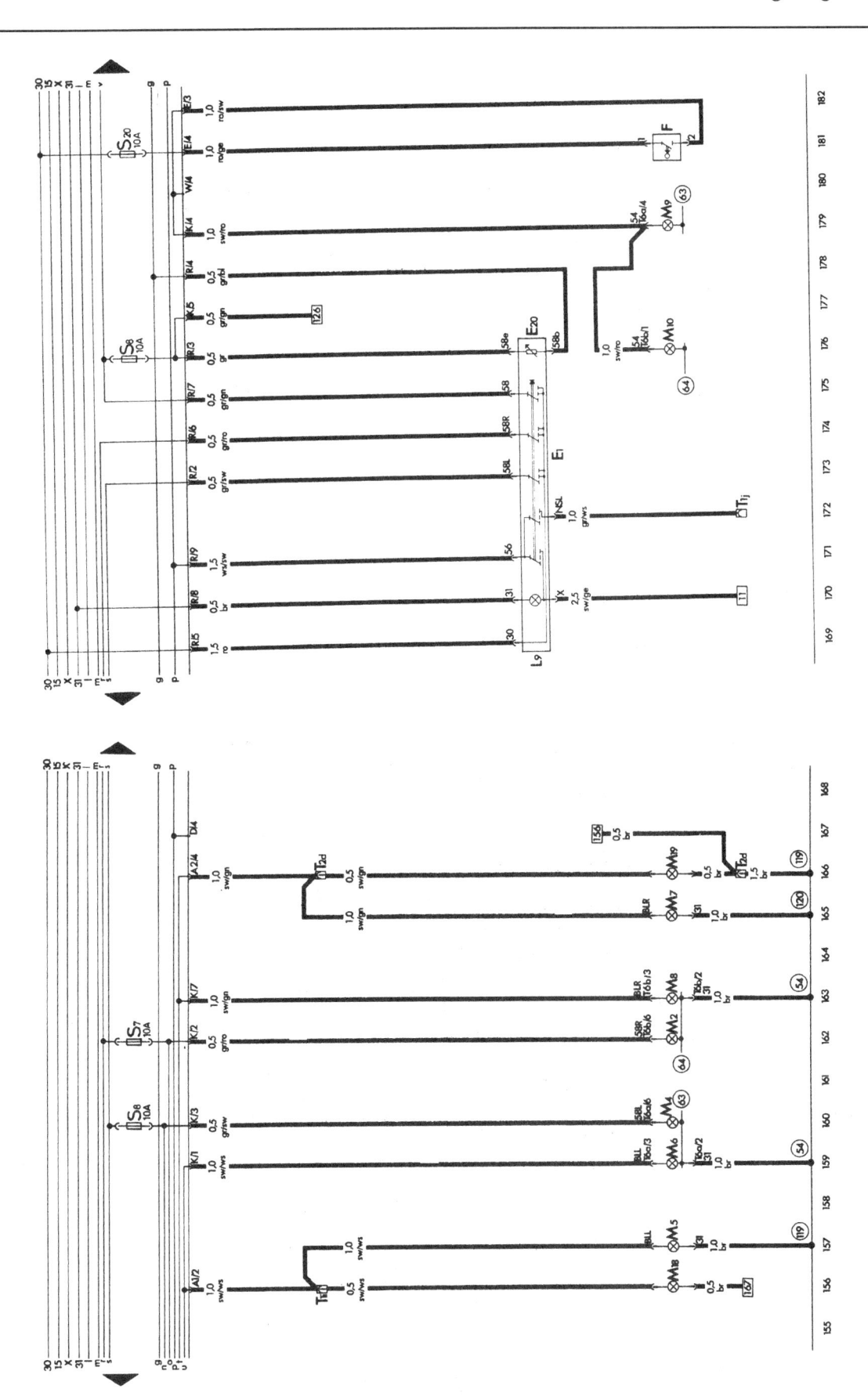

Diagram 61 Direction indicators and tail lights - 1.6 and 1.8 carburettor models, from January 1989

12•52 Wiring diagrams

Diagram 64 Rear foglight and heated windscreen washer jets - 1.6 and 1.8 carburettor models, from January 1989

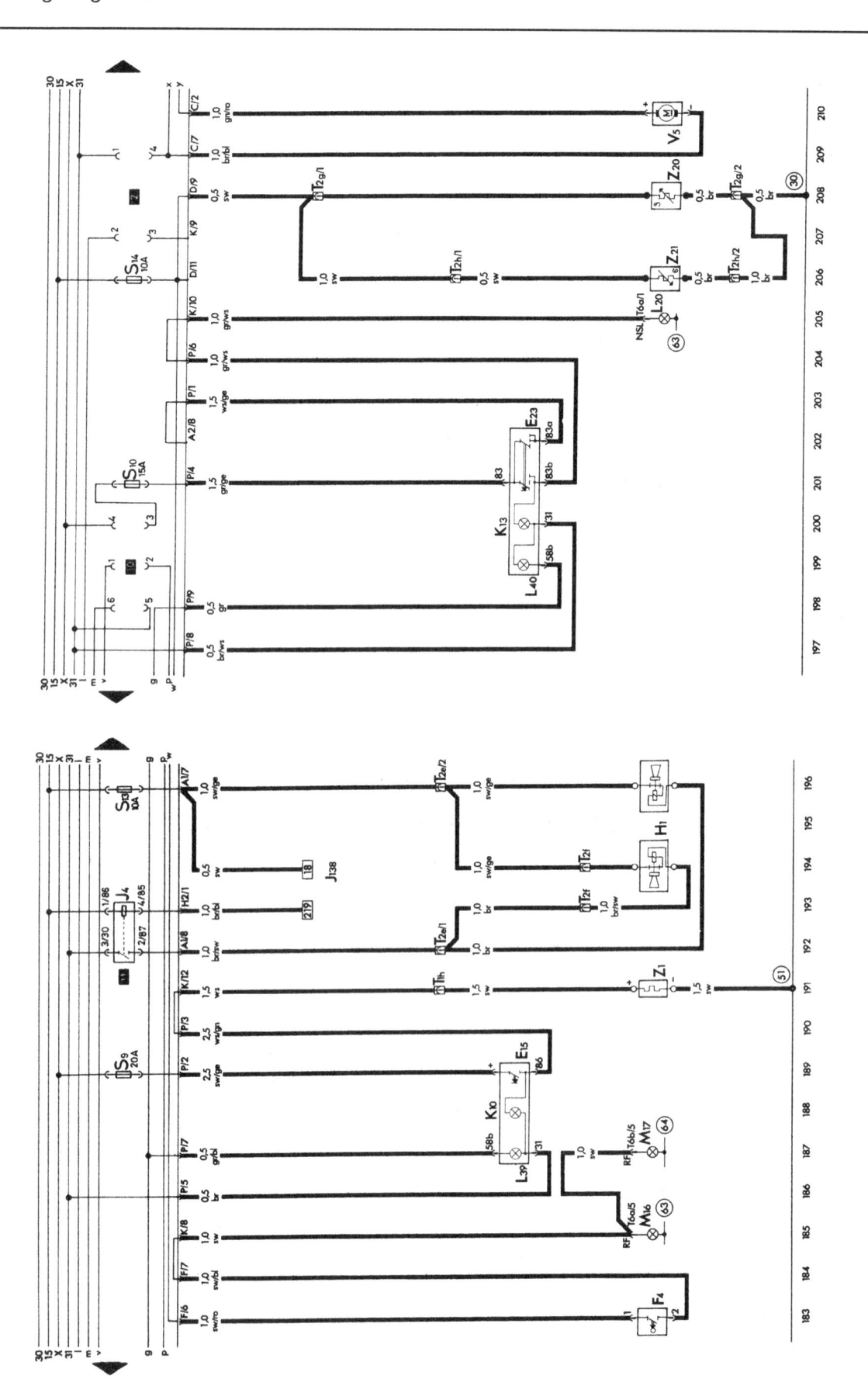

Diagram 63 Reversing lights, heated rear window and dual tone horn - 1.6 and 1.8 carburettor models, from January 1989

Wiring diagrams 12•53

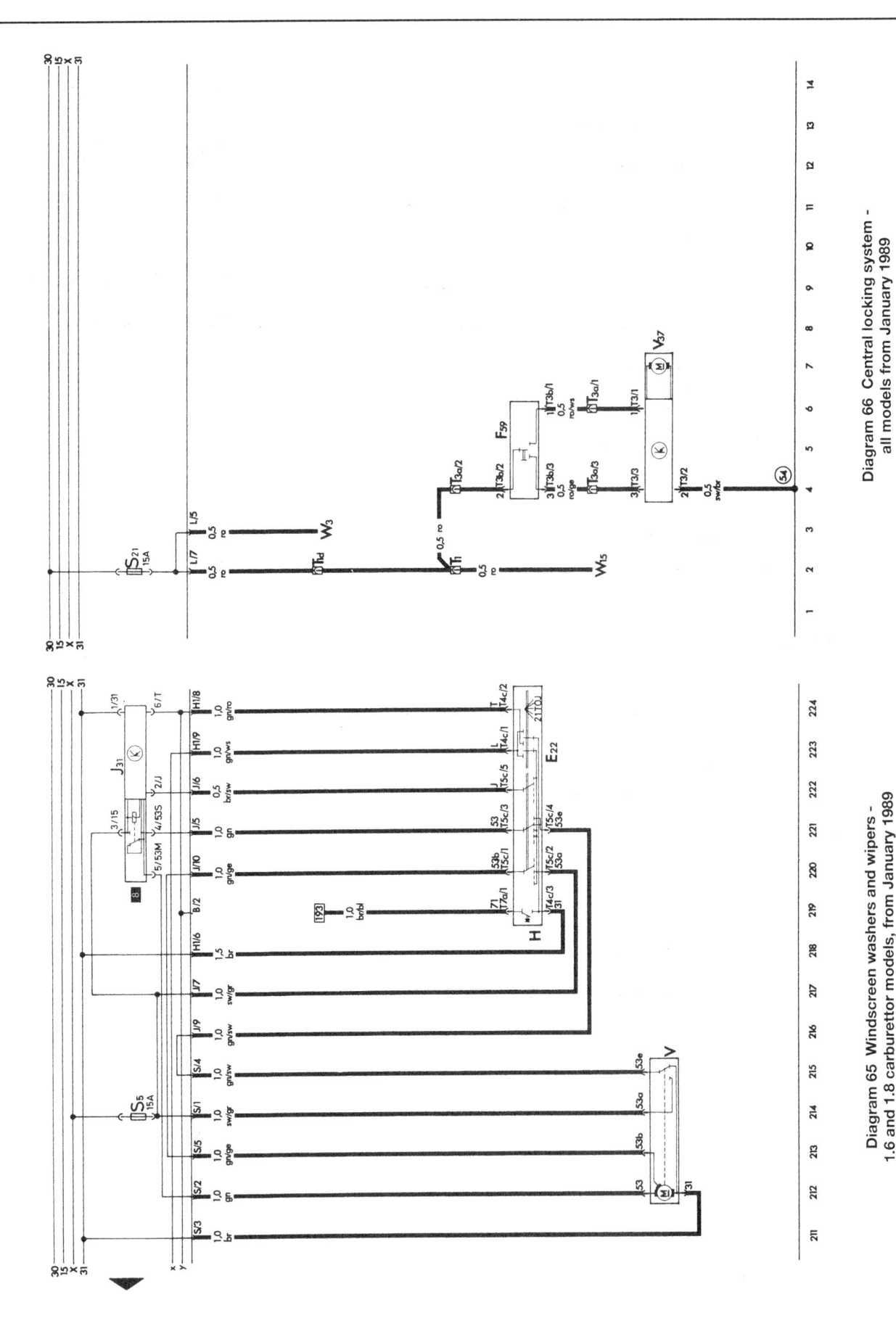

Diagram 66 Central locking system - all models from January 1989

Diagram 65 Windscreen washers and wipers - 1.6 and 1.8 carburettor models, from January 1989

12•54 Wiring diagrams

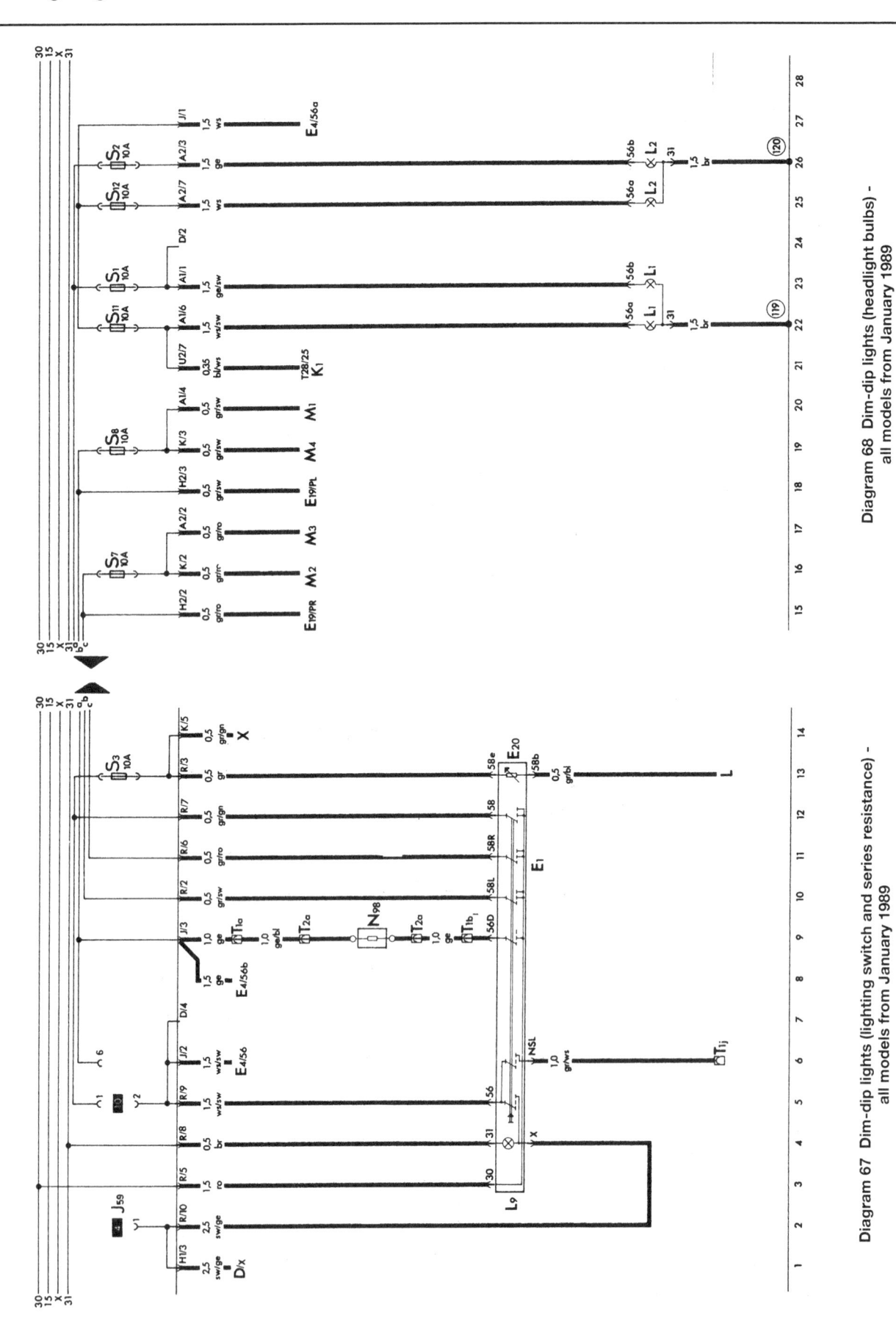

Diagram 67 Dim-dip lights (lighting switch and series resistance) - all models from January 1989

Diagram 68 Dim-dip lights (headlight bulbs) - all models from January 1989

Wiring diagrams 12•55

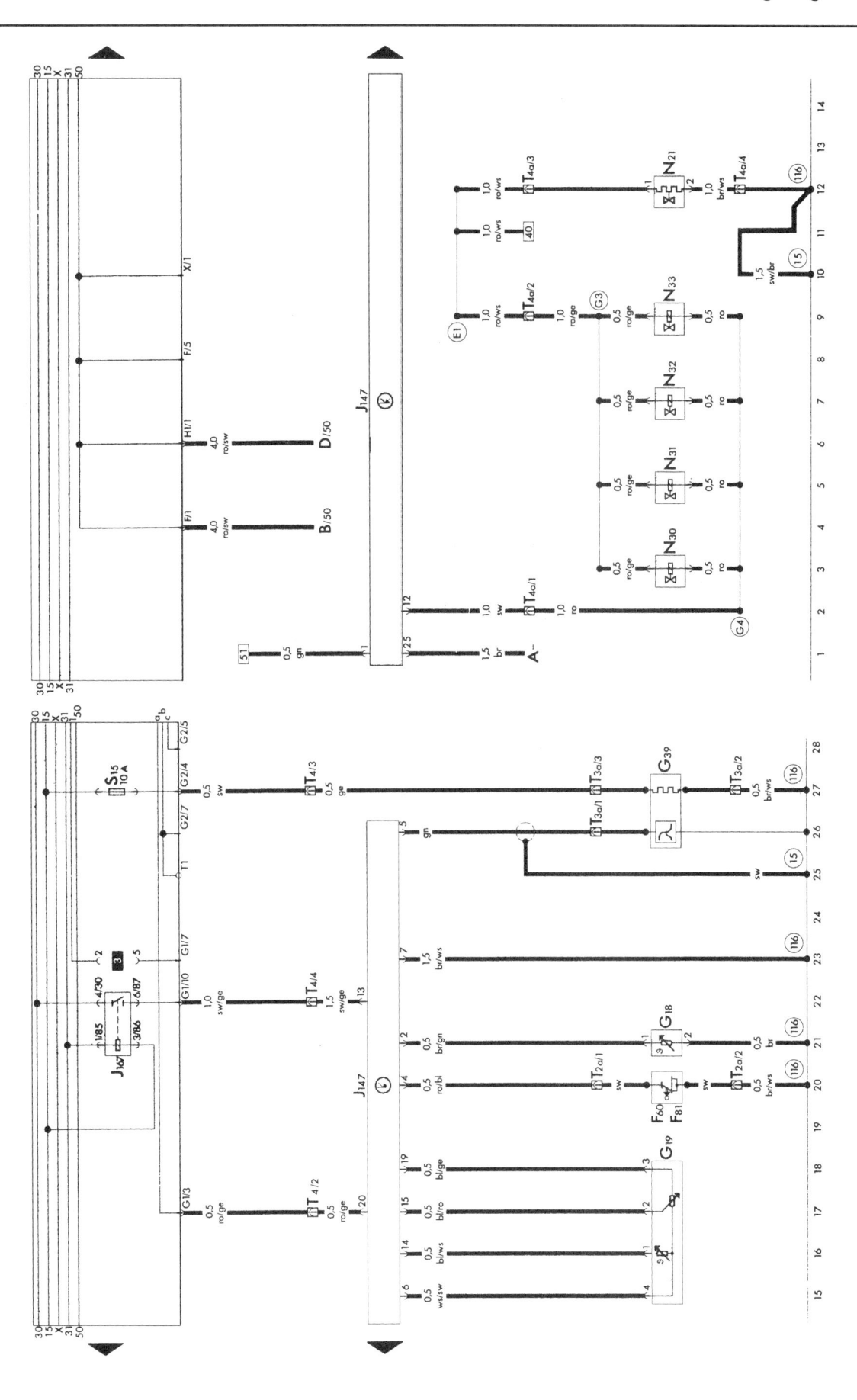

Diagram 70 Digijet control unit and injectors - 1.3 (code NZ) models

Diagram 69 Digijet control unit and sensors - 1.3 (code NZ) models

12•56 Wiring diagrams

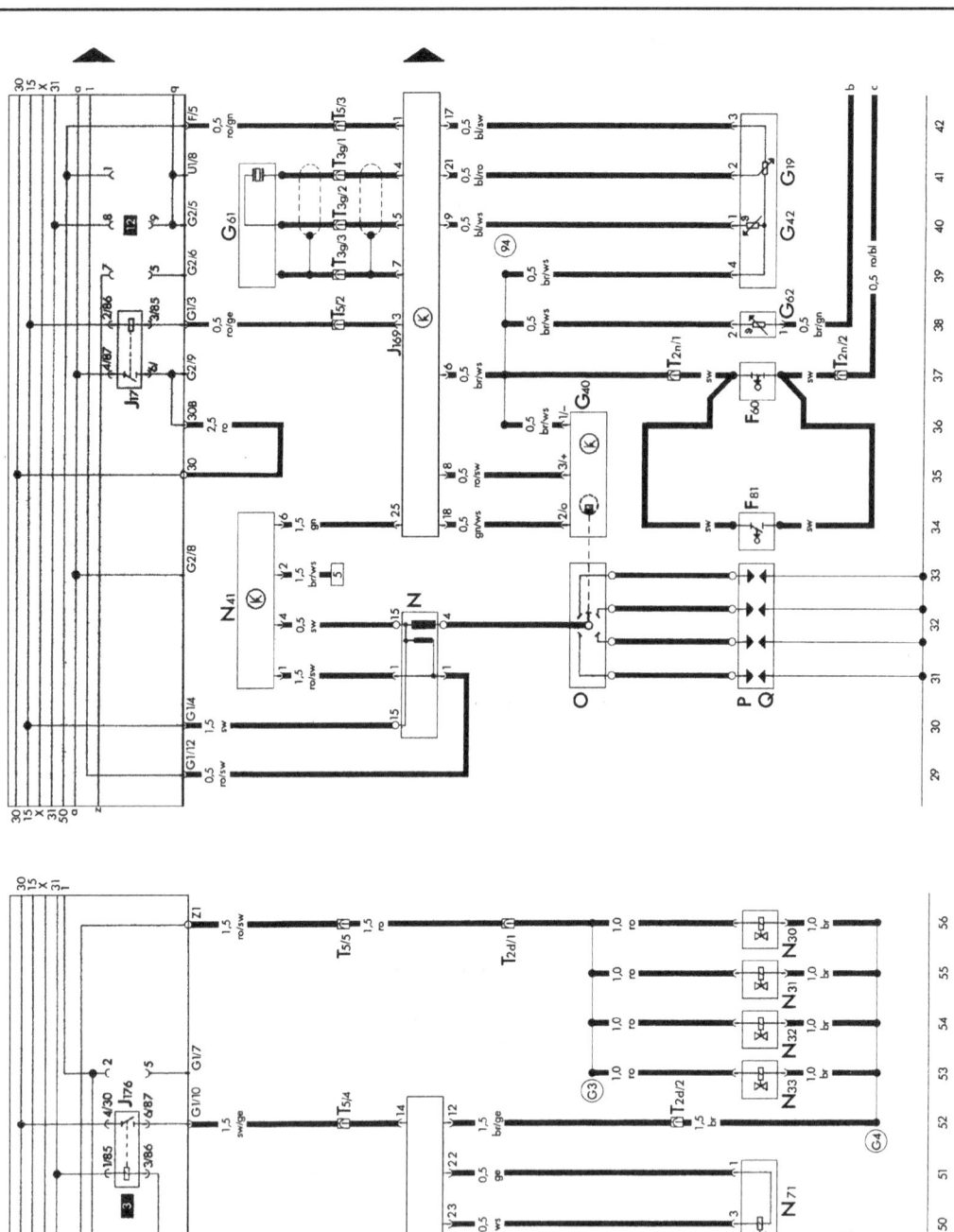

Diagram 72 Digifant ignition system - later 1.8 models

Diagram 71 Digifant fuel system - later 1.8 models

Reference REF•1

Dimensions and weights .REF•1
Conversion factors . . . . .REF•2
Buying spare parts . . . . .REF•3
Vehicle identification . . . . .REF•3
General repair procedures . . . . .REF•4
Jacking and vehicle support . . . . .REF•5

Tools and working facilities . . . . .REF•6
MOT test checks . . . . .REF•8
Fault finding . . . . .REF•12
Glossary of technical terms . . . . .REF•20
Index . . . . .REF•25

Dimensions and weights

Note that vehicle kerb weights for later models have increased marginally over those given below. Further information can be obtained from a VW dealer

Dimensions
Overall length:
  Golf . . . . .3985 mm
  Jetta . . . . .4315 mm
Overall width:
  Golf . . . . .1665 mm
  Jetta . . . . .1665 mm
Overall height:
  Golf . . . . .1415 mm
  Golf GTi . . . . .1405 mm
  Jetta . . . . .1415 mm
Wheelbase:
  All models . . . . .2475 mm
Turning circle:
  All models . . . . .10.5 m

Weights (approximate)
Kerb weight:
  Golf Base model . . . . .837 kg
  Golf C and C Formel E:
    Manual . . . . .847 kg
    Automatic . . . . .867 kg
  Golf GL:
    Manual . . . . .892 kg
    Automatic . . . . .912 kg
  Golf GTI . . . . .1003 kg
  Jetta C . . . . .897 kg
  Jetta CL Formel E . . . . .897 kg
  Jetta GL:
    Manual . . . . .922 kg
    Automatic . . . . .952 kg
Maximum trailer load – with brakes:
  1.05 litre . . . . .800 kg
  1.3 litre . . . . .1000 kg
  1.6 and 1.8 litre . . . . .1200 kg
Maximum roof rack load:
  All models . . . . .75 kg

Conversion factors

Length (distance)
Inches (in)	x 25.4	= Millimetres (mm)	x 0.0394	=	Inches (in)
Feet (ft)	x 0.305	= Metres (m)	x 3.281	=	Feet (ft)
Miles	x 1.609	= Kilometres (km)	x 0.621	=	Miles

Volume (capacity)
Cubic inches (cu in; in^3)	x 16.387	= Cubic centimetres (cc; cm^3)	x 0.061	=	Cubic inches (cu in; in^3)
Imperial pints (Imp pt)	x 0.568	= Litres (l)	x 1.76	=	Imperial pints (Imp pt)
Imperial quarts (Imp qt)	x 1.137	= Litres (l)	x 0.88	=	Imperial quarts (Imp qt)
Imperial quarts (Imp qt)	x 1.201	= US quarts (US qt)	x 0.833	=	Imperial quarts (Imp qt)
US quarts (US qt)	x 0.946	= Litres (l)	x 1.057	=	US quarts (US qt)
Imperial gallons (Imp gal)	x 4.546	= Litres (l)	x 0.22	=	Imperial gallons (Imp gal)
Imperial gallons (Imp gal)	x 1.201	= US gallons (US gal)	x 0.833	=	Imperial gallons (Imp gal)
US gallons (US gal)	x 3.785	= Litres (l)	x 0.264	=	US gallons (US gal)

Mass (weight)
Ounces (oz)	x 28.35	= Grams (g)	x 0.035	=	Ounces (oz)
Pounds (lb)	x 0.454	= Kilograms (kg)	x 2.205	=	Pounds (lb)

Force
Ounces-force (ozf; oz)	x 0.278	= Newtons (N)	x 3.6	=	Ounces-force (ozf; oz)
Pounds-force (lbf; lb)	x 4.448	= Newtons (N)	x 0.225	=	Pounds-force (lbf; lb)
Newtons (N)	x 0.1	= Kilograms-force (kgf; kg)	x 9.81	=	Newtons (N)

Pressure
Pounds-force per square inch (psi; lbf/in^2; lb/in^2)	x 0.070	= Kilograms-force per square centimetre (kgf/cm^2; kg/cm^2)	x 14.223	=	Pounds-force per square inch (psi; lbf/in^2; lb/in^2)
Pounds-force per square inch (psi; lbf/in^2; lb/in^2)	x 0.068	= Atmospheres (atm)	x 14.696	=	Pounds-force per square inch (psi; lbf/in^2; lb/in^2)
Pounds-force per square inch (psi; lbf/in^2; lb/in^2)	x 0.069	= Bars	x 14.5	=	Pounds-force per square inch (psi; lbf/in^2; lb/in^2)
Pounds-force per square inch (psi; lbf/in^2; lb/in^2)	x 6.895	= Kilopascals (kPa)	x 0.145	=	Pounds-force per square inch (psi; lbf/in^2; lb/in^2)
Kilopascals (kPa)	x 0.01	= Kilograms-force per square centimetre (kgf/cm^2; kg/cm^2)	x 98.1	=	Kilopascals (kPa)
Millibar (mbar)	x 100	= Pascals (Pa)	x 0.01	=	Millibar (mbar)
Millibar (mbar)	x 0.0145	= Pounds-force per square inch (psi; lbf/in^2; lb/in^2)	x 68.947	=	Millibar (mbar)
Millibar (mbar)	x 0.75	= Millimetres of mercury (mmHg)	x 1.333	=	Millibar (mbar)
Millibar (mbar)	x 0.401	= Inches of water (inH$_2$O)	x 2.491	=	Millibar (mbar)
Millimetres of mercury (mmHg)	x 0.535	= Inches of water (inH$_2$O)	x 1.868	=	Millimetres of mercury (mmHg)
Inches of water (inH$_2$O)	x 0.036	= Pounds-force per square inch (psi; lbf/in^2; lb/in^2)	x 27.68	=	Inches of water (inH$_2$O)

Torque (moment of force)
Pounds-force inches (lbf in; lb in)	x 1.152	= Kilograms-force centimetre (kgf cm; kg cm)	x 0.868	=	Pounds-force inches (lbf in; lb in)
Pounds-force inches (lbf in; lb in)	x 0.113	= Newton metres (Nm)	x 8.85	=	Pounds-force inches (lbf in; lb in)
Pounds-force inches (lbf in; lb in)	x 0.083	= Pounds-force feet (lbf ft; lb ft)	x 12	=	Pounds-force inches (lbf in; lb in)
Pounds-force feet (lbf ft; lb ft)	x 0.138	= Kilograms-force metres (kgf m; kg m)	x 7.233	=	Pounds-force feet (lbf ft; lb ft)
Pounds-force feet (lbf ft; lb ft)	x 1.356	= Newton metres (Nm)	x 0.738	=	Pounds-force feet (lbf ft; lb ft)
Newton metres (Nm)	x 0.102	= Kilograms-force metres (kgf m; kg m)	x 9.804	=	Newton metres (Nm)

Power
Horsepower (hp)	x 745.7	= Watts (W)	x 0.0013	=	Horsepower (hp)

Velocity (speed)
Miles per hour (miles/hr; mph)	x 1.609	= Kilometres per hour (km/hr; kph)	x 0.621	=	Miles per hour (miles/hr; mph)

Fuel consumption*
Miles per gallon (mpg)	x 0.354	= Kilometres per litre (km/l)	x 2.825	=	Miles per gallon (mpg)

Temperature
Degrees Fahrenheit = (°C x 1.8) + 32   Degrees Celsius (Degrees Centigrade; °C) = (°F - 32) x 0.56

It is common practice to convert from miles per gallon (mpg) to litres/100 kilometres (l/100km), where mpg x l/100 km = 282

Buying spare parts

Spare parts are available from many sources, including maker's appointed garages, accessory shops, and motor factors. To be sure of obtaining the correct parts, it will sometimes be necessary to quote the vehicle identification number. If possible, it can also be useful to take the old parts along for positive identification. Items such as starter motors and alternators may be available under a service exchange scheme - any parts returned should always be clean.

Our advice regarding spare part sources is as follows.

Officially-appointed garages

This is the best source of parts which are peculiar to your car, and which are not otherwise generally available (eg badges, interior trim, certain body panels, etc). It is also the only place at which you should buy parts if the vehicle is still under warranty.

Accessory shops

These are very good places to buy materials and components needed for the maintenance of your car (oil, air and fuel filters, spark plugs, light bulbs, drivebelts, oils and greases, brake pads, touch-up paint, etc). Components of this nature sold by a reputable shop are of the same standard as those used by the car manufacturer.

Besides components, these shops also sell tools and general accessories, usually have convenient opening hours, charge lower prices, and can often be found not far from home. Some accessory shops have parts counters where the components needed for almost any repair job can be purchased or ordered.

Motor factors

Good factors will stock all the more important components which wear out comparatively quickly, and can sometimes supply individual components needed for the overhaul of a larger assembly (eg brake seals and hydraulic parts, bearing shells, pistons, valves, alternator brushes). They may also handle work such as cylinder block reboring, crankshaft regrinding and balancing, etc.

Tyre and exhaust specialists

These outlets may be independent, or members of a local or national chain. They frequently offer competitive prices when compared with a main dealer or local garage, but it will pay to obtain several quotes before making a decision. When researching prices, also ask what "extras" may be added - for instance, fitting a new valve and balancing the wheel are both commonly charged on top of the price of a new tyre.

Other sources

Beware of parts or materials obtained from market stalls, car boot sales or similar outlets. Such items are not invariably sub-standard, but there is little chance of compensation if they do prove unsatisfactory. In the case of safety-critical components such as brake pads, there is the risk not only of financial loss but also of an accident causing injury or death.

Second-hand components or assemblies obtained from a car breaker can be a good buy in some circumstances, but this sort of purchase is best made by the experienced DIY mechanic.

Vehicle identification

Modifications are a continuing and unpublicised process in vehicle manufacture, quite apart from major model changes. Spare parts manuals and lists are compiled upon a numerical basis, the individual vehicle identification numbers being essential to correct identification of the component concerned.

When ordering spare parts, always give as much information as possible. Quote the vehicle model, year of manufacture, chassis and engine numbers as appropriate.

The *vehicle identification plate* is located within the engine compartment, on the right-hand inner wing (see illustration). There is also a *vehicle identification sticker* on the left-hand side of the luggage compartment rear panel which contains the VIN, engine/gearbox code letters and paint/trim codes.

The *chassis number* is stamped on the top of the engine compartment rear bulkhead.

The *engine number* is stamped into the cylinder block/crankcase (see illustrations).

Other identification numbers or codes are stamped on major items such as the gearbox, final drive housing, distributor, etc. These numbers are unlikely to be needed by the home mechanic.

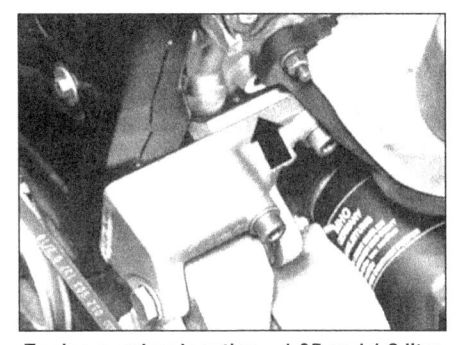

Identification number locations in the engine compartment

1 Vehicle identification plate
2 Engine number
3 Chassis number

Engine number location – 1.05 and 1.3 litre

Engine number location – 1.6 and 1.8 litre

General repair procedures

Whenever servicing, repair or overhaul work is carried out on the car or its components, observe the following procedures and instructions. This will assist in carrying out the operation efficiently and to a professional standard of workmanship.

Joint mating faces and gaskets

When separating components at their mating faces, never insert screwdrivers or similar implements into the joint between the faces in order to prise them apart. This can cause severe damage which results in oil leaks, coolant leaks, etc upon reassembly. Separation is usually achieved by tapping along the joint with a soft-faced hammer in order to break the seal. However, note that this method may not be suitable where dowels are used for component location.

Where a gasket is used between the mating faces of two components, a new one must be fitted on reassembly; fit it dry unless otherwise stated in the repair procedure. Make sure that the mating faces are clean and dry, with all traces of old gasket removed. When cleaning a joint face, use a tool which is unlikely to score or damage the face, and remove any burrs or nicks with an oilstone or fine file.

Make sure that tapped holes are cleaned with a pipe cleaner, and keep them free of jointing compound, if this is being used, unless specifically instructed otherwise.

Ensure that all orifices, channels or pipes are clear, and blow through them, preferably using compressed air.

Oil seals

Oil seals can be removed by levering them out with a wide flat-bladed screwdriver or similar implement. Alternatively, a number of self-tapping screws may be screwed into the seal, and these used as a purchase for pliers or some similar device in order to pull the seal free.

Whenever an oil seal is removed from its working location, either individually or as part of an assembly, it should be renewed.

The very fine sealing lip of the seal is easily damaged, and will not seal if the surface it contacts is not completely clean and free from scratches, nicks or grooves. If the original sealing surface of the component cannot be restored, and the manufacturer has not made provision for slight relocation of the seal relative to the sealing surface, the component should be renewed.

Protect the lips of the seal from any surface which may damage them in the course of fitting. Use tape or a conical sleeve where possible. Lubricate the seal lips with oil before fitting and, on dual-lipped seals, fill the space between the lips with grease.

Unless otherwise stated, oil seals must be fitted with their sealing lips toward the lubricant to be sealed.

Use a tubular drift or block of wood of the appropriate size to install the seal and, if the seal housing is shouldered, drive the seal down to the shoulder. If the seal housing is unshouldered, the seal should be fitted with its face flush with the housing top face (unless otherwise instructed).

Screw threads and fastenings

Seized nuts, bolts and screws are quite a common occurrence where corrosion has set in, and the use of penetrating oil or releasing fluid will often overcome this problem if the offending item is soaked for a while before attempting to release it. The use of an impact driver may also provide a means of releasing such stubborn fastening devices, when used in conjunction with the appropriate screwdriver bit or socket. If none of these methods works, it may be necessary to resort to the careful application of heat, or the use of a hacksaw or nut splitter device.

Studs are usually removed by locking two nuts together on the threaded part, and then using a spanner on the lower nut to unscrew the stud. Studs or bolts which have broken off below the surface of the component in which they are mounted can sometimes be removed using a stud extractor. Always ensure that a blind tapped hole is completely free from oil, grease, water or other fluid before installing the bolt or stud. Failure to do this could cause the housing to crack due to the hydraulic action of the bolt or stud as it is screwed in.

When tightening a castellated nut to accept a split pin, tighten the nut to the specified torque, where applicable, and then tighten further to the next split pin hole. Never slacken the nut to align the split pin hole, unless stated in the repair procedure.

When checking or retightening a nut or bolt to a specified torque setting, slacken the nut or bolt by a quarter of a turn, and then retighten to the specified setting. However, this should not be attempted where angular tightening has been used.

For some screw fastenings, notably cylinder head bolts or nuts, torque wrench settings are no longer specified for the latter stages of tightening, "angle-tightening" being called up instead. Typically, a fairly low torque wrench setting will be applied to the bolts/nuts in the correct sequence, followed by one or more stages of tightening through specified angles.

Locknuts, locktabs and washers

Any fastening which will rotate against a component or housing during tightening should always have a washer between it and the relevant component or housing.

Spring or split washers should always be renewed when they are used to lock a critical component such as a big-end bearing retaining bolt or nut. Locktabs which are folded over to retain a nut or bolt should always be renewed.

Self-locking nuts can be re-used in non-critical areas, providing resistance can be felt when the locking portion passes over the bolt or stud thread. However, it should be noted that self-locking stiffnuts tend to lose their effectiveness after long periods of use, and should then be renewed as a matter of course.

Split pins must always be replaced with new ones of the correct size for the hole.

When thread-locking compound is found on the threads of a fastener which is to be re-used, it should be cleaned off with a wire brush and solvent, and fresh compound applied on reassembly.

Special tools

Some repair procedures in this manual entail the use of special tools such as a press, two or three-legged pullers, spring compressors, etc. Wherever possible, suitable readily-available alternatives to the manufacturer's special tools are described, and are shown in use. In some instances, where no alternative is possible, it has been necessary to resort to the use of a manufacturer's tool, and this has been done for reasons of safety as well as the efficient completion of the repair operation. Unless you are highly-skilled and have a thorough understanding of the procedures described, never attempt to bypass the use of any special tool when the procedure described specifies its use. Not only is there a very great risk of personal injury, but expensive damage could be caused to the components involved.

Environmental considerations

When disposing of used engine oil, brake fluid, antifreeze, etc, give due consideration to any detrimental environmental effects. Do not, for instance, pour any of the above liquids down drains into the general sewage system, or onto the ground to soak away. Many local council refuse tips provide a facility for waste oil disposal, as do some garages. If none of these facilities are available, consult your local Environmental Health Department, or the National Rivers Authority, for further advice.

With the universal tightening-up of legislation regarding the emission of environmentally-harmful substances from motor vehicles, most vehicles have tamperproof devices fitted to the main adjustment points of the fuel system. These devices are primarily designed to prevent unqualified persons from adjusting the fuel/air mixture, with the chance of a consequent increase in toxic emissions. If such devices are found during servicing or overhaul, they should, wherever possible, be renewed or refitted in accordance with the manufacturer's requirements or current legislation.

Note: It is antisocial and illegal to dump oil down the drain. To find the location of your local oil recycling bank, call this number free.

OIL CARE — FOLLOW THE CODE
OIL BANK LINE
0800 66 33 66
www.oilbankline.org.uk

Jacking and vehicle support REF•5

The jack supplied with the vehicle tool kit should only be used for changing the roadwheels - see *"Wheel changing"* at the front of this Manual. When using the jack, position it on firm ground and locate its head in the relevant vehicle jacking point **(see illustration)**.

When carrying out any other kind of work, raise the vehicle using a hydraulic (or "trolley") jack, and always supplement the jack with axle stands positioned under the vehicle jacking points **(see illustration)**.

Always use the recommended jacking and support points. Never work under, around or near a raised vehicle unless it is properly supported.

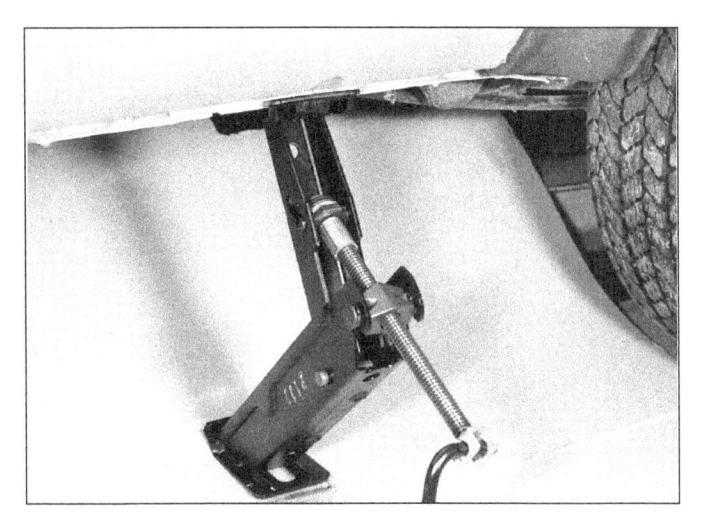

With jack base on firm ground, locate jack head into vehicle jacking point

Alternative jack location point at front (A) and rear (B) using hydraulic jack

REF•6 Tools and working facilities

Introduction

A selection of good tools is a fundamental requirement for anyone contemplating the maintenance and repair of a motor vehicle. For the owner who does not possess any, their purchase will prove a considerable expense, offsetting some of the savings made by doing-it-yourself. However, provided that the tools purchased meet the relevant national safety standards and are of good quality, they will last for many years and prove an extremely worthwhile investment.

To help the average owner to decide which tools are needed to carry out the various tasks detailed in this manual, we have compiled three lists of tools under the following headings: *Maintenance and minor repair*, *Repair and overhaul*, and *Special*. Newcomers to practical mechanics should start off with the *Maintenance and minor repair* tool kit, and confine themselves to the simpler jobs around the vehicle. Then, as confidence and experience grow, more difficult tasks can be undertaken, with extra tools being purchased as, and when, they are needed. In this way, a *Maintenance and minor repair* tool kit can be built up into a *Repair and overhaul* tool kit over a considerable period of time, without any major cash outlays. The experienced do-it-yourselfer will have a tool kit good enough for most repair and overhaul procedures, and will add tools from the *Special* category when it is felt that the expense is justified by the amount of use to which these tools will be put.

Maintenance and minor repair tool kit

The tools given in this list should be considered as a minimum requirement if routine maintenance, servicing and minor repair operations are to be undertaken. We recommend the purchase of combination spanners (ring one end, open-ended the other); although more expensive than open-ended ones, they do give the advantages of both types of spanner.

- Combination spanners:
  Metric - 8 to 19 mm inclusive
- Adjustable spanner - 35 mm jaw (approx.)
- Spark plug spanner (with rubber insert) - petrol models
- Spark plug gap adjustment tool - petrol models
- Set of feeler gauges
- Brake bleed nipple spanner
- Screwdrivers:
  Flat blade - 100 mm long x 6 mm dia
  Cross blade - 100 mm long x 6 mm dia
  Torx - various sizes (not all vehicles)
- Combination pliers
- Hacksaw (junior)
- Tyre pump
- Tyre pressure gauge
- Oil can
- Oil filter removal tool
- Fine emery cloth
- Wire brush (small)
- Funnel (medium size)
- Sump drain plug key (not all vehicles)

Repair and overhaul tool kit

These tools are virtually essential for anyone undertaking any major repairs to a motor vehicle, and are additional to those given in the *Maintenance and minor repair* list. Included in this list is a comprehensive set of sockets. Although these are expensive, they will be found invaluable as they are so versatile - particularly if various drives are included in the set. We recommend the half-inch square-drive type, as this can be used with most proprietary torque wrenches.

The tools in this list will sometimes need to be supplemented by tools from the *Special* list:

- Sockets (or box spanners) to cover range in previous list (including Torx sockets)
- Reversible ratchet drive (for use with sockets)
- Extension piece, 250 mm (for use with sockets)
- Universal joint (for use with sockets)
- Flexible handle or sliding T "breaker bar" (for use with sockets)
- Torque wrench (for use with sockets)
- Self-locking grips
- Ball pein hammer
- Soft-faced mallet (plastic or rubber)
- Screwdrivers:
  Flat blade - long & sturdy, short (chubby), and narrow (electrician's) types
  Cross blade – long & sturdy, and short (chubby) types
- Pliers:
  Long-nosed
  Side cutters (electrician's)
  Circlip (internal and external)
- Cold chisel - 25 mm
- Scriber
- Scraper
- Centre-punch
- Pin punch
- Hacksaw
- Brake hose clamp
- Brake/clutch bleeding kit
- Selection of twist drills
- Steel rule/straight-edge
- Allen keys (inc. splined/Torx type)
- Selection of files
- Wire brush
- Axle stands
- Jack (strong trolley or hydraulic type)
- Light with extension lead
- Universal electrical multi-meter

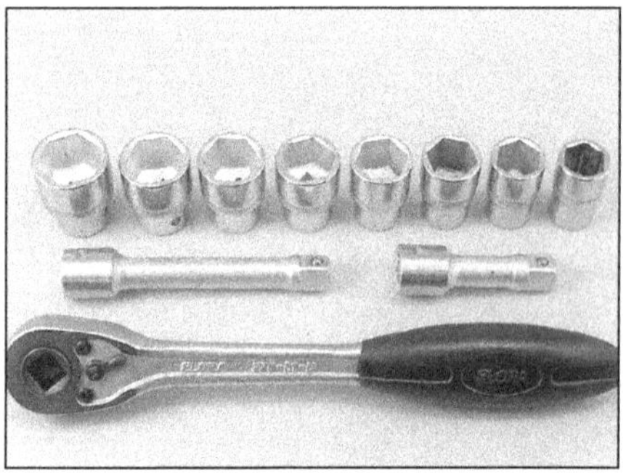

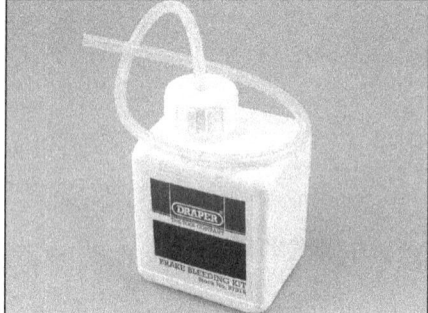

Sockets and reversible ratchet drive

Brake bleeding kit

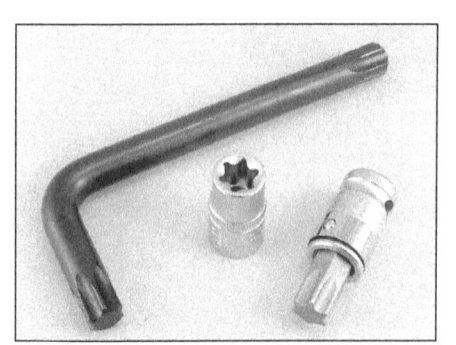

Torx key, socket and bit

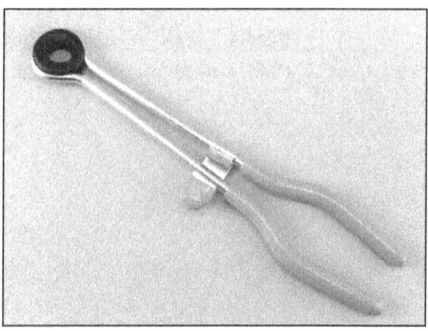

Hose clamp

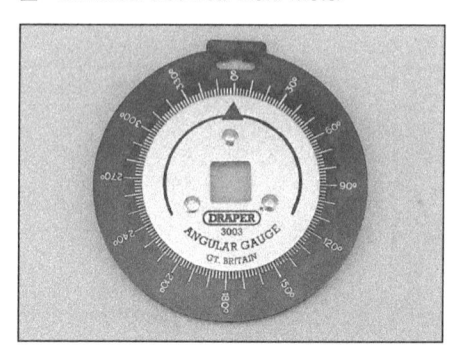

Angular-tightening gauge

Tools and working facilities   REF•7

Special tools

The tools in this list are those which are not used regularly, are expensive to buy, or which need to be used in accordance with their manufacturers' instructions. Unless relatively difficult mechanical jobs are undertaken frequently, it will not be economic to buy many of these tools. Where this is the case, you could consider clubbing together with friends (or joining a motorists' club) to make a joint purchase, or borrowing the tools against a deposit from a local garage or tool hire specialist. It is worth noting that many of the larger DIY superstores now carry a large range of special tools for hire at modest rates.

The following list contains only those tools and instruments freely available to the public, and not those special tools produced by the vehicle manufacturer specifically for its dealer network. You will find occasional references to these manufacturers' special tools in the text of this manual. Generally, an alternative method of doing the job without the vehicle manufacturers' special tool is given. However, sometimes there is no alternative to using them. Where this is the case and the relevant tool cannot be bought or borrowed, you will have to entrust the work to a dealer.

- ☐ Angular-tightening gauge
- ☐ Valve spring compressor
- ☐ Valve grinding tool
- ☐ Piston ring compressor
- ☐ Piston ring removal/installation tool
- ☐ Cylinder bore hone
- ☐ Balljoint separator
- ☐ Coil spring compressors (where applicable)
- ☐ Two/three-legged hub and bearing puller
- ☐ Impact screwdriver
- ☐ Micrometer and/or vernier calipers
- ☐ Dial gauge
- ☐ Stroboscopic timing light
- ☐ Dwell angle meter/tachometer
- ☐ Fault code reader
- ☐ Cylinder compression gauge
- ☐ Hand-operated vacuum pump and gauge
- ☐ Clutch plate alignment set
- ☐ Brake shoe steady spring cup removal tool
- ☐ Bush and bearing removal/installation set
- ☐ Stud extractors
- ☐ Tap and die set
- ☐ Lifting tackle
- ☐ Trolley jack

Buying tools

Reputable motor accessory shops and superstores often offer excellent quality tools at discount prices, so it pays to shop around.

Remember, you don't have to buy the most expensive items on the shelf, but it is always advisable to steer clear of the very cheap tools. Beware of 'bargains' offered on market stalls or at car boot sales. There are plenty of good tools around at reasonable prices, but always aim to purchase items which meet the relevant national safety standards. If in doubt, ask the proprietor or manager of the shop for advice before making a purchase.

Care and maintenance of tools

Having purchased a reasonable tool kit, it is necessary to keep the tools in a clean and serviceable condition. After use, always wipe off any dirt, grease and metal particles using a clean, dry cloth, before putting the tools away. Never leave them lying around after they have been used. A simple tool rack on the garage or workshop wall for items such as screwdrivers and pliers is a good idea. Store all normal spanners and sockets in a metal box. Any measuring instruments, gauges, meters, etc, must be carefully stored where they cannot be damaged or become rusty.

Take a little care when tools are used. Hammer heads inevitably become marked, and screwdrivers lose the keen edge on their blades from time to time. A little timely attention with emery cloth or a file will soon restore items like this to a good finish.

Working facilities

Not to be forgotten when discussing tools is the workshop itself. If anything more than routine maintenance is to be carried out, a suitable working area becomes essential.

It is appreciated that many an owner-mechanic is forced by circumstances to remove an engine or similar item without the benefit of a garage or workshop. Having done this, any repairs should always be done under the cover of a roof.

Wherever possible, any dismantling should be done on a clean, flat workbench or table at a suitable working height.

Any workbench needs a vice; one with a jaw opening of 100 mm is suitable for most jobs. As mentioned previously, some clean dry storage space is also required for tools, as well as for any lubricants, cleaning fluids, touch-up paints etc, which become necessary.

Another item which may be required, and which has a much more general usage, is an electric drill with a chuck capacity of at least 8 mm. This, together with a good range of twist drills, is virtually essential for fitting accessories.

Last, but not least, always keep a supply of old newspapers and clean, lint-free rags available, and try to keep any working area as clean as possible.

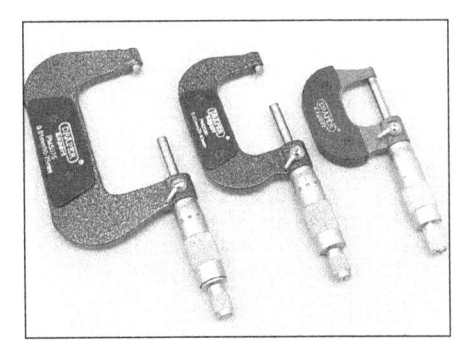

Micrometers

Dial test indicator ("dial gauge")

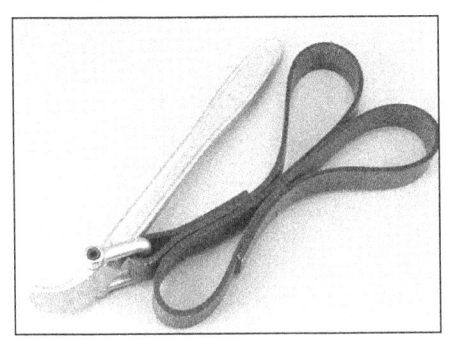

Strap wrench

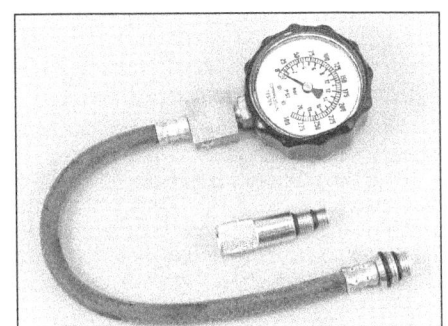

Compression tester

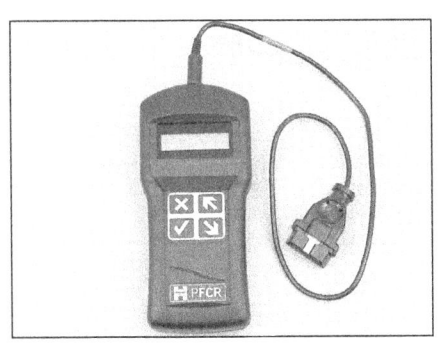

Fault code reader

REF•8 MOT test checks

This is a guide to getting your vehicle through the MOT test. Obviously it will not be possible to examine the vehicle to the same standard as the professional MOT tester. However, working through the following checks will enable you to identify any problem areas before submitting the vehicle for the test.

Where a testable component is in borderline condition, the tester has discretion in deciding whether to pass or fail it. The basis of such discretion is whether the tester would be happy for a close relative or friend to use the vehicle with the component in that condition. If the vehicle presented is clean and evidently well cared for, the tester may be more inclined to pass a borderline component than if the vehicle is scruffy and apparently neglected.

It has only been possible to summarise the test requirements here, based on the regulations in force at the time of printing. Test standards are becoming increasingly stringent, although there are some exemptions for older vehicles.

An assistant will be needed to help carry out some of these checks.

The checks have been sub-divided into four categories, as follows:

1 Checks carried out **FROM THE DRIVER'S SEAT**

2 Checks carried out **WITH THE VEHICLE ON THE GROUND**

3 Checks carried out **WITH THE VEHICLE RAISED AND THE WHEELS FREE TO TURN**

4 Checks carried out on **YOUR VEHICLE'S EXHAUST EMISSION SYSTEM**

---

1 Checks carried out **FROM THE DRIVER'S SEAT**

Handbrake

☐ Test the operation of the handbrake. Excessive travel (too many clicks) indicates incorrect brake or cable adjustment.
☐ Check that the handbrake cannot be released by tapping the lever sideways. Check the security of the lever mountings.

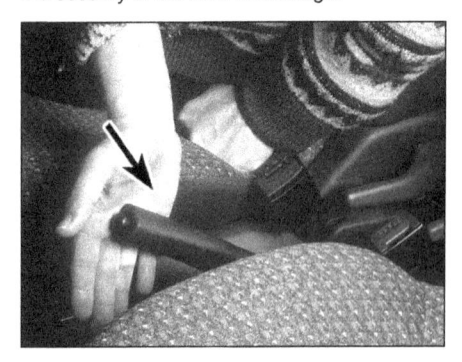

Footbrake

☐ Depress the brake pedal and check that it does not creep down to the floor, indicating a master cylinder fault. Release the pedal, wait a few seconds, then depress it again. If the pedal travels nearly to the floor before firm resistance is felt, brake adjustment or repair is necessary. If the pedal feels spongy, there is air in the hydraulic system which must be removed by bleeding.

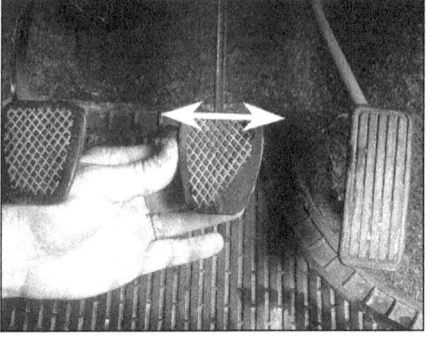

☐ Check that the brake pedal is secure and in good condition. Check also for signs of fluid leaks on the pedal, floor or carpets, which would indicate failed seals in the brake master cylinder.
☐ Check the servo unit (when applicable) by operating the brake pedal several times, then keeping the pedal depressed and starting the engine. As the engine starts, the pedal will move down slightly. If not, the vacuum hose or the servo itself may be faulty.

Steering wheel and column

☐ Examine the steering wheel for fractures or looseness of the hub, spokes or rim.
☐ Move the steering wheel from side to side and then up and down. Check that the steering wheel is not loose on the column, indicating wear or a loose retaining nut. Continue moving the steering wheel as before, but also turn it slightly from left to right.
☐ Check that the steering wheel is not loose on the column, and that there is no abnormal movement of the steering wheel, indicating wear in the column support bearings or couplings.

Windscreen, mirrors and sunvisor

☐ The windscreen must be free of cracks or other significant damage within the driver's field of view. (Small stone chips are acceptable.) Rear view mirrors must be secure, intact, and capable of being adjusted.

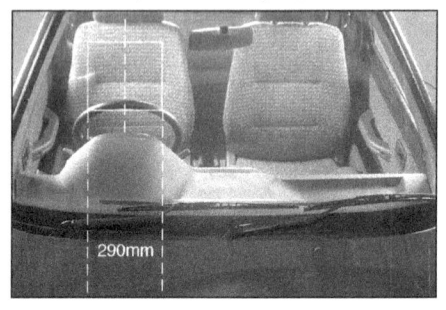

☐ The driver's sunvisor must be capable of being stored in the "up" position.

MOT test checks REF•9

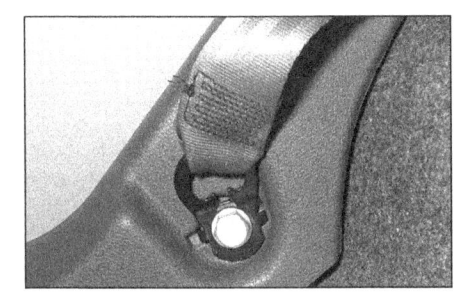

Seat belts and seats

Note: *The following checks are applicable to all seat belts, front and rear.*

☐ Examine the webbing of all the belts (including rear belts if fitted) for cuts, serious fraying or deterioration. Fasten and unfasten each belt to check the buckles. If applicable, check the retracting mechanism. Check the security of all seat belt mountings accessible from inside the vehicle.

☐ Seat belts with pre-tensioners, once activated, have a "flag" or similar showing on the seat belt stalk. This, in itself, is not a reason for test failure.

☐ The front seats themselves must be securely attached and the backrests must lock in the upright position.

Doors

☐ Both front doors must be able to be opened and closed from outside and inside, and must latch securely when closed.

2 Checks carried out WITH THE VEHICLE ON THE GROUND

Vehicle identification

☐ Number plates must be in good condition, secure and legible, with letters and numbers correctly spaced – spacing at (A) should be at least twice that at (B).

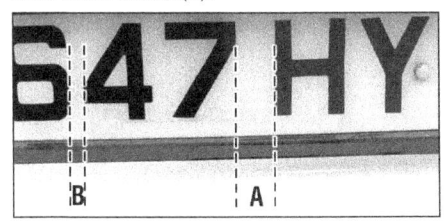

☐ The VIN plate and/or homologation plate must be legible.

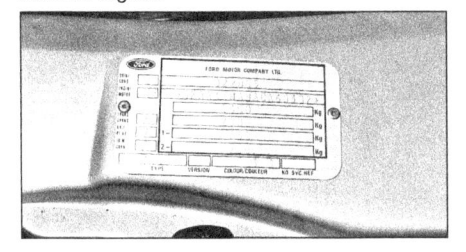

Electrical equipment

☐ Switch on the ignition and check the operation of the horn.

☐ Check the windscreen washers and wipers, examining the wiper blades; renew damaged or perished blades. Also check the operation of the stop-lights.

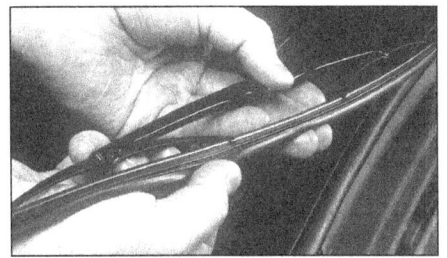

☐ Check the operation of the sidelights and number plate lights. The lenses and reflectors must be secure, clean and undamaged.

☐ Check the operation and alignment of the headlights. The headlight reflectors must not be tarnished and the lenses must be undamaged.

☐ Switch on the ignition and check the operation of the direction indicators (including the instrument panel tell-tale) and the hazard warning lights. Operation of the sidelights and stop-lights must not affect the indicators - if it does, the cause is usually a bad earth at the rear light cluster.

☐ Check the operation of the rear foglight(s), including the warning light on the instrument panel or in the switch.

☐ The ABS warning light must illuminate in accordance with the manufacturers' design. For most vehicles, the ABS warning light should illuminate when the ignition is switched on, and (if the system is operating properly) extinguish after a few seconds. Refer to the owner's handbook.

Footbrake

☐ Examine the master cylinder, brake pipes and servo unit for leaks, loose mountings, corrosion or other damage.

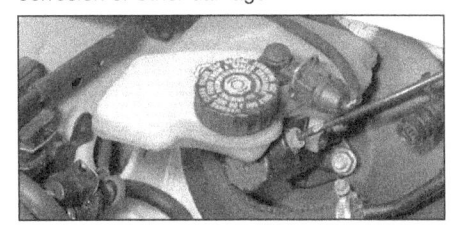

☐ The fluid reservoir must be secure and the fluid level must be between the upper (**A**) and lower (**B**) markings.

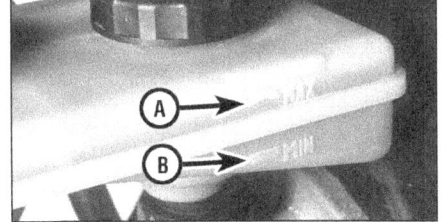

☐ Inspect both front brake flexible hoses for cracks or deterioration of the rubber. Turn the steering from lock to lock, and ensure that the hoses do not contact the wheel, tyre, or any part of the steering or suspension mechanism. With the brake pedal firmly depressed, check the hoses for bulges or leaks under pressure.

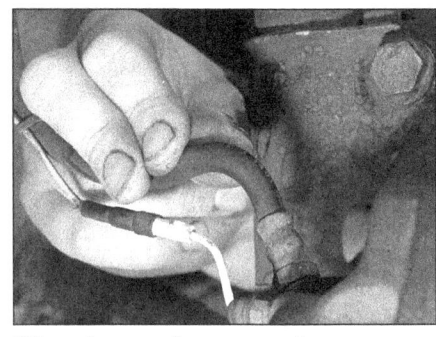

Steering and suspension

☐ Have your assistant turn the steering wheel from side to side slightly, up to the point where the steering gear just begins to transmit this movement to the roadwheels. Check for excessive free play between the steering wheel and the steering gear, indicating wear or insecurity of the steering column joints, the column-to-steering gear coupling, or the steering gear itself.

☐ Have your assistant turn the steering wheel more vigorously in each direction, so that the roadwheels just begin to turn. As this is done, examine all the steering joints, linkages, fittings and attachments. Renew any component that shows signs of wear or damage. On vehicles with power steering, check the security and condition of the steering pump, drivebelt and hoses.

☐ Check that the vehicle is standing level, and at approximately the correct ride height.

Shock absorbers

☐ Depress each corner of the vehicle in turn, then release it. The vehicle should rise and then settle in its normal position. If the vehicle continues to rise and fall, the shock absorber is defective. A shock absorber which has seized will also cause the vehicle to fail.

REF•10 MOT test checks

Exhaust system

☐ Start the engine. With your assistant holding a rag over the tailpipe, check the entire system for leaks. Repair or renew leaking sections.

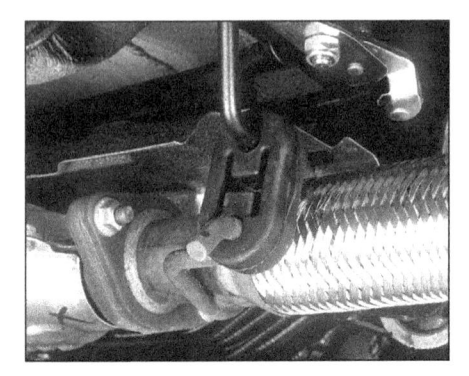

3 Checks carried out WITH THE VEHICLE RAISED AND THE WHEELS FREE TO TURN

Jack up the front and rear of the vehicle, and securely support it on axle stands. Position the stands clear of the suspension assemblies. Ensure that the wheels are clear of the ground and that the steering can be turned from lock to lock.

Steering mechanism

☐ Have your assistant turn the steering from lock to lock. Check that the steering turns smoothly, and that no part of the steering mechanism, including a wheel or tyre, fouls any brake hose or pipe or any part of the body structure.

☐ Examine the steering rack rubber gaiters for damage or insecurity of the retaining clips. If power steering is fitted, check for signs of damage or leakage of the fluid hoses, pipes or connections. Also check for excessive stiffness or binding of the steering, a missing split pin or locking device, or severe corrosion of the body structure within 30 cm of any steering component attachment point.

Front and rear suspension and wheel bearings

☐ Starting at the front right-hand side, grasp the roadwheel at the 3 o'clock and 9 o'clock positions and rock gently but firmly. Check for free play or insecurity at the wheel bearings, suspension balljoints, or suspension mountings, pivots and attachments.

☐ Now grasp the wheel at the 12 o'clock and 6 o'clock positions and repeat the previous inspection. Spin the wheel, and check for roughness or tightness of the front wheel bearing.

☐ If excess free play is suspected at a component pivot point, this can be confirmed by using a large screwdriver or similar tool and levering between the mounting and the component attachment. This will confirm whether the wear is in the pivot bush, its retaining bolt, or in the mounting itself (the bolt holes can often become elongated).

☐ Carry out all the above checks at the other front wheel, and then at both rear wheels.

Springs and shock absorbers

☐ Examine the suspension struts (when applicable) for serious fluid leakage, corrosion, or damage to the casing. Also check the security of the mounting points.

☐ If coil springs are fitted, check that the spring ends locate in their seats, and that the spring is not corroded, cracked or broken.

☐ If leaf springs are fitted, check that all leaves are intact, that the axle is securely attached to each spring, and that there is no deterioration of the spring eye mountings, bushes, and shackles.

☐ The same general checks apply to vehicles fitted with other suspension types, such as torsion bars, hydraulic displacer units, etc. Ensure that all mountings and attachments are secure, that there are no signs of excessive wear, corrosion or damage, and (on hydraulic types) that there are no fluid leaks or damaged pipes.

☐ Inspect the shock absorbers for signs of serious fluid leakage. Check for wear of the mounting bushes or attachments, or damage to the body of the unit.

Driveshafts (fwd vehicles only)

☐ Rotate each front wheel in turn and inspect the constant velocity joint gaiters for splits or damage. Also check that each driveshaft is straight and undamaged.

Braking system

☐ If possible without dismantling, check brake pad wear and disc condition. Ensure that the friction lining material has not worn excessively, (A) and that the discs are not fractured, pitted, scored or badly worn (B).

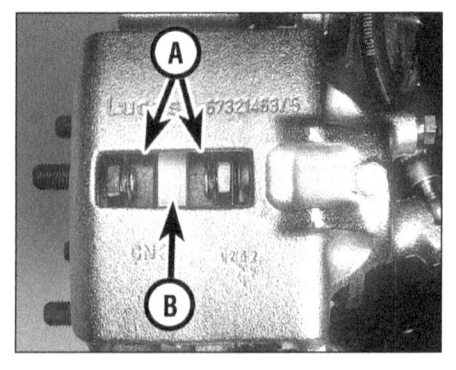

☐ Examine all the rigid brake pipes underneath the vehicle, and the flexible hose(s) at the rear. Look for corrosion, chafing or insecurity of the pipes, and for signs of bulging under pressure, chafing, splits or deterioration of the flexible hoses.

☐ Look for signs of fluid leaks at the brake calipers or on the brake backplates. Repair or renew leaking components.

☐ Slowly spin each wheel, while your assistant depresses and releases the footbrake. Ensure that each brake is operating and does not bind when the pedal is released.

MOT test checks REF•11

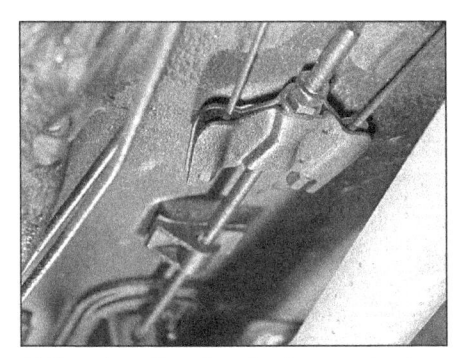

☐ Examine the handbrake mechanism, checking for frayed or broken cables, excessive corrosion, or wear or insecurity of the linkage. Check that the mechanism works on each relevant wheel, and releases fully, without binding.

☐ It is not possible to test brake efficiency without special equipment, but a road test can be carried out later to check that the vehicle pulls up in a straight line.

Fuel and exhaust systems

☐ Inspect the fuel tank (including the filler cap), fuel pipes, hoses and unions. All components must be secure and free from leaks.

☐ Examine the exhaust system over its entire length, checking for any damaged, broken or missing mountings, security of the retaining clamps and rust or corrosion.

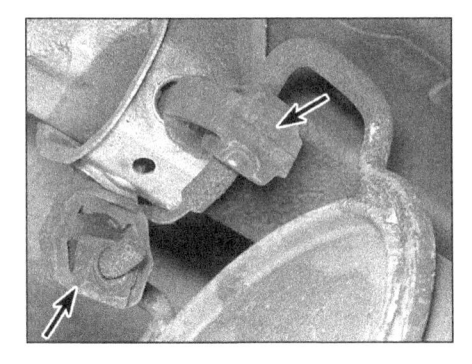

Wheels and tyres

☐ Examine the sidewalls and tread area of each tyre in turn. Check for cuts, tears, lumps, bulges, separation of the tread, and exposure of the ply or cord due to wear or damage. Check that the tyre bead is correctly seated on the wheel rim, that the valve is sound and properly seated, and that the wheel is not distorted or damaged.

☐ Check that the tyres are of the correct size for the vehicle, that they are of the same size and type on each axle, and that the pressures are correct.

☐ Check the tyre tread depth. The legal minimum at the time of writing is 1.6 mm over at least three-quarters of the tread width. Abnormal tread wear may indicate incorrect front wheel alignment.

Body corrosion

☐ Check the condition of the entire vehicle structure for signs of corrosion in load-bearing areas. (These include chassis box sections, side sills, cross-members, pillars, and all suspension, steering, braking system and seat belt mountings and anchorages.) Any corrosion which has seriously reduced the thickness of a load-bearing area is likely to cause the vehicle to fail. In this case professional repairs are likely to be needed.

☐ Damage or corrosion which causes sharp or otherwise dangerous edges to be exposed will also cause the vehicle to fail.

4 Checks carried out on YOUR VEHICLE'S EXHAUST EMISSION SYSTEM

Petrol models

☐ Have the engine at normal operating temperature, and make sure that it is in good tune (ignition system in good order, air filter element clean, etc).

☐ Before any measurements are carried out, raise the engine speed to around 2500 rpm, and hold it at this speed for 20 seconds. Allow the engine speed to return to idle, and watch for smoke emissions from the exhaust tailpipe. If the idle speed is obviously much too high, or if dense blue or clearly-visible black smoke comes from the tailpipe for more than 5 seconds, the vehicle will fail. As a rule of thumb, blue smoke signifies oil being burnt (engine wear) while black smoke signifies unburnt fuel (dirty air cleaner element, or other carburettor or fuel system fault).

☐ An exhaust gas analyser capable of measuring carbon monoxide (CO) and hydrocarbons (HC) is now needed. If such an instrument cannot be hired or borrowed, a local garage may agree to perform the check for a small fee.

CO emissions (mixture)

☐ At the time of writing, for vehicles first used between 1st August 1975 and 31st July 1986 (P to C registration), the CO level must not exceed 4.5% by volume. For vehicles first used between 1st August 1986 and 31st July 1992 (D to J registration), the CO level must not exceed 3.5% by volume. Vehicles first used after 1st August 1992 (K registration) must conform to the manufacturer's specification. The MOT tester has access to a DOT database or emissions handbook, which lists the CO and HC limits for each make and model of vehicle. The CO level is measured with the engine at idle speed, and at "fast idle". The following limits are given as a general guide:

At idle speed -
   CO level no more than 0.5%
At "fast idle" (2500 to 3000 rpm) -
   CO level no more than 0.3%
   (Minimum oil temperature 60°C)

☐ If the CO level cannot be reduced far enough to pass the test (and the fuel and ignition systems are otherwise in good condition) then the carburettor is badly worn, or there is some problem in the fuel injection system or catalytic converter (as applicable).

HC emissions

☐ With the CO within limits, HC emissions for vehicles first used between 1st August 1975 and 31st July 1992 (P to J registration) must not exceed 1200 ppm. Vehicles first used after 1st August 1992 (K registration) must conform to the manufacturer's specification. The MOT tester has access to a DOT database or emissions handbook, which lists the CO and HC limits for each make and model of vehicle. The HC level is measured with the engine at "fast idle". The following is given as a general guide:

At "fast idle" (2500 to 3000 rpm) -
   HC level no more than 200 ppm
   (Minimum oil temperature 60°C)

☐ Excessive HC emissions are caused by incomplete combustion, the causes of which can include oil being burnt, mechanical wear and ignition/fuel system malfunction.

Diesel models

☐ The only emission test applicable to Diesel engines is the measuring of exhaust smoke density. The test involves accelerating the engine several times to its maximum unloaded speed.

Note: *It is of the utmost importance that the engine timing belt is in good condition before the test is carried out.*

☐ The limits for Diesel engine exhaust smoke, introduced in September 1995 are:

Vehicles first used before 1st August 1979:
   Exempt from metered smoke testing, but must not emit "dense blue or clearly visible black smoke for a period of more than 5 seconds at idle" or "dense blue or clearly visible black smoke during acceleration which would obscure the view of other road users".

Non-turbocharged vehicles first used after
   1st August 1979: 2.5m-1
Turbocharged vehicles first used after
   1st August 1979: 3.0m-1

☐ Excessive smoke can be caused by a dirty air cleaner element. Otherwise, professional advice may be needed to find the cause.

REF•12 Fault finding

Engine

- [ ] Engine fails to rotate when attempting to start
- [ ] Engine rotates but will not start
- [ ] Engine difficult to start when cold
- [ ] Engine difficult to start when hot
- [ ] Starter motor noisy or excessively rough in engagement
- [ ] Engine starts but stops immediately
- [ ] Engine idles erratically
- [ ] Engine misfires at idle speed
- [ ] Engine misfires throughout the driving speed range
- [ ] Engine hesitates on acceleration
- [ ] Engine stalls
- [ ] Engine lacks power
- [ ] Engine backfires
- [ ] Oil pressure warning light illuminated with engine running
- [ ] Engine runs-on after switching off
- [ ] Engine noises

Cooling system

- [ ] Overheating
- [ ] Overcooling
- [ ] External coolant leakage
- [ ] Internal coolant leakage
- [ ] Corrosion

Fuel and exhaust system

- [ ] Excessive fuel consumption
- [ ] Fuel leakage and/or fuel odour
- [ ] Excessive noise or fumes from exhaust system

Clutch

- [ ] Pedal travels to floor - no pressure or very little resistance
- [ ] Clutch fails to disengage (unable to select gears)
- [ ] Clutch slips (engine speed increases with no increase in vehicle speed)
- [ ] Judder as clutch is engaged
- [ ] Noise when depressing or releasing clutch pedal

Manual gearbox

- [ ] Noisy in neutral with engine running
- [ ] Noisy in one particular gear
- [ ] Difficulty engaging gears
- [ ] Jumps out of gear
- [ ] Vibration
- [ ] Lubricant leaks

Automatic transmission

- [ ] Fluid leakage
- [ ] Transmission fluid brown, or has burned smell
- [ ] General gear selection problems
- [ ] Transmission will not downshift (kickdown) with accelerator pedal fully depressed
- [ ] Engine will not start in any gear, or starts in gears other than Park or Neutral
- [ ] Transmission slips, shifts roughly, is noisy, or has no drive in forward or reverse gears

Driveshafts

- [ ] Clicking or knocking noise on turns (at slow speed on full lock)
- [ ] Vibration when accelerating or decelerating

Braking system

- [ ] Vehicle pulls to one side under braking
- [ ] Noise (grinding or high-pitched squeal) when brakes applied
- [ ] Excessive brake pedal travel
- [ ] Brake pedal feels spongy when depressed
- [ ] Excessive brake pedal effort required to stop vehicle
- [ ] Judder felt through brake pedal or steering wheel when braking
- [ ] Brakes binding
- [ ] Rear wheels locking under normal braking

Suspension and steering

- [ ] Vehicle pulls to one side
- [ ] Wheel wobble and vibration
- [ ] Excessive pitching and/or rolling around corners or during braking
- [ ] Wandering or general instability
- [ ] Excessively stiff steering
- [ ] Excessive play in steering
- [ ] Tyre wear excessive

Electrical system

- [ ] Battery will not hold a charge for more than a few days
- [ ] Ignition warning light remains illuminated with engine running
- [ ] Ignition warning light fails to come on
- [ ] Lights inoperative
- [ ] Instrument readings inaccurate or erratic
- [ ] Horn inoperative or unsatisfactory in operation
- [ ] Windscreen/tailgate wipers inoperative or unsatisfactory in operation
- [ ] Windscreen/tailgate washers inoperative or unsatisfactory in operation
- [ ] Electric windows inoperative or unsatisfactory in operation
- [ ] Central locking system inoperative or unsatisfactory in operation

Introduction

The vehicle owner who does his or her own maintenance according to the recommended service schedules should not have to use this section of the manual very often. Modern component reliability is such that, provided those items subject to wear or deterioration are inspected or renewed at the specified intervals, sudden failure is comparatively rare. Faults do not usually just happen as a result of sudden failure, but develop over a period of time. Major mechanical failures in particular are usually preceded by characteristic symptoms over hundreds or even thousands of miles. Those components which do occasionally fail without warning are often small and easily carried in the vehicle.

With any fault finding, the first step is to decide where to begin investigations. Sometimes this is obvious, but on other occasions a little detective work will be necessary. The owner who makes half a dozen haphazard adjustments or replacements may be successful in curing a fault (or its symptoms), but will be none the wiser if the fault recurs and ultimately may have spent more time and money than was necessary. A calm and logical approach will be found to be more satisfactory in the long run. Always take into account any warning signs or abnormalities that may have been noticed in the period preceding the fault - power loss, high or low gauge readings, unusual smells, etc - and remember that failure of components such as fuses or spark plugs may only be pointers to some underlying fault.

The pages which follow provide an easy reference guide to the more common problems which may occur during the operation of the vehicle. These problems and their possible causes are grouped under headings denoting various components or systems, such as Engine, Cooling system, etc. The Chapter and/or Section which deals with the problem is also shown in brackets. Whatever the fault, certain basic principles apply. These are as follows:

Fault finding REF•13

Verify the fault. This is simply a matter of being sure that you know what the symptoms are before starting work. This is particularly important if you are investigating a fault for someone else who may not have described it very accurately.

Don't overlook the obvious. For example, if the vehicle won't start, is there petrol in the tank? (Don't take anyone else's word on this particular point, and don't trust the fuel gauge either!) If an electrical fault is indicated, look for loose or broken wires before digging out the test gear.

Cure the disease, not the symptom. Substituting a flat battery with a fully charged one will get you off the hard shoulder, but if the underlying cause is not attended to, the new battery will go the same way. Similarly, changing oil-fouled spark plugs for a new set will get you moving again, but remember that the reason for the fouling (if it wasn't simply an incorrect grade of plug) will have to be established and corrected.

Don't take anything for granted. Particularly, don't forget that a `new' component may itself be defective (especially if it's been rattling around in the boot for months), and don't leave components out of a fault diagnosis sequence just because they are new or recently fitted. When you do finally diagnose a difficult fault, you'll probably realise that all the evidence was there from the start.

Engine

Engine fails to rotate when attempting to start
- [ ] Battery terminal connections loose or corroded ("*Weekly checks*").
- [ ] Battery discharged or faulty (Chapter 5).
- [ ] Broken, loose or disconnected wiring in the starting circuit (Chapter 5).
- [ ] Defective starter solenoid or switch (Chapter 5).
- [ ] Defective starter motor (Chapter 5).
- [ ] Starter pinion or flywheel ring gear teeth loose or broken (Chapters 2 and 5).
- [ ] Engine earth strap broken or disconnected (Chapter 5).

Engine rotates but will not start
- [ ] Fuel tank empty.
- [ ] Battery discharged (engine rotates slowly) (Chapter 5).
- [ ] Battery terminal connections loose or corroded ("*Weekly checks*").
- [ ] Ignition components damp or damaged (Chapters 1 and 5).
- [ ] Broken, loose or disconnected wiring in the ignition circuit (Chapters 1 and 5).
- [ ] Worn, faulty or incorrectly gapped spark plugs (Chapter 1).
- [ ] Choke mechanism sticking, incorrectly adjusted, or faulty (Chapter 4).
- [ ] Major mechanical failure (eg camshaft drive) (Chapter 2).

Engine difficult to start when cold
- [ ] Battery discharged (Chapter 5).
- [ ] Battery terminal connections loose or corroded ("*Weekly checks*").
- [ ] Worn, faulty or incorrectly gapped spark plugs (Chapter 1).
- [ ] Choke mechanism sticking, incorrectly adjusted, or faulty (Chapter 4).
- [ ] Other ignition system fault (Chapters 1 and 5).
- [ ] Low cylinder compressions (Chapter 2).

Engine difficult to start when hot
- [ ] Air filter element dirty or clogged (Chapter 1).
- [ ] Choke mechanism sticking, incorrectly adjusted, or faulty (Chapter 4).
- [ ] Carburettor float chamber flooding (Chapter 4).
- [ ] Low cylinder compressions (Chapter 2).

Starter motor noisy or excessively rough in engagement
- [ ] Starter pinion or flywheel ring gear teeth loose or broken (Chapters 2 and 5).
- [ ] Starter motor mounting bolts loose or missing (Chapter 5).
- [ ] Starter motor internal components worn or damaged (Chapter 5).

Engine starts but stops immediately
- [ ] Insufficient fuel reaching carburettor (Chapter 4).
- [ ] Loose or faulty electrical connections in the ignition circuit (Chapters 1 and 5).
- [ ] Vacuum leak at the carburettor or inlet manifold (Chapter 4).
- [ ] Blocked carburettor jet(s) or internal passages (Chapter 4).

Engine idles erratically
- [ ] Incorrectly adjusted idle speed and/or mixture settings (Chapter 1).
- [ ] Air filter element clogged (Chapter 1).
- [ ] Vacuum leak at the carburettor, inlet manifold or associated hoses (Chapter 4).
- [ ] Worn, faulty or incorrectly gapped spark plugs (Chapter 1).
- [ ] Uneven or low cylinder compressions (Chapter 2).
- [ ] Camshaft lobes worn (Chapter 2).
- [ ] Timing belt incorrectly tensioned (Chapter 2).

Engine misfires at idle speed
- [ ] Worn, faulty or incorrectly gapped spark plugs (Chapter 1).
- [ ] Faulty spark plug HT leads (Chapter 1).
- [ ] Incorrectly adjusted idle mixture settings (Chapter 1).
- [ ] Incorrect ignition timing (Chapter 1).
- [ ] Vacuum leak at the carburettor, inlet manifold or associated hoses (Chapter 4).
- [ ] Distributor cap cracked or tracking internally (Chapter 1).
- [ ] Uneven or low cylinder compressions (Chapter 2).
- [ ] Disconnected, leaking or perished crankcase ventilation hoses (Chapters 1 and 4).

Engine misfires throughout the driving speed range
- [ ] Blocked carburettor jet(s) or internal passages (Chapter 4).
- [ ] Carburettor worn or incorrectly adjusted (Chapters 1 and 4).
- [ ] Fuel filter choked (Chapter 1).
- [ ] Fuel pump faulty or delivery pressure low (Chapter 4).
- [ ] Fuel tank vent blocked or fuel pipes restricted (Chapter 4).
- [ ] Vacuum leak at the carburettor, inlet manifold or associated hoses (Chapter 4).
- [ ] Worn, faulty or incorrectly gapped spark plugs (Chapter 1).
- [ ] Faulty spark plug HT leads (Chapter 1).
- [ ] Distributor cap cracked or tracking internally (Chapter 1).
- [ ] Faulty ignition coil (Chapter 5).
- [ ] Uneven or low cylinder compressions (Chapter 2).

REF•14 Fault finding

Engine (continued)

Engine hesitates on acceleration
- [ ] Worn, faulty or incorrectly gapped spark plugs (Chapter 1).
- [ ] Carburettor accelerator pump faulty (Chapter 4).
- [ ] Blocked carburettor jets or internal passages (Chapter 4).
- [ ] Vacuum leak at the carburettor, inlet manifold or associated hoses (Chapter 4).
- [ ] Carburettor worn or incorrectly adjusted (Chapters 1 and 4).

Engine stalls
- [ ] Incorrectly adjusted idle speed and/or mixture settings (Chapter 1).
- [ ] Blocked carburettor jet(s) or internal passages (Chapter 4).
- [ ] Vacuum leak at the carburettor, inlet manifold or associated hoses (Chapter 4).
- [ ] Fuel filter choked (Chapter 1).
- [ ] Fuel pump faulty or delivery pressure low (Chapter 4).
- [ ] Fuel tank vent blocked or fuel pipes restricted (Chapter 4).

Engine lacks power
- [ ] Incorrect ignition timing (Chapter 1).
- [ ] Carburettor worn or incorrectly adjusted (Chapter 1).
- [ ] Timing belt incorrectly fitted or tensioned (Chapter 2).
- [ ] Fuel filter choked (Chapter 1).
- [ ] Fuel pump faulty or delivery pressure low (Chapter 4).
- [ ] Uneven or low cylinder compressions (Chapter 2).
- [ ] Worn, faulty or incorrectly gapped spark plugs (Chapter 1).
- [ ] Vacuum leak at the carburettor, inlet manifold or associated hoses (Chapter 4).
- [ ] Brakes binding (Chapters 1 and 9).
- [ ] Clutch slipping (Chapter 6).

Engine backfires
- [ ] Ignition timing incorrect (Chapter 1).
- [ ] Timing belt incorrectly fitted or tensioned (Chapter 2).
- [ ] Carburettor worn or incorrectly adjusted (Chapter 1).
- [ ] Vacuum leak at the carburettor, inlet manifold or associated hoses (Chapter 4).

Oil pressure warning light illuminated with engine running
- [ ] Low oil level or incorrect grade ("Weekly checks").
- [ ] Faulty oil pressure switch (Chapter 12).
- [ ] Worn engine bearings and/or oil pump (Chapter 2).
- [ ] High engine operating temperature (Chapter 3).
- [ ] Oil pressure relief valve defective (Chapter 2).
- [ ] Oil pick-up strainer clogged (Chapter 2).

Engine runs-on after switching off
- [ ] Idle speed excessively high (Chapter 1).
- [ ] Faulty anti-run-on solenoid (Chapter 4).
- [ ] Excessive carbon build-up in engine (Chapter 2).
- [ ] High engine operating temperature (Chapter 3).

Engine noises

Pre-ignition (pinking) or knocking during acceleration or under load
- [ ] Ignition timing incorrect (Chapter 1).
- [ ] Incorrect grade of fuel (Chapter 4).
- [ ] Vacuum leak at the carburettor, inlet manifold or associated hoses (Chapter 4).
- [ ] Excessive carbon build-up in engine (Chapter 2).
- [ ] Worn or damaged distributor or other ignition system component (Chapter 5).
- [ ] Carburettor worn or incorrectly adjusted (Chapter 1).

Whistling or wheezing noises
- [ ] Leaking inlet manifold or carburettor gasket (Chapter 4).
- [ ] Leaking exhaust manifold gasket or pipe to manifold joint (Chapter 1).
- [ ] Leaking vacuum hose (Chapters 4, 5 and 9).
- [ ] Blowing cylinder head gasket (Chapter 2).

Tapping or rattling noises
- [ ] Faulty hydraulic tappets (Chapter 1 or 2).
- [ ] Worn valve gear or camshaft (Chapter 2).
- [ ] Worn timing belt or tensioner (Chapter 2).
- [ ] Ancillary component fault (water pump, alternator etc) (Chapters 3 and 5).

Knocking or thumping noises
- [ ] Worn big-end bearings (regular heavy knocking, perhaps less under load) (Chapter 2).
- [ ] Worn main bearings (rumbling and knocking, perhaps worsening under load) (Chapter 2).
- [ ] Piston slap (most noticeable when cold) (Chapter 2).
- [ ] Ancillary component fault (alternator, water pump etc) (Chapters 3 and 5).

Cooling system

Overheating
- [ ] Insufficient coolant in system ("Weekly checks").
- [ ] Thermostat faulty (Chapter 3).
- [ ] Radiator core blocked or grille restricted (Chapter 3).
- [ ] Electric cooling fan or thermostatic switch faulty (Chapter 3).
- [ ] Pressure cap faulty (Chapter 3).
- [ ] Timing belt worn, or incorrectly tensioned (Chapter 2).
- [ ] Ignition timing incorrect (Chapter 1).
- [ ] Inaccurate temperature gauge sender unit (Chapter 3).
- [ ] Air lock in cooling system (Chapter 1).

Overcooling
- [ ] Thermostat faulty (Chapter 3).
- [ ] Inaccurate temperature gauge sender unit (Chapter 3).

External coolant leakage
- [ ] Deteriorated or damaged hoses or hose clips (Chapter 1).
- [ ] Radiator core or heater matrix leaking (Chapter 3).
- [ ] Pressure cap faulty (Chapter 3).
- [ ] Water pump seal leaking (Chapter 3).
- [ ] Boiling due to overheating (Chapter 3).
- [ ] Core plug leaking (Chapter 2).

Internal coolant leakage
- [ ] Leaking cylinder head gasket (Chapter 2).
- [ ] Cracked cylinder head or cylinder bore (Chapter 2).

Corrosion
- [ ] Infrequent draining and flushing (Chapter 1).
- [ ] Incorrect antifreeze mixture or inappropriate type (Chapter 1).

Fault finding REF•15

Fuel and exhaust system

Excessive fuel consumption
- [ ] Air filter element dirty or clogged (Chapter 1).
- [ ] Carburettor worn or incorrectly adjusted (Chapter 4).
- [ ] Choke cable incorrectly adjusted or choke sticking (Chapter 4).
- [ ] Ignition timing incorrect (Chapter 1).
- [ ] Tyres under-inflated ("Weekly checks").

Fuel leakage and/or fuel odour
- [ ] Damaged or corroded fuel tank, pipes or connections (Chapter 1).
- [ ] Carburettor float chamber flooding (Chapter 4).

Excessive noise or fumes from exhaust system
- [ ] Leaking exhaust system or manifold joints (Chapter 1).
- [ ] Leaking, corroded or damaged silencers or pipe (Chapter 1).
- [ ] Broken mountings causing body or suspension contact (Chapter 1).

Clutch

Pedal travels to floor - no pressure or very little resistance
- [ ] Broken clutch cable (Chapter 6).
- [ ] Faulty clutch pedal self-adjust mechanism (Chapter 6).
- [ ] Broken clutch release bearing or fork (Chapter 6).
- [ ] Broken diaphragm spring in clutch pressure plate (Chapter 6).

Clutch fails to disengage (unable to select gears)
- [ ] Faulty clutch pedal self-adjust mechanism (Chapter 6).
- [ ] Clutch friction plate sticking on transmission input shaft splines (Chapter 6).
- [ ] Clutch friction plate sticking to flywheel or pressure plate (Chapter 6).
- [ ] Faulty pressure plate assembly (Chapter 6).
- [ ] Transmission input shaft seized in crankshaft spigot bearing (Chapter 2).
- [ ] Clutch release mechanism worn or incorrectly assembled (Chapter 6).

Clutch slips (engine speed increases with no increase in vehicle speed)
- [ ] Faulty clutch pedal self-adjust mechanism (Chapter 6).
- [ ] Clutch friction plate friction material excessively worn (Chapter 6).
- [ ] Clutch friction plate friction material contaminated with oil or grease (Chapter 6).
- [ ] Faulty pressure plate or weak diaphragm spring (Chapter 6).

Judder as clutch is engaged
- [ ] Clutch friction plate friction material contaminated with oil or grease (Chapter 6).
- [ ] Clutch friction plate friction material excessively worn (Chapter 6).
- [ ] Clutch cable sticking or frayed (Chapter 6).
- [ ] Faulty or distorted pressure plate or diaphragm spring (Chapter 6).
- [ ] Worn or loose engine or gearbox mountings (Chapter 2).
- [ ] Clutch friction plate hub or transmission input shaft splines worn (Chapter 6).

Noise when depressing or releasing clutch pedal
- [ ] Worn clutch release bearing (Chapter 6).
- [ ] Worn or dry clutch pedal bushes (Chapter 6).
- [ ] Faulty pressure plate assembly (Chapter 6).
- [ ] Pressure plate diaphragm spring broken (Chapter 6).
- [ ] Broken clutch friction plate cushioning springs (Chapter 6).

Manual gearbox

Noisy in neutral with engine running
- [ ] Input shaft bearings worn (noise apparent with clutch pedal released but not when depressed) (Chapter 7).*
- [ ] Clutch release bearing worn (noise apparent with clutch pedal depressed, possibly less when released) (Chapter 6).

Noisy in one particular gear
- [ ] Worn, damaged or chipped gear teeth (Chapter 7).*

Difficulty engaging gears
- [ ] Clutch fault (Chapter 6).
- [ ] Worn or damaged gear linkage (Chapter 7).
- [ ] Incorrectly adjusted gear linkage (Chapter 7).
- [ ] Worn synchroniser units (Chapter 7).*

Jumps out of gear
- [ ] Worn or damaged gear linkage (Chapter 7).
- [ ] Incorrectly adjusted gear linkage (Chapter 7).
- [ ] Worn synchroniser units (Chapter 7).*
- [ ] Worn selector forks (Chapter 7).*

Vibration
- [ ] Lack of oil (Chapter 1).
- [ ] Worn bearings (Chapter 7).*

Lubricant leaks
- [ ] Leaking driveshaft oil seal (Chapter 7).
- [ ] Leaking housing joint (Chapter 7).*
- [ ] Leaking input shaft oil seal (Chapter 7).*

*Although the corrective action necessary to remedy the symptoms described is beyond the scope of the home mechanic, the above information should be helpful in isolating the cause of the condition so that the owner can communicate clearly with a professional mechanic

REF•16 Fault finding

Automatic transmission

Note: *Due to the complexity of the automatic transmission, it is difficult for the home mechanic to properly diagnose and service this unit. For problems other than the following, the vehicle should be taken to a dealer service department or automatic transmission specialist.*

Fluid leakage

☐ Automatic transmission fluid is usually deep red in colour. Fluid leaks should not be confused with engine oil, which can easily be blown onto the transmission by air flow.

☐ To determine the source of a leak, first remove all built-up dirt and grime from the transmission housing and surrounding areas, using a degreasing agent or by steam-cleaning. Drive the vehicle at low speed, so that air flow will not blow the leak far from its source. Raise and support the vehicle, and determine where the leak is coming from. The following are common areas of leakage:
a) *Fluid pan (transmission sump).*
b) *Dipstick tube (Chapter 7).*
c) *Transmission-to-fluid cooler fluid pipes/unions (Chapter 7).*

Transmission fluid brown, or has burned smell

☐ Transmission fluid level low, or fluid in need of renewal (Chapter 1).

General gear selection problems

☐ The most likely cause of gear selection problems is a faulty or poorly-adjusted gear selector mechanism. The following are common problems associated with a faulty selector mechanism:

a) *Engine starting in gears other than Park or Neutral.*
b) *Indicator on gear selector lever pointing to a gear other than the one actually being used.*
c) *Vehicle moves when in Park or Neutral.*
d) *Poor gear shift quality, or erratic gear changes.*

☐ Refer any problems to a VW dealer, or an automatic transmission specialist.

Transmission will not downshift (kickdown) with accelerator pedal fully depressed

☐ Low transmission fluid level (Chapter 1).
☐ Incorrect selector adjustment (Chapter 7).

Engine will not start in any gear, or starts in gears other than Park or Neutral

☐ Faulty starter inhibitor switch (Chapter 7).
☐ Incorrect selector adjustment (Chapter 7).

Transmission slips, shifts roughly, is noisy, or has no drive in forward or reverse gears

☐ There are many probable causes for the above problems, but the home mechanic should be concerned with only one possibility - fluid level. Before taking the vehicle to a dealer or transmission specialist, check the fluid level and condition of the fluid as described in Chapter 1. Correct the fluid level as necessary, or change the fluid and filter if needed. If the problem persists, professional help will be necessary.

Driveshafts

Clicking or knocking noise on turns (at slow speed on full lock)

☐ Lack of constant velocity joint lubricant (Chapter 8).
☐ Worn outer constant velocity joint (Chapter 8).

Vibration when accelerating or decelerating

☐ Worn inner constant velocity joint (Chapter 8).
☐ Bent or distorted driveshaft (Chapter 8).

Braking system

Note: *Before assuming that a brake problem exists, make sure that the tyres are in good condition and correctly inflated, the front wheel alignment is correct and the vehicle is not loaded with weight in an unequal manner*

Vehicle pulls to one side under braking

☐ Worn, defective, damaged or contaminated front or rear brake pads/shoes on one side (Chapter 1).
☐ Seized or partially seized front or rear brake caliper/wheel cylinder piston (Chapter 9).
☐ A mixture of brake pad/shoe lining materials fitted between sides (Chapter 1).
☐ Brake caliper mounting bolts loose (Chapter 9).
☐ Rear brake backplate mounting bolts loose (Chapter 9).
☐ Worn or damaged steering or suspension components (Chapter 10).

Noise (grinding or high-pitched squeal) when brakes applied

☐ Brake pad or shoe friction lining material worn down to metal backing (Chapter 1).
☐ Excessive corrosion of brake disc or drum, especially if the vehicle has been standing for some time (Chapter 1).
☐ Foreign object (stone chipping etc) trapped between brake disc and splash shield (Chapter 1).

Excessive brake pedal travel

☐ Faulty master cylinder (Chapter 9).
☐ Air in hydraulic system (Chapter 9).

Fault finding REF•17

Braking system (continued)

Brake pedal feels spongy when depressed
- [ ] Air in hydraulic system (Chapter 9).
- [ ] Deteriorated flexible rubber brake hoses (Chapter 1 or 9).
- [ ] Master cylinder mounting nuts loose (Chapter 9).
- [ ] Faulty master cylinder (Chapter 9).

Excessive brake pedal effort required to stop vehicle
- [ ] Faulty vacuum servo unit (Chapter 9).
- [ ] Disconnected, damaged or insecure brake servo vacuum hose (Chapter 9).
- [ ] Primary or secondary hydraulic circuit failure (Chapter 9).
- [ ] Seized brake caliper or wheel cylinder piston(s) (Chapter 9).
- [ ] Brake pads or brake shoes incorrectly fitted (Chapter 1).
- [ ] Incorrect grade of brake pads or brake shoes fitted (Chapter 1).
- [ ] Brake pads or brake shoe linings contaminated (Chapter 1).

Judder felt through brake pedal or steering wheel when braking
- [ ] Excessive run-out or distortion of front discs or rear drums (Chapter 9).
- [ ] Brake pad or brake shoe linings worn (Chapter 1).
- [ ] Brake caliper or rear brake backplate mounting bolts loose (Chapter 9).
- [ ] Wear in suspension, steering components or mountings (Chapter 9).

Brakes binding
- [ ] Seized brake caliper or wheel cylinder piston(s) (Chapter 9).
- [ ] Incorrectly adjusted handbrake mechanism or linkage (Chapter 1).
- [ ] Faulty master cylinder (Chapter 9).

Rear wheels locking under normal braking
- [ ] Rear brake shoe linings contaminated (Chapter 1).
- [ ] Faulty brake pressure regulator (Chapter 9).

Suspension and steering

Note: *Before diagnosing suspension or steering faults, be sure that the trouble is not due to incorrect tyre pressures, mixtures of tyre types or binding brakes*

Vehicle pulls to one side
- [ ] Defective tyre ("*Weekly checks*").
- [ ] Excessive wear in suspension or steering components (Chapter 10).
- [ ] Incorrect front wheel alignment (Chapter 10).
- [ ] Accident damage to steering or suspension components (Chapter 10).

Wheel wobble and vibration
- [ ] Front roadwheels out of balance (vibration felt mainly through the steering wheel) (Chapter 10).
- [ ] Rear roadwheels out of balance (vibration felt throughout the vehicle) (Chapter 10).
- [ ] Roadwheels damaged or distorted (Chapter 10).
- [ ] Faulty or damaged tyre (Chapter 10).
- [ ] Worn steering or suspension joints, bushes or components (Chapter 10).
- [ ] Wheel nuts loose (Chapter 1).

Excessive pitching and/or rolling around corners or during braking
- [ ] Defective Hydragas units and/or dampers (where fitted) (Chapter 10).
- [ ] Broken or weak suspension component (Chapter 10).
- [ ] Worn or damaged anti-roll bar or mountings (Chapter 10).

Wandering or general instability
- [ ] Incorrect front wheel alignment (Chapter 10).
- [ ] Worn steering or suspension joints, bushes or components (Chapter 10).
- [ ] Roadwheels out of balance (Chapter 10).
- [ ] Faulty or damaged tyre (Chapter 10).
- [ ] Wheel nuts loose (Chapter 1).
- [ ] Defective Hydragas units and/or dampers (where fitted) (Chapter 10).

Excessively stiff steering
- [ ] Lack of steering gear lubricant (Chapter 10).
- [ ] Seized track rod balljoint or suspension balljoint (Chapter 10).
- [ ] Incorrect front wheel alignment (Chapter 10).
- [ ] Steering rack or column bent or damaged (Chapter 10).

Excessive play in steering
- [ ] Worn steering column universal joint(s) or intermediate coupling (Chapter 10).
- [ ] Worn steering track rod balljoints (Chapter 10).
- [ ] Worn steering gear (Chapter 10).
- [ ] Worn steering or suspension joints, bushes or components (Chapter 10).

Tyre wear excessive

Tyres worn on inside or outside edges
- [ ] Tyres under-inflated (wear on both edges) ("*Weekly checks*").
- [ ] Incorrect camber or castor angles (wear on one edge only) (Chapter 10).
- [ ] Worn steering or suspension joints, bushes or components (Chapter 10).
- [ ] Excessively hard cornering.
- [ ] Accident damage.

Tyre treads exhibit feathered edges
- [ ] Incorrect toe setting (Chapter 10).

Tyres worn in centre of tread
- [ ] Tyres over-inflated ("*Weekly checks*").

Tyres worn on inside and outside edges
- [ ] Tyres under-inflated ("*Weekly checks*").

Tyres worn unevenly
- [ ] Tyres out of balance ("*Weekly checks*").
- [ ] Excessive wheel or tyre run-out ("*Weekly checks*").
- [ ] Defective Hydragas units and/or worn dampers (where fitted) (Chapter 10).
- [ ] Faulty tyre ("*Weekly checks*").

REF•18 Fault finding

Electrical system

Note: *For problems associated with the starting system, refer to the faults listed under "Engine" earlier in this Section*

Battery will not hold a charge for more than a few days

- ☐ Battery defective internally (Chapter 5).
- ☐ Battery electrolyte level low (Chapter 1).
- ☐ Battery terminal connections loose or corroded ("*Weekly checks*").
- ☐ Alternator drivebelt worn or incorrectly adjusted (Chapter 1).
- ☐ Alternator not charging at correct output (Chapter 5).
- ☐ Alternator or voltage regulator faulty (Chapter 5).
- ☐ Short-circuit causing continual battery drain (Chapter 12).

Ignition warning light remains illuminated with engine running

- ☐ Alternator drivebelt broken, worn, or incorrectly adjusted (Chapter 1).
- ☐ Alternator brushes worn, sticking, or dirty (Chapter 5).
- ☐ Alternator brush springs weak or broken (Chapter 5).
- ☐ Internal fault in alternator or voltage regulator (Chapter 5).
- ☐ Broken, disconnected, or loose wiring in charging circuit (Chapter 12).

Ignition warning light fails to come on

- ☐ Warning light bulb blown (Chapter 12).
- ☐ Broken, disconnected, or loose wiring in warning light circuit (Chapter 12).
- ☐ Alternator faulty (Chapter 5).

Lights inoperative

- ☐ Bulb blown (Chapter 12).
- ☐ Corrosion of bulb or bulbholder contacts (Chapter 12).
- ☐ Blown fuse (Chapter 12).
- ☐ Faulty relay (Chapter 12).
- ☐ Broken, loose, or disconnected wiring (Chapter 12).
- ☐ Faulty switch (Chapter 12).

Instrument readings inaccurate or erratic

Instrument readings increase with engine speed

- ☐ Faulty voltage regulator (Chapter 12).

Fuel or temperature gauge give no reading

- ☐ Faulty gauge sender unit (Chapters 3 or 4).
- ☐ Wiring open circuit (Chapter 12).
- ☐ Faulty gauge (Chapter 12).

Fuel or temperature gauges give continuous maximum reading

- ☐ Faulty gauge sender unit (Chapters 3 or 4).
- ☐ Wiring short-circuit (Chapter 12).
- ☐ Faulty gauge (Chapter 12).

Horn inoperative or unsatisfactory in operation

Horn operates all the time

- ☐ Horn push either earthed or stuck down (Chapter 12).
- ☐ Horn cable to horn push earthed (Chapter 12).

Horn fails to operate

- ☐ Blown fuse (Chapter 12).
- ☐ Cable or cable connections loose, broken or disconnected (Chapter 12).
- ☐ Faulty horn (Chapter 12).

Horn emits intermittent or unsatisfactory sound

- ☐ Cable connections loose (Chapter 12).
- ☐ Horn mountings loose (Chapter 12).
- ☐ Faulty horn (Chapter 12).

Windscreen/tailgate wipers inoperative or unsatisfactory in operation

Wipers fail to operate or operate very slowly

- ☐ Wiper blades stuck to screen, or linkage seized or binding (Chapter 12).
- ☐ Blown fuse (Chapter 12).
- ☐ Cable or cable connections loose, broken or disconnected (Chapter 12).
- ☐ Faulty relay (Chapter 12).
- ☐ Faulty wiper motor (Chapter 12).

Wiper blades sweep over too large or too small an area of the glass

- ☐ Wiper arms incorrectly positioned on spindles (Chapter 12).
- ☐ Excessive wear of wiper linkage (Chapter 12).
- ☐ Wiper motor or linkage mountings loose or insecure (Chapter 12).

Wiper blades fail to clean the glass effectively

- ☐ Wiper blade rubbers worn or perished ("*Weekly checks*").
- ☐ Wiper arm tension springs broken or arm pivots seized (Chapter 12).
- ☐ Insufficient windscreen washer additive to adequately remove road dirt film ("*Weekly checks*").

Fault finding REF•19

Electrical system (continued)

Windscreen/tailgate washers inoperative or unsatisfactory in operation

One or more washer jets inoperative

- [ ] Blocked washer jet (Chapter 12).
- [ ] Disconnected, kinked or restricted fluid hose (Chapter 12).
- [ ] Insufficient fluid in washer reservoir ("*Weekly checks*").

Washer pump fails to operate

- [ ] Broken or disconnected wiring or connections (Chapter 12).
- [ ] Blown fuse (Chapter 12).
- [ ] Faulty washer switch (Chapter 12).
- [ ] Faulty washer pump (Chapter 12).

Washer pump runs for some time before fluid is emitted from jets

- [ ] Faulty one-way valve in fluid supply hose (Chapter 12).

Electric windows inoperative or unsatisfactory in operation

Window glass will only move in one direction

- [ ] Faulty switch (Chapter 12).

Window glass slow to move

- [ ] Incorrectly adjusted door glass guide channels (Chapter 11).
- [ ] Regulator seized or damaged, or in need of lubrication (Chapter 11).
- [ ] Door internal components or trim fouling regulator (Chapter 11).
- [ ] Faulty motor (Chapter 12).

Window glass fails to move

- [ ] Incorrectly adjusted door glass guide channels (Chapter 11).
- [ ] Blown fuse (Chapter 12).
- [ ] Faulty relay (Chapter 12).
- [ ] Broken or disconnected wiring or connections (Chapter 12).
- [ ] Faulty motor (Chapter 12).

Central locking system inoperative or unsatisfactory in operation

Complete system failure

- [ ] Blown fuse (Chapter 12).
- [ ] Faulty relay (Chapter 12).
- [ ] Broken or disconnected wiring or connections (Chapter 12).

Latch locks but will not unlock, or unlocks but will not lock

- [ ] Faulty master switch (Chapter 12).
- [ ] Broken or disconnected latch operating rods or levers (Chapter 11).
- [ ] Faulty relay (Chapter 12).

One motor fails to operate

- [ ] Broken or disconnected wiring or connections (Chapter 12).
- [ ] Faulty motor (Chapter 12).
- [ ] Broken, binding or disconnected latch operating rods or levers (Chapter 11).
- [ ] Fault in door latch (Chapter 11).

Glossary of technical terms

A

ABS (Anti-lock brake system) A system, usually electronically controlled, that senses incipient wheel lockup during braking and relieves hydraulic pressure at wheels that are about to skid.

Air bag An inflatable bag hidden in the steering wheel (driver's side) or the dash or glovebox (passenger side). In a head-on collision, the bags inflate, preventing the driver and front passenger from being thrown forward into the steering wheel or windscreen.

Air cleaner A metal or plastic housing, containing a filter element, which removes dust and dirt from the air being drawn into the engine.

Air filter element The actual filter in an air cleaner system, usually manufactured from pleated paper and requiring renewal at regular intervals.

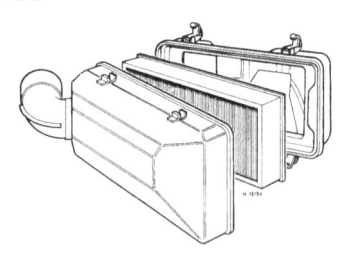

Air filter

Allen key A hexagonal wrench which fits into a recessed hexagonal hole.

Alligator clip A long-nosed spring-loaded metal clip with meshing teeth. Used to make temporary electrical connections.

Alternator A component in the electrical system which converts mechanical energy from a drivebelt into electrical energy to charge the battery and to operate the starting system, ignition system and electrical accessories.

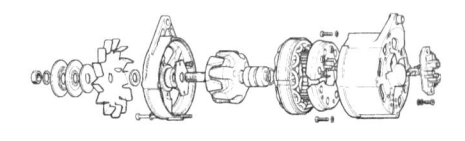

Alternator (exploded view)

Ampere (amp) A unit of measurement for the flow of electric current. One amp is the amount of current produced by one volt acting through a resistance of one ohm.

Anaerobic sealer A substance used to prevent bolts and screws from loosening. Anaerobic means that it does not require oxygen for activation. The Loctite brand is widely used.

Antifreeze A substance (usually ethylene glycol) mixed with water, and added to a vehicle's cooling system, to prevent freezing of the coolant in winter. Antifreeze also contains chemicals to inhibit corrosion and the formation of rust and other deposits that would tend to clog the radiator and coolant passages and reduce cooling efficiency.

Anti-seize compound A coating that reduces the risk of seizing on fasteners that are subjected to high temperatures, such as exhaust manifold bolts and nuts.

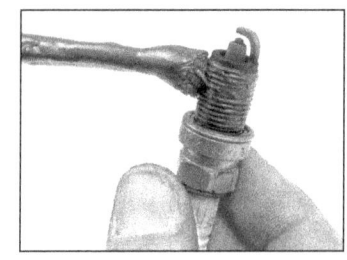

Anti-seize compound

Asbestos A natural fibrous mineral with great heat resistance, commonly used in the composition of brake friction materials. Asbestos is a health hazard and the dust created by brake systems should never be inhaled or ingested.

Axle A shaft on which a wheel revolves, or which revolves with a wheel. Also, a solid beam that connects the two wheels at one end of the vehicle. An axle which also transmits power to the wheels is known as a live axle.

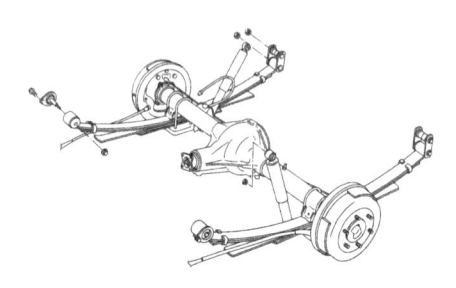

Axle assembly

Axleshaft A single rotating shaft, on either side of the differential, which delivers power from the final drive assembly to the drive wheels. Also called a driveshaft or a halfshaft.

B

Ball bearing An anti-friction bearing consisting of a hardened inner and outer race with hardened steel balls between two races.

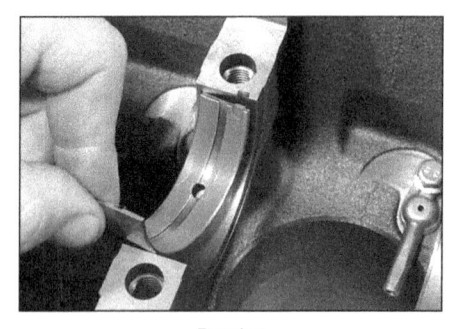

Bearing

Bearing The curved surface on a shaft or in a bore, or the part assembled into either, that permits relative motion between them with minimum wear and friction.

Big-end bearing The bearing in the end of the connecting rod that's attached to the crankshaft.

Bleed nipple A valve on a brake wheel cylinder, caliper or other hydraulic component that is opened to purge the hydraulic system of air. Also called a bleed screw.

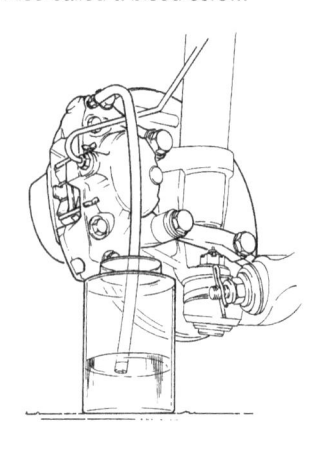

Brake bleeding

Brake bleeding Procedure for removing air from lines of a hydraulic brake system.

Brake disc The component of a disc brake that rotates with the wheels.

Brake drum The component of a drum brake that rotates with the wheels.

Brake linings The friction material which contacts the brake disc or drum to retard the vehicle's speed. The linings are bonded or riveted to the brake pads or shoes.

Brake pads The replaceable friction pads that pinch the brake disc when the brakes are applied. Brake pads consist of a friction material bonded or riveted to a rigid backing plate.

Brake shoe The crescent-shaped carrier to which the brake linings are mounted and which forces the lining against the rotating drum during braking.

Braking systems For more information on braking systems, consult the *Haynes Automotive Brake Manual*.

Breaker bar A long socket wrench handle providing greater leverage.

Bulkhead The insulated partition between the engine and the passenger compartment.

C

Caliper The non-rotating part of a disc-brake assembly that straddles the disc and carries the brake pads. The caliper also contains the hydraulic components that cause the pads to pinch the disc when the brakes are applied. A caliper is also a measuring tool that can be set to measure inside or outside dimensions of an object.

Glossary of technical terms REF•21

Camshaft A rotating shaft on which a series of cam lobes operate the valve mechanisms. The camshaft may be driven by gears, by sprockets and chain or by sprockets and a belt.

Canister A container in an evaporative emission control system; contains activated charcoal granules to trap vapours from the fuel system.

Canister

Carburettor A device which mixes fuel with air in the proper proportions to provide a desired power output from a spark ignition internal combustion engine.

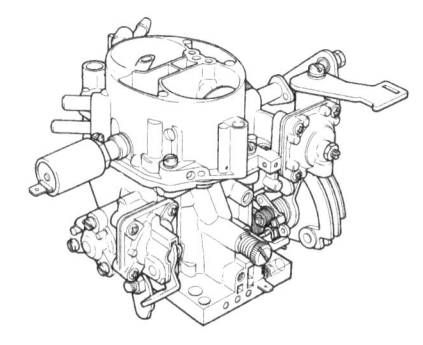

Carburettor

Castellated Resembling the parapets along the top of a castle wall. For example, a castellated balljoint stud nut.

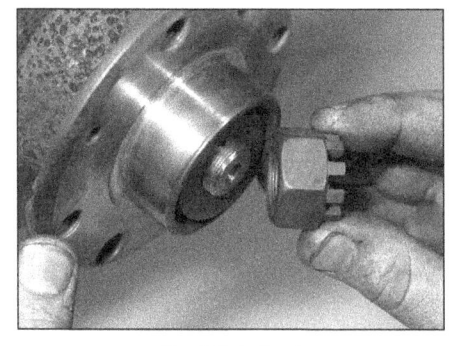

Castellated nut

Castor In wheel alignment, the backward or forward tilt of the steering axis. Castor is positive when the steering axis is inclined rearward at the top.

Catalytic converter A silencer-like device in the exhaust system which converts certain pollutants in the exhaust gases into less harmful substances.

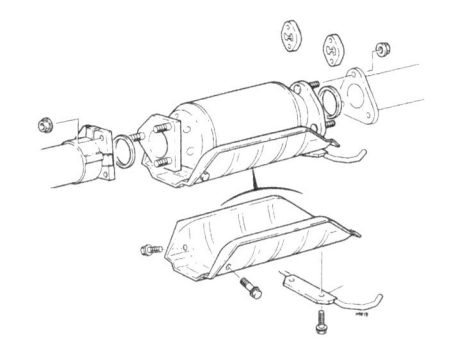

Catalytic converter

Circlip A ring-shaped clip used to prevent endwise movement of cylindrical parts and shafts. An internal circlip is installed in a groove in a housing; an external circlip fits into a groove on the outside of a cylindrical piece such as a shaft.

Clearance The amount of space between two parts. For example, between a piston and a cylinder, between a bearing and a journal, etc.

Coil spring A spiral of elastic steel found in various sizes throughout a vehicle, for example as a springing medium in the suspension and in the valve train.

Compression Reduction in volume, and increase in pressure and temperature, of a gas, caused by squeezing it into a smaller space.

Compression ratio The relationship between cylinder volume when the piston is at top dead centre and cylinder volume when the piston is at bottom dead centre.

Constant velocity (CV) joint A type of universal joint that cancels out vibrations caused by driving power being transmitted through an angle.

Core plug A disc or cup-shaped metal device inserted in a hole in a casting through which core was removed when the casting was formed. Also known as a freeze plug or expansion plug.

Crankcase The lower part of the engine block in which the crankshaft rotates.

Crankshaft The main rotating member, or shaft, running the length of the crankcase, with offset "throws" to which the connecting rods are attached.

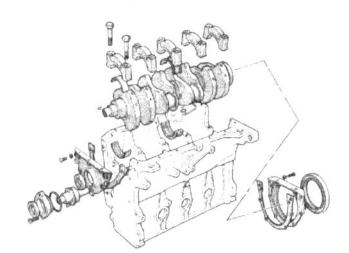

Crankshaft assembly

Crocodile clip See Alligator clip

D

Diagnostic code Code numbers obtained by accessing the diagnostic mode of an engine management computer. This code can be used to determine the area in the system where a malfunction may be located.

Disc brake A brake design incorporating a rotating disc onto which brake pads are squeezed. The resulting friction converts the energy of a moving vehicle into heat.

Double-overhead cam (DOHC) An engine that uses two overhead camshafts, usually one for the intake valves and one for the exhaust valves.

Drivebelt(s) The belt(s) used to drive accessories such as the alternator, water pump, power steering pump, air conditioning compressor, etc. off the crankshaft pulley.

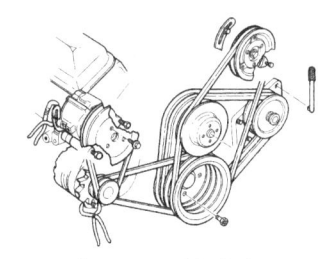

Accessory drivebelts

Driveshaft Any shaft used to transmit motion. Commonly used when referring to the axleshafts on a front wheel drive vehicle.

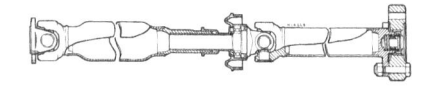

Driveshaft

Drum brake A type of brake using a drum-shaped metal cylinder attached to the inner surface of the wheel. When the brake pedal is pressed, curved brake shoes with friction linings press against the inside of the drum to slow or stop the vehicle.

Drum brake assembly

Glossary of technical terms

E

EGR valve A valve used to introduce exhaust gases into the intake air stream.

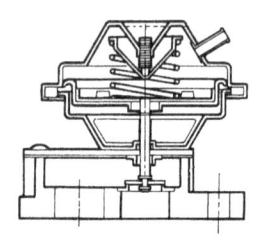

EGR valve

Electronic control unit (ECU) A computer which controls (for instance) ignition and fuel injection systems, or an anti-lock braking system. For more information refer to the *Haynes Automotive Electrical and Electronic Systems Manual*.

Electronic Fuel Injection (EFI) A computer controlled fuel system that distributes fuel through an injector located in each intake port of the engine.

Emergency brake A braking system, independent of the main hydraulic system, that can be used to slow or stop the vehicle if the primary brakes fail, or to hold the vehicle stationary even though the brake pedal isn't depressed. It usually consists of a hand lever that actuates either front or rear brakes mechanically through a series of cables and linkages. Also known as a handbrake or parking brake.

Endfloat The amount of lengthwise movement between two parts. As applied to a crankshaft, the distance that the crankshaft can move forward and back in the cylinder block.

Engine management system (EMS) A computer controlled system which manages the fuel injection and the ignition systems in an integrated fashion.

Exhaust manifold A part with several passages through which exhaust gases leave the engine combustion chambers and enter the exhaust pipe.

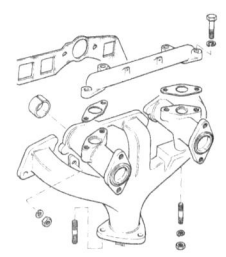

Exhaust manifold

F

Fan clutch A viscous (fluid) drive coupling device which permits variable engine fan speeds in relation to engine speeds.

Feeler blade A thin strip or blade of hardened steel, ground to an exact thickness, used to check or measure clearances between parts.

Feeler blade

Firing order The order in which the engine cylinders fire, or deliver their power strokes, beginning with the number one cylinder.

Flywheel A heavy spinning wheel in which energy is absorbed and stored by means of momentum. On cars, the flywheel is attached to the crankshaft to smooth out firing impulses.

Free play The amount of travel before any action takes place. The "looseness" in a linkage, or an assembly of parts, between the initial application of force and actual movement. For example, the distance the brake pedal moves before the pistons in the master cylinder are actuated.

Fuse An electrical device which protects a circuit against accidental overload. The typical fuse contains a soft piece of metal which is calibrated to melt at a predetermined current flow (expressed as amps) and break the circuit.

Fusible link A circuit protection device consisting of a conductor surrounded by heat-resistant insulation. The conductor is smaller than the wire it protects, so it acts as the weakest link in the circuit. Unlike a blown fuse, a failed fusible link must frequently be cut from the wire for replacement.

G

Gap The distance the spark must travel in jumping from the centre electrode to the side electrode in a spark plug. Also refers to the spacing between the points in a contact breaker assembly in a conventional points-type ignition, or to the distance between the reluctor or rotor and the pickup coil in an electronic ignition.

Gasket Any thin, soft material - usually cork, cardboard, asbestos or soft metal - installed between two metal surfaces to ensure a good seal. For instance, the cylinder head gasket seals the joint between the block and the cylinder head.

Gasket

Gauge An instrument panel display used to monitor engine conditions. A gauge with a movable pointer on a dial or a fixed scale is an analogue gauge. A gauge with a numerical readout is called a digital gauge.

H

Halfshaft A rotating shaft that transmits power from the final drive unit to a drive wheel, usually when referring to a live rear axle.

Harmonic balancer A device designed to reduce torsion or twisting vibration in the crankshaft. May be incorporated in the crankshaft pulley. Also known as a vibration damper.

Hone An abrasive tool for correcting small irregularities or differences in diameter in an engine cylinder, brake cylinder, etc.

Hydraulic tappet A tappet that utilises hydraulic pressure from the engine's lubrication system to maintain zero clearance (constant contact with both camshaft and valve stem). Automatically adjusts to variation in valve stem length. Hydraulic tappets also reduce valve noise.

I

Ignition timing The moment at which the spark plug fires, usually expressed in the number of crankshaft degrees before the piston reaches the top of its stroke.

Inlet manifold A tube or housing with passages through which flows the air-fuel mixture (carburettor vehicles and vehicles with throttle body injection) or air only (port fuel-injected vehicles) to the port openings in the cylinder head.

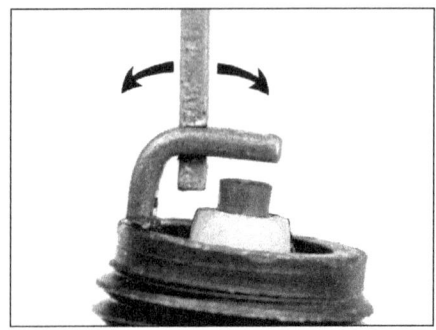

Adjusting spark plug gap

Glossary of technical terms REF•23

J

Jump start Starting the engine of a vehicle with a discharged or weak battery by attaching jump leads from the weak battery to a charged or helper battery.

L

Load Sensing Proportioning Valve (LSPV) A brake hydraulic system control valve that works like a proportioning valve, but also takes into consideration the amount of weight carried by the rear axle.

Locknut A nut used to lock an adjustment nut, or other threaded component, in place. For example, a locknut is employed to keep the adjusting nut on the rocker arm in position.

Lockwasher A form of washer designed to prevent an attaching nut from working loose.

M

MacPherson strut A type of front suspension system devised by Earle MacPherson at Ford of England. In its original form, a simple lateral link with the anti-roll bar creates the lower control arm. A long strut - an integral coil spring and shock absorber - is mounted between the body and the steering knuckle. Many modern so-called MacPherson strut systems use a conventional lower A-arm and don't rely on the anti-roll bar for location.

Multimeter An electrical test instrument with the capability to measure voltage, current and resistance.

N

NOx Oxides of Nitrogen. A common toxic pollutant emitted by petrol and diesel engines at higher temperatures.

O

Ohm The unit of electrical resistance. One volt applied to a resistance of one ohm will produce a current of one amp.

Ohmmeter An instrument for measuring electrical resistance.

O-ring A type of sealing ring made of a special rubber-like material; in use, the O-ring is compressed into a groove to provide the sealing action.

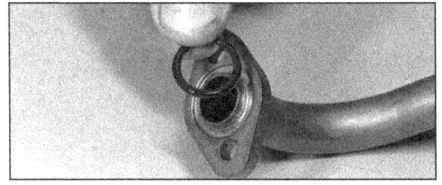

O-ring

Overhead cam (ohc) engine An engine with the camshaft(s) located on top of the cylinder head(s).

Overhead valve (ohv) engine An engine with the valves located in the cylinder head, but with the camshaft located in the engine block.

Oxygen sensor A device installed in the engine exhaust manifold, which senses the oxygen content in the exhaust and converts this information into an electric current. Also called a Lambda sensor.

P

Phillips screw A type of screw head having a cross instead of a slot for a corresponding type of screwdriver.

Plastigage A thin strip of plastic thread, available in different sizes, used for measuring clearances. For example, a strip of Plastigage is laid across a bearing journal. The parts are assembled and dismantled; the width of the crushed strip indicates the clearance between journal and bearing.

Plastigage

Propeller shaft The long hollow tube with universal joints at both ends that carries power from the transmission to the differential on front-engined rear wheel drive vehicles.

Proportioning valve A hydraulic control valve which limits the amount of pressure to the rear brakes during panic stops to prevent wheel lock-up.

R

Rack-and-pinion steering A steering system with a pinion gear on the end of the steering shaft that mates with a rack (think of a geared wheel opened up and laid flat). When the steering wheel is turned, the pinion turns, moving the rack to the left or right. This movement is transmitted through the track rods to the steering arms at the wheels.

Radiator A liquid-to-air heat transfer device designed to reduce the temperature of the coolant in an internal combustion engine cooling system.

Refrigerant Any substance used as a heat transfer agent in an air-conditioning system. R-12 has been the principle refrigerant for many years; recently, however, manufacturers have begun using R-134a, a non-CFC substance that is considered less harmful to the ozone in the upper atmosphere.

Rocker arm A lever arm that rocks on a shaft or pivots on a stud. In an overhead valve engine, the rocker arm converts the upward movement of the pushrod into a downward movement to open a valve.

Rotor In a distributor, the rotating device inside the cap that connects the centre electrode and the outer terminals as it turns, distributing the high voltage from the coil secondary winding to the proper spark plug. Also, that part of an alternator which rotates inside the stator. Also, the rotating assembly of a turbocharger, including the compressor wheel, shaft and turbine wheel.

Runout The amount of wobble (in-and-out movement) of a gear or wheel as it's rotated. The amount a shaft rotates "out-of-true." The out-of-round condition of a rotating part.

S

Sealant A liquid or paste used to prevent leakage at a joint. Sometimes used in conjunction with a gasket.

Sealed beam lamp An older headlight design which integrates the reflector, lens and filaments into a hermetically-sealed one-piece unit. When a filament burns out or the lens cracks, the entire unit is simply replaced.

Serpentine drivebelt A single, long, wide accessory drivebelt that's used on some newer vehicles to drive all the accessories, instead of a series of smaller, shorter belts. Serpentine drivebelts are usually tensioned by an automatic tensioner.

Serpentine drivebelt

Shim Thin spacer, commonly used to adjust the clearance or relative positions between two parts. For example, shims inserted into or under bucket tappets control valve clearances. Clearance is adjusted by changing the thickness of the shim.

Slide hammer A special puller that screws into or hooks onto a component such as a shaft or bearing; a heavy sliding handle on the shaft bottoms against the end of the shaft to knock the component free.

Sprocket A tooth or projection on the periphery of a wheel, shaped to engage with a chain or drivebelt. Commonly used to refer to the sprocket wheel itself.

Starter inhibitor switch On vehicles with an

REF•24 Glossary of technical terms

automatic transmission, a switch that prevents starting if the vehicle is not in Neutral or Park.
Strut See MacPherson strut.

T

Tappet A cylindrical component which transmits motion from the cam to the valve stem, either directly or via a pushrod and rocker arm. Also called a cam follower.
Thermostat A heat-controlled valve that regulates the flow of coolant between the cylinder block and the radiator, so maintaining optimum engine operating temperature. A thermostat is also used in some air cleaners in which the temperature is regulated.
Thrust bearing The bearing in the clutch assembly that is moved in to the release levers by clutch pedal action to disengage the clutch. Also referred to as a release bearing.
Timing belt A toothed belt which drives the camshaft. Serious engine damage may result if it breaks in service.
Timing chain A chain which drives the camshaft.
Toe-in The amount the front wheels are closer together at the front than at the rear. On rear wheel drive vehicles, a slight amount of toe-in is usually specified to keep the front wheels running parallel on the road by offsetting other forces that tend to spread the wheels apart.
Toe-out The amount the front wheels are closer together at the rear than at the front. On front wheel drive vehicles, a slight amount of toe-out is usually specified.
Tools For full information on choosing and using tools, refer to the *Haynes Automotive Tools Manual*.
Tracer A stripe of a second colour applied to a wire insulator to distinguish that wire from another one with the same colour insulator.
Tune-up A process of accurate and careful adjustments and parts replacement to obtain the best possible engine performance.
Turbocharger A centrifugal device, driven by exhaust gases, that pressurises the intake air. Normally used to increase the power output from a given engine displacement, but can also be used primarily to reduce exhaust emissions (as on VW's "Umwelt" Diesel engine).

U

Universal joint or U-joint A double-pivoted connection for transmitting power from a driving to a driven shaft through an angle. A U-joint consists of two Y-shaped yokes and a cross-shaped member called the spider.

V

Valve A device through which the flow of liquid, gas, vacuum, or loose material in bulk may be started, stopped, or regulated by a movable part that opens, shuts, or partially obstructs one or more ports or passageways. A valve is also the movable part of such a device.
Valve clearance The clearance between the valve tip (the end of the valve stem) and the rocker arm or tappet. The valve clearance is measured when the valve is closed.
Vernier caliper A precision measuring instrument that measures inside and outside dimensions. Not quite as accurate as a micrometer, but more convenient.
Viscosity The thickness of a liquid or its resistance to flow.
Volt A unit for expressing electrical "pressure" in a circuit. One volt that will produce a current of one ampere through a resistance of one ohm.

W

Welding Various processes used to join metal items by heating the areas to be joined to a molten state and fusing them together. For more information refer to the *Haynes Automotive Welding Manual*.
Wiring diagram A drawing portraying the components and wires in a vehicle's electrical system, using standardised symbols. For more information refer to the *Haynes Automotive Electrical and Electronic Systems Manual*.

Index REF•25

Note: References throughout this index are in the form - "Chapter number"•"page number"

A

Accelerator cable:
 carburettor models - 4A•8
 fuel injection models - 4B•5
Accelerator pedal - 4A•9
Air cleaner element - 1•20
 carburettor models - 4A•4
 Digijet fuel injection - 4E•2
 K-Jetronic fuel injection - 4B•4
 Mono Jetronic fuel injection - 4D•2
Air cleaner unit, carburettor models - 4A•4
Air conditioning:
 compressor - 3•11
 drivebelt - 1•13, 3•11
 system check - 1•11
Air inlet duct, Mono Jetronic fuel injection - 4D•2
Air inlet pre-heater, Mono Jetronic fuel injection - 4D•2
Airflow meter:
 Digifant fuel injection - 4F•4
 Digijet fuel injection - 4E•3
 K-Jetronic fuel injection - 4B•8
Airflow sensor plate and control plunger, K-Jetronic - 4B•7
Alternator:
 brushes - 5D•3
 drivebelt - 1•13, 5D•3
 removal and refitting - 5D•3
 testing - 5D•3
 voltage regulator - 5D•3
Antifreeze concentration check - 1•14
Automatic air cleaner temperature control:
 carburettor models - 4A•4
 Digifant fuel injection - 4F•2
Automatic transmission - 7B•1 et seq
Automatic transmission:
 fluid renewal - 1•22
 fluid level check - 1•18
 removal and refitting - 7B•4
Auxiliary air valve, K-Jetronic - 4B•6

B

Battery:
 charging - 5D•2
 check - 0•15, 1•11
 maintenance - 5D•2
 removal and refitting - 5D•2
Body electrical systems - 12•1 et seq
Body protective and decorative trim fittings - 11•13
Bodywork and fittings - 11•1 et seq
Bonnet:
 lock - 11•4
 removal, refitting and adjustment - 11•4
 release cable - 11•4

Boot lid:
 removal, refitting and adjustment - 11•6
 lock and lock cylinder - 11•6
Brakes:
 calipers - 9•4
 check - 1•10
 discs - 9•6
 drums - 9•9
 fluid level check - 0•12
 fluid renewal - 1•22
 pads - 9•2
 pad and rear shoe lining check - 1•19
 pressure regulator - 9•10
 shoes - 9•7
Braking system - 9•1 et seq
Bumpers - 11•11
Buying spare parts - REF•3

C

Camshaft:
 1.05 and 1.3 litre pre-August 1985 - 2A•8, 2A•14, 2A•16
 1.05 and 1.3 litre post August 1985 - 2B•2, 2B•3, 2B•4, 2B•5
 1.6 and 1.8 litre 8 valve - 2C•9
 1.8 litre 16 valve - 2D•3
Capacities - 0•17
Carburettor:
 overhaul - 4A•10
 removal and refitting - 4A•9
 adjustments:
  1.05 litre engine - 4A•14
  1.3 litre engine - 4A•17
  1.6 & 1.8 litre engines - 4A•18
Catalytic converters - 4B•3
Central locking system - 11•10
Centre console - 11•15
Choke cable, 1.05 litre engine - 4A•9
Cigarette lighter - 12•12
Clutch - 6•1 et seq
Clutch:
 adjustment - 6•2
 cable - 6•2
 inspection - 6•7
 operation check - 1•17
 pedal - removal and refitting - 6•4
 release mechanism - 6•8
 removal and refitting - 6•5
Coil:
 contact breaker type - 5A•6
 transistorised type - 5B•7
Cold acceleration enrichment system, K-Jetronic - 4B•6
Cold start valve and thermotime switch, K-Jetronic - 4B•6
Combination switches - 12•7
Condenser, contact breaker type - 5A•4

Index

Contact breaker point: - 1•12
   renewal and adjustment - 1•14, 5A•4
Contents - 0•2
Control unit:
   Digifant fuel injection - 4F•4
   fully electronic type - 5C•2
Conversion factors - REF•2
Coolant level check - 0•11
Coolant pump - 3•7
Cooling fan and motor - 3•6
Cooling, heating and air conditioning systems - 3•1 et seq
Cooling system:
   draining, flushing and filling - 3•4
   electrical switches - 3•8
Courtesy light switches - 12•8
Crankshaft and bearings:
   1.05 and 1.3 litre pre-August 1985 - 2A•10, 2A•12, 2A•13, 2A•15
   1.6 and 1.8 litre 8 valve - 2C•13, 2C•15, 2C•17
CV joint and boot check - 1•18
Cylinder block/crankcase:
   1.05 and 1.3 litre pre-August 1985 - 2A•13
   1.6 and 1.8 litre 8 valve - 2C•16
Cylinder head:
   1.05 and 1.3 litre pre-August 1985 - 2A•7, 2A•9, 2A•16, 2A•17
   1.05 and 1.3 litre post August 1985 - 2B•2, 2B•3, 2B•5
   1.6 and 1.8 litre 8 valve - 2C•11, 2C•18
   1.8 litre 16 valve - 2D•4

D

Diaphragm pressure switch, K-Jetronic - 4C•4
Dimensions - REF•1
Direction indicators - 12•6
Distributor:
   contact breaker type - 5A•5
   fully electronic type - 5C•3
   transistorised type - 5B•4, 5B•6
Door:
   handles - 11•9
   lock - 11•9
   rattles - 11•4
   removal and refitting - 11•9
   striker adjustment - 11•9
   trim panel - 11•7
Drive flange oil seals - 8•4
Driveshafts - 8•1 et seq
Driveshaft:
   dismantling and reassembly - 8•2
   removal and refitting - 8•1
Dust and pollen filter - 11•18

E

Electrical systems check - 0•15
Electrically-operated door mirror motor - 12•12

Engine:
   adjustments after major overhaul - 2A•18, 2B•8, 2C•19
   ancillary components refitting - 2A•18, 2C•19
   ancillary components removal - 2A•6, 2C•8
   dismantling - 2A•6, 2C•8
   electrical system check - 1•11
   examination and renovation - 2A•12, 2C•15
   reassembly - 2A•14, 2C•17
   refitting - 2A•18, 2C•19
   removal - 2A•4, 2C•5
Engine/gearbox separation and reconnection - 2A•5, 2C•8
Engine oil and filter renewal - 1•16
Engine oil level check - 0•11
Engine repair procedures:
   1.05 and 1.3 litre - pre August 1985 - 2A•1 et seq
   1.05 and 1.3 litre - post August 1985 - 2B•1 et seq
   1.6 and 1.8 litre 8 valve - 2C•1 et seq
   1.8 litre 16 valve - 2D•1 et seq
Evaporative fuel control system, Digijet fuel injection - 4E•5
Exhaust manifold:
   carburettor models - 4A•21
   fuel injection - 4B•12
Exhaust system inspection, removal and refitting: - 1•17
   carburettor models - 4A•22
   fuel injection, 8 valve engines - 4B•12
   fuel injection, 16 valve engines - 4C•5
Exterior mirrors - 11•11

F

Facia panel - 11•15
Facia switches - 12•7
Facia trim panel - 12•11
Fault Finding - REF•12 et seq
   automatic transmission - REF•12, REF•16
   braking system - REF•12, REF•16
   clutch - REF•12, REF•15
   cooling system - REF•12, REF•14
   driveshafts - REF•12, REF•16
   electrical system - REF•12, REF•18
   engine - REF•12, REF•13
   fuel and exhaust system - REF•12, REF•15
   manual gearbox - REF•12, REF•15
   suspension and steering - REF•12, REF•17
Fluid leakage check - 1•11
Flywheel, 1.05 and 1.3 litre - 2A•10, 2A•14, 2A•16, 2C•16
Footbrake pedal - 9•12
Front anti-roll bar - 10•5
Front foglight bulb and unit - 12•5
Front seats - 11•16
Front suspension, camber adjustment - 10•5
Front suspension strut - 10•4
Front wheel bearing:
   renewal - 10•6
   bearing housing - 10•5

Index

housing liner - 11•12
Front wing - 11•13
Fuel accumulator, K-Jetronic - 4B•10
Fuel hose and union check - 1•19
Fuel and exhaust systems:
   carburettor models - 4A•1 et seq
   Digifant fuel injection - 4F•1 et seq
   Digijet fuel injection - 4E•1 et seq
   K-Jetronic fuel injection for 8 valve engines - 4B•1 et seq
   K-Jetronic fuel injection for 16 valve engines - 4C•1 et seq
   Mono Jetronic fuel injection - 4D•1 et seq
Fuel filler gravity valve, carburettor models - 4A•8
Fuel filter renewal - 1•21, 4B•10
Fuel gauge sender unit - 4A•8
Fuel injectors:
   Digifant fuel injection - 4F•3
   Digijet fuel injection - 4E•3
   K-Jetronic fuel injection - 4B•7
   Mono Jetronic fuel injection - 4D•3
Fuel lift pump, K-Jetronic - 4B•9
Fuel metering distributor, K-Jetronic fuel injection - 4B•8
Fuel pressure regulator, Digifant - 4F•3
Fuel pump:
   carburettor models - 4A•6
   Digifant fuel injection - 4F•4
   K-Jetronic - 4B•9
   Mono Jetronic - 4D•5
Fuel reservoir, carburettor models - 4A•7
Fuel system control linkage - 1•11
Fuel tank:
   carburettor models - 4A•7
   fuel injection models - 4B•10
Fuses - 12•1, 12•2, 12•3

G

Gearbox:
   oil level check - 1•17
   overhaul - 7A•7
   removal and refitting - 7A•5
Gearchange and consumption gauge - 12•11
Gearshift mechanism - 7A•2
General information and precautions:
   automatic transmission - 7B•1
   body electrical systems - 12•2
   bodywork and fittings - 11•1
   braking system - 9•2
   carburettor models - 4A•4
   clutch - 6•2
   cooling, heating and air conditioning systems - 3•2
   Digifant fuel injection - 4F•1
   Digijet fuel injection - 4E•2
   driveshafts - 8•1
   electrical fault-finding - 12•3
   engine, 1.05 and 1.3 litre pre-August 1985 - 2A•3
   engine, 1.05 and 1.3 litre post August 1985 - 2B•2
   engine, 1.6 and 1.8 litre, 8 valve - 2C•5
   engine, 1.8 litre, 16 valve - 2D•3
   ignition system - contact breaker type - 5A•2
   ignition system - fully electronic type - 5C•1
   ignition system - transistorised type - 5B•2
   K-Jetronic fuel injection, 8 valve engines - 4B•2
   K-Jetronic fuel injection, 16 valve engines - 4C•2
   manual gearbox - 7A•2
   Mono Jetronic fuel injection - 4D•2
   starting and charging systems - 5D•2
   suspension and steering - 10•2
General repair procedures - REF•4
Glossary of technical terms - REF•20

H

Hall sender:
   fully electronic type - 5C•2
   transistorised type - 5B•4
Handbrake:
   cables - 9•12
   lever - 9•11
Hazard flasher system - 12•6
Headlamp bulbs and headlamps:
   alignment - 1•19, 12•4
   range control - 12•5
   removal and refitting - 12•4
Heat exchanger/fresh air box - 3•9
Heater and fresh air blower unit - 3•9
Heater controls - 3•8
Hinge and catch lubrication - 1•20
Horn - 12•12
HT leads, distributor cap and rotor arm:
   contact breaker type - 5A•4
   fully electronic type - 5C•2
   transistorised type - 5B•4
Hydraulic bucket tappets:
   free travel, 1.05 and 1.3 litre - 2B•7
   free travel, 1.6 and 1.8 litre 8 valve - 2C•19
Hydraulic pipes and hoses - 9•10
Hydraulic system, bleeding - 9•10

I

Identifying leaks - 0•9
Idle speed and mixture adjustment:
   Digifant fuel injection - 4F•2
   Digijet - 4E•3
   K-Jetronic, 8 valve engines - 4B•4, 4B•5
   K-Jetronic, 16 valve engines - 4C•2
   Mono Jetronic fuel injection - 4D•3
Idle speed boost (air conditioned models) - 4B•4
Idle speed stabilisation system:
   Digifant fuel injection - 4F•2
   K-Jetronic fuel injection, 16 valve engines - 4C•4
Idle switch control valve, Mono Jetronic - 4D•3

Index

If your car won't start - 0•6
Ignition switch/steering column lock - 12•7
Ignition system:
 contact breaker type - 5A•1 et seq
 fully electronic type - 5C•1 et seq
 transistorised - 5B•1 et seq
Ignition timing: - 1•15
 contact breaker type - 5A•6
 fully electronic type - 5C•3
 transistorised type - 5B•7
Increased idling speed valve (air conditioned models) - 4B•4
Injector unit housing, Mono Jetronic - 4D•4
Inlet air pre-heater, Digijet - 4E•3
Inlet manifold:
 carburettor models - 4A•21
 K-Jetronic, 8 valve engines - 4B•10
 K-Jetronic, 16 valve engines - 4C•5
Inlet manifold preheating, carburettor models - 4A•20
Instrument panel - 12•8
Intensive maintenance - 1•10
Intermediate shaft - 2C•14, 2C•16, 2C•18
Introduction:
 to roadside repairs - 0•6
 to Routine maintenance - 1•10
 to the VW Golf & Jetta - 0•4
 to Weekly Checks - 0•10

J

Jacking and vehicle support - REF•5
Jump starting - 0•7

L

Light bulbs - 12•5
Light, direction indicator and horn check - 1•11
Lock, hinge and latch mechanism check - 1•10
Loudspeakers - 12•16
Lubricants and fluids - 0•16
Luggage compartment light switches - 12•8

M

Maintenance and Servicing - 1•1
Maintenance procedures - 1•10
Maintenance schedule - 1•5, 1•6
Major body damage - 11•4
Manual gearbox - 7A•1 et seq
Master cylinder - 9•9
Minor body damage - 11•2
MOT test checks - REF•8
Multi-function indicator - 12•11

O

Oil capacities - 0•17
Oil cooler - 2C•15
Oil filter:
 1.05 and 1.3 litre - 2A•12
 1.6 and 1.8 litre - 2C•15
 mounting, 1.6 and 1.8 litre - 2C•15
Oil pressure warning switches - 12•8
Oil pump:
 1.05 and 1.3 litre pre-August 1985 - 2A•11, 2A•13, 2A•15
 1.05 and 1.3 litre post August 1985 - 2B•4, 2B•5
 1.6 and 1.8 litre - 2C•12, 2C•16
Oil seals, 1.6 and 1.8 litre - 2C•15
Oil types - 0•16
Overrun cut-off:
 Digifant fuel injection - 4F•4
 K-Jetronic fuel injection, 16 valve engines - 4C•4

P

Pistons and connecting rods:
 1.05 and 1.3 litre - 2A•12, 2A•13, 2A•15
 1.6 and 1.8 litre 8 valve - 2C•13, 2C•16, 2C•18
 1.8 litre 16 valve - 2D•4
Power steering fluid:
 draining and refilling - 10•14
 level check - 0•12
Power steering pump:
 removal, refitting and drivebelt adjustment - 10•14
 drivebelt(s) check - 1•13
Pre-throttle valve clearance, Digijet - 4E•4
Pressure relief valve, K-Jetronic - 4B•9

R

Radiator - 3•5
Radiator grille - 11•5
Radio/cassette player - 12•15
Rear axle beam - 10•8
Rear brake:
 cylinder - 9•8
 drum - 9•9
 shoes - 9•7
Rear hub bearings - 9•7, 10•8
Rear seat - 11•17
Rear suspension strut and coil spring - 10•7
Rear window wiper motor - 12•13
Relays - 12•3
Routine Maintenance and Servicing - 1•1 et seq
Routine Maintenance procedures - 1•10 et seq
Routine Maintenance schedule - 1•5, 1•6

Index

S

Safety First! - 0•5
Screen/headlamp washer fluid check - 0•12
Seat belts - 1•10, 11•17
Selector cable, automatic transmission models - 7B•3
Slow running adjustment - 1•17
Spark plug renewal - 1•14
    contact breaker type - 5A•4
    fully electronic type - 5C•2
    transistorised type - 5B•2
Spark plug type - 1•3
Specifications:
    1.05 and 1.3 litre pre-August 1985 engine - 2A•1
    1.05 and 1.3 litre post August 1985 engine - 2B•1
    1.6 and 1.8 litre 8 valve engine - 2C•1
    1.6 and 1.8 litre 16 valve engine - 2D•1
    automatic transmission - 7B•1
    body electrical systems - 12•1
    bodywork and fittings - 11•1
    braking system - 9•1
    carburettor fuel system - 4A•1
    clutch - 6•1
    contact breaker type ignition system - 5A•1
    cooling, heating and air conditioning systems - 3•1
    Digifant fuel injection - 4F•1
    Digijet fuel injection - 4E•1
    driveshafts - 8•1
    electronic type ignition system - 5C•1
    K-Jetronic fuel injection - 16 valve engines - 4C•1
    K-Jetronic fuel injection - 8 valve engines - 4B•1
    manual gearbox - 7A•1
    Mono Jetronic fuel injection - 4D•1
    routine maintenance - 1•2
    starting and charging systems - 5D•1
    suspension and steering - 10•1
    transistorised type ignition system - 5B•1
Speedometer cable - 12•12
Starting and charging - 5D•1 et seq
Starter motor - 5D•4
Steering column - 10•9
Steering gear:
    adjustment - 10•12
    bellows - 10•10
    check - 1•19
    removal and refitting - 10•12
Steering lock - 10•10
Steering wheel - 10•8
Sump - 2A•11, 2A•16
Sump and oil pump, 1.6 and 1.8 litre engine - 2C•12
Sunroof:
    guide rails cleaning and lubrication - 1•21
    removal, refitting and adjustment - 11•14
Suspension and steering - 10•1 et seq
Suspension check - 1•20
Switch unit:
    electronic type - 5C•2
    transistorised type - 5B•4

T

Tailgate - 11•5
Thermostat - 3•6
Throttle damper, Mono Jetronic - 4D•4
Throttle stop, Digifant - 4F•3
Throttle valve switch:
    Digifant fuel injection - 4F•2
    Digijet fuel injection - 4E•3
    K-Jetronic fuel injection, 16 valve - 4C•4
Tie-rods and balljoints - 10•11
Timing belt and sprockets:
    1.05 and 1.3 litre pre-August 1985 - 2A•10, 2A•14, 2A•18
    1.05 and 1.3 litre post August 1985 - 2B•4
    1.6 and 1.8 litre 8 valve - 2C•8, 2C•17, 2C•18
    1.8 litre 16 valve - 2D•3
Timing belt renewal - 1•22
Tools and working facilities - REF•6
Towing - 0•9
Track control arm - 10•6
Transmission - *See* **Manual gearbox** or **Automatic transmission**
Transmission stall test (automatic) - 7B•4
Tyre condition and pressure check - 0•14
Tyre pressures - 0•17

U

Underbonnet check points - 0•10

V

Vacuum servo unit - 9•12
Valve clearance check: - 1•12
    pre-August 1985 1.05 and 1.3 litre - 2A•18
    pre-August 1985 1.6 and 1.8 litre 8 valve - 2C•18
Vehicle exterior and interior maintenance - 11•1
Vehicle identification - REF•3
Vehicle underbody check - 1•20

W

Warm-up valve, K-Jetronic - 4B•6
Warning lamp cluster - 12•7
Weights - REF•1
Wheel alignment - 10•15
Wheel changing - 0•8
Window regulator - 11•10
Windows - 11•11
Windscreen washer system - 12•15
Windscreen wiper:
    linkage - 12•15
    motor - 12•13
    arms - 12•12
    blades - 0•13, 12•12
Wiring Diagrams - 12•16, 12•17 et seq

Notes

Notes

Preserving Our Motoring Heritage

The Model J Duesenberg Derham Tourster. Only eight of these magnificent cars were ever built – this is the only example to be found outside the United States of America

Almost every car you've ever loved, loathed or desired is gathered under one roof at the Haynes Motor Museum. Over 300 immaculately presented cars and motorbikes represent every aspect of our motoring heritage, from elegant reminders of bygone days, such as the superb Model J Duesenberg to curiosities like the bug-eyed BMW Isetta. There are also many old friends and flames. Perhaps you remember the 1959 Ford Popular that you did your courting in? The magnificent 'Red Collection' is a spectacle of classic sports cars including AC, Alfa Romeo, Austin Healey, Ferrari, Lamborghini, Maserati, MG, Riley, Porsche and Triumph.

A Perfect Day Out

Each and every vehicle at the Haynes Motor Museum has played its part in the history and culture of Motoring. Today, they make a wonderful spectacle and a great day out for all the family. Bring the kids, bring Mum and Dad, but above all bring your camera to capture those golden memories for ever. You will also find an impressive array of motoring memorabilia, a comfortable 70 seat video cinema and one of the most extensive transport book shops in Britain. The Pit Stop Cafe serves everything from a cup of tea to wholesome, home-made meals or, if you prefer, you can enjoy the large picnic area nestled in the beautiful rural surroundings of Somerset.

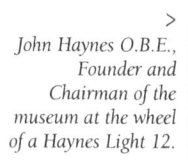

John Haynes O.B.E., Founder and Chairman of the museum at the wheel of a Haynes Light 12.

Graham Hill's Lola Cosworth Formula 1 car next to a 1934 Riley Sports.

The Museum is situated on the A359 Yeovil to Frome road at Sparkford, just off the A303 in Somerset. It is about 40 miles south of Bristol, and 25 minutes drive from the M5 intersection at Taunton.

Open 9.30am - 5.30pm (10.00am - 4.00pm Winter) 7 days a week, *except Christmas Day, Boxing Day and New Years Day*

Special rates available for schools, coach parties and outings Charitable Trust No. 292048